ALEXANDER ELIOT, an authority on Greek history, mythology, and art, has written 14 books, including *Earth, Air, Fire and Water; Socrates; The Concise History of Greece; Creatures of Arcadia;* and *The Universal Myths*. He is the editorial consultant for this guidebook.

BERYL BIGGINS, a longtime resident of Athens, has written guides to Athens, Istanbul and the Aegean coast of Turkey, and the Dodecanese islands. She is a contributing editor to an English-language magazine in Athens.

JEFFREY CARSON has lived on the island of Paros since 1970 and teaches art history at the Aegean Center for the Arts. The author of four books, he also is an art-book reviewer and occasional tour leader in Greece.

JOHN CHAPPLE has lived in Greece since 1969, working as a writer and editor of books about Greece for Lycabettus Press in Athens.

JANE WINSLOW ELIOT was brought up in Europe and met her husband, Alexander, when she was at *Time* magazine. They raised their children abroad, spending several years in Greece, and return there frequently. She has written guidebooks to Greece and contributed to *Travel & Leisure, Atlantic,* and *Horticulture* magazines.

ELIZABETH BOLEMAN HERRING is publishing editor of *The Southeastern Review: A Quarterly Journal of the Humanities in the Southeastern Mediterranean* and a columnist for *The Athenian: Greece's English Language Monthly*. Herring is also a professor of journalism at Southeastern College in Athens and the author of four books.

DIANA FARR LADAS, a resident of Greece since 1972, is a free-lance writer, translator, and editor. Author of a travel guide to Corfu and the Ionian islands, she is also an editor of the *Chandris Hotels Magazine*.

J. A. LAWRENCE is an American who has lived in Athens for 15 years. She writes science fiction, children's books, and historical fiction and has contributed to several guidebooks on her adopted country. She has co-authored a guide to Athens, produced a compendium of information for newcomers intending to live in Greece, and written a guide to Cyprus.

SHERRY MARKER has travelled regularly to the Peloponnese since 1975. She has contributed articles on Greece to *Travel & Leisure* and the *New York Times* and has published several guidebooks on Greece.

CONNIE SOLOYANIS, a former New Yorker, has lived in Athens for decades and covers it for periodicals in the United States and Greece. He is a member of the Society of American Travel Writers.

NIKOS STAVROULAKIS is a native of Crete and returns there frequently. He is the director of the Jewish Museum of Greece and teaches Byzantine and Ottoman history at a college in Athens.

TOM STONE, a 20-year resident of Greece currently living in Thessaloniki, is the author of guides to Greek food and wine and to the island of Patmos. He has published short stories and a novel, as well as many articles in Greek periodicals.

THE PENGUIN TRAVEL GUIDES

AUSTRALIA

CANADA

THE CARIBBEAN

ENGLAND & WALES

FRANCE

GERMANY

GREECE

HAWAII

IRELAND

ITALY

LONDON

MEXICO

NEW YORK CITY

PORTUGAL

SAN FRANCISCO &
NORTHERN CALIFORNIA

SPAIN

TURKEY

THE PENGUIN GUIDE TO GREECE 1991

ALAN TUCKER
General Editor

PENGUIN BOOKS

PENGUIN BOOKS

Published by the Penguin Group
Viking Penguin, a division of Penguin Books USA Inc.,
375 Hudson Street, New York, New York 10014, U.S.A.
Penguin Books Ltd, 27 Wrights Lane,
London W8 5TZ, England
Penguin Books Australia Ltd, Ringwood,
Victoria, Australia
Penguin Books Canada Ltd, 2801 John Street,
Markham, Ontario, Canada L3R 1B4
Penguin Books (N.Z.) Ltd, 182–190 Wairau Road,
Auckland 10, New Zealand

Penguin Books Ltd, Registered Offices:
Harmondsworth, Middlesex, England

First published in Penguin Books 1990
This revised edition published 1991

1 3 5 7 9 10 8 6 4 2

Copyright © Viking Penguin,
a division of Penguin Books USA Inc., 1990, 1991
All rights reserved

ISBN 0 14 019.934 9
ISSN 1043-4607

Printed in the United States of America

Set in ITC Garamond Light
Designed by Beth Tondreau Design
Maps by David Lindroth
Illustrations by Bill Russell
Fact-checked in Greece by Michael House
Transliteration by Louise D. Townsend
Edited by Lisa Leventer

Except in the United States of America, this
book is sold subject to the condition that it
shall not, by way of trade or otherwise, be lent,
re-sold, hired out, or otherwise circulated
without the publisher's prior consent in any form
of binding or cover other than that in which it
is published and without a similar condition
including this condition being imposed on the
subsequent purchaser.

THIS GUIDEBOOK

The Penguin Travel Guides are designed for people who are experienced travellers in search of exceptional information that will help them sharpen and deepen their enjoyment of the trips they take.

Where, for example, are the interesting, isolated, fun, charming, or romantic places within your budget to stay? The hotels and resorts described by our writers (each of whom is an experienced travel writer who either lives in or regularly tours the city, region, or islands of Greece he or she covers) are some of the special places, in all price ranges except for the lowest—not the run-of-the-mill, heavily marketed places on every travel agent's CRT display and in advertised airline and travel-agency packages. We indicate the approximate price level of each accommodation in our description of it (no indication means it is moderate), and at the end of every chapter we supply contact information so that you can get precise, up-to-the-minute rates and make reservations.

The Penguin Guide to Greece 1991 highlights the more rewarding parts of Greece so that you can quickly and efficiently home in on a good itinerary.

Of course, the guides do far more than just help you choose a hotel and plan your trip. *The Penguin Guide to Greece 1991* is designed for use *in* Greece. Our Penguin Greece writers tell you what you really need to know, as well as what you can't find out so easily on your own. They identify and describe the truly out-of-the-ordinary restaurants, shops and crafts, activities, sights, and beaches, and tell you the best way to "do" your destination.

Our writers are highly selective. They bring out the significance of the places they cover, capturing the personality and underlying cultural resonances of a town or region—making clear its special appeal. For exhaustive detailed coverage of local attractions, we suggest that you also use a supplementary reference-type guidebook, such as a Blue Guide, along with the Penguin Guide.

The Penguin Guide to Greece 1991 is full of reliable and timely information, revised each year. We would like to know if you think we've left out some very special place.

> ALAN TUCKER
> *General Editor*
> *Penguin Travel Guides*
>
> 375 Hudson Street
> New York, New York 10014
> or
> 27 Wrights Lane
> London W8 5TZ

CONTENTS

Overview	5
Useful Facts	12
Bibliography	30

THE MAINLAND

Athens	39
Getting Around	69
Accommodations	71
Athens After Dark	75
Shops and Shopping	93
Attica: Day Trips from Athens	101
The Classical Tour: Delphi, Olympia, Epidaurus	113
The Peloponnese	138
Epirus	194
Thessaly	222
Northern Greece	246

THE ISLANDS

The Sporades	335
Skiathos	336
Skopelos	343
Alonnisos	348
Skyros	352
The Ionian Islands	361
Corfu	364
Lefkada	375
Kefallonia	382
Ithaca	391

ix

CONTENTS

 Zakynthos   394
 Kythira   402

The Argo-Saronic Gulf Islands   **408**
 Aegina   408
 Poros   416
 Hydra   420
 Spetses   422

The Cyclades   **427**
 Andros   432
 Tinos   439
 Mykonos   445
 Delos   452
 Syros   455
 Naxos   462
 Paros   471
 Siphnos   480
 Milos   486
 Santorini   493

Crete   **506**

The Dodecanese   **562**
 Rhodes   564
 Kastellorizo   574
 Kasos, Karpathos, and Chalki   577
 Symi, Tilos, and Nisyros   586
 Kos   594
 Astypalaia   602
 Kalymnos   604
 Leros   609
 Patmos   612

The Northeastern Aegean Islands   **625**
 Ikaria   629
 Samos   638
 Chios   651
 Lesvos   669
 Limnos   678

Chronology   **688**

Index   **711**

MAPS

Greece	2
Athens	44
Plaka, Syntagma, and Kolonaki	58
Attica	102
Classical Tour	114
The Peloponnese	140
Epirus	196
Thessaly	224
Northern Greece	247
Thessaloniki	252
Western Macedonia	278
Eastern Macedonia	296
Thrace	319
Skiathos and Skopelos	337
Alonnisos and Skyros	349
The Ionian Islands	362
Corfu	365
Lefkada	376
Kefallonia and Ithaca	384
Zakynthos and Kythira	395
The Argo-Saronic Gulf Islands	410
The Cyclades	428
Andros	433
Tinos and Mykonos	440
Syros	456
Naxos	463
Paros and Siphnos	472
Milos and Santorini	487
Eastern Crete	517
Western Crete	536
Rhodes	565
Karpathos and Kasos	578
Symi, Tilos, and Nisyros	588

Kos and Astypalaia	595
Kalymnos, Leros, and Patmos	606
Ikaria, Fourni, and Samos	630
Chios	652
Lesvos	670
Limnos	679

THE PENGUIN GUIDE TO GREECE 1991

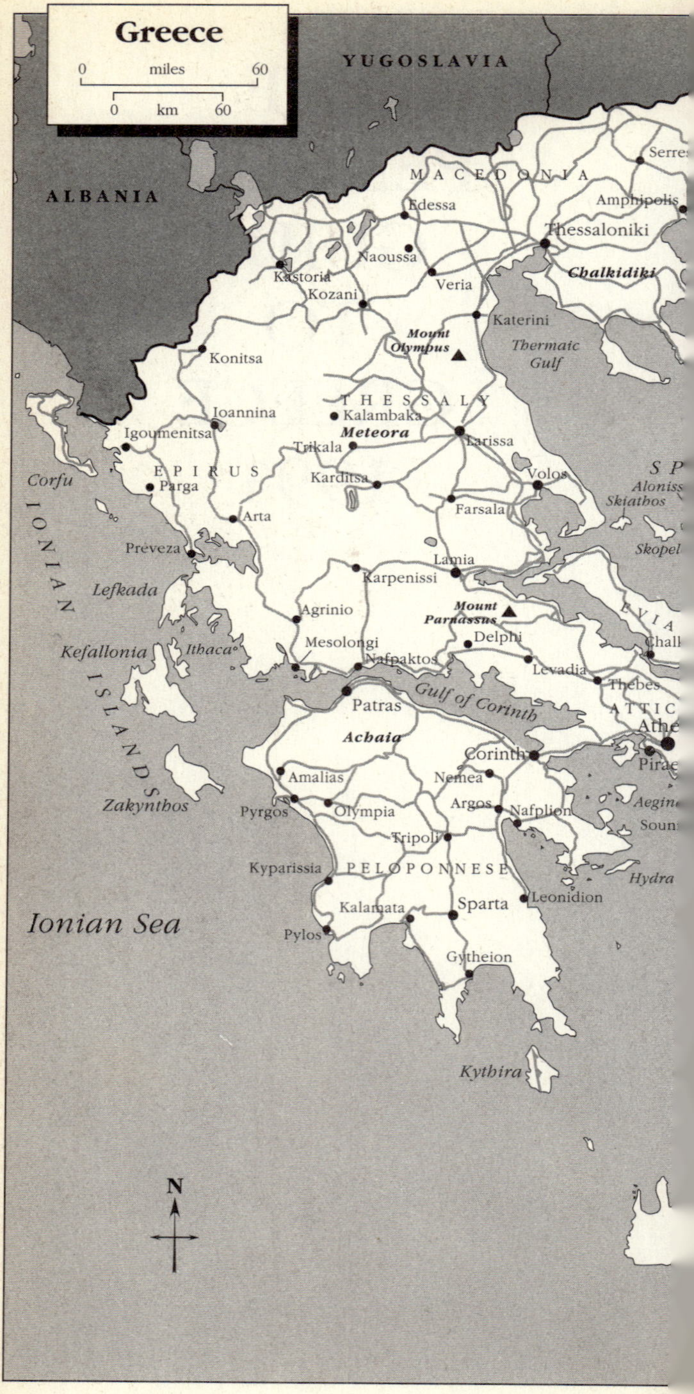
Greece
0 miles 60
0 km 60
YUGOSLAVIA
ALBANIA
MACEDONIA
Serres
Amphipolis
Edessa
Thessaloniki
Naoussa
Chalkidiki
Kastoria
Veria
Kozani
Katerini
Mount Olympus
Thermaic Gulf
Konitsa
THESSALY
Ioannina
Kalambaka
Meteora
Igoumenitsa
Larissa
Trikala
EPIRUS
Corfu
Parga
Karditsa
Volos
Alonisos
Skiathos
Arta
Farsala
Skopelos
IONIAN ISLANDS
Preveza
Lamia
Karpenissi
Lefkada
Mount Parnassus
EVIA
Agrinio
Delphi
Chalkis
Kefallonia
Ithaca
Mesolongi
Nafpaktos
Levadia
Thebes
Patras
Gulf of Corinth
ATTICA
Athens
Achaia
Corinth
Piraeus
Amalias
Nemea
Zakynthos
Pyrgos
Olympia
Argos
Nafplion
Aegina
Sounion
Tripoli
Kyparissia
PELOPONNESE
Hydra
Leonidion
Sparta
Kalamata
Ionian Sea
Pylos
Gytheion
Kythira
N

ULGARIA
TURKEY
Xanthi
THRACE
Komotini
Alexandroupolis
Kavala
Sea of Marmara
Thasos
Samothrace
Mount Athos
Limnos
Troy
NORTHEASTERN AEGEAN ISLANDS
ADES
Lesvos
TURKEY
eyros
Aegean Sea
Chios
Colophon
Ephesus
Andros
Samos
avrio
Kea
Tinos
Ikaria
Mykonos
Miletus
Syros
nos
Delos
Patmos
Naxos
Leros
Paros
riphos
Bodrum
Kalymnos
Siphnos
Halicarnassus
CYCLADES
Amorgos
Kos
os
Ios
Astypalaia
Nisyros
Symi
Rhodes
DODECANESE
Tilos
Santorini
Anafi
Chalki
Lindos
Sea of Crete
Rhodes
Karpathos
ania
TO KASTELLORIZO (MEGISTI)
CRETE
Herakleion
Rethymno
Knossos
Kasos
Ierapetra
Libyan Sea

OVERVIEW

By Alexander Eliot

Alexander Eliot received a Guggenheim Fellowship for Studies of Greece and the Middle East as Spiritual Cradles of the Western World. An authority on Greek history, mythology, and art, he has written 14 books, including Earth, Air, Fire and Water; Socrates; The Concise History of Greece; Creatures of Arcadia; *and* The Universal Myths.

Greece is not a destination in which to live like pampered guests, sitting and tippling with servants all around, watching staged entertainments, feasting on caviar, romancing to soft music, and floating in heated pools. In other words, it's not your ordinary vacation spot, by any means. This is not to say that Greece lacks excellent tourist facilities, or that the country fails to offer an unstinting abundance of sun, sea, and sporting activity. The point is that Greece gives you all this and then begins to work on your psyche at a much deeper level.

First, there's the many-faceted loveliness of the place. Moving beyond the Athenian metropolis, which has the strengths and weaknesses of most crowded historic capitals, you'll find that the rest of Greece remains a rock garden of extremes, among them the tragic gloom of Mycenae, the purity of Delos, the melodrama of Santorini, and the exaltation of Parnassus. There are also the tall villages and spring torrents of Arcadia, the rippling Thessalian plain, and finally, in Lord Byron's words, "the isles of Greece, the isles of Greece, where burning Sappho loved and sung." What do these places have in common?

The light. The clear Greek light is born, disports itself, and dies in glory every day. The golden mountains, purple valleys, lilac islands, and white villages alike resemble theater sets for the drama enacted by daylight itself. All things touched by this light become startlingly vivid; you feel as if you are seeing objects entire for the first time since childhood. Colors also are clearer here. The blue and white of the Greek flag appear reflected everywhere, as background to the red clay soil, the sparse, dusty green foliage, the yellow broom, the black olives, the gray-gold stones, and the rainbow seas of sunset.

Greece is crisscrossed with mountain ranges and laterally split by the Gulf of Corinth. It has more than 1,400 islands of all sizes (169 of which are inhabited). Greece has brief land borders with Albania, Yugoslavia, Bulgaria, and Turkey, but her chief neighbor is the sea. Natural resources are few, and only a tenth of the country's 50,000 square miles is suitable for farming. Sheep and goats crop the high, dry ground.

Although Greece isn't much larger than Scotland or New England, it's so chopped up, so various, and so crammed with wonders that you can't begin to cover it in a single visit. Almost everybody starts in Athens, where more than a third of Greece's nearly ten million people now reside, and goes on from there.

Athens is smoggy and traffic-clogged, but that's true of most great metropolises today. This is still the only place to get a quick fix on Greek culture, both ancient and modern. And it's surprisingly inexpensive, with luxury hotels at moderate prices, marvelous late-night feasting in the Plaka district for very little money, and good shopping. Not to visit the Acropolis would be perverse, and if you are the least bit concerned with history and art you should look into Athens's great museums as well.

Day trips from Athens to surrounding **Attica** make sense if your time is limited. You can go by taxi or tour bus to **Daphni** for its marvelous Byzantine church; to **Eleusis** for its otherworldly mystery; and to Poseidon's beautiful temple remains at **Cape Sounion** for the sunset. You can also take day cruises to the nearby **Argo-Saronic Gulf** islands of **Aegina, Poros, Hydra,** and **Spetses.**

Then comes a difficult choice: Shall it be the mainland or the islands? And after that: Which part of the mainland, and which islands? This will depend upon your tastes and the time at your disposal. In general, the mainland offers more history and art, while the islands are strongest in hedonistic pleasures, but there's a lot of overlap. For instance, the mainland has many marvelous beaches and some luxury resorts, and the islands include numerous important centers of Classical, Byzantine, and Crusader culture.

The mainland first. After Athens itself, the most popular

mainland option is to make a **Classical Tour** of **Delphi**, **Olympia**, and **Epidaurus**, stopping at points in between. This can be done by tour bus, but we recommend a rented car (or car and driver, if you're feeling flush). This one-week round-trip journey from Athens casts an ellipse around central Greece, the Gulf of Corinth, and the northern Peloponnese. It's your best introduction to the glory that was Greece. We've included a special chapter to outline this tour.

A second option is to explore the **Peloponnese** by car. In the course of a week or two (depending on how far you go), you would see many of the items on the Classical Tour as well as ancient **Corinth**, **Nemea**, King Agamemnon's **Mycenae**, Cyclopean **Tiryns**, the romantic remains of Medieval **Mystra**, the austere **Mani** country, Gibraltar-like **Monemvasia**, and more.

Still a third possibility is to drive north onto the flat plains of **Thessaly**, cut west to **Meteora's** towering rock fountain, where monasteries perch like storks' nests on chimney pots, then continue west through Metsovo in lofty **Epirus**, with its 191 stone bridges, three of which date back to the 13th century. In Epirus is the romantic city of **Ioannina**, brooding upon its emerald waters, and nearby is **Dodona**, site of the earliest oracle, where Zeus often spoke through the rustling leaves of an oak grove. Beyond Dodona lies the ferry to Corfu, where, after less than a week all told, you can turn in your car and become a beachcomber.

A fourth mainland option (the variants are numberless) is to base yourself in **Thessaloniki**, Greece's second city and the capital of Macedonia, and explore the still-mysterious, comparatively tourist-free reaches of northern Greece. **Mount Olympus** and **Mount Athos** cast long shadows over this region, which is closely identified with King Philip II of Macedon and his son, Alexander the Great. Local archaeological research has yielded finds that date back to 7000 B.C., including stone foundations for brick dwellings and shrines containing ceramic images of a fat fertility goddess. The Stone Age farmers who made those things had no knowledge of the wheel, and they produced neither weapons nor fortifications. Might theirs have been the blissful "golden age" of ancient legend?

And now the islands. For more than half the travellers to Greece, the pull of the islands proves irresistible. A highly recommended way to check them out, especially on a first visit, is by cruise ship (or better yet, if you can afford it, by chartered yacht). There's a whole range of island cruises in large vessels and small, lasting from a few days to a week or more, that are especially popular with newcomers (see Useful Facts, below). The favored stops are Santorini, Herakleion (in Crete), Rhodes, Patmos, and, of course, Mykonos.

After cruising, then what? You can fly Olympic, bounce by hydrofoil, or idle by ferryboat to dozens upon dozens of seagirt destinations. It's no easy matter to choose from among them all. Return visitors often opt for a single island, which makes sense. Here we'll discuss them group by group.

The easiest lot to identify is the **Ionian** chain off the western coast, stretching from flowery **Corfu** in the north (opposite southern Albania) down through **Ithaca** (Odysseus's long-sought home) before tailing off to **Kythira** in the far south, below the Peloponnese. Generally speaking, the Ionian islands are more luxuriant than their Aegean counterparts. The people seem relatively laid back; for instance, they never beat their olive trees, they just wait for the fruit to fall. The fine hand of the conquering Venetians, followed by the cool British (Gladstone was Lord High Commissioner of the Ionians for a while), may have had something to do with this.

As for the **Sporades**, the very word means "scattered," so it's hardly surprising that those islands lie dispersed like seeds across the Aegean, beginning north of Evia and off the coast of Thessaly. Favored among them are steep-sloped, pine-studded **Skiathos**, **Skopelos**, and **Skyros**, as well as rustic **Alonnisos**.

The **Dodecanese** islands are very much dominated by **Rhodes**, a big old favorite off the southwest coast of Turkey. Dodecanese means "twelve islands," yet there are actually 14 in this rather widely scattered group, including one, **Kastellorizo**, that's literally off the map of Greece. Perhaps loveliest of them all is **Patmos**, where Saint John the Divine (or John the Writer, as the Greeks call him) composed his harrowing Revelation.

Then come the forested, vineyarded, and sizable islands of the northeastern Aegean, where winter can be cold and wet. **Chios**, **Limnos**, craggy **Samos**, unspoiled **Ikaria**, and convivial **Lesvos** (a.k.a. Lesbos) all have much to offer. Take the rich wine of Samos, famous from ancient times. Immortal Hera, wife to Zeus, had a vast temple on Samos, and one of its 134 columns still stands. Samos offers the added advantage of day ferries to nearby Turkey. (The political differences between the two nations are not permitted to interfere with their touristic truce.) Lesvos is the largest and most popular island of this group. Our word "lesbian" derives from Lesvos, where lived the eloquently poignant female poet Sappho.

The **Cyclades** are the most popular islands of all, and their bare beauty is regarded as being typically Greek. True to their name, which means "forming a circle," these rocky outcroppings in the blue Aegean, crowned with white Cubist towns, create a rough oval stretching southeastward from the central mainland and the large, relatively undeveloped island of Evia. **Andros** in the north and **Santorini** in the south are the poles of the Cyclades' slantwise ellipse. At its center lie sacred **Delos**, the birthplace of Apollo and Artemis, and her profane sister-island, ever-glamorous **Mykonos**, the playpen of today's instant immortals.

The first inhabitants of the Cyclades were Stone Age entrepreneurs in the mining and working of obsidian. The Bronze Age brought huge demand for the ingredients of bronze, namely, copper and tin. By 3000 B.C. Cycladians were venturing westward all the way to Spain in search of those metals, for trade with Egypt and Sumer. Thus did the first of many successive Greek cultures act as middleman between Asia, North Africa, and still-barbarous Europe. The purity and rigor of Cycladic marble carvings, to be seen at Athens and elsewhere, call to mind the work of such modern masters as Constantin Brancusi, Alberto Giacometti, and Ben Nicholson.

The large island of **Crete**, which defines the Aegean's southern boundary, is where the first major Greek culture came into existence, sometime before 1900 B.C. At the start of our century, Sir Arthur Evans discovered what was probably the ancient Cretan capital at Knossos. Not many archaeologists are privileged to unearth a lost civilization. He called this one "Minoan," after the legendary Cretan king Minos. The evidence Evans excavated indicates that the Minoans fashioned a giant thalassocracy, or sea empire, that extended far and wide around the Mediterranean. No weapons from the earliest times have been found. It seems that the Minoans prospered not by force of arms but through merchant-marine enterprise alone. What effectively finished them was the greatest natural disaster ever to occur in a civilized area: the volcanic eruption of the island of Santorini around 1500 B.C., an explosion so violent it joggled three continents. Because Crete lies not far south of Santorini, her cities were tumbled and her all-important merchant navy destroyed.

Greece gets great word-of-mouth advertising and has a very high rate of repeat travellers. One theory credits this not so much to the country's softer charms as to its mentally healing, nerve-settling powers. Strained by the rigors of modern life, some people have found Greece to be just the place to straighten out their priorities.

In Greece the physical actualities are vivid. Faced with them, you'll find that the computer readouts in your head dissolve like snowflakes on a hot stove. Yet whatever you may know of classical Greek myth, literature, and philosophy endures, because it creates a perfect fit with the scene itself. Who remembers the table of the elements learned in high school physics? Who can forget the four "elements"—earth, air, fire, and water—that were known to the great pre-Socratic cosmologists?

It's often asked how people can afford to keep going back to Greece. Distance makes this a fairly expensive country to reach, especially for North Americans and Australians, but once you're here everything's a bargain. Thus the wonderful cruises, deluxe hotels, and posh island resorts are generally within your grasp. Moreover, even the most modest accommodations are clean, comfortable, and tasteful, as a rule. In short, a brief visit might be extravagant, but for longer vacations Greece makes economic sense.

Another frequent question concerns the food. Isn't it monotonous, and a bit oily, too? That's possible. But the grilled fish and baby lamb, the pastas with eggplant, the artichokes, the wild greens (*ágria horta*), and the thick, homemade yogurt with honey (*yaoúrti me meli*) are outstanding. Follow your nose to the most aromatic tavernas. It's customary to select from what's on view rather than from the menu, and if there's too much olive oil for you, do what the Greeks do: Call for lemon and squeeze a few slices over everything.

Greece has no "great" native wines on which to fritter away your funds, but her local varieties are sure to please adventurous wine lovers. Be sure to sample the much-maligned resinated wines called *retsína*—the perfect supplement to a snack beneath a pine tree by the sea. Shakespeare's "malmsey" wine came from Monemvasia, in the Peloponnese. It is said to have resembled the strong rosé wine of Santorini today, which washes things down quite nicely.

When Tsannis Tzannetakis was chosen as prime minister in the summer of 1989 to head the then-interim government, he kept the tourism portfolio for himself. "Not only is tourism a major source of foreign exchange," Tzannetakis explained, "but more significantly, it's a means of promoting our culture and heritage." The best of that heritage belongs to the world at large; Greek ideals of democracy, dialectics, medicine, and sport drive us to this day.

No wonder Greece bid hard to host the Olympic games of 1996, the 100th anniversary of the modern Olympics. Meanwhile, legislation to improve hotel standards, open more casinos, and create air charters is pending in Parliament. One hopes that reform of the Greek Archaeological Service will follow. There's been too much rebuilding of the classical ruins, scrubbing down ancient statuary, and repainting old icons and frescoes. What for? Presumably to make things "more accessible to tourists," in the Disney sense. Improved museum display and personnel attitudes would better promote Greek culture.

Classical Greek ruins may be encountered on many a Mediterranean shore, but most of them are here. There's never been a more creative culture than Greece of the sixth through the fourth centuries B.C. It could be argued that no country ever slept longer than Greece did under Roman, Byzantine, Venetian, Frankish, Catalan, and Turkish rule, yet she kept her language miraculously intact while nurturing the Greek Orthodox religion. The Medieval Christian art and architecture to be found at Daphni, Osios Loukas, Meteora, and Mount Athos, for instance, carry much the same spiritual force as the country's pagan remains.

The present nation came into existence piece by piece during the 19th and 20th centuries. Her finest hour to date occurred in 1940, when a small but fierce Greek force decisively hurled an Italian invasion well back into Albania. There was no stopping the Nazi blitzkrieg that followed, but Greek guerilla resistance to the German occupation was heroic. Afterward, however, the desperately impoverished, half-starved populace fell into an extremely vicious civil war.

The very same thing had happened during Greece's Golden Age. Her successful defense against Persia (so glowingly described by Herodotus) was followed by the suicidal Peloponnesian Wars, which drew this comment from Thucydides: "Moderation was despised as weakness. Prudence became cowardice . . . Guilelessness, the chief characteristic of a noble nature, was laughed to scorn and disappeared."

These are not unfamiliar phenomena today. Yet you can develop guileless relationships with many Greeks on their native ground. Obviously, not all travellers care to be friends. Greeks find that odd, but they're compassionate about it. If you make no advances, they rarely will either, but they're usually ready and often speak English. Moreover, if you've taken the trouble to learn a little Greek you'll be amazed at how far it stretches. Your new friends will jolly you along, increasing your vocabulary by leaps and bounds.

Philoxenía, or hospitality, is part of the Greek tradition. Natives claim with justice that there's been far less terrorism in Greece than in Italy, Germany, France, or Spain, and they point with pride to their extremely low crime rate. (Women, native or foreign, can walk practically anywhere at night.) Finally, they note with satisfaction that many foreigners of Greek descent now see fit to invest in the homeland.

Beyond Athens, social life centers on the village well, the sidewalk café, the open-air market, and the evening stroll (*volta*). Conversation comes peppered with personal questions, salted with good-natured evasions, buttered with one-up wit. It's also oiled with gossip and vinegared with argument. Pride, prejudice, and flashing anger lie close beneath the surface of Greek courtesy. So do love and joy.

USEFUL FACTS

When to Go

April through June and September and October are the choice months, just before and just after the high tourist season, when it is easier to get a room, rent a boat, and find a highway relatively free of traffic. The weather is usually clear and comfortable, warm enough for swimming. The sometimes strong *meltémi* winds of summer stop blowing in the fall, making yachting and sailing particularly good. Fresh fruits and vegetables are abundant. In spring there are the wildflowers, the trees in bloom, everything reawakening with that special vibrancy hot countries possess.

That said, Greece in summer, particularly on the islands, is also a joy. There are the water sports, the outdoor living, the smashing beauty, the fun. It's crowded, that's all, and tempers get frayed, especially when there is not always enough to go around—particularly hotel rooms. In the winter months from November through March the sacred sites are cool and unfrequented, museums are uncluttered by tours, and streets are walkable. Even the islands can be wonderful in winter. By February the almond trees are in bloom (something to see against the snowy peaks of Parnassus), and by March fields are glowing with many of the country's 6,000 species of wildflowers.

Entry and Exit Documents

Entry: If you are a tourist going for under four months, a valid passport will suffice. This covers nationals from the European Community (EC), the United States, Canada, Australia, and New Zealand. For these countries Greece requires neither a visa nor any medical shots.

Exit: Be sure to have valid statements from antiques shops showing the authenticity of your purchases. Anything made before 1830 (or thereabouts) will not be permitted out without special clearance from the National Archaeological Museum, 1 Tositsa Street, Athens. For antiques dated after 1830 you must approach the Byzantine Museum at Vasilissis Sophias and Rigilis. However, shops may legitimately sell antiques to foreigners, many of whom live in the country on a semipermanent basis; travellers need to check things out pretty carefully before buying an antique they wish to take home. Customs is strict about this.

Arrival at Major Gateways by Air

Olympic Airways flies to Athens and Thessaloniki from most of the world's major airports. You can also get direct flights year-round on EC carriers and SAS to Rhodes and Crete and to Corfu in summer. Rhodes is a free port, so you will go through customs once you're back in Athens.

British Airways and Air Caledonia fly to Athens from Great Britain; Air Canada and Canadian Airlines International from Canada; and Pan Am and TWA fly nonstop to Athens from the United States (TWA flies nonstop only in summer; at other times there is a stop in Rome).

The Thessaloniki airport has direct flights in summer from most EC countries and via Scandinavian Airways. Direct can sometimes mean a stop at Athens, but that depends on long-distance schedules at the time.

Olympic Airways provides regular flights to 22 islands during the summer and to all major islands winter and summer.

Upon arrival in Athens you are not more than 20 minutes from Syntagma Square, the center of town. You are also on the highway to the major beach resorts. Taxis will get you to the main square for between 500 and 600 drachmas, regular shuttle buses to Syntagma Square for less. If the taxi driver does not put down the meter, you might pay as much as 4,000 drachmas, so make sure it's down when you begin.

Some hotels offer shuttle service—sometimes. It is all rather small-time and slightly disorganized, but at least there is not far to go to find transportation. Both taxis and buses wait out in front of the arrivals terminals.

Arrival by Boat
If you arrive by cruise ship, you will dock in Piraeus, the Mediterranean's busiest port, where customs formalities are minimal. It is about 16 km (10 miles) to Athens (about 15 to 20 minutes) and will cost about 1,500 drachmas by cab, because fares are legally doubled from the port. There is also a little subway train that takes you to Omonia Square in about 20 minutes, and there are buses.

If you are entering Greek waters in your own yacht or other small boat, entry documents are required. There are 27 entry-exit ports where you must show your logbook (good for one year) and have your passport stamped. If you do not already have a logbook, one can be issued at the time of your arrival.

Arrival by Train
Trains from Europe go to Thessaloniki, 400 km (250 miles) north of Athens, where you must transfer if you are proceeding to Athens. (It is preferable to continue by air.) Trains to Thessaloniki come from London, Paris, Oslo, Lisbon, Helsinki, and Moscow, and offer sleeping-car compartments. Less accommodating trains run from Istanbul. Since Greece does not have an interesting or extensive rail network, a Eurailpass will not save you time or money.

Arrival by Car
The most popular entryway is by ferry from Brindisi, in southern Italy. The ferry goes overnight to Igoumenitsa, in Epirus, and to Patras, in the Peloponnese. Ferries are usually crowded but efficient. You might be lucky enough to get a cabin if you arrive at the boat early—which you must do if you want to ensure a place for your car.

The other entryway by car is on International Highway 192 through Yugoslavia.

A valid driver's license from your country or an international driver's license is required.

Around Greece by Car
By far the best way to get around on the mainland is by hiring a car and driver or driving yourself. The alternative is the tour bus, no longer an especially pleasant way to travel. The arterial roads are good for the most part, but it's never advisable to get far off the primary and secondary highways, because minor roads can deteriorate pretty fast into dust-

covered rocks. The secondary highways are shared with mopeds, donkeys, carts, pedestrians, motorcycles, and trucks, requiring your full attention; they are not always well marked or well serviced.

Distances between desirable destinations do not seem great when you are driving in Greece. On the other hand, ill-marked turnoffs, hidden country tavernas, and little-known but still important sites are all reasons to go at a reasonable pace so as not to miss anything.

Traffic can be congested in Athens, but it then thins out on the main highways, except on Sundays. (To control automobile pollution, Athens has instituted a plan whereby cars with license numbers ending in odd numbers drive on odd-numbered days, while those ending in even numbers drive on even-numbered days. This system does not apply on weekends or official holidays or during the month of August. Whether it diminishes pollution is debatable.) Impossible parking still makes having a car in Athens out of the question; use one only to get out of the city. The same is true, although not to the same degree, in Thessaloniki.

Around Greece by Air

Olympic Airways is the only carrier permitted to make domestic flights in Greece. Olympic provides extensive and reliable service to the major cities and some 22 islands. Major islands such as Crete, Rhodes, and Corfu have frequent flights all year round. Fares are kept low, to slow migration to the mainland, but are changeable. Among the destinations you can reach by air from Athens are: Thessaloniki, Corfu, Kefallonia, Paros, Zakynthos, Ioannina, Skiathos, Limnos, Chios, Samos, Kos, Rhodes, Lesvos (Mytilini), Kythira, Chania, Herakleion, Santorini, Mykonos, and Karpathos. See the Getting Around sections for individual destinations for more details.

Getting Around the Islands by Boat

The first thing to know is that getting around the islands by boat is not easy. It is glorious fun, however, and can be the best part of a vacation.

Cruising. For first-time visitors, the easiest way to go is to take one of the luxurious cruise ships from Piraeus that stop at several major islands, often including Crete, Santorini, Rhodes, Patmos, and Mykonos, and often in Turkey as well. The ships are well appointed, the spirit of the crew exceptionally welcoming and good-natured, the stops important. The main Greek luxury lines are Sun Line and Epirotiki. Then there is Swans Hellenic, with its renowned on-board lecture program led by famous British dons. There is also a new entry in this watery field, the sumptuous and expensive Sea Goddess Cruises. Cycladic Lines boats take day trips to the Argo-Saronic Gulf islands; Ionian Sea Lines services the Ionian group.

Varied schedules give all travellers an opportunity to dip their toes in the dramatic crystal colors of the Aegean and Ionian seas. There are fancy, far-flung seven-day cruises that cost 200,000 to 400,000 drachmas per person, double occupancy; three- to four-day central island cruises on less imposing but equally friendly ships, costing upwards of 69,000 drachmas; and one- to two-day trips to the Argo-Saronic Gulf and Ionian islands that are comparably inexpensive. The only drawback to cruising is that you often feel left with too little time to savor the magic. First-time visitors, however, can get a wonderful overview, returning another day to spend time on the islands of their choice.

There are also many worthwhile air-cruise packages. Check with your travel agent or with the cruise companies, which have offices in most major cities of the world. Contact:

Cycladic Cruises: In Greece, 81 Patission Street, Athens, 104 34, Tel: (01) 822-9468; in the U.S., c/o Hellastours, Inc., 1100 Glendon Avenue, Suite 1746, Los Angeles, CA 90024, Tel: (213) 208-8700, (800) 624-7533 (in California), or (800) 824-8535; in Canada, c/o Triaena Holidays, 543 Danforth Avenue, Toronto, Ontario M4K 1P7, Tel: (416) 461-0727.

Epirotiki Lines: In Greece, Epirotiki Building, 87 Akti Miaouli, Piraeus, 185 35, Tel: (01) 452-6641, Fax: (01) 413-3814; in the U.S., 551 Fifth Avenue, New York, NY 10176, Tel: (212) 599-1750 or (800) 221-2470, Fax: (212) 687-0241.

Sun Line Cruises: In Greece, 3 Iasonos Street, Piraeus, 185 37, Tel: (01) 452-3417 or 322-8883, Telex: 241044 SUNL GR; in the U.S., 1 Rockefeller Plaza, Suite 315, New York, NY 10020, Tel: (212) 397-6400 or (800) 872-6400; in Canada, Tel: (800) 368-3888.

Royal Cruise Line: In Greece, 81 Akti Miaouli, Piraeus, 185 38, Tel: (01) 451-9553; in the U.S., 1 Maritime Plaza, San Francisco, CA 94111, Tel: (415) 956-7200 or (800) 227-5628 (U.S. and Canada).

Mediterranean Sun Cruises and **Mediterranean Sun Line Ferry Ltd.**: In Greece, 5 Sachtouri Street, Piraeus, 185 36, Tel: (01) 452-4804, Telex: 211825 MSLS GR, Fax: (01) 452-4873.

Another option is the yacht-like ships of **Viking Yacht Cruises**. These vessels take roughly 35 passengers and cruise the Cyclades. Although the ships are clean and comfortable, the whole adventure is bare bones, more like a bunch of friends out for a picnic. But some lovely places are visited, and everyone has a great time with the friendly officers and crew, who have no space in which to maintain a lordly distance. Contact Viking Yacht Cruises in the U.S. (there is an economic advantage to making arrangements through the U.S.) at 6 Turkey Hill Road South, Westport, CT 06880; Tel: (203) 226-7911 or (800) 341-3030.

Yachting. For anywhere between 15,000 and 750,000 drachmas you can rent a yacht or caïque under the direction of a Greek captain and crew—or take one out on your own, if you meet sailing qualifications. This is not so expensive if you consider sharing the cost among six friends. A yacht is the most magical way to experience the islands: picnics in secluded coves, stops at out-of-the-way places, docking at fashionable marinas, enjoying plenty of fresh food and wine, all at your own pace, subject only to the vagaries of the weather. For more information, contact the **Greek Yacht Brokers and Consultants Association** at 36 Alkyonis Street, Paleo Phaleron, Athens, 175 61; Tel: (01) 981-6582.

Flotilla. Several companies offer the opportunity to sail your own small craft within a group of six or seven vessels, watched over by a Greek captain who knows the local winds and water. Subject to his agreement, you go off from the group as far as you like but meet up at designated ports by specified times. It is a safe, companionable way to go, with the added zest of a little adventure. For information, contact the Greek Yacht Brokers and Consultants Association (see above).

Ferries. If getting there is all you want to do, you can try swimming—or a Greek ferry. Either way you have as good a chance of reaching your destination; Greek ferries are what made Odysseus hardy. There are several new ones that are air-conditioned; even so, anyone without the stomach of an islander stays up on deck. Some serve whole meals, others soft drinks and potato chips. Whatever you read in books and magazines about ferries and their schedules, the main thing to remember is that most of it won't work on the spot. No Greek harbor master will entrust himself and his livelihood to the sea if there is the slightest chance of rough weather. The strong *meltemi* winds of summer are notorious. Some storms are predictable, but when there is any doubt the vessel just doesn't go. To make matters more difficult, there will be several unmarked offices on islands, each dealing with a different ship's schedule. Islanders never seem to be sure who is handling which boat that week. You may want to go to Samos but, after a week of trying, take the ship to Kos instead, waving at the one to Samos chugging in as you leave port.

As you cross the Gulf of Corinth at Rion or take similar short ferry trips, there are no bounds to the awe you feel as you watch your car snuggled in among several two-trailer trucks loaded with soft drinks and other provisions. Less than a centimeter separates your frail vehicle from utter annihilation. There are ferries galore to take, some 50 of them at last count, to Crete, Rhodes, Corfu, Samos, the Sporades, the Cyclades, and more. Fortunately, most islands are too small to warrant a car for a short visit, and local taxis are not that expensive.

Be assured that it would be foolhardy to take a ferry at the end of your trip when you are trying to get to the airport for a flight home. You might have been told that you could fly to one island, say Crete, take a ferry to another, for instance Santorini, and fly from there. But since you're depending on the ferry to get you to Santorini, you can't quite be sure you will make your flight out of that island. And you'll never get back to the mainland by air without a reservation in the ever-lengthening high season.

To sum up: If you have plenty of time, the stomach of a Greek sailor, and enough money to cover stay-overs, then by all means plan on ferries. If, however, you haven't planned, but there you are in Samos, say, and there is the ferry to Chios, which has an easily found caïque that chugs to Turkey, then jump on (Rhodes, Kos, Chios, Samos, and Patmos have connections with Turkey year-round).

In the following chapters you will find more detailed information on how to get around specific island clusters (the Cyclades, the Sporades, the Dodecanese, etc.). There are regular ferries plying Greek waters day and night. One sure thing can be said for them—they are cheap. You probably will be able to find your way onto one or two. Your best bet is to sit at a harbor café with a glass of something and keep asking anyone who will listen. Someone's bound to know something sooner or later.

Hydrofoil. Several clusters of islands now have hydrofoil service (passengers only): the Argo-Saronic Gulf islands, the Dodecanese, the Cyclades, and the Sporades. These vehicles pound against the waves summer and winter. For information contact Flying Dolphins, 8 Akti Themistokleous, Piraeus, 185 36; Tel: (01) 452-7107. (Again, see specific sections for further details.)

Catamaran. There is one more way to get from one

island to another during the tourist season: the catamaran—
a quick, fairly large vessel used primarily for daily excursions such as the one from Rhodes to Symi. If the water is rough, the ride can be bumpy or even cancelled; if not, it is smooth as a cloud.

Ships and Ferries to Turkey. The western coast of Turkey has become a prime tourist destination, welcoming visitors from several Greek islands: Chios (one hour to Çesme), Samos (two hours to Kuşadası, the port for Ephesus), Patmos (three hours to the ruins of Milos, five and a half hours to Kuşadası), Rhodes (four hours to Bodrum), and Kos (one hour to Bodrum). Check with local tourist organizations or wander the waterfront to see what itineraries are available during your visit (they are posted on large slates). The main thing to remember: You must return with your group or risk difficulties with officialdom of both countries.

Around Greece by Walking/Bus/Moped

On the Islands. You might opt for a moped. Although the roads may be potholed and narrow, it is a pleasant way to get about. Buses are harrowing but sometimes offer the only way to proceed. Of course, you may be in luck and get one of the few taxis available. There are lovely walks, both short and long, good for most visitors.

On the Mainland. Walking requires some careful planning, as distances may be deceptive. The main concern in wilder areas is shepherd dogs trained to protect their flocks. Be sure the shepherd has seen you and signaled his dog before you venture near the sheep. These dogs are trained to obey only their masters.

Local Time

Greek standard time is ahead of London by two hours, New York by seven hours, and Los Angeles by ten hours, and is behind Sydney by seven hours. Daylight saving time is in effect from the last Sunday in March to the first Sunday in September.

Traditional Settlements

Greece has been changing its ideas about tourism in the past few years, no longer building ugly blocks of boring white rectangles to act as receptacles for tour groups. The new effort is to retain and maintain the beautiful Greek landscape travellers have come so far to enjoy. Elounda Mare on Crete, where 30 bungalows share some 18 swimming pools, and Steps of Lindos on Rhodes, built in the form of a small Greek mountain village, are two examples of environmentally interesting luxury hotels. Part of this new approach includes a Greek National Tourist Organization program to remodel old buildings such as towers in the Mani, wooden houses on Mount Pelion, and entire small villages on Santorini. By inducing locals to remain, the villages are kept as authentic as possible. The attractively renovated houses are provided with modern conveniences, including kitchen facilities, for week- or month-long stays. Eight settlements are in full operation, the first phase of the program. For information contact the Greek National Tourist Organization: EOT Diefthynsi Ekmetalefseos, 2 Amerikis Street, Athens, 105 64; Tel: (01) 322-3111.

Currency

The drachma is the Greek unit of currency. At press time the exchange in Greece was 145 drachmas per U.S. dollar, 275 drachmas per English pound sterling, 135 drachmas per Canadian dollar, and 125 drachmas per Australian dollar.

Drachma denominations are 1, 2, 5, 10, 20, and 50 in coin; and in bills, 50 (blue), 100 (reddish), 500 (green), 1,000 (brownish), and 5,000 (blue).

The currency does not fluctuate rapidly, and there is no black market. Many merchants, however, prefer foreign cash and are willing to bargain their merchandise accordingly. Currency will be exchanged at your hotel or by a friendly shopkeeper at a fair rate.

In general, bills over 500 drachmas cannot be exchanged once you have left the country, although some banks may make exceptions and exchange even 1,000-drachma bills.

Telephoning

Hellenic Telecommunications Organization (OTE) offers a cheap alternative to telephoning from your hotel, which may add a large surcharge, including fees for uncompleted calls, to your bill. OTEs are located conveniently, often in post offices. The country code for Greece is 30; the city code for Athens is 01 (all Greek city codes begin with zero, which should be omitted when telephoning Greece from outside the country).

Electric Current

The basic power supply is 220 volts AC. On a very few islands the current is 110 volts DC. North American appliances will require transformers or built-in converters in either case.

Business Hours

Banks are open from 8:00 A.M. to 2:00 P.M. Mondays through Fridays. Some banks are open for foreign currency exchange at other times.

In Athens, main central post offices are open Mondays through Fridays from 7:30 A.M. to 7:30 P.M. Those in immediate suburbs close at 2:15 P.M.

Some international businesses, particularly shipping, have begun to keep European hours, working through the hot midday. This will vary from company to company and also from season to season.

Except for the mid-afternoon siesta, nothing is fixed in bronze in Greece. Shops are supposed to be open approximately from 8:00 A.M. to 2:00 P.M. on Tuesdays, Thursdays, and Fridays, then close during the hot mid-afternoon and reopen from about 5:30 to 8:30 P.M. On Mondays, Wednesdays, and Saturdays, shops stay open between 8:30 A.M. and 2:30 P.M. Most will then close for the rest of the day. In winter shops may be open all day, but this is under review. Many shops push their opening hours into the afternoon; others do not.

The only place that does not respect the mid-afternoon closing is the kiosk, where you can get help, directions, and newspapers, and always make a phone call.

It is a serious breach of etiquette to call anyone during the mid-afternoon siesta. In fact, the police may be called if people become offensively noisy during that time.

Holidays

Greek Orthodox Easter falls on the first Sunday after the first full moon following the spring equinox and Passover. It does not always coincide with Western Christianity's Easter, which does not include Passover in its calculations (they coincide every four years). During the ten days of Greek Easter it seems as if most of Greece is out on the roads and filling the hotels, taking part in somber, candle-lit processions, setting off fireworks, and eating out. The celebration is particularly moving on the islands and in remote villages. With so many people having left the city, it is a festive and yet tranquil time to visit Athens.

Anastenária (May 21) takes place in three villages just a little north of Thessaloniki. After careful preparation, participants dance barefoot on live coals. Although the ceremony dates back before Christianity, the dancers carry icons of Saints Helen and Constantine. (See the chapter on northern Greece for more information.)

Throughout Greece local festivals take place continually

as people celebrate their region's particular saints and events. There are also seasonal ones, such as wine festivals, and celebrations peculiar to certain islands, such as Sponge Week on Kalymnos and the Feast of the Virgin on Tinos. Check with your hotel on arrival to see what is happening during your visit. You will be welcome, whatever the event.

Credit Cards

Most major international credit cards are welcomed throughout Greece.

For Further Information

The Greek National Tourist Organization is a primary source of information, with offices around the world: **Athens Headquarters**, 2 Amerikis Street, Athens, 105 64, Tel: (01) 322-3111; **Athens Information Center**, Information Desk, National Bank of Greece, 2 Karageorgi Servias Street (on Syntagma Square), Athens, 105 63, Tel: (01) 322-2545; **New York**, Olympic Tower, 645 Fifth Avenue (fifth floor), New York, NY 10022, Tel: (212) 421-5777; **Los Angeles**, 611 West Sixth Street (suite 2998), Los Angeles, CA 90017, Tel: (213) 626-6696; **Canada**, 1233 Rue de la Montagne, Montreal, QC H3G 1Z2, Quebec, Tel: (514) 871-1535; **England**, 8 Conduit Street, London, W1R DOJ, Tel: (071) 734-5997.

A new service has been initiated this year: direct bookings from the U.S. to Greece for all domestic flights and for reservations at hotels. It is provided by the California Hotel and Conference Reservation Center; Tel: (800) 736-5717 or, in California, (714) 534-2642.

Another useful telephone number is that of the Greek Chamber of Hotels, which will find the number of any hotel in Greece; in Athens, Tel: (01)323-7193.

Language

The most astonishing thing about the Greek language is its power of survival. The Greek of Homer is to modern Greek (a 28-century span) what the English of Chaucer is to modern English (a 6-century span). For many centuries people were assumed to be Greek if they spoke Greek. Even today, if you speak it somewhat easily, the feeling remains that you must somehow be Greek.

While language is deeply entwined with national identity, a traveller can get by with no Greek at all. English is being taught as the second language in schools, and people who want to get ahead in the tourist industry go to special language academies.

USEFUL FACTS

There are two modes of modern Greek: *katharévousa,* an artificial pure Greek created for the emerging modern Greek state in the 19th century, and the rich vernacular called *demotikí,* which takes many of its words from the Middle East, Europe, and even America. Demotiki is now taught in all schools and universities. Although katharevousa was disestablished after the fall of the colonels' junta in 1967, many writers published in academic papers, newspapers, and official pronouncements continue to use katharevousa. But ever since the great poet and novelist Nikos Kazantzakis (1885–1957) broke the ice, Greek literature has used demotiki.

Despite the daunting look of Greek, it is easy to learn enough to read a street sign and to say good morning (*kaliméra*) or thank you (*efharistó*). You will seem much less terrifying to the Greeks, and they will seem friendlier to you.

First, a few basic words and phrases that will help even on a brief visit:

Please	Parakaló
Thank you	Efharistó (pronounced "efhah-reestoh," accented on the "oh")
Yes	Málista/Neh (colloquial)
No	Óhee (tip your head, not your hand, slightly back)
It doesn't matter	Then birázi
Excuse me	Signómee
All right	Entáxi
Good	Kalá
Very good	Polée kalá
Nothing, thank you	Típote, efharistó
The bill	To logariasmó
How are you?	Ti kánete? (polite, plural)/Ti káneis? (familiar, singular)
What is your name?	Pos sas léne?
Good morning	Kaliméra
Good afternoon/evening	Kalispéra
Good night	Kaliníchta
Slow	Sigá, sigá
Fast	Grígora
Your health (hello)	Yásas (polite, plural)/yásou (familiar, singular)
Big	Megálo
Small	Meecró
Hot	Zestó
Cold	Créeo

USEFUL FACTS

The alphabet also is beautiful, fun to learn, and helpful to know. With a little imagination you might be able to make out menus, some newspaper headlines, and many signs; very often a mysterious word deciphered turns out to be one already familiar. *ΜΠΑΡ,* for instance, means "bar."

Here is the Greek alphabet and tips on pronunciation.

Upper case	Lower case	Name	Pronunciation
Α	α	alpha	aah
Β	β	beta	v
Γ	γ	gamma	g (as in goats), y
Δ	δ	delta	th (as in then)
Ε	ε	epsilon	e (as in red)
Ζ	ζ	zeta	z
Η	η	eta	e (as in weed)
Θ	θ	theta	th (as in thin)
Ι	ι	iota	ee
Κ	κ	kappa	k
Λ	λ	lambda	l
Μ	μ	mu	m
Ν	ν	nu	n
Ξ	ξ	xi	ks
Ο	ο	omicron	o (as in log)
Π	π	pi	p
Ρ	ϱ	rho	r
Σ	σ	sigma	s
Τ	τ	tau	t
Υ	υ	upsilon	ee
Φ	φ	phi	f
Χ	χ	chi	h, kh (like the Spanish *j*)
Ψ	ψ	psi	ps
Ω	ω	omega	o (as in photo)

Combinations

αι	e as in red
ει, οι, υι	e as in tree
ου	oo as in moo
αυ	af
ευ	ef
γγ	ng (as in hungry)
γκ	hard g (ng inside a word)
ντ	d (nd inside a word)
μπ	b (mb inside a word)

Note on Transliteration

Transliteration of both ancient and modern Greek spelling is in transition from a rather parochial, idiosyncratic, and too often latinized ("Icarus" for "Ikaros") form to a simpler, more international style favored by the Greeks themselves.

However, because many Classical Greek names are so familiar in their anglicized versions, we have retained some of the traditional and most common transliterations: Aristotle, Sophocles, and Acropolis for Aristotelis, Sophoklis, and Akropolis.

Since the accent in Greek does not change the sound, merely the stress, we have accented only when a word is first introduced. We only accent two-syllable words when the accent is on the second syllable. We do not accent ancient place names since standard English forms do not usually match either ancient or modern Greek pronunciations and spellings.

—*Jane Winslow Eliot*

Outstanding Characteristics of the Greek Islands

The words "Greek island" have been so abused by advertisers and travel agents and mythologized by poets that expectations are likely to become confused. All the islands are indeed worth visiting—but not for the same reasons. The Ionian islands, which run down the mainland's west coast, are green islands, and are affected by their proximity to Italy. The Cyclades, clustered in the Aegean, are dry and more Classical, while the Dodecanese are quite varied and are influenced by nearby Turkey. The Argo-Saronics, in the quieter waters between Athens and the Peloponnese, are sophisticated and wealthy. The scattered Sporades, popular with Greeks, have woods as well as beaches, while four of the five northeastern Aegean islands are magically haunted by echoes of Classical Greece. And Crete is a veritable continent unto itself. The English are most attracted to Corfu, the Germans to Naxos, the Swedes to Rhodes, the Greeks to Tinos.

This chart is intended to serve as a summary of each island's **most notable characteristics**. The bigger, better-developed islands have almost everything, while some of the smaller ones perhaps offer just swimming and walking and good fresh fish. To choose wisely you must read on.

	SPORADES	Skiathos	Skopelos	Alonnisos	Skyros	*IONIANS*	Corfu	Lefkada
Sand beaches		●	●	●	●		●	●
Black sand beaches								
Pebble beaches		●	●					
Black pebble beaches								
No beaches								
Windsurfing		●	●				●	●
Scuba diving							●	●
Geological interest								
Mountainous landscape			●		●		●	●
Wooded/green		●	●	●			●	●
Arid								
Good walking/hiking		●	●	●			●	●
Auto/motorbike							●	●
No autos								
Bicycling								●
Local small boat transportation		●	●	●	●			
Picturesque villages							●	●
Exceptional architecture			●				●	
Modern day religious interest								
Special foodstuffs					●		●	●
Well known local wine								●
Island crafts			●		●			●
Neolithic interest								
Minoan/Mycenaean interest								
Classical interest								
Medieval interest					●		●	●
Venetian interest					●		●	●
Luxury facilities		●					●	
Shopping		●	●				●	
Very developed		●					●	
Less developed				●	●			●
Heavily touristed		●					●	
Nightlife		●					●	
Yacht facilities		●	●	●	●		●	●

Kefallonia	Ithaca	Zakynthos	Kythira	ARGO-SARONICS	Aegina	Poros	Hydra	Spetses	CYCLADES	Andros	Tinos	Mykonos	Delos	Syros	Naxos	Paros	Siphnos
•		•	•		•	•		•		•	•	•		•	•	•	•
	•						•							•			
													•				
		•			•	•	•	•		•		•			•	•	•
		•										•					
•		•								•	•				•	•	
•	•	•			•		•	•		•	•				•	•	•
		•	•			•		•									
			•				•					•	•	•			
	•		•		•		•	•		•					•	•	
•		•	•							•	•	•		•	•	•	
							•						•				
		•			•	•									•		
	•	•			•	•	•	•		•		•		•		•	•
							•					•	•		•	•	•
							•							•			
											•						
•		•			•					•				•	•		
•		•								•						•	
	•	•									•	•				•	•
														•			
					•	•					•		•		•	•	•
•	•	•	•		•					•	•				•		
•		•	•											•	•	•	
					•							•					
							•					•					
		•			•							•			•	•	
•	•		•				•			•	•			•			•
		•			•		•	•				•			•	•	•
							•					•			•	•	
•	•	•			•	•	•	•		•	•	•		•	•	•	•

	Milos	Santorini	*CRETE*	*DODECANESE*	Rhodes	Kastellorizo	Kasos	Karpathos
Sand beaches	●	●	●		●			●
Black sand beaches								
Pebble beaches		●					●	
Black pebble beaches		●						
No beaches						●		
Windsurfing	●	●	●		●			
Scuba diving			●	●				
Geological interest	●	●	●			●		
Mountainous landscape			●	●			●	●
Wooded/green			●					
Arid						●		
Good walking/hiking		●	●				●	
Auto/motorbike	●	●	●		●			
No autos								
Bicycling								
Local small boat transportation	●	●				●		●
Picturesque villages		●	●		●			●
Exceptional architecture		●			●			
Modern day religious interest		●	●					
Special foodstuffs								
Well known local wine		●	●					
Island crafts			●					
Neolithic interest	●							
Minoan/Mycenaean interest	●	●	●					
Classical interest	●	●	●		●			
Medieval interest			●		●			
Venetian interest			●					
Luxury facilities		●	●		●			
Shopping		●			●			
Very developed		●	●		●			
Less developed	●					●	●	●
Heavily touristed		●	●		●			
Nightlife		●	●		●			
Yacht facilities	●		●		●	●	●	●

	Chalki	Symi	Tilos	Nisyros	Kos	Astypalaia	Kalymnos	Leros	Patmos	*NORTHEASTERN AEGEANS*	Ikaria	Samos	Chios	Lesvos	Limnos	*NORTHERN GREECE*	Thasos	Samothrace
	•	•	•		•	•		•	•		•	•	•	•	•		•	
		•		•									•					
			•	•			•		•			•						
													•					
																		•
					•				•		•	•	•	•	•		•	
				•			•		•		•	•		•				
					•		•		•		•	•		•			•	•
								•				•		•			•	
		•		•					•						•			
		•	•	•		•		•	•		•	•	•	•			•	•
												•		•			•	
			•		•			•					•					
•	•						•		•			•	•				•	
		•		•			•				•			•			•	
		•							•				•	•				
									•					•				
	•		•										•		•			
					•							•						
	•							•				•	•	•				
															•			
						•								•				
				•							•	•	•	•		•	•	
				•		•			•			•	•	•				
					•								•					
				•							•		•				•	
				•							•	•					•	
•			•	•		•	•	•		•				•				•
				•				•			•						•	
				•				•			•							
	•	•		•	•	•	•	•		•	•	•	•			•		

BIBLIOGRAPHY

KEVIN ANDREWS, *Castles of the Morea*. Good survey of Byzantine, Frankish, Turkish, and Venetian fortresses situated in the wilds of the Peloponnese—but only part of the story. The rest is recounted in the book below.

———, *The Flight of Ikaros*. Firsthand impressions by a young American writer in Greece; mainly about Greeks at war with themselves before, during, and after the civil conflict of 1947 to 1949. Impressively honest and still relevant portrait of the modern Greek character.

MANOLIS ANDRONIKOS, *The Royal Graves at Vergina*. Authoritative account by the archaeologist who uncovered these Macedonian tombs.

J. T. BENT, *Aegean Islands: The Cyclades, or Life Among the Insular Greeks*. Originally published in 1884, this is a learned, anecdotal account, a marvelous book on the islands.

JOHN BOARDMAN, JASPER GRIFFIN, OSWYN MURRAY, EDS., *The Oxford History of the Classical World: Greece and the Hellenistic World* (1986). A selection of illustrated survey articles by experts in their fields on various aspects—myth, art, philosophy, etc.—of Archaic, Classical, and Hellenistic Greece. Up-to-date, articulate, always interesting.

C. M. BOWRA, *The Greek Experience*. A superb survey of the central concepts of Classical Greek religion, art, thought, and society.

———, *Periclean Athens*. A short study of Athens in the fifth century B.C. by one of the preeminent historians of the ancient world.

THOMAS BULFINCH, *The Age of Fable*. First published in 1855, this bowdlerized classic did much to popularize Greek, Roman, and Celtic mythology and is still widely read in schools as an introduction to the subject. Included as part of the collection called *Bulfinch's Mythology*.

WALTER BURKERT, *Greek Religion* (1977). From prehistory and the Minoan–Mycenaean Age to the "philosophical religion" of the pre-Socratics, Plato, and Aristotle. Includes discussions of the rituals, the sanctuaries, the various mystery religions, the gods (among them the so-called chthonic gods), and the oracles. Translated into English from the German.

BIBLIOGRAPHY

A. R. BURN, *The Pelican History of Greece*. Up-to-date, intelligent, entertaining, and slanted toward hard fact as opposed to wishful speculation.

JOHN CAMPBELL AND PHILIP SHERRARD, *Modern Greece*. The best account of modern Greece yet written, even though it stops with the ascension of the colonels' junta in 1967. Deals with its historical origins and developments, religion and literature, politics and social mores in sensitive, perceptive depth.

JOHN CHADWICK, *The Decipherment of Linear B*. A fascinating account of the work of Ventris and Chadwick in breaking the mysteries of the script known as Linear B. Full of suspenseful moments, at times it reads like a detective story.

———, *The Mycenaean World*. This is a highly readable general survey that covers every aspect of Mycenaean life.

NICHOLAS CHEETHAM, *Medieval Greece*. Useful, very readable history of a highly complicated period: post-Crusades, when a shifting balance of power between East and West was constantly changing the map of Greece.

ROBERT AND KATHLEEN COOK, *Southern Greece, An Archaeological Guide*. A brief but thorough and engagingly written guide to the major archaeological and historical sites of Attica, Delphi, and the Peloponnese. Excellent maps and plans.

F. M. CORNFORD, *Before and After Socrates*. The best short introduction to the Classical Greek philosophers, especially Socrates, Plato, and Aristotle.

———, *From Religion to Philosophy: A Study in the Origins of Western Speculation*. This distinguished historian of ancient philosophy uses anthropological and sociological insights as well as historical analysis to relate earlier Greek religious ideas to the later philosophies about which we know much more. In the process he illuminates both Greek religion and philosophy.

———, *The Mysterious Horses of Skyros*. The author argues that the small Skyrian ponies are the horses portrayed in the Elgin Marbles.

JOHN CROSSLAND AND DIANA CONSTANCE, *Macedonian Greece*. A bit out of date (1982) but extremely well researched, obviously at first hand, and lovingly written; a well-balanced blend of hard facts and subjective insights.

S. I. DAKARIS, *Dodona*. The site guide written by the excavator. The English translation is a little rough, but the information is clear on the ancient site of the oracle in Epirus, second in importance only to the one in Delphi.

RAE DALVEN, *The Jews of Ioannina*. Fascinating history and description of this unique Jewish community in Greece, the Romaniots, Greek-speaking Jews believed to have settled in Epirus at the time of Alexander the Great (356 to 323 B.C.) or perhaps before.

GUY DAVENPORT, TRANS., *Archilochos, Sappho, Alkman*. Three ancient island poets elegantly translated.

MARC S. DUBIN, *Greece on Foot, Mountain Treks and Island Trails*. Detailed descriptions of how and where to walk in Greece.

GERALD DURRELL, *My Family and Other Animals*. Hilarious account of the Durrells on pre–World War II Corfu, crammed with natural history of the island.

LAWRENCE DURRELL, *The Greek Islands*. Personal memories of the major Greek islands, from Corfu to Crete to Samothrace. Somewhat dated (1977) in terms of everyday facts, but rich in timeless observations on myth, folklore, ambience, and flora and fauna. Many fine photographs.

———, *Prospero's Cell*. Beautifully written memoir, a guide to the landscape and manners of Corfu before everyone went to see what the Durrells were raving about.

ALEXANDER ELIOT, *Concise History of Greece*. From the beginning through the 1970s.

———, *Earth, Air, Fire and Water*. An exploration of Greek life and legend and the author's own elemental philosophy of life.

ORIANA FALLACI, *A Man*. Passionate, thinly disguised novelization of the life and death of Alekos Panagoulis, the man who tried to assassinate the head of the Greek colonels' junta, written by the renowned Italian journalist who became his lover. Also a chilling portrait of the forces that maintained the dictatorship and survived its fall.

MANOS FALTAITS, *Skyros*. A history of the island from the time of Achilles to the present.

PATRICK LEIGH FERMOR, *Mani*. Fascinating description of this strange corner of the Peloponnese and its legends and people.

———, *Roumeli*. Superb ruminations on various aspects of northern Greece, especially Meteora and the Sarakatsanoi nomads, as well as on the Greek character in general.

ARTHUR FOSS, *Epirus*. A bit dated (1978), but a thorough presentation of the area.

JOHN FOWLES, *The Magus*. A mysterious, labyrinthine descent into the terrors of existential freedom, set in contemporary Greece, with superb evocations of the country and its people based in part on Fowles's observations as a teacher on the island of Spetses.

ROBIN LANE FOX, *Alexander the Great*. Perhaps the best modern book on the great conqueror. See also his *In Search of Alexander,* an excellent coffee-table version.

JOHN FREELY, *Crete* (1989). This is a good *vade mecum* in that Freely has gone to great pains to incorporate his own vast reading as well as his keen response to the nuances of the island.

KIMON FRIAR, *Modern Greek Poetry*. Superb anthology from Cavafy and Kazantzakis to Seferis, Elytis, and Gatsos et al., by the renowned translator of Kazantzakis's *The Odyssey: A Modern Sequel*.

NICHOLAS GAGE, *Eleni* (1983). A moving account of the heroism of the author's mother during the Greek Civil War (1947 to 1949) in the mountains of Communist-occupied northern Greece.

JAMES GRAHAM, *The Palaces of Crete* (1987). An excellent detailed guide to the palaces of Knossos, Phaistos, and more. Illustrated.

MICHAEL GRANT, *The Rise of the Greeks*. Excellent, recently published (1987) general survey of the diverse and often neglected worlds of pre-Classical Greece (c. 1000 to 490 B.C.), demonstrating that Greece was not only Athens, Sparta, and Corinth.

———, *The Classical Greeks* (1989). Continues the story of the previous volume up until the accession of Alexander the Great in 336 B.C.

ROBERT GRAVES, *The Greek Myths*. A weaving together of all the numerous variants of the Greek myths into a cohesive narrative, retold, annotated, and interpreted with wit and erudition by one of the great literary and iconoclastic minds of the 20th century. Invaluable to scholars, a delight to the general reader.

PETER GREENHALGH AND EDWARD ELIOPOULOS, *Deep into Mani*. A practical, up-to-date companion to Fermor's *Mani* for exploring this region of the Peloponnese. Fine descriptions and excellent photographs.

HERODOTUS, *The Histories*. These "researches" (*historia*) into the causes of the Persian wars with Athens, written by a contemporary of Pericles, also include fascinating descriptions of exotica observed by Herodotus on his travels throughout the Mediterranean world during the fifth century B.C.

HOMER, *Iliad*. The story of several weeks in the tenth and final year of the Trojan War, when Achilles' sulking anger over Agamemnon's taking of his concubine eventually causes the death of both his best friend, Patroklos, and the Trojan hero, Hector. Densely poetic, rich in metaphor, humanity, and divinities, it was the Classical Greeks' equivalent of a bible.

———, *Odyssey*. Odysseus's ten-year voyage home following the conclusion of the Trojan War, his adventures with the Cyclops, Sirens, etc. A rousing adventure story much different in character from the *Iliad*.

M. C. HOWATSON, ED., *The Oxford Companion to Classical Literature* (1989). This is about Greek, Hellenistic, and Roman literature, as the title says, but it is also about history, myth, religion, philosophy, music, and much more. It's in dictionary format, and you'll find yourself dipping into it again and again for anything to do with the ancient Classical world. Illustrated.

HUXLEY AND TAYLOR, *The Flowers of Greece and the Aegean*. An excellent field guide to the flowers and vegetation of the country. It is finely illustrated and is an invaluable companion on long walks through the countryside and mountains.

WERNER JAEGER, *Paideia: The Ideals of Greek Culture*. Illuminating, highly readable three-volume study of the development of the Greek mind, from Homer through Plato.

NIKOS KAZANTZAKIS, *Freedom or Death*. Also known as *Captain Michalis*, this story of a Cretan revolt against Ottoman rule in the late 19th century is a vivid, colorful picture of Crete at the time of the author's childhood.

———, *The Odyssey: A Modern Sequel*. His masterpiece, a 33,333-line epic poem brilliantly translated into rich American hexameters by Kimon Friar. Odysseus, the embodiment of the *élan vital*, pursues his destiny beyond Ithaca to the ends of the earth.

———, *Report to Greco*. His autobiography or, rather, self-portrait. Passionate, poetic, dealing with the themes of his literary works, in a "report" to one of his spiritual mentors, the Cretan-born painter, El Greco. Good descriptions of Crete and of visits to various Greek monasteries, particularly Mount Athos.

———, *Zorba the Greek*. The most accessible of his works for a Western audience. A great story with colorful characters set mainly in Crete in the early 20th century. The two main characters, the earthy Zorba and the intellectual, Europeanized narrator, embody the conflicting sides of what Kazantzakis saw as both his and man's eternal battle with himself.

RICHMOND LATTIMORE, *The Poetry of Greek Tragedy* and *Story Patterns in Greek Tragedy*. Brief, provocative, highly informative studies of the basic elements of Greek tragedy from the playwrights to hamartia and hubris by the best of modern translators and editors.

J. C. LAWSON, *Modern Greek Folklore and Ancient Greek Religion*. Rich in accounts of witches, werewolves, and other denizens of Cretan mountains and valleys.

WILLIAM LEAKE, *Travels in the Morea*. An early-19th-century account by an observant traveller.

———, *Travels in Northern Greece*. Colonel Leake was the British consul in Ioannina during Ali Pasha's rule.

LESLIE A. MARCHAND, ED., *Lord Byron: Selected Letters and Journals*. Brilliant, pungent, erudite: the next best thing to meeting the man himself. Volumes 1 and 11 deal with his two trips to Greece (1809 to 1810 and 1823 to 1824).

H. MELLERSH, *The Destruction of Knossos*. A highly readable work on the Minoan period as well as an examination of Knossos's palaces and the excavations.

HENRY MILLER, *The Colossus of Maroussi*. In 1939, with Europe in flames, Miller visited Lawrence Durrell and found the indomitable spirit of man in the light, landscape, and people of ancient and modern Greece. Perhaps his finest book, this certainly is one of the best personal views of the country ever written.

WILLIAM MILLER, *The Latins in the Levant*. Published in 1908, this remains the classic work on the Frankish occupation of Greece.

JOHN JULIUS NORWICH, *Byzantium: The Early Centuries*. Highly readable first volume (1989) of a planned three-volume history of the empire. Entertaining and enlightening.

ALEXANDROS PAPADIAMANTIS, *The Murderess*. One of Greece's foremost 19th-century novelists writes about the darker side of life on Skiathos.

APOSTOLOS PAPAGIANNOPOULOS, *Monuments of Thessaloniki*. The best small-format guide to Thessaloniki, well translated, with color photographs and a clear map.

I. A. PAPANGELOS, *Chalkidiki*. Small-format paperback chock-full of detailed information, maps, and color photographs covering all aspects of the area, including Mount Athos.

PAUSANIAS, *Guide to Greece*. Pausanias made his travels in the second century A.D., when many of the ancient temples were still in use. His guide is a fundamental reference work for modern archaeologists and fascinating reading for the more casual visitor.

J. D. S. PENDLEBURY, *The Archaeology of Crete*. An essential work for understanding the Minoan period.

F. E. PETERS, *The Harvest of Hellenism*. Alexander the Great and the Greek culture he spread throughout the Near East.

DILYS POWELL, *An Affair of the Heart*. A moving account of an Englishwoman's experiences with Greece and archaeology, particularly at Knossos, before and after World War II.

MICHAEL PRATT, *Britain's Greek Empire*. An account of what happened in the Ionian islands during British rule.

PANDELIS PREVELAKIS, *The Tale of a Town*. A wonderfully evocative picture of Rethymno by one of Crete's finest modern writers.

GEORGE PSYCHOUNDAKIS, *The Cretan Runner*. Translated and with an introduction by Patrick Leigh Fermor. Personal account by Cretan guide and message carrier for British guerrillas, including Fermor, hiding in Cretan mountains during Nazi occupation. A vivid, earthy, very Cretan memoir.

MARY RENAULT, *The King Must Die* and *The Bull from the Sea*. Absorbing novels of prehistorical Athens and Crete centering around the myth of Theseus, Athens's first king, and his escape from the Minotaur in the labyrinth of Knossos.

———, *The Alexander Trilogy*. From the wild Macedonian mountains of Alexander the Great's childhood to the labyrinthine intrigues that followed his death, an epic and entertaining three-volume novelization of his life and times. Renault's *The Nature of Alexander*, an essay on the man with superb color photographs, is an excellent companion to the novels.

COLIN RENFREW, *The Emergence of Civilization: The Cyclades and the Aegean in the Third Millennium B.C.* A very good standard account.

G. M. A. RICHTER, *A Handbook of Greek Art*. If you want only one book on ancient Greek art, get this one.

STEVEN RUNCIMAN, *Byzantine Style and Civilization*. The best short treatment of the subject by one of its unquestioned masters.

J. A. SAKELLARAKIS, *A Guide to the Herakleion Museum*. Written by the director of the museum, this is an essential book if you wish to understand some of the riches contained within the museum collections.

TIM SALMON, *The Mountains of Greece, a Walker's Guide*. Detailed descriptions of how and where to walk in the Greek mountains.

VINCENT SCULLY, *The Earth, the Temple, and the Gods*. This is an exciting book that connects the locations of temples with the roles of the gods.

GEORGE SEFERIS, *Collected Poems*. An excellent annotated translation by Edmund Keeley and Philip Sherrard. Spare and beautiful verse that powerfully evokes the Greek landscape by perhaps the country's most noted poet.

TIM SEVERIN, *The Jason Voyage*. Entertaining story of a real-life voyage with good background material linking the Argonaut story with present-day Volos and elsewhere.

L. S. STAVRIANOS, *The Balkans Since 1453*. And up to 1956. A hefty account, lucidly written, of this still-volatile area.

I. F. STONE, *The Trial of Socrates*. The noted journalist's provocative assertion that Socrates was an antidemocratic elitist and thus justifiably condemned to death by Athenians. Engrossing, persuasive, and illuminating, whether or not you finally agree.

RICHARD STONEMAN, *A Literary Companion to Travel in Greece*. A compilation of travel pieces, poetry, and literature written over the centuries about many places in Greece. Requires a taste for 18th- to 19th-century English, but has an excellent, informed introduction and commentaries.

THUCYDIDES, *The Peloponnesian War*. Unfinished at the time of his death, but still the best account of the war between Sparta and Athens ever written. Brilliantly recorded by an Athenian general cashiered after a defeat at Amphipolis, who then travelled throughout Greece, including Sparta, and got both sides of the story.

VASSILIS VASSILIKOS, *Z*. A novel about the famous 1963 political assassination in Thessaloniki, which became an international *cause célèbre* through the Costa-Gavras film by the same name starring Yves Montand.

EMILY VERMEULE, *Greece in the Bronze Age*. A scholarly, technical book, but well written and even funny.

TIMOTHY WARE, *The Orthodox Church*. Excellent introduction to both the history of the Greek Orthodox church and the ways of its faith and worship.

———, *The Orthodox Way*. A compelling presentation of Orthodox beliefs.

MARTIN YOUNG, *Corfu and the Other Ionian Islands*. A bit out of date, but a very impressive survey of the islands.

EDUARD ZELLER, *Outlines of the History of Greek Philosophy*. One of the clearest surveys of Greek thought, from the pre-Socratics to the ascendancy of the Roman Empire.

—*John Chapple and Tom Stone*

ATHENS

By Jane Winslow Eliot

Jane Winslow Eliot was brought up in Europe and met her husband, Alexander, when she was a researcher/reporter at Time *magazine. They raised their children abroad, spending several years in Greece, and return there frequently. She has written a guidebook to Greece and contributed to* Travel & Leisure, Atlantic, *and* Horticulture *magazines.*

Every city, created as it is by its own people, is distinctive. What, then, distinguishes Athens from other smog-filled, sulfur-fumed, traffic-congested cities of the world?

In a short history of the planet, Athens would get a chapter. Probably all Western nations could claim Athens as part of their heritage, and its influence can be traced far to the East. During the great age of the city, from the eighth through the fourth centuries B.C., the Greeks' gods touched down on Earth and became human, while Athenians, in turn, strove to become god-like. For some few glorious centuries they met, and the fire that blazed from Athens lit the otherwise dark stage of history, igniting the hearts of humankind.

So a tour of Athens takes the traveller over more levels of history than most city tours. First it leads through the contemporary urban terrain and over the stones of past ones. Then it points back through history, setting the grid of facts upon which the flowers of human endeavor have climbed. On yet another level a guide to Athens must include those stories and myths that people tell to make a difference in their lives. Athens was rich in strange yet revealing stories; the myths of gods, goddesses, demigods, nymphs, and satyrs were its special means to make understandable puzzling aspects of the world of nature and human nature.

In flat historical terms Athens might leave a traveller

unmoved, or at best wondering what all the shouting is about. That statue in the National Archaeological Museum—is it Zeus or just another well-kept, middle-aged thunderbolt-thrower? Understanding what went into the ancient city is crucial to understanding Athens today.

The story of Athens begins in Neolithic times, some 5,000 years ago. It fused with the rest of Greece for a while, as civilizing influences came from the islands and from farther east. Later the Doric invasion from the north brought fresh spirit; new gods touched down. Then, some 2,700 years ago, Athens exploded in glory onto the world stage. There is still no good explanation as to why this happened. After a thousand years the pagan era, one of the most inventive in human history, came to an end. The amazing originality of the city, however, found new ways to channel its spirit, welcoming a new god, shaping new values with the insight of old ones. The Christian Bible was filtered through Greek to come out as we know it. Greek literature, philosophy, and art opened the door for the Italian Renaissance. Then came the Turks, and for 400 years the Greek religion, language, and traditions were maintained by the Greek Orthodox church.

The Turks fortified the Acropolis, then settled down on its north side. An uneasy truce ensued. Finally, in 1821, the Greek people declared their War of Independence. Seven years later the Peloponnese was indeed free. (Athens was freed in 1833 and was made the capital of modern Greece in 1834.) It would take more than another century for the Greek nation we know today to become an independent unit. True independence would be achieved piecemeal and never peacefully. Internal struggles racked the nation. Out of practice in the heady atmosphere of liberty, the Greeks were first pressured by the great European powers to accept a foreign king. In due course, however, what was the Royal Palace became the House of Parliament. Despite the ravages of World War II and the devastation of civil war, Greece industrialized and internationalized. It became a full-fledged member of the European Community, from which flows a good deal of vitally needed economic support. Both right wing and left have moved closer to the center. Greek politics, although still somewhat volatile, are parliamentarian.

Greater Athens contains more than a third of the nation's population; some three and a half million of the ten million Greeks live here. Geographically it's a gateway to the Middle East, but Greeks see themselves with both feet planted firmly in Europe. Soon new economic and political changes will bind EC members together even more firmly. In the meantime, the last 20 years of government have encouraged some 80 percent of the people to own their own apartments or homes. That makes for stability. Greek revolutionaries become lambs when they have to fix a leaking roof or plant a vegetable garden—much less gather the drachmas to add another floor to the house.

The traveller's Athens revolves around a small area of a city whose greatness extends over time rather than space. It is easy to get hold of. To understand the layout of Athens, imagine the part of main interest as a sailing ship: On the bridge you will find Syntagma Square, which is as it should be, Syntagma being the center of most travellers' activity. Directly north, at the tip of the mast, rather like a flag, unfurls one of the world's greatest sculpture collections, the National Archaeological Museum, spanning some 5,500 years of Greek civilization. Just northeast of Syntagma you will find fashionable Kolonaki, like color in the jib, the boom of the boat being the two main streets, Panepistimiou and Stadiou, which lead from Syntagma to working Athens's Omonia Square. The bow points east up Vasilissis Sophias Avenue, or embassy row, and farther on bends north to the swank suburb of Kifissia on the gentle slopes of Mount Penteli. The real treasure, the hill of the Acropolis, is stored in the hold, along with the ancient Agora and the old town, Plaka. The anchor chain dangling south is Syngrou Avenue, a freeway-like stretch that leads to beaches, seaports, and airports.

MAJOR INTEREST

Acropolis: Parthenon, Temple of Athena Nike,
  Erechtheion, museum, ancient theaters
National Archaeological Museum
Agora: Stoa of Attalos, Hephaisteion
Plaka, old town
Lycabettus Hill: Fabulous views
Syntagma Square: Parliament, cafés
Kolonaki Square: Shops, galleries
Small museums: Benaki, Goulandris Museum of
  Cycladic Art, Byzantine Museum, National Gallery,
  Jewish Museum

Ancient Athens is like a theme park, the theme being political freedom. Its greatest art, its greatest monuments, even its early human-size and very human-passioned gods reflect this.

The beginnings of democracy as we know it in the West can be traced to sixth- and fifth-century B.C. Athens. In the little city-state named Athens, which comprised the city itself and the land of Attica around it, each citizen was a member of the Assembly and could cast a vote. Citizens were compelled by law to do jury duty, to take their places in the Assembly, to cast their votes—and to attend the theater. Surprising as this last obligation seems, the plays were quite instructive. Theater was like an ancient public school. In each case citizens were paid to perform their civic duties, losing their allowance if they failed to show.

A time trip through the remains of ancient Athens gives the traveller a chance to relive the most glorious years of Greek history, a history that now belongs to the world. Athenian ideals and achievements pushed the West in directions that people the world over still long to follow.

The Acropolis is home to all that. Climb up to the **Propylaea**, the massive entrance gate that guards the sacred rock, and see what all the shouting is about. About halfway up, pick a spot with a panoramic view of the sea; before entering the sacred precinct, stop to look around. From this vantage point you can take in several historic places, all with stories that together illuminate the events that took place during the thousand years of what Edgar Allan Poe termed "the glory that was Greece."

THE ACROPOLIS AND ANCIENT ATHENS

Salamis

Stop on the marble path to the Parthenon and look out over the water: There to the right, just beyond the port of Piraeus, is the quiet island of Salamis (Salamína), which, although Greeks visit often, has very little other than history to attract foreigners. One day, though, in the early years of the fifth century B.C., the emperor of all the Persians and most of the known world, Xerxes, the Great King of Kings, sat on a marble throne high on a cliff outside Athens at Egaleo, overlooking the narrow waters between himself and the little island. There was to be a sea battle between his troops and the Athenian army. Some 1,000 fully manned Persian triremes rode the waves. A Persian victory was prophesied. The great oracle of Delphi had stated flatly, when pressed, that Athens would be saved only by "a wooden wall." A wooden barricade had defended the Acropolis, but the emperor's troops had burned that, along with the rest of the abandoned city. (Athens's inhabitants had all moved to Salamis before Xerxes' attack.) Xerxes could still see smoke drifting across the blue sky.

No less a traitor than Themistocles, the general of the Athenians, had advised Xerxes to block both entrances to the strait. According to Themistocles' secret message, the Greeks were terrified and planned to slip away before dawn. Now all the Persians had to do was to seal them up in the strait and attack. It would give Xerxes great pleasure to wipe away the historic stain of Persia's defeat at Marathon.

Themistocles, however, was not a traitor. Being a good pupil of Athena, he would use trickery to confound Xerxes. Themistocles trusted a wooden wall of a sort other than the one the Delphic oracle had seemed to mean—his navy, consisting of 380 light, easily maneuverable ships armed with sharp brass battering rams at their prows.

Xerxes watched now as some Greek ships turned tail, scudding swiftly away. Behind them the Persian navy lumbered majestically. Once the Persian ships stood packed like caviar in the narrow straits, Themistocles gave a signal. The Greek ships whirled about and jammed their brass prows into the hulls of Xerxes' ships. By nightfall most of the Persian vessels were at the bottom of the Saronic Gulf.

There's a story that when Xerxes descended upon empty Athens, he found no ordinary wine left behind. The Athenians had deliberately spoiled it for him by putting pine resin in the wine casks. Returning victorious after Salamis, the Athenians naturally broke out the wine. Tasted in the flush of victory, it did not seem so bad. Hence comes *retsína,* that oddly delicious wine that is so characteristically Greek.

The victory of free citizens over an empire of slaves made Athens the cynosure of Greece. Pericles, its elected leader in the next generation, inspired the Athenians to build a sumptuous temple to the goddess Athena, their special protector. The Parthenon, here on the Acropolis, was to be the city's crowning glory.

Areopagus

Just across from the Acropolis rises a famous old hill known as the Areopagus. (It's really just a slightly dangerous rock to climb, fun if your shoes have rubber soles.) The story goes that Ares, god of war, was tried here for murder by his fellow

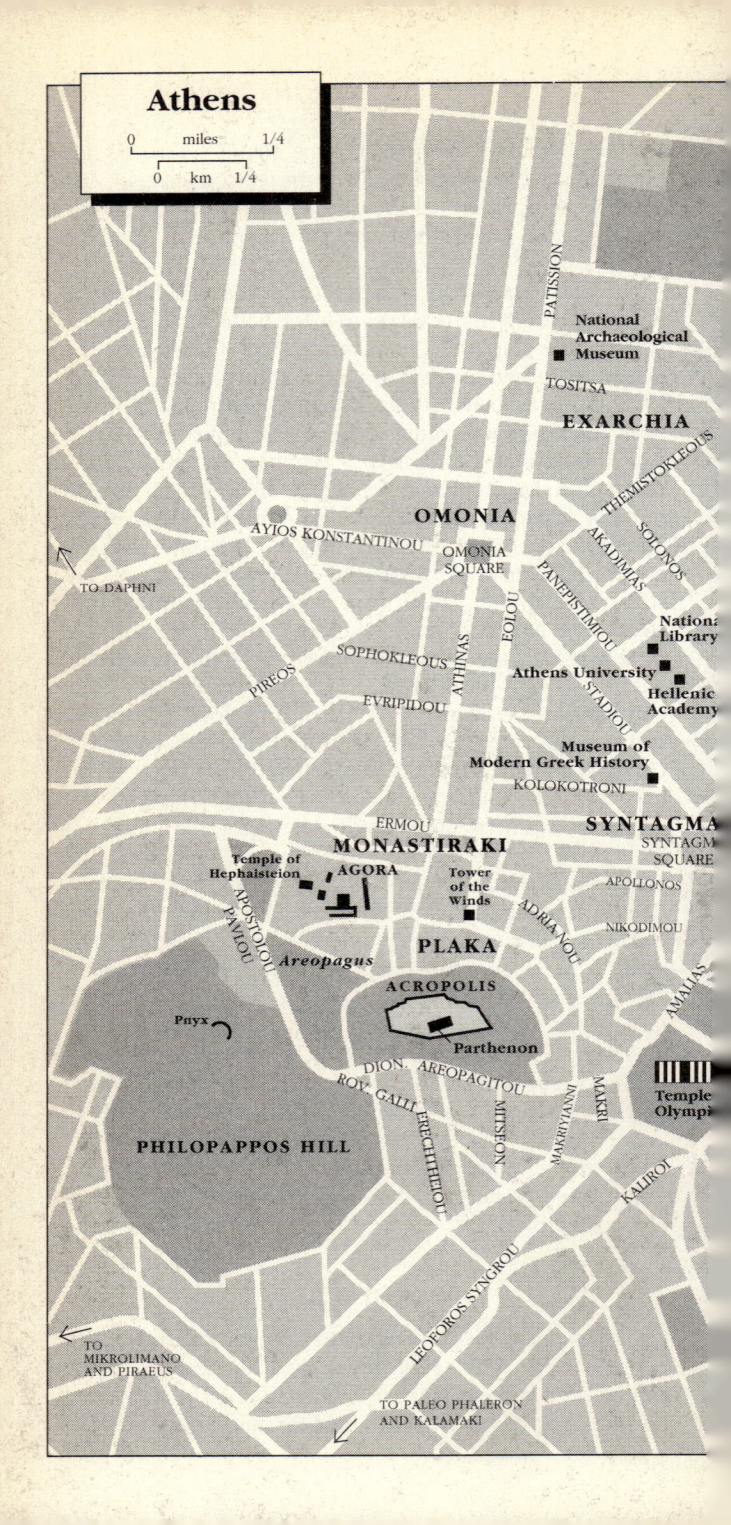

Athens

0 miles 1/4
0 km 1/4

- National Archaeological Museum
- PATISSION
- TOSITSA
- **EXARCHIA**
- **OMONIA**
- AYIOS KONSTANTINOU
- OMONIA SQUARE
- TO DAPHNI
- THEMISTOKLEOUS
- SOLONOS
- AKADIMAS
- PANEPISTIMIOU
- National Library
- Athens University
- Hellenic Academy
- PIREOS
- SOPHOKLEOUS
- ATHINAS
- EOLOU
- EVRIPIDOU
- STADIOU
- Museum of Modern Greek History
- KOLOKOTRONI
- ERMOU
- **MONASTIRAKI**
- **SYNTAGMA**
- SYNTAGMA SQUARE
- APOLLONOS
- NIKODIMOU
- Temple of Hephaisteion
- AGORA
- Tower of the Winds
- ADRIANOU
- **PLAKA**
- APOSTOLOU PAVLOU
- *Areopagus*
- **ACROPOLIS**
- Parthenon
- Pnyx
- DION. AREOPAGITOU
- ROV. GALLI ERECHTHEIOU
- MITSEON
- MAKRIYIANNI
- MAKRI
- AMALIAS
- Temple Olympi[eion]
- **PHILOPAPPOS HILL**
- LEOFOROS SYNGROU
- KALLIROI
- TO MIKROLIMANO AND PIRAEUS
- TO PALEO PHALERON AND KALAMAKI

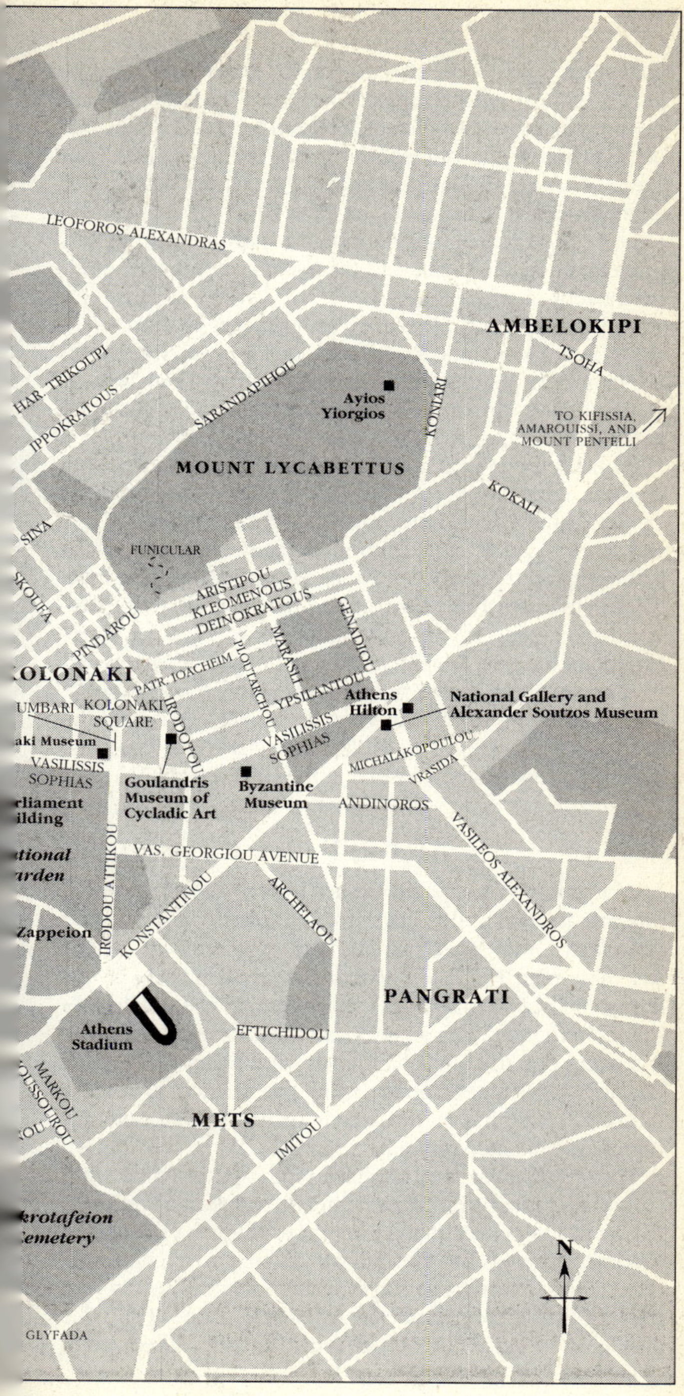
LEOFOROS ALEXANDRAS
AMBELOKIPI
TSOHA
HAR. TRIKOUPI
IPPOKRATOUS
SARANDAPIHOU
Ayios Yiorgios
KONIARI
TO KIFISSIA, AMAROUISSI, AND MOUNT PENTELLI
MOUNT LYCABETTUS
KOKALI
SINA
FUNICULAR
SKOUFA
ARISTIPOU
KLEOMENOUS
DEINOKRATOUS
GENADIOU
PINDAROU
MARASLI
PLOUTARCHOU
KOLONAKI
PATR. IOACHEIM
YPSILANTOU
Athens Hilton
National Gallery and Alexander Soutzos Museum
KOLONAKI SQUARE
IRODOTOU
VASILISSIS SOPHIAS
MICHALAKOPOULOU
VRASIDA
Goulandris Museum of Cycladic Art
Byzantine Museum
ANDINOROS
IRODOU ATTIKOU
VAS. GEORGIOU AVENUE
VASILEOS ALEXANDROS
ARCHELAOU
KONSTANTINOU
Zappeion
PANGRATI
Athens Stadium
EFTICHIDOU
MARKOU
METS
IMITOU
N
GLYFADA

gods; thus it is not surprising that this became the seat of justice, known as the Hill of Curses (*arai*). Later it also became the seat of Athens's early government of aristocrats, descendants of the original ten tribes of the city-state. Because of abuses, the aristocrats were eventually stripped of all their powers by Solon the Lawgiver and retained only the right to protect the constitution. The power to make and implement laws was put into an assembly composed of all the citizens of Athens.

The dynamics of these early experiments in representative government underwent considerable refinement over the centuries, developing by trial and error. Their lessons were not lost on the founders of the American form of government.

Probably the most famous person to appear on the Areopagus was Saint Paul the Apostle. It is believed that when he came to Athens he went right down to the Agora, as Socrates was wont to do in earlier times. There he began to talk to whoever would listen. The Stoic and Epicurean philosophers were particularly interested and brought Paul up to the Areopagus to speak to the Assembly, for, as the King James Version of the New Testament reports: "All the Athenians and strangers which were there spent their time in nothing else, but either to tell or to hear some new thing." Dionysius the Areopagite, for one, listened and believed. He was Paul's first convert to "the Unknown God" in the skeptical city.

Pnyx

Just beyond the Areopagus toward the sea rises a small hill that the ancients called "the crowded place," or Pnyx. And crowded it was. After 500 B.C. this is where the Athens Assembly met. The Assembly comprised all citizens of Athens, some 30,000 males. They were paid for the privilege of being there. Sometimes they were fined for nonattendance if matters of particular importance were being considered. Because a 5,000-person minimum was needed to make a quorum, often that many citizens had to squash onto the bleachers built atop the hill.

The Pnyx is located on peaceful, pine-planted Philopappos Hill, where walking the mostly unmarked paths is a lovely way to wait for the sunset on the Parthenon. There is a small, tree-shaded *kafeneío,* but the hill lends itself to picnics, too. (Legend has it that the prison in which Socrates spent his last days is somewhere near the center of Philopappos Hill.) The excellent sound-and-light performance (see Athens After

Dark, below) is viewed from the old Pnyx amphitheater. To reach the park go straight instead of turning right off Areopagitou in front of the Herodes Atticus theater.

Herodes Atticus and Dionysus Theaters

On the southern flank of the Acropolis sits the second-century A.D. Herodes Atticus amphitheater (*odeion*), visible on your right as you walk up to the ticket booth. Named for a famous art patron of the period, the Herodes Atticus is open as a tourist site during the day, but the best way to experience it fully is to attend an evening performance here. Athens puts on a special summer festival that includes ballets and symphonies as well as Greek tragedies and comedies (see Athens After Dark, below). If you visit the city during the festival months, you should set aside at least one evening for this wonderful theater. It is a splendid place to see any kind of performance, and the acoustics, as usual in Greek amphitheaters, are excellent. Sitting out on a warm summer evening overlooking the lights of Athens, watching the stars appear in the darkening sky, you will feel the ghosts of centuries moving in the shadows.

The theater that the Greeks of the Golden Age actually attended is just east of the Herodes Atticus and is dedicated to the god Dionysus, patron of the unsettling art of drama. The worship of Dionysus, whose rituals introduced wine making to Greece, began in Attica in the tenth century B.C. In ancient Greece the major festival of Anthesterion took place each year in February, when the previous year's vintage was opened and dedicated to Dionysus. This was a highly charged, passionate religious ceremony. First a goat was sacrificed (the word *tragedy* means "song of the goat"). Next, devotees masquerading as goats would sing and dance, chanting in unison dithyrambs, or hymns, that induced a kind of wild ecstasy. After the consumption of meat and drink came the Odes of the Comos (from which the word *comedy* derives), obscene songs and spontaneous political satires that amused the throng. They were sung as a procession of men pranced about with grotesque phallic symbols. Sometimes the rituals of Dionysus got out of hand, and dreadful things happened. It was not surprising that as Athens became more urbanized the wild orgies were modified. Around the sixth century B.C. Thespis, with the backing of the tyrant Pisistratus, took the outlandish rituals and formalized them into real theater. They still contained the dark passions of the earlier Dionysiacs, but now the intoxicating ceremonies were enacted on stage. Thus was the earliest theater on the Acropolis dedicated to the god Dionysus.

The Theater of Dionysus was originally built of wood; not until the fourth century B.C. was it rebuilt in stone. Although Plato says that it seated 30,000 people, modern scholars estimate that a maximum 17,000 could have squeezed in. Here the great tragedians Aeschylus, Sophocles, and Euripides saw their work produced. Each wrote perhaps a hundred plays, which were presented in cycles of three, with a satyr play thrown in to round off the day. Athenian citizens, as mentioned earlier, were paid to attend; it was deemed important even then to have an educated populace in order to maintain a strong democracy.

Aeschylus and Sophocles, both working at the beginning of the fifth century B.C., dominated the scene. Later, when Athens began undertaking adventures that were to lead her into perversions of power and ultimate disasters, the skeptical and bitterly ironic Euripides placed his work before the public. He eventually left Athens for the court of the Macedonian king.

Temple of Athena Nike

Despite the depredations of time, the exquisite little Temple of Athena Nike, floating to the south of the Propylaea, remains delectable as a succession of reconstructions. Built in 427 B.C. on a Mycenaean bastion, it celebrates a victory (*nike*) that came late.

The artist who adorned Nike's temple with bas-reliefs came up with a good explanation for the goddess's tardiness: The strap of her sandal had come untied. She stopped to fix it, and that's what delayed her. Thirteen pieces of the frieze that encircled the temple are now in the Acropolis Museum. In separate scenes the artist depicts Nike approaching the beleaguered city, losing her sandal, bending to tie it back on, hurrying through the air, her delicate garments lightly pressed against her beautiful body, and finally landing on tiptoe, half breathless, to be welcomed by Athena.

Nike's temple has not been allowed to enjoy its well-earned peace. Among numerous unhappy incidents, in 1686 the Turks took it apart to use the site for military purposes. It was reconstructed according to drawings after Greek independence was achieved. In 1936 the temple was again dismantled, this time so the foundations could be reinforced.

Just over 50 years later it is being subjected to the same process all over again.

Erechtheion

This so-called Old Temple, which faces the north flank of the Parthenon along the Sacred Way, is a strange building in both appearance and history. Dedicated to Athena, Poseidon, and the ancient earth figure Erechtheus, it is built on two levels— the late-sixth-century structure atop earlier foundations— and lacks aesthetic unity. In our time the structure has been restored with dead-white blocks of marble mortised in among the remaining aged blue-gray limestone, and the former glorious **caryatids** (figures of women on whose heads rests the porch roof) have been replaced with cast versions. The originals may be found huddled in the Acropolis Museum. Stripped, debased, pockmarked, and forlorn, the building is nonetheless clothed in mystery by its puzzling legends.

The first and oddest is the story that Hephaestus, the lame god of the forge, once tried to take Athena by force, and she pushed him off. As he fell, his seed impregnated the earth goddess Gaia, who as a result gave birth to Erechtheus (sometimes called Erechthonius). Gaia's odd offspring had a snake's tail. She gave him to Athena as a foster child, and Athena, in turn, entrusted him to King Kecrops of Athens. The infant was to be kept in a basket that was never to be uncovered. But it was opened, of course, and here the story blurs. Some say there was only a serpent, or two serpents, inside. In any case, the two princesses who had peeked went mad and leaped to their deaths from a cliff on the Acropolis. The nebulous Erechtheus, serpentine son of Gaia, Athena, and Hephaestus, was given a place of worship in the Old Temple.

In time, as the primeval chthonic gods (that is, gods of the earth) were replaced by the Olympian pantheon, a new legend attached itself to the Erechtheion.

This myth concerns a struggle between Athena, goddess of reason, and her shaggy uncle Poseidon, god of the sea (and of earthquakes). Standing on the Acropolis beside the Old Temple in the presence of Zeus and the other gods, these two great deities contended for Attica. Poseidon, in his direct way, struck the rock with his trident. Instantly a saline spring burst forth. Athena, more agriculturally minded, tapped the earth with her foot, causing an olive tree to grow from the stony ground. Victory was declared hers. An olive tree still graces the spot where the struggle is said to have occurred.

The Parthenon

The Parthenon is not so much marble as idea. It shows how true, alive, and balanced thought can be. In ancient times the temple was dedicated to Athena, the goddess of wisdom and the virgin protector of Athens.

Built in the middle of the fifth century B.C., the Parthenon was the dream of Pericles, whom Thucydides called "the first of Athenians." He held sway over his fellow citizens from the time he came to power until his death 32 years later.

His vision of a rebuilt Acropolis, brilliant with the best that Athenian craftsmen could produce, came at a moment of internal peace in Athenian affairs. After the Persians were defeated at Salamis and retreated from Greek territory once and for all, Athens prospered. Toward the middle of the century funds in the Athenian treasury had reached a handsome 5,000 talents—enough to buy 30 million man-hours of skilled labor. With this wealth at the disposal of the assembly, Pericles gained a good deal of popularity by exhorting the citizens to dispense large amounts. Thanks to this statesman-politician, Athens already possessed a powerful and well-kept navy that was in virtual command of the Aegean. This adventure in empire, going as it did against the precepts of rights and freedoms written into the Athenian constitution, would soon weaken Athens dangerously. But meanwhile the ambitious Pericles wished to bedeck his city, to make it the magnificent center of his growing power, and at the same time to spread some of the surplus funds among the citizens.

There were voices of dissent, of course, but once the plan was agreed to the city proceeded boldly. The Acropolis was cleared and the temples that had been smashed by the Persians were lovingly replaced with new ones. The new foundations for the Parthenon were laid on top of the remains of an older temple to the goddess Athena. (Some of the sculptures from this earlier structure are preserved in the Acropolis Museum.) From then on, the city's most important and impressive religious ceremonies would take place in the Parthenon. It also served as the city treasury.

Kallikrates and Iktinos, both architects, designed the Parthenon under the supervision of Phidias, who was in charge of public works. (Kallikrates also designed the Temple of Athena Nike.) Phidias is said to have conceived all the sculptures on the friezes, metopes, and pediments that circled the upper walls inside and out. Legends of the gods, stories of the ancients, and depictions of the procession of the Great Panathenaia were subjects for these carvings. (The most ancient and revered of Athenian festivals, the Panathenaia was a week-long celebration with chariot and horse races, athletic competitions, musical contests, dancing, torch and trireme races, and poetry recitals. The festival culminated in the grand procession so beautifully depicted in the sculptures of the Parthenon.) Phidias delegated the work to many other sculptors under his direction, but he completed the chryselephantine statue of Athena Parthenos himself.

Set on a wooden frame, this was a 38-foot statue of the virgin goddess constructed from the city's store of ivory and gold. It was the largest statue ever made of these precious materials. The ivory was used for the face, hands, and arms, while the clothes were sheets of pure gold. Phidias, later accused of stealing a portion of the gold, arranged to have it unbolted and weighed. Not an ounce was missing from the ton of gleaming metal, so back it went. (Annoyed with his accusers, the sculptor hastened to Olympia to create an equally magnificent ivory-and-gold statue of Zeus.) The splendid statue of Athena was set inside the Parthenon, where it shone in golden brilliance as it caught the first rays of the midsummer sun.

The Parthenon was built in the austere Doric style but was lighter and slimmer than earlier Doric temples. The source of this apparent lightness can be traced to some subtle construction methods. Tradition holds that all the columns of the building bulge slightly, a feature known as entasis. Brought into harmony with the curve of the human eye, their lines seem straighter yet more vigorous than perfectly vertical shafts, which in contrast appear concave. The thickness of the parabolic bulge can be as much as four inches, as on the floor, or almost invisible to the naked eye, as in some of the flutings. In addition, all the pillars lean inward at an angle of less than one degree. Of course, little of this is true of the areas that have been reconstructed, since such subtlety died with the builders of the Parthenon. Some conservators already dismiss the existence of these old calculations.

The builders of the Parthenon employed a host of small contractors to chisel its many stones and capitals, and it thus displays a wonderful variety within sameness, as trees do in a forest. The play of light and shadow flowing down along the extra-deep flutings of the columns makes for constantly changing motion in perfect stillness.

The columns' capitals, also created in the severe Doric mode, might be abstractions of the human head: Instead of cushioning the weight of the roof, they channel it to other parts of the structure as if it were thought. The column is like the human body, or a tree, standing firmly. It brings the strength of the ground up through the capital to meet the pediment, where the gods live, and transfers the weight of the pediment down through the capital to bedrock.

In the midst of the modern city's asphalt and concrete, the Acropolis, with its Parthenon, stands as a shining citadel to an ideal. Freedom—spiritual, intellectual, and political—was the Greek promise the Parthenon still lets no one forget. Over the centuries visitors have come here to plumb its mysteries, retrue their energies, and reaffirm their hopes. There is bitter irony in the fact that the Parthenon's completion took place as Athens itself was eating up the little islands of the Aegean and beginning its long slide into a war that would bring it ultimately to ruin—and a sleep of centuries. The world went on, seemingly untouched by the great Athenian experiment, settling back into little kingdoms and warring empires. The Parthenon, however, stood firm, a beacon in the dark. Her columns rose above the Attican plain, attesting to an ideal that would not die.

The Parthenon has changed over two and a half millennia. It has been transformed in ways that have appealed to many, but to others these intrusions appear to be nothing less than catastrophic. In the sixth century A.D. the temple was turned into a Christian church, dedicated first, appropriately, to Ayia Sophia (Holy Wisdom), then to the Virgin Mother of God (Theotokos). Alterations were made, particularly to the east end, for the new form of worship. During the Turkish occupation an exquisite mosque was built into the Parthenon. At another time a Turkish garrison stored explosives here. When attacking Venetians bombarded the Acropolis in 1687, an unfortunate hit set the explosives off like fireworks, and the temple suffered considerably. Fourteen columns, friezes, and entablature were blown to pieces, and a group of horses on the west pediment was smashed on the rocks below.

Further damage was done by Lord Elgin in his self-appointed task of "protecting" Phidias's lovely carvings. In the early 19th century the famous (or infamous) British diplomat was given permission by the Turks to take what he wanted from the ruins. Over a period he removed almost all the sculptures. There are a few rather badly damaged pieces still to be seen in the Acropolis Museum, and part of the inner frieze, also in bad condition, is still *in situ;* the rest, to the continuing irritation of the Greeks, is on view in the British Museum in London. Against all odds (as in their battle against the Persians), the Greeks have been demanding their return. Byron is said to have written roughly of the good Briton:

> Noseless himself, he brings home noseless blocks,
> To show at once the ravages of time and pox.

And:

> First on the head of him who did this deed
> My curse shall light—on him and all his seed.

Once they had won their independence from the Turks, the Greeks set about restoring the Acropolis to its previous Classical simplicity. For good or ill, this meant getting rid of the accretions of centuries. Sadly, however, they could not recover the wondrous statue of Athena, or the beautiful marbles Lord Elgin took, or the splendor of the paraphernalia of ritual.

The changes brought about by the archaeologists and restorers are as controversial as any in the long history of the building's transformations. According to Yannis Stavrakakis, a technical assistant to the Parthenon Restoration Office, he and his colleagues have had to dismantle the work of previous 20th-century restorers because much of it was done with concrete molds and iron bands that leached into the marble, causing it to expand and break. Pollution has also played a part, causing a kind of marble death that has made the columns begin to crumble beneath their own weight. All the weakened stones will have to be replaced with "healthy" ones; some of these have been gathered from fragments found on the Acropolis, and some new blocks have been taken from the ancient quarries at Penteli, where stones for the original building were cut. This time around the columns will be repaired with titanium clamps and dowels, to be mortared into the rosy Penteli marble, unfortunately with a white cement.

The most recent elements that have changed the Parthenon are air pollution and tourism. Efforts are being made in Athens for stricter smog control through curbs on industry, dispersion of factories to the far provinces, and restrictions on automobile use. These have made a little headway against the problem, but much more will have to be done. As for tourism, literally millions of people have tramped across the monument's vulnerable marble floors, too many of them in boots and high heels. Now the restored ruins can be seen only from the outside, mantled in ugly scaffolding and guarded by a huge steel crane.

The Parthenon was built not to measure but to "measured thought." No matter what anyone does to it, or has done, the old temple-church-mosque, restored or unrestored, glows with potent energy, silent and magnificent. To see the ruins of the Parthenon is to see transforming powers at work. The missing parts have passed not into thin air but into human consciousness.

Acropolis Museum

This is one of the best small museums of the world. Dusty and ill kept, it nonetheless contains some very important sculptures and is well worth a visit.

Among the sculptures not to be missed are the early-sixth-century B.C. pediment depicting Herakles wrestling, probably with Achelous, the river god, from an earlier parthenon; the sixth-century B.C. Moschophoros, a man carrying a calf; the loping hound; the *korai,* statues of maidens dedicated to Athena; metopes from the Parthenon interior frieze depicting the Panathenaia, left over from Lord Elgin's grab; slabs from the parapet of the Temple of Athena Nike, including the famous image of Nike fixing her sandal; and the caryatids, the 22-foot-high columns in the form of women carrying baskets, which once upheld the Erechtheion's porch.

The following little-known story sheds light on the incredibly life-like hound sculpture: There was once a hunting dog named Laelaps who could catch anything that ran. But there was also a fox who could outrun anything. Inevitably they became joined in a chase that went on all day. Laelaps could not quite catch his prey, but the fox could never quite escape, either. Finally, Hephaestus turned both animals into statues.

The carved hound's thick neck, enlarged rib cage, and extreme light-footedness were characteristic of a Greek breed of wild dog that used to run free in the mountains. These have been mostly rounded up now and are found only in the most remote places.

AGORA

The history of the Athenian Agorá, the ruins of which occupy the flattish area below the northwest slope of the Acropolis, can be traced back some 5,000 years to Neolithic times. Archaeologists from the American School of Classical Studies have been excavating and reconstructing here for decades, laying bare the palimpsest of millennia. If you descend from the Acropolis you'll see on your right the blinding white reconstruction of the **Stoa of Attalos**. It replicates what archaeologists think was the arcade of shops built in the second century B.C. by Attalos II, king of Pergamon. It's now a museum housing the Agora finds. (Two blocks to the right of the stoa, and not part of the Agora proper, is the **Roman forum**, begun by Julius Caesar and finished by Hadrian.) The central, flat area facing the Stoa of Attalos was once bounded on three sides by stoas, porticoed arcades fronting covered market stalls. In between are the foundations of gymnasia, council chambers, law courts, and other civic and commercial buildings.

On the west side, looming over the Agora proper, stands the somber Temple of Hephaestus, or **Hephaisteion** (still called the Theseion on some maps), the best-preserved Classical temple in Greece. Hephaestus, god of the forge, overseer of technology and crafts, was the son of Zeus and Hera. He is said to have tried to rape Athena, the virgin goddess of reason herself, but she repulsed the attack. Another legend says that Athena married Hephaestus, and that the fine arts grew from their union.

Hephaestus was an old god. The ancients had known the science of metallurgy for thousands of years, using it to forge armor, construct chariots, and make utensils. For centuries they had also been fascinated by mechanics. During temple initiations, such as the famous one at Eleusis (see the chapter on Attica, below), dramatic effects were achieved by mechanical means. Doors opened seemingly by themselves, objects moved without visible means, colored lights caused lurid effects, hideous apparitions arose from nowhere, dolphins leaped, thunder pealed, statues spoke. These devices were moved by steam, fire, pulleys, wheels, and other mechanical devices—all this activity under the guidance and protection of Hephaestus the cripple, whose temple overlooked the busy life of commerce and law in the Agora. The temple was turned into a church in the fifth century A.D.

Across the hot and dusty center, behind the law courts and the civic offices, near the lower slopes of the Areopagus, stand the remains of the prison where Socrates probably held court after he was condemned to death on charges of corrupting the youth of Athens. More vivid than any ruin are Plato's evocations of this disheveled old philosopher, in cloak and sandals, hurrying about the Agora, debating with other learned men, teaching, talking, arguing.

PLAKA

Plaka, the old town, is just east of the Agora, and after a visit to the Classical sites the outdoor tavernas of this lively maze of streets can be refreshing. The Acropolis, which overhangs Plaka, keeps coming into view; by watching for it you'll always find your way. Plaka stretches about a mile across the northern flank of the Acropolis, making it very easy to navigate here even at night.

Furthermore, almost all roads lead to Plaka, especially from Syntagma (see below). With your back to Parliament you can go left out of the square on Philellinón Street; then, before the top of the hill, a right on Nikodímou will lead to Plaka. Or you can go down any of the three good shopping roads that lead west out of Syntagma: Perikléos, Ermoú, or Mitropóleos. Then, when you get near the new cathedral, a left on Mnisikléos will get you to Plaka. (Mitropoleos also leads to the famous flea market of **Monastiráki**, a place filled to overflowing with artifacts in the ever-inventive Greek tradition.) Even Athena Street (Athinás), which leads down from Omónia Square, will take you to lower Ermou and on to Plaka.

Plaka itself is the most pleasant place in Athens to buy Greek handicrafts and souvenirs. The old town is also the most enchanting spot for outdoor tavernas and restaurants. It is always festive, particularly at night and on holidays. The narrow, winding streets usually stream with strollers, Greek and foreign alike, and some of the friendliest charcoal-grill places you'll ever find lie scattered along Plaka's hillside.

Plaka is the oldest continually inhabited town in Europe and was an important site even in prehistoric times. When the Turks settled here, they probably chose the site to avoid the swampy areas west and southwest of the Acropolis. It is said that when the palace of King Otto (Greece's first monarch, a Bavarian chosen by a London conference) was being planned, the engineers strung a rope from Plaka down through what is now Syntagma and hung hunks of raw meat along it at intervals. After some time the meat was examined for maggots; the place where the fewest maggots were found got the palace—the site of today's Parliament.

After the War of Independence the area around Plaka was settled literally overnight. Because the city fathers failed to agree on a formal building plan, impatient Athenians simply chose their own parcels of land and put up their houses, illegally, at night. The instigator of this practice was a builder from Anáfi, hence the name for the topmost part of Plaka, Anafiótika.

For a while in the 1960s and 1970s, Plaka was taken over by rowdy touristic restaurateurs who vulgarized the area. It has since reverted to the graciously bohemian ways of old.

Tower of the Winds

The Tower of the Winds is almost the first ancient building you come to as you walk down the west side of Plaka from the Acropolis. It stands east of the Roman market, overlooking the ruins.

The octagonal Tower of the Winds is a first-century B.C. landmark, built by the astronomer Andronicus. Its famous external bas-reliefs show the winds coming from the eight cardinal directions. There used to be a bronze weather vane that, when moved by the slightest breeze, pointed to the relief against which the wind was blowing. The building also once housed a water clock. No one knows precisely what this looked like. It may have had a clock face with an hour hand or it may have featured a revolving celestial globe. Either way, the clock was moved by water released from a reservoir at a regular rate so that it gradually lowered a float attached to the cogged clock wheels. Such a device dates back to Athens's Golden Age. Marvelous as it may seem, it was not without its detractors. Plato once remarked disparagingly that "lawyers are driven by the water clock"; Aristotle said that the length of a drama should be determined by its plot, "and not the water clock."

SYNTAGMA SQUARE

If Athens has a center, it is Sýntagma, a.k.a. Constitution, Square. Here are located the Parliament building and the city's most important tourist services. Around Syntagma (currently undergoing extensive renovation) cluster the Greek National Tourist Organization, American Express, Pan Am, TWA, and Olympic Airways. Circling the square is a necklace of noisy traffic (everyone in Athens seems to have an automobile). One of the few taxi stands in the city is located on the east side of the square. You can find it by looking for the largest and most restless crowd of people.

From the top of Syntagma, the **Parliament** building looks down majestically upon the ever-changing scene. Completed in 1842, the building was originally built as a royal

Plaka, Syntagma, and Kolonaki

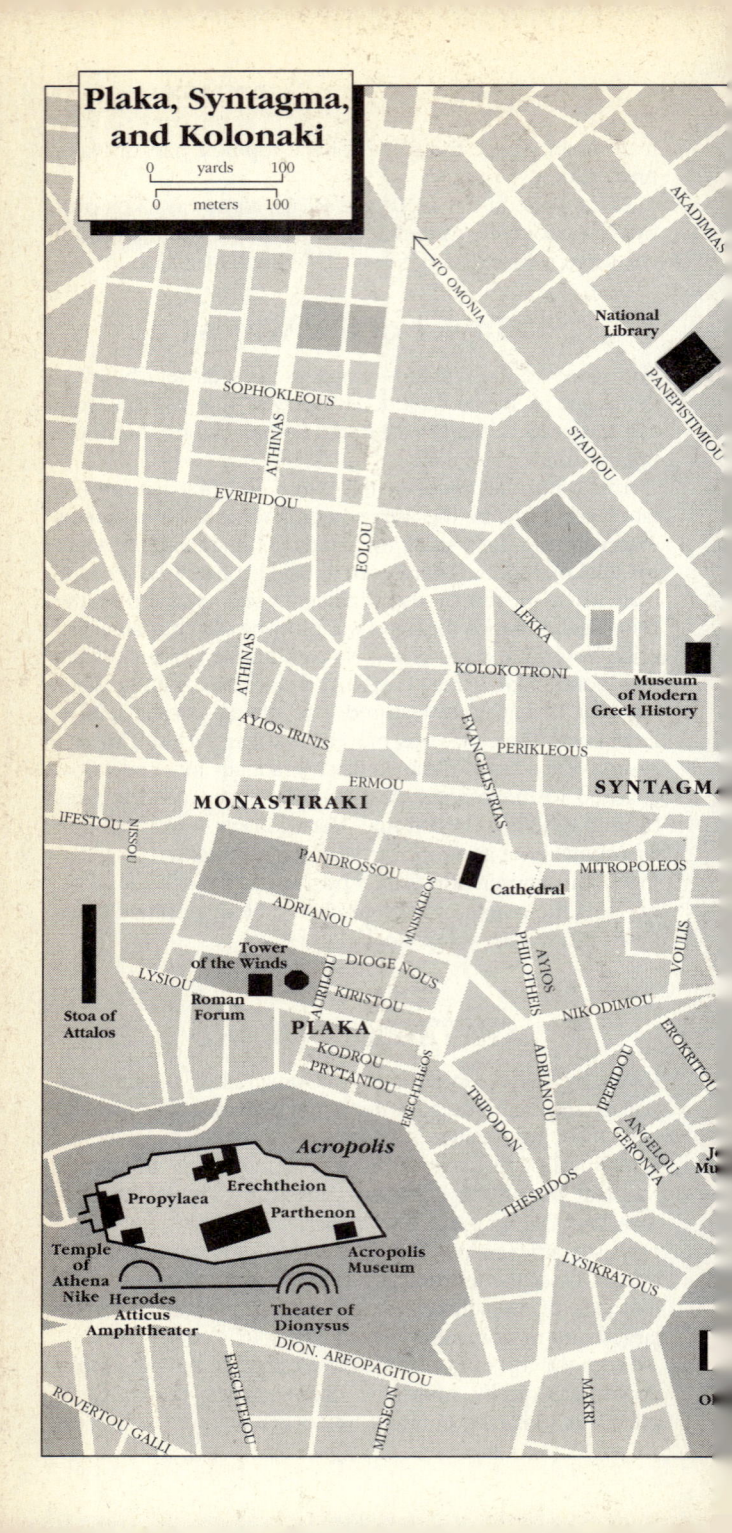

EXARCHIA

IPPOKRATOUS
SKOUFA
DIDOTOU
MASSALIAS
SOLONOS
SINA
OMIROU
ANAGNOSTOPOULLOU
TSAKALOF
AMERIKIS
DIMOKRITOU
VOUKOURESTIOU
PINDAROU
IRAKLITOU

Athens University

Hellenic Academy

Mount Lycabettus

FUNICULAR

KOLONAKI

HARITOS
PATR. IOACHEIM
KRIEZOTOU
ZALOKOSTA
KANARIS
KOLONAKI SQUARE
KOUMBARI
IRODOTOU
N. DOUKA

Benaki Museum

Goulandris Museum of Cycladic Art

VASILISSIS SOPHIAS

SYNTAGMA SQUARE

Parliament Building

AMALIAS AVENUE

PHILELLINON

VAS. GEORGIOU AVENUE

Presidential Palace

National Garden

IRODOU ATTIKOU

AMALIAS AVENUE

Zappeion

LEOFOROS OLGAS

KONSTANTINOU AVE.

of Zeus

N

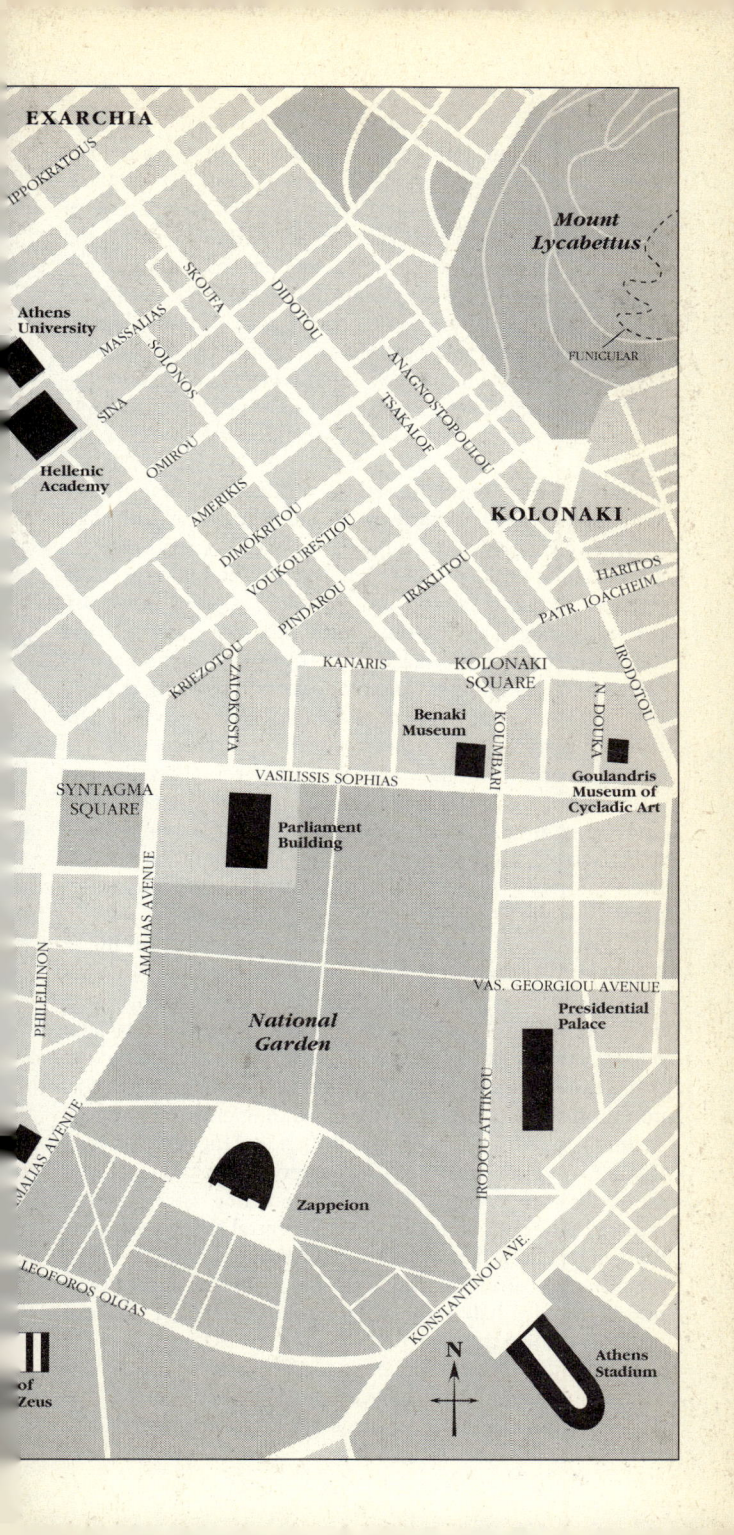

Athens Stadium

palace for the Bavarian king Otto (Othon), first monarch of Greece, who reigned for almost 30 years, from 1834 to 1862.

Almost from the start Otto's front door was the scene of parades and demonstrations. On September 3, 1843, the Athenians gathered in front of the palace, calling for a constitution. It was not enough to promise it; the beleaguered Otto had to have the charter drawn up and signed before the boisterous populace would disperse. The square takes its name from that day, *sýntagma* meaning "constitution." Ultimately Otto was forced to abdicate. A Danish royal, backed by international powers, ascended the throne in his stead.

Otto I will be remembered for at least one thing: He instituted the bizarre **changing of the guard** that still takes place on Syntagma in front of Parliament (every hour on the hour, though flexible in heat waves). With guns at hand, dressed in white skirts, pleated blouses, and pompom-decorated boots, two strong young men, specially selected for height, high-step in a jerky yet rhythmical fashion across the usually scorching pavement to replace two others high-stepping out of the shade of two wooden sentry boxes. The ceremony recalls the mating dance of very eccentric ostriches. (For anyone interested in such ceremonies, there is also a changing of the guard outside the Presidential Palace on Irodou Attikou, and an elaborate one accompanied by a military band every Sunday morning in front of Parliament. Every morning at 8:00 a detachment of guards also raises the flag on the Acropolis.)

As the new capital of Greece (so designated in 1834), Athens prospered. The first four-horse carriage was imported, the first stove appeared, the first bathrooms were installed. A grand private mansion, the Dmitriou, was built on the northwest corner of the square; it would later become the historic Grande Bretagne hotel. The street it cornered on was declared the fast-expanding city's new official boundary until a city plan could be adopted. But just as in Plaka, no overall building plan was ever accepted, and people built wherever they wanted, erecting unauthorized houses in the dark of night. (Outside central Athens, the same thing happens today. When enough houses crop up in an unauthorized location, the residents of the new neighborhood call city hall requesting paved roads and modern utilities—which they get.)

Back in the 19th century balls and festivities made the city a cheerful place. Not that everything was serene: In one decade alone there were 21 changes of government. While

Greece was still struggling, her newfound nationalism produced some serious side effects—and some nonsensical ones. Greek scholars, for example, insisted on pulling down the new opera house so that Athenians would concentrate on their Classical heritage through Greek drama rather than enjoy pageantry and vocal virtuosity.

KOLONAKI

On your imaginary map of Athens, Kolonáki is found just above the bow of the ship. Sitting on the southern slope of Mount Lycabettus, it is within easy walking distance of Syntagma Square. Kolonaki is the fashionable, expensive part of Athens, slightly staid and respectable. There is good shopping up here (see Shops and Shopping, below), and some good restaurants (see Athens After Dark, below), most of which have been serving travellers for decades. Kolonaki centers on its main square, a pleasant site half surrounded by outdoor cafés that offers an enjoyable ambience for dinner or afterward.

In the area you will find galleries showing works by modern Greek artists and some international ones. Stop in to get a glimpse of yet another dimension of contemporary Athens.

LYCABETTUS

This charming destination, just northeast of the heart of the city, shouldn't be missed. The tallest hill in Athens, Lycabettus (Lykavittós) is only 910 feet high and makes for an easy outing. You can climb up through Kolonaki to Aristipou Street and find the entrance to the funicular, or you can cab it to the funicular and ride to the top in comfort. (Children love the funicular.) At the top is a 360-degree panorama of Athens and Attica. To the north you can see in the distance splendid Mount Pentéli, which gave its rosy marble to the Parthenon. Apartments and tavernas sprout on Penteli, where asphodels (sacred flowers from Elysian fields) used to grow. The most fashionable Athenians have moved onto her petticoats, their villas crowding together to form a busy hemline pattern. The cool mountain towns of Ekáli, Drosiá, and Kifissiá, all to the north of Athens, have become stylish suburbs and are popular places to go for long Greek lunches on Sundays and holidays.

Those two mountains nearer the city that you see are Mount Parnis, to the north, and Mount Hymettos (Imittós), to the east. Parnis has an international gambling casino plunked right at its top (see Athens After Dark), and Mount Hymettos has been famous since ancient times for its thick, thyme-flavored honey, which, on fresh yogurt, is still one of the best treats of the land.

Looking south toward the sea you'll see the Acropolis, and farther along to the right is Piraeus, the busiest Mediterranean port. In the distance, like two sunbathing turtles, float Salamis and Aegina islands.

Lycabettus at one time marked the city limits, but today Athens continues to push outward to the edges of Attica. Little white apartment buildings wash up the flanks of mountains the way surf breaks on the shore. There is no end to the building mania. If someone runs out of money, he merely leaves the next floor unfinished until enough capital is gathered to carry on.

Atop Lycabettus, visit the tiny 19th-century **church of Ayios Yiórgios**, where Yiorgios Nikolakopoulos, an artist steeped in the Greek Orthodox spirit, is repainting the insides. He seems to be capturing that elusive, rather mystical quality that is too often missing from the work of many contemporary craftsmen.

There is also a **café-restaurant** up here, with a panoramic view, some steps down from the church.

The walk down the hill is pleasant if you have the time. You wind down through a small pine grove, a favorite haunt of lovers at night. If you are staying at the St. George Lycabettus hotel, you are in luck. The path leads right by its door.

VASILISSIS SOPHIAS AVENUE

Vasilíssis Sophías is a wide avenue that leads east from Syntagma, then bends north to Amaroussi, Kifissia, and Ekali on Mount Penteli. It can also take you to the national highway, leading to Thebes and northern Greece. East along Vas. Sophias stand the American Embassy, the Hilton Hotel, the National Garden, and four small museums worth a visit: the Goulandris, Benaki, Byzantine, and National Gallery (the Modern Art Museum). A single morning and afternoon will give you a taste of some 5,000 years of Greek art.

These four museums are located between Syntagma

Square and the American Embassy and are within walking distance of both. If you are coming from Syntagma, much of the walk can be done in the fragrant quiet of the **National Garden** just behind Parliament. All four museums have a decidedly eccentric aspect, the Goulandris and the Benaki probably because they were formed as personal collections. Opening and closing times for all museums are erratic and need to be checked; also, the museums are often subject to strikes and reconstructions.

Benaki Museum

Located on the corner of Koumbári Street and Vas. Sophias, this wonderful house and all its contents are Antoine Benaki's legacy to the state. The collection offers the traveller a fascinating, if puzzling and jumbled, rundown of Greek and Middle Eastern history through pictures, documents, clothes, and everyday utensils. The colorful displays include objects from Persia, Byzantium, Turkey, Thrace, Macedonia, and other parts of Greece, some pieces dating back to 3000 B.C. Note the evidence they give of the differences as well as the remarkable similarities between the cultures of Asia Minor and Greece. The visit provides a good overview of Greek artifacts that will enable you to better judge objects offered for sale in antiques shops. The museum itself sells replicas of some of the works exhibited. Tel: 361-1617; closed Tuesdays.

Goulandris Museum of Cycladic Art

The Goulandrís Museum, on Neophýtou Doúka just north of Vas. Sophias, is a pleasantly designed three-story edifice devoted chiefly to the display of Cycladic art. Five thousand years ago the Cycladic islands were the center of Greek civilization, constituting a bridge between the more advanced culture of Asia Minor and the still primitive Greek mainland. The smooth, modern-looking figural sculptures this civilization left behind, however, tell us little about what went on in Cycladic life. The collection includes objects from prehistoric times up to the fourth century B.C. This quiet, cool museum offers a restful interlude and the opportunity to admire the simple, haunting elegance of Cycladic art. Tel: 724-9706; closed Tuesdays and Sundays.

Byzantine Museum

The Byzantine Museum, occupying the Villa Ilíssia at 22 Vas. Sophias, used to be one of the most important small museums of the world. Sometimes the entire museum is open, sometimes only part. It houses some very fine mosaics and Byzantine sculptures plus a dazzling iconostasis, or altar screen, and what was once the most beautiful icon collection anywhere. Masses of marvelous jewel-like paintings once gleamed in ill-lit rooms. Now, bright lights and scientific cleaning have shined the icons up to the glossiness of a magazine page. There are fashions in museum conservation as there are in artistic styles; it seems these days you need to become a connoisseur of both. Tel: 721-1027; closed Mondays.

National Gallery and Alexandros Soutzos Museum

This museum, just opposite the Hilton on the corner of Vas. Sophias and Konstantínou avenues, houses a permanent collection of Greek artists' work from the 16th century on. Special shows are frequently mounted; in 1989 the museum featured an odd but interesting exhibition called "Mind and Body," which was designed to convince the Olympic Committee that Greece should host the 100th-birthday celebration of the modern games. Tel: 721-1010; closed Mondays.

AMALIAS AVENUE

Amalías is essentially the eastern boundary of Plaka, a speedy thoroughfare running along the National Garden. The Garden's paths lead into the **Záppeion**, a large building in its own graceful garden. Here films are shown (in English) and conferences held. To the right, across Olgas Street, lie the open spaces of the **Temple of Olympian Zeus**, the largest temple in Greece. It was built in Roman times in imperial grandeur, so it seems out of sync with the rest of ancient Greece. Still, if you are staying nearby it is worth wandering through, particularly in the early morning or late afternoon.

One of the most endearing museums in Athens is the **Jewish Museum**, about halfway down the south side of Amalias at number 36 on the quiet third floor of an old office building. It was begun by and is still under the direction of

Nikos Stavroulakis, artist and scholar (and contributor of the section on Crete in this guidebook). Stavroulakis has created a tranquil atmosphere in which to present an extraordinarily artistic capsule of the 2,500-year history of Greek Jews. Tel: 323-1577; closed Saturdays.

METS AND PANGRATI

Across Konstantinou Avenue from the Zappeion and behind the old sports stadium (dating from 330 B.C., it was restored between 1896 and 1906 for the Olympic Games, but is hardly ever used), lies the area known as Mets, and, just north of it, Pangrati. These places are difficult to characterize: Not so scruffy as Omonia, they can be interesting to walk through, as they are particularly Greek, with some lovely pre–World War II houses still to be found among the jumble of recently constructed buildings. For the most part neither area has been set up for tourists; rather, they are for Greeks going about the business of daily life. During the day you might do some nontourist-style shopping, and there are some pleasant *kafeneíos* to sit at, but Athenian traffic takes much of the pleasure out of walking. At night the area's excellent tavernas and discos attract a younger crowd (see Athens After Dark).

OMONIA SQUARE

Omónia Square is well up the mast of our imaginary sailing ship. Northwest of Syntagma, it is the other great square of Athens, a hot and hurried one with limited appeal to the short-term visitor. You might drive through it on your way to the National Archaeological Museum. Encircled by jammed sidewalks, Omonia Square is blessed with a splashing fountain at its heart. This is working Athens, whose side streets are your best bet for souvlakia and other fast food, which in Greece means stand-up grills. The two streets that link Omonia to Syntagma are Stadíou and Panepistimíou; the National Library, Athens University, and the Hellenic Academy are located along Panepistimiou. Stadiou, which features the excellent **Museum of Modern Greek History** (housed in the Old Parliament), is otherwise better for shopping. Buses and cars, however, make both streets unpleasant to walk along. Be careful not to get stuck in Omonia

NATIONAL ARCHAEOLOGICAL MUSEUM

The National Archaeological Museum is the proud flag on our ship of state. It's located on Patission Street, which spokes north out of Omonia Square. The pleasant garden out front has a good snack bar-café.

This is one of the most important sculpture museums in the world, and as museums go it is relatively easy to negotiate. The collection goes back to Neolithic times (3500–2500 B.C.), thus spanning some 5,500 years. In a fairly consistent trajectory over these five millennia, the collection makes it possible to see the subtle changes in style wrought by Greek civilization as it matured from early religious consciousness to the almost decadent sophistication of the last days of the Hellenistic age.

The most efficient way to proceed is to leave the earliest years until last. This means you should save the great gallery of Mycenaean and Minoan artifacts, with its side rooms of Neolithic and Cycladic art, until the very end. After getting your ticket, turn to the entrance on your left. Here you will begin your visit with some impressive archaic figures from the eighth, seventh, and sixth centuries B.C. The outsize figures of young men such as those in gallery 8 were once designated as images of Apollo, but in the present demythologizing mode of museum thinking they are called simply *kouroi,* meaning "young men." They have an eager energy, as if they were ready to step off into the unknown.

Gallery 15 contains the museum's crown jewels: the bas-relief of **Demeter and Persephone-Kore** and the awesome bronze statue of **Zeus** (sometimes called Poseidon), which has a claim to being one of the most magnificent in the world.

The god stands in the center of the room, poised as if to throw a thunderbolt. Zeus was father of the gods, lustful, irritable, pleasure-loving—and fickle. With a deep sense of joy, he went about impregnating goddesses, nymphs, and mortal women at will. He was responsible for the twins Apollo and Artemis, the hero Herakles, and the goddess Athena, among many others. The name Zeus may be translated as "life." The figure's light-footedness and farsightedness convey the wide-ranging interests of the god.

The label "Poseidon" is sometimes attached to this figure, but the sea god Poseidon is traditionally depicted in Greek art as a shaggy, slightly soft-muscled man with a trident, a three-pronged fishing spear meant for thrusting. Fishermen in the Mediterranean still use the trident; they stand very still, poised for a quick downward motion. This bronze god, on the other hand, is throwing, not thrusting. Nor is there any other indication he is Poseidon—he was merely called that because he was found in the sea off Artemission. He stands at the center of the room where there is always a crowd like a dust storm at his feet—that is, until some time around 4:00 when the tour buses take off. Circle him then, until you find the spot where he seems to be throwing his thunderbolt right at you.

The marble bas-relief from Eleusis, on a side wall in the same room, represents Demeter and her daughter, Persephone, or Kore. (*Kore* means "young girl," or "daughter," in Greek.) With the goddesses is Triptolemos, prince of Eleusis, where Demeter's sanctuary stood. The goddesses are shown giving seed corn to the serious young Triptolemos, whose mission, like that of an early Johnny Appleseed, was to disseminate the art of grain cultivation to humankind.

The museum contains an interesting copy of the lost Athena from the Parthenon, the captivating bronze *Boy on a Horse,* and some amusing Pan figures. There is also a collection of small Greek bronzes that have been cleaned and shined to look as if they could be on sale in a tourist shop. The lovely, soft green patina of some 2,500 years has been carefully picked off. At best these bronzes look 19th century. Unfortunately, the accumulation of centuries, once removed, cannot be replaced—except by centuries. If you do go in, note the small Zeus from Dodona poised to hurl a thunderbolt.

Upstairs are vases. Greek vases are an acquired taste that can lead to an addiction. Until you get hooked, just keep looking.

Also upstairs is a pretty restoration of the few bits of fresco found at Santorini, survivors of the volcanic explosion that ripped the island's heart out sometime between 1500 and 1000 B.C. This was one of the greatest catastrophes that ever rocked civilization. As with most reconstructions, this one tells you as much about contemporary archaeological thinking as it does about the ancients. Peering closely, you can discern how few are the fragments left from the past (these were found after World War II), and how the rest have been executed in the Art Nouveau style fashionable at the turn of the 20th century.

Back downstairs is the life-size bronze Apollo that workers found when digging up a Piraeus street in 1959.

To complete the sequence of major sculptures before getting lost amid the mass of jewelry, daggers, cups, and the like in the large Mycenaean gallery, move swiftly through the rooms of Hellenistic sculpture, most of which need not detain you on a first visit. Hellenistic art, roughly that which came after Alexander the Great until the Greco-Roman period, lacks the firmness of intent that was so skillfully merged with artistry in earlier times. Greek sculpture slowly became imbued with a softer, even decadent, impulse. By the late fourth century B.C., the great age of the Greek adventure was coming to a close.

This tendency is marvelously portrayed in the life-size bronze *Youth of Antikythera,* cast around 340 B.C. and found in the sea in 1900. Sometimes called *The Ballplayer,* the figure stands with one hand outstretched as if to catch a baseball. In a way, this masterpiece of Hellenistic art completes the development of Greek sculpture. Fine pieces continued to be produced, but none of this descriptive power.

Now you might either hurry ahead or retrace your steps to enter the great Mycenaean Hall. This is like dropping into a king's treasure house. Everything lies scattered in cases about the room. Probably the most famous objects are two Minoan masterpieces, golden goblets found at Vaphio. Before Demeter taught farming, ancient man had domesticated the wild bull and had gone from hunter to cattleman, a major advance in human development. The goblets depict the capture and taming of the bull in exquisite detail and display the finest of workmanship. Indeed, the art of working gold seems to have reached its highest point in the most ancient times.

For sheer drama and gold weight, the place of honor goes to the treasure from Mycenae. The great Minoan civilization on the islands overlapped the heights of Mycenaean civilization on the mainland. This grandiose era (2000–1100 B.C.) saw the building of the great palaces on Crete, the catastrophe of Santorini, and the storied Trojan War. Agamemnon, king of Mycenae, was the overall commander of the Greek forces in that contest. The 19th-century German archaeologist Heinrich Schliemann, who found much of the gold displayed in this gallery, believed this was so, and he spent his life and wealth on a dream that changed the way we think of ancient Greece. In effect, he transformed much of myth into history simply by digging. Schliemann first excavated Troy, finding the remains of the legendary city immortalized by Homer. Then he dug at Mycenae, unearthing what tradition has long held to be the site of Agamemnon's citadel and beehive tomb.

Galleries 29 and 30 take you even farther back, to the Cycladic age, around 2500 B.C. This was the time of Early Minoan civilization on Crete and a thousand years before the great volcanic explosion on Santorini. Finds include the same objects that still predominate in our culture: kitchen utensils, tools, weapons, and jewelry. Perhaps more compelling are the mysterious-looking statues. Made of white Parian marble, these smooth, elongated figures, mostly of women, were executed with little identifying detail in a simple, almost abstract style.

The museum sells some books and cards, but for good reproductions your best bet is back out on Stadiou. Tel: 821-7717.

GETTING AROUND

Getting In
Olympic Airways and TWA have direct flights to Athens from New York (TWA flies nonstop only in summer; at other times there is a stop in Rome). Olympic Airways and Air Canada fly direct from Toronto. Olympic Airways, British Airways, and Air Caledonia have direct flights to Athens from London. The Athens airport is a 20-minute cab ride from Syntagma Square, the center of town. (See also Arrival at Major Gateways by Air, in Useful Facts, above.)

Taxis
Most Athenian taxi drivers are honest businessmen. They tend to own their own cabs and can find their way around the maze of Athens with elegant wizardry. When they seem to detour, it is usually through the quickest, if not the shortest, route. Usually—once you get a taxi—you can just sit back and relax.

Yet you must remember that there are almost ten million people in Greece, more than three and a half million of whom live in greater Athens. Greeks have added a democratic wrinkle to gridlock. Taxi fares are deliberately kept down so that low-income Athenians unable to find room on buses will still have some means of locomotion. This bit of social consciousness might seem to give you an advantage—taxis are so much cheaper than expected. But wait till you try competing as a taxi hailer with the master queue-bargers of the world.

Taxi fares are regulated in a complex style. Small, legal additions to the base fare are seldom posted. Then, too, there will be official changes. Mostly you will be told the truth. But figure approximations: The fare, for instance, starts at about 50 drachmas, with a minimum of 240 drachmas regardless of what the meter says. Add 50 drachmas for each bag, plus 50 for nighttime. Waiting is metered, but you would be wise to promise extra to prevent others from kidnapping your cab. On certain holidays, taxis can charge extra again (ten days at Easter, Christmas, and New Year).

A cabbie will accept other passengers to share your taxi if they are going in the right direction for him. This works both ways. At a busy intersection, call out your destination. Maybe a cab will stop—but be alert to others who may jump ahead of you. Plant your feet firmly on the ground and stick your elbows out. When you share a cab, both customers pay the full fare.

There is a way out of the taxi problem in some areas of town: the radio cab. Your restaurant waiter or hotel concierge will call one for you. The cab will usually charge 150 drachmas for coming and sometimes takes a quarter of an hour to arrive.

Doormen at the hotels along Syngrou, such as the Marriott, the Inter-Continental, and the Chandris, can sometimes catch you a cab out front, and sometimes not. They will call a radio taxi, of course, if you prefer. The Hilton and the deluxe hotels around Syntagma are relatively reliable places to catch cabs.

Syntagma has one of the few official taxi stands, and one of the longest queues. But when they're empty, taxis head toward Syntagma as seagulls to the setting sun.

Trolleys and Buses

There are blue and green buses, and there are trackless yellow trolleys run by electric overhead cables. Clean, roomy, and direct, these vehicles have been upgraded, and some beautiful ones from Hungary now ply the better parts of town. But there are not enough, so the first rule is, try not to use buses and trolleys at rush hour.

For trolleys and buses you must buy your ticket at a kiosk. Ask your hotel for a schedule and directions to the nearest kiosk that sells tickets (not all do). You get on at the back or the middle, where you will find a machine into which you insert your ticket to cancel it. Sometimes a conductor will come by to make sure you have done so. People with passes get on in front and don't always use the little machine, so don't follow their example. And watch your wallet, as in any crowded situation.

Buses, and particularly trolleys, are a viable alternative to taxis if your destination is fairly direct, such as up and down Vasilissis Sophias, Stadiou, or Syngrou streets.

Walking

If you are just visiting Athens for a few days while staying at a midtown hotel, walking is a very pleasant way of getting around—except at midday in summer.

You can walk from Syntagma through Plaka up to the Acropolis and down again, enjoying every minute of the way. The swank Kolonaki district is an easy walk from the Hilton and also from Syntagma Square. Walking the back streets from Syntagma down to the National Archaeological Museum lets you see a lot of Athens. Quaint, tree-shaded squares, odd shops, and residential areas beat the boulevards polluted by taxis and buses.

If you want to visit the little museums on Vas. Sophias, you can walk from Syntagma through the relatively unpolluted air of the National Garden almost to the Byzantine Museum. All four museums (the Goulandris, the Benaki, the Byzantine, and the National Art Gallery) stand within a few blocks of one another, and the garden makes the walk pleasant.

ACCOMMODATIONS

The following hotels are indicated as being *deluxe* (very reasonable by international standards, from 10,000 to 32,000 drachmas for a double), *first class* (pleasant hotels that always seem to satisfy their customers; under 10,000 drachmas for a double), or *pensions* ("B category" hotels with special charm; under 7,000 drachmas).

The telephone country code for Greece is 30; the city code for Athens is 01; when calling Athens from outside the country, omit the zero.

Deluxe

Athenaeum Inter-Continental. Equally convenient to the airport and Piraeus, the 559-room Athenaeum is nonetheless only five minutes away from the center of Athens with regular shuttle-bus transportation provided. It's got all the major conveniences of a deluxe hotel: air-conditioning, double-glazed soundproof windows, direct dialing, and shops. In addition, it boasts an art gallery and an art-filled lobby.

89–93 Syngrou Avenue, Athens, 117 45. Tel: 902-3666; Telex: (21) 221554 ATH GR; Fax: 921-7653.

Astir Palace. Centrally located on the corner of Vas. Sophias and Panepistimiou Street (directly across the street from the Grand Bretagne), the austere Astir Palace (the flagship of the locally famed Astir chain) was built during the last decade for government officials on parliamentary business. The rooms on the left side (facing Parliament) have a view of the Acropolis as well as of the parades, processions, and political demonstrations in Syntagma Square. The higher up you are the better.

"The Astir Palace hotel cannot be bought—or sold," says its manager, Mr. Sabbatos. This enigmatic remark has a story. It seems that when the foundations for the hotel were being dug, construction workers came upon some ancient walls. Work halted for a year while deliberations took place on how to proceed. In the end the hotel was not allowed to build upon the ruins. And so, well lit and safe behind a glass partition, the ruins can now be seen from your table in the tranquil, air-conditioned dining room named **Apokalypsis**—which means "revelation." "It certainly was that," says Sabbatos flatly. Above the ruins is empty space—90 feet of it between the hotel and the avenue, ensuring that the hotel's 59 rooms and 20 suites are wrapped in quiet. In such a busy central location, this is a considerable plus—and the rooms are priced accordingly.

1 Vas. Sophias, Athens, 105 64. Tel: 364-3112; Telex: (21) 222380 APAT GR; Fax: 364-2825.

Grande Bretagne. The majestic Grande Bretagne stands just diagonally across the street from Parliament overlooking Syntagma Square and all its varied activities. The most famous and historic of Athens hotels, it has maintained the highest standards since it first opened its doors in 1874. Back then it boasted 80 rooms and two of the first bathrooms ever installed in the young capital.

That was only the beginning. The Grande Bretagne (or GB, as it is familiarly known) continues to be the traditional home away from home for hosts of famous visitors, remaining discreetly impressive in its role as spectator to history all the while. Enlarged and upgraded many times over the years, the hotel has all modern conveniences, including minibars, fax machines, royal bathrooms, double-glazed windows to keep out noise, and satellite television. From the front rooms and suites, particularly the upper stories, there is a splendid view of the Acropolis.

Syntagma Square (1 King George Street), Athens, 105 63. Tel: 323-0251; Telex: (21) 5346; Fax: 322-8034.

Athens Hilton. The Athens Hilton, directly across busy Konstantinou Street from the National Gallery, was the first of the modern deluxe hotels to be built in the city. Its restaurants and pools are meeting haunts of Athenians as well as guests. The air-conditioned rooms have fabulous views of Athens (try to get one overlooking the Acropolis), color television, and marble baths with all the trimmings; rooms on the south side are especially luxurious. The hectic lobby is chock-full of shops, tourist information desks, and business services.

46 Vas. Sophias, Athens, 106 76. Tel: 722-0201; Telex: (21) 5808; Fax: 721-3110.

Ledra Marriott. Out of the center of town on Syngrou Avenue (but with a regular shuttle bus to the airport, the Acropolis, and Syntagma Square), the Ledra Marriott has all the usual amenities of a deluxe hotel: air-conditioning, sound-proofing, beauty salons, color television, and shops. It also has three restaurants: the **Kona Kai** (Polynesian), the **Ledra Grill** (international), and the **Zephyros** (open all day). The restaurants and the **Crystal Lounge** (with its famous 1,000-droplet crystal chandelier) have become popular meeting places for Athenians. May through September the **Panorama Bar** serves dinner by the rooftop swimming pool.

115 Syngrou Avenue, Athens, 117 41. Tel: 934-7711; Telex: (21) 223466 MAR GR; Fax: 935-8603.

St. George Lycabettus. Perched on the side of Mount Lycabettus in fashionable Kolonaki, this 150-room establishment is the best hotel for the unhurried traveller, the person who likes to savor a trip rather than just "do" it. Try for a fourth-floor corner room with a southern exposure for perhaps the best view in Athens. Although deluxe in category, the St. George Lycabettus has a quiet, family-owned atmosphere. From its small but perfectly situated swimming pool you can look up Mount Lycabettus and out to Athens, the Acropolis, and the sea. The formal **Grand Balcon** dining room overlooks twinkling nighttime Athens, and a charming restaurant downstairs called The Snack is open all day. There are also shops and a beauty parlor.

2 Kleomenous Street, Athens, 106 75. Tel: 729-0711; Telex: (21) 4253; Cable: MANTZOTEL; Fax: 729-0439.

First Class
Amalia. Centrally located, just around the corner from Syntagma, the Amalia faces the wonderful National Garden. It is also near the romantic Temple of Zeus and not far from the Mets and Pangrati areas. Front rooms are rather noisy. Shuttle buses to the airport stop almost directly out front.

10 Amalias Avenue, Athens, 105 57. Tel: 323-7301; Telex: (21) 5161; Fax: 323-8792.

Electra Palace. A large, old (1970s) hotel with a roof garden, swimming pool, and parking. Several stories higher than allowed nowadays, it offers some spectacular views. At the northern edge of Plaka, it is well within walking distance of the Acropolis and Plaka.

18 Nikodimou Street, Athens, 105 57. Tel: 324-1401; Telex: (21) 6896; Fax: 324-1875.

Parthenon. Within walking distance of the entrance to the Acropolis and far enough from the bustle of Syntagma and Plaka to be quiet without being out of touch. It, too, has a pleasant garden. Air-conditioned, with restaurant and garage.

3 Makri Street, Athens, 117 42. Tel: 923-4594/8.

Pensions
Adonis. Located on a pedestrian street in Plaka, this little hotel has been newly constructed by a Greek who used to run the Annapolis Hilton. He keeps his place like a jewel. ("It is mine, after all," he explains.) It has one of the nicest roof gardens in Athens and a smashing close-up view of the Acropolis as well as Lycabettus, with all Athens spread like a topographical map in between. It is "B category," but in this case such categorizing is more of a tourist ministry technicality.

3 Kodrou Street, Athens 105 58. Tel: 324-9737.

Akropolis House. Across the street from the Adonis and from **Amorgos**, one of the most interesting antiques shops in the city, this hotel has kept its old style intact, with old wallpaper, old furniture, and old pictures in its old downstairs lobby and tiny breakfast room. The rooms, though, have been modernized.

6–8 Kodrou Street, Athens 105 58. Tel: 322-2344.

ATHENS AFTER DARK

After an exciting daytime of filling the soul from the cornucopia of antiquities and monuments of a glorious past, travellers will find that Athens after dark offers a dazzling nightlife with practically endless possibilities to titillate and refresh the body. And during the long summer, which stretches from May through October, it's almost all outdoors, especially dining.

The after-dark gamut includes an impressive array of restaurants, nightclubs, bars, *bouzoúki* clubs, discos, and even boisterous Greek hard-rock concerts, all to be taken in at a leisurely pace. Also not to be overlooked are the ubiquitous tavernas—with or without live music and song. It should be noted from the outset that dining in Greece usually takes place after sunset—any time after 9:00 P.M. at the very earliest, until midnight or later. Indeed, you may well find that if you arrive even a few minutes before nine, the place you've chosen is still closed. Hotels serve earlier if you cannot hold out.

Whenever you venture out of walking distance for an evening on the town, we suggest that when you are ready to call it a night you ask your waiter to call a radio taxi for you. This will cost you a mere 250 drachmas extra (paid to the driver) and ensures a ride to your hotel.

For film fans there are opportunities to catch up with the big hits missed during the previous winter season. These are rerun, screened outdoors with Greek subtitles. Foreigners are advised to sit fairly close to the screen, for often the sound track is turned down low to avoid complaints from neighboring residents.

For those who enjoy listening to the Greek language, the theater in Athens is quite active, and adaptations of American, English, and Russian plays as well as musicals and topical satires are staged outdoors in summer and indoors at other times.

The **Athens Festival**, which takes place between early June and mid-September, hosts a mixture of local and internationally famed troupes performing opera, ballet, plays, and concerts in the all-marble, open-air Herodes Atticus Theater, an impressive and discreetly restored structure snuggled at the base of the Acropolis. Originally built in the second century A.D., it is named for the Greek benefactor who paid the bill. Details of programs and tickets for the festival and other special concerts are available from your hotel concierge, travel agent, and Greek National Tourist Organization offices both in Athens and abroad.

After a performance at the Athens Festival you can avoid the usual hectic scramble for taxis—of which there is an acute shortage at such times, when some 5,000 people pour out of the theater—by dining at one of the recommended tavernas nearby. Very often you will find the performers of the night having supper at these places. The **Strofi**, at 25 Rovértou Galli, is but one block away, almost in a beeline downhill from the entrance of the Herodes Atticus. It offers Greek cuisine in a rooftop setting, with the illuminated Parthenon as a backdrop.

Another possibility, one block to the east of the Strofi at 46 Erechtheíou Street, is **The Symposium**, with somewhat more elegant dining in an attractive courtyard. The atmosphere is romantic and the menu *nouvelle*. (Making reservations before the theater is recommended; Tel: 922-5321.)

Three blocks to the east of the Strofi, at 20 Mitséon Street, is **Socrates Prison**, an inexpensive taverna that spills out onto the narrow sidewalk. Simple Greek fare is served here. Another choice is to stroll to the nearby Plaka (see below) and eat at one of its many spots.

For a capsule history of Athens, the **sound-and-light** presentation at the Acropolis is recommended. There are hour-long shows every night after sunset (except when the moon is full) in various languages. Your hotel concierge can inform you when English is scheduled. The "theater" is the Pnyx, the semicircular hillside terrace where the Athens Assembly met after 500 B.C.

Afterward dine at the nearby **Dionysos** (43 Rovertou Galli Street; Tel: 923-3182), a rather elegant place owned by the Greek National Tourist Organization (but operated by a private company) that offers combinations of Greek and international dishes. You can also enjoy cocktails here earlier and see a "silent" version of the sound-and-light show.

Wine- and fun-lovers will enjoy the **Daphní Wine Festival**, which takes place at the western edge of the sprawling city in a pine-wooded setting adjacent to the famed Byzantine church of Daphní (which has some brilliant mosaics) and the less-known mental institution. (Daphni is about a half-hour ride from the center of Athens; see the chapter on Attica, below.) Running roughly from July through September, the festival offers unlimited samplings of some 60 wines of Greece along with a wide variety of dining choices, Greek entertainment, and dance music, all at different pavilions.

Amid the stands of barrels scattered about, patrons are served by young women in national costumes. You buy a sampling glass and a carafe on entry—and impose your own limit on refills.

Originally this festival was devised to help get rid of old wine at the time of "stomping" (pressing) the new. Although Greek wineries are now concerned with vintage, the festival still carries on because of its popularity. Sometime during the festival a "celebrity" wine pressing is held in a huge vat, with diplomats and local beauties baring their legs and stomping away.

DINING

You may experience some confusion the first time you study a Greek menu—every item has two prices listed next to it. What these figures represent are the basic price of the item (the smaller one) and the price you are actually billed (on the right), which includes the service charge. If an item on the menu does not have a price, it is not available.

The service charge brings up the subject of tipping. Since this charge can be as high as 18 percent, any "tip" need not be a percentage of the total bill. Greeks usually leave up to 200 drachmas per person in a fairly nice place, and perhaps 100 drachmas per person at the average neighborhood taverna. It should be noted that the waiter gets whatever tip is put in the dish or small tray on which the bill is presented. An extra tip of 100 drachmas should be left on the table, out of the dish, for the busboy.

In general all bills in tavernas are honest. Indeed, sometimes the waiter makes up the bill according to what you confirm you had. Naturally there's the occasional error in arithmetic, especially if it's done hurriedly at the table. Just check the figures and total, and no one will get upset.

While you ponder what to order, the grammatical and spelling errors on some menus may provide some amusing entertainment. Some favorites are "children on the spit" (for chicken); "small bullets" (for pullets); "smocked cheese" (for smoked); "kid in the oven" (for goat); "salad with herpes" (for herbs); "compost" (compote); "smashed potatoes"; and, too, the statement of responsibility at the bottom: "All on the menu under the police control to the prices overcharged."

If you have trouble figuring out a dish, the waiter will gladly lead you to the kitchen or a window display to let your eyes make the choice. Many places have conveniently placed the kitchen near the entrance just for this purpose. And no one objects if you use the finger-pointing method, as it limits mistakes and misunderstandings.

Hardly anyone visits Greece for the food, but its simplicity and variety can be a pleasant surprise. For centuries Greek cooking has been basically anything grilled over charcoal, especially meat and seafood. Until recently, practically all tavernas placed the grill immediately outside their premises to create an atmosphere pungent with the smell of good cooking to entice patrons inside, and usually the owner tended the grill personally. For a variety of reasons many of the grills have now been moved inside, so following your nose may no longer be the most reliable method.

There is, however, the "Connie Cat Theory" on how to find a good taverna: Follow the cats. Every taverna has its regulars. Invariably this feline family guards its territory well from any stray, would-be intruders. If a cat at a taverna should be noisy and persistent in making its presence known and, horror of horrors, use its paws to do so—and if said cat hungrily devours just about anything thrown at it, it is advisable not to enter the establishment or, if you're already seated, to leave the place pronto.

If, on the other hand, the cats are orderly, wait to be recognized quietly and unobtrusively at a discreet distance, and scorn this and that random tidbit, then you can relax. A good taverna spoils cats that wait patiently for their favorite food, and serves them only when they are invited to dine.

Something else to be wary about: When a Greek encounters a rather slick façade on a taverna, he invariably passes up the place. A taverna must appear somewhat run-down to be any good, as proof that the test of time has deemed it so. And there are some classic examples, especially in Plaka. By what barometer is a taverna a taverna and a restaurant a restaurant? There are those who believe a taverna becomes a restaurant when the management replaces the paper table coverings with ones of cloth (and, coincidentally, raises prices). But even when this happens, some owners like to use both labels.

Whenever you dine in a taverna or restaurant, be apprised that there are three ways to upset your waiter (and all other patrons): (1) Drink your beer from the bottle; (2) Ask for fruit before your main course; (3) Request tea after dinner.

There is never a rush in a taverna—for the patron, that is. You can dawdle over a plate of boiled spinach or baked beans, sipping your beer or wine as long as you like, no matter how long the waiting line for tables gets. Don't become upset, however, if the waiter takes his time getting to your table to take your order; he will in good time. If you're ignored after the initial serving and want something, do not hesitate to make noise to attract attention. This is not considered rude.

Note, too, that if you like steak (or any other meat) less than well done, be very specific and firm. The average cook lives in the belief that all meat should be thoroughly burned.

Tavernas that do not provide "house entertainment" sometimes permit itinerant musicians to do a bit, collect tips, and then leave. (There is one aged violinist known in the tavernas of Plaka whom most people tip *not* to play.)

With your taverna meal you may sample *retsína,* the unique-tasting wine of Greece. Even though many insist that retsina appeals only to Greek peasants and English tourists, it does seem to please some others. There are several stories as to its origin. One is that Greek peasants, anxious not to have their Turkish overlords drink all the good wine, put resin in it to make it distasteful, and then got used to the taste. Another, more likely, story is that the wine was originally fermented and stored in pinewood barrels that had not been aged. Net result: Resin seeped into the wine. Retsina varies in taste and strength, with some individual tavernas making their own and offering delightfully light versions. In most places it is served *heema* (by the carafe).

Some Greek food may prove heavy for visitors' digestion, mainly from the lavish use of olive oil, especially in frying. Certain renditions of *moussaká* settle in the stomach like concrete. It might be advisable in the warmer months to feast on an appetizing assortment of *mezédes,* along with the ever-popular Greek salad, *souvláki* (grilled chunks of meat or fish on a stick), or plain pieces of meat. If you desire feta cheese or onions on your Greek salad, in most places you must request these ingredients.

Among the assortment of mezedes are three standard and tasty dips: *tzatzíki* (a combination of grated or diced cucumber, yogurt, and garlic); *taramosaláta* (fish roe with boiled potato, soaked white bread, finely chopped onion, oil, and lemon); *melitzánosalata* (eggplant—aubergine—with grated onion, ripe tomato, oil, and vinegar). Somewhat less common is *fava* (mashed yellow beans mixed with olive oil and topped with a sprinkling of fresh onion). Among others: *yígantes* (lima beans), *keftédes* (meatballs), *piperiés* (fried peppers in oil), *dolmádes* (meat and rice wrapped in vine leaves; another version is wrapped in cabbage leaves), *horta* (anything from spinach to dandelion greens, and all very tasty), and *bekrí mezé* (beef bits cooked in tomato spiced with cinnamon).

Grilled mezedes include *oktapódi* (bits of octopus) and *kalamári* (squid, cooked with spinach or grilled), *sykotákia* (bits of fried liver), *tyrópita* (cheese pie), *spanakópita* (spinach pie), and *batsária* (boiled beets). Certain tavernas have specialties for which they are noted.

Among main dishes are the standard souvlaki (as described above), *arní youvétsi* (lamb with macaroni, tomato, and spices cooked in an earthen casserole), *garídes youvétsi* (shrimp cooked with tomato and feta cheese in a casserole), *arní lemonáto* (lamb cooked with spinach and lemon sauce), *paidákia* (lamb chops), and *yemistá* (peppers and tomatoes stuffed with meat, rice, and spices).

The average dessert served in a taverna is a tray of peeled fruit and/or yogurt with honey and nuts, and usually no coffee. Greeks customarily enjoy their dessert and coffee at a second place—a *kafeneío* (sweet shop).

A bit of incidental intelligence: The Greek Orthodox monasteries of the Byzantine era had their cooks decked out in high white hats to distinguish them from the black-hatted monks. This is the origin of the chef's hat.

Syntagma and Kolonaki

There are several places in and around central Sýntagma for quick or leisurely, and early, dining. Among these is the **Delphi**, at 13 Nikis Street. Service is efficient and the menu is broad and inexpensive.

Nearby at 5 Philellinón Street is the **Syntrivani tou Syntagmatos** (Fountain of Syntagma), featuring a small fountain in a courtyard around which tables are grouped under an awning. Inexpensive.

Definitely more upscale is **Gerofinikas**, with the old palm tree from which it gets its name still growing in the center of the indoor premises. Here you get to choose your meal by the finger-pointing method when your waiter escorts you to a display. 10 Pindárou Street; Tel: 362-2719.

These three are basically indoors, and both Delphi and Gerofinikas are air-conditioned. If you prefer, as do most Greeks, to eat outdoors, you can do so just a few blocks away in Kolonaki, the fashionable section of Athens (Gerofinikas is in this neighborhood). A tiny park in the center of the main square shelters the single, ancient column from which the area gets its name—*kolonáki* means "small column." In the upper corner of this square is a cluster of tavernas, one distinguished from the next by its chairs and tablecloths. All are covered with awnings to provide shade during the daytime.

Part of the scene here is people-watching, and sure enough, local celebrities do parade by when they are not themselves among the onlookers. Of the five places in the area, the two farthest away from the center—the **Kolonaki Tops** and the **Lykovrisi** (Wolf's Stream)—are recommended for drinks, tasty mezedes, and full meals. A specialty of both is the stuffed peppers and tomatoes with a side order of oven-baked potatoes. A little upscale is the popular **G. B. Corner** of the Grande Bretagne Hotel, on Constitution Square: a cozy, three-level place to have drinks, snacks, full meals (Greek and otherwise) or coffee and cake.

Plaka

Many after-dark pleasures are concentrated in Plaka. This is the oldest quarter of Athens, a fascinating and colorful hodgepodge of 19th-century houses, Greek and Roman ruins, and Byzantine churches, all spilling down the northern slope of the Acropolis. Certain of the winding, narrow streets have been converted into pedestrian malls, so you no longer have to be constantly wary of vehicular traffic.

If you haven't been to Athens in more than five years, be apprised that the glaring neon signs and blaring music of discos are gone—officially banished. There are still bars, tavernas, and nightclubs, but their external appearance is more sedate.

There are dozens upon dozens of tavernas in Plaka. Many serve fresh food, and you can't go wrong if you order a simple Greek salad or the like for a snack. The places listed for Plaka have been established for at least decades (one of them is a century old) and have long proven to be reliable.

By far the most popular taverna in Plaka (for both locals and visitors) is the now-historic (over half a century old) **Xinos**, at 4 Angélou Gerónta Street. It looks (and is) somewhat run-down; the walls need painting badly, but doing so would cover the old "Plaka art," which invariably depicts happy cartoon figures. The food is good here, and moderately priced. Casserole dishes are notable, and the waiter will tell you of any specials for the day. The trio of serenading guitarists has been playing together here for more than two decades and offers both Greek and international favorites, as does the kitchen. When the strolling trio plays for your table, tipping should be discreet—either by slipping a bill into a convenient pocket or shaking hands (without standing up). This rule applies for house guitarists-singers in other places as well.

Consisting of three small rooms, Xinos expands outdoors in the warmer months into its small courtyard by removing one wall. Many a taverna takes down a wall or two or moves into a courtyard or, if possible, onto the roof. The alternative is to close down for the hot summer. Xinos is closed Saturdays, Sundays, and during the month of July. It's best to book ahead; Tel: 322-1065.

Another, albeit smaller, standby is **Zafiris**, at 4A Thespídos Street, where the menu concentrates on game and stuffed chicken. Athenians who "never" go to Plaka will admit they patronize Zafiris (and Xinos). Here in the crowded, somewhat dilapidated premises, you dine next to famed shipowners or former ministers. Zafiris is tucked away in a side street, disguised as a closed shop. Because it cannot "move" outdoors, it evades the summertime tourist crowds by closing. Tel: 322-5460.

One spot of interest is **To Gerani**, or Ouzeri Kouklis, at 14 Trípodon Street. An *ouzerí* usually serves only mezedes—snacks to have with an ouzo—but you can make quite a delightful and filling meal of them. Here, as you sip the national drink, you can dine on a fine assortment. Located in an old house that might be called quaint, To Gerani's walls are decorated with vintage turn-of-the-century photographs that include a few "naughty" studies of nude women of the time. There are several levels: the street, the veranda, and the upper balconies. Indoors is as comfortable as out.

Along with your drinks—usually ouzo, served in miniature glass mugs and best mixed with water—your waitress will bring some eight tasty mezedes on a large tray. In addition to these are two specialties: sausages, which you cook (or burn) at your table, and smoked herring, which is also set afire in a dish on your table. No individual plates are served, so you eat Greek style, sticking your fork into whatever *mezé* looks appetizing—and do be sure to work your way around the assortment. To Gerani is inexpensive and is popular with the younger crowd.

If you are still hungry, cross the street. Almost opposite is the **Tsekouras Taverna** (3 Tripodon Street; Tel: 323-3710). You step down into the premises of a covered indoor courtyard painted all white, including the tree trunks. Wine barrels line one wall, and an old jukebox stands silent. Tsekouras has been serving for more than 70 years and specializes in *stifádo* (stew of hare or veal with whole onions, tomato, and spices) and snail dishes. The cook is the husband of the proprietress.

If you would like to see "Plaka art" in its most complete form, try **Stamatopoulos**, at 26 Lysíou Street (Tel: 322-8722). In business for a healthy 107 years and featuring an attractive garden for summer, Stamatopoulos has a quartet of musicians-singers. Specialties include fish and meat kebabs, and veal in casserole. The wall paintings are not as old as the taverna.

The **Aerides** (Winds) **Taverna**, at 3 Aurilou Street (Tel: 322-6266), is special in that it directly faces the lovely first-century B.C. Tower of the Winds. Offering simple, light fare at tables in the street, it's inexpensive and is open from breakfast to late supper.

A little more elegant is the **Hermion**, at 15 Pandróssou Street (Tel: 324-6725). More of a restaurant, it features a combination of Greek and Continental cooking and boasts two spacious (for Plaka), pleasant gardens and air-conditioned indoor premises.

One spot dating from 1898 (as evidenced by the faded wooden sign over the door) is the **Taverna Psara**, at 16 Erechtheos Street at the corner of Erokritou. Family owned and operated, it features fresh fish (a rarity in Plaka), including the popular *barboúni* (red mullet) charcoal grilled; a specialty is grilled kalamari. Psara seats 30 inside and 30 outdoors under a shady tree. Good for lunch while experiencing Plaka, this place shows its age. Tel: 325-0285.

Plaka Tavernas with Shows

An old standby is **Yeros tou Morea**, at 27 Mnisikléos Street (Tel: 322-1753), a veteran of more than 60 years, with good Greek fare and a floor show. Members of the audience are invited to join the Greek dances at the end of the show. An open-air establishment with grapevines hanging overhead, Yeros tou Morea is closed from early December through March.

The **Dionysos** (not to be confused with the GNTO restaurant of the same name opposite the Acropolis), at 21 Mnisikleos Street (Tel: 322-7589), features a Greek floor show along with typical Greek cuisine. Its rooftop provides a panoramic view of the city, including the Acropolis and Mount Lycabettus.

Seven Brothers, at 3–5 Hill Street (Tel: 323-8287), has a floor show, including a belly dancer who rushes from club to club to appear in three places a night.

There's one *bouzoúki* club in Plaka, the **Perivoli T'oura-**

nou (Heaven's Garden), at 19 Lysikrátous Street (Tel: 323-5517), just opposite Hadrian's Arch. (Our subsequent comments on bouzouki in general apply here.)

Seafood

If fish is your dish, then dining in **Mikrolímano** (Little Port)—which old-timers may remember as Tourkolímano (Turkish Port)—is a must. It's only a 20- to 30-minute ride from central Athens; any cabbie will know where to take you if you merely say "Meekroleémahno." Down toward the seaport of Piraeus, this sheltered yacht harbor is lined with seafood restaurants, one adjacent to the other. Reservations are unnecessary. With the water gently lapping at your feet and the yachts moored and docked seemingly at touching distance, this is a seductive setting.

The procedure is to select a table and have the waiter escort you to the indoor premises (across the street) to pick your fish or lobster from a set of metal drawers full of ice. Practically all lobster nowadays is frozen—gone are the days when the waiter would "walk" your lobster for you. Much of the fish is frozen, too.

Here are two simple freshness tests for fish (aside from the nasal appraisal): (1) Look into its eyes; if they're clear, okay, but if clouded, nay. (2) Push a finger against the fish; if the spot reshapes as soon as you remove your finger, okay, but if an indentation remains, move on to the next offering.

At fish tavernas/restaurants, each dish served will have a small slip of paper on it. This records the weight and price of the dish. Save these scraps to check the bill. Often the waiter will not have a duplicate set for his accounting.

Fresh fish (along with friendly and courteous service) can always be found at **Canaris**, at 50 Akti Koumoudouroú Street (Tel: 417-5190), one of the older establishments, and at the **Kokkini Varka**, on the same street at number 18 (Tel: 417-5853), which has a small fishing smack suspended from its ceiling. A third reliable in this lineup of seafood places is **Zephyros**, at number 48 (Tel: 417-5152).

Some insiders, including several Greek shipowners, prefer a place a few minutes' drive from Mikrolimano (or a 10- to 15-minute walk along the seafront toward Athens), the **Dourabeis**, at 29 Athínas Dilavéri Street (Tel: 412-2092), which faces out toward the sea. Here you will find not only fresh fish but also an unusual (and large) salad offering that includes radishes, lettuce, leeks, green onions, and Salonika peppers.

For an experience and a variety of seafood offerings,

Vassilena's, in Piraeus at 72 Etolikoú Street (Tel: 461-2457), is a delight. Situated in a renovated grocery store (with tins of tomato paste and the like as decor), it utilizes the rooftop in summer. There is no menu as such; instead, a series of at least 16 dishes is served, and the end of the parade is usually heralded by soup. (It is good to be ravenously hungry when you trek to Vassilena's.) The concentration is on seafood, but not exclusively, and it is surprisingly inexpensive. In the days of Greece's monarchy, the royal family ate here regularly. George Vassilena is the son of the founder, and his chief cook is the son of the original chief cook as well.

You can also dine regally on fish outside of Mikrolimano. One of the most noted spots is the **Bouillabaisse**, at 28 Zissimopoulou Street in Amphithéa (Tel: 941-9082), about halfway to the airport from central Athens. Freshly caught fish is on display, and the first customers get first picks—the catch of the day dwindles as the night wears on. Meals open with the house soup, after which the restaurant was named. Bouillabaisse operates year round and is one of the few places that has room for car parking.

Another fine spot is just down the street at number 24: the **Botsaris**, where you can make the soup a main course (Tel: 941-3022).

Closer to the center of Athens is **The Anthropos**, at 13 Archeláou Street, near the Truman statue in Pangráti (Tel: 723-5914). The premises are colorful, with scores of pictures of local and international celebrities dining here. Anthropos boasts top-grade seafood and other specialties, and the outdoor surroundings are reminiscent of the Greek isles. It's usually closed for two or three months in the summertime, depending on the whim of the owner, Takis.

Dining at Large

If you are in a mood to sample regional cooking and you have a healthy appetite, take a taxi to **Apaggio**, a real "find" of a taverna at 8 Megístis Street in Kalamáki, a neighborhood on the outskirts of Athens. Apaggio is owned and operated by Angeliki Maniaki, who has three women from various parts of Greece in her kitchen creating original dishes. The menu changes daily and is announced at each table by Angeliki herself.

Samplings include lamb cooked with prunes and almonds; beef smothered in special spicy sauce and served with feta-stuffed hot peppers; spicy shrimp *youvétsi;* lamb with cheese wrapped in pastry; eggplant (aubergine) stuffed with cheese, ham, and peppers; and onion pie. This place is high on gourmet eating, with gourmand portions, and very reasonably priced. Hardly anyone gets a table without a reservation; Tel: 983-9093.

Myrtia, at 32 Trivonianou Street (south of the Zappeion, between the Stadium and the cemetery), is another of the best-known tavernas of Athens, complete with serenading guitarists and regularly patronized by top officials and visiting celebrities (all of whom have their pictures on the bamboo-covered walls). There is no menu as such; food is presented, and it is good. It's best to go with a minimum of four people, even six, to do justice to the heaping portions. First comes a set of mezedes, followed by dishes piled high with beef, chicken, lamb, and pork. Reservations recommended; Tel: 902-3633. (For those who may be familiar with this favorite after 45 years, it has moved some 150 yards from its old location and is now off Markou Moussourou.)

Around the corner on Markou Moussourou is the **Mets Bar**, which is named after the area. The Mets is an attractively decorated and surprisingly spacious place, with marble-topped tables and a long, three-sided bar. Though primarily for gabbing and drinking, it does have a good variety of snacks and main dishes. Mets is popular with younger Athenians.

Across the street and a little farther downhill, at 3 Markou Moussourou, is the **Manesis Taverna**—without music, but lower priced than Myrtia. You can dine in a tree-shaded courtyard. The waiter brings you a large trayful of sample offerings to help you make the decision. Tel: 922-7684.

A few steps farther down, at number 1, is **Memories**, a delightful spot with a magnificent view of the Acropolis and Mount Lycabettus, both of which are illuminated at night. Memories offers a fine selection on the upscale menu (both Greek and international dishes; the Chateaubriand is tender and succulent). Memories also has good cheek-to-cheek dance music. Reservations are necessary for dining (Tel: 922-5712) but not for sitting or standing at the bar—or dancing. Closed Sundays and from May 15 through September 15. If you're in the mood for more frenetic dancing, there is a disco in the basement of the same building and another, smaller one up top. Both are very popular and packed.

One taverna that is consistently good and always open on Sunday evenings is **Themistocles**, at 31 Vas. Georgíou B Avenue in Pangrati, near the Caravel Hotel. Themistocles serves good Greek fare, including a fine *bekrí mezé,* lamb in lemon sauce, and meatballs. Signs posted on the white-washed walls and trees of the gardens request that patrons not talk loudly or sing after 11:00 P.M., so as not to disturb the neighborhood's residents. Tel: 721-9553.

Another good spot for dining in the winter is the **Remezzo**, at 6 Haritos Street in nearby Kolonaki, with a superb kitchen, a varied menu, and a good ambience. Remezzo is an "in" place to rub elbows with shipowners, politicians, and other celebs, and it features top pianists and singers. In summer the Remezzo transforms into a popular disco on the island of Mykonos, home of the genial host, Maky Zouganelli.

Balthazar, at 27 Tsoha Street on the other side of Lycabettus from Remezzo, is not far from the U.S. Embassy, closer to the Australian. Situated in a renovated mansion, Balthazar has a fine menu. Outdoors there is a big drinking area consisting of a bar, tables, and a dance floor. A little removed in the back is a sheltered dining area with much greenery. Tel: 644-1215.

Foreign Restaurants

Athens and environs have a host of fine foreign restaurants. The great majority do not compare too favorably with those of New York, London, or Paris, but they do provide relief from the Greek taverna offerings.

We've already mentioned some places that feature dishes other than Greek. In addition there is quite a rash of Chinese restaurants. The Greeks have discovered the wok—but not the subtleties of cooking with it. Most of the Chinese food here would not be missed, but there are a couple of exceptions.

The **Far East**, at 7 Stadíou Street (at the end of the stoa) right off Syntagma Square, is top-grade in all respects and could compete internationally. It features Chinese, Korean, and Japanese specialties; the premises and service are super. Best to reserve; Tel: 323-4996.

High on the list of satisfying dining experiences is the **Kona Kai** of the Ledra Marriott, on Syngrou Avenue. The breathtaking setting includes a wall-size panorama of a Polynesian paradise, a waterfall, pools, and queen bamboo chairs. The menu includes Polynesian, Chinese, and Japanese specialties. The last has its own special tables and chefs. The selection of exotic drinks is extensive. Tel: 934-7711.

The dining experience in Athens is at the **Bajazzo**, situated in a stately 1920s house at 35 Ploutarchou Street, one of the quaint "stairway" streets of the Kolonaki area. The attractive premises comfortably accommodate some 30 patrons in the main dining room and another ten in a private-party salon. Chef-owner Klaus Feuerbach (who once served as specialty chef to the Shah of Iran) creates dishes for the day, all unusual combinations such as chicken with snails, curry in banana, shrimp with watermelon, sliced duck imbedded with sour cherries complemented by cauliflower-stuffed zucchini. This is the type of place where you sip Kir Royale. Reservations are essential; Tel: 729-1420.

Probably the best Italian restaurant in Athens is **Boschetto**, situated in the pleasant block-size park in front of the Evangelismos Hospital (across from the Athens Hilton). It has no official street address, but it is at the crossroads of Vasilíssis Sophías Avenue and Genádiou Street. In the warmer months dining is outdoors on an inviting, tree-shaded veranda. The carpaccio, seafood salad, and *spaghetti al mare,* as well as the various pastas, are recommended. The Boschetto also has that "elegant" touch of no prices listed on the ladies' menu. Reservations a must; Tel: 721-0893.

Da Bruno, at 46 Ayíou Alexándrou Street in Páleo Pháleron, near Glyfáda (Tel: 981-8959), also offers very fine Italian cuisine, including a good selection of pasta dishes, but in more mundane premises. Here you can grill your own steak at table on a hot stone. It's about a 20-minute taxi ride from the center of town.

If you have a craving for pasta, the Athens Hilton's **Byzantine Café** features a wide assortment (buffet style) along with other Italian delights every Wednesday. Tel: 722-0201. (Both the Athens Hilton and the Ledra Marriott hotels feature evening dining, buffet style, by their swimming pools during the summer. Both also feature dance music.)

Prunier, at 63 Ypsilántou Street in Kolonaki, is really French, with frogs' legs, snails, and the like liberally laced with garlic. Tel: 722-7379.

The Balalaika, at 38 Andinoros Street (practically next to the Hotel Caravel), is Russian from its doorman to its balalaika music to its caviar. Strictly czarist. Tel: 724-6287.

Maralinas, at 11 Vrasída Street (behind the Hilton), has delicious Lebanese cuisine and belly dancers. It's really more of a jumping nightclub than restaurant, but hosts Amin and Azra are glad to make suggestions. Tel: 723-5425.

For German fare, there is the tiny (seats no more than 40) **Delicious** restaurant at 6 Zalokósta Street, just off Syntagma Square. Delicious calls itself a restaurant, but it is more a delicatessen with a surprisingly large menu of mainly original dishes. Chef-owner Gunther Heerd and his wife are a team, sharing duties as cook, manager, waiter, and so forth.

Gunther will prepare special "surprises" with advance notice. Tel: 363-8455. Unfortunately Delicious closes from the end of May through mid-October.

The **Curry Palace**, at 38B Poseidónos Avenue in Kalamaki (in the outskirts of Athens), offers Indian-Pakistani cuisine, including vegetarian menus. Tel: 983-8889.

BARS

Athens is not a city where you go to the neighborhood pub just to drink. Unlike Americans and British, Greeks drink not for the sake of drinking but to socialize, and in most instances they'll snack while sipping.

A host of little, cozy-appearing bars spotted around town, mostly near major hotels and in central Syntagma Square, exist for the lonely seeking female companionship. Behind the Hilton, for example, there is a row of no fewer than four, all with female bartenders and "attendants"—and, usually, solitary customers. Prices are as steep as the customer is anxious or drunk. In the main these places are to be avoided.

There are still some pimps working around central Syntagma Square who invite the single, foreign-looking male or duo to have a drink in a cozy bar. Let it suffice to say that these characters work on commission for inducing the people they lure into a bar or club to be hustled.

Women travelling alone in Athens will no doubt come across the plentiful supply of caballeros (*kamákia*). They are very active around Syntagma and nearby Kolonaki, as well as around the Acropolis and Plaka. You don't have to look for them—they'll find you. Nowadays they are willing to share a day of culture before an evening of dining and fun (on the visitor). Some of the kamakia now carry identification cards that attest they are free of AIDS.

One quaint place is the **Apotsos**, at the end of the arcade at 10 Panepistimíou Avenue, two blocks from Syntagma Square. A throwback to the 1930s and 1940s, Apotsos is decorated with posters, old biscuit-tin covers, calendars, and the like from that period. Replete with overhead fans and rush-bottom chairs, it's a bit noisy and has a colorful set of regulars, including press and politicians, and features an extensive menu of hot snacks. A meal here is half a dozen mezedes. Try the *saganáki* (fried cheese), *keftédes* (meatballs), *yígantes* (lima beans), *bekrí mezé* (bits of beef in sauce of tomato and cinnamon), as well as the ever-present Greek salad. The Apotsos is open for late lunch or early cocktails but not for dinner.

Half a block away from the Apotsos, around the immediate next corner, is the **Athenaeum**, at 8 Amerikís Street. The entrance may not be inviting or even suggest a restaurant inside, but do venture in. It appears to be a private club, but it is not. The Athenaeum features a cozy, quiet bar and both a light buffet and a menu for heartier meals. In deference to the Greek passion for dining outdoors in warmer months, the Athenaeum closes from June 15 through September 15.

If you'd like to witness a spectacular sunset (pollution permitting) while imbibing your cocktails, get yourself atop Mount Lycabettus. That's the sharp-peaked mount in the center of the Attica plains, in view from almost all points of central Athens. You can look down at the Acropolis from this vantage point, which is topped with a white, cake-like church. There's a funicular to help you get to the top, or you can walk. Once the sun has set, be advised that there are many far better places to dine than at the café here.

In general the leading hotel bars are comfortable and attractive but bear New York and London prices. Among the more pleasant are those of the Athens Hilton—both the newly renovated **Pan Bar** and the rooftop **Galaxy** (which also is a good vantage point for a sometimes brilliant sunset)—the two bars of the Grande Bretagne, and those of the Ledra Marriott and Athenaeum Inter-Continental hotels. The last has an indoor Viennese sidewalk café. All feature live piano music. A panoramic view of the city can also be had from the rooftop bar-restaurant of the St. George Lycabettus hotel.

BOUZOUKI

Bouzoúki (plural, *bouzoúkia*) describes a form of entertainment, a musical instrument, a music, a dance, and a spirit that is rather Greek-peasant. The music and instrument developed in Greek communities in Asia Minor and moved to Greece in the 1920s when Greece and Turkey, apparently exhausted by waging war on each other, effected an exchange of populations instead of bullets. The actual instrument started as a mandolin, but with a harder tone and an elongated stem. Bouzoukia in Greece, unlike those abroad, rarely feature belly dancers, which are strictly Anatolian. Certain Greek nightclubs among those mentioned earlier feature belly dancers because the customers expect them.

Bouzouki songs have no religious connotations, even though they sound similar to American spirituals. They are laments of a hard life (originally in Turkey, later in Greece), unrequited love, and the like. Sophisticates never "go to the bouzoukia," as the Greek expression puts it, and you will see hardly any tourists at one. Laborers and the so-called lower-class politicians and civil servants make up the basic audience.

But there are exceptions. If you happen to like music blastingly loud, decibels louder than disco; if you like to have a table of laborers boisterously drown out the star singers; if you like to have a dish of substandard food (generally unappetizing souvlaki with teaspoons of peas and diced carrots) put in front of you—bouzouki may be for you. Many regulars disdain any food, although it is automatically included in the bill.

The show never starts before midnight, and the presentation is a row of singers and musicians, all seated, each performing in turn while remaining seated. At any given moment it can be a guessing game as to who is singing.

Rarely nowadays will you see *spasta*—the smashing of plates. It is passé. Some time ago the government discouraged the practice as being barbaric, and bouzouki club owners very quickly discovered that more profits could be reaped with less mess if they used flowers instead of plates. Thus, patrons are badgered by persistent waiters to buy small bowls of flowers, which are meant to be thrown at the performers who please the audience; those who really please are literally "showered" with flowers. If you buy enough for a shower, the waiter will go onstage during the performance, point to you, and then shower the singer with your blossoms. A table for four at a bouzouki club can cost some 50,000 drachmas (including the inedible dinner—and there are rarely any substitutions), but the flower tab can easily more than double that.

You can hear bouzouki music (whether you want to or not) perhaps more gently in almost any regular nightclub or even in the numerous piano bars around town. You can also tell when it is midnight, because usually that hour signals the start of bouzouki in the program.

Syngrou Avenue, the main boulevard from Athens center to the airport and to Piraeus, has perhaps a dozen bouzouki clubs. The **Iphigenia**, at 201 Syngrou Avenue (Tel: 934-9444), is one of the few where *spasta* is still alive: Patrons may break plates here. Special dishes that shatter easily are used, and you pay for what you break. If you present a good argument here (and perhaps break enough plates), you might be able to convert the obligatory food charges to booze.

The Playboy, at 137 Syngrou (Tel: 934-8587), offers a perceptibly lighter, maybe even palatable, bouzouki program. Closed from April to September.

DANCING

Aside from those mentioned above, here are some places with particularly good dance music. The **Neraida**, at 2 King George Avenue in Kalamaki, has for years reigned as the queen of nightclubs, with both indoor and outdoor premises. It features a floor show, bouzouki, and top Greek entertainers, but offers time out for dance sessions. The food is somewhat better than average bouzouki quality.

Yesterday's, at 3 November 17th Street in Eliópoulis (en route to the airport, just beyond the East Terminal), features American music along with a good menu. Winter only.

The **Sixties**, at 42 Poseidon Avenue in Paleo Phaleron, a seaside resort about 8 km (5 miles) southwest of Athens, has good dance music, pleasant surroundings, and fine international cuisine.

On the Rocks, on Souniou Street in Várkiza (Tel: 897-1763), provides good dance music and menu in beautiful, romantic surroundings. It's a 30- to 45-minute, 1,400-drachma taxi ride out of town beyond the beaches of Vouliagmeni. Also out Vouliagmeni way (past the airport and Glyfada) is the **Nine Muses**, situated in the Astir Hotel complex, with good dance music (Tel: 896-4024).

Copacabana, at 4 Kaliroi Street (near the center of Athens, within view of the Olympian Zeus temple), features a floor show, usually of foreign acts, including magician, comedian, singers, and dancers. It also has "hostesses."

LEGAL GAMBLING

If you feel like some gambling, Athens has a casino situated high atop Mount Parnis to the north, more than a half-hour drive from the center of the city. Getting there includes a cable-car ride offering a bird's-eye view of Athens below you. Supervised by Casinos Austria, this is the second-largest casino in Europe after Madrid's; it offers American and French roulette, blackjack, *punto banco,* and chemin de fer. You can also dine here, and there's a 135-room hotel attached, should you choose to sleep over.

Be aware that 95 percent of the patrons are Greeks, who gain admittance by presenting a copy of their tax returns attesting that they earned at least 700,000 drachmas; foreigners gain admission by presenting their passports and 950 drachmas. The 52 tables are ordinarily crowded to the point of standing room only. Bets range from 200 to 20,000 drachmas, with chips representing up to one million drachmas (U.S. $7,000).

To export any winnings, you must have declared foreign currency on your arrival at Athens Airport. Otherwise, if you're lucky at the tables, you may be swimming in drachmas.

One-way taxi fare from central Athens is about 3,000 drachmas. If you have a car, do *not* drive up to the casino; take the cable car, which takes only a few minutes. Otherwise you face a journey of well over an hour along a tortuous and dangerous road.

—*Connie Soloyanis*

SHOPS AND SHOPPING

Athens is caught—quite comfortably, for the Greeks—between East and West: between the bedlam of the "Turkish" bazaar at Monastiraki, with its overpowering sound, smell, and attendant sensory overload, and the air-conditioned, minimalist enclaves of Gucci, PentheRoudakiS, and, good heavens, even Laura Ashley in the upscale Kolonaki district. Shoppers may slide along this East-West continuum at will and bring home the best of both—a quirky and schizophrenic harvest, but one uniquely Athenian.

Most visitors will find everything they want in the rough triangle formed by Monastiráki, Kolonáki (Plateía Philikís Etaireías), and Omónia squares. Athens's finest boutiques are located in the Kolonaki area, on Skoufá, Tsakálof, and Patriárchou Ioacheím streets. From Sýntagma down to Monastiraki, Ermoú and Mitropóleos streets are lined with solidly middle-class merchants and mini department stores. Between Omonia and Kolonaki, the long boulevards of Stadíou, Panepistimíou, and Akadimías all feature clothing, book, music, and shoe stores. In a warren of streets around Monastiraki Square, on Pandróssou, Adrianoú, and Iféstou streets, is the bazaar, or flea market, whose heart may be pinpointed at tiny Plateía Avyssinías (Abyssinia Square).

Shopping in Athens is best done on foot, on crowded pavements more often than not potholed and uneven. The jostling and smog consumption at street level are modern Athenian realities foreign visitors must take in stride. There is little danger of street theft, even in the recesses of the bazaar. Travellers' checks and major credit cards are accepted by most merchants throughout the city, though paying in cash may often lower a marked price significantly. Return visitors should note that the haggling and bargaining of yesteryear are no longer *de rigueur* in Greece; even in the bazaar set prices are usually firm.

Shop hours are a source of irritation for locals and visitors alike, as successive governments have not decided, once and for all, how "European" the Greek work week should be. At present most merchants are open daily except Sundays; on Mondays, Wednesdays, and Saturdays shops are generally open from 8:30 A.M. to 2:30 P.M.; on Tuesdays, Thursdays, and Fridays they are open from 8:00 A.M. till 2:00 P.M. and from 5:30 until 8:30 in the evening. You will find that these schedules are subject to change. Pharmacies and banks are on different schedules. Shops catering primarily to tourists, and the omnipresent kiosks, may be open at all hours. Shops in the flea market (except those selling antiques) are open on Sunday mornings. The fine antiquarians and galleries also step to a different drummer; some galleries may close during the summer months. The National Tourist Organization office on Syntagma Square and the concierges at better hotels may be of assistance in sorting out this scheduling. It is annoying to hike several miles downtown and brave the crowds in the flea market only to find the shop you've come to visit closes early on Saturdays.

Jewelry

Athenian jewelry—especially the 22-karat creations in saffron-colored "Greek" gold—is justifiably famous the world over. The country's "Ambassador of Gold," **Ilias Lalaounis**, a fourth-generation goldsmith originally from Delphi, offers more than 25 collections of jewels at his several Athens shops. Each collection is inspired by a distinctive period in Greek history, Persian or Islamic art, prehistoric idols, Greek flora and fauna—even Schliemann's drawings of ornaments found at Troy. The main Lalaounis store is located at 6 Panepistimiou Street. Gold and silver stores are also located at the **Athens Tower** in Ambelókipi, a neighborhood in the northeastern part of Athens. Be sure to see Lalaounis's gold and silver tea services and other household objects.

The other great name in Greek gold is **Zolotas**, the only jeweler permitted by the Greek government to copy the treasures in the archaeological museums of Athens and

Thessaloniki as well as the Benaki Museum. Zolotas's main store is at 10 Panepistimiou Street.

Probably the most creative and exciting work in Athenian gold being done today is by the designers of **Fanourakis**, a jeweler with shops at 23 Patriarchou Ioacheim in Kolonaki and on the pedestrian walkway at 2 Evangelístrias, running between Ermou and Kolokotróni streets. Fanourakis, a Cretan goldsmith, has trademark floral pieces in 22- and 18-karat gold, with or without imaginatively cut jewels; a special new line of work treats gold like fine fabric, folding and knotting it.

Foreigners may buy from the better-known Lalaounis and Zolotas; Athenian society frequents Fanourakis and others—such as **Michalis**, with shops at 7 Perikléous (near Evangelistrias and parallel to Ermou) and 2 Voukourestíou, and on the fifth floor at 15 Amerikís downhill from Kolonaki; **Xanthopoulos**, at 4 Voukorestiou; **J. Vourakis & Fils**, who represent Piaget in Athens, at 8 Voukourestiou and 9 Stadiou; and, of course, **PentheRoudakiS**, whose work may be seen at 19 Voukourestiou and around the corner at 5 Tsakalof.

Another highlight of Greek jewelry is the so-called *Yaniátika,* named for the city of Ioannina in Epirus, whose silversmiths are famous for perfecting the scorched, filigree, and braided-silver techniques incorporated in this work. Shops featuring this jewelry and other silver items such as worry beads, picture frames, cigarette boxes, and candelabra are located on and just off Lekka Street in the city center. It's worth comparing prices here. **Nikolaos Dragatsis**'s shop at 21 Lekka is a good place to start.

Art and Antiques
Visitors should know that it is expressly forbidden to remove any object, however "insignificant," from an archaeological site. Permits are required for exporting antiquities of any sort, so it is best to deal only with reliable and experienced antiquarians.

In this area there are no longer any "bargains" in Athens. The days of picking up icons or ancient coins for a song ended some 30 years ago. Still, for those interested in folk-art items—embroideries, shadow puppets (*Karagöz* dolls), carved wooden furniture, and the like—prices are still within reason. For less finicky consumers, beautiful modern copies of ancient works are readily available at a fraction of the cost of the originals.

For true antiques—ancient, Byzantine, and later vintage—

there are several stores of interest in the **Monastiraki** bazaar proper and five in the city center. (Note: Phone numbers are supplied, as you would do well to call for shop hours or appointments.)

Sirapian Dikran's comprehensive antiques shop, located in the very heart of Monastiraki's flea market at 31 Ifestou Street (Tel: 321-2579), represents a cornucopia of treasures from the classic to the Turkish and includes mementos of World War II. **George Goutis**'s shop nearby at 47 Pandrossou Street (Tel: 321-3212) is another rich emporium, with leather Karagöz dolls and national costumes suspended from the rafters, amber and carnelian seal stones, and traditional Greek jewelry and coins in glass cabinets. **Eleni Martinou**, at 50 Pandrossou Street (Tel: 321-3110), is the best-known antiquarian in the district and a fount of information. Her shop is located at the old entranceway to the Roman agora, where today street merchants display the distinctive, bright woven textiles from Metsovo, another good buy.

Just north of Monastiraki, at 17 Athinas Street (Tel: 321-0285), is **Ioannis Kostandoglou**'s shop, another impressive selection of Greek antiques. Kostandoglou has a more upscale shop at 20 Voukourestiou Street (Tel: 362-6238), also a good place to find icons, jewelry featuring coins, charms against the evil eye, and Byzantine artifacts. (This second shop is appropriately called **Mati**, which means "eye.")

A very special store is **Anthes**, a little "brownstone" at 24 Pindarou Street in Kolonaki (Tel: 363-6951). Here is antique furniture (they ship) from the last three centuries, along with paintings, marble architectural elements, and some exquisite modern work in metal. (Special visitors may be honored with a grand tour of the premises, and here see how best to use these Greek antiques in a modern setting.)

Zoumboulakis Galleries, with the main showroom on Kolonaki Square (Tel: 360-8278) and a more intimate gallery at 7 Kriezótou Street just a few blocks to the west (Tel: 363-4454), is famed for fine multiples (numbered editions of fine prints and sculptures), prints, posters, and antiques, and is probably Athens's best-known art dealer. Those interested in the finest of modern Greek art—the work of Tsarouchis, Mytaras, Moralis, Fassianos, et al.—should not miss this gallery. Those interested in antiques should contact Mrs. Zoumboulakis herself for an appointment.

Stamp and coin enthusiasts should seek out **Paul G. Pylarinos**'s shops at 7–9 Sophokléous Street, up toward Omonia Square, and 6 Stadiou Street (Tel: 321-0577). The owner is the publisher of the monthly *Collectors' Review*.

Near Syntagma Square, at 4 Amalias Avenue, is the posh, pricey **Galerie Antiqua**, with Greek and international antiques ranging from carved island furniture to Chinese porcelain (Tel: 323-2220).

Retro
A recent trend in European capitals is "retro shopping" at stores specializing in late-19th- and early- to mid-20th-century clothing, costume jewelry, and household objects. There are several such shops worth visiting in Athens.

Berlin, down the steps at 10A Didótou Street in the Exárchia area just northwest of Kolonaki, is often ransacked to outfit period-piece productions on stage or television. Boxes, linens, dolls, military uniforms, postcards, and hats are all available, much of the material German. **Nostalgia**, close by at 44 Sina Street, and **Ranga Paranga**, at 23 Sina, both specialize in retro clothing. (There is a tendency in Athens for shops carrying certain types of wares to cluster together: Hence the many shoe shops on Kanáris Street, the jewelers on Voukourestiou, etc.)

In the Plaka area, **Galerie Iró**, at 12 Iperídou Street, combines antiques with retro items. Across the street the **Clockwork Monkey Collectors' Corner**, at 17 Iperidou, offers cigarette lighters, watches, posters, boxes, buttons, pens, and mechanical toys.

E. & P. Sokara's **Antiques**, at 1 Nissoú Street (Tel: 325-4051) in the heart of the flea market, is another center for retro enthusiasts, with antique linens and crystal thrown in for good measure.

Handicrafts, Museum Shops, Ecclesiastical Shops
Some kinds of shopping are best done in Athens and nowhere else. Two stores feature the very best in modern copies of traditional Greek handicrafts.

The **National Welfare Organization**'s shop at 135 Vasilíssis Sophías in Ambelokipi is worth the taxi ride out from the city center, as here, under one roof, the buyer may purchase *flokáti* rugs, tapestries (see those based on the work of the modern Greek painters Ghika and Tsarouchis), needlepoint, hand-knotted and handwoven rugs, ceramics, and copper items—all authentic. Another store is located downtown at 6 Ipatias Street in Plaka.

The **Center of Hellenic Tradition**, in Monastiraki, is located upstairs in the arcade at 59 Mitropoleos Street/36 Pandrossou Street. Sculpture, jewelry, carved furniture, ceramics, and textiles, all of high quality, are available here. A charming *kafeneío* is also located on the premises—a nice place to collapse for coffee, with a view of the Parthenon.

Some of the best buys in Athens are at the museum shops. The **National Archaeological Museum**, on Patission Street, has a large basement showroom where excellent copies of ancient Greek statuary and Byzantine icons may be purchased. Buyers may even ship home a life-size (more than six feet) bronze copy of the famous 450 B.C. statue of Zeus-Poseidon if they so desire.

The **Benaki Museum**, at 1 Koumbári Street, and the **Goulandris Museum of Cycladic Art**, at 4 Neophýtou Doúka Street, have excellent "Western-style" museum shops. The former features icons, copies of ancient and Byzantine jewelry, recordings, and cards. The latter offers copies of Cycladic sculpture. If you have only one shopping day in Athens, visit the Benaki (closed Tuesdays).

In the warren of streets on the Plaka side of the cathedral, notably Ayios Philothéis and Ayios Andréas streets, visitors will find Athens's icon painters and ecclesiastical suppliers. All the elaborate trappings of the Orthodox rite may be had here, from vestments heavy in gold thread to pectoral crosses, votive offerings in gold or silver (*támata*), silver-chased icons, brass candle stands, and incense and oil lamps.

This wealth of church goods may be attractive to the more secular shopper. Elizabeths, Catherines, Anthonys, and so on may also want to commission modern icons of their saintly namesakes. The **Philokalia** shop at 38 Voulis Street in Plaka has Greek Orthodox books in several languages, incense, Byzantine music on cassettes and records, cards, and reasonably priced icons.

Compendium Ltd., at 28 Nikis Street, off Syntagma Square, is the city's most complete and user-friendly bookstore, replete with guidebooks and Penguins. Both **Reymoundos**, at 18 Voukourestiou Street, and **Eleftheroudakis**, at 4 Nikis Street, are the best places for art and gift books.

Kolonaki

A walk through the city's poshest shopping district may deplete the checkbook, but shoppers seeking quality knockoffs of Paris's latest fine shoes and bags, in addition to Athens's branches of Europe's elite designer boutiques, should give Tsakalof Street a day or so.

Tsakalof is the main thoroughfare for upscale shopping, beginning at Kolonaki Square proper. At 2 Tsakalof is **Omega**, featuring fine shoes, next to **Mocassino**, at number 4, which carries a younger line of men's and women's shoes, as well as bags. Across the pedestrian walkway at number 5 is the Melathron Shopping Mall, which houses **Gucci**, **Penthe-RoudakiS**, the **Pagoni** tie shop, the **Silver Center** (for silver services), **Ozz** (silver jewelry), and **Filippo's** (menswear).

Farther down Tsakalof at number 13 is **Ritsi** for men; the women's and children's Ritsi is located at number 23. **Trussardi**, Italy's equivalent of France's Hermès, sells upscale clothing and accessories. It's located at 15 Tsakalof, just across from the popular Everest snack bar.

Turn left down Iraklítou Street and find Kolonaki's best hair salon at number 12—**Giel Haute Coiffure**—just above the punk clothing boutique **Remember**.

Off Tsakalof to the left at 21 Pindarou Street is **Plekta Lanari** for fine, reasonably priced designer knitwear for women. To the right up Pindarou at number 38 is **Pop Eleven**, the city's most complete record shop. Listen to work by George Dalaras, Ross Daly, Vassilis Tsitsanis, Haroula Alexiou, and Sotiria Bellou, for starters. Next door is **Kiara**, for some of Athens's loveliest feminine ready-to-wear, plus Gianni Versace swimwear.

Back on Tsakalof at number 30 is **Sarella**, with less expensive women's ready-to-wear and the latest northern European styles. To the left, down Voukourestiou Street at number 25A, is **Anastasia/Siba**, with romantic Italian designs in satin, pearls, and lace: expensive but exquisite evening wear. (Siba has another shop in Exarchia at 40 Ippokrátous Street.)

Haute Couture

It should be noted that Athens has its own significant designers with small but ardent followings. **Athena Andreadi**—sort of a Greek answer to Ralph Lauren—maintains an atelier at 57 Deinokrátous Street; Tel: 724-2642 for an appointment. **Polatof**, with designer ready-to-wear and ready couture, is located at 25 Voukourestiou Street. **Parthenis**'s *outré* black-and-white shockers can be found at 17 Nikis Street and at 20 Dimokritou and Tsakalof streets. **Aslanis**, noted for fine craftsmanship and color à la St-Laurent, is at 16 Anagnostopoúlou and Iraklitou streets. **Loukia Haute Couture** is upstairs at 24 Kanaris Street; downstairs you will find her prêt-à-porter collections. Tel: 362-7334 for appointments.

Miscellaneous

In closing, here are some oddities: **Leskhi**, at 19 Pindarou Street, is a fine bookbinder; **Sportif**, at 6 Voukourestiou Street, has men's articles, including some quite nice Greek briar pipes; **Stavros Melissinos**—the "Poet-Sandalmaker"—

at 89 Pandrossou Street is the only place to purchase sandals; and the **Nasiotis** family's book emporium in the arcade at 24 Ifestou Street is a must for bibliophiles.

If you break a heel—and you will—stop in at **Takouni Expres** (1 Skoufa Street; 12 Voulis Street; 5 and 13 Ippokratous Street in the arcades), and if you want anything a department store back home has to offer, **Minion**, at 13 Patissíon Street near Omonia Square, is your best bet.

For chocolate truffles stop in at **Aristokration**, at 6 Voukourestiou Street (one shop away from Voulgaridou). For pistachio and other exquisite baklava trek out to **Farouk Hanbali** in Ambelokipi at 4 Messenias Street, near the church of Ayia Triada.

Greek wines are the country's best-kept secret, but they do not travel well and are best consumed during your stay. Pick up ouzo and Metaxa "brandy"—preferably Seven Star—at the duty-free shop at the airport on your way home.

A final note: Those who've bought too much to stuff in existing luggage can pick up an extra bag at **Panagiotopoulos Leather and Travel Goods**, 20 Mitropoleos Street near Syntagma.

—*Elizabeth Boleman Herring*

ATTICA
DAY TRIPS FROM ATHENS

By Jane Winslow Eliot

For all of its world-shaking history, the peninsula known as Attica, pointing southeast into the Aegean Sea, seems a minute and insignificant piece of land. It is bounded by Mount Parnis in the northwest, Amfiaráeion in the northeast, Mégara in the west, and the sea elsewhere. Attica is the setting for both Athens, the capital of Greece, and Piraeus, its international port. Greater Athens has nibbled at the rocky promontory (in fact, that's what *attica* means), creating a hot, dusty megalopolis where once was a magnificent land like no other.

Still, pockets of Attica's magnificence remain, reason enough to go out into the harsh but wondrous landscape. The only sensible way to go is by car. Bicycles are too dangerous; walking is too hot. There are day tours by the dozen, but nowadays these are too speedy and crowded for real fun. If that's the only way you can get to Sounion, though, give it a whirl. You don't have to stick with the crowd once you arrive. If you don't drive, taxis can be hired for the trip or by the day.

Depending on the amount of time available, you will want to spoke out from Athens the 70 km (40 miles) southeast to Sounion, the 10 km (6 miles) west to Daphni, the 40 km (26 miles) northeast to Marathon, the 22 km (15 miles) northwest to Eleusis, the 10 km (6 miles) southwest to Piraeus, and the 10 km (6 miles) east to Paenia and the Vorres Museum. Buses leave Athens every 15 minutes from Plateía Eleftherías and take about 20 minutes to go to Daphni, 45 minutes to Eleusis. Sounion and Daphni are worth outings of their own, but Eleusis is better as a stop-off on your way to

Attica

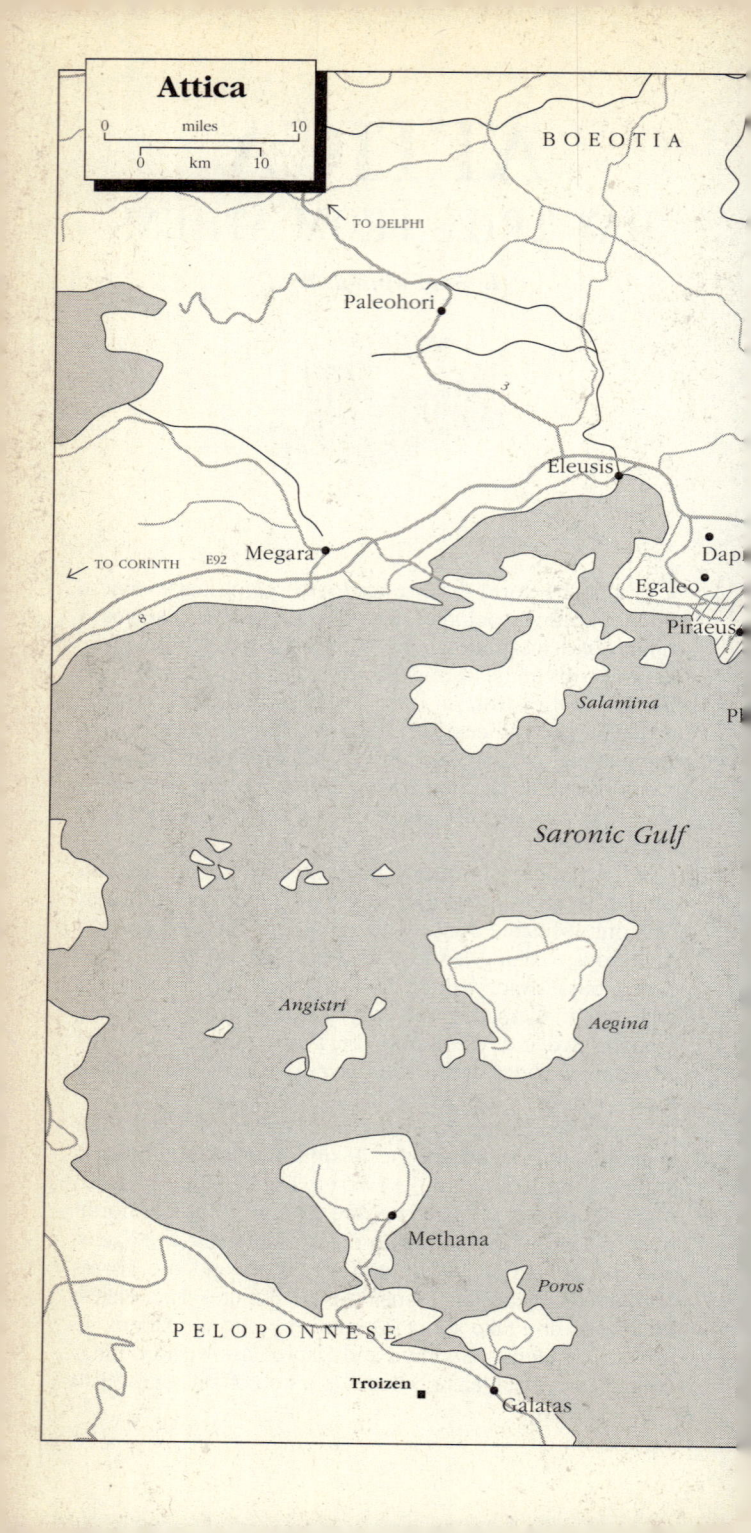

0 — miles — 10
0 — km — 10

BOEOTIA

TO DELPHI

Paleohori

Eleusis

TO CORINTH E92

Megara

Dap

Egaleo

Piraeus

Salamina

Pi

Saronic Gulf

Angistri

Aegina

Methana

Poros

PELOPONNESE

Troizen

Galatas

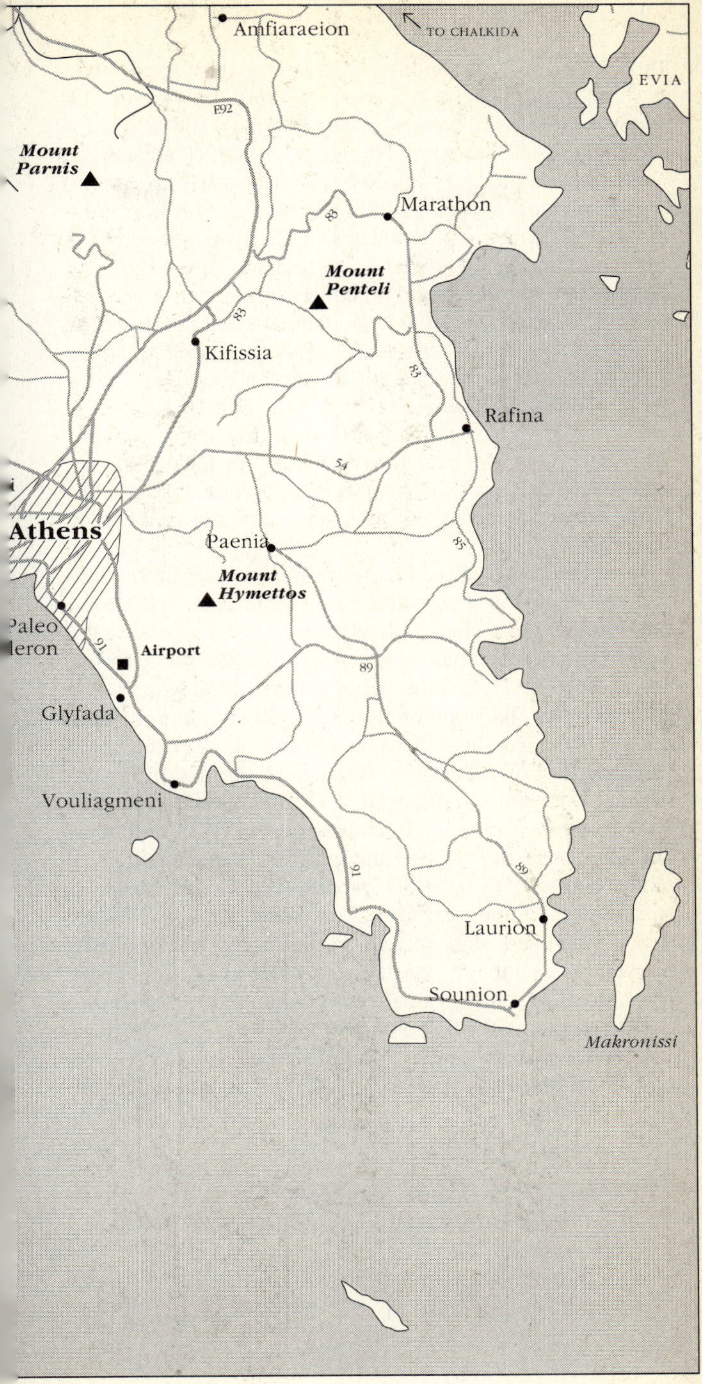
Amfiaraeion
TO CHALKIDA
EVIA
E92
Mount Parnis
Marathon
83
Mount Penteli
83
Kifissia
83
Rafina
54
Athens
Paenia
85
Mount Hymettos
Paleo
Airport
91
89
Glyfada
Vouliagmeni
91
89
Laurion
Sounion
Makronissi

Delphi or the Peloponnese; Marathon is best done on a daylong swing around the coast of Attica. The Vorres Museum is no more than a two-hour outing by car or taxi for those interested in a rundown of modern Greek artists.

On a jaunt around the coast of Attica, you'd go out the southern coast on the Poseidon Highway, maybe stop at the resorts of Glyfada and Vouliagmeni for a swim among the rich and famous, then head on to Sounion to see the great Temple of Poseidon. An hour later you're on your way north around the east coast of Attica to **Rafína**, a delightful seaside port with good fish restaurants and interesting quayside activity—an amusing place for lunch. Refreshed, you drive on up to Marathon, only another 20 km (12 miles).

From Marathon you might choose to head up to Chalkída and swing over the bridge to the island of **Evia** (Euboea), which is quite pretty in the north and central areas. The roads are good and so are the many seafood tavernas along the coast.

Another choice would be to turn inland at Marathon onto the well-engineered road that leads up to **Ekáli** and **Drosiá** on **Mount Pentéli**. Here, in fragrant pine groves, are some of the great grill tavernas where you can relax for a typical Greek evening. The fashionable suburb of **Kifissiá**, which sprawls down the slope of Mount Penteli, ten minutes back on the main road to Athens, offers any number of choice restaurants and tavernas (try **Vassilis** on the main Kifissia–Athens road; the excellent kitchen attracts Athenian regulars), as well as some fine accommodations. The **Pentelikon** is a luxurious hotel, with restaurants, bars, a swimming pool, tennis courts, a gym, and a garden. The **Grand Chalet** is small but charming, also with a restaurant. Many of Kifissia's streets are lined with ancient trees shading beautiful old houses and well-tended gardens. However, given the horrendous Athenian traffic, it's hard to recommend Kifissia on its own as an outing for first-time visitors.

On your swing around Attica, unless there is traffic, you're now less than half an hour from Syntagma Square in Athens.

MAJOR INTEREST

Temple of Poseidon at Sounion
Luxury resorts at Glyfada and Vouliagmeni
Marathon
Daphni: Byzantine mosaics
Sacred site of Eleusis

Vorres Museum: modern Greek art
Piraeus

TO SOUNION

The southern coast from Paleo Phaleron (just outside Athens) south to Soúnion, a distance of 72 km (45 miles), is the watery playground of Athens. Almost every sort of water sport imaginable can be tried in comfort along these rocks and beaches. The farther from Athens you go, the clearer the water. The highway (the Poseidon) is always in sight of the sea, which is of a remarkable blue-green color, and pine trees offer pleasant picnic spots along the way.

Glyfáda, a resort just beyond the airport, is still a little too close to Athens. (However, it has **Psaropoulos**, an old and great—and infinitely slow—fish restaurant.) **Vouliagméni**, another 10 km (6 miles) to the south, is another story. It is simply the most attractive resort on the mainland, with several good hotels, some very fine restaurants, and one of Greece's fanciest marinas. The Astir chain has a luxury complex here on the beach, with three hotels that attract the rich and famous from all over the world. The **Aphrodite** is the newest, most intimate, and least expensive, and has the most to offer, including a doctor on the premises. The **Arion** has lovely bungalows as well as a main building geared for conventions, while the **Nafsika** is large and secluded, built in the early 1970s in a grand enough manner. The **Greek Coast Hotel** is on a much less lavish scale and very much smaller, with only 55 rooms.

The entire beautiful coast is lined with small beaches, marinas, piers, and restaurants. Development thins out toward Sounion, with villas dotting the hills somewhat more sparsely. Sounion itself has a small, first-class hotel—the **Aigaion**—built on its southern slopes, out of the wind. If you stay here, try for rooms with a view of the Temple of Poseidon.

What makes this coast memorable, however, is the journey back through time that you can make nowhere else. For here are the remains of one of the loveliest temples in Greece: On the tip of the southern coast of Attica at Sounion, beyond the beaches, beyond the villas, stands the lovely fifth-century B.C. **Temple of Poseidon**. For centuries its shining columns have stood like beacons for ships at sea. The promontory is dangerous in stormy weather, but the temple signals safety in its little harbor and promises shelter from the strong north gales. When the winds are blowing you'll indeed see large ships and small huddled below the temple.

It is said that this is the headland where the legendary hero Theseus set off to Crete in hopes of slaying the Minotaur, the monstrous half man, half bull that lived deep inside a labyrinth from which no victim had ever emerged. Ariadne, daughter of the king of Crete, befriended Theseus and showed him the means of escape. Theseus did as she advised, slew the monster, and got away. After many adventures he came within sight of Cape Sounion once again. But Theseus forgot the promise he had made to his father, Aegeus, the king of Athens: If he survived his ordeals, he was to signal his safe return by hoisting white sails in place of the black ones that had served him throughout the journey. Alas, when Aegeus saw black sails on the horizon, he flung himself over the cliff in despair. According to one romantic tradition, this is how the Aegean Sea got its name.

The temple that stands so stunningly on the promontory could belong to no one but Poseidon, earthshaker and god of the sea, who once contended with the goddess Athena for all of Attica. Myths allow for many interpretations, but it's known that in Attica's early days the sailors and fishermen along this coast struggled for precedence over the farmers and vinedressers of the interior. By the close of the sixth century B.C., of course, the townspeople of Athens had won out over both groups.

In the golden fifth century B.C. the fruits of sea and land trade combined to help make Athens great. Newly opened silver mines at Laurion, some three miles from Sounion, brought untold wealth as well, some of which helped build this wonderfully sited temple to Poseidon. The graceful structure was most probably designed by the same man who built the Temple of Hephaestus in the Agora, a building that rests heavy on the earth in contrast to the way this one balances joyfully on its rocky base, its slender columns drawing delicate white lines against deep-blue sea and sky.

Once Athenian sea power had dwindled to nothing, pirates made Cape Sounion their watery province for a while. Today luxury cruise ships, expensive yachts, and colorful fishing boats peacefully crisscross the Saronic Gulf. At sunset the scene is especially enchanting.

MARATHON

Marathon, 40 km (26 miles) northeast of Athens, is not much more than a splendid place to daydream about the past. It also has a white-sand beach that stretches in a flat crescent for some three miles. There's even a good place to stay, the **Golden Coast Hotel**, which is open from April to October and offers a taverna, swimming pool, tennis courts, and air-conditioning. If all has gone well, when you arrive in Marathon it'll be the right time for an afternoon swim.

It was at Marathon in 490 B.C. that a small army of freedom-loving Greeks stopped an onslaught from enslaved Asia. A hundred thousand men may have descended on Marathon, and the Greek defenders numbered about 10,000.

Darius, emperor of Persia, held sway from the Hindus River all the way to Ethiopia. He had experienced no trouble in swallowing whole towns and even nations at a gulp, so why not little Greece?

The Persians sailed their massive fleet south toward Athens. Bent on defending their families and their land against slave-soldiers with nothing to gain or lose, the Athenian citizen-soldiers waited on the western slopes of Mount Penteli, overlooking Marathon's white sand.

As the Persian soldiers began to disembark, the Athenian troops strung out to create a long front line, waiting until the enemy was dispersed. Then the Athenians leveled their long spears and charged silently down the slope. The enemy's arrows and wicker shields were no match for the unstoppable charge that crashed their line. Athenian troops advanced on both flanks to the water's edge, cutting the trapped Persian force to shreds. The Persian fleet pulled away, leaving some 6,400 dead on the alien shore and seven vessels captured. The Greeks had lost only 192 soldiers. The might of imperial Asia had been stopped cold. The victory at Marathon was democracy's first big one. When it was all over, Pheidippides, a runner, undertook to bring the news to Athens. He ran the 26-odd miles at breakneck speed, arriving with barely enough breath to gasp *"Hierete!"*—"Rejoice!" The word is still used as a familiar greeting, and the run itself has given us our modern marathon. An undistinguished mound and a small museum commemorate the battle.

Writing more than 2,000 years later, Lord Byron distilled the essence of the battle in a famous poem:

> The mountains look on Marathon—
> And Marathon looks on the sea;
> And musing there an hour alone,
> I dreamed that Greece might still be free;
> For standing on the Persians' grave,
> I could not deem myself a slave.

DAPHNI

The most important Byzantine church in Attica is to be seen at the monastery of Daphní, about 10 km (6 miles) from Syntagma Square right off the main highway to Corinth. The church is well marked and easy to find. Whether you are going to or coming from the city, bent on a longer journey, try not to be too hurried to stop here.

The monastery was first built and fortified in the sixth century A.D. on the site of an old temple to Apollo. It is named for the sacred laurel tree (*daphne*) that once grew here. The present church was built in the 11th century and dedicated to the Dormition of the Virgin. Architecturally its most remarkable feature is the majestic dome, some 27 feet in diameter and 50 feet high. Resting on an eight-sided base, the dome virtually caps the entire church. A hypnotic Pantokrator stares down at you from its center.

The church contains some of the most beautiful Byzantine mosaics in Greece. Although not all have survived the centuries, the ceilings and upper walls are still blazing with archangels, saints, prophets, martyrs, bishops, and monks. The topmost panels tell stories of Christ and the Virgin. The four most astonishing adorn the squinches right under the dome, including an austere Annunciation, a Nativity, and, on the southwest, one of the finest mosaics ever conceived—the Baptism of Christ. Here, the Savior stands naked in crystal-clear water up to his chest while angels hover with delicately colored towels and an intense John the Baptist leans to perform the rites.

Surpassing the Baptism in complexity is the Transfiguration, in which Christ is shown taking on the shape of divine light in the presence of Moses, the prophet Ilias, and three of His disciples, Peter, James, and John.

The church has been restored in a discreet, old-fashioned way. The surviving mosaics were delicately reaffixed, while the rest has been left cleaned and protected.

ELEUSIS

After spending some time in Greece, you may begin to ask yourself: What is the difference between a sacred site and a museum or a church?

Eleusis (Elevsína), about 45 minutes west of Athens, is an interesting example of the difference. In a dirty, sprawling industrial town of some 18,000 people lies the **Sanctuary of the Earth Mother Demeter** at the base of a tiny conical hill. (There aren't any special tavernas in the town. It's best to eat at sparkling seaside Mikrolimano—see Piraeus, below, or Athens After Dark, above—on the way here.)

Once in the sanctuary you can hardly see the sky for smog; the earth for vast, mole-like excavations; or the sea for spilled petroleum, blackened freighters, gas-drilling platforms, and the like. Five acres of dusty digging disfigures the flat plain, adding little to anyone's knowledge about the place. It is easy to see why the site is no longer popular.

On the right at the base of the hill is the **Cave of Hades**, which was once taken to be the entrance to the underworld. The great **Propylaea** lies in ruins almost straight ahead, and behind it are the imposing remains of the Temple of Demeter, beyond which a little path curves up the tiny hill to a small but exquisite **museum**. There are some lovely objects inside, particularly the little lady caught in stone while running for joy against a stiff *meltémi* wind. Farther up the hill are modern ruins of a World War II bunker and a clock tower (broken), and a wide view of the ravaged plain and desecrated bay.

Demeter's legend is familiar to many from childhood. One day Demeter's beautiful daughter, Persephone, was playing in the flower-filled fields of Eleusis, when Hades kidnapped her and took her to his dark, glittering realm. Demeter was frantic. She asked the other gods and goddesses for help, but no one lifted a hand.

So she stopped all things from growing. Soon she was told where Persephone was hidden. Realizing the game was up, Hades gave his young captive three pomegranate seeds to eat as a way to make her return to him at least three months of every year. Happy mother and daughter were reunited and vegetation returned to the earth, as it does each spring.

Today at the site of this story all is quiet, empty, and still—not at all the way it was in ancient times, when the exciting final night of the Great Panathenaia took place in

Eleusis. For hundreds of years festivals were celebrated here at planting and harvest time; by the fifth century B.C. as many as 30,000 people would joyfully walk the 14 miles from Athens by torchlight to gather at this site each September. Following almost two weeks of solemn ceremonies conducted in Athens, initiates and acolytes would at last return to Eleusis for the final revelation. Plays were presented at the temple, with awesome theatrical effects produced by ingenious mechanical devices, colored lights, and thunderous noises. Chants and songs were sung while incense and the smoke of burning sacrifices filled the air.

In ancient times a sacred site was both a religious place and an educational one where people chosen for initiation into a profession would undertake training. To learn the mysteries of medicine, for instance, one was expected to spend time at Hippocrates' center on Kos; one trained in agriculture at Demeter's sites, in smithing and technology at Hephaestus's sanctuaries, and in sailing at Poseidon's; at Olympia one tested the limits of physical excellence and endurance. Initiates pledged service to their fellows and vowed never to reveal anything. At Eleusis initiates would learn farming techniques, returning home with skills as well as seeds. They were taught to respect the gods, count on the seasons, and rely on themselves.

So how does that make Eleusis a sacred site? It was not so much the professional secrets, the sacred teachings, the purifications and traditions, the chants and melodramas, or incense and candles that clinched it. There were other things to learn, "awesome mysteries," as Hesiod sang in his hymn to Demeter, "which no one may in any way transgress or pry into or utter, for deep awe of the gods checks the voice." The final "awesome" revelation was not to be divulged on pain of death. What makes Eleusis particularly intriguing is that its central mystery has not been revealed to this day.

THE VORRES MUSEUM

About 25 minutes up Vasilissis. Sophias and out on Messógion Street you'll begin to notice signs directing travellers to Paenía, a little town just east of Athens that has two attractions: the **Cave of Paenia** and the **Vorres Museum**. The cave is hard to find and worth looking for only if you have already seen everything else in Athens. It is not in the same league with the spectacular ones down south in the Mani peninsula and up north near Ioannina. In addition, the drive out across the once-famous Attican vineyards is strewn with dumps and blocked by traffic.

The Vorres Museum, on the other hand, offers an almost complete rundown of modern Greek art, and for some travellers that will be reason enough to make the drive.

Housed on six beautifully kept acres, the museum has two parts. One is an array of Greek artifacts, rugs, furniture, clothes, jewelry, and the like, placed as if in a real Greek home. The other is a massive collection that includes works by most of the best 20th-century Greek artists. In general, modern Greek painters and sculptors hold their own pretty well. It's a shame that so few are known outside their own country.

The museum (Tel: 644-2520) is open only on Saturdays and Sundays, from 10:00 A.M. to 2:00 P.M., the very worst days to drive anywhere in Attica. Go by taxi if you can; it will cost about 1,000 to 1,500 drachmas.

PIRAEUS

A subway leaves Omonia Square for Piraeus and can be recommended over buses, except at rush hour, when nothing is recommended. The best way to cover the 10 km (6 miles) southwest is still by taxi. Cab drivers know their way around the port and where the cruise ships are docked.

Piraeus is a series of busy harbors. The main reason to go there is to leave the mainland—by cruise, yacht, sailboat, ferry, or hydrofoil. There is one harbor, well separated from ferries and cruise docks, where you will find some of the best fish restaurants in Greece: **Mikrolímano**. This is an idyllic place to dine, a tiny harbor crowded with small pleasure craft of all shapes and sizes. On a promontory to one side is the ultra-posh Royal Yacht Club, nostalgically named, since Greece has no monarchy. There are more than 20 fish restaurants crowded side by side in a semicircle around the water's edge. Each has its loyal customers who return regularly. Try the **Canaris**, almost in the center. An air of suppressed excitement as well as beauty suffuses little Mikrolimano. If you like the glamour of boating, this is the nicest spot around Athens to go for lunch or dinner (see also Athens After Dark).

The harbor of Zea is where the larger private yachts and cabin cruisers are docked—a dazzling display. (It is also home to a small but excellent naval museum that incorporates part of the ancient walls.) Note the caïques (rhymes with *sky-eeky*), high-pooped, yacht-like vessels designed to navigate the erratic rhythms of Aegean waves. For anyone going to the Argo-Saronic Gulf islands or the Peloponnese, this is the harbor where you will find Flying Dolphin's yellow-and-black hydrofoils to take you there.

For ferries to the other Aegean islands and Crete, the Poseidon Quay is your point of departure. Make sure you find your ship before you dispense with your taxi.

Piraeus is a working city of half a million people. Home port for the Greek Navy, it is also the base for its merchant ships. More passengers traipse on and off pleasure craft here than at any other port in the world. Except at Mikrolimano, though, don't expect Piraeus to have quaint or restful places to spend your time.

GETTING AROUND

Getting around Attica can be about as enervating as any driving there is. The province has become one vast suburb. There is a movement to disperse new commercial enterprises throughout the rest of Greece, which should ease the pressures on Athens in the future. But too much of the land already has been gobbled up by mostly unplanned building.

A subway train transports commuters up to Kifissia and down to Piraeus. Buses inch along both ways through some of the worst traffic anywhere and are not recommended. You can, if you have the heart of a kamikaze pilot, rent a car and drive yourself, but taking a taxi is less harrowing. Taxis make it easy to get to the resort hotels along the Sounion coast and up to cool mountains. For about 1,500 drachmas a taxi will get you to and from the Vorres Museum in Paenia. Full-day and half-day tours to Sounion are possible. Check with your hotel concierge; many hotels now have helpful tourist information and reservation desks in their lobbies.

ACCOMMODATIONS REFERENCE

- **Aigaion.** Sounion, 195 00. Tel: (0292) 392-00.
- **Astir Palace Hotels: Aphrodite, Arion, Nafsika.** Vouliagmeni, 166 71. Tel: (01) 896-0211; Telex: (21) 5013; Fax: (01) 896-2582.
- **Golden Coast Hotel.** Marathon, 190 07. Tel: (0294) 921-02.
- **Grand Chalet.** 38 Kokinara Street, **Kifissia**, 145 62. Tel: (01) 808-4837; Telex: (22) 3818.
- **Greek Coast Hotel.** 8 Panos Street, **Vouliagmeni**, 166 71. Tel: (01) 896-0302.
- **Pentelikon.** 66 Deligiani Street, Kefalari, **Kifissia**, 145 62. Tel: (01) 808-0317; Telex: (22) 4649.

THE CLASSICAL TOUR

DELPHI, OLYMPIA, EPIDAURUS

By Alexander Eliot

The word "Classical" is a catchall, of course, because it can be applied to practically all Greek and Roman antiquities. What preceded the Classical era in Greece were the Bronze Age, Cycladic, Minoan, and Mycenaean cultures followed by the Archaic so-called Iron Age of troubles and warring Dorians. The Classical Greeks themselves dated their era from the founding of the Olympic games in 776 B.C. The first Classical poet, Homer, lived and sang at about that time.

When Greco-Roman Christianity triumphed at Constantinople and vitalized the Byzantine Empire from there, the Classical era faded. Doom came slowly, however. In A.D. 361 the last pagan emperor, Julian the Apostate, sent an emissary to request a prophecy from the renowned Oracle of Delphi. The emissary found a single priest of Apollo at the site, spoke with him, and brought back this message: "Tell the King the fair hall has fallen to the ground. No longer has Apollo a hut, nor a prophetic laurel, nor a spring that speaks. Even the water of speech is quenched." That marked the end, after a little more than a millennium.

The creative apogee of Classicism came early, during the sixth, fifth, and fourth centuries B.C. Philosophers from Heraclitus to Aristotle, poets from Pindar to Menander, sculp-

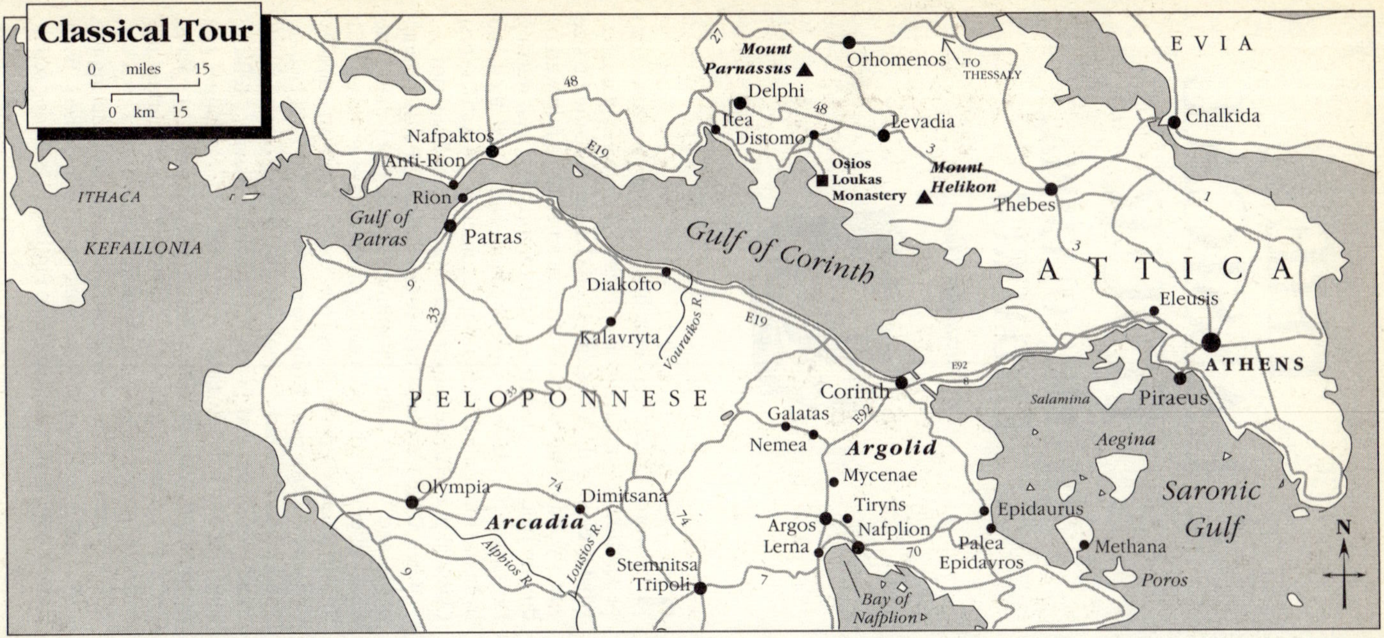
Classical Tour
0 miles 15
0 km 15
EVIA
Chalkida
Orhomenos
TO THESSALY
Mount Parnassus
Delphi
Itea
Distomo
Levadia
Osios Loukas Monastery
Mount Helikon
Thebes
Nafpaktos
Anti-Rion
Rion
Gulf of Patras
Patras
ITHACA
KEFALLONIA
Gulf of Corinth
ATTICA
Eleusis
ATHENS
Piraeus
Salamina
Aegina
Saronic Gulf
Methana
Poros
Diakofto
Kalavryta
Vouraikos R.
E19
E92
PELOPONNESE
Corinth
Galatas
Nemea
Argolid
Mycenae
Tiryns
Argos
Nafplion
Lerna
Epidaurus
Palea Epidavros
Bay of Nafplion
Olympia
Dimitsana
Arcadia
Alphios R.
Lousios R.
Stemnitsa
Tripoli
N

tors from Phidias to Praxiteles, and architects from Iktinos to Polyclitus all lived within that time span. Moreover, most men of genius in those days lived and worked within the small ellipse that encloses Athens, Delphi, Olympia, and Epidaurus. That's why it's still possible to zero in on the best of Classical culture by spending a few days in Athens and then making a circuit of the three other sites mentioned.

Every day, in fact, fleets of sleek, air-conditioned tour buses depart, or rather belch away, from Athens, bound for Delphi, Olympia, Epidaurus—or all three in sequence. They're crammed with Europeans, for the most part, people who've come to Greece for some experience of ancient history, not just a holiday. These tourists seem to be largely content with what they get—a grueling schooling.

You can't go home again, home to the roots of Western culture, by tour bus. First, because swarming along in a tightly scheduled, junk-fed culture cluster is so wearisome. Second, because the locust-like cicerones generate little more than forgettable facts. Still, you've not seen Greece unless you've made the standard "Classical Tour." The foundations of your own cultural inheritance are here. If ancient Athens was a living laboratory of democratic procedure, Delphi was the first independent, internationally respected think tank, Olympia was the first world center for sport, and Epidaurus was the first world-famous medical clinic, for physical and mental problems alike.

So our advice is to read up, rent a car, and go it on your own. Make a one-week circuit of Classical Greece. You'll start from Athens, spend two nights at Delphi, two more at Olympia, and a final two at Nafplion (near Epidaurus) before heading back to Athens again. Along the way you'll have paused at Osios Loukas, Tiryns, Mycenae, Nemea, and ancient Corinth. (See also the chapter on the Peloponnese, which includes regular coverage of sites there.) This one-week spin calls for less than two days (four leisurely half-days) of actual driving.

February through May and September and October are the ideal seasons. Remember, Greek spring really starts early in February when the almond trees bloom. March and April are especially heavenly here: You'll find the land literally carpeted with wildflowers, although wool sweaters may still be in order. If summer is the only time you can get away, don't let that stop you. Just follow these three suggestions: Check in ahead of the crowds, sightsee early mornings and late afternoons, and tune out during the hot, top-lit noontime.

Maps come with your car, and signposting is adequate, so

we won't dwell too much on directions here. Athens traffic is notoriously sticky, but once you get on National Highway 1 and head northward you'll fairly fly the first 70 km (43 miles) to the second turnoff for Thebes. From there on, don't worry about route numbers; follow the destination signs. From Thebes to Levadia is another 45 km (28 miles); then there's a winding 30-km (19-mile) climb over the shoulder of Mount Parnassus to Delphi. Total: 145 kilometers, or some 90 miles. You can afford to drive slowly, and once you're off the main highways you should keep an eye peeled for sheep, goats, bikes, juggernaut buses, and rogue trucks. But even with the side trip to Osios Loukas that we recommend, you'll do no more than three and a half hours of actual driving on your first day.

We suggest two nights at each stop so that you'll get to know the sites in different lights and conditions, see most things twice, and even begin to feel somewhat at home. That's what the bus tours can't give you, and it's tremendously important. Driving from Delphi to Olympia on your third morning, you'll begin by dropping down to the dismally polluted port of Itea on the Gulf of Corinth. The winding, dull, but well-engineered coast road westward from there to Nafpaktos covers 98 km (61 miles). Plowing patiently on through Nafpaktos's traffic jams, you'll reach Anti-Rion to catch one of the frequent small ferries south across the gulf to Rion; it's a nice half-hour ride. From Rion to Olympia is not much more than 100 km (62 miles) on a dull, traffic-heavy highway with one bad bottleneck: Patras. Altogether, the distance covered on your third morning will have been under 240 km (150 miles), probably in less than four hours.

Driving east from Olympia on your fifth morning, you'll cross the mountains of Arcadia on a still narrowly winding road, with glorious views at every hairpin turn and a few poignantly old-fashioned villages clinging to the cliffs. We strongly suggest pausing for Greek coffee in one of the village cafés, and stopping again to picnic in the high wilderness. This 100-km (62-mile) stretch will be accomplished all too soon. Then you're on a major highway for about another 50 km (31 miles) through Tripoli to Nafplion, your base for seeing Epidaurus.

Your seventh and last day involves the same amount of actual driving; it too will run about 150 km, or some 93 miles. But as you proceed northward on the Corinth road from Nafplion you'll be turning off to visit **Mycenae**, then **Nemea**, then ancient **Corinth** itself (these three sites are not actually discussed here, but in the chapter on the Peloponnese, below). After that you'll have a clear run across the isthmus and eastward to Athens again. Because of the stops you're making, this will be a full final day. (It had better not be a Sunday, because the traffic flooding into Athens late Sunday afternoons is fierce.)

MAJOR INTEREST

Osios Loukas Monastery
Katholikon and Panayia churches

Delphi
Sacred precinct
Museum (*Charioteer*)

Olympia
Sacred precinct
Museum (west pediment, metopes)

Tiryns
Corbeled galleries
West staircase

Epidaurus
Sacred precinct
Amphitheater

OSIOS LOUKAS MONASTERY

On the first morning of your tour, sweep right by the Classical remains at Thebes and Levadia, which are not of compelling interest. About 21 km (13 miles) after Levadia, as you approach Mount Parnassus (and Delphi) through an increasingly grand, rugged landscape, you'll find yourself close to the ancient crossroad where the tragic hero Oedipus unwittingly destroyed his own father.

Here there's a turnoff from route 48 to the left, signposted Osios Loukas. Swing south along the slow, little road, remembering that this requires a totally different driving rhythm from the one that you've been on. The idea is to break your trip an hour short of Delphi—not that you'll find anything remotely Classical about Osios Loukas. It's just that this happens to be one of the most beautiful Byzantine monuments in existence; a little inconsistency won't hurt.

On the way you will pass through the village of Dístomo, where Nazi troops martyred 218 men, women, and children in 1944, reducing Distomo to a ghost town. It was eventually rebuilt and the village square dedicated to Franklin D. Roosevelt. (The square is now called Ethnikí Antístasis, or National Resistance.)

Osios Loukás Monastery, which faces the steep slope of Mount Helikon, was a prime rallying point in the long Greek struggle against Turkey. Here, in 1780, the freedom fighter Andreas Androutsos made a brilliant stand against the Turks, finally escaping with all his men. It was here, too, in 1821, that Bishop Isaias blessed the weapons of the freedom fighters and proclaimed the beginning of the Greek War of Independence in the area. This rocky region has always bred warriors.

But at the monastery you'll encounter no reminders of human savagery. This place always appears bathed in fragrant peacefulness. It nestles amid almond groves halfway down a hill that overlooks a hidden valley of red earth, yellow corn, and silver-green olives. Ancient plane trees generously shade the broad flagstone terrace, where a friendly old hound dozes the day away. Osios Loukas himself (Saint Luke the Stiriot, a local tenth-century hermit, not the Evangelist) still seems to bless the place.

Born near Delphi of well-to-do parents, Loukas disappeared into the wilderness while still a youth. Having no formal vocation, he assumed monk's raiment only because a pair of pilgrims on their way to Rome gave it him. Like Saint Francis of Assisi, Loukas also healed the afflicted and communed with animals. His way of life was blameless, yet dangerous. Alone and weaponless, he naturally took to his heels whenever armed bands appeared. The small wars that racked Greece in his day forced the saint from one hideaway to another, until he reached this remote site.

Here he gathered a few disciples and began, they say, to prophesy in the Delphic way. Byzantine bigwigs were so impressed by Loukas's oracular powers that they undertook to build a beautiful monastery around him.

Osios Loukas died on February 7, 953, just as his beloved almond trees were coming into blossom. Two years later, according to his first disciple and biographer, the first of the two churches here was completed. Ever since then Osios Loukas has been a place of pilgrimage.

The **Kathólikon** and the smaller **Panayía** churches stand joined, sharing a wall and inner door within the small monastery enclosure. The moment you step inside you'll sense the magnitude of their mystery. Multicolored marble, cipollino, gold, porphyry, frescoes, mosaics, carvings, columns, capitals, arches, domes—all quietly fountain up and around you in such a way that you can't take in more than a fraction of what's here.

DELPHI

For about a thousand years people came to Delphi in the firm conviction that the sun god Apollo knew everything—and that his Delphic oracle could not lie. Hellenic kingdoms and city-states did their banking here, in the form of gifts to the god together with temple treasuries and sculptural monuments. This terraced ledge of **Mount Parnassus** held an incredible amount of glorious Greek art and architecture. It still looks down upon a deep gorge of silvery olive trees and up to a pair of mighty cliffs that seem about to clap hands in the sun.

The *Homeric Hymn to Pythian Apollo* relates that the sun god selected Delphi as the place where he would "... build a glorious temple to be an oracle for men ... both they who dwell in rich Peloponnesos and the men of Europe, and from all the wave-washed isles, coming to question me.

"But nearby was a sweet flowing spring, and there with his strong bow the lord, son of Zeus, killed the bloated great she-dragon, a fierce monster, wont to do great mischief to men ... Wherefore the place is now called Pytho, and men call the lord Apollo by another name, Pythian, because on that spot the power of piercing Helios made the monster rot away."

Possibly this myth celebrates the ascendance of the burning rays of reason over the dark subconscious. Most interpreters go further still, suggesting that the triumph of logic over Nature herself is implied. But this seems unlikely; the ancient Greeks revered the natural world—as we often don't.

Consider the stinking, big-time bauxite operation that is not only gouging out foothills between Delphi and the coast but is also turning the nearby gulf port of Itea into a cesspool. You can sometimes smell something fishy, and you'll often sense the presence of a smoggy blur at Delphi today. But just a bit of the bauxite-dragon's tail is visible from Apollo's temple. It's a covered trench that snakes down the formerly pristine gorge below.

The **Vouzas** hotel in town is most convenient to the sacred precinct, and it's got stupendous views. The **Amalia**, however, at the far end of town, is quieter, more comfortable, and friendlier as well. Both of these depend upon the tour-bus trade, and so the personnel suffer considerable attrition from confused or unhappy lodgers. The Amalia is part of a chain, whereas the Vouzas appears to be family owned. Yet the people at the Amalia keep smiling, while those at Vouzas sometimes fall into snits.

Recommended tavernas at Delphi are **Zorba's**, with a nice garden and great olive oil, and **Grigori's**, with a starlit terrace, a party spirit, and a fabulous grill. For shopping visit the family-style **Wholesale** place opposite Zorba's. It really is much cheaper than the relatively swank shops that flank the main drag below.

But the small village is really beside the point. Stroll down the highway to the sacred precinct. Visit all of it, without trying to keep it all straight. Smell the flowers and the pines. Enjoy the caressing winds. Like a gigantic ear of stone, Delphi tends to magnify natural sounds. Some birds around here trill like bicycle bells, others chirp like clinking coins.

Look up and you'll notice a pair of eagles wheeling overhead. That's a promise; you never fail to find them here. According to legend the first pair was released by the god Zeus, one atop the eastern Caucasus range and the other on Mount Atlas in northwest Africa. One eagle flew east, the other west, and they met here, at the world's center.

Pilgrims coming here would begin by washing their hands in the Castalian spring, which flows from between the cliffs above. (That's where the carcass of the she-monster rotted away, purified in death.) Having been ritually cleansed, each suppliant would make a generous offering and hand in a question for the oracle. During the next few days or weeks of waiting, he'd have a look around while getting to know the priests of the place. In this way much information from the far ends of the earth was fed into the oracle's collective intelligence.

Apollo regularly provided nervous institutions with amoral, cold-temperature contingency analyses and prophecies. In that sense Delphi resembled a modern think tank. But the god also welcomed individual seekers, giving them wonder, challenge, delight, and fear in about equal measure.

To get a sense of the whole thing, pass the museum and walk along the south fence of Apollo's precinct until you reach the curve of the road and, on your left, the Castalian spring. Take advantage of a quiet moment to clamber 10 or 20 yards up the gorge and dip your hands in the water trickling from the rock face. The cliffs above seem to lean in as witnesses; it's still an awesome experience.

Then cross the road and dip down into the **Sanctuary of Athena Pronaia** (Athena Standing Before the Temple), which occupies a very narrow ledge between the gorge below and the beetling cliffs above. It seems the goddess chose a dangerous post to defend here. In 480 B.C. a thunderous avalanche at this spot buried the vanguard of a Persian raiding party and frightened the remainder away. That rock slide was doubtless man-made, but others followed in the fourth century B.C. and again in 1905. Here you'll see what was one of the earliest Classical temples, ruins dating from the mid-seventh century B.C. Here too is a partly restored fourth-century B.C. *tholos,* or round temple, which must have been exquisite in its day.

Regaining the road once more, retrace your steps to the left until you reach the gate of Apollo's sacred precinct, and turn in. You'll find yourself at the start of a pedestrian **sacred way**, which mounts in looping fashion to Apollo's temple above. Tour guides shepherd their charges slowly up the slope, with frequent pauses to expatiate upon the stone foundations of long-vanished glories. The excellent, reasonably priced, illustrated catalogue available at the site lists no fewer than 54 items of antiquarian importance in the area. If your interest is not so detailed it may suffice to recognize that your ascent was once bordered with rank upon rank of statuary and miniature temples crammed with votive offerings from far-flung Greek islands and city-states.

The retaining wall of polygonal boulders that shores up the foundations of the **Temple of Apollo** has its own quiet magnificence. According to legend the first temple here was built of laurel, the second of beeswax and feathers, the third purely of bronze. Because legend seldom prevaricates altogether, we may suppose that temporary open-air altars were erected in those materials. The first Classical temple was erected here during the mid-seventh century B.C. That was destroyed by fire and replaced in the sixth century. The same thing happened again 200 years later.

The present remains of the fourth-century temple yield no clue to the location or the workings of Apollo's oracle. (Conceivably, some fanatic late pagan or early Christian piously destroyed whatever evidence there may have been.) But literary sources suggest the following scenario during a visit to the oracle: The pilgrim descended alone into the sun god's smoky underground sanctuary. There he would encounter a middle-aged priestess wearing a girlish costume. She was known, intriguingly enough, as the Pythia—being somehow connected with the she-monster of old. We're told that this strange personage sat enthroned, in a seeming trance, upon a tripod. Presumably a covered basin or a tray of some sort rested on the tripod, and the priestess perched atop that. She would address the suppliant directly and very briefly in a deep, throbbing voice, for Apollo spoke through her.

From prehistoric days until the time of Emperor Hadrian, perhaps a thousand suppliants a year went down to brave the Pythia. She removed blood pollution from murderers and dispatched military expeditions. She oversaw the founding of shrines, temples, and even cities in far corners of the Mediterranean world. She established and confirmed hundreds of new religious rituals. She elevated certain mortals to semi-divine status. And many were the men to whom she gave weird, wonderful, but confusing counsel.

King Croesus of Lydia lavished a ton of gold and silver on the oracle, plus gold coins (among the first ever struck) for every native Delphian. Croesus's billion-dollar question: Should he or should he not invade Persia? "March," Apollo advised, "and you'll destroy a great empire." So Croesus invaded, only to lose all. The Persian emperor Cyrus made him a court slave, then benevolently offered to grant Croesus's dearest wish.

"Master," Croesus responded, "let me send these chains to the god of the Greeks, whom I most honored, and ask him if he is accustomed to cheat his benefactors."

So that was done, whereupon the Pythia gently explained that "the wise thing would have been to send again to inquire which empire had been meant, Cyrus's or his own. But as he misinterpreted what was said, and made no second inquiry, he must admit the fault to have been his."

These facts were reported by the world's first historian: Herodotus. Many famous tales of Delphic utterances come down to us on his authority. Others we have from Plutarch, Pausanias, and similarly reputable sources. Their accounts were believed by their contemporaries and reattested down the centuries.

Someone once asked the Pythia if any man was wiser than Socrates. "No man!" she replied. What about women? Was any woman wiser than Socrates? If so, the Pythia kept that information to herself.

The enquirer hastened home to Athens to give Socrates the news. The philosopher found it deeply disturbing. As he later explained: "I said to myself, What can the god mean? What is the interpretation of his riddle? For I know that I have no wisdom, small or great."

Socrates proceeded to scour Athens high and low in

hopes of finding someone wiser than himself—to no avail. His conclusion: The oracle was irrefutable. "The man is wisest," it meant, "who, like Socrates, knows that his wisdom is in truth worth nothing."

To complete your own tour of the sanctuary, take the path leading beyond the temple and on up to the small concert **amphitheater**, where contests in music and poetry were once held. From here it's a short climb through pine woods to the **stadium**, center of the Pythian games that Delphi used to host. Classical Greece adored athletic contests, so the Olympic games alternated with others here, at Nemea, and at the Isthmus of Corinth.

Descending again to exit the sanctuary, don't fail to look into the **Delphi Museum** along the path to your right. You may feel with some justice that museums are barbarous and exhausting places, but you can't begin to grasp the cool, natural splendor of Classical statuary without their help. That's especially so in Athens, at Olympia, and here. Among the marble bas-reliefs that may catch your eye is a frieze from the Treasury of Siphnos that depicts a running battle between helmeted giants and gigantic gods; it dates from the late sixth century B.C. Other masterpieces, perhaps a quarter-century later, are the Theseus and Herakles metopes from the Treasury of the Athenians.

But the greatest gem in the museum is undoubtedly the *Charioteer*.

In 478 B.C. King Polyzalus of Sicilian Gela entered a four-horse chariot in Delphi's Pythian games. Having won the race, Polyzalus presented Delphi with a life-size bronze monument depicting his victorious horses, chariot, and charioteer. A little over a century later, in 373 B.C., an earthquake-triggered avalanche pulverized the monument—all except for the charioteer.

The Delphians set up a temple where the avalanche had rolled, but first they reverently interred the surviving bronze charioteer under their new building's foundations. Now why should the people of that far-off period conduct what amounted to holy burial for a broken fragment of a mere athletic monument? Not out of ignorance or superstition. On the contrary, the Classical Greeks understood that any true work of art had its own spiritual force and inherent dignity, and was worthy of obsequy. French archaeologists unearthed the *Charioteer* in 1896, and it soon became the acclaimed centerpiece of the Delphi Museum's collection.

OLYMPIA

The new highway shoots you into Olympia without warning. It's still pretty much a one-street town, entirely oriented to tourism. (For additional coverage and information concerning Olympia's hotels and eating places, see the Peloponnese section.) Here, as at Delphi, the sacred precinct and the adjacent museum are really all that matter. They're so rich in aesthetic satisfactions and historical associations that you should make a quick visit on the afternoon of your arrival, and spend the whole next day there as well.

The sacred site, known as the **Altis**, is grassy, flowery, and peaceful, dominated by the low, cone-shaped **Hill of Cronus**. There, in prehistoric times, stood altars to pre-Olympian deities, including Cronus and Rhea (the parents of Zeus) and Gaia, Mother Earth. Dorian invaders from Thessaly mastered this area sometime before 1000 B.C., bringing Zeus worship and imposing a suitably altered mythology upon the land. They even named a pair of neighboring mountains Olympus and Ossa in memory of their native region.

Aristotle informs us that Iphitus, king of the city-state of Elis, made a pact with Lycurgus, king of Sparta, that led to the founding of the Olympic games on a Panhellenic scale in the year 776 B.C. Their pact was inscribed on a bronze disk that hung in the Olympian Temple of Hera. Elis was proverbially rich in cattle and philosophers. A rancher's paradise tucked away in the northwestern corner of the Peloponnese, it never achieved anything like the power of Sparta. Indeed, Elis's chief distinction was that it included Olympia within its borders, hosted the Olympic games, and served to keep that all-important festival free of politics. It is true that neighboring Pisa elbowed the Elians out for brief periods, and that eventual Roman conquest left them only nominal control of the games. However, the political neutrality and festival responsibility of Elis were recognized and respected century after century.

Here mild weather holds sway, with a good deal of winter rain. The Altis occupies an undulant meadow where two rivers, the Alpheios and the Kladeos, come together. As you wander these bucolic acres, with their marble platforms and tumbled stones, it's difficult to imagine how grand things must have been. Dozens of colonnaded and richly adorned buildings and thousands of statues stood here in ancient times. This was a religious shrine, an athletic hall of fame, a place of training and administration, and, finally, an adjunct to the games themselves. The **stadium** lies just beyond the Hill of Cronus on your left. The still unexcavated **hippodrome** is not far to the right of that.

The foundations of the **Temple of Hera** were laid in the mid-seventh century B.C., and are thus among the oldest remaining examples of Classical architecture that Greece has to offer. The original superstructure of wood and terracotta was gradually replaced with stone as the centuries passed. This temple stood for no fewer than 1,000 years. It once contained a statue of Hera enthroned, with her husband, Zeus, standing meekly at her side.

The **Temple of Zeus** was built between 470 and 456 B.C. at the superb peak of Classicism, in the glow that followed the successful defense of Greece against Persia. It had six enormous columns front and back, plus 13 down the sides, all of the local conchiferate stone covered with a fine coat of lime. More than 210 feet long and over 90 feet wide, this was the largest temple in the Peloponnese. It contained a gigantic gold-and-ivory chryselephantine statue by Phidias depicting Zeus enthroned. Purists complained that the statue's 40-foot scale was off, pointing out that if the figure were to stand up, it would destroy the temple roof. But the consensus held that Phidias had created the Seventh Wonder of the World. "The other Wonders we admire," the historian Arrian noted. "This one we reverence as well. It's a great misfortune for anyone not to see this before he dies." During the fourth century A.D. Christian Byzantine conquerors removed the monument to Constantinople. Soon afterward it was destroyed by fire.

The Games

The first travel writer was the Greek Pausanias, who lived in the second century A.D. By then the grandeur of the Roman Empire embraced and overshadowed the glory that was Greece. Yet the vast majority of Greek cultural institutions and monuments survived intact. So Pausanias's extremely thorough *Description of Greece* covers incredibly rich ground. By great good fortune, this text has come down to us complete. His account is a gold mine for scholars and a Bible for archaeologists. Here's the passage that tells of how the Olympic games began:

> The Elian antiquaries say that Cronus first reigned in heaven, and that a temple was made for him at Olympia by the men of that age, who were named the Golden Race. They say that when Zeus was born, Rhea committed

the safekeeping of the child to the Idaean Dactyls [whose] names were Herakles, Paeonaeus, Epimedes, Iasius, and Idas. Now Herakles, as the eldest, set his brethren to run a race, and crowned the victor with a branch of wild olive . . .

The Idaean Herakles is therefore reputed to have been the first to arrange the games, and to have given them the name Olympic. He made the rule that they should be celebrated every fourth year . . . Some say that Zeus here wrestled with Cronus himself for the kingdom; others that he held the games in honor of his victory over Cronus. Among those who are said to have gained victories is Apollo. They say that he outran Hermes in a race, and vanquished Ares in boxing . . .

"Many a wondrous sight may be seen, and not a few tales of wonder may be heard in Greece," Pausanias concludes, "but there is nothing on which the blessing of God rests in so full a measure as the rites of Eleusis and the Olympic games."

A more down-to-earth but still mythological account of how the games began is that they were instituted as memorial rites of Pelops, the man for whom the Peloponnese (Pelops's Island) is named. It seems he won control from the tyrant Oenomaus in a race at Olympia.

Princess Hippodamia ("horse tamer") was King Oenomaus's daughter. Thirteen suitors in turn had begged the old man for her hand. In each case, Oenomaus had offered what seemed a sporting challenge: "Take my daughter in your chariot on the road to Corinth. I'll sacrifice a ram to Zeus and then chase after you. If you cross the border ahead of me, Hippodamia is yours. If I catch you first, however, you're a dead man."

The tyrant's chariot team was the fastest in the land. It must have depressed the princess, riding home again with her bloody-handed dad 13 times in a row. So when Pelops turned up, she helped him cheat by tampering with Oenomaus's chariot wheels. In mid-pursuit the wheels flew off and Oenomaus was dragged to his death.

The first Olympics on actual record occurred in 776 B.C. The last of the ancient Olympics (the 293rd) took place no fewer than 1,169 years later, in A.D. 393, when the Byzantine emperor Theodosius I abolished all pagan festivals. (In A.D. 426 Theodosius II went further still, ordering the destruction of all pagan temples.)

Athletes of the Classical age were at least as fiercely competitive—not to say combative—as our own. They too had everything to gain. Along with their victory wreaths of wild olive, the winners were showered with civic honors, victory odes, free meals, monuments, tax breaks, sinecures, hero worship, and enduring fame. Losers took nothing; the line was sword-sharp. And that wasn't the only downside. For all its wonders, Classical culture was dreadfully repressive to women. At Olympia none was permitted to appear— not even in the stands! Individual male excellence being the point, team play, too, was excluded.

Every four years Elis would send out "truce-bearers of Zeus the thunder god" to issue invitations all the way from southern Epirus to northern Africa and from Massilia (Marseille) in the west to Trebizond in the east. On average a thousand athletes and their trainers showed up, along with some 45,000 spectators. For the occasion a one-month "truce of Greece" was proclaimed, during which anyone who made war or molested travellers was subjected to heavy fines payable at Olympia.

In the reign of the pharaoh Psammetichus, Elis sent an embassy requesting Egypt's sages to suggest possible improvements in the Olympic games. The honor and prestige of Elis would be better served, Egypt counseled, if the state were to confine its role in the games to that of host and referee. After careful consideration, Elis rejected this advice. Her citizens had proved to be fair umpires even when their own sons were involved, so they saw no need to bar future generations of Elians from the joys and strains of competition. Their decision nicely illustrates the old Hellenic spirit of competition, strife, and justice, too.

The Olympics were part sport, part religion, and part World's Fair. They took place over a five-day period during the first or second full moon after the summer solstice. The schedule varied somewhat down the centuries, of course, but here's its general pattern. The first day was given over to greetings, meetings, and oath-takings, plus a special sacrifice to "Zeus, Averter of Flies." No one knows what that sacrifice was or how it worked, but Aelian assures us that all resident flies either perished or buzzed off, "purely out of respect for the god."

The chief oath-taking occurred in the Council House beneath a frightening bronze image of Zeus, god of oaths, bearing thunderbolts in both hands. It was customary, Pausanias tells us, "for the athletes, their fathers and brothers, and also the trainers, to swear upon the cut pieces of a boar that they will be guilty of no foul play in respect to the Olympic games. The athletes take an additional oath, that for ten successive months they have strictly observed the rules of training... I forgot to ask what they do with the boar after the athletes have taken the oath..."

We'll never know. Pausanias goes on to say that Zeus's thunderbolts did fall from time to time. Sixteen miscreants were compelled to erect expensive statues that carried inscriptions detailing their sins—namely, bribe-taking, arriving late for the games, and running away at the last moment. One would-be scofflaw's inscription confessed that the Delphic Oracle had ordered him to cough up.

Apparently fines were frequent. On top of that, many participants—athletes and judges alike—were publicly flogged for conspiracy, unseemly shenanigans, spoilsport activities, or false starts. ("It's better to be whipped," Themistocles of Athens once remarked, "than left at the post.")

The second morning opened with a procession to the hippodrome followed by chariot and horse racing. The hippodrome was a track shaped like the outside rim of a paper clip. The starting gates, accommodating no fewer than 44 chariots, were built in the form of a ship's prow. An eagle representing Zeus and a dolphin representing either Poseidon or Apollo crowned this much-admired structure.

When the trumpets sounded for the race to begin, the eagle ascended on a long piston while the dolphin dived from its height. At the same time, the starting ropes were reeled in—back to front so that the teams toward the back of the V were released first, giving all chariots an even start.

Ahead lay 12 double laps, or about nine miles containing 23 sharp turns. The charioteers leaned forward like ski jumpers, shaking their reins and cracking their whips, never touching the handrails of their flashing, flimsy vehicles except in dire emergency. It's on record that in one such contest at Olympia, a single chariot out of a field of 40 crossed the finish line.

Trotting races and mule-cart races used to follow the chariot event, but they were soon discontinued in favor of flat racing as we now know it.

The third morning at Olympia began with a procession to the altar of Zeus, followed by the ritual sacrifice of a whole herd of oxen. The aroma of ox bones wrapped in burning fat wafted to the gods. Then the athletic competitions resumed. The meat was saved for victory banquets.

The third afternoon was given over to boys' events: footracing, wrestling, and boxing. It sometimes happened that fathers and their sons won championships at the same Olympics, but only Diagoras of Rhodes and his sons scored a triple win. In 464 B.C. Diagoras won the boxing crown, his eldest son was the victor in the pancration (a contest involving both boxing and wrestling), and his younger son outboxed all other boys. When the children carried their father around the arena on their shoulders, many spectators wept.

The fourth day began just after sunrise with a "long race" of slightly under three miles. Our marathon run is a modern invention, although one inspired by an incident in Athenian history. When Athens defeated the invading Persians at Marathon beach, a famous runner named Pheidippides was dispatched to tell the home folks the news. He covered the roughly 26-mile distance at top speed, and then, gasping out the word "Rejoice!" at Athens's gates, happily fell dead. ("Rejoice!" is still a favorite form of greeting in Greece: HAIR-et-eh.)

After the "long race" came a dash down the length of the stadium and back, some 400 yards. Instead of squatting at the start, the runners stood upright with their feet planted five or six inches apart in shallow-grooved limestone blocks. Vase paintings show that their running form was much the same as our own.

The 400-yard dash was followed by the climactic 200-yard sprint. This meant bursting off the starting line to reach the far end of the stadium in an all-out explosive effort. The Greeks honored runners above all other athletes; they named each Olympiad for the fastest man there, the 200-yard winner.

"Nothing gets riches," cracked the comic playwright Aristophanes, "like contests in music and athletics!" What made that humorous was the fact that such contests were held strictly for amateurs. However, victorious native sons were very well rewarded. Moreover, if a victor's home town happened to be poor, he could always switch—but usually at some cost. For instance, when Stotades of Crete changed his allegiance to the bustling merchant city of Ephesus in Ionia, the Cretans banished him. And when Astylos of Krotona removed himself to a sports-mad tyrant's court in luxurious Syracuse, his old admirers back home bitterly pulled down the statue they had raised to him and turned his former town house into a prison.

For high-stepping arrogance, the sprinter Eubotas beat them all. He turned up at Olympia with a life-size bronze statue of himself in his baggage. Never before, and never again, did an Olympic champion dedicate his own monument on the very day he won.

The so-called heavy sports took up the afternoon of the fourth day. In ascending order of violence, these comprised wrestling, boxing, and pancration.

Classical wrestling was clean-cut and elegant. It permitted no torture holds and required no going to the mat. The object was simply to throw one's opponent down while keeping one's own feet, three times out of five. Surviving representations show the standard throws you might expect: cross-hip, headlock, body press, heave, flying mare. The referee is right there in the vase paintings, too, carrying a long knobby stick with which to punish participants for infractions.

Philostratus tells us that the great wrestler Milo earned a unique monument at Olympia, a statue depicting him with a discus beneath his feet and a pomegranate in his right hand. The champion used to stand on a greased discus and challenge all comers to push him off. He would also hold a pomegranate in his delicate steely grip and dare the world to try to break its skin, let alone take it away from him. Tradition asserts that he proved unbudgeable and unbeatable.

Boxing followed the wrestling. The vase paintings show big fellows bellying up to each other, swaybacked, with their fists cocked at eye level. They rather resemble John L. Sullivan, "the Strong Boy from Boston," opposing Gentleman Jim Corbett in an old sporting print. In ancient times prizefighting was much rougher than it is today—but at least Greek rules did not permit hitting below the neck.

There were no boxing gloves. Instead, contestants wrapped their fists in 12-foot strips of rawhide, which added lethal weight plus greatly increased cutting power. No rounds were called, no rest allowed, and no points scored. To parry blows must have been bruising; to slip them, contestants would snake their heads and shoulders about. Thus did Hippomachos take the crown at three successive Olympics without receiving a single blow. Melanchomas topped that; he never struck a blow but defended himself so well that his opponents finally dropped from exhaustion! The poet Lucilius wrote a satiric epitaph on a similar champion. In Dudley Fitts's translation it reads:

> To Apis the Boxer
> His grateful opponents have erected
> This statue
> Honoring him
> Who never by any chance hurt one of them.

Nonetheless, severe damage and even death must have occurred often in the Olympic ring. Apollonius's epic *Voyage of Argo* describes a legendary match in which "the mingled din of knuckles knocking upon horribly grating teeth and jaws resembled the incessant pounding in a shipyard where planks are being joined and hammered home on the reluctant bolts."

Boxing matches concluded in either knockout or surrender. This created a special problem for Spartan athletes, whose most hallowed boast was: "A Spartan never surrenders." Sparta smartly forbade her sons to box or practice the pancration. When blood and teeth began to fly, these most warlike Greeks stood apart, pale with frustration.

Glaucus, the greatest of all Olympic pugilists, discovered his destiny by accident when he was about 16. His father's plowshare had fallen out of its haft. Unthinkingly, the youth drove the blade firmly in again with a sidearm swipe of his fist. After witnessing this show of strength the boy's father began training him for the Olympics. But Glaucus almost lost his first Olympic contest. Badly outboxed, he stood cut, dazed, and bleeding and was about to fall when his father yelled out: "Son, mend the plow!" Glaucus immediately righted himself and demolished his opponent with a single chopping blow.

The pancration came next. Tales concerning the pancration itself are too brutal to go into here. The word *pancration* means "all powers." It stood for bare-handed, catch-as-catch-can single combat. Ear biting, eye gouging, and finger breaking were standard moves. Mutilating one's opponent was praiseworthy, whereas surrender was sissy. What could have induced sane men to play in such a way? The Greek physician and anatomist Galen was one who warned of the price: lameness, toothlessness, impotence, blindness, addled brains, and premature old age.

The cool of the evening brought a last, 400-foot race run by athletes wearing helmets and carrying heavy shields. In the early days they also wore metal shin guards, or greaves. Classic battle tactics called for a good deal of running, both toward and away from the action. So this final event of the Olympics gave warriors a chance to shine.

"Come back with your shield, or on it!" Spartan mothers were supposed to have said while hurrying their sons off to war. To come back on your shield meant D.O.A.; presumably that was better than suffering the undying shame of having lost your shield. Not everyone agreed, though. In the mid-seventh century B.C. the Ionian pirate and poet Archilochus put his own case like this (translation by Sir William Maris):

> A perfect shield bedecks some Thracian now.
> I had no choice: I left it in a wood.
> Ah, well, I saved my skin, so let it go!
> A new one's just as good.

The fifth and last day of the Olympics was given over to ceremonies and celebrations of which almost nothing is known. On the final night the stars looked down upon a solemn procession of the victors, followed by a great open-air banquet at which victory odes were sung. At dawn tents and market booths were folded up and a thousand campfires doused.

Olympia Today

Olympia today is a gentle ruin and a provocative museum, with a floating population of bemused tourists and a small, tourist-oriented town attached. The **museum** at Olympia is fairly new and spaciously arranged. It's always been renowned for its vast collection of small bronzes found at the site, with items from Archaic times (c. 660–480 B.C.) down through the entire Classical era. Unfortunately, however, this incredibly rich horde has now been scrubbed down.

Bronze statuary develops a greenish patina, a sort of second skin, as it weathers over the course of years and centuries. The *Charioteer* at Delphi, for instance, has some of this. It's always been regarded as a good thing, a pleasant-hued protective coating that nature and the tender hand of time provide. But now some scientists assert that in rare instances the patina is conducive to "cancer of the bronze." Therefore, as a prophylactic measure, they say, it's not a bad idea to strip the patina away. In the Olympia Museum there's one bronze object left that escaped the chemical holocaust, a cauldron dating from the eighth century B.C.

If the holocaust of bronzes is especially painful, further shocks follow. The greatest single work here is the **west pediment** from the Temple of Zeus. It represents a brawl between lustful centaurs and Lapith warriors, with Lapith women as the prize. The piecing together and arrangement of these shattered figures has always been controversial. It never seemed quite right, but now it looks all wrong after a new curatorial team decided to switch the major brawlers all about.

Still, if you close your eyes to the ensemble and open them to the telling details of this stupendous pediment, it will stir your heart. According to Pausanias the artist was "Alkamenes, a contemporary and apprentice of Phidias and only second to him as a sculptor." Alkamenes brought hot, swirling, sensual energy to this crucially important masterpiece, yet bathed the entire struggle in compassion, too.

Pausanias mentions having seen "Hermes bearing the babe Dionysos, a work of Praxiteles in stone," at Olympia. This piece was found, and it's in the museum. Until fairly recently it was the major attraction, partly because of Praxiteles' fame as the greatest of late Classical sculptors, partly for its inherent delicacy of sentiment and modeling. But some find the statue disappointing now. The restoration of the damaged legs is still problematical. Then too, taste has changed. To the modern eye, force beats delicacy.

The equally famous large ceramic known as *Zeus Abducting Ganymede* has become something of a gay icon. (Ganymede, a Trojan prince, was Zeus's only homosexual fling.) But some things about it don't quite fit. First, the object in the left hand of Zeus does not remotely resemble his characteristic thunderbolt. Second, this Zeus wears a cap and his beard is neatly trimmed short. You'll not find that in any genuine representation of the father-god. Nor will you discover elsewhere the passionless rushing quality that imbues this figure. There's nothing lustful about him, that's for sure.

Nor is Ganymede seductive. Because of a break in the ceramic, the sex of the "abducted" party remains unclear. He, or she, fairly flies along, neither struggling nor coy, in the crook of the god's right arm. Conceivably, this ceramic shows the god Hermes, Guide of Souls, capped and gowned as he was often depicted, hastening along with the spirit of a dead person. Note that his captive also carries a rooster, symbol of resurrection.

The marble **metopes** in the main gallery, showing the labors of Herakles, remain untouched; they are absolutely inspiring and beyond all praise. This is still a great museum. However, Olympia's most compelling attractions are outside.

There you can experience some of the spirit of ancient Olympia: Run in the stadium; arm wrestle in the Temple of Hera; rest among the stones of the workshop of Phidias. Climb the small Hill of Cronus; use the benches in the shade of whatever pines remain. Read the inscriptions that identify this ruin or that, but don't attempt to sort out precisely what happened at what spot. The moist, soft breeze, the ship-like clouds, the broken columns crisp with fossilized seashells, the nightingales, the poppies and the asphodels all help to induce a feeling of time travel. As you seem to unscroll, a whole millennium of high sport spills out before you.

TIRYNS

Having driven east from Olympia over high Arcadia (see The Peloponnese), crossed the central plateau, and wound down the escarpment overlooking the bay of Nafplion, you'll enter the low, fertile region known as the Argolid, Greece's fruit basket.

On your right you'll see a turnoff to **Lerna**, a very ancient settlement at the place where Herakles is said to have destroyed the nine-headed monster, Hydra. Continuing around the bay, you'll see a left-hand fork leading to **Argos**, the town for which the whole region is named. For a time ancient Argos ruled the plain from its cone-shaped hill. The Argive shrine of Aphrodite remained a place of pagan pilgrimage well into Byzantine Christian days. (For more on Lerna and Argos, see The Peloponnese.)

A little farther on comes Tiryns, next to the road from Argos to Nafplion on the left-hand side and well signposted. When Homer described Tiryns as "wall-girt" he was understating the case. These walls, encompassing a low hill, were mostly constructed during the 13th century B.C. About a thousand yards in circumference, they're 30 to 60 feet thick and built of unmortared boulders weighing tens of tons apiece. How were those boulders ever wrestled into position? Speculation is rife, but nobody really knows; the secret of such architecture had been lost before the Golden Age of Greece began. The Classical Greeks called the surviving buildings of this kind "Cyclopean," meaning that Tiryns and its ilk must have been built by a race of Titans, or Cyclops.

In its heyday, when the bay extended this far inland, Tiryns stood at the water's edge. The city must have resembled a titanic sea turtle, barnacled with palaces and lying prone across a deep underground spring. It was here that Herakles was born. This site has practically no recorded history—it belongs to legend; yet the remains are as real and solid as can be. For all these reasons it is strongly recommended that you pause here for an hour.

Explore the "corbeled" galleries, or tunnels, in the walls, whose seemingly Gothic arches are actually formed of huge stone slabs leaning inward under enormous pressure. Parts of these tunnels are brilliantly polished, but not by the hand of man. Many, many generations of shepherds sheltered their woolly flocks here, and the sheep naturally rubbed against the stones.

Climb the curved, stone west staircase, which was designed to frustrate unwelcome guests and to fill the welcome ones with awe; and pace the foundations at the summit. You're looking out upon Greece now, from a standpoint of more than 3,000 years ago.

Nafplion lies just a few minutes beyond Tiryns, where you'll be relaxing for the next two nights; see The Peloponnese for details.

EPIDAURUS

The 50 km (31 miles) east from Nafplion to Epidaurus (Epídavros) used to be a lovely drive, but now it's built up and traffic clogged. Allow about an hour.

In the second century A.D., when Pausanias came to Epidaurus, it was still a working clinic, hospital, and health spa combined. His description shows that it remained steeped in religious observance as well.

Kindly Asklepios—Apollo's son by a mortal princess—was born in the region, and here he virtually invented medicine. People revered him as the *soter,* or savior. They said his final triumph was bringing Hippolytus back from the dead. For that interference with the natural order of things Zeus transfixed Asklepios with a thunderbolt.

The myth points to an interesting dichotomy in pagan religion. The priests of Zeus and his harsh, passionate Olympians coexisted uneasily with an older, humbler stream of pagan faith that centered on nature. Not for Asklepios were the lightning, eagles, peacocks, spears, and crested helmets of snowy Olympia. His own familiars were of the earth—the loyal, wound-licking dogs and the harmless golden-brown serpents native to sunny Epidaurus. Asklepios employed these animals, as well as herbs gathered along the mountain flanks and the pure springs watering his shrine, to implement cures.

Here is Pausanias's description of the place: "The sacred grove ... is surrounded by mountains on every side. Within the enclosure, no birth or death takes place ... The image of Asklepios ... is of ivory and gold. The god is seated on a throne, grasping a staff in one hand, and holding the other over the head of a serpent. A dog crouches at his side. On the throne are carved in relief the deeds of Argive heroes:

Bellerophon killing the Chimera and Perseus after he has cut off the Medusa's head."

Note that the triumphs depicted on Asklepios's throne were not over human adversaries but concerned a winged monster and one that turned people to stone—creepy, disease-like entities, in other words.

"Over against the temple," Pausanias continues, "is the place where the suppliants of the god sleep. Near it is a round building of white marble... worth seeing. It contains a picture of Love by Pausias: The god has thrown away his bow and arrows; he's picked up a lyre instead. Here too is another painting by Pausias, which represents Drunkenness imbibing from a crystal goblet. In the picture you can discern not only the crystal goblet but also a woman's face through it."

(No Greek mural painting from the Golden Age survives. Descriptions like this one help us understand why the ancients placed mural art on a par with sculpture.)

"Tablets stood within the enclosure," Pausanias reports. "In my time six were left. On these tablets are engraved the names of men and women who have been healed by Asklepios, together with the disease from which each suffered, and the manner of the cure. The inscriptions are in the Doric dialect. Apart from the others stands an ancient tablet with an inscription stating that Hippolytus dedicated twenty horses to the god...

"In the Epidaurian sanctuary there is an amphitheater which in my opinion is most especially worth seeing. It is true that the amphitheater at Megalopolis in Arcadia is much bigger... but for symmetry and beauty what architect could vie with Polyclitus? It was none other than Polyclitus who made this theater, and the round building as well."

Of all the things Pausanias describes, only the foundations of the round building, or *tholos,* and the amphitheater remain. The cellar floor of the tholos, with its oddly maze-like arrangement of marble slabs, was formerly of special interest and a favorite subject for photographs, but during the past few years it has been covered up and closed to the public, with no reason given.

The **amphitheater** remains wide open and welcoming against its grassy hill. This is really the whole object of your visit to Epidaurus. Dating from the fourth century B.C., the theater is an architectural masterpiece beyond compare. Just feel how the structure cups the air, and how lightly it contains the people—up to 14,000, in fact. Operas and other events are frequently held here.

Classical literature provides many instances of hypochondria, psychosomatic illness, and outright madness, all of which were treated at Epidaurus. How? That's a question without a clear answer. After Hippocrates, who claimed direct descent from Asklepios, drugs doubtless played an increasing role in the medicine practiced here. Hypnosis, also. But the chief healer may have been sleep, with serpents as cold companions to induce dreams of a seemingly divine nature.

For simple internal ailments the water of the local springs was heartily prescribed—and with good reason, according to modern chemical analysis: Epidaurian water closely matches the mineral count of bottled spring water from Evian, France. Native visitors make a point of drinking from, and washing at, the water tap outside the little museum.

The museum itself can be skipped. Its very narrow galleries, clogged with screeching tour groups, can quickly dissipate the peace you've gained from the site as a whole, and there's nothing in particular to see. Athens's National Archaeological Museum has appropriated all the best things found here.

By imperial Roman times some 300 Asklepian shrines and hospitals had been founded around the Mediterranean. Clearly the doctors of that day must have done something right. Their Asklepian attitude—of loving care and reverence for individual life—was in sharp contrast to the cynicism that had overtaken pagan civilization, opening the way for Christianity.

Driving back to Athens on the final day of your Classical tour, you'll naturally want to stop at Mycenae, Nemea, and ancient Corinth. They're well signposted and all within minutes of the highway. For guidance to all three places, see the chapter on the Peloponnese, below.

ACCOMMODATIONS REFERENCE
For accommodations in other areas discussed in the Classical Tour, see The Peloponnese, below.

▶ **Amalia**. Apolonos, **Delphi**, 330 54. Tel: (0265) 821-01.
▶ **Vouzas**. 1 Pavlou and Friderikis, **Delphi**, 330 54. Tel: (0265) 822-32.

THE PELOPONNESE

By Sherry Marker

Sherry Marker has been travelling regularly to the Peloponnese since 1975. She studied archaeology at the American School of Classical Studies in Athens and has written several guidebooks and contributed articles on Greece to Travel & Leisure *magazine and the* New York Times.

Many who come to the Peloponnese (Pelopónnisos) because of half-remembered legends—of Agamemnon and Clytemnaestra, Menelaus and Helen, Herakles and the Nemean lion, Olympic victors and Spartan warriors—discover unexpected worlds. There's the world of Byzantium: the palace and churches of Mystra, the fortress of Monemvasia, and the frescoed chapels that dot the bleak landscape of the Mani. There are Crusaders' castles in Arcadia and Messenia, where French knights in armor jousted before courtiers, and fortresses such as Koroni and Methoni, once the "twin eyes" watching over Venice's sea empire. On seemingly inaccessible crags and cliffs stand monasteries possessing icons that escaped Turkish plunder during the Greek War of Independence. There is even a sprinkling of mosques and Turkish fortresses that survived Greek reprisals once the war was won. Throughout the Peloponnese are neglected stands of mulberry trees that once nourished silkworms and supported a silk industry so prosperous that during the Middle Ages the entire area was known as The Morea, from the Greek for "mulberry."

Much of the Peloponnese was devastated in the War of Independence and repeatedly damaged by subsequent earthquakes; in consequence, modern Corinth, Argos, Tripoli, and Megalopoli have little but their ancient names and sites to recommend them. The two largest towns—Patras and Kalamata—are engulfed in a building frenzy that makes them almost unrecognizable to anyone born there before the 1960s. Yet in the hill towns and upland plains of Arcadia and Laconia there are slate- and tile-roofed villages with cobbled streets, blessedly free of the flat-topped houses and office buildings proliferating elsewhere faster than Hydra's heads. Nowhere in Greece are there finer villages, more imposing ancient and Medieval sites, grander mountains, lovelier coves and seaside hamlets—or, it must be admitted, nastier towns and cities.

All this makes the Peloponnese a bit elusive. Even the name is odd: It means "the island of Pelops." And yet the Peloponnese, joined to the mainland by the narrow Isthmus of Corinth until the canal was dug, was not an island at all. Chances are that the name Peloponnese reflects the ancient Greek perception that this was a distinct world apart from mainland Greece. As for Pelops, he was the son of Tantalus, the king of Lydia. For obscure reasons Tantalus served up his son to the Olympian gods concealed in a stew. The gods spotted the dead child and brought him back to life, but not before Demeter had taken a bite from Pelops's shoulder.

Fitted out with a new ivory shoulder, Pelops wooed the daughter of the king of Elis; their marriage produced the ill-fated House of Atreus and much of the mythology, history, and art of the Peloponnese. Homer celebrated the House of Atreus in the *Iliad,* and Aeschylus wrote about Pelops's grandson, Agamemnon, and his bloody homecoming to Mycenae in plays still performed at the theater of Epidaurus, just 48 km (30 miles) from Mycenae.

Nothing is very far apart in the Peloponnese, which is only 132 miles long and 134 miles wide. The Peloponnese would make an excellent Rorschach test: Just what *does* it look like? A top-heavy trident? A trident with a thumb? A dinosaur's footprint? A mulberry leaf? The briefest of geography lessons may help: This southernmost extension of the Balkan peninsula is separated from mainland Greece by the Gulf of Corinth and bounded by three seas: the Aegean to the east, the Ionian to the west, and the Sea of Crete to the south. The Peloponnese ends in three long prongs, flanked by the Messenian and Laconian gulfs, with Cape Gallo to the west, Cape Matapan in the center, and Cape Malea to the east.

For administrative purposes, the Peloponnese is divided into seven districts, or nomes, which correspond quite

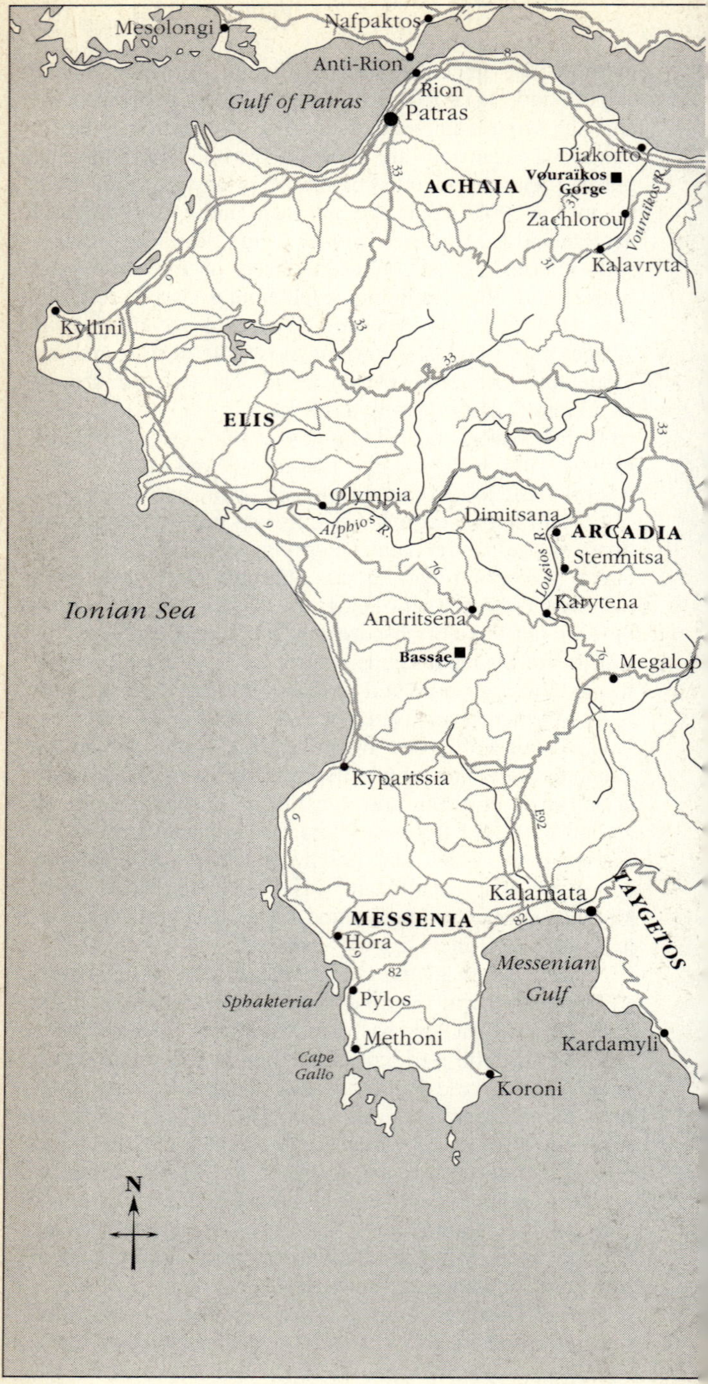
Mesolongi
Nafpaktos
Anti-Rion
Rion
Patras
Gulf of Patras
Diakofto
Vouraïkos Gorge
ACHAIA
Zachlorou
Vouraïkos R.
Kalavryta
Kyllini
ELIS
Olympia
Alphios R.
Dimitsana
ARCADIA
Stemnitsa
Lousios R.
Karytena
Andritsena
Bassae
Megalop
Ionian Sea
Kyparissia
E92
Kalamata
TAYGETOS
MESSENIA
Hora
Messenian Gulf
Sphakteria
Pylos
Methoni
Cape Gallo
Koroni
Kardamyli
N

The Peloponnese
0 miles 22
0 km 22
Itea
Gulf of Corinth
ATTICA
Lake Vouliagmeni
Megara
Peracbora
E92
Corinth Canal
Loutraki
CORINTHIA
Corinth
Isthmia
Salamina
Galatas
ARGOLID
TO ATHENS
Nemea
Mycenae
Epidaurus
Palea Epidavros
Aegina
Argos
Tiryns
Methana
Myloi
Nafplion
Poros
Lerna
Drepano
Tripoli
Tolon
Kastraki
Galatas
Gulf of Argolis
Ermioni
Porto Heli
Hydra
Spetses
PARNON MOUNTAINS
Leonidion
LACONIA
Sparta
Mystra
Kiparissi
Yeraki
Eurotas R.
MOUNTAINS
Yerakas
Itilo
Gytheion
Kelefa
Limeni
Monemvasia
Areopolis
Caves of Dirou
Laconian Gulf
Mani
Neapolis
Yerolimena
Vathia
Cavo Grosso
Porto Kaio
Cape Malea
Cape Matapan
Kythira

closely to the ancient regions; as you travel about, you'll see roadside signs announcing these divisions. If you spend much time here, you'll come to appreciate that the nomes are not arbitrary, but reflect cultural as well as geographical distinctions. The **Argolid** occupies the eastern thumb of the Peloponnese, with **Corinthia** taking in the northeast, while **Achaia** and **Elis** sprawl north and west to the Ionian Sea above **Messenia** in the southwest; **Laconia** occupies the southeast, with **Arcadia** at the very center of the Peloponnese. These divisions seem straightforward, but—as any visitor can attest—Greece is nothing if not complicated. Two examples: A small portion of the nome of Corinthia extends across the Isthmus of Corinth onto the mainland, and the islands off the eastern and southern coasts of the Peloponnese (Hydra, Poros, Spetses, and Kythira) are administered by the nome of Piraeus.

To take in the major Peloponnesian sites, you might go from Athens to Corinthia and the Argolid for Corinth, Epidaurus, Mycenae, Tiryns, Nemea, Lerna, and Nafplion; then head inland and south to Laconia for Sparta, Mystra, and Yeraki; then down to Monemvasia, the Mani peninsula, and the Caves of Dirou; cross to Messenia and the west coast (where the finest beaches are), past Koroni and Methoni and up to Pylos; continue up the west coast to Elis for Olympia—perhaps with a side trip into the pastoral valleys of Arcadia, so beloved of the ancient poets; and end with an extraordinary train trip along the Vouraïkos river in Achaia.

If you come to Greece on one of the ferry boats from Italy, you can just as easily begin your tour at Patras. If you're coming from central Greece on the shuttle service across the Gulf of Corinth, you can start at Rion. There are good roads in the Peloponnese even through the mountains, and superb beaches along the coast. Travel in the spring or fall and you'll see more crocuses and poppies than tourists.

The contemporary Greek writer Dragoumis said, "A pot of basil may symbolize the soul of a people better than a drama of Aeschylus." Virtually every house in the Peloponnese has its basil: There's basil planted in old olive-oil cans and in clay pots whose shape hasn't changed much since Agamemnon's day. The scent of all that basil and of the oregano that grows wild on the hills *is* the Peloponnese, just as the heather on the hill is Scotland and the aroma of nutmeg and cinnamon is Grenada.

This is the world of farmers on donkeys returning from their fields at dusk, fishermen landing their catch on harbor quays at dawn, and shepherds on remote hillsides suddenly calling out, "Where you from? You from Chicago? I used to work there; now I'm home." In the Peloponnese there's no need to choose between the glory that was Greece and today's pleasures: It's all there, to be enjoyed, savored, and recollected over glasses of pungent retsina and cups of the sweet sludge the Greeks call coffee.

MAJOR INTEREST

Agamemnon's Mycenae
Leonidas's Sparta
Byzantine Mystra and Monemvasia
Frankish and Turkish castles
Nafplion, the first capital of independent Greece
Patras and Corinth, gateways to the Peloponnese

Monuments and museums: Olympia, Corinth, Mycenae, Pylos

Temples and theaters: Bassae, Nemea, Epidaurus, Argos

Arcadian villages

Wonders natural (the Caves of Dirou and the Langada Pass) and man-made (the Corinth Canal and the tower villages of the Mani)

Quintessential Greek landscape of sea and mountains

Beaches: Gytheion and Pylos

Greece's sweetest eggplants and tomatoes, Easter lamb and winter artichokes, fish large (tunny) and small (gopes), and Kalamata olives

Food and Wine of the Peloponnese

Greek food does not have striking regional contrasts. Certain basic ingredients—olive oil, eggplant, feta cheese, and lamb—are as characteristic of Macedonia as of the Peloponnese. Some dishes, however, *are* distinctively Peloponnesian, and to find them it's best to avoid places with signs that say "tourist restaurant," especially near major archaeological sites such as Olympia, Corinth, and Mycenae. By and large such restaurants serve overcooked veal, soggy vegetables, bland crème caramel, lukewarm beer, and expensive bottled wine rather than local retsina from the barrel.

Just around the corner from the new "tourist restaurant" there's often a small taverna where you will almost certainly find at least one waiter who knows enough English to help you order. Menus in "English" are not always an immediate help. "Pork shops" and "neat balls" may be easy enough to decipher, but to find out what a "grass hill" (summer greens) or "inkstand" (squid) is, you may want to follow Greek custom and have a look in the kitchen.

That's where you'll find *kounoupídi kapamá* (a cauliflower dish), said to have originated in Kalamata, or grilled *pitsoúnia, ortýkia,* or *pérdikes* (pigeons, quail, or partridges), once almost a daily dietary staple in the Mani. Other Peloponnesian specialties include *psari à la spetsiósa* (fish baked with tomato sauce), *moskári kapamá* (veal with wine and spices), and *kounéli stifádo* (rabbit with tiny onions and vinegar). Surprisingly, the *stifado* (sometimes made with beef instead of rabbit) is not at all sour, perhaps because a cinnamon stick is tucked into the casserole.

Much of the Peloponnese is a rich farming area, and Greeks agree (insofar as they ever agree on anything) that the sweetest eggplants are from Argos, the tastiest quinces from Corinth, and the richest olives from Kalamata. The region's agricultural wealth offers considerable seasonal variety, although the severe drought of 1990 substantially diminished many crops (fruit and citrus trees, lettuce, and tomatoes were badly hit)—and noticeably elevated prices.

Most Greeks base their menus on what's plentiful at the local market and resist the blandishments of imported and frozen foods. If you're in the Peloponnese in the spring, there's tender lamb and glorious artichokes in *avgolémono* (egg-lemon) sauce; in summer, real *horiátiki saláta* (Greek salad to you) with juicy tomatoes, fistfuls of black olives, mounds of feta cheese, and lashings of olive oil, topped off with oregano. In autumn there's game and in winter the *fasólia* and *revíthia* (beans and chick peas), which are Lenten staples.

Whatever the season, you'll inhale the aroma of lambs and goats roasting over charcoal. The historian William Miller noted that "in proportion to its population, Greece has more goats than any other country; there are 119 goats to every 100 Greeks." That's a lot of goats—as anyone who drives in the Peloponnese discovers on those occasions when it's sensible to cede the right of way to a goatherd. Year round, you'll get well acquainted with garlic, oregano, rosemary, and thyme, and the green-gold olive oil that calls out for astringent local retsina wine. While you're coming to terms with retsina, sample some of the nonresinated vintages from the region's largest winery, Achaia Clauss, based near Patras. Patras also produces some of the most popular brands of ouzo.

Greeks take their food as seriously as the French do—but in a very different way. Whereas the French argue passionately about the influence of one recipe or region on another, Greeks want you to know that their cuisine is *their* cuisine. Just suggest to most Greeks that their food owes a lot to Turkish cuisine but reveals a strong Italian influence, and you'll bring any conversation to a momentary standstill, followed by several hours of high-decibel argumentation and table thumping.

CORINTHIA AND THE ARGOLID

Corinthia and the Argolid, which stretch across the northeast Peloponnese, offer a daunting amount to see; there's no area in Greece as rich in history and mythology, none with more antiquities and monuments, ranging from the third-millennium B.C. palace at Lerna to the 18th-century mosque used as the first Parliament house of newly independent Greece at Nafplion. The land here is unusually hospitable, with none of the abrupt mountains and sinuous valleys of most of the Peloponnese. Instead there are olive and citrus groves, wheat fields, and grape arbors that spread inland to the encircling mountains and down to the sea.

There's so much to take in here that some package-tour buses leave Athens in the morning, rumble across the Corinth Canal into ancient Corinth, barrel through the plain beneath Acrocorinth to Mycenae, streak to Epidaurus, and end up for the night at Nafplion—after a stop at Tiryns. It's all perfectly reasonable for anyone wanting to get a sense of what it must have been like to be on the march with Julius Caesar, but others may prefer to heed a Greek injunction and proceed *sigá, sigá*—"slowly, slowly." (See also the Classical Tour chapter, above, which covers some of these places in a one-week circuit.)

It's not easy to go slowly on the journey from Athens to the Corinth Canal: Choosing between the old coast road and the new toll road that begins beyond the malodorous *banlieue* of Eleusis is a bit like choosing between Scylla and Charybdis. The old road offers vertiginous twists alternating with traffic jams in once-pleasant seaside towns, while the new road serves as a race course for buses and trucks straddling the dividing line. It's enough to make travellers nostalgic for the mythical days when the greatest hazard on the Athens–Corinth road was the giant Skiron, who robbed the unwary and flung them over the cliffs to his accomplice, a carnivorous sea turtle.

When French engineers completed the four-mile-long **Corinth Canal** in 1893 after 11 years of work, they finished a job that only two particularly megalomaniacal Roman emperors—Caligula and Nero—had previously attempted. Cape Matapan, at the tip of the Peloponnese, was so feared that smaller ships, emptied of their cargo, were dragged over the isthmus on wooden runners, then reloaded before continuing. (Some signs of the ancient slipway, the *diolchos,* are still visible west of the canal.) Until the canal was built, ships sailing between Athens's port of Piraeus and Italy had to round Cape Matapan, adding 200 miles to their journey. Ironically, by the time the canal was finished commercial vessels could negotiate Matapan with little danger, and many were too large for the canal, which was increasingly used primarily by pleasure craft and small cruise lines.

The canal is always in a hubbub, with local buses disgorging passengers, gypsies peddling corn dolls, kiosks selling foreign-language newspapers, and garish souvenir shops (most with acceptable toilet facilities) trading in trinkets. For many years a camel was tethered beside one of the canal's *souvláki* stands; its unexplained disappearance gave pause to all who had ever dined on the chewy fare served there and speculated as to its precise nature. The bridge is usually lined with spectators hoping to see a ship *not* make it through the 75-foot-wide canal.

Perachora

It's tempting when you reach the Corinth Canal to speed on into the Peloponnese, but if you do you'll miss one of the most magical spots in Greece: the eighth-century B.C. **Sanctuary of Hera** at Perachóra. Part of the magic comes from Perachora's associations with the brilliant young English archaeologist Humfry Payne, who excavated here in the 1930s, died tragically young, and is buried at Mycenae. His widow, the English film critic Dilys Powell, has written two evocative memoirs of their years at Perachora: *An Affair of the Heart* and *The Traveller's Journey Is Done*.

An intermittently paved road runs to the site, 32 km (20 miles) north of the canal on the northern shore of the Gulf of Corinth. En route you'll pass through **Loutráki**, once a fashionable spa and now a sprawling resort where Greeks enjoy the hot springs. The road continues to the melancholy village of Perachora before reaching **Lake Vouliagméni**, with its cluster of fish tavernas. The ancient site is beneath the lighthouse at the tip of the hooked peninsula northwest of the lake.

Like Lato in Crete, Perachora is a gem of a site: There are views across the blue waters of the gulf to the distinct mound of Acrocorinth and the seemingly endless mountains of the Peloponnese. The site is tiny, unexpected, often deserted (but not on summer weekends, when youths—many with transistor radios—come here to swim off the rocks in the miniature harbor beneath the sanctuary). There are the remains of two temples, several cisterns and stoas, as well as a modern chapel on ancient foundations.

Ancient Corinth

On summer days it seems that the ambient aphorism "See Corinth and die" might easily refer not to the city's legendary pleasures but to the effects of the crowds and the heat. It's a good idea *not* to drive as close to the site as possible, lest you find yourself trapped by tour buses when you finish your visit; instead, park on the outskirts of the village of ancient Corinth, with its string of souvenir shops and interchangeable restaurants. Both modern Corinth (3 km/2 miles from the canal) and the ancient site (5 km/3 miles from the modern town) are clearly signposted on the main Athens–Patras road. If you're travelling by car, you can bypass modern Corinth altogether, but if you arrive by bus or train you'll continue from the modern town to the ancient site by bus or taxi.

Corinth might have gone the way of Athens and Sparta—a brief burst of glory, followed by centuries of decline—had it not been for Julius Caesar, who refounded the city Rome had destroyed a century earlier. As the administrative center for Achaia, Corinth had its heyday under the Romans, with an astonishing 300,000 citizens and perhaps 400,000 slaves. The **Excavation Museum** documents the wealth of Roman Corinth with an extensive collection of statues of imperial figures and of mosaics, including one depicting a sunburned Pan piping to several besotted heifers.

From the eighth century B.C. Corinth managed an overseas empire, founding colonies in Italy, exporting black-figure pottery around the Mediterranean, and managing the Isthmian Games at home. (The Excavation Museum at ancient

Corinth has splendid examples of the pottery, and a fine museum on the Isthmian Games 8 km/5miles away at Isthmia makes up for a less than dazzling site.) Such success might suggest that the Corinthians were mere workaholics, but in fact they were sufficient bons vivants to cause other Greeks to say, "Not all are lucky enough to visit Corinth." The most famous courtesan in antiquity was Lais, who was wooed by the philosopher Diogenes and was but the best known of the city's pleasures, which included thousands of prostitutes who dedicated their efforts to the goddess Aphrodite. (Ask to see the locked room at the Excavation Museum containing anatomical votive objects from the Asklepieion that will convince you of how seriously Corinthians took their pleasures.) One who came to Corinth and was not amused by its pleasures was Saint Paul, who worked here as a tentmaker in A.D. 51 and 52, irritating the neighbors with his relentless proselytizing. Paul successfully pleaded his case to the Roman governor Gallio at the elevated *bema* on the south side of the forum.

The excavations at ancient Corinth suggest the raw size of this aggressive commercial and governmental center. When the traveller and writer Pausanias stopped here in the second century A.D., he commented that "Corinth has plenty of baths," and seemed to have had as much trouble telling them apart as the rest of us. It has to be admitted that two Greek monuments, the Doric **Temple of Apollo**, with 7 of its massive 38 columns still standing, and the arcaded **Fountain of Peirene**, largely remodeled by the Romans, are Corinth's most evocative buildings. It somehow seems fitting that Americans, who have perfected and successfully exported the shopping mall and coined the term "bureaucratese," should be the excavators of this Roman progenitor of international commercialism and big government.

A good road runs from the excavation site up to **Acrocorinth**, the massive humped mountain south of the ancient site. The well-preserved fortifications here protected Corinth and stopped generations of invaders from penetrating into the Peloponnese. Especially in summer, you'll probably want to drive up (the walk takes at least an hour) and save your energy for exploring the summit, with its pleasant jumble of Byzantine chapels and cisterns, Frankish fortifications, a Venetian belvedere, and Turkish mosque and houses; a small café at the summit (not always open; bring water) sells soft drinks and snacks. When the relentless 19th-century traveller Colonel William Leake came here, he wrote that "the view comprehends perhaps a greater number of celebrated objects than any other in Greece." Leake not only saw the mountains of central Greece and Attica, but caught as well the distinct gleam of the Parthenon about 50 miles away on the Acropolis. The Parthenon was perfectly visible from Acrocorinth until quite recently, when the Athenian *nefos* (smog) shrouded it, along with the Attic hills. Still, the headland of Perachora (in Greek, "the land beyond") usually stands out clearly beyond the Gulf of Corinth.

Nemea

This splendid site is located in a lush valley just west of the Corinth–Argos road about midway between the towns. It is almost always deserted, and when you suddenly see the three columns of the **Temple of Zeus**, you might almost think you'd discovered it yourself. The Nemean games took place near the **Sanctuary of Zeus** from the sixth to the third century B.C. One legend says that Herakles founded the games after dispatching the Nemean lion, the first of the Twelve Labors, which made him the favorite hero of the Peloponnese. Time telescopes at Nemea, where a massive sixth-century A.D. Christian basilica and cemetery sit below the fourth-century B.C. Doric Temple of Zeus.

It's a cliché that the Greeks had an unerring eye for picking perfect spots for their temples and sanctuaries; Nemea's American excavators honored the tradition by placing their superb new museum here so that it overlooks the site, vineyards, and olive groves. The museum welcomes visitors with a display of drawings and writings by early travellers. Pausanias, who remarked rather irritably that "the temple of Nemean Zeus is worth seeing, except that the roof has collapsed," would certainly approve of the scale model of the site and partial reconstruction of the temple roof. Photographs of athletic scenes on Greek vases re-create events that took place in the hillside stadium. A fine exhibit displays coins found here, making the point that the games drew spectators from Greek cities as far away as Italy and Asia Minor.

Herakles himself is still remembered locally in the popular "Blood of Herakles" wine, which is sold at roadside stands and served at two modest tavernas at Chani Aneste, just off the Corinth–Argos road in the Derbenákia Pass, at the former site of a Turkish wayfarers' inn. Several shady plane trees and a gushing spring make this the best place for a snack between Corinth and Mycenae.

Mycenae

About 10 km (6 miles) south of the Nemea turnoff, a signposted road runs 2 km (about a mile) east to the little village of Mycenae (Mikínes), itself several kilometers before the ancient site. The village has the usual roadside attractions (souvenir stands, restaurants, anonymous hotels), but one of these modest hotels has a glorious past: the rebuilt **Belle Helene**, where Mycenae's first excavator, the great German archaeologist Heinrich Schliemann, lived. The original hotel was destroyed a decade ago in a fire, but the owners (including brothers named Agamemnon and Menelaus) saved the guest register, which was filled with the signatures of such famous visitors as Claude Debussy and Virginia Woolf. An overnight stay here and an evening walk up to the citadel is the best way to take in the landscape, which can't have changed much since the bonfires flashed across the hills, signaling that Troy had fallen to Agamemnon. Just out of sight behind the hills is the **Argive Heraion**, where Agamemnon and Menelaus took the oaths of the Greek Host to recapture Helen and destroy Troy.

If possible, see Mycenae out of season or early in the morning, before multitudes of tourists swarm up the ramp beneath the Lion Gate into the citadel. Whatever the season, wear rubber-soled shoes and take a hat (a good idea at most sites). Mycenae's polished rocks are treacherous, and the only shade is in the underground secret cistern and the *tholos* (circular tombs) named for Atreus, Clytemnaestra, and Aegisthus.

The English philhellene Robert Liddell summed up Mycenae's enduring magic: "Mycenae is one of the most ancient and fabulous places in Europe. I think it should be visited first for the fable, next for the lovely landscape, and thirdly for the excavations." The landscape is deceptive: Blink, and you might almost miss Mycenae from the Corinth–Argos road. Yet from the citadel itself it's clear that this hummock framed by twin mountains and set off by deep ravines spies on any movement in the plain of Argos. Like Tiryns, just outside Nafplion, and Pylos, across the Peloponnese in Messenia, Mycenae occupies a height no greater than its might demanded.

As to Mycenae's "fable," today it belongs not only to Agamemnon but also to Heinrich Schliemann, himself an almost mythical figure. A sickly child, Schliemann left school at 14 and worked as a grocer's apprentice for five years, then set off for Venezuela as a cabin boy, but was shipwrecked and washed ashore on the coast of Holland. He made a fortune in indigo, travelled to America (where he became a citizen), and then set off to do what he'd intended all along: prove that Homer knew as much of history as of poetry. In rapid succession, Schliemann excavated Troy's burned citadel (his overly hasty methods destroying much of Homer's Troy in the process), then set off for Mycenae, Homer's "Mycenae, rich in gold," where the massive Lion Gate and mysterious subterranean tombs had preserved the memory of Troy's destroyer.

"I have looked upon the face of Agamemnon bare," Schliemann reportedly cabled the king of Greece in 1876, when he found a gold burial mask in a grave on Mycenae's citadel. When another grave revealed the corpses of three women and two babies, one of them wrapped in a gold sheet, Schliemann remembered Cassandra, her two handmaidens, and her infant twins—all murdered here by Agamemnon's wife, Clytemnaestra. And as for Clytemnaestra herself, Schliemann gave her name to a tomb found outside the citadel walls. And why was Clytemnaestra's tomb outside the walls? Greek tradition was clear on that point: Clytemnaestra was buried away from the rest of the royal family in punishment for killing Agamemnon.

So many spectators flocked to Mycenae to catch a glimpse of the 14 kilos of gold Schliemann found that the militia was called out to protect both gold and excavators. And it wasn't just the gold that was stunning: For generations scholars had questioned whether Homer, in the late 8th century B.C., could have known anything about the 13th-century B.C. world of the Trojan War. Everything Schliemann found—gold cups, jewelry, elaborately wrought inlaid swords and daggers, bronze armor—could have been made to order from Homer's descriptions. Homer's "Mycenae, rich in gold," Agamemnon and Clytemnaestra, Helen and Troy—all were plucked from the world of mythical figures like Herakles and the Nemean lion and revealed to be history preserved in poetry across four centuries.

Schliemann concentrated on Mycenae's graves and tombs, but excavation since his time has revealed that Mycenae was more than an isolated palace but less than a town, with a scattering of houses and workshops around the royal residence. Unfortunately, only low foundations remain on the irregular citadel slopes, with no traces of the brightly painted walls, ceilings, and floors whose reconstructions remind many of Minoan palace decoration. You'll find it much easier to unravel the Mycenaean palaces at Tiryns and Pylos. Still, inventory tablets written in the ancient script known as Linear B give tempting suggestions of what Mycenae's palace must have looked like, with furniture worthy of Versailles, including "an ebony chair with ivory braces worked with stags' heads and men and little calves" and "an ebony footstool inlaid with ivory butterflies."

Much has been lost, but four monuments would make the journey here worthwhile even without the knowledge that this was the home of the ill-fated House of Atreus. There's Mycenae's encompassing circuit of **defense walls**, so immense that later Greeks called them "Cyclopean," imagining that only giants could have built them. Then there is the **Lion Gate**, one of the earliest examples of monumental sculpture in Western art, a stark statement of Mycenae's power. And there's the mysterious **grave circle**, just inside the Lion Gate. Was Agamemnon buried here? Schliemann thought so, although scholars today disagree; many think that the kings buried here lived well before Agamemnon.

Finally, there is the **Treasury of Atreus**, also known as the Tomb of Agamemnon, an enormous, domed "beehive" tomb tunneled deep into a hillside; its great size and incredibly exact masonry make it the most impressive monument to survive from the Mycenaean era. The tomb may have been contemporary with the Lion Gate; certainly its entrance, with one of the two lintel stones weighing in at 120 tons, is every bit as monumental. Inside, soaring into the shadows to a height of more than 40 feet, is the great vault—the largest known vault built before the Pantheon was raised more than a thousand years later. The interior walls were richly decorated with bronze rosettes, and once your eyes are accustomed to the darkness you should be able to see some of the nails that once held them in place; you'll certainly see the swooping swallows that make their nests here. This tomb was robbed in antiquity, but what was found elsewhere gives an idea of the golden treasures that may have been placed in the small side chamber that is almost hidden in the tholos wall.

If you want an idea of Mycenae's strength, consider this: The *rosso antico* marble used to decorate the façade of the Treasury of Atreus probably came from quarries on Cape Matapan, at the farthest end of the Peloponnese. The seas off Matapan were so fierce that later generations of Greeks dragged their ships across the Isthmus of Corinth to avoid them—but the Mycenaeans sailed home with a cargo of marble.

The most important finds from Mycenae, including all the gold, the inlaid sword and dagger blades, most of the pottery, figurines, and reconstructed frescoes, are on display in the National Archaeological Museum in Athens. Some finds, including the marvelous terra-cotta idols from the Cult Center in the Citadel House, are in the Nafplion Museum. Travellers stopping in London can see architectural fragments from the Treasury of Atreus in the British Museum.

Nafplion

Looking out on the severe Arcadian mountains, this little port on the Gulf of Argolis is easily the loveliest town in the Peloponnese, a stroller's delight offering a welcome break from the rigors of touring. There's even a miniature castle in the harbor, the 15th-century **Bourtzi** (Islet Fortress), whose fairy-tale appearance belies its history. This was once the home for executioners who dared not live ashore near the families of their victims. Small boats ply back and forth from the quay on excursions to the Bourtzi.

Náfplion's harborside is lined with cafés and restaurants; the century-old **Poseidon** restaurant, with casks of retsina stacked along one wall, has simply prepared fresh fish, as does the nearby **Savvouras** restaurant. Fish-loving Athenians travel to Nafplion for lunch or dinner at Savvouras—not, however, because seafood is any cheaper here than in Athens. Indeed, fishing throughout the Mediterranean is very thin, so fishermen must charge a lot in order to make a living.

Off the harbor, narrow side streets with cascades of bougainvillaea have attractive art galleries and legitimate crafts shops along with the usual souvenir shops. One of the nicest galleries is at 6 Athan. Siokou Street, where **Konstantine Beslemes** sells jewels and paintings on old wood, including delightful harbor scenes. (This gallery, like many in Nafplion, is closed in winter.) Odós Staikopoúlou Street also has several small antiques shops that sell old bread stamps and dowry chests, and contemporary crafts shops offering wooden reproductions of the figures from Greek shadow plays. At **The Enotion** on Odos Staikopoulou you can see (and buy) Iannis Kokkoris's marvelous reproductions of figures used in the Karagöz shadow theater. The Karagöz plays, featuring the bumptious Karagöz, who outwits all enemies, used to be one of the great delights of visitng Greece. Now performances are few and far between, but Iannis Kokkoris puts on shows for The Peloponnesian Folklore Foundation. A few doors away, the **Perasma Gallery** sells nontraditional wooden Karagöz figures.

The lower town has several pleasantly old-fashioned hotels, of which the best is the **King Otto** (with perhaps the most elegant staircase in the Peloponnese). The more sybaritic may prefer the **Xenia Palace** hotel, one of the few luxury hotels in the Peloponnese, sited high above town beneath the final heights of the Palamídi Fortress. (A road now spares visitors the climb up 857 rock-cut steps to the Palamidi's summit.) The Xenia Palace resists tours, and its international clientele includes Athenian gentry taking breaks from the *nefos* (smog) and heat. There's a pool, and rooms have spectacular views of the Bourtzi.

The Greek National Tourist Organization manages a rocky beach below the Palamidi, and there are opportunities to swim outside town at **Tolón**, **Drépano**, and **Kastráki**. Tolon and Drepano are in the throes of overdevelopment, which makes swimming on the beach beneath the Bronze Age site of Asine at Kastraki particularly pleasant. All of these beaches can be reached by bus or taxi from Nafplion.

Over the centuries Venetians, Franks, and Turks contended for possession of Nafplion, and it's easy to see why. Aside from the town's charms, the harbor is excellent and is well guarded by the 700-foot-high Palamidi cliff. Thanks to its largely Venetian fortifications (the Lion of Saint Mark is in evidence in several places), Nafplion almost alone in the Peloponnese escaped destruction during the War of Independence (1821 to 1828). Furthermore, Nafplion was Greece's first capital after the war, which gained it a clutch of Neoclassical buildings that are more than usually elegant for a town this size.

Constitution Square, just behind the harbor, has two well-preserved mosques, a startling bank with pseudo-Minoan columns, and the excellent **Odyssey** book and newspaper shop with a wide selection of English titles ranging from the classics to paperback best sellers. At the foot of the square stands a Venetian depot turned **Archaeological Museum**. The arsenal's thick walls make it cool even in the heat of summer, and the Mycenaean collection, with a full suit of bronze armor and a boar's-tusk helmet, is a delight. Less famous but equally entrancing are the gesticulating terra-cotta idols from Mycenae and the eerie bust known as the *Lord of Asine*.

Just off Constitution Square, on Vassíleos Alexándrou, a 19th-century mansion houses the absolutely stunning collection of the **Peloponnesian Folklore Foundation**, which won the European Small Museum of the Year award in 1981. Dioramas and life-size photographs show scenes of village life: mothers and daughters spinning, farmers at work, silk and cotton weaving, and a wide-eyed young couple on their wedding day. The collection of costumes is second only to that at Athens's Benaki Museum. In addition, there's a shady garden courtyard and coffee shop, and a superb gift shop with examples of weaving, embroidery, and recordings of traditional Greek music. Next door the **Nafplion Art Gallery** gives a glimpse of trends in contemporary Greek and European art.

Two of Nafplion's best restaurants are moments away from both museums: the **Hellas Restaurant** (best at lunch), at the foot of Constitution Square, and **Ta Phanaria** (excellent for dinner), just off the square on Odos Staikopoulou. Summer crowds sometimes overwhelm the staff at the Hellas, while Ta Phanaria is usually much less frantic. Both restaurants have an unusual variety of dishes, usually including *dolmádes* (stuffed grape leaves) in egg-lemon sauce. Anyone who's still hungry can try an extravagant *Tsikágo* ice cream sundae at **The Pink Panther**, on Odos Staikopoulou, or a honey-laden baklava at the sweet shop by the Agamemnon Hotel on the quay.

A stroll through the narrow streets above Constitution Square leads past several Turkish fountains and two interesting churches. The first, **Saint Spyrídon**, on Odós Kapodístriou, is much visited by Greeks as the spot where Kapodistrias, the first governor of the independent state of Greece, was assassinated in 1831. The second, the Catholic **church of the Metamorphosis**, seems to encapsulate Nafplion's intricate history: It was built by the Venetians, converted into a mosque by the Turks, and later reconsecrated as a Catholic church. The church has an ornamental wooden doorway with an inscription listing various philhellenes, including "nephews" of George Washington, and Lord Byron, who "died that Greece might yet be free."

Nafplion's charms have not gone unrecognized, and in high season there are often more tourists than locals in most of the harborside cafés. Still, the side streets belong primarily to the Nafpliots, who seem to have a sweet tooth exceptional even for Greeks. On summer evenings families indulge in "submarines," the ice-water-and-vanilla sweet that alternately slakes and revives thirst. The town is at its most magical at twilight, when the clamor of church bells sends the swifts swooping above the crumbling mosques while the Lion of Saint Mark watches from the Venetian battlements.

It's perfectly possible with a little doubling back to see anything in Corinthia and the Argolid as an excursion from

Nafplion, although you'll probably stop at Corinth and Mycenae on the way there. Epidaurus is a major excursion, but Ayia Moni, Argos, Lerna, and Tiryns can be combined as a day trip, with time left over for a swim. In summer the Flying Dolphin hydrofoil (known locally as "Tō Flying") offers connections from Nafplion to Spetses, Hydra, and Poros, as well as down the coast to Monemvasia, and back to Piraeus.

Epidaurus

It's easy to understand why this pine-scented grove was one of the most important healing spas in antiquity. The **sanctuary** was an ancient version of Baden-Baden grafted onto Lourdes: Baths, rest hostels, and, of course, the theater, restored the flesh as well as the spirit. Sacred serpents, quartered in the mysterious *tholos,* played a significant but unknown part in the healing rites.

The spectacle at Epidaurus's fourth-century B.C. **theater**, a 14,000-seat arena, rivals opera performances at Rome's Baths of Caracalla or Verona's amphitheater. Few experiences can be grander than seeing a play performed where it was seen more than 2,000 years ago. Epidaurus (Epídavros) is one of the few places in Greece where things usually begin on schedule: If all goes well, the play starts precisely as the sun dips beneath the mountains behind the stage. The theater's acoustics are legendary: A whisper is clearly audible from the topmost seats, while louder tests conducted by less courteous tourists—shouts of "Can you hear me?"—might almost be heard at Mycenae.

The plays are given in either ancient or modern Greek, but program notes have English plot synopses, and the Odyssey bookshop in nearby Nafplion usually stocks translations. The spectacle itself needs no translation, and a great deal of the fun comes from watching Greeks in the audience hiss Clytemnaestra's villainy, roar with laughter at Aristophanes' antics, and cheer through their tears when Electra recognizes her lost brother, Orestes, by the childhood scar above his eye. The dictatorship of the Colonels understood the power of ancient drama and forbade performances of Sophocles' *Antigone,* lest the story of individual conscience in conflict with autocracy inflame citizens against the regime.

A good road (signposted from Nafplion) winds 30 km (19 miles) through sere hills from Nafplion to Epidaurus. The ideal way to visit Epidaurus is to spend some time at the sanctuary, then return for an evening performance at the theater (weekends June through September). You could while away some time at one of the beaches nearby at **Paleá Epídavros**, **Méthana**, and **Galatás**. If you're coming from Nafplion, it's better to leave your car behind and come with one of the theater excursions that bus you to and from Epidaurus: Driving unfamiliar twisting roads at night in the company of 13,999 other spectators eager to get home is not a relaxing end to an evening at the theater. If you have the time, stay overnight at the **Xenia Hotel** just outside the sanctuary precincts, but be sure to make a reservation well in advance and check in before the performance. The hotel is small, and rooms are at a premium during the theater season.

(See also the Classical Tour chapter above for more on Epidaurus.)

Ayia Moni

Most Greek monasteries and convents are not easy to get to—the contemplative life demands isolation—which makes a visit to Ayía Moní Areias, just outside Nafplion, particularly attractive. (To visit Ayia Moni take the Epidaurus road one kilometer out of town to the signposted right turn; the convent is another 2 km up the side road. Don't go in the middle of the day, when the nuns, like most Greeks, have their siesta.) Ayia Moni is on the site of the spring where Hera is said to have bathed once a year to restore her virginity, in the vain hope of rekindling Zeus's ardor. The nuns will show you the spring, which they have dammed up to create a goldfish pond more than ample enough for Hera's purposes. The convent church dates to 1149 and is architecturally the best example of its period in the area; the frescoes are not old. Inside is the holy icon, which you will be told was *acheiropoitós,* not made by human hands, the discovery of which led to the building of the convent.

A rich Greek-American gave money to restore a wing of the convent that burned in the 1930s. He was guided here from his home in Chicago, the nuns say, by the Virgin and Saint Michael, whom he recognized by their heavenly aroma. The nuns, who seem equally at home with legends of Hera and Saint Michael, sell lovely embroidery. Ayia Moni, particularly charming in the soft light of late afternoon, seems a world away from the sophisticated bustle of Nafplion.

Tiryns

If Homer and Schliemann hadn't made Mycenae loom so large in the imagination, Tiryns, just a few kilometers north of Nafplion on the Argos road, would have far more visitors. As it doesn't, Tiryns, with its compact citadel, is far easier to explore than its famous neighbor. Before the coast silted up, Tiryns was much closer to the seashore, and it has been suggested that this city was the Piraeus of Mycenae—the port for its powerful neighbor.

Homer called Tiryns "well walled," and when you walk the 2,400-foot circuit, 25 feet thick at the base, you'll see why. Pausanias found Tiryns's walls (which would have risen twice as high as what remains) "no less marvelous" than the pyramids of Egypt, and stated unequivocally that this was the work of giant Cyclopes. Who else, asked Pausanias, could have moved stones (some weighing 14 tons) "so huge that a pair of mules would not even begin to budge the smallest." Almost better than the walls are the subterranean corbeled vaults and storage chambers, rubbed smooth by the generations of sheep that sheltered here after Tiryns fell, along with Mycenae, during the unexplained wave of disasters—invasions? civil wars?—that ended the Mycenaean world around 1200 B.C.

(See also the Classical Tour chapter above for more on ancient Tiryns.)

Lerna

There are three reasons to go to Lerna. First, the short drive west from Nafplion offers Felliniesque scenes of would-be swimmers seemingly floating through the knee-high shallows of the Argolic Gulf. Gypsy encampments sprawl across the fields, and women in brightly colored costumes chase half-naked children along the beach.

Then, just south of Myloi (Myli) on the Tripoli road, there's the **House of the Tiles**, a third-millennium B.C. "palace" whose foundations are completely preserved. The site is covered by a protective roof, which makes the palace's size crystal clear. Pottery from as far away as Troy and Niš (the Yugoslav birthplace of Constantine the Great) has been found here, another reminder of the far-ranging trade routes that existed long before the Trojan War. Outside the House of the Tiles are the lovingly preserved foundations of a tiny Neolithic house. How dark and cramped life must have been! Today, surrounded by citrus groves, Lerna is magical—a spot, like Perachora, where the present drops away.

The final reason to come here is less than a mile away at Myloi, where you'll find a string of souvlaki stands. Try the **Lerna**, in a shaded hollow beneath the main road, with its small playground, a pond of thunderous frogs, a few recently unearthed ancient remains, and the best souvlaki and fried potatoes for miles around.

Argos

If Homer were choosing an epithet for this place today, surely it would be "Abysmal Argos." (You can get to Argos from Nafplion either along the main road past Tiryns or by following the coast road to Myloi, then turning right [north]; either way, the trip takes less than half an hour.) Argos was one of the most powerful cities in antiquity, boasting twin acropolises, but because the modern town was built over the ancient one and has been repeatedly ravaged by earthquakes, there's little to be seen of the city that dominated the Argolid for so long. The remains of the fourth-century B.C. theater suffer by comparison with the theater at Epidaurus but are worth a glance. Still, there's only one real reason to grit your teeth and hazard Argos's traffic-glutted streets: the excellent archaeological **Museum of Argos**, with its impressive bronze armor from the Geometric period, a marvelous seventh-century B.C. pottery fragment showing Odysseus blinding Polyphemos, and a tortoiseshell lyre worthy of Apollo. Finally, there's the tiny (but impressively round-bottomed) terra-cotta "goddess," found at Lerna, whose date of ca. 4000 B.C. makes it one of the oldest representational figures found in the Peloponnese. En route to the museum, partisans of folk art will enjoy the advertising signs above the bus station in Argos's main square.

Happily, ancient Argos is best seen from its principal acropolis, the **Lárissa**, which is encircled by a Medieval castle incorporating ancient walls; there's even enough shade under the battlements for a picnic. (A road leads up to the Larissa from the Tripoli bypass.) From the Larissa, the Sanctuary of Apollo and Athena is clearly visible on Argos's lesser acropolis, the shield-shaped Aspis. Farther below, part of the ancient agora stands out, although the theater is hidden in the hillside. The view from the Larissa is one of the most spectacular in Greece, taking in the full sweep of the Argolid, the gulf, the mountains of Arcadia, the cliffs above Nafplion, and the plain beneath Tiryns and Mycenae.

LACONIA
Sparta

Sparta (Sparti) has one of the most dramatic sites in the Peloponnese. Spread along the Eurotas river, it lies in the center of the great bowl of the Vale of Laconia, which is itself encircled by the massive Parnon and Taýgetos mountain ranges. Snowcapped well into summer, Taygetos (pronounced Tah-YEE-geh-tos) looks precisely like a child's drawing of a mountain: jagged peaks rising precipitously from the ground line. With Taygetos closing off the westward horizon, causing an early and abrupt sunset, there is no place in Greece where you feel farther from the sea, or more isolated.

Sparta is an anomaly: For once, the modern town has more charm than the negligible ancient remains, thanks to Greece's first king, Otto, who decided in 1834 to return Sparta to some semblance of its former grandeur. Otto took his responsibilities seriously, if eccentrically, and disconcerted his new subjects by putting aside his Western suits and affecting the *foustanélla,* or Greek kilt. Be that as it may, in Sparta Otto ordained a proper European town, with a tidy grid plan bisected by two wide boulevards, and a central *plateía* (square). Earthquakes have leveled most of Otto's Neoclassical buildings, although a number of arcaded shops, the attractively restored Neoclassical town hall, the venerable **Hotel Menelaion** (still Sparta's best hotel), and the **Archaeological Museum** on Daphnoú Street remain. (The museum deserves a visit for its terra-cotta masks, Roman mosaics, and the splendid fifth-century B.C. marble bust that is thought to depict the great Spartan hero Leonidas.)

Sparta is an energetic town, with shops and restaurants crammed into every inch of space. Food here is about what you'd expect from the descendants of people who prided themselves on surviving on a diet of gruel, but the basement taverna facing the Archaeological Museum is perfectly adequate, and tables placed outdoors on the sidewalk have a view of a rose garden and assorted ancient statues. In winter, *loukoumádes,* the quintessential Greek sweet (deep-fried pastry drenched in honey and coated with cinnamon), are sold at the coffee shop across from the museum; even Greeks usually find this Platonic ideal of the caloric too sweet for summer consumption.

Sparta's main attraction is its particularly vigorous evening *volta* (promenade) in the main plateia, which you can take in from a ringside seat at one of the cafés in front of the town hall. Soon after 8:00 P.M. a buzz of conversation begins as first one or two people, then clusters of three and four, and finally all of Sparta begins to walk the length of the plateia, turn, and walk back again. And again. And again.

Young men walk together, twirling worry beads or (more fashionably) car keys, outdoing one another in nonchalance; young women stroll along, pausing to fuss over one another's hairdos, darting glances at the young men. Parents are omnipresent to monitor nascent courtship. Occasionally groups stop and greet each other with ritual exclamations of pleasure. Sparta is truly a provincial capital par excellence: It's not hard to imagine a local Emma Bovary sighing at the prospect of passing yet another evening here greeting the same neighbors she sees night after night.

The Spartan volta is one of the great spectator sports in Greece, but the fact remains that it's not easy to warm to the ancestors of the people you see walking today. The best that can be said of the original Spartans is that their reputation for courage was justified: Sparta and heroism were synonymous after Leonidas and his band of 300 stood alone against the Persian forces at Thermopylae. Still, perhaps it's just as well that almost nothing remains of ancient Sparta (also called Lacedaemon). Plato sneered at it, declaring that it was like "an army camp, not a people who live in a town," and Thucydides was all too prescient when he wrote that if Sparta were ever "to become desolate, and the temples and the foundations of the public buildings were left, no one in future times would believe that this had been one of the preeminent cities of Greece."

Perhaps the best place to meditate on the difference between the Athenian and Spartan spirit is on the outskirts of town at the ruined **Sanctuary of Artemis Orthia**, where Spartan boys were whipped to prove their manhood. Plutarch described the scene: "The boys who are flogged all day on the altar of Artemis Orthia often remain blithe and cheerful unto death; they vie with each other to see which of them can best and longest endure the blows. The victor is held in the highest esteem..."

It's worth taking a stroll at sunset to the sparse remains on Sparta's low acropolis, if only for the stunning view of Taygetos. During the Byzantine era the theater was systematically raided for building material for homes, churches, and defense walls in Mystra. Much of what was left was destroyed in the 18th century by the mad antiquarian Abbé Fourmont, who hired workmen to raze Sparta's antiquities in his search for inscriptions. "For a month now," he wrote, "I have been engaged in the entire destruction of Sparta ... it is a quarry of inscribed marble, which I must excavate without scruple ... overturning its walls and temples ... not leaving one stone on another ... Imagine, if you can, how happy this makes me!"

Mystra

The 8-km (5-mile) drive from Sparta west to Mystrá (well signposted) is one of the most alluring in Greece, winding through citrus groves and along the reedy banks of the Eurotas river. All the way Mystra operates like a magnet, pulling the eye toward its odd, conical hill set off on a spur from Taygetos's lower slopes. Slowly, the honey-colored peak reveals an entire deserted Medieval city: Castle ramparts appear, the shells of great houses, and everywhere red-tiled church roofs, shimmering like so many poppies on a hillside. Inside, it's endlessly seductive to wander through what one Byzantinist described as "Mystra's picturesque incoherence": down streets and lanes, through archways and gates, past the high walls of once stately homes towering above the ruins of more than 2,000 modest houses. At every turn there are new views across the Vale of Laconia; the finest ones can be had from the cathedral, the Palace of the Despots, and, of course, the summit.

Mystra is as large as many Italian Renaissance hill towns (20,000 lived here under Byzantine rule, and as many as 42,000 under the Venetians, when this was a center of the silk industry). There's a lower and an upper entrance to the site. Parking at the bottom of the hill makes it possible to see Mystra in ascending order, then slump back down to your car. Rubber-soled shoes are advised, although Greek matrons seem to feel duty-bound to confront Mystra in high heels.

Mystra exists because in 1249 William II de Villehardouin built a fortress and palace here in an attempt to hold together the Peloponnesian empire his Frankish ancestors had seized from the Greeks after the Fourth Crusade in 1204. But William failed; defeated and captured at the battle of Pelagonia in 1259, he had to turn over Mystra, along with Monemvasia and the Castle of Maina. A daring escape attempt ensued but was thwarted at the last minute when a Greek soldier recognized William's legendary buck teeth.

Starting in 1348, Michael Cantacuzenus, son of the emperor John VI, began to build the enormous **Palace of the Despots** on a plateau on the slopes below Villehardouin's castle. Successive Byzantine emperors realized Mystra's strategic importance, made it capital of the Despotate of the Morea, and sent their heirs here for some imperial training. This made Mystra second in importance to Constantinople itself. Various despots added to the palace, which continued to grow until Mystra fell to the Turks in 1460. The palace's once-extensive east wing is now a jumble of ruins, including the remains of a small mosque. Still, enough remains of the massive west wing, with its vaulted ground-level rooms and third-story throne room, to suggest the palace's original splendor.

In the century before Byzantium fell, just at the time of the creative explosion of the Trecento and early Quattrocento in Tuscany and Umbria, Mystra was home to a renaissance in arts and learning that blazed like a comet, only to be extinguished by the long years of Turkish rule. The court attracted scholars and literati, painters, and architects from Macedonia, Crete, and even Italy. As a result, Mystra's churches were decorated in something of an international style, with hints of the color and modeling of Giotto and Duccio.

Mystra's churches are its principal glory, and there's nowhere in Greece to get a better sense of the complex variety of Byzantine church architecture. Most combine the basilica form with the Greek cross, add on a few extra domes, and sometimes throw in a bell tower for good measure. From the outside the churches are jewel-like, thanks to an ornate mixture of stone and bricks that is often compared to cloisonné work. Inside, all is dim, with pale light filtering down onto a profusion of ornament from tiny, lozenge-shaped windows high in the central dome. While architects in the West vied with one another to let more and more light into their churches, the builders at Mystra placed their windows not for maximum light but for maximum mystery.

Within these churches shapes take form slowly, and any view of the altar itself is blocked by an ornately carved iconostasis (altar screen), perhaps wood, perhaps marble, almost certainly multicolored. Floors have multicolored paving slabs and columns are of variegated marble, each with an elaborately carved capital that differs from its neighbor. Everywhere, on every inch of wall space, frescoes tell the story of the liturgy, under the often unnerving eye of Christ the Pantokrator and the gentler gaze of Mary from the dome. These paintings were, as the early church fathers said, the "books of the illiterate," and the faithful knew just where to look to see the Nativity and Christ's early years, the Miracles, the martyrs and church fathers, and the final horrors of Judgment Day.

The whole may well be greater than the sum of the parts at Mystra, but take along a map and stop first at the oldest church, the 14th-century **cathedral of Ayios Dimítrios**, with its breezy courtyard alive with flowers and a welcome fountain. A marble plaque with the double-headed eagle of Byzantium commemorates the coronation here of Constantine Paleologos, the last emperor of Byzantium, who died fighting on the ramparts when Constantinople fell to the Turks in 1453.

Near the remains of the **Episcopal Palace** next to the cathedral is a **museum** with architectural fragments on the ground floor and stunning icons and fresco fragments upstairs. The museum is the easiest place to get a good idea of Mystra's famous coloristic detail and expressionism up close—as you'll discover when you crane to see details high up in domes and spandrels in Mystra's churches.

Above the cathedral is the Brontochion monastery complex, which has two churches, modest **Ayioi Theodóri**, with its central dome, and the extravagant **Panayía Hodegétria**, with its exuberant profusion of domes. The frescoes in both churches have recently been restored to something close to their original brilliance and luminosity. The warrior saints in Ayioi Theodori are certainly splendid, but the Hodegetria frescoes have been revealed to be among Mystra's finest. At last it's possible in the scenes of the Miracles of Jesus to see the delicate pinks and greens, the exquisite facial modeling using white brushstrokes, and the lightness of the figures. What could be more unlike the stiff mosaics of Ravenna and Daphni than these airy angels?

Wonderful though these churches are, two more are even finer: the **Pantánassa Monastery**, yet higher up the slopes, and the little **Perívleptos Monastery**, with its 14th-century frescoes, a short walk downhill from the Pantanassa. The great Byzantinist David Talbot Rice awarded laurels to the Pantanassa, calling its frescoes "the very flower of late Byzantine art." Now restored, they gleam with new color showing the impressionistic modeling of figures.

Be warned: The frescoes in the lower registers are late, and insignificant; you'll get a crick in your neck looking up at the higher, 15th-century frescoes, but it's worth it. *The Raising of Lazarus* (with one bystander fastidiously holding his nose against the grave stench) is stunning, and the startled figures in the Ascension perfectly capture the moment of awe when Christ's tomb is found empty. Looking like some extravagant pastry, with its mound of domes, the Pantanassa is altogether lovely. This is still an active convent, and nuns selling embroidery are often in evidence.

The highest ramparts, reached after a stiff climb, offer views of all Mystra from a site so romantic that Goethe placed the meeting of Helen and Faust here. Although Mystra itself was never lost, the memory of its former glory was obscured for centuries. Something so grand, locals thought, must have been built by their heroic ancestors, not by their Byzantine forefathers. When the French traveller Pouqueville visited Mystra in 1799, his local guide claimed that this was ancient Sparta, and identified all the monuments Pausanias mentions: the acropolis, the agora, and the remains of the Temple of Artemis. Finally, gesturing to the Palace of Despots, the guide pronounced it the home of Menelaus and Helen—a chronological error of only two and a half millennia!

(If you want to visit Mystra early in the morning before the site becomes hot and crowded, consider staying at the **Hotel Byzantion** in the modern hamlet of Mystra just below the site.)

If you're not heading south from Sparta to Yeraki, Monemvasia, or the Mani (as we do), but west to Koroni and Methoni, Pylos, and Olympia via Kalamata, you'll take the **Langáda Pass** from Laconia into Messenia. The road, although adequate, is narrow, with hairpin bends, and deservedly ranks as one of the great scenic routes in the Peloponnese. There's a small café at the summit, with splendid views. (It's only 60 km/37 miles from Sparta to Kalamata, but allow several hours for the drive itself, mostly to stop and enjoy the scenery.) This is the route Telemachus took from Nestor's Palace at Pylos when he came to Sparta in search of news of his peripatetic father, Odysseus.

Monemvasia

Ninety-five kilometers (59 miles) southeast of Sparta by way of Yeraki (see below), Monemvasía, nicknamed "the Gibraltar of Greece," juts out of the sea on the easternmost prong of the Peloponnese. From a distance the black rock looks like a petrified sea monster, and it is one of a number of places in Greece of which it can be said that seeing is not altogether believing. The monasteries of the Meteora are equally improbable. If you're lucky enough to come here by boat, you'll find yourself bending over backward trying to take in this Medieval city, which plummets down sheer slopes. It seems that residents should have to go about with grappling hooks so as not to tumble into the sea. But it's not so. What makes Monemvasia so special is that, unlike Mystra, there *are* residents: only a handful year round, but at Christmas and Easter, weekends, and from May through October, the town comes alive. Restaurants and shops along the main street open their doors, and in August the Athenians and foreigners who have been buying up and restoring old houses come for "the season."

A humped island only 1,600 yards long and half again as wide, Monemvasia is connected to the mainland by a slender causeway (the *moni emvasis,* "one entrance," of its name). If you have a car you can drive across the causeway and park outside the city gate, although places are at a premium in high summer, when it makes better sense to park on the mainland and walk or take a taxi over. If you walk, console yourself with the thought that the first settlement here was on the summit, which is approached by a much steeper path. Just as you give up hope of reaching your destination you're confronted by a Venetian gate in a massive wall. Inside lies Monemvasia.

You can easily see the town's highlights in a day. Begin with the most difficult. Turn left at the first lamppost for the ascent along a slithery stone path to the citadel begun by the Byzantines in the 6th century and greatly augmented by the Venetians when they held Monemvasia from 1464 to 1540. The summit is crowned by the **church of Ayia Sophía**, perched on the edge of the cliffs 880 feet above the sea. Ayia Sophia's mixed architecture perfectly symbolizes Monemvasia's complex history. The town's Byzantine rulers built the domed church no later than the 13th century, and when the Venetians came they added a two-story loggia. When the Turks replaced the Venetians a century later, they turned Ayia Sophia into a mosque, whitewashed the frescoes, and inserted a *mihrab* (arched niche) in the southern wall to indicate the direction of Mecca.

From the citadel, on the very top of the rock, it's obvious why Greeks, Franks, Venetians, and Turks contended for Monemvasia: It commands the sea passages from east to west. From the 8th century on, almost every ship that sailed from Italy to the Levant or down to Crete and Africa put in here, and in the 14th century, while Mystra dominated the Morea's culture, Monemvasia was its commercial center. Fleets from the west sailed here with goods for the Levant and sailed home with hogsheads of Monemvasia's most famous product, the prized malvasia wine (Shakespeare's malmsey), the Champagne of the Middle Ages. Understandably, when Monemvasia fell to the Turks, locals burned their vineyards rather than let them fall to the enemy. Many fled rather than live under Turkish rule; some took vine cuttings with them to the Aegean islands. Today the amber-colored wine of Santorini is thought to be closest in taste to the famous malmsey.

From Ayia Sophia you can wander the line of the defense walls through a desert land of desiccated shrubs and broken walls, past the ruins of aristocratic houses with enormous communal cisterns that allowed Monemvasia to hold out for three years and more under siege. Monemvasia was never taken by assault, only by siege and starvation; the residents were reduced to eating rats on occasion. This is a wild place, and it's something of a relief to return to the pleasures of the lower town and wander with no particular plan down narrow alleys and through vaulted passages. You're bound to pass a number of small churches (most are locked) and will eventually come across the **church of Christos Elkómenos** in the main square. Like Ayia Sophia, Christos Elkomenos was built by the Byzantines and remodeled by the Venetians, who placed a Lion of Saint Mark on the Episcopal Palace next door. Just across from the church are the remains of a low-domed mosque, which for years has been rumored to be on the verge of opening its doors as Monemvasia's museum.

Monemvasia's charms are such that more is truly better, and if you're suffering from hotel burnout by the time you get here, take heart: A number of traditional houses have been carefully restored as hotels. The finest is the **Malvasia**, with rooms and apartments in a number of restored buildings scattered between several locations on the rock. Rooms in the Malvasia's main building have refrigerators but no cooking facilities; breakfast is served in the morning, and soft drinks and snacks are available during the day at a small café. Throughout the Malvasia's holdings, every detail—from the traditional beamed ceilings, massive door locks, and wood shutters to the rag rugs and handwoven bedspreads—is just right. (Service is very casual, but sufficiently cordial to make amends.) In what must have been a considerable coup, the Malvasia has recently restored the Stellakis house, one of the grandest mansions in Monemvasia and one of only three houses remaining with balconies over the sea. You might want to request a suite here when you make a reservation and indulge in a fantasy that you're staying in your own Greek home.

This is the kind of place that makes you think that you really *could* write that novel. Until then, it's hard to imagine a nicer locale in which to spend time resting, reading the works of Monemvasia's famous poet, Ioannis Ritsos, swimming off the rocks, and peeking into your neighbors' garden courtyards. (If you can't get a room at the Malvasia, try the smaller and less elegant **Hotel Byzantino**, with nicely restored rooms in several old houses.) Best of all is the moment every afternoon when the day-trippers depart and the light that made the Turks call this the "violet rock" arrives.

Then it's time for a stroll to the **Byzantion** café to listen to classical music and write a few postcards, and look into **Ioanna Angelatou**'s shop next door, where you will find good reproductions of traditional Greek crafts (embroideries and ceramics) and a few genuinely old items (bread stamps and copper). Soon it's time to decide whether to indulge in some escapist spaghetti alla carbonara at **To Kanoni**, or have more traditional Greek fare sitting under the fig tree at **Matoula's**, looking out on the sea and down at the innumerable cats that sit quietly by the tables, hoping for the occasional fish head or french fry. Not that these are the only restaurant choices: There's a string of tavernas with better-than-average food along Monemvasia's main street.

A leisurely stay here also makes it possible to take in the rock's complicated history under Greek, Frankish, and Venetian rulers (for details, pick up a copy of the excellent local guidebook, *Monembasia: The Town and Its History*). By the time of the Greek War of Independence, only 350 families lived on the rock. They supported themselves by exporting the dye used to color Turkish fezzes red. After independence many residents moved across to the mainland, and Monemvasia was well on its way to becoming a genuine ghost town. Today it is enjoying a renaissance while managing to preserve its integrity.

(The mainland village of Yéfyra, or "Bridge," at the foot of the causeway, has a bank, telephone, and post offices. The Malvasia travel agency—good English spoken—offers a variety of local day trips and can get you seats on the Flying Dolphin service to Piraeus—via Leonidion, Hydra, Spetses, and Poros—and Kythira, and a ferry to Crete. There are hotels and restaurants in Yefyra, but the only reason to stay here is if you can't get a room on the rock.)

Yeraki

If Mystra and Monemvasia have whetted your appetite for Medieval Greece, consider a distinctly off-the-beaten-path excursion that can be done from either of the better-known sites. Allow the better part of a day, not because you're going far (Yeraki is 40 km/25 miles southeast of Sparta) but because you'll have to "find the guard with the keys of the churches," seldom as brisk an operation as some guidebooks imply.

The best way to find the guard is to stop for a coffee at the village square and let it be known that you want to see either Yiorgos Koures or Yiorgos Tsipoura, who alternate as guards (*phýlakes*) for Yeraki's splendid, recently restored but seldom visited Byzantine churches. If neither guard is in the square, locals will help you run one of them down. Be warned: Although four churches are in the village, another three are on the steep ascent to the Frankish fortress just outside town, and both guards set a brisk pace. (A gratuity is appropriate.)

Yeráki is the name both of a tumbledown village and of the Medieval fortress (clearly visible from the village) that guarded the road from Mystra to Monemvasia. If you're visiting the fortress on your own, follow the main road out of Yeraki 4 km (2.5 miles) and then turn left onto the signposted, partially paved road that runs to the foot of Medieval Yeraki. From there a short, steep walk past ruined houses and churches brings you to the summit.

Medieval Yeraki is a miniature Mystra, with frescoed churches, clusters of house walls, splendid crenellated defense walls, and, on clear days, a view of the sea 20 miles away. After deciphering the Byzantine and Venetian building periods at Monemvasia's churches of Ayia Sophia and Christos Elkomenos, you'll recognize that the citadel **church of Ayios Yiórgos** was built by the Byzantines, then remodeled by their successors, in this case the Franks, who added pointed arches and icon niches.

You're not likely to encounter anyone else at Yeraki, and it's easy to feel that this bit of Medieval Greece is yours alone. If you like to picnic, try the shaded forecourt of Ayios Yiorgos. Otherwise, there are usually excellent country *loukánika* (sausages), fluffy *keftédes* (meatballs), and mountain retsina at Yeraki's **Alana** restaurant on the main square. Don't be surprised if locals ask where you're from and why you're here; after all, you're no longer in tourist Greece.

THE MANI

The Mani, the region at the very tip of the Peloponnese in both Laconia and Messenia, is something of an acquired taste, like ouzo or retsina: harsh and unforgettable. Despite a good, new circular road from Gytheion to Areopolis and Yerolimena (which makes it possible to drive the peninsula in a day) and a sprinkling of hotels, the Mani is little visited, perhaps because it has no antiquities, certainly because it was almost unreachable for so long. The entire peninsula is a 30-mile-long projection of Taygetos that juts out into the sea like the central prong of a bent trident. Outer, or Messenian, Mani includes the west coast from the Bay of Itilo north to Kalamata; Deep Mani lies south of the pass from Itilo in the west to Gytheion on the east coast, and is itself divided into Inner Mani along the Messenian Gulf and Lower Mani along the Laconian Gulf. Outer Mani can be beguiling, with good beaches and fertile fields along the coast, but Deep Mani is bewitching, a bleak lunar landscape dominated by the Kakávouna (Evil Mountains), which run south of Areopolis as far as Cape Matapan (also known as Tenaros). Since the Mani is not well known, some background information may be useful.

All the Mani, but especially Inner Mani, is a world unto itself, utterly unlike anything else in Greece. Punctuating its bizarre landscape is an architecture as symbiotic with the land as the rock monasteries of Cappadocia, the *trulli* of Apulia, or the Hopi Indian cave dwellings of the American Southwest. The Mani's distinctive tower houses are as one with the barren landscape: Villages of gray stone towers rise on sere hills backed by mountains with no hint of vegetation. Sometimes it seems that the only thing in the Mani that isn't petrified is the sky, which in winter becomes as harsh as the landscape itself. No place in Greece can be hotter in summer, when the fierce wind that blows down from the mountains all year contends with the parching *Livas* gales that rush across the sea from North Africa. Still, if you count discovery as one of the greatest pleasures of travel, and want to see an unusual corner of Greece, this is the place for you.

When Colonel Leake came here in 1806 he was told there were about 130 tower villages, a population of 30,000, and upward of 10,000 muskets. The Maniots, like the Highland Scots, prized valor and poetry and regarded themselves as nature's noblemen (the dominant Mavromichalis family boasted that its great beauty came from having a mermaid in the family tree). Outsiders regarded the Maniots as boorish outlaws, as Sir George Wheler commented in 1682: "The Maniotes are famous Pirates by sea, and Pestilent Robbers by Land." Many suggested that the name "Mani" came from the locals' *manía,* or fierce anger. That didn't offend the Maniots one bit: When Napoleon Bonaparte proved his mettle, Maniots remembered that some of their number had emigrated generations earlier to Corsica and claimed Napoleon as their own.

Today no more than 5,000 live in the Mani; entire villages are virtually deserted except for the few old people who remain. This is the most conservative part of the Peloponnese (you may see nostalgic pictures displayed of the exiled king Constantine), and men in shorts or women in slacks should expect to raise eyebrows. (What to do? Women in skirts can count on getting their legs lacerated by thornbushes and thistles in the countryside; perhaps skirts for town and slacks for walks would be a good compromise.)

The Mani has always existed on the fringes of history (even the ubiquitous Dorians never got here), although it was surprisingly well populated in the Mycenaean era, when three towns sent ships to fight with Agamemnon at Troy. Still, the area was insignificant during Classical antiquity, and so isolated that Christianity made no significant inroads until well into the 9th century. This was the last pagan stronghold in Greece. Yet once Christianity arrived it took deep roots, and an astonishing number of churches were built here between the 10th and 14th centuries. Searching them out is one of the great pleasures of travel in the Mani.

Not surprisingly, there are few relics of the Frankish and Venetian empires. Like almost everyone else, they left the Mani alone after building the ritual fortress or two. The Venetians, however, took note of the quails that paused by the million near Matapan en route from northern Europe to Africa. Every spring shiploads of pickled quails were exported from Porto Kaio (the Venetian Porto Quaglio, or Port of the Quails) to become delicacies for Venetian dinner tables. Eventually the quails changed their flight pattern, and few are to be seen today.

No one ever conquered the Mani, but through the centuries this was a last refuge for successive waves of Greeks fleeing invaders—Goths, Vandals, and Huns, and later, Slavs and Turks. Many, including a good number of Slavs, intermarried and stayed—a topic best avoided here, as in the rest of the Peloponnese, where implications of Slavic ancestry are not appreciated. Better to remember that the fall of Constantinople brought a wave of refugees here who were considered sufficiently grand that they became an instant local aristocracy known as "Nyklians," although no one seems to know why. The Nyklians quickly erected the three- and four-story tower houses that became the Mani's most distinctive architectural feature, and just as quickly began the blood feuds that dominated life here until this century.

Almost anything could start a feud, which, once begun, could continue for years, ending only in absolute destruction or total surrender for one clan, complete victory for another. By day the men fought, by night they rebuilt their towers. Colonel Leake found this description of life in the Mani in a manuscript he discovered at Mystra: "One defends his tower against another, or pursues his neighbor. One has a claim upon another for a murdered brother, another for a son, another for a father, another for a nephew." Leake concluded dryly that "To pull down the adversary's house is generally the object and end of the war." Women (whose principal role was to bear sons, colloquially known as "guns") were allowed out to tend the crops and the wounded and to bury the dead. One legacy remains of all this bloodshed: the dirges, or *mirológia,* which Maniot women still sing.

Even the Turks, mindful of the Maniot reputation for ferocity, gave up the idea of governing here, and appointed locals to govern for them. The greatest was Petrobey Mavromichalis of Areopolis (known as Black Michael, a member of the family descended from the mermaid). Unknown to his Turkish masters, Mavromichalis was a secret member of the clandestine liberation movement Philikí Etaireía. Mavromichalis led the Mani against the Turks in the Greek War of Independence during the early 1820s—and, once independence was won, turned against the new Greek government. When Mavromichalis was imprisoned in Nafplion, his relatives journeyed there and assassinated Greece's new governor, Kapodistrias, first shooting him as he left church, then slashing him with the Maniot weapon of choice, the *yataghan,* a hefty scimitar.

This wasn't the last time the Mani expressed its displeasure with national rule: When King Otto sent troops to pacify the area, the Maniots regarded the Greek soldiers as simply another group of foreign invaders. They captured most, and then delighted in ransoming them back to what was, obviously only nominally, the government of the Mani itself. Armed resistance to national rule ended in this century, but the Mani continued to live according to its own traditions, ignoring governmental edicts mandating compulsory education and other alien ideas. It's often said that the Middle Ages, which lasted longer in Greece than in most of Europe, continued here virtually into this century.

Into the Mani

There's only one "tourist" destination here: the Caves of Dirou, just south of Areopolis on the western coast (see below). A popular day trip for Greeks, the site is worth visiting if you are partial to caves or curious to take a bit of your holiday to observe Greeks on theirs. The Mani's deeper pleasures—tower villages, small Byzantine chapels, isolated beaches, and the fierce landscape—deserve several days, and draw few visitors other than hardy German campers. This will change as word gets out about how easy the new road and hotels have made travel, but until then you can have the best of both worlds and enjoy the comforts of an incipient tourist industry while encountering few tourists. If you're planning to scout out the churches and tower villages, bring water, binoculars, walking shoes, and Peter Greenhalgh and Edward Eliopoulos's *Deep into Mani*, an invaluable help. Whatever you do, be sure to read Patrick Leigh Fermor's classic, *Mani*.

If you're coming into the Mani from Sparta, you'll arrive first at **Gýtheion**, just as Helen and Paris did when they eloped from Sparta. (Gytheion is an easy 46-km/28.5-mile run south on the good asphalted road from Sparta.) According to Homer, the two spent their first night together on the islet of Kranaë (today's Marathónisi) in Gytheion's harbor. Before continuing to Troy, Paris erected a shrine to the Aphrodite of Erotic Love; when Menelaus recaptured Helen, he tore it down and in its place erected statues of Themis (Justice) and Praxidica (Punishment). Gytheion looks almost like an island village, with its stepped side streets and a crescent of houses built up against a hillside. Boats for Kythira and Crete leave from Gytheion, guaranteeing enough year-round traffic to keep several of the harborside tavernas open all year; in August there's also a modest three-day drama festival at Gytheion's small Roman theater.

When you set out into the Mani from Gytheion you may be surprised at the lush citrus groves and sandy beaches outside town. The landscape is gentle, and there are even cows grazing in green fields along the banks of the river Sminos. Soon enough you'll get a taste of the barren Mani landscape, as the road begins to writhe through the only pass from the east to the west coast. You'll know you're on your way when you see the ruins of the Frankish **Castle of Passava** and notice clusters of towers on the nearby hills. The road travels under the brow of Mount Pentadáktylos (so named because the range resembles five gnarled fingers) until it reaches the squat Turkish fortress of **Kelefá**; north lies Messenian Mani, with Areopolis and Inner Mani to the south. Kelefa watches over Areopolis's minuscule port, Limeni, and the deep Bay of Itilo.

Messenian Mani is lush and fertile, its sinuous corniche running above superb beaches through hamlets dotted with small Byzantine chapels to **Kardamýli**, where Patrick Leigh Fermor lives. In *Mani* Fermor wrote that Kardamyli was "too inaccessible and there is too little to do there, fortunately, for it ever to be seriously endangered by tourism." Today there's a string of tourist shops on the main street and tavernas (**Lilla's** has the most varied menu) overlooking the beach, but Kardamyli is far from "spoiled." Certainly almost no one stops at the tenth-century **church of Ayios Nikólaos Kambinári** (recently restored), south of Kardamyli at Platsa; a pity, as both the architectural ornament outside, including ancient blocks, and the frescoes inside are splendid, and there's an ideal picnic spot in the pine grove beside the church.

South of the fortress of Kelefa is the Mani's only real town, **Areópolis**, appropriately named after the god of war. Areopolis is a dour place. One of its odd features is the **church of the Taxiárchoi** (the Archangels), which boasts primitive carvings of martial saints and zodiac signs. The church is obscured by its own campanile and penned in by the severe towers that make Areopolis shadowy even at midday. One tower, just beyond the church of the Taxiarchoi, has been converted into the **Kapetanakou Tower Hotel** by the Greek National Tourist Organization. The tower, approached by a stone path, is flanked by the fruits of a valiant attempt at a small garden—nothing except prickly pears grows easily in the Mani. Several rooms have sleeping lofts reached by ladders, and most have cool stone floors covered by multicolored rag rugs *koureloúdes*). Breakfast is served in a low-ceilinged room with benches and tables, handwoven cushion covers, and rag rugs. If you want to buy examples of the traditional handwoven koureloudes, present yourself at the kiosk across from the three restaurants in the square on the outskirts of town, and ask the proprietor if you can see his wife Kyria Vasiliki's handicraft.

Areopolis is one of three Maniot towns where you can

spend a night in a tower house. Two others are the tiny village of **Stavri** (on Cavo Grosso, the rounded cape on the Mani's west coast that bulges into the sea between the gulfs of Mezapos and Yerolimena; see below), where you will find the **Tsitsiris Castle Hotel**; and, farther south on the peninsula, the nearly deserted village of **Váthia**, where in 1989 the GNTO converted 12 towers into the **Vathia Tower Hotel** in an effort to provide superior accommodations and revitalize the local economy. Although the hotels are not far apart, there's so much to see in the Mani that a night in each would still leave you wanting to return.

All three hotels have traditional decorations and, happily, modern comforts, and any would have been greatly appreciated by Colonel Leake, who described the wretched night he spent in a genuine tower house in 1806. There were, Leake wrote, "mattresses and blankets... piled up in one corner of the room; all the rest of the family furniture is hung around the walls or stowed away in wooden boxes, ranged around; the floor consists of loose boards, and, never undergoing ablution, harbours myriads of fleas in winter, and bugs in summer." One thing hasn't changed since Leake's day: The wind howls all night.

Twelve kilometers (7.5 miles) south of Areopolis are the enormous **Caves of Dirou**, Glyfáda and Alepótrypa, with their subterranean lakes. (On summer weekends the caves are mobbed; if you're determined to go, buy a tour ticket in Glyfada for the first available tour and then relax on the beach, where there are tavernas.) These, the largest known caverns in Greece, are an important archaeological site where significant finds of pottery, obsidian, and human bones from Neolithic and even earlier times have been made. (Some of the finds are on view in the museum in Sparta.) The "Schliemann" of the caves was a local dog that disappeared into a sinkhole and returned home three days later covered with red clay, arousing the curiosity of a local spelunking archaeologist, Anna Petrocheilou.

Tours (currently only of Glyfada) are conducted in a string of boats reassuringly roped together and are normally narrated in Greek, but guides usually point out fantastic clumps of stalactites and stalagmites nicknamed The Cathedral, The Dragon's Lair, and The Sunken Ship. After a half-mile journey by boat you have the opportunity to walk about a bit on dry ledges deep within the cave. Despite interior lighting, the caves are suitably Stygian; there are rumors that giant eels live in the black depths. If you don't test the cavern's famous echo, someone else probably will.

Nonspelunkers will be glad to head on south toward the harbor of **Yeroliména** and into the stretch of the Mani that features several of the finest tower villages, including **Kita** and **Nomia**. As Patrick Leigh Fermor wrote, the two villages present "a vision as bewildering as the distant skyline of Manhattan or that first apparition of gaunt medieval skyscrapers that meets the eye of the traveller approaching San Gimignano across the Tuscan plain." Almost at their best from afar, both are melancholy places to wander and seem to be inhabited primarily by enormous spiders, prickly pears, and goats. In summer it's not uncommon to find anomalous family groups of the very old and the very young here; the missing generations are off at work in Athens, having sent the grandchildren or even great-grandchildren "home" for the holidays.

The west coast is also where you'll find the Mani's finest Byzantine chapels, some far out on the bulge of Cavo Grosso. Seeing the Mani chapels, secret shrines neglected for years, is as startling as happening upon a clutch of Cotswold or Burgundian churches hidden in the countryside. There are few experiences more unnerving than coming upon one of these abandoned, perhaps roofless chapels endowed with rich fresco cycles, elaborate cloisonné brickwork, and architectural ornament of intertwined flowers and vines and whimsical beasts. If you find some of the better-preserved churches locked, be thankful, not irritated: In recent years unscrupulous antiques dealers have carted off icons, hacked out sections of frescoes, and prized out carvings. If you want to see the locked churches, go to the Demarchion, or city hall, in Areopolis and ask for the guard (*phýlakas*), Leonidas Demopoulos, who has the keys and is free many afternoons. A gratuity is appropriate.

If you go on your own, remember that almost all chapels that are not in villages are hard to find, camouflaged by their settings on slopes and in ravines and further disguised by decay, which makes several of the simple, barrel-vaulted structures resemble abandoned sheep sheds. It's easy to get lost; keep an eye out for the stands of cypress trees that flank some churches. It seems clear that the builders took a malevolent pleasure in choosing places that would test the devotion of any who came to worship—and then reward them with yet another example of the Greek genius for marrying architecture to landscape. No less impressive than the Temple of Apollo at Bassae or the palace at Mycenae, these small chapels were conceived with an uncanny eye for the perfect site.

If you can go to only a few churches, head for **Stavri**, just north of the tower villages of Kita and Nomia and reached from the main Areopolis–Yerolimena road by a signposted side road running out onto Cavo Grosso. The 12th-century **church of Episkopí**, which has a worthy fresco cycle, is set high on a slope above the bay. Below, the domed **church of Vlachérna** stands on the seacoast near an isolated farm where improbable oxen graze in the fields—a fantastic sylvan landscape that seems lifted from a Pompeiian wall painting. All around, just out of sight, are more towers, more Byzantine chapels, all waiting to be discovered anew. Some of the finest churches are at **Ano Boularioi**, 25 km (15.5 miles) south of Areopolis and signposted off the Areopolis–Yerolimena road a few kilometers north of Yerolimena. Ano Boularioi is noted for its several magnificent towers; here you will find the 11th-century **church of Ayios Strategós**, which has an elaborate fresco cycle, and **Ayios Panteleímon**, a primitive chapel crouched on a slope just out of town. If you think that the strange figures in the Ayios Panteleimon frescoes look more Middle Eastern than Greek, you're right: Monks from Asia Minor evidently built this church.

If you've brought your hiking boots, you may want to set aside half a day and head down to **Porto Kaio** at the tip of the Mani peninsula to walk out to **Cape Matapan**, the southernmost point in mainland Greece, past the remains of the **Temple of Poseidon** under the little chapel of Asomatioi. (Porto Kaio is some 40 km/25 miles south of Areopolis, and the walk from Porto Kaio to Cape Matapan takes at least an hour each way.) Matapan is so remote that the ancient Greeks thought it must have an entrance to the underworld; one of Herakles' Twelve Labors brought him here to capture the three-headed guard dog, Cerberus. After battling the nine-headed Lernean Hydra, Herakles was ready for Cerberus and choked him into submission, protected by his lion-skin cloak—all that remained of the man-eating Nemean lion. That took care of Cerberus, but Matapan's dire reputation lingered: From antiquity until the last century, pirates attacked vessels struggling to round the cape and preyed on shipwrecks.

MESSENIA
Methoni and Koroni

The fortresses of Methoni, on the Ionian Sea, and Koroni, on the Messenian Gulf—on either side of the westernmost

Peloponnesian prong—were Venice's first holdings in Greece, and were so important that they were known as the "twin eyes of the empire." As always, the Ottoman sultan coveted Venice's holdings, and some of the bloodiest sieges in Greek history took place here. On the afternoon of August 9, 1500, the Turks slaughtered Methoni's 7,000-man Venetian garrison. The Venetians got their revenge in 1685, killing all 1,500 Turks defending Koroni. Afterward, the conquerors filed into the citadel church and sang a *Te Deum* of thanksgiving.

It makes sense to see the two citadels on one excursion, and the 35-km (22-mile) drive through the rolling hills of the peninsula that separates them seems almost more Arcadian than Arcadia itself. If you're heading from Areopolis to Pylos, you can skirt the horrors of Kalamata 76 km (47 miles) north of Areopolis and continue 29 km (18 miles) south to Koroni. Then head across the peninsula to Methoni, just 12 km (7.5 miles) south of Pylos. This makes for a long day; you may prefer to visit the fortresses as an excursion from Pylos itself.

Although Methoni and Koroni were long linked in history and both were frequented by ships of trade and pilgrims en route to the Holy Land, the two couldn't be more different today. Methoni is very much the ruined fortress, with an undistinguished modern village, while Koroni is a surprising oasis of flowers and trees, with an active convent and whitewashed houses inside the fortress walls and a delightful seaside village below. In short, Methoni should be seen for its Venetian fortress—the best preserved in the Peloponnese—and Koroni for its present-day charms.

Imposing from a distance and daunting from within, **Methóni** is immense, enveloping a 100-foot peninsula. The castle is protected from its landward side by a deep moat crossed by an arched bridge that ends at massive walls pierced by a monumental Venetian gate. Inside sprawls an overgrown maze of lowering parapets, vaulted passages, musty cisterns, projecting artillery bastions, and the confused remains of a cathedral. Methoni is a palimpsest of Peloponnesian history evidenced by its Lions of Saint Mark, some incised on the walls, others tumbled to the ground; a Turkish bath; and three pillboxes built by German and Italian forces during World War II. The most agreeable belvedere is the little Bourtzi castle just offshore, even though it's somewhat disconcerting to remember that this is where the 7,000 Venetian defenders were hacked to death.

Throughout the Middle Ages a town of several thousand

inhabitants sprawled inside Methoni's walls; almost no early travellers had a good word for the place, complaining of intense squalor and the persistent stench of pigs. A German pilgrim who stopped here in 1483 after visiting the Holy Land reported that more than 6,000 pigskins filled with lard were shipped off to Venice during his short visit. Methoni's most famous visitors were the great Spanish writer Cervantes, who was brought here as a galley slave by the Turks after the battle of Lepanto in 1571, and the French poet Chateaubriand, who began his Grand Tour here in 1806. Chateaubriand seems to have spent his time walking the ramparts and taking in the splendid views, which are still the best reasons to come.

Koróni's fortifications are almost as grand as Methoni's, especially the east wall above the sea, which seems molded to the cliffs. The road into the fortress runs up from the town through an imposing gateway with a pointed arch (do *not* attempt to drive up). Inside, a cluster of whitewashed houses lines a cobblestoned path leading to the convent of Ierá Moní Timíou Prodrómou, where nuns sell embroideries, pray, and tend the flowers in the convent cemetery. It's all a pleasant contrast to Methoni's weedy summit, especially in the late afternoon, when locals stroll up to watch the sunset and admire the distant peaks of Taygetos and the Mani.

Beneath the fortress, modern Koroni is a delight of stepped side streets, brightly painted houses with elaborate wrought-iron balconies, and a scattering of elegant Neoclassical buildings. The harbor (with several modest hotels and fish tavernas serving good local wine) may be saved from overdevelopment by the fact that there's really nowhere to spread except inland. In the 12th century the Arab geographer Edrisi described Koroni as "a small town with a large fort over the sea"—precisely what makes it so appealing today.

Pylos

Homer calls Mycenae "rich in gold" and Tiryns "well walled," but Pylos is "sandy Pylos, rich in cattle." Homer's description conjures up a peaceful sylvan scene—just what you'll find today at **Nestor's Palace** at Pylos, situated on a low plateau (Epáno Englianós) above the fertile plain of Messenia, about 17 km (11 miles) north of the modern town of Pylos. While Agamemnon met a bloody homecoming at Mycenae and Odysseus roamed the seas, prolonging his adventures and delaying his homecoming to his patient wife, Penelope, Nestor lived in contented old age at Pylos, happily reminiscing about his youthful cattle-rustling exploits or the great days at Troy. It seems just the spot for the garrulous old king whose lengthy speeches (inevitably beginning with "That reminds me . . ." or "Well, when I . . .") feature in both the *Iliad* and the *Odyssey*. Nestor is the first great bore in literature, somehow more endearing than irritating as he offers unsolicited advice to all who will listen—and many who try not to.

In the *Odyssey* Nestor has a captive audience, Odysseus's young son, Telemachus, who comes seeking news of his father. Telemachus learns a lot more about Nestor than he does about Odysseus, but the scenes of Nestor's hospitality to Telemachus—a superb banquet, followed by a delicious hot bath administered by Nestor's daughter and handmaidens—are among the poem's most delightful moments. It was particularly frustrating, then, that Pylos was lost for so long, although most ancient writers and modern scholars had theories on where it must have been. In 1939 the American archaeologist Carl Blegen came here to excavate because a number of *tholos* had been found in the area.

In an almost unbelievable stroke of luck, Blegen's initial trial trench struck the palace archives, revealing the first of more than 600 clay tablets inscribed in the mysterious script that became known as Linear B. It was a moment as heady and astonishing as Schliemann's discovery of the gold of Mycenae or Lord Carnarvon's first glimpse of King Tut's tomb. But what did the tablets say? And in what language? No one knew, until the brilliant young English architect Michael Ventris, perhaps the quintessential gifted amateur, beat the scholars at their own game. In 1952 Ventris deciphered the tablets and proved that they were written not in some strange, unknown tongue, but in the earliest known form of Greek—thus proving that Greek had been a written language far longer than anyone had imagined.

Some 30 years of excavation (during which Blegen himself became coeval with Nestor, and many came to think of the palace as Blegen's, not Nestor's) revealed an elaborate two-story palace complex, with royal apartments and workshops surrounding a large central room (the *megaron*). Unlike Mycenae and Tiryns, Pylos had no defense walls, and its low hill is hardly an acropolis. It seems a very peaceable kingdom indeed—and evidently was, until the terrible day in about 1200 B.C. when the palace burned to the ground, leaving scorch marks on the surviving walls.

When Telemachus came here he did just what you will: He walked through the main entrance past the sentry box, through the series of courtyards, and into the great central megaron, with its enormous hearth. The megaron probably had a second-story balcony where the women of the palace might have spied on visitors. The walls were gaily frescoed, the floors brightly inlaid; the whole scene must have been exceptionally merry.

Nestor and Telemachus drank many toasts, and probably used a new cup each time: Thousands of drinking vessels were found in the storerooms off the megaron. Just a few feet away is the king's bathroom, where Telemachus may well have had his bath; Blegen used to point out to visitors the little step by the tub and, with the sympathy of one elderly man for another, suggested that it was added when Nestor began to have trouble getting in and out of his bath.

Without the drama of "blood-soaked Mycenae," sandy Pylos, cooled by breezes, is the most magical Mycenaean site. Below it are the rich farm fields and vineyards that once supplied the palace, echoing with the sound of hoes and workers whistling their insistent monotonous threnodies. Even the hideous corrugated metal protective roof over the site cannot spoil its beauty. It's easy to see why Nestor headed home so quickly after Troy fell, and left the wandering to Odysseus.

Many finds from Pylos, including ingeniously restored frescoes, are on view at the small museum in Hora, just 4 km (2.5 miles) north of the ancient site; others are in Athens's National Archaeological Museum.

Modern Pylos, 17 km (11 miles) south of the palace, is a village on the verge of abandoning itself to overdevelopment; fortunately the harbor and main square are unaffected. At present this is still a pleasant place to spend a night, in part because there are not enough hotels to draw many tours. (Two hotels under joint management are good: the **Karalis Beach Hotel**, on a shady promontory overlooking the harbor, and the **Hotel Karalis**, overlooking both town and harbor. There are good seafood restaurants along the quay.)

The fortresses of **Paleókastro** and **Neókastro** (Old and New Castle) guard Pylos's harbor, the finest on the Peloponnese's west coast. This was the scene of the battle of Navarino in 1827, when a combined French, Russian, and British armada defeated the Turkish fleet. The battle, which was decisive in winning Greece's independence, should never have taken place: The allies' mandate was simply to contain the Turks. Inevitably shots rang out, and when the fighting stopped, 6,000 Turkish sailors were dead. The grateful citizens of Pylos erected a monument to the three admirals in the arcaded town square behind the harbor.

The harbor's mouth is blocked by the slender island of Sphaktería, where the Athenians blockaded a Spartan force during the Peloponnesian War. Desperate for supplies, the Spartans bribed locals to swim underwater at night, towing skins and gourds filled with food. On the 72nd day of the siege the Spartans surrendered. "Of all the events of this war," Thucydides wrote, "this came as the greatest surprise to the Hellenic world; for men could not conceive that the Lacedaemonians would ever be induced by hunger or any other compulsion to give up their arms, but thought that they would keep them until they died, fighting as long as they were able." The Spartans, of course, went on to win the war.

ELIS

Olympia

"There are enough irksome and troublesome things in life; aren't things just as bad at the Olympic festival? Aren't you scorched there by the fierce heat? Aren't you crushed in the crowd? Isn't it difficult to freshen yourself up? Doesn't the rain soak you to the skin? Aren't you bothered by the noise, the din and other nuisances? But it seems to me that you are well able to bear and indeed gladly endure all this, when you think of the gripping spectacles you will see." A commentator on the most recent Olympic games? No, the philosopher Epictetus in the second century A.D., after a visit to the original games.

Epictetus was but one of thousands of spectators from the entire Greek world who streamed into Olympia in the heat of summer for five days every fourth year between the first recorded games in 776 B.C. and the last in A.D. 393. The crowds were so immense that by sunrise of the first day there wasn't room for one more spectator. There were no women. Pausanias tells us that "on the road to Olympia before you cross the Alphios River ... there is a precipitous mountain with high rocks ... where the laws of Elis hurl down any woman detected entering the Olympic assembly, or even crossing the Alphios on the forbidden days." Only one woman is known to have escaped: Pherenike, who came disguised as her son's trainer. Discovered, she was spared out of deference to her dead husband, father, and brother—

all Olympic victors. Thereafter trainers entered the precinct nude, to prevent other deceptions.

Olympia (Olymbía) is so vast that it's almost impossible to believe its precise location was unknown for more than a thousand years, and that it was the chance find of a lucky traveller. The temples were toppled by earthquakes, while whole buildings and even statues were chopped up to make new buildings by early Christian squatters. The magnificent head of Apollo from the pediment of the Temple of Zeus was used in a house wall as if it was a mere fieldstone. Repeated earthquakes and flooding finally drove settlers away from Olympia; much of what was left was preserved under mud and silt. The epicene **Hermes of Praxiteles**, enjoying a room to himself as today's star of the site's museum collection, spent 14 centuries under ten feet of mud beside the Temple of Hera.

There's really no modern parallel for Olympia, where sports events alternated with religious observances in a mélange that could take place today only if the World Series and Christmas coincided and were observed in a complex combining a cathedral with Yankee Stadium, flanked by government buildings, hotels, offices for the clergy, and training camps. Perhaps that's why Olympia reveals itself slowly; it's easy to enter the site, stroll a bit, enjoy the breezes rustling through the pines, only to realize that you have no concrete idea of what you've seen. Several suggestions may help. (Olympia is least crowded first thing in the morning, at lunchtime, and in the late afternoon; there's a snack kiosk but no restaurant by the site.)

When you arrive at ancient Olympia you'll find that it, like Caesar's Gaul, is divided into three parts: First comes the museum, where you'll park, and where you *should* begin (but probably won't, out of eagerness to see the site). More about the museum later. Once you enter the site you pass some recently excavated Roman baths (not at all what you came to Olympia to see) and, more encouragingly, remains of part of the athletic and administrative complex. With a site map you can make out the ancient gymnasiums, wrestling arenas, swimming pools, hotels for trainers and guests, stoas (halls or pavilions), and assembly buildings. A few more steps and you reach Olympia's third and most impressive section: the **Altis**, or sacred grove, with the massive **Temple of Zeus**, the appropriately smaller **Temple of Hera**, and various small shrines to gods, heroes, and men, including the Peloponnese's first hero, Pelops, and one of its many conquerors, Philip V of Macedon.

There's no need for a map to spot the fifth-century B.C. Doric Temple of Zeus, where the Olympic flame was (and still is) lit before the games. Along with the Temple of Apollo at Delphi, this was one of the most impressive temples in Greece, even though its massive columns now lie scattered on the ground. While Delphi's surround is wild, Olympia's is gentle. Is there—was there ever—a lovelier Classical site than this? In antiquity, as today, the sanctuary was shaded with plane trees, poplars, oaks, and pines, but Olympia's most famous tree was the *kotinos kallistephanos,* the "olive beautiful for its crowns," from which the victors' wreaths were made; an olive tree marks the spot where the original grew by Zeus's temple. The best way to let Olympia soak in is to sit on one of the fallen columns near the olive tree, preferably with a copy of Pausanias's account of Olympia. The pine trees smell wonderful, and the soporific hum of summer cicadas is louder here than anywhere in Greece.

Romantic? Yes, but lest you be carried away by all those gray columns, so pure and severe, remember that much of the temple and its sculpture were painted in a profusion of colors that today would probably cause more gasps of shock than admiration. Nor, perhaps, would every visitor enjoy stepping back in time for the highlight of the religious observances during the games: the slaughter and roasting of 100 oxen at the great altar of Zeus.

The ancient **stadium** where many events took place has been carefully restored; legend says that Herakles himself paced off the race course, and many visitors puff up and down it so that they can boast of running at Olympia. One who ran here probably wished he hadn't: Charmos, the long-distance runner who, according to the Palatine Anthology, finished seventh in a field of six. "A friend," we are told, "ran alongside him shouting, 'Keep going, Charmos!' and although fully dressed, beat him. And if Charmos had had five friends, he would have finished twelfth."

Olympia was chockablock with dedications: Victorious athletes offered votive bronzes; proud home towns erected marble or bronze statues of the victors; cities and warriors gave armor from famous battles (Miltiades, victor over the Persians at Marathon, sent his helmet). Much of what once was here can be seen in the superb **Excavation Museum.** As the collection makes clear, Olympia would have made almost any other place in Greece look bare. There was hardly a square inch of ground without a statue, hardly a space on a temple wall for another dedication—although the Roman general Mummius managed to squeeze in 21 gilded shields on the metopes of the Temple of Zeus after he sacked Corinth in 146 B.C.

This is a museum where it's almost impossible to pick one favorite piece. Would it be the terra-cotta statue of a smug Zeus carrying off his demurely anticipatory cup-bearer, Ganymede? One of the delicate bronze horses, snarling griffins, or the maternal griffin nursing her young? The marble Nike (Victory) of Paionios, who seems to float in space? Only the best was good enough for Olympia: The fifth-century B.C. sculptor Phidias set up shop here to make the chryselephantine statue of Zeus that was one of the Seven Wonders of the World. So much ivory was used in the statue that the antiquarian Philo of Byzantium thought that God had made elephants so Phidias could make the Zeus. The statue's fame proved its undoing; it is believed that an emperor carted it off to adorn Constantinople, where it perished in a fire.

The museum's central room displays the sculpture from the Temple of Zeus, set against the walls to suggest its original placement on the temple. The west pediment shows the battle of the noble Lapiths and brutish Centaurs. Apollo oversees the conflict, which was symbolic of the struggle between civilization (for which read Greece) and the forces of darkness (the barbarian world). The east pediment and the metopes (which showed the Twelve Labors of Herakles) are reminders of two conflicting stories of how the games began. Some said Herakles initiated them to celebrate finishing one of his Twelve Labors, diverting the Alphios river to cleanse King Augeas's stables. We do not know what so preoccupied the king, but his stables, quartering more than 500 bulls, had not been cleaned for 12 years; Herakles did it in a day. The metopes show some of the Twelve Labors.

Others thought that Pelops, not Herakles, founded the Olympic games to commemorate a chariot race that won him the hand of the daughter of the king of Pisa. It should be mentioned that Pelops won the race by loosening the king's chariot pins so that a wheel fell off. Not very sporting, but Pelops got off scot-free, although his descendants in the the ill-fated House of Atreus did not fare so well. The east pediment shows the contest of Pelops. Pelops may have been the first, but he was certainly not the last to cheat in an Olympic event: When the emperor Nero raced here he fell from his chariot, climbed back in, finished last, and had himself declared winner. Justly, after his death Nero's name was stricken from the victors' list.

Remember what Epictetus said, and don't be too hard on the straggling modern village of Olympia. It must have had the same souvenir shops, hotels, and restaurants in antiquity that it does today, appearing somnolent out of season and erupting into a frenzy for the games. There's a small museum here of the modern Olympics, which were inspired by the French nobleman Pierre de Courbetin (whose heart, fittingly, is buried in Olympia). The Elgin Marbles aren't the only part of their heritage most Greeks want returned: An energetic lobby tried to bring the new Olympics back to Greece in 1996, in time for their 100th anniversary.

Olympia finally has a good in-town hotel, the **Altis**, with an exceptionally attractive group of art galleries, shops, and cafés on the ground level—not to mention the best book shop in the Peloponnese. Just around the corner is the unusually adventurous **Praxiteles** restaurant, with terrific retsina—what more can you ask for? If the answer is "a swimming pool," try the **Amalia** hotel just out of town. The Amalia requires demi-pension (half-board), and you'll have to forego the delicious *mezédes* (hors d'oeuvres) at the Praxiteles (which opened a modest hotel in 1989). The family-run **Spiliopoulos** restaurant enjoys a shady sidewalk location on Dumas Street and offers fine provincial Greek cuisine prepared and served with loving care.

(See also the Classical Tour chapter above for more on ancient Olympia.)

ACHAIA
Patras

Patras, overlooking the Gulf of Patras just west of the opening of the Gulf of Corinth, is the largest city in the Peloponnese and the third largest in Greece, and has, alas, none of the charms of Athens or Thessaloniki. Almost the entire town has a built-yesterday look, primarily because it's growing nearly as fast as Athens and with even less evidence of planning. Like Athens's Piraeus, this is a place for arrivals and departures; Byron arrived in Greece here, and if you take the Italy–Greece ferryboat, so might you. If you leave Greece from Patras you may find that you have more time here than you expected: The ferryboats are not noted for their punctuality. What follows is not meant to lure you to Patras, but to help you pass the time if you're stuck here.

The first thing to do is to get away from the waterfront, where ticket agents contend for customers and dazed travellers try to find ships for Italy or trains and buses to Athens amid trucks unloading cargo in the street. The Patras waterfront has none of the redeeming features of Piraeus, with its old markets and coffeehouses, although people who remember prewar Patras say it was lovely. They may be right: Take a look at the fresco of old Patras, with its elegant arcaded streets (precious few remain), in the **cathedral of Ayios Andréas**, just off the waterfront. According to legend the cathedral is on the spot where Saint Andrew was crucified; the saint's head, which spent five centuries in exile in Rome, is encased in an elaborate gold reliquary near the altar. The church itself is an architectural horror, and the little park outside, with several cafés, is as good a place as any to speculate on why almost every church in Greece built before this century is just right—and virtually every one since all wrong.

Patras produces most of Greece's ouzo and a good deal of wine, much of it at the Achaia Clauss winery in the hills outside town—which would be a nice spot to visit anywhere and is an irresistible escape from Patras. On the way out of town you can drive (cautiously) up very steep streets to the Kastro, a mélange of Byzantine, Frankish, Venetian, and Turkish walls on the ancient acropolis. There are fine views over the sea and across the Gulf of Corinth, and the streets beneath the Kastro are as close to Old World charm as you'll get in Patras.

The **Achaia Clauss winery** seems to have wandered into Greece from Bavaria; indeed, the Clauss family was German. Visiting dignitaries get to see wine being made, but others must content themselves with visiting the caves filled with enormous barrels of the sweet Mavrodaphne dessert wine—just *how* sweet you'll find out when you get your free sample. The wine was named for the first Clauss's wife, Daphne, who died young and had the beautiful black eyes (*mavra matia*) that are so often celebrated in Greek love songs.

If you have to spend the night in Patras, the best bet is to get away from the din of the harborside and head for Rion. If you stay at the enormous **Porto Rio Hotel** on the beach, you can have a swim followed by a good fish dinner at one of the nearby tavernas. If you're heading north into central Greece, Rion is also the place to catch the ferry across the Gulf of Corinth to Anti-Rion.

The Rack-and-Pinion Railroad from Diakofto to Kalavryta

If you're devoted to mountain driving, you can head inland from Patras and worm your way through the mountains to Kalavryta and the monastery of Ayia Lavra. You'd see some beautiful scenery on some fairly alarming roads, but you'd miss one of the most exciting excursions in the Peloponnese: the rack-and-pinion narrow-gauge railroad from Diakofto on the Gulf of Corinth through the Vouraïkós gorge to Kalavryta. It's an easy 45-km (28-mile) run on the main coast road from Patras to Diakofto. **Diakoftó** itself is a pleasant seaside village, a good place for lunch and a swim—something that can't be said about many towns along the Gulf of Corinth these days.

The 24-km (15-mile) train ride takes about an hour and a half, passing through tunnels, over viaducts marginally wider than the train itself, and along streams; passengers "ooh" and "aah" and Greek women ward off danger by repeatedly making the sign of the cross. If possible, break your journey deep in the gorge at the village of **Zachloroú**, which straddles the Vouraïkos river, and catch a taxi or walk on to the **Megaspileon Monastery** (completely rebuilt after a fire in 1934, but with some good icons), which was built, as its name suggests, deep in a cave. After you visit the monastery you can continue on to Kalavryta on a later train.

Kalávryta is a name well known throughout Greece. In 1943 the Germans herded 1,463 men into the schoolhouse, machine-gunned them, and torched the town. The hands of the tower clock still stand at 2:34, the time of the massacre. For years Kalavryta was a village of women in black—mothers, widows, and sisters of the slain. Today it is rebuilt, repopulated, and lively, producing a rose jam much beloved by Greeks and profiting from visitors who come to see the restored **Ayía Lavra Monastery** (also torched by the Germans), 7 km (4 miles) out of town. Greeks visit Ayia Lavra much as Americans go to Lexington and Concord, to see where their country's revolution began.

ARCADIA

The ancient and Medieval sites in the Peloponnese are so seductive that it's tempting, especially on a brief visit, to rush from pillar to post (or temple to castle). There's a real danger of heading home thinking of the Peloponnese as a series of grand, disconnected monuments and missing much of the sheer pleasure of the countryside and villages. If you're willing to sacrifice the seaside and the fast coastal motorway, try to take a day or two to head inland from Olympia to Arcadia—whose name, like that of Camelot, suggests a lost world of rustic bliss. Both for the landscape and for a cluster of villages between Olympia and Tripoli, Arcadia is well worth a visit.

The Greek poet Theocritus set his pastoral verses in Sicily, but when the Roman poet Virgil sat down to write pastorals he used Arcadia, far off in the Peloponnese, as the setting. Clearly distance lends romance to a spot, but why, out of all Greece, did Virgil choose Arcadia (which he'd never seen) as the setting for his lovelorn shepherds to pipe mournful ditties amid the rocks and rills? Probably the fact that Pan and his pipes came from here had a lot to do with Virgil's choice; in any event, Virgil made Arcadia and the pastoral synonymous. Most people forgot what Virgil had ignored: that the ancient Greeks had viewed the Arcadians not as romantic rustics but as country bumpkins, jeering that they lived on a diet of acorns in their inhospitable mountain fastness.

Over the centuries the myth of Arcadia as a land of milk and honey grew, making this remote mountain district a favored setting for bucolic verse and art. When the 17th-century French painter Poussin depicted idealized shepherds in flowing robes no shepherd ever wore, he placed the scene in Arcadia by showing the shepherds contemplating a tombstone inscribed *Et in Arcadia Ego*. The implication was that death (the ultimate reality), symbolized by the tombstone, could intrude even into Arcadia, the fabled land of pastoral bliss (the ultimate fantasy). The myth of Arcadia was pervasive: Keats wrote in his "Ode on a Grecian Urn" of Arcady's "leaf-fring'd" legends and "wild ecstasy."

As it happens, poets and painters were instinctively right to pick Arcadia—an unusually green place for Greece—to symbolize the enchantments of the countryside. This is the best-watered section of the Peloponnese, and mountain torrents really *do* bubble down hills in springtime. In summer, when the rest of Greece is parched, milky-green rivers flow along reedy banks, and all winter the mountain peaks have snow, and villages are sometimes cut off from the outside world.

In *The Republic* Plato said that the ideal city should be small enough that all the citizens would recognize one another. When you see the Arcadian mountain villages you'll know he was right. Each one is a Shangri-la, and together they have some of the most distinctive traditional architecture in Greece. Tall rectangular houses, usually built perpendicularly into hillsides, have red-tile roofs and elegant windows and doors, often with marble lintels. Most Arcadian villages were settled in antiquity and prospered during the Middle Ages, and again during the last century; little has been built since, hence their charm.

Even **Andrítsena**, about 60 km (37 miles) southeast of Olympia along a spectacular mountain road, seems unruffled by the tourists who come to see the fifth-century B.C. **Temple of Apollo at Bassae**, the most remote and austere of such monuments. A visit to Bassae, majestic in its mountain isolation, should be one of the highlights of any Peloponnesian journey. Unfortunately the temple has been in the throes of restoration for some years, and although the obtrusive metal scaffolding has been removed, a new protective tent was popped over Bassae in 1989, making it look as if P. T. Barnum had just passed through.

Andritsena, however, retains its magic: Mountain springs bubble out of pipes imbedded deep in the ancient plane trees that shade the main square and rush out of the four spouts of an 18th-century public fountain. The local bread and wine are delicious, the rugs for sale along the main street are indigenous and hand-loomed, and the loudest sound for miles around—the poets would approve—is usually distant sheep bells on the hills.

Twenty kilometers (12.5 miles) east of Andritsena, Medieval **Karýtena**, with its vaulted passages and arched Frankish bridge, is considerably prettier than its image on the 5,000-drachma note. From Karytena another 20 km north on a vertiginous mountain road brings you to **Stemnítsa**, a yet more remote spot clinging to a hillside. How does anyone make a living here? Some of the answers are given at the local **Folklore Museum**, which features displays of costumes, home life, and farm tools. A hundred years ago Stemnitsa, like nearby Tripoli, was a center for metalwork, turning out tools and many of the sheep bells that still echo across Arcadia. The real pleasure of Stemnitsa, however, is not in the museum, but the village, with its handsome three- and four-story stone houses and several frescoed churches scattered about. The tiny **basilica of Trión Ierárchon**, on a plateia just below Stemnitsa's main street, has the best-preserved frescoes. The walk up to the Kastro past the crumbling chapels of Profítis Ilías and Panayía Vaferon offers fine views of the village and countryside. There's even a good small hotel, the **Trikolonion**; the structure itself is a handsome traditional stone building, although the rooms have simple modern furnishings.

Just north of Stemnitsa, **Dimitsána**, the oldest Arcadian village, is the loveliest of the lot, sprawling across two hills dotted with trees, high above the Lousios river. Its imposing houses rise to four and five stories along cobblestoned streets, and, as at Stemnitsa, there are a number of surprisingly elegant churches with Western-style campaniles, relics of the days when this was an important Medieval citadel. Just outside town, the modern **Hotel Dimitsana** is well situated for walks in the countryside. Greeks know Dimitsana's name because of its most famous son, Archbishop Germanos, who raised the standard of rebellion against the Turks in 1821 at the monastery of Ayia Lavra in Kalavryta.

GETTING AROUND

You can get to the Peloponnese by plane from Athens, arriving in Kalamata in the south, but you'll probably drive here or come by train, boat, or bus. You can go virtually anywhere by bus, but expect to get familiar with bus stations as you wait for connections. The train runs from Athens to Corinth, Diakofto, Patras, Pyrgos, Kyparissia, and Kalamata; or to Corinth, Mycenae, Argos, Tripoli, and Kalamata. Again, expect to travel at a leisurely pace. By boat you'll arrive at Patras coming from Italy or Crete, although some boats from Crete dock at Gytheion. The Flying Dolphin hydrofoil from Piraeus has a number of stops on the east coast of the Peloponnese (Methana, Ermioni, Porto Heli, Leonidion, Kyparissi, Yerakas, Monemvasia, and Neapolis), but service is limited outside of summer. This should be an efficient way to travel but isn't, since you can buy only point-to-point tickets. It's perfectly possible, for example, to buy a ticket from Piraeus to Hydra, planning to spend the night and continue on to Monemvasia, only to discover that there are no seats available for several days.

The vagaries of public transportation are such that travel by car is your best option, especially if you're on a fixed schedule. Most roads are asphalted, and Greek auto mechanics, should you have any problems, are geniuses. One thing to keep in mind: The route numbers that appear on many maps almost never appear on road signs and are never used in giving directions. You'll find most roads uncrowded except on summer weekends, when Athenians stream into the

Peloponnese; try not to be on the road from Athens on a Friday afternoon, or heading to Athens on a Sunday after lunchtime.

Major car-rental firms (Hellas, Avis, Hertz) have offices in Athens and Patras; some Peloponnesian towns have local car-rental firms. If you're using a major company, compare prices and try to make a reservation before you leave home, especially if you'll be travelling during the summer. Be sure to factor in the healthy surcharges for insurance and V.A.T.

There are a number of one-day to one-week coach tours in the Peloponnese run by such firms as Hellastours, CHAT, and American Express, which you can book at home or in Athens. Guides are usually knowledgeable, hotels comfortable, and buses air-conditioned, and this isn't a bad way to get an idea of what you'd like to explore later on your own.

ACCOMMODATIONS REFERENCE

▶ **Altis.** Olympia, 270 65 Elis, Peloponnese. Tel: (0624) 231-01/02 or 224-59.

▶ **Amalia Hotel Olympia.** Olympia, 270 65 Elis, Peloponnese. Tel: (0624) 221-90.

▶ **Belle Helene.** Mycenae, 212 00 Argolid, Peloponnese. Tel: (0751) 662-25 or 664-34.

▶ **Hotel Byzantino.** Kastro, **Monemvasia**, 230 70 Laconia, Peloponnese. Tel: (0732) 613-51 or 615-62/63; Fax: (0732) 613-31.

▶ **Hotel Byzantion.** Vasilissis Sophias, **Mystra**, 231 00 Laconia, Peloponnese. Tel: (0731) 933-09.

▶ **Hotel Dimitsana. Dimitsana**, 221 00 Arcadia, Peloponnese. Tel: (0795) 315-18/19/20.

▶ **Kapetanakou Tower Hotel.** Areopolis, 230 62 Laconia, Peloponnese. Tel: (0733) 512-33.

▶ **Hotel Karalis.** 26 Kalamatas Street, **Pylos**, 240 01 Messenia, Peloponnese. Tel: (0723) 229-60/80; Telex: 252 185 HOKA GR.

▶ **Karalis Beach Hotel. Pylos**, 240 01 Messenia, Peloponnese. Tel: (0723) 230-21/22; Telex: 252 185 HOKA GR.

▶ **King Otto.** 3 Farmakopoulou Street, **Nafplion**, 211 00 Argolid, Peloponnese. Tel: (0752) 275-85.

▶ **Malvasia Hotel.** Kastro, **Monemvasia**, 230 70 Laconia, Peloponnese. Tel: (0732) 611-13, 614-35, or 613-23.

▶ **Hotel Menelaion.** 65 K. Paleologou Street, **Sparta**, 231 00 Laconia, Peloponnese. Tel: (0731) 221-61/63.

▶ **Porto Rio Hotel.** Rio-Patras, 265 00 Achaia, Peloponnese. Tel: (061) 992-102 or 992-212; Telex: 312207 GR; Fax: (061) 992-115.

▶ **Praxiteles**. 7 Spiliopoulou, **Olympia**, 270 65 Elis, Peloponnese. Tel: (0624) 225-92.
▶ **Hotel Trikolonion. Stemnitsa**, 221 00 Arcadia, Peloponnese. Tel: (0795) 812-97.
▶ **Tsitsiris Castle Hotel. Stavri**, 230 71 Laconia, Peloponnese. Tel: (0733) 542-97.
▶ **Vathia Tower Hotel. Vathia**, 230 71 Laconia, Peloponnese. Tel: (0733) 542-44.
▶ **Xenia Hotel. Epidaurus**, 210 52 Argolid, Peloponnese. Tel: (0753) 220-05.
▶ **Xenia Palace**. Akronafplia, **Nafplion**, 211 00 Argolid, Peloponnese. Tel: (0752) 289-81/82/83; Telex: (0298) 154 XENI GR.

EPIRUS

By John Chapple

John Chapple has been living in Greece since 1969, working as a writer and editor for Lycabettus Press on books about Greece.

Epirus (Ipiros) is Greece's large northwestern corner, bordered on the west by the Ionian Sea and on the east by the Pindos mountains and Thessaly. To the south it extends approximately halfway down the Ambracian Gulf, and to the north is Albania, an important influence past and present. Its area is vast—3,553 square miles—and most of it mountainous, so a visit requires considerable selectivity. Tourism is relatively undeveloped, for most travellers entering Greece from Italy at the port of Igoumenitsa head directly down to Athens and other better-known destinations, leaving Epirus for more enterprising souls. But if you take the time to explore this region, you will come to appreciate its beautiful coast, inland plains, and mountains, which become increasingly dramatic the farther you head inland.

Our coverage presents the most frequented route first, down the coast toward the south. Then we discuss the inland plain cities of Ioannina and Arta. If you are going to explore Epirus, go directly to Ioannina, an interesting city to visit and the best base from which to see the areas to its north and south. Arta, so far south that it should be visited separately, is probably best to see on your way down to or up from Athens. The mountains, the glory of Epirus, are presented next, beginning with the mountain villages of Zagoria and ending in the town of Metsovo, from which you can continue on to Thessaly (see below) or retrace your path to Ioannina and head south from there.

MAJOR INTEREST

Strong sense of history and tradition
Remote landscapes and villages

Medieval Parga

Nekromanteion: Oracle of the Dead

Oracle of Zeus at Dodona

Ioannina
The walled city
The island
Regional cuisine

Zagoria
Stunning mountain landscapes
Traditional villages
Hiking in the Pindos mountains

Mountain village of Metsovo

THE COAST

Igoumenítsa, a ten-hour ferry ride from Otranto, Italy, and a two-hour ferry ride from Corfu, became a port only after the boundary between Albania and Greece was set in 1923. With the growth of tourism in Greece since World War II, it has become a major transit center. The majority of visitors to Corfu, unless they fly, take the ferry from Igoumenitsa, and, conversely, the port serves as a major point of entry to mainland Greece. Hotels, restaurants, and ticket agencies are here in abundance, and there are buses to Ioannina, Athens, and virtually anywhere else in the country. (If you are continuing from Igoumenitsa by bus, have your travel agency arrange for you to take a ferry that lands in good time for your bus connection.) Most of the population is of Albanian stock, and they are prospering on the transit trade. Your interest, once here, is to move on, although having lunch at one of the dockside restaurants is a pleasant way to ponder your journey's next step.

Parga

Parga, 50 km (31 miles) south of Igoumenitsa, is a picturesque Medieval port town. Some Mycenaean remains have been found in the area, and Octavius (later called Augustus) mar-

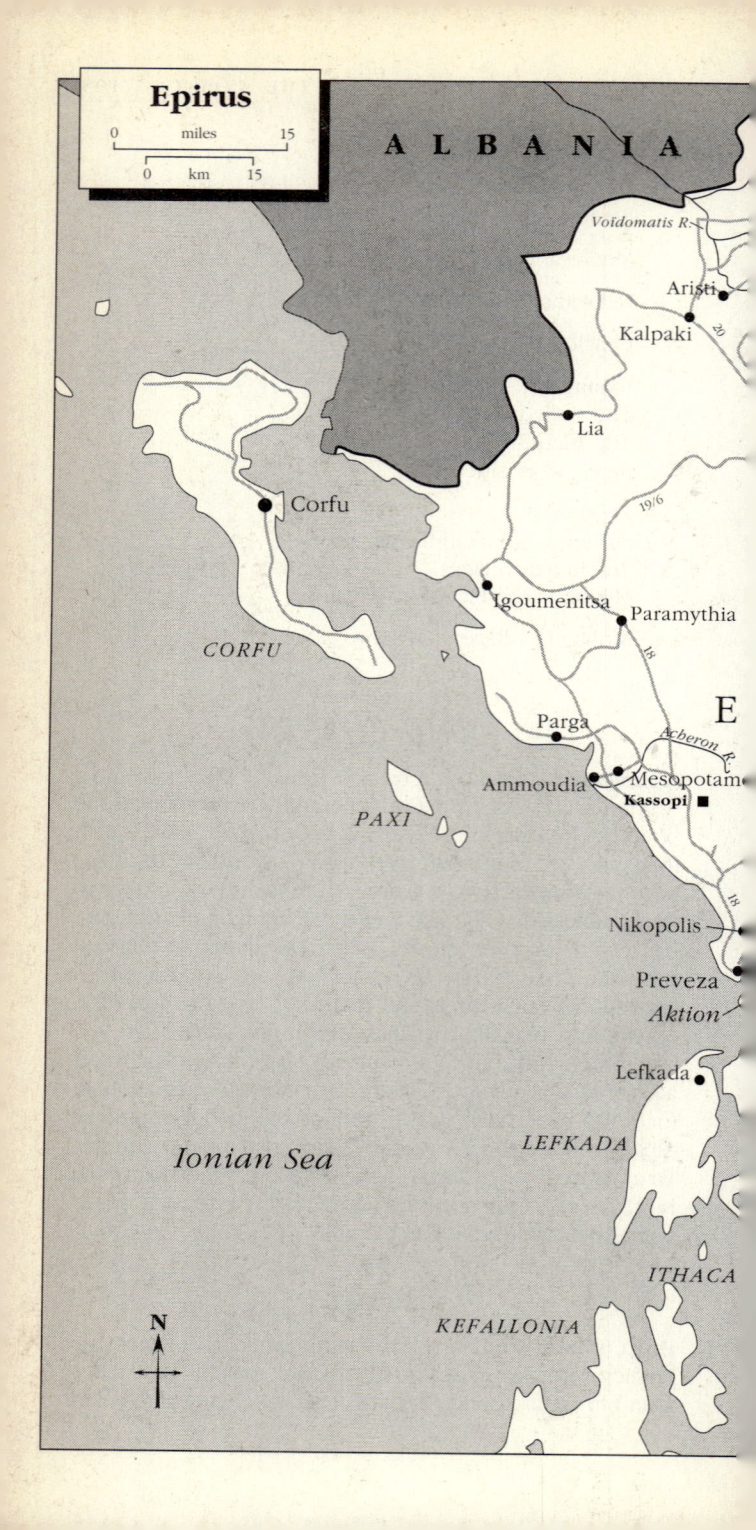

Epirus

0 — miles — 15
0 — km — 15

ALBANIA

Voïdomatis R.

- Aristi
- Kalpaki
- Lia
- Corfu

CORFU

- Igoumenitsa
- Paramythia
- Parga

E

Acheron R.

- Ammoudia
- Mesopotam
- **Kassopi**

PAXI

- Nikopolis
- Preveza
- *Aktion*
- Lefkada

LEFKADA

Ionian Sea

ITHACA

KEFALLONIA

N

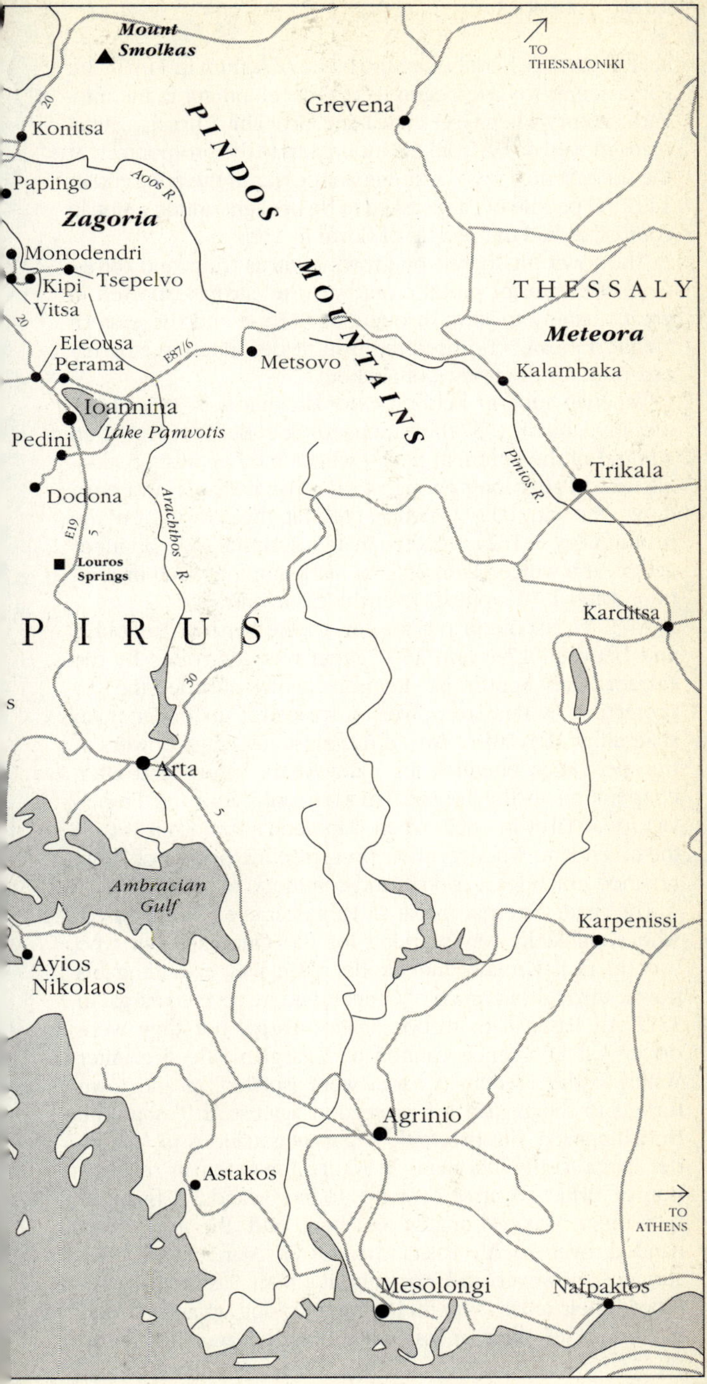

Mount Smolkas
TO THESSALONIKI
Grevena
PINDOS MOUNTAINS
Konitsa
Papingo
Aoos R.
Zagoria
Monodendri
Tsepelvo
Kipi
Vitsa
THESSALY
Meteora
Eleousa
Perama
E87/6
Metsovo
Kalambaka
Ioannina
Lake Pamvotis
Pedini
Pinios R.
Trikala
Dodona
Arachthos R.
E19
Louros Springs
PIRUS
Karditsa
Arta
Ambracian Gulf
Karpenissi
Ayios Nikolaos
Agrinio
Astakos
TO ATHENS
Mesolongi
Nafpaktos

shaled his fleet here before the battle of Actium in 31 B.C. But Parga seems to have begun its real development in the mid-14th century when Greek-speaking, probably Christian, Albanians moved down from the mountains to the promontory. At the time, Venice was the dominant power in the area, and in 1401 the people of Parga asked to be brought under Venetian control, as had the people of Corfu in 1386.

The town prospered by growing citrus fruits and olives. One of the major citrus crops was the citron, exported in great quantity to Jews throughout Europe and the eastern Mediterranean, who used the fruit to decorate the tabernacles built for the festival of Sukkoth.

Venetian support held off Ottoman attacks in 1452, 1475, and 1499, but in 1537 the famous Kheir el-din Barbarossa, an admiral of the Ottoman fleet—whose mother was Greek—captured Parga long enough to destroy its castle and burn down the city. The Venetians rebuilt the fortress on the promontory in 1624, as noted in an inscription over an inner gate near a winged Lion of Saint Mark. Another such inscription, dated 1701, appears over the castle entrance.

In 1797 Napoleon put an end to the Venetian republic, and between 1798 and 1807 Parga was controlled by the extraordinary Septinsular Republic, which afforded the city protection by Russian power but placed it under Ottoman suzerainty. Here were two of the most autocratic powers in Europe, bitter enemies for many years before and after, cooperating in the Ionian. It lasted only until the French victory at Tilsit in 1807, when Napoleon's star again was in the ascendant. Whoever their protector, the people of Parga retained much local control and continued to prosper.

The main external threat to Parga came to be Ali Pasha, who supposedly was working for the Ottomans but who was, in fact, virtually independent. He was extending his power throughout much of Greece, and he coveted Parga. In 1812 Ali Pasha sent troops against Parga, but they were driven off by French cannon and Pargian rifle fire. After Waterloo the French in Parga were isolated, so the town turned to the British for protection against Ali Pasha. The British agreed, but promptly began negotiations to surrender Parga to the Ottomans in return for Ottoman recognition of British control over the Ionian islands. A financial settlement was eventually reached, and the town was handed over to Ali Pasha's troops in March 1819. The Pargians, however, did not submit to Ali Pasha. They removed their icons from their churches, dug up and burned the bones of their ancestors, and sailed away to Corfu, leaving empty the town Ali Pasha had desired for so many years.

Ali Pasha had a house built on the coast and peopled Parga with Muslims. It was, however, his last triumph, for the sultan turned against him and he was killed three years later. The Muslims remained in Parga under Ottoman rule until the Greeks gained control throughout Epirus in 1913.

Today the Venetian fortress still dominates the headland between two bays. On the east the Medieval town runs from the saddle below the fortress down to the water, where open-air fish restaurants fill the quay. The street running from the quay is filled with tourist shops selling jewelry, clothing, fast food, and film. The better shops, such as **Porta** and **Nostos**, which sell jewelry and clothing, are directly behind the restaurants. Facing the quay is a string of small rocky islands that protect the bay. The largest has a whitewashed chapel dedicated to the Virgin Mary, another chapel dedicated to Saint Nikolas, and a small fort built by the French in 1808. You can swim from the beach here or, if you want less company, in the smaller bay along the shore to the east.

Immediately west of Parga is a large, beautiful sandy beach known as **Valtos**. The road to it winds up along the steep slopes behind the town among tall olive trees. The black nets spread out in autumn to collect the olive crop are left rolled up beneath the trees for most of the year, looking like so many giant roots. The public road to Valtos beach runs right down to the middle of the beach, so everybody in town who wants to get there does. There are two large restaurants just behind the beach, one providing music over loudspeakers suspended from the trees. This is a fine place to go if you have small children and like company.

The best way to enjoy Parga, however, is to stay at the **Lichnos Beach Hotel**, just outside of town. This hotel, a campground, and a few apartments control the only access road down to the beach, so you don't have everybody with wheels here. In addition to the main building, the hotel has bungalows in a lemon orchard running down to the sandy shore, a good idea well carried out. It is peaceful here, and beautiful.

Excursion boats leave for the island of **Paxi** from Parga's central pier. The boats leave at 9:30 in the morning and take approximately one hour and 15 minutes to reach Paxi, where they stay until 4:00 P.M. A very small, relatively undeveloped island with only a few towns, it attracts a regular British clientele on holiday who enjoy the nothing-to-do atmosphere found in this picturesque setting. (See the Corfu section below for more on Paxi.) You can also take a boat to the Nekromanteion (discussed below) at 9:30 in the morning. This excursion takes one hour to reach the Acheron river at Ammoudia, from which you must walk about 20 minutes to reach the ancient site. The boat returns to Parga after two hours, stopping at Lichnos beach so you can swim, and delivers you back to Parga at 4:00 P.M.

Nekromanteion

On a hill behind the village of **Mesopótamos**, 37 km (23 miles) south of Parga, is the Nekromanteion, the Oracle of the Dead. Archaeological opinion does not entirely agree that this is, in fact, the Nekromanteion, although the site does fit Herodotus's description, which says it is in the land of the Thesprotians on the banks of the Acheron, one of the four ancient rivers entering the underworld.

If you're driving from Parga, turn right after 10 km (6 miles), following the sign that reads "61 km to Preveza." At Ammoudia turn left at the sign saying "Athens 430 km"; Mesopotamos is 2 km (about a mile) farther on. As you enter the village there is a sign pointing left up a gravel road to the Nekromanteion.

Most of the remains visible on the site date to the 3rd or 4th century B.C. A small 18th-century church stands on top of the ruins, and the remains of an 18th-century house serve as the guard's room. A map carved in stone and set on a pedestal near the guard's room provides some help in understanding the ruins. The most impressive remains here are the large polygonal wall you pass on your right on the way to the underground barrel-vaulted chamber and the chamber itself. Metal stairs descend to the room, where it will take some time to get used to the poor light. (The floor is uneven, so watch your step.)

You can well imagine this chamber as the place where people came to ask questions of the dead. It seems to fit Homer's description of Odysseus visiting Hades and sacrificing to the spirits of the dead, and Herodotus's tale of Periandros, the tyrant of Corinth, communicating with the spirit of his dead wife at the Nekromanteion.

The Acheron river enters the Ionian just below Mesopotamos at the village of **Ammoudiá**, which means "sands"—and indeed, there is a fine sand beach here. The narrow river, navigable for a few hundred yards, is the destination of Parga tours advertising trips to the Nekromanteion.

Kassopi and Zalongo

The inland route (18) south from Mesopotamos runs through some villages and along a relatively uninteresting mountain road. The new highway along the shore (39) is a pleasanter and faster drive. If you take the shore route, turn east 17 km (10.5 miles) north of Preveza and then, after 2 km (a little over a mile), north (left) again onto route 18. The sign for the village of Kamarina and ancient Kassopi is 5 km (3 miles) north, on the right.

Ancient **Kassopi**, the capital city of the Kassopaian tribe in the fourth century B.C., is 5 km (3 miles) from the turn off route 18, 2 km beyond the village of Kamarina. A small sign on the left of the road at the apex of a hairpin turn to the right indicates the site, a two-minute walk away through tall pine trees. The city was built on a lovely shallow bowl of a plateau 1,600 feet high, with steep cliffs rising behind it to the north. To the south there is a fine view down over the Ionian Sea and the Ambracian Gulf. The extensive ruins are overgrown, but many structures can be found with the help of a large metal site plan on the wall of the guard's house to the right inside the entrance. At its most prosperous, Kassopi probably had a population of about 9,000.

The 16th-century **monastery of Zálongo** is approximately 300 yards due east, at the foot of the cliff beneath the towering cement statue of women dancing and holding hands. This statue commemorates one of the more desperate acts of resistance to Ali Pasha, the final act in the 15-year struggle of the Souliots, a tribe of Christians from the region of Souli, to keep their independence.

The last siege, which cost Ali Pasha dearly, lasted throughout the summer of 1803. Finally, left without water, the Souliots agreed to negotiate surrender with Ali Pasha's commander, his son Veli. After a formal surrender was signed guaranteeing Souliot safety, about 2,000 of the Souliots started toward Parga and the remaining 1,000 headed for Preveza. Six men, led by a man known as "Last Judgment" Samuel, barricaded themselves in the fort of Kunghi and blew it up as Ali Pasha's troops approached. Veli attacked the Souliots going to Parga, but they managed to reach the city safely. The Souliots heading toward Preveza were attacked and massacred in the monastery of Zalongo. About 60 women and children escaped up the mountain; however, when they reached the top the women threw their children over the cliff and then, dancing traditional Souliot dances, jumped over themselves.

The monastery is now a peaceful place. Stairs behind it lead up to the cliff edge where the women jumped.

Nikopolis

Nikópolis (Victory City), 5 km (3 miles) north of Preveza, lies on the northern side of the narrow entrance to the Ambracian Gulf. The town was built by Augustus after his victory over Antony and Cleopatra in 31 B.C. in the battle of Actium, the Latin name for the peninsula of Aktion, which constitutes the southern shore of the entrance to the Ambracian Gulf. Here Augustus settled both his veterans and the people who were scattered in many, by then poor, Epirot cities, including the people of nearby Kassopi. The new city gave him strategic control over ships moving between mainland Greece and Italy. Saint Paul apparently spent the winter of A.D. 64 in Nikopolis and wrote his Epistle to Titus here.

From the north, the first indications of Nikopolis are the ruins of a Roman bath, which you will pass on the right side of the road just before the left turn toward Arta and Ioannina. (The first road sign says "Arta 44 km" to the left and then, 50 yards farther on, another sign says "Ioannina 96 km" to the left, indicating the same road.) From the intersection you can see the remains of a large Roman theater a few hundred yards down the road to the left, below the village of Smyrtoúla. Before the battle of Actium, Augustus pitched his camp on the hill above the village so he could observe the ships fighting. Today you can see the foundation stones of a large victory monument he built on the summit.

The main ruins of Nikopolis are the Roman **city walls**, which lie ahead toward Preveza. After 200 yards the road curves around the end of this impressive structure, with its three bands of brick. About halfway along as you follow the wall is a sign on the right side of the road identifying ancient Nikopolis, opposite which are the ruins of the early Christian basilica of Ayios Alkýsonos, with its large rectangular portal. Another 80 yards farther up on the right is a small sign in Greek pointing to the odeum, which lies 150 yards down a dirt road that passes through an arch in the city wall. The odeum, a small theater, is in much better condition than the large Roman **theater**. Return to the paved road and go another 100 yards to the right toward Preveza. Just before the sign that points the way to Mítikas, watch carefully for the somewhat obscure entrance to the archaeological site. Here you will find a small **museum** with Roman sculpture and the ruins of another early Christian basilica, that of Ayios Doumétios. Both this church and Ayios Alkysonos have fine mosaics, but they are covered with protective layers of sand and cannot be seen.

Préveza is the town you pass through, quickly, to take the ten-minute ferry ride over to Aktion. It was ruled, in turn, by the Venetians, Ottomans, Venetians, French, and Ali Pasha, remaining under Ottoman control until captured by the Greeks in 1912. On the southern point, below the ferry landing, is a large Venetian fort.

IOANNINA

Ioánnina (Yánnina), 92 km (57 miles) east of Igoumenitsa via E-19 (route 6), is a busy commercial center, right on the main trade route from the east over the Pindos mountains from Thessaly and easily accessible from the north, south, and west. The walled city is situated on a rectangular rocky peninsula that juts into Lake Pamvotis (also called the Lake of Ioannina). The earliest written evidence that the city existed—with a fortress and a permanent population—is a late-seventh-century reference to a bishop of Ioannina. The name Ioannina seems to derive from a sixth-century Byzantine church, of which no remains can be seen, built on the peninsula by the emperor Justinian.

The city's history is complex: Invading Bulgars, Slavs, Normans, Serbs, Albanians, and Turks all challenged Byzantine rule in Ioannina, successfully on many occasions. After the Crusaders captured Constantinople in 1204, some of the refugee Byzantine nobility established the Despotate of Epirus in hopes of resurrecting the Byzantine Empire. Nicaea, not Epirus, succeeded in expelling the Crusaders from Constantinople, but the Despotate of Epirus continued its struggle for ascendancy. The conflict ended only in 1264 when Michael VIII Paleologos brought enough military force to convince Michael II of Epirus to submit.

After the butcherous Serbian ruler Thomas Preloumbos was killed in 1384, the people of Ioannina turned for help to Esau Buondelmonte, the Florentine ruler of Kefallonia, and he turned to the Ottomans. Buondelmonte became a vassal of the Ottoman sultan and brought an Ottoman army to protect Ioannina from Albanian siege. His successor, Carlo Tocco, also was able to hold off the Albanians only by allying himself with the Ottomans. When Tocco died in 1429 his realm was contested by his nephew and his three illegitimate sons. Sultan Murad II wanted no more bickering and sent Sinan Pasha, governor of the Ottoman European provinces, to take control.

Ioannina withstood the Ottoman siege throughout the summer of 1430 until Sinan Pasha pledged that the people could keep all their property and would have no religious restrictions. Ioannina accepted these terms and remained under Ottoman rule for 482 years.

Until the late 16th century the Ottoman Empire was a growing force, the provider in many ways of a tolerant, stable environment. What sticks in the mind, however, is the long decline, particularly in the 18th and 19th centuries, when the empire's subjects longed to be free of what had become arbitrary and corrupt rule. In Ioannina the dominant figure in this context is Ali Pasha, who ruled the city from 1788 until 1822.

Assessing Ali Pasha is as complex a task as any in modern Greek history. Some contemporary Greek nationalist opinion reduces him to a murderous Turk and Muslim, and would expunge him from the records. Murderous he certainly was, for he admitted to having caused the deaths of 30,000 people. He was a Turk, however, only in that he was descended from one on his father's side six generations earlier. All the other genes were Albanian. His Albanian followers, known as Skipetars, were the core of his military strength, although he used anyone—English, French, or Greek—to his advantage. Many Greeks who later became prominent in the War of Independence or the independent Greek government had served Ali Pasha. As for being a Muslim, neither he nor his Skipetars seem to have taken much interest in religion.

Intelligent and brave, but venal, violent, and unprincipled, Ali Pasha was the embodiment of egocentricity run amok, "the worst unhung criminal in Europe," as a contemporary English visitor observed. Nonetheless, under Ali Pasha's control Ioannina flourished; thanks to his interest in commerce, he even built a road to Preveza and kept it cleared of bandits.

Ioannina is still thriving, and at first glance it appears to be just a large provincial town bent on trade. If you look a little beneath the surface, however, you will find some very interesting things. But first things first: There is more demand than there are hotel rooms, so book your accommodations in advance. Both the **Olympic** and the **Galaxy** hotels in the center of town are pleasant and friendly, but the price difference between them and the more luxurious **Xenia Hotel**, off the main street, Dodóni, is minimal, and the Xenia's restaurant has the deserved reputation of being the best in town. Once you are in Ioannina, a visit to the Greek National Tourist office helps. The staff is enthusiastic and helpful, and will gladly supply you with maps and useful advice. They will also help you select hotels anywhere in Epirus and head you in the right direction if you want to rent a car. You can contact the office at 2 Napoléontas Zervá, Ioannina, 452 32 Epirus; Tel: (0651) 250-86.

You're in for some pleasant surprises concerning food in Ioannina. The fresh trout available on the island (see below) is simply prepared, very good, and very inexpensive—reason enough to go, particularly for lunch. You also should sample what Greeks call *gastra,* available only in Epirus, most easily in Ioannina. A gastra is, literally, a heavy cast-iron top in the shape of a cone, perhaps three feet in diameter with a perimeter lip about two inches high. A fire is built on a flat hearth and the gastra suspended over it from a hook until the metal becomes red hot. Then the coals are shoveled aside and a baking dish containing either lamb or goat is placed on the hearth. The gastra is lowered onto the baking dish, which it fits tightly, and the ashes are shoveled onto the gastra. The meat is then left to cook for two hours; the juices remain, resulting in meat as tender as you ever are likely to eat.

Two good restaurants in the area serve gastra. The first, which calls itself simply **The Gastra**, is 6 km (4 miles) from town on the right side of the road past the airport, just before the left turn for the road to Igoumenitsa. The second, **Diogenes**, is one kilometer farther on after taking that left turn, on the far edge of the first village, Eleoúsa. Both have prompt, courteous service, and the prices are most reasonable.

The Walled City

The walled city on the peninsula is the obvious focus for any visitor to Ioannina. The approach to it from the national tourist office goes near the **Archaeological Museum**, which features well-displayed finds from throughout ancient Epirus. Across Dodoni Avenue and farther down toward the water is the **bazaar**, with narrow streets and closely packed shops retaining something of Ioannina's Medieval commercial atmosphere. Ioannina has long been famous for its metalwork, and here you can purchase fine silver objects, notably filigree, less expensively than elsewhere in the area.

Inside the wall are the quiet streets and small houses of old Ioannina. On Justinian Street, a narrow cobblestone way adjacent to the city wall to the left as you enter the Big Gate, is the **Old Synagogue**, surrounded by a high wall. The approximately 80 Jews living in Ioannina today are all who remain of a once-thriving Romaniot—not Sephardic— community with roots in Greece dating at least to the third century B.C. (For more about the Romaniots, read *The Jews of Ioannina,* by Rae Dalven; see the Bibliography.)

Follow signs to the municipal museum housed in the early-17th-century **mosque of Aslan Pasha**. Entering through the thick walls and passing piles of cannonballs along the way up to the museum, you are reminded of Ioannina's military strength. The view from the heights is commanding. The museum displays material from the Greek War of Independence and the 1913 campaign, which finally expelled the Turks from Epirus.

In the southern corner of the walled city stands the **Fetiye Mosque**, left in a state of decay, which Ali Pasha had built for his grave. Outside the mosque you can clearly see two unmarked graves, one containing the remains of his first wife, Eminé, the other containing the headless remains of Ali Pasha. His head, buried in Istanbul by the Albanian community there, rests beneath the marvelously ironic inscription: "Here lies the head of Ali Pasha, who labored 40 years for the cause of Albanian independence."

As you approach the Fetiye Mosque you will see on your right the recently reconstructed building now housing the Ioannina department of Byzantine antiquities. In the early 19th century Ali Pasha's palace stood on this site. In the 1860s the Ottomans tore down Ali Pasha's palace and built a military hospital in its place. This building, in turn, was torn down by the Greeks in 1958 and a palace was built in 1964 as a summer residence for King Paul. It was never used, however, and was abandoned after the royal family left Greece in 1967.

The Island

Don't miss the island in **Lake Pamvótis**. Boats leave from the shore below the city walls every half hour, and the trip takes only ten minutes. Towering sycamores shade the landing, along which are four unpretentious restaurants, great pleasures of Ioannina. There are two other restaurants inland, just before the entrance to the monastery of Ayios Panteleimonas (called the Ali Pasha museum on the island signs). The food is the same in all of these restaurants, but you might be most comfortable in the shade of the sycamores at the **Pamvotis** restaurant to the far left as you land on the island, or in either of the two inland establishments, the **Thomas** or the **Propodes**.

Frogs' legs, eels, crayfish, and trout are the traditional fare. Every restaurant has at least one large glass tank holding your lunch. The lake has a serious pollution problem, so stay away from the frogs and the large fish, which are caught by the island fishermen. The trout, however, are raised in clear mountain streams and are delicious grilled. The eels are also tasty but are considerably more expensive.

The path from the shore forks shortly beyond the restaurants; the one to the right goes to the **monastery of Ayios Nikólaos ton Philanthropinón** near the top of the hill. The walls inside the 16th-century church are covered with frescoes that are in considerably better condition than most you will see in Greece, and few of such quality are this accessible. (A flashlight is useful, in any case.) In the outer narthex, just to the left of the entrance, note especially the images of seven Greek philosophers—Plato, Apollonius, Solon, Aristotle, Plutarch, Thucydides, and Cheilon—all of whom lived well before Christ.

Signs to the monastery read "Secret School," for the monks held classes here; throughout the long Ottoman occupation of Greece the church played a fundamental role preserving Greek culture. The school probably was not secret, though, since the Ottomans generally tolerated Orthodox Christianity and the Greek language; non-Muslim subjects were free to follow their own faith and ways as long as they accepted Islamic authority and paid the requisite taxes. Ali Pasha, in fact, encouraged Greek education, and it is highly unlikely that he did not know about the island school, thanks to his many spies.

The path turning to the left leads to the **monastery of Ayios Panteleímonas**, where Ali Pasha was killed. When the Ottoman army besieged the city, Ali Pasha decided to defend only the walled city and his palace, the **Litharitza** (a partial reconstruction, occupied by a café, is on the site in the park near the Archaeological Museum). Presumably to keep the city's wealth from falling to the attackers, he had his Skipetars loot and then burn the city. After 18 months Ali Pasha's forces were reduced to only 100 men. In January 1822 he agreed to confer with the Ottoman commander, Khurshid Pasha, on the island.

Instead, Khurshid Pasha sent an execution squad. The

assassins fired up through the ceiling of the ground floor, mortally wounding Ali Pasha. Today the bullet holes remain clearly visible in the floorboards of the upper room. When Ali Pasha died his supporters stopped resisting. The attackers dragged Ali Pasha's body to the top of the stairs—where you now buy your entrance ticket—and cut off his head; they then displayed it around town on a silver tray for three days.

SOUTH OF IOANNINA

Dodona

In a beautiful bowl of a valley just 21 km (13 miles) southwest of Ioannina is Dodona, site of the Oracle of Zeus. Dodona is the oldest oracle in Greece, used probably since the early Bronze Age. According to a fourth-century B.C. text, in antiquity the sanctuary was not walled but surrounded by bronze cauldrons set on tripods. The cauldrons touched one another, and all vibrated when one of them was struck. Prophecies were made on the basis of the sound of the vibrating cauldrons. Later they were made from the sound of the rustling leaves of the sacred oak tree.

The first Hellenic tribe in Epirus, the Thesprotians, settled in the area early in the Middle Helladic period (1900 to 1600 B.C.), and are mentioned by Homer as serving Zeus of Dodona. After the Trojan War, in the 12th century B.C., another Hellenic tribe, the Molossians, moved into Epirus, forcing the Thesprotians to the south and east over the Pindos mountains into Thessaly, although the sanctuary of Dodona remained under Thesprotian control until the end of the fifth century B.C.

It was Olympias, the daughter of Molossian King Neoptolemos (370 to 368 B.C.), who married Philip II of Macedonia and became the mother of Alexander the Great. The most famous Molossian king was Pyrrhos (297 to 271 B.C.), whom we know for his costly victory over the Romans in 279 B.C. Pyrrhos's rule was nonetheless a bright era for Epirus, one of political expansion; new cities were founded and many buildings were constructed. The **theater** (restored), which can seat 18,000 and is the most impressive—indeed, virtually the only—structure on the site today, was built during his reign.

During the wars between the Macedonian kingdom and the Romans, the southern Epirot tribes, led by the Molossians, sided with Macedonia. After the Romans defeated the last Macedonian king, Perseus, in 168 B.C., they turned against those Epirots who had opposed them, destroying 70 cities and carrying away 150,000 people as slaves. Late in the first century B.C., the Greek cities of Epirus, particularly those in the south, were reduced to villages. Dodona was deserted.

Augustus and other Roman emperors supported the sanctuary, which continued to function at least until the mid-fourth century A.D. and probably until the reign of the emperor Theodosius (347 to 395). Theodosius, however, moved to stamp out pagan practices; in A.D. 391 the sacred oak was cut down, and, either to unearth suspected treasure or to completely uproot the heathen symbol, the ground beneath it was excavated down to bedrock. Dodona, maintaining its ties to things sacred, became the seat of a bishopric. In the fifth or sixth century a basilica was built on the site of the sanctuary with material from the ancient buildings. Gothic invasions, however, made life untenable in Dodona, and the inhabitants moved to the new city the emperor Justinian established in the early sixth century on the peninsula jutting into Lake Pamvotis.

The Louros Springs and the 1912–1913 Army Headquarters

South of Ioannina, 29 km (18 miles) on the Arta road (route 5/E 19), are the Louros Springs, a round pool approximately 80 yards in diameter. The pool's water supplies a trout farm behind a **taverna**, which, of course, has a ready supply of fresh trout. The abundant water also is used for washing, in three large holes set in the taverna's front porch and in two other holes carved out of the rock farther on. With such a powerful flow of water it is easy, without soap, to wash the deep-pile *flokáti* rugs; a sign declares readiness to wash anything from rugs to sheets.

From the front of the taverna a road continues past an abandoned state trout farm up to the pool itself, which you can drive around. Just above the pool is a National Tourist Organization (EOT, in Greek) restaurant, with the large letters **EOT** below the eaves. Although established by the National Tourist Organization, the restaurant is run by the Panouklias family and everything about it is in good taste, including the wood-paneled Epirot decor and the food. Upstairs are four attractive guest rooms.

Two kilometers back toward Ioannina on the left side of

the road is a small sign in Greek worth heeding: "Army Camp 1912/13," which you can understand by the date. It points down the road toward the inn that served as army headquarters for the Epirus campaign during the first Balkan War. Now an army memorial, it is maintained by two conscripts completing their national service. There is no literature available on the site, and whether or not one of the conscripts speaks English when you visit will be the luck of the draw, but don't miss this gem.

Except for the statues across the road facing the inn, the building and surrounding fields can't have changed much since the Balkan Wars, although perhaps the inn is now cleaner. Two of the three rooms on the second floor contain various memorabilia of Crown Prince Constantine, commander of the Greek army, and of other major participants, along with some contemporary paintings of the campaign. The third room has the meat of the matter, for here on the wall is displayed a large contour map explaining the battle for Ioannina.

The map shows Ioannina protected by a semicircular ring of mountains. The city was defended by 30,000 Turkish troops commanded by Essat Pasha; the Greek attackers numbered 6,000. Named for the heights where the fiercest fighting took place, the battle of Bizaniou lasted six weeks, from January 10 until February 21, 1913. After an extended heavy artillery bombardment, on February 19 Crown Prince Constantine concentrated his fire on Mount Bizaniou. Expecting a frontal assault, the Turks moved some of their troops from the western heights for reinforcement, but the Greeks attacked the western heights in three prongs, eventually meeting at the village of Pedini, near Dodona. The main bodies of both armies remained fiercely engaged to the east, on the heights of Mount Bizaniou.

Crown Prince Constantine had ordered these contingents to wait at Pedini, but Major Ioannis Velisariou led 300 men to the village of Ayios Ioánnis, adjacent to Ioannina, where he overpowered the Turkish resistance and cut the telephone lines. This convinced Essat Pasha that the Greek army was there in force, and he surrendered to Velisariou. The battle on Mount Bizaniou raged on until Velisariou returned to the inn with Turkish officials. The next morning Essat Pasha formally surrendered his sword to Prince Constantine. The Crown Prince immediately returned it to the Turkish commander, who had been his classmate and friend at the Berlin War College. Major Velisariou was commended for his bravery but demoted for disobedience.

Arta

Arta is 73 km (45 miles) south of Ioannina, too far to be included comfortably in a day trip from Ioannina. Visit it on your way down to Athens; the main, inland route south from Ioannina runs through Arta. If you are following the coast, turn east for Arta from ancient Nikopolis, above Preveza.

Arta, an agricultural and industrial center, is the second-largest city in Epirus and the former capital of the Despotate of Epirus, as evidenced by the large 13th-century **castle** that stands to the north near the Arachthos river. What will most likely interest the contemporary visitor are the four-arched stone bridge, built early in the 16th century, and the extraordinary church of the Parigoritissa, built in 1285.

The **stone bridge** is on the northern edge of the city, parallel to the modern bridge as you drive into Arta from Ioannina or the coast. Its foundations date to the Hellenistic period. According to folk myth, each day's work fell down at night until the master builder sacrificed his beautiful wife by having her built, alive, into the foundations. (Similar myths concerning bridges are common throughout southeastern Europe.)

The **church of the Parigorítissa** (Virgin Mary the Consoler) is near the center of town. Soon after you pass over the modern bridge, turn right immediately before the bronze statue of a Greek soldier. A road sign with an arrow pointing to the right reads "Center" and "Hospital." Continue for about one kilometer until you reach the sign for the village of Koméno (15 km/9.5 miles to the right). On the far side of the street is an arched, one-story Ottoman building that now serves as a café. The church can be seen about 100 yards diagonally up to the right from this intersection.

Built on the hill, the church dominates the scene as you approach. It boasts two rows of double windows and a 70-foot-high central dome that is supported at two levels by columns on cantilevers and decorated with a mosaic of Christ the Pantokrator. The combined effect of great height, a relatively small floor space, columns that seem to float, and illumination from the numerous windows is both impressive and beautiful.

There are one 14th-century and four other 13th-century Byzantine churches in Arta, most of them near the castle walls; walking through the narrow streets among the old houses to find them is a pleasant experience. If you want to stay overnight in Arta, choose the **Xenia** hotel, a modern cement building inside the castle, with a fine view.

NORTH OF IOANNINA

In the village of **Pérama**, just 4 km (2.5 miles) north of Ioannina on the road to Metsovo, is an extensive limestone cave, through which visitors are taken in small groups. Historically more interesting is the small village of **Kalpáki**, 35 km (22 miles) north of Ioannina via route 20, where the Greek army stopped the Italian advance in the winter of 1940–1941. This was an extraordinary, heroic accomplishment by a small country against its much larger neighbor, and it did wonders for Greek self-respect. On the left (west) side of the road are busts of King George II, the prime minister and dictator Ioannis Metaxas, and the army commander Alexandros Papagos. On the right side of the road, next to the small museum, is a bust of Colonel Mordechai Frizis, a Jewish colonel killed by the Italians during the Greek advance north of the present Albanian border.

The Germans nullified this success by invading Greece through Bulgaria, completely overrunning the country by the end of May 1941. The occupying German forces were harassed by either the Communist-led resistance movement or the rightist resistance group led by the Epirot general, Napoleon Zervas. Rivalry between the political left and right continued in a bloody civil war after the Germans withdrew. Today it still affects Greek politics, although on much more civil terms.

If you enjoy literary sites, you may want to visit **Liá**, southwest of Kalpaki, approximately 15 km (9 miles) north of the Igoumenitsa road. This village is the setting for Nicholas Gage's *Eleni*, the story of his mother's struggle to protect her children during the civil war.

Konitsa

About 20 km (12.5 miles) north of Kalpaki, the road (still route 20) rises for a few miles, then drops down into a beautiful valley where the Voïdomátis and Aóos rivers join after cutting spectacular gorges through the Pindos mountains. The small town of Kónitsa, just past the mouth of the Aoos gorge, is where Ali Pasha's mother was born. The Greek army garrison here withstood a violent three-week attack in the winter of 1947–1948 from the Communists, who wanted to make Konitsa their capital.

There are post-Byzantine churches and Ottoman remains in and around Konitsa, and even hot mineral springs at the nearby village of **Kavasíla**. But the main reason to visit Konitsa is to see the Aoos gorge; the late-19th-century, single-arch stone bridge, which stands in startling contrast to the modern bridge built parallel to it; and, from afar, the Stomiou Monastery. Here you get the first idea of the beauty for which the Pindos mountains are so renowned. There is also an unpretentious riverside **taverna**, the only one for miles, where you can have fresh fried trout; it has no posted name, just a sign in Greek indicating that there's a taverna on the south bank of the Voïdomatis river about 2 km (about a mile) south of Konitsa. You will find this establishment 200 yards off the main road, down a dirt road parallel to the river.

The Aoos river breaks from the mountains just south of Konitsa after cutting a spectacular **gorge** between Mount Smólikas, the highest peak in the Pindos mountains, and Mount Gamíla. The 1870 **stone bridge** near the modern road commands attention. Note the small bell beneath the apex of the arch, which rings with any strong wind to warn travellers about the danger of being blown off. There are 191 stone bridges scattered throughout Epirus, most of them built in the 18th or 19th century but some in the 16th or 17th century. Three are dated to the 13th century. As you travel along they will suddenly appear next to the road, often seeming to connect only one footpath with another, but standing nonetheless as eloquent evidence of the vitality of trade.

Two hundred yards south of the Aoos river a rough macadam road turns up to the right and runs parallel to the main road. When it reaches the river the macadam stops, the road becoming a bulldozed track that turns up the gorge toward **Stomíou Monastery**, built in 1774. You can see the white building high up on the right side of the gorge almost as soon as you pass the old stone bridge; to reach it on foot takes a little more than an hour. The views of the gorge on the way up and, of course, from the monastery itself, are beautiful, with the often snow-capped Mount Smolikas in the distance. Though the monastery is maintained, there are no monks there full-time. Sadly, the modern repairs have been done with not very artfully applied cement.

ZAGORIA

Approximately 30 km (19 miles) north of Ioannina is the collection of 46 Pindos mountain villages known as Zagória,

Zagóri, or Zagorohória. The landscape is rugged and beautiful, with forests, peaks dropping down abruptly to fast-moving streams, and stone villages blending into the terrain. From one of the villages, **Monodéndri**, you can see directly down into the **Vikos gorge**, one of the most spectacular canyons in Greece. Today there are roads, most of them paved, but until quite recently you could reach these villages only on four feet or two. You can get to most of them by bus, but buses are slow and you will have to wait where the bus drops you for several hours at least, or even until the next day, unless you are prepared to walk. If you do not have a car, rent one in Ioannina. By paved road there are two separate routes into Zagoria and the Pindos mountains from the valley along which the Ioannina–Konitsa road (route 20) runs: the northern route and the southern; we discuss both below.

Earning a living in these remote villages has always been as difficult as the land is beautiful. In the late 18th century there was a spurt of economic activity when Greek ships were permitted to sail under the Russian flag, giving a major boost to Greek commerce. From their flocks of sheep and goats the mountain villagers produced wool thread, which was carried down to Thessaly and woven into cloth. Among the main items made from this cloth were sailors' capes, which were as close to waterproof as could be. Wool thread was exported in bulk by caravans heading east toward the Ottoman capital and northwest to Budapest and Vienna. In the winter the flocks were moved down to the valleys near Ioannina or to the low plains of Thessaly, and in the spring were moved back up to the mountains. This transhumant, or seasonal herding, activity has been going on since antiquity over the same routes without fundamental change until this generation. Now the flocks are vastly smaller than the 10,000 or more they used to number, and the animals are transported in trucks.

Another source of income was the construction trade. Craftsmen's guilds of masons, wood-carvers, and painters from the mountains travelled throughout the Balkans to construct anything from private homes to churches to bridges. In later years the men from Zagoria worked in the Austro-Hungarian empire, much as the *Gastarbeiter* have been working in Germany since the 1950s. The men went off to work and the women and children stayed in the villages. In this century, particularly since World War II and the Greek Civil War, the central government paid little heed to Zagoria, and the village youth left. In the last few years, however, government policy toward Zagoria has warmed, and there is considerable support, notably from the National Tourist Organization, to enliven the villages at least during the summer months. Still, some villages have been abandoned altogether and many have only small, elderly populations.

For all that, Zagoria is fascinating, both because it makes you aware of an ancient way of life most of us have never encountered and because the scenery is stunning. Unless you intend to drive back to Ioannina to spend the night in a hotel there, make arrangements to stay in Zagoria beforehand. Although you might find a room anywhere that someone is willing to rent, only 6 of the 46 Zagoria villages have hotels: Aristi, Papingo, Vitsa, Monodendri, Tsepelovo, and Skamneli. These hotels are pleasant but basic. Don't go to Zagoria for luxury accommodations and gourmet dining. Go for the mountain trails, as many people do—but not so many that you are likely to feel anything like the crush that is standard for much of lowland Greece during the summer season. Here you can get away.

Hiking in the **Pindos** mountains is exhilarating. It takes you much closer to the land and its people than most visitors even dream possible, but you must prepare for it properly. If hiking is your interest, you should get one or both books written by experienced climbers in the Pindos: *Greece on Foot,* by Marc S. Dubin, and *The Mountains of Greece,* by Tim Salmon. If you can find them nowhere else, these books can be purchased in Athens at the store called **Pindos** at 4A Alexandras Avenue (Tel: 01-821-4971). Don't go on the trails without them.

Northern Route into Zagoria

The best-known village on the northern route into the Pindos mountains and Zagoria is Papingo, or Megalo (Big) Papingo, one of the oldest in the area—it is mentioned in Byzantine records of 1352. The turnoff to it from the main road (route 20) is to the east, 4 km (2.5 miles) north of Kalpaki. Ten kilometers (6 miles) from route 20 up into the Pindos toward Papingo is the village of **Arísti**, with one small, functioning hotel and one large hotel under construction. The functioning hotel, with ten rooms and a restaurant, is run by the pleasant **Zeses** family. Three kilometers (2 miles) below the village the road passes over a small stone bridge (built in 1873) that crosses the Voïdomatis river. By the bridge the water forms a pool deep enough to swim in—quickly, for the water is cold—and you can walk up the right bank through a lovely stand of sycamore trees. If the weather is warm you'll find campers with tents along the stream. After a few hundred yards the path peters out on a small rock ledge, from which you must either jump into the water or retrace your steps.

From the river the road climbs steeply up 20 hairpin turns. Stop at one of the turns and look back across the narrow gorge at the **Spiliótissa** monastery, dedicated to the Dormition of the Virgin. Its church was built in 1665.

Once you have passed the hairpin turns you will reach **Megálo Pápingo** after about a 20-minute drive. On your right is the extraordinary **Vikos gorge**, named after the village of Vikos across the valley as you drive up toward Papingo. The heights above the gorge reach more than 4,500 feet above sea level, and the drop straight down to the Voïdomatis river is 3,000 feet.

In Megalo Papingo the **National Tourist Organization** runs a small hotel occupying several old houses, faithfully rebuilt in the traditional style. The manager, Byron Papageorgiou, is from Papingo and is generous with his knowledge of the area. **Koulis Christodoulou**, who runs a store-café-restaurant on the far side of the square, also has rooms to rent, as does **Kalliope Ranga**.

A marvelous small hotel has recently been opened by **Nikos Saxonis** on the road past Koulis Christodoulou's store. Two of the buildings were reconstructed under Nikos's supervision, and the third he designed and built in tune with the village's architecture. Each room is an almost perfect mix of traditional architecture, modern conveniences, and beautiful taste. He and Poly, both of whom speak English fluently, provide bed and breakfast, not other meals, but the breakfast is fresh and delicious.

If you want to use the Hellenic Alpine Club's shelter up on the mountain, make arrangements with Koulis Christodoulou. Across from his store is a small, pleasant restaurant. Kyria Kalliope, as the proprietress is known, also runs a small restaurant in the courtyard of her house, about 30 yards before the National Tourist Organization hotel.

Megalo Papingo and **Mikró** (Little) **Pápingo** are just 4 km (2.5 miles) apart. Approximately halfway between them, where the road takes a sharp right turn after a small ravine, is a small sign that says "Kolymbíthres," here meaning a swimming hole. Leave your car and walk up the narrow path to the left above the stream. After the path bends to the right, you will see a wall with a door that sometimes dams the stream, forming the very cold pool. The rock walls of this narrow little valley have been smoothed by the seasonal torrents, and you can work your way perhaps a hundred yards upstream.

Mikro Papingo has two small, comfortable hotels, the **Agnanti** and the **Dias**. Both are tastefully built and decorated in the traditional style.

You can take a great variety of hikes from Papingo; consult the Dubin and Salmon books. Perhaps the best-known hike is the one up to **Drakólimni**—Dragon Lake—on Mount Gamíla. It takes two and a half hours to reach the Hellenic Alpine shelter on Mount Astrakas, at 6,400 feet; Drakolimni, at 6,726 feet, is about one and a half hours farther on. One edge of the lake is about 15 yards from a straight drop down to the river.

Southern Route into Zagoria

The southern route to Zagoria turns east from the Ioannina–Konitsa road 19 km (12 miles) north of Ioannina, where there is a clearly marked sign to Monodendri. The road turns immediately up from the valley into the mountains and leads to a great number of villages, but you should head for **Monodéndri**, 19 km from the turn. Monodendri has three small hotels: the **Vikos Guest House** by the lower square, and the Dimitris **Daskalopoulos** and **Zarkadas** hotels by the upper square. The Vikos Guest House is the largest, with private bath; all are modern and clean. The Daskalopoulos Hotel is the most unusual, for it occupies a small, 500-year-old building, with the original wooden beams. Its proprietor, Dimitris Daskalopoulos, is generous and outgoing. Monodendri also has two small restaurants, one on the lower and one on the upper square, both offering straightforward, simple fare. The restaurant on the upper square tends to be less crowded.

From the lower square walk down about 15 minutes to the **monastery of Ayía Paraskeví**, built in 1412. Follow the signs up the path running along the side of the Vikos gorge. It's about a 1,600-foot drop from the path straight down to the Voïdomatis river. The path continues perhaps 300 yards to a cave villagers once used as a refuge, and at one point narrows over a short wooden bridge. Take care, for there is no retaining barrier. The view is extraordinary, but you won't enjoy it if you get dizzy.

For an even better view from the top of the gorge, take the sometimes-paved road up past Monodendri for 7 km (4.5 miles). At about 5 km you will begin to see unusual piles of striated limestone. When the road ends, walk down the stone path leading to the edge of the gorge. At certain points the cliffs drop 3,000 feet down to the water. The Voïdomatis river runs for about five miles before joining the Aoos river near Konitsa.

Where else you go depends upon how much you want to drive down beautiful mountain valleys to visit traditional villages and lovely 17th- and 18th-century arched stone bridges. If you go to **Kipi**, for instance, three such bridges will evoke the region's past for you. If you go on to **Tsepélovo** you will see more of them, plus a lovely 18th-century church, though you will have to find the caretaker to let you in. **Dílofo** has a marvelous village square with a towering sycamore tree. During the summer a small restaurant is open here; it's one of the places where you can try the traditional Zagoria dish *alevrópitta,* made of flour, cheese, and eggs.

METSOVO

Métsovo, 56 km (35 miles) northeast of Ioannina (the drive via route 6/E 87 up seemingly innumerable hairpin turns takes one hour), is an anomaly, a bustling Greek mountain village of approximately 3,000 people at 3,792 feet above sea level. Elsewhere in the Greek mountains the villages cling to a tenuous existence, but this one, populated by Vlachs, enjoys unusual vitality. (The Vlachs are a non-Greek people whose ancestors settled in Greece in antiquity.) One of the first things you notice about Metsovo is that there are many small children, unlike in Zagoria. The village's location on the main pass between Epirus and Thessaly helps, as does the infusion of money from villagers who have made fortunes abroad—but clearly these people have learned how to keep their way of life going in the modern world.

Tourism also helps, but it is in scale and is far from the only source of income. Although there are 12 hotels in Metsovo, make reservations before you go. All are family-run and pleasant. The **Apollon Hotel**, run by the Boubas family, is right by the central square and has indoor parking. The **Victoria Hotel**, run by Tassos Vadevoulis, has a commanding view down the mountain. It's on the secondary, not the main road, and has adequate parking space. The hospitality and comfort of these hotels will bring home the fact that you are in the Greek extension of the Alps.

The food in Metsovo is good if simple. Try the **Taverna To**

Spitiko—home-cooking taverna—on the right side of the main road a short way below the Bitouni Hotel. Thirty yards past the square on the road going out and down (not up) to the south is another pleasant taverna. The **Rocco** restaurant and bar is one block behind the Apollon Hotel. Wherever you eat, try the locally produced red wine, Katoi, if you can find it—it's in demand and not always available.

This Vlach village has lived off its flocks of sheep and goats for centuries; the animals are still very much a part of Metsovo life, as you can see from the many cheeses for sale, including the local smoked specialty called Metsovone. Wood carving, weaving, and embroidery are also traditional occupations, resulting in goods that fill the shops all along the main street down to the square. The best weaving and embroidery can be found at the **Metsovo Folk Art Cooperative**, about 50 yards above the Egnatia Hotel, a place well worth a visit whether you buy or not. You can still see elderly men and women wearing the traditional costumes, particularly on Sundays (notice the women's heavily embroidered aprons).

Approximately 50 yards up from and roughly parallel to the main road is the reconstructed **Tosítsa family mansion**, now a museum, worth visiting for the house itself and the various articles of 19th-century mountain housekeeping. The spring, for example, is in the front room. People are guided through in groups, so the door may be shut when you arrive. Even if a group has just started, you won't have to wait more than 20 minutes.

On the far side of the square is the **Metsovo Art Museum**, housing paintings donated by Metsovo's best-known son, Evangelos Averoff. All the canvases displayed were painted by Greeks and are likely to raise considerably your opinion of the country's artists.

Metsovo has two monasteries you should visit. The first is the **monastery of the Panayía** (the Virgin Mary), which is still functioning. Ask for directions and visiting hours from the small newspaper-magazine shop in the square on the left (north) as you come down the main road. The monastery is about a 15-minute walk away, down the road to the left of the square, below the village on the banks of the Arachthos river. It was founded in the 17th century, and for the last 15 years has been beautifully maintained by one nun. The buildings are as lovely as the setting.

The **monastery of Ayios Nikólaos**, founded early in the 14th century and rebuilt about 1700, is also down near the Arachthos river, but below the south side of the village. By foot, take the lower road heading down out of the southwest corner of the square and follow the wooden signs. If you are driving, take the upper road from the same corner of the square. You will have to park your car and walk approximately 80 yards up the grassy slope to the monastery. Long blackened from smoke, the interior walls and ceiling were restored in 1960 by the Tositsa Foundation. Stunning frescoes are now visible, and the church is lighted so you can easily see them.

If you leave Metsovo for Thessaly you will traverse the Katára pass, 5,540 feet above sea level. Stakes considerably higher than the roof of your car are there to mark the road during heavy snowfalls.

GETTING AROUND

If you don't land in Epirus by ferry at Igoumenitsa, you can reach Ioannina by bus from Athens on any one of the 11 buses that leave throughout the day. The trip takes seven hours. For information, ask someone who speaks Greek to call the national bus system, KTEL, in Athens; Tel: (01) 512-9363. Buses are also available from Thessaloniki; Tel: (031) 512-444.

It is far better to fly into Ioannina. From Athens there are daily flights (50 minutes) and from Thessaloniki two flights a week (40 minutes). From Ioannina you can travel by bus to virtually all the villages and towns in Epirus, but buses are not a practical means of transportation if you don't speak Greek and are operating on anything resembling a schedule. Instead, rent a car from one of the agencies in Ioannina, and talk with the National Tourist Organization there about where to stay, particularly if you go up into the mountains. The roads are in good condition and well marked. Note that the route numbers on many maps and included in this text for easy reference are not, in fact, posted on the roads themselves.

ACCOMMODATIONS REFERENCE

▶ **Agnanti Hotel.** Mikro Papingo, 440 16 Epirus. Tel: (0653) 411-23.

▶ **Apollon Hotel.** Metsovo, 442 00 Epirus. Tel: (0656) 418-44.

▶ **Koulis Christodoulou.** Megalo Papingo, 440 16 Epirus. Tel: (0653) 411-38.

▶ **Dimitris Daskalopoulos Hotel.** Monodendri, 440 17 Epirus. Tel: (0653) 612-33.

- Dias Hotel. **Mikro Papingo**, 440 16 Epirus. Tel: (0653) 411-08.
- Galaxy Hotel. **Ioannina**, 452 21 Epirus. Tel: (0651) 250-56.
- Kalliope Ranga. **Megalo Papingo**, 440 16 Epirus. Tel: (0653) 410-81.
- Lichnos Beach Hotel. **Parga**, 480 60 Epirus. Tel: (0684) 312-57.
- Louros Springs Hotel. P.O. Box 1027, **Ioannina**, 451 10 Epirus. Tel: (0654) 712-02.
- National Tourist Organization Hotel. **Megalo Papingo**, 440 16 Epirus. Tel: (0653) 411-25.
- Olympic Hotel. **Ioannina**, 452 21 Epirus. Tel: (0651) 222-33.
- Nikos Saxonis Hotel. **Megalo Papingo**, 440 16 Epirus. Tel: (0653) 416-15.
- Victoria Hotel. **Metsovo**, 442 00 Epirus. Tel: (0656) 417-71.
- Vikos Guest House. **Monodendri**, 440 17 Epirus. Tel: (0653) 612-32.
- Xenia Hotel. **Arta**, 471 00 Epirus. Tel: (0681) 274-13.
- Xenia Hotel. **Ioannina**, 452 21 Epirus. Tel: (0651) 250-87.
- Zarkados Hotel. **Monodendri**, 440 17 Epirus. Tel: (0653) 612-05.
- Zeses Hotel. **Aristi**, 440 16 Epirus. Tel: (0653) 411-47.

THESSALY

By Tom Stone

Tom Stone first visited Greece in 1959 and has lived continuously in the country since 1970. He is the author of Tom Stone's Greek Handbook, The Greek Food & Drink Book, *and* Patmos, *a history of and guide to the island. He has had short stories and a novel published in the United States, and articles of local interest have appeared in Greek periodicals.*

Thessaly (Thessalía) seems a place between places, a huge amorphous plain couched between central Greece and Macedonia, Epirus and the north Aegean Sea, through which travellers have passed for eons on their way to somewhere else—Athens or Macedonia, Europe or the Bosphorus. For centuries the area was locked, as it were, into isolated obscurity by its two notoriously narrow border passes, Thermopylae in the south and the Vale of Tempe in the north. Its coastline was so inhospitable that the Athenians didn't even bother to man it against the Persian invasions, and the mountain range on its western border, the Pindos, was also forbidding (even today it often becomes impassable in winter). Indeed, the apostle Paul was said (in a fifth-century addendum to the Acts of the Apostles) to have "neglected" Thessaly on his first missionary journey to Greece, bypassing it on his way from Veria to Athens.

Visitors today still do the same, sadly unaware that not far from the main road (national highway E 92) and railway lines are some of the most stunningly beautiful areas in all of Greece: the phantasmagorical mountains and monasteries of the Meteora, at the foothills of the Pindos mountains to the west; the major port city of Volos and the attendant wonders of Mount Pelion to the east, whose summit is crowned by a ski resort, its eastern base fringed with Capri-like beaches, and its slopes swathed in great natural splendor; and to the north, the Vale of Tempe, a narrow, lush gorge dividing Mount Ossa from Olympus, home of the gods.

MAJOR INTEREST

Volos
Archaeological Museum
Exhibition of works by the folk artist Aristides Laoudi
Seaside promenade

Mount Pelion
Drive through its lush mountain landscape; sea views
Villages of Makrinitsa, Zagora, Milies, Vizitsa
Beaches of Horefto and Milopotamos
Skiing at Agriolefkes

The Meteora
Unique landscapes
Monasteries, their settings and Byzantine art
Villages of Kalambaka and Kastraki

Vale of Tempe

THE PLAIN

Until about two million years ago the Thessalian plain was an immense lake (and even in Herodotus's time was purported to have been so by local tradition). Geological upheavals then drained the water and, in so doing, exposed the huge conglomerate formations on its shores and bed that now form the strange landscape of the Meteora. The alluvial land plain that was left is one of the most fertile in Greece, yielding grains, tobacco, fruit, and rice as well as providing excellent grazing land for horses, cattle, and sheep.

It was this plain that attracted Neolithic farmers, now believed to have first settled here with their matriarchal cultures in about 7000 B.C., having crossed into Greece via the Bosphorus from Asia. One of the earliest Neolithic settlements that dotted the plain, and the most complete yet discovered, was **Sesklo**, located near the present-day port of Volos on the Pagasitlikos Bay. (A beautifully presented exhibition in the Volos Archaeological Museum details finds from this era from all over Thessaly and includes maps, photographs of sites, and a display illustrating daily life and work in a typical Neolithic settlement.)

It was sometime during this period that tribes of cen-

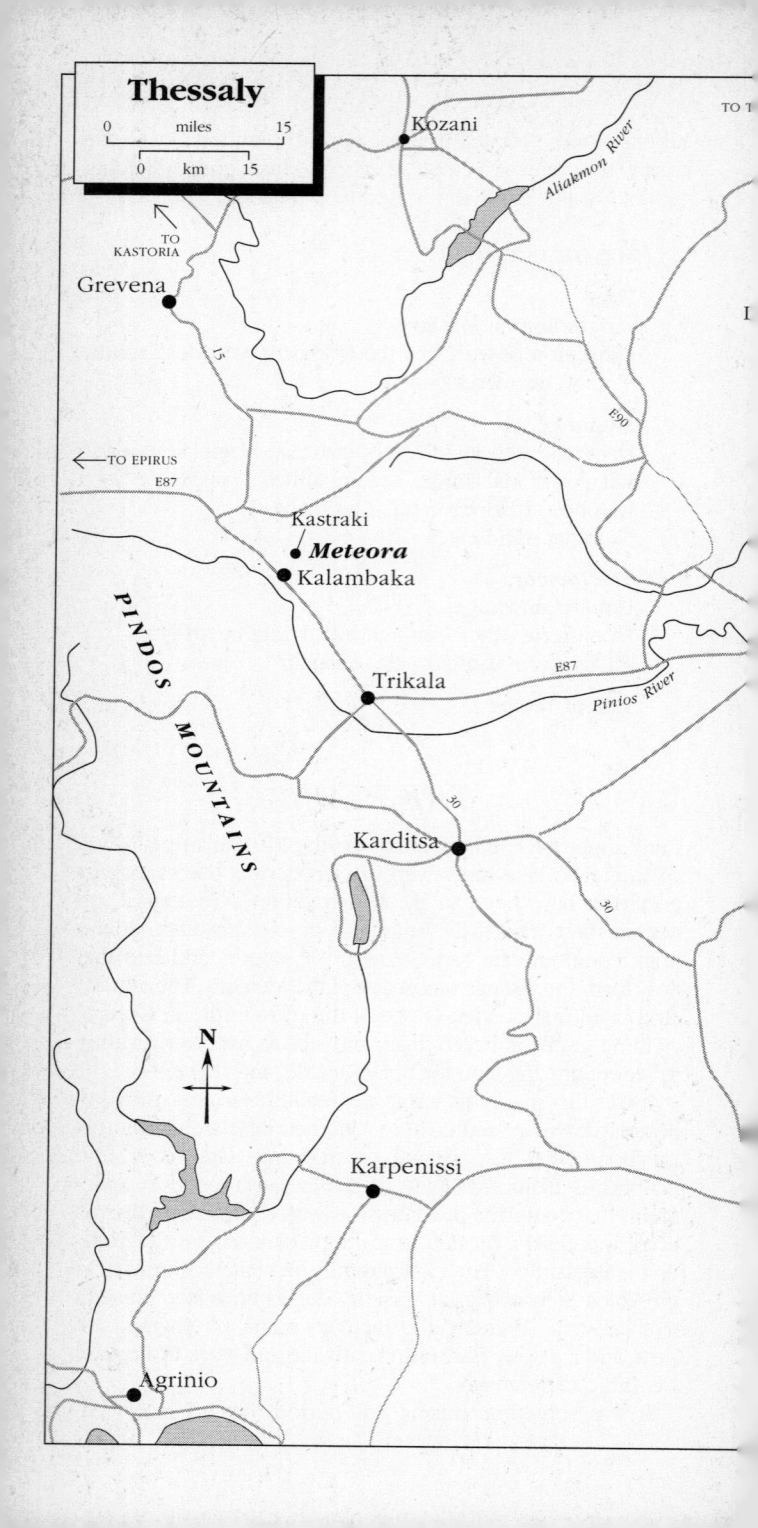

Thessaly

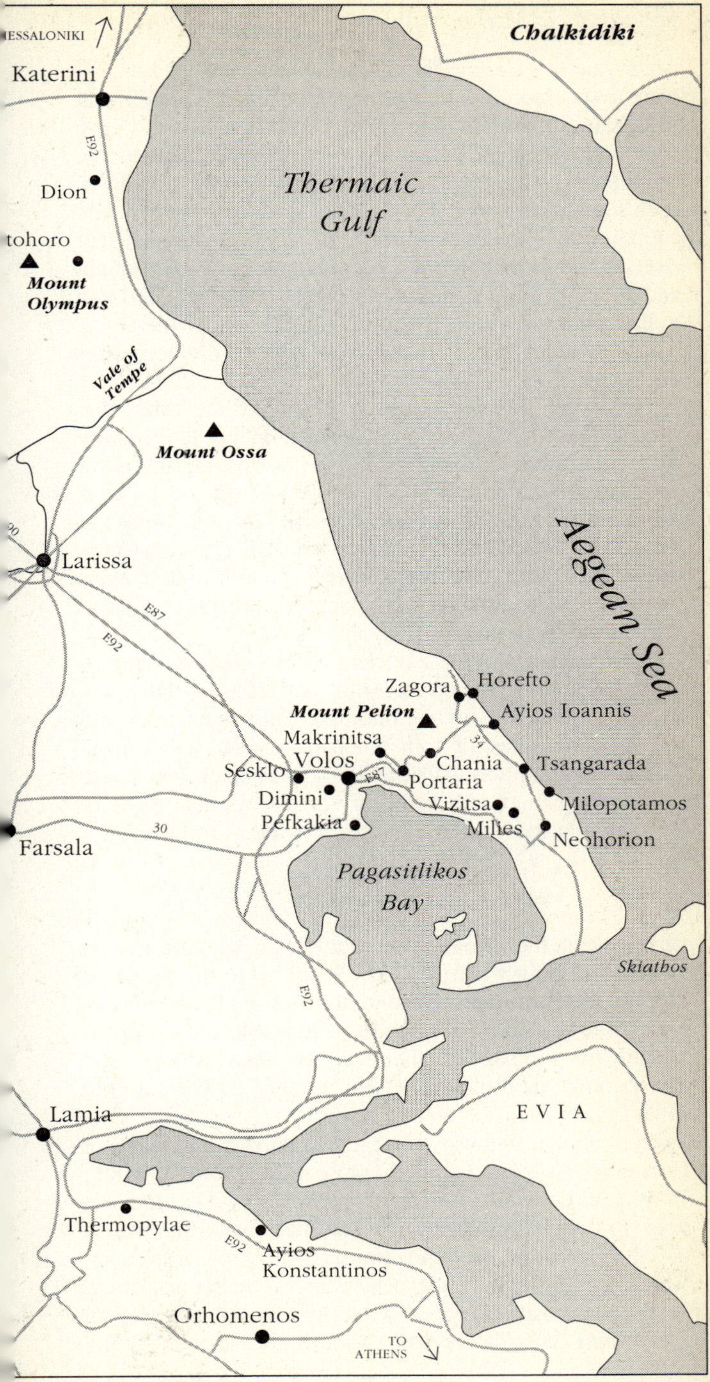

ESSALONIKI
Chalkidiki
Katerini
E92
Dion
Thermaic
Gulf
tohoro
Mount
Olympus
Vale of
Tempe
Mount Ossa
Aegean Sea
Larissa
E87
E92
Zagora
Horefto
Mount Pelion
Ayios Ioannis
Makrinitsa
34
Volos
Chania
Sesklo
E87
Portaria
Tsangarada
Dimini
Vizitsa
Milopotamos
Pefkakia
Milies
Neohorion
30
Farsala
Pagasitlikos
Bay
Skiathos
E92
EVIA
Lamia
Thermopylae
E92
Ayios
Konstantinos
Orhomenos
TO
ATHENS

taurs—a race of beings thought to be half man, half horse—were first rumored to be roaming the plain. It is not difficult to imagine how migrating tribes, reaching the tops of the surrounding mountains, could perceive Thessalian horse breeders crossing the lowlands on their steeds far below as such strange creatures. Whatever the case, both the centaurs and Thessaly's horses became renowned throughout ancient Greece, the former figuring prominently in Greek thought and literature and art, the latter playing a duly celebrated role in the armies of Philip II and his son, Alexander the Great, whose wonder horse, Bucephalus, was of the legendary Thessalian stock.

The name Thessaly comes from one of the tribes that overran the Neolithic communities in about the 12th century B.C., when waves of migrants pressed down from the north and east on their way—such as people do today—to a supposed paradise farther south. These "Thessali" were the tribe from which sprang various baronial clans that controlled the countryside from centers such as Larissa (a word of non-Greek origin meaning "citadel" or "king's place") and created the quasi state of Thessaly.

Of the remains of these ancient centers—Larissa, Pherae, Tricca, Krannon, Pharsalos, Arne, and Elatea—little now exists of interest to anyone but a specialist in the area; and the modern cities of today's plain—Larissa, the capital, Trikala, and Karditsa—are market towns much less intent on servicing the needs of history or visitors than those of the plain's farmers and the transport of their produce.

Larissa

Lárissa sits in the virtual center of the plain, with the seaport of Volos an hour's drive (57 km/35 miles) to the southeast and the Meteora rocks at the foothills of the Pindos mountains an hour and a half (80 km/50 miles) to the west. It is roughly two-thirds of the way between Athens and Thessaloniki via the E 92, a total distance of 510 km (320 miles).

The national highway, route E 92, skirts the suburbs of Larissa, which is just as well, because there is little reason to stop in this crowded, bustling commercial city—except, perhaps, to catch a bus elsewhere. The spacious central plateia and the Alkazár park, on the opposite side of the Pinios river, which runs through the city center, offer refreshing places to relax and perhaps have a sip of the city's prized *tsípouro* with *mezedákia* (hors d'oeuvres). Tsipouro, the schnapps of the north, is a cousin to ouzo but is not flavored with anise; somewhat smoother than ouzo and slightly sweet, it, too, clouds a little when water is added. Near and north of the square are the remains of a Classical temple and a Byzantine fortress, the **Froúrion**. A short walk down Eleftheríou Venizélou Street is the **Archaeological Museum**. Housed in a small and somewhat dilapidated former mosque, it contains finds dating from Paleolithic to Imperial Roman times, a sadly desultory display of Larissa's rich history.

In the fifth century B.C. Larissa was the home of the most powerful of the Thessalian ruling families, the Aleuadai, who supported Xerxes during his attempt to conquer Athens in 480 B.C. This losing cause, plus rivalries with other families of Thessaly, weakened the entire alliance, which then came under Spartan domination in the Peloponnesian Wars.

A century later, a revived Thessaly under the leadership of an opposing city, Pherai, became an important and imposing force in Pan-Greek politics. In 370 B.C. Pherai's leader, Jason, was assassinated just as he was assembling a large army for purposes that will never be known, although it is assumed to have been an attempt at hegemony over all of Greece. This goal was then left to be achieved by the man the Aleuadai called in for help in regaining power from Pherai: Philip II, king of Macedon.

In 197 B.C. the invading Romans freed Thessaly from Macedonian control, and it has remained a distinct political entity ever since. Because of the flatness of its plain and strategic central position in the country, however, not to mention the richness of its soil, Thessaly remained an irresistible battleground for armies, including those of Caesar and Pompey at Pharsala in A.D. 48; the Franks, Bulgarians, Byzantines, and Ottomans; and the Nazis and Greek Civil War guerillas, the latter two engaging in conflicts that made targets even of Meteora's monasteries.

The bus station for the Meteora (via Trikala) is on the south side of the city near the railway station. On the north side, just two blocks down Olympou Street from the Archaeological Museum, is the bus station for Volos–Mount Pelion, our next destination.

VOLOS

While primarily a center of commerce involved with the export of Thessaly's goods, Volos has recently, under a

Communist mayor popular with all colors of Greece's political spectrum, undergone a civic refurbishment that makes it one of the most attractive port cities in the country. It is situated on the Pagasitlikós Bay at the base of the mountainous Pelion peninsula, which separates the bay from the north Aegean Sea.

While the layout and architecture of the city as a whole are functional and uninspired, most of it having been built after earthquakes virtually leveled the old town in 1954 and 1955, the waterfront area has now been made into a seaside promenade (Argonáfton Street) more than a mile long that is a delight to both the eye and the soul. There are parks, playgrounds, a quayside dotted with excellent modern sculptures, an aquarium in the works, and a narrow-gauge railway on which will run the prewar, bright-red little train (called the *traináki* by the locals) that once connected Volos with the villages on the east side of the Pelion peninsula.

At its western end, near the landing stage for ships to and from the Sporades, the promenade features a long line of spacious outdoor cafés. At the eastern end, in the area named Anavros, is a small, tree-shaded beach replete with old-fashioned fish tavernas. The two best of these are **Ta Palia Kalamakia** (The Old Bamboo Canes), which serves only fish, and **O Nestoras**, which serves fish and a host of other freshly grilled and prepared dishes. The promenade is also the site of the city's best hotel, the modern **Xenia**, which has one side directly on the sea and the other facing the promenade's park. It is currently undergoing extensive renovation, much delayed by the government's lack of financing. The **Park Hotel**, just off the seafront park, is of the anonymous international style of the 1970s, well appointed, glass-and-marble comfortable, with some rooms facing the park. Two sister hotels, the **Hotel Galaxy** and the **Hotel Kypseli**, the latter on a corner of the western promenade, sit side by side in the center of town, bordering a quiet, traffic-free side street. Built in the early 1960s and with some rooms without bath, the Galaxy and Kypseli are nevertheless well kept and serviceable.

The **Archaeological Museum** (on the corner of the promenade and Athanasáki Street) has, as mentioned earlier, an excellent display of Neolithic finds. It is also home to an unmatched collection of painted grave *stelai* from the Hellenistic period and finds from the Mycenaean, Protogeometric, Geometric, Classical, and Roman eras. Equaling the Neolithic display in interest and quality of presentation is a reconstruction of burials from all these periods, complete with skeletons and various offerings and personal possessions of the deceased. But perhaps the best aspect of the museum is the extremely clear and educational way in which everything is arranged. The exhibitors obviously had schoolchildren very much in mind, a great boon to anyone who is still a "child" in this area.

The self-designated **Folk Museum**, just down the road (18 Plastíras Street), is equally impressive but for utterly the opposite reasons. Set in the home of its creator, the 86-year-old folk artist Aristides Laoudi, it is a jam-packed, floor-to-ceiling explosion of paintings, collages, and sculptures that have burst forth from this true phenomenon of a man since he was hospitalized in 1981 and lay in bed looking for something to do with his hands. A former furniture maker, Laoudi took up painting and produced primitive-style works that rank with the best of their kind. They are part of a local tradition that includes works by the great primitive master Theophilos (1878–1934), some of whose murals can be seen in the villages of Mount Pelion, just above Volos. But don't bother to bargain for a purchase with Aristides. He doesn't sell, he just paints.

At night the entire promenade, from the docks and coffee shops along its western end to the tavernas and beach on the east, becomes a concourse for what seems to be all of Volos out for a walk. The best restaurant in the center of town, **Petros Dzafolias**, is at the far end of the western promenade at 40 Argonafton (Argonauts) Street, just opposite the berth for the Flying Dolphin. Opened in 1970 by its eponymous owner, who still runs the place with a family friend, the restaurant serves only grilled meats and refuses to open for lunch, lest the quality of its evening service and cooking be compromised. The "other best," the **Remvi**, is on the eastern side just beyond the Archaeological Museum, at 22 Nikos Plastiras. Run by two brothers, Remvi is a venerable Volos favorite, spacious and unpretentious, with tables indoors and out. Its specialties are grilled meats and fish, its decor plain white tablecloths.

Three kilometers (2 miles) to the southwest, across the harbor from the promenade and the bronze statue of the ship *Argo,* lies the bayside area of **Pefkákia**, site of the third-century B.C. city of Demetrias and the sixth-century B.C. city of Pagasai. This is also said to be the location from which the legendary Argonauts embarked on their voyage in search of the Golden Fleece in the second millennium B.C.

It was from here in 1984 that the writer-sailor Tim Severin launched his full-scale model of the *Argo* in an adventurous attempt to prove that such a craft could have made it through the daunting currents of the Bosphorus up to the Black Sea. Severin and others believe that Pefkakia may have been the very place where the original boat was built and set sail. Thanks to his success and the continuing efforts of archaeologists, there is increasing speculation that Jason may have been an actual historical figure.

But even if nearby Pefkakia did not have such a legendary connection, it would still be worth the short taxi ride solely for its breathtaking view of Volos at night, with the lights of Mount Pelion rising like constellations around the unseen villages of Makrinitsa to the left and Portaria (see below) to the right. Two discotheques occupy this wonderful location: the **Burgi** (open only in summer), closer to the water and built entirely on outdoor terraces, and **Ratatouille**, higher up and open winter and summer. Although not quite as "heavenly" as it is at night, the view by day can be enjoyed from the neighboring beach of **Alikés**, where there are two tavernas, the local favorite being **Souipas**.

MOUNT PELION

In ascending this mountain the visitor takes abrupt leave of both the modern world and the Mycenaean heroic age, and is borne upward in time and space to the era of Ottoman rule in the 16th and 17th centuries. It is a startling transition, with no line of demarcation between the end of Volos and the beginning of the mountain along the street leading up it, Eleftheriou Venizelou (and very few signs either naming Pelion or showing you how to get there). But suddenly, one of the characteristic timber-framed mansions of the area rises in stately splendor beside the road going up, and it is clear that some sort of time capsule has been entered.

There are several ways of viewing Pelion, which is actually more a range than a single mountain, rising to its peak of 5,415 feet near the ski run of Agriolefkes and descending gradually toward the southern end of the peninsula. You can either begin at that end, leaving Volos along the coast road to the south and working upward from the village of Milies or Neohóri around the eastern seacoast, ascending to the peak and then dropping down into Volos, or vice versa, as in the description that follows.

Either of these routes, if done in a proper, leisurely manner with stops for lunch, walks, and perhaps a swim, takes a full day, at least nine to ten hours. A less rigorous alternative would be to go up the mountain from Volos, drop straight down the other side to the beach of Horefto (or Ayios Ioannis or Milopotamos—more on these beaches below), and come back again over the same route in the late afternoon, when the sun is setting in the western plains below and beyond Volos.

Mount Pelion was first settled in its present form when the Ottomans took long-term possession of it after 1453. Because one of the few freedoms the Turks allowed was that of religion, much of the Christian population either joined monasteries or huddled around them for protection. And because monasteries were established mainly in remote, mountainous areas for the purpose of solitude, Pelion became the site of some of the many new Greek communities that sprang up during the Turkish occupation.

The town houses clustered near the monasteries have a distinctive architecture that identifies them as primarily defensive dwellings. Here families lived on the lighter, upper floors of wood and plaster; the lower floors, made of thick stone and having narrow slits for windows, were generally used for storage, cooking, and preserving food. But later, as the Greeks and Turks learned to coexist and the Greeks began to use the harbor below as a center of commerce, the purpose and architectural style of the houses became less defensive and more outwardly luxurious, displaying wealth rather than guarding it and resulting in the magnificent mansions that you see today.

While there are scatterings of groups of these houses all over the Pelion range, the finest concentration is found in the village of **Makrinítsa**, a 30-minute drive up from the center of Volos.

If you are driving on your own rather than taking a local or tour bus, be aware that the villages and turnoffs on the mountain come up quite suddenly on this continually curving road, leaving very little time to make a decision about whether or not to stop. Therefore it is best to have a specific destination in mind and eyes on the lookout for the necessary signposts, some of which are very misleading, as are maps and local guidebooks.

For example, while most maps indicate that the turnoff—to the left—for Makrinitsa comes before the village of Portaria, it actually comes in the middle, as the main road curves right just after the town's gas station. A five-minute drive then takes you to the lush, tree-shaded parking area just outside the village—if, that is, the road is not packed with cars and tour buses.

Nevertheless, the village is worth the visit, no matter how many tourists and souvenir shops crowd the lanes. Of particular interest in summer is the spacious village square shaded by huge plane trees and surrounded by various cafés and a restaurant, the **Exostis**. Perched on the edge of a bluff, both the restaurant and the square offer a marvelous view of Volos below; here is a perfect spot for lunch or a sunset ouzo.

Also of interest in the square is a mural by the folk artist Theóphilos on the wall of the small café **Diamantis**. The painting depicts the death of Katsantonis, one of the great Robin Hood–like heroes of the resistance against the Turks. The café is unfortunately too small for more than two or three tables and does not serve food, so a quick glimpse of the mural is usually all you can get before being conducted to a table outdoors.

Frescoes by Theophilos can also be seen in the **church of Ayia Triáda**, up the hill through the village along a path that begins behind the church in the main square. Also in this direction is the 18th-century **monastery of Panayía Makrinítissa**, around which the town was originally built.

If that sunset ouzo is still being contemplated—or even if it is not—you might consider spending the night in Makrinitsa. The Greek National Tourist Organization has splendidly renovated, and is renting rooms in, three of Makrinitsa's traditional mansions (*archontiká*): the Mousli, Xiradaki, and Sisilianou guesthouses. These have only a limited number of beds (15) and are naturally prized accommodations, so reservations should be made days if not months in advance.

The **Xiradáki** and **Mouslí** houses (to the east and west of the main square, respectively) offer spectacular views of Volos and its bay; the **Sisiliánou** house is situated directly above the square and is higher than the other two, but its view is somewhat obstructed by plane trees. All three houses were lovingly restored following the earthquakes of 1954 and 1955, with the decor styled in keeping with the original. Each is built according to the same basic design, which includes a walled garden, where breakfast is served when weather permits (other meals are not offered); a reception-living-dining room on the ground floor, formerly the site of work and storage space; and guest rooms with a common bath on the first floor where once were sewing rooms and the kitchen. Last but not least is the upper floor, the most luxurious part of the house, where the master and his wife would receive their guests and where the study and master bedroom were located. The rooms on this floor have the best views. In addition, each has a newly installed private bathroom—an entirely forgivable anachronism. During the winter season there is central heating for visitors who come to Pelion for skiing and holiday fun. These tend to be Athenians who can afford the relatively upscale prices of the archontika plus the cost of the trip itself. In summer the clientele is somewhat more international.

Upon leaving Makrinitsa you will be sorely (and quite rightly) tempted to make an immediate stop in the lovely square of **Portariá**. The village is known for its wine and cheese and is also the starting point for a three-and-a-half-hour hike up to one of the highest peaks on Pelion, the 5,077-foot Pliesídi, where there existed in antiquity a temple of Zeus Akraios and the cave said to be that of the centaur Chiron.

Chánia is another 25 minutes up the mountain (magnificent views) and is the resort town for the ski center **Agrioléfkes**. The culinary specialty of the village (actually that of all Volos and Pelion) is a dish called *spetsofái,* a kind of Greek *piperiade* made of sausages, green pepper, and puréed tomatoes and seasoned with paprika, tasty and filling anytime and wonderfully warming in winter.

The trip down the tortuous and often rain-crumbled road on Pelion's eastern side is one of the most stunning in all of Greece. There are streams and small waterfalls, and tunnel after tunnel of forest so thick that the air turns green—or greenish white, if a passing low-hanging cloud happens to envelop the mountain slope. Below, visible in brief snatches and coming closer with every curve, is the Aegean coastline.

The village of **Zagorá**, about a 25-minute drive down from Chania, is considerably rougher than the villages on the Volos side of the mountain, but not without its charms, including a large tree-shaded square with a beautiful Pelion-style 18th-century church.

Horeftó, the port village of Zagora, is about another 15 minutes away but on a road with tighter curves, if that's possible. Nevertheless, its sandy beach, luminous sea, and as yet not overdeveloped ambience make it seem, particularly after the twisting and turning, like Tahiti. There are several recently constructed but charmingly low-key rooming houses that can be booked from agencies in Volos—the **Erato** pension, the **Hotel Katerina**, and the house of the **Dimitroulia Brothers**, all facing the beach. Caïques float in the harbor, trees line the beach road, children play in the dusty street—all in all an attractively sleepy atmosphere.

There is a bus from Volos once during the week and also on Saturdays and Sundays.

Ayios Ioánnis, about 30 minutes south along the beautifully verdant road from Zagora (route 34), is similar to Horefto but somewhat more developed. There are numerous cafés and tavernas, various small hotels, jet skis for rent, and a large camping area at the far end of the beach. Nevertheless, it still retains a certain charm from its past as a simple fishing village, a characteristic that is particularly evident when you are dining on the home cooking of the **Ostria** taverna. Situated among the trees just to the left of the last curve of the only road that descends into the village (park there first and then walk back), the Ostria specializes in a "pie" filled with wild greens (*hortópita*) and offers excellent general fare. The kitchen will also prepare special orders of anything within reason if given a day or two's warning. The Ostria has a wonderful view of the sea from its tree-shaded, flower-bedecked outdoor dining area. Tel: (0426) 313-31.

In utter contrast to the development of Ayios Ioannis are the singular beaches at **Milopótamos**, about an hour and a quarter's drive south on route 34. On the way, in the village of **Tsangaráda**, is the charming *plateía* of Ayía Paraskeví. To the left and down a small road turning off the main one at a roadside taverna, the plateia is covered by and barely contains, with its church, an ancient plane tree some 49 feet in diameter. In the shade of the tree is a small café with tables where a pause can be wonderfully refreshing.

The turnoff for Milopotamos comes immediately after the village of Tsangarada. A curving 7-km (4.5-mile) road leads down to and abruptly ends at a small, walled promontory overlooking the sea. At the top are two tavernas and a parking area. Some 325 feet below, on either side of the promontory, are two cliff-enclosed beaches. The one on the left, i.e., to the north, is the most beautiful and can be easily viewed from the top of the promontory as well as from the taverna that perches on the cliff edge behind it. Stairs lead from this taverna down to the beach, which seems too spectacular to be real, looking as though it had been fixed up by a film company to resemble Capri and then left there once the movie-making was over. Framed by a tight, U-shaped curve of rocks, it is covered with fine white sand on which the crystal-clear turquoise sea swells, breaks, and recedes. At the far end a natural arch in the rocks points through to more sea and the rugged coast to the north.

In contrast, the beach to the south, which is not visible

from either the promontory or the taverna above, is much wider and covered with stones. But not ordinary stones—smooth, white, sensuously rounded ones of varying shapes and sizes arrayed in waves, looking as if they belonged to a dream about a landscape by Dali.

The drive back to Volos along route 34 and around the southern flank of the Pelion range is long (about one and a half to two hours), but again, spectacular, with a large section of it curving around sheer drops to ravines and to the sea below—fortunately on a comfortingly good and reasonably wide road.

The Makrinitsa-like village of **Vizítsa** and its companion town of **Miliés** are about a 45-minute drive southwest of Milopotamos. You'll come to Milies first, the actual living center of the two; Vizitsa now exists only for its beauty, having been recently resurrected by the tourist bureau's renovation of its lovely mansions as guesthouses. There are four of these—**Yeroulánou**, **Katsanáki**, **Kyriakópoulou**, and **Kontou**—with capacities ranging from 8 to 29 beds and similar in layouts, furnishings, and rustic elegance to the houses in Makrinitsa described above. Kontou, located the highest up, has the best of the generally excellent views.

Aside from its cheese bread (*tyrópsomo*), Milies is particularly famous for its role in the revolution against the Turks. Its school is noted for having kept the Greek passion for freedom alive during the occupation, which did not end until 1881 in Thessaly, 49 years after Athens and the rest of the southern mainland had been freed. Milies is also the birthplace of well-known members of the secret Philikí Etaireía society, most particularly Anthimos Gazis, who raised the flag of revolt in Thessaly on May 1, 1821, in Milies' church of the Taxiarches. Built in 1741, this structure is typical of the post-Byzantine style of the period.

On the half-hour drive along the coast road back to Volos are a number of small villages and summer resort towns, all with good beaches, a surprisingly clean sea (considering their proximity to Volos), camping facilities, and fine tavernas. Along the seaside promenades in this area a time-honored nightly ritual takes place: *nymfopázaro*—"bride bargaining" would be the literal if somewhat clumsy translation—in which parents of eligible young women take their daughters for a stroll so that they might be perused and chatted up by parents of equally eligible young sons. Though slowly dying out in much of Greece, this custom still maintains a strong foothold here.

THE METEORA

From Mount Pelion to Thessaly's other famous heights—the Meteora—you must travel westward, across the entire Thessalian plain to the village of Kalambaka at the foothills of the Pindos mountains, a pleasant 144-km (89-mile) drive through rolling farmland on a well-surfaced two-lane asphalt highway, route E 87.

The weirdly beautiful natural phenomenon called the Meteora is a cluster of immense perpendicular rock formations rising, in some instances, to heights of more than 2,000 feet, grouped within an area of about two square miles just to the north of Kalambaka. Some 600 years ago Byzantine monks began erecting monastic communities atop these odd megaliths. "Monasteries of the air," Patrick Leigh Fermor described them, while aptly calling the rocks themselves "the insane mountains of the Meteora" (see Bibliography).

In recent years **Kalambáka**, which sits astride route E 87, has sprouted a plethora of tourist shops, fast-food eateries, cafés, pubs, tavernas, restaurants, rooming houses, and hotels minuscule and grand. The best of the latter are the luxurious **Divani Motel**, just on the eastern outskirts of Kalambaka, its swimming pool facing route E 87 on the right as you arrive from Trikala; the new and more intimate **Hotel Antoniadi**, across the road from the Divani; and the tiny, utterly delightful **Hotel Meteora**, situated on the western outskirts of Kalambaka just under the looming rock face that hides the village from the Meteora proper. This last hotel, lovingly cared for by its owner, Nikos Gekas, has eight simply furnished rooms, all with showers, and most with a magnificent view of both the rock face and the Thessalian plain spread out below. It is a favorite of foreign embassy staff from Athens as well as many other devoted clientele, and therefore should be booked at least a month in advance.

Of the same name, **The Meteora** is Kalambaka's best and most intriguing taverna. It is located near the hotel on the village's "second square" (it has no name other than that: "*ee déftheri plateía*"), where the road for the Meteora branches off to the northwest from the E 87. The owner of the taverna, Haris Gertsos, has a passion for collecting things, particularly wine and beer bottles, and has consequently lined the walls of his establishment with an extraordinary display of these and other items from floor to ceiling—and wherever else he can find a spot. The food is supervised with a similarly cheerful passion by his wife, Katie. It's basic Greek fare, but of good quality and variety.

This second square tends to be the natural center of activity for visitors to Kalambaka. In front of the Meteora taverna is a taxi stand where cabs can be hired for trips to as many of the Meteora's monasteries as you wish, while one block south of the square is Kalambaka's bus station, where morning and midday coaches leave for the first of the Meteora's monasteries, Great Meteoron (see below). From here you can also catch buses for Trikala, Ioannina and the rest of Epirus, Grevena in Macedonia, and various Thessalian villages. On the western side of the square is Kalambaka's only foreign newsstand and, a few blocks to the north (see the small signposts on the northwest corner), the 12th-century **cathedral of the Dormition** (called *paliá mitrópolis*—"old cathedral"—by the locals). The cathedral has very good frescoes by three Cretan artists, including the great Theophanes, and a magnificent marble pulpit indicative of the stature of this church, and the area, during the Byzantine era.

Finally, the second square is where you catch the local bus (labeled "Trikala" because it goes there later) for Kalambaka's sister village of **Kastráki**, surprisingly still the best-kept secret of the area. Not only is the village beautiful in itself, but it is from here that the spectacular impact of the Meteora becomes truly apparent.

For this reason, Kastraki—2 km (about a mile) northwest of the second square on the Meteora road—is best approached on foot by way of a side road signposted "Old Habitation of Kastraki," which branches to the right off the Meteora road about half a kilometer outside of Kalambaka, just opposite a roadside taverna. This detour—also possible by car on a new asphalt surface—leads around the foot of the first Meteora rocks visible after you leave Kalambaka. Here, in natural caves scooped by erosion out of the sides of the pinnacles, you can see the remnants of abandoned monastic habitations as well as, lower down, rock-walled stables still in use.

After an easy 20-minute walk, the road leads into the "Old Habitation," i.e., the upper, original area of Kastraki that is now its poorest neighborhood. From here the village cascades downward to the Meteora–Kalambaki road in a tumble of rustic, tree-nestled, red-tiled roofs, with one of the rough cement-paved streets wide enough to take a modern car, even through some difficult turns.

While proudly still the domain of donkeys and roosters and

to some extent disdainful of the gross commercialism of Kalambaka, Kastraki is nevertheless allowing a certain number of tourist facilities to penetrate its privacy without marring (so far) its beauty. There are a small number of rooms for rent, with the **Hotel Kastraki** (actually a small, knickknack-cluttered private house) being the most venerable, and the "super lux" rooming house of John and Gregory **Ziogas**, recently of Las Vegas, the newest and best equipped. Both are next to each other on the Meteora road about half a kilometer past the fork that leads to the central square of the village. Also on the main road, about 200 yards before this fork and on the Kalambaka side of Kastraki, is an excellent campground, the **Vlachos Kastraki**, which boasts both a swimming pool filled from artesian wells and newly installed tiled and stainless steel washing and toilet facilities that would not look out of place in the swankiest of modern hotels. There are several tree-shaded tavernas along this main road, all of equal quality. The one most favored by people from Kalambaka, however, is **Boufidis's**, on the Meteora road just north of the village.

Also north of the village is the small **chapel of Ayios Yiórgos Mándilas** (St. George of the Kerchief), built in a shallow cave up in the rock formation east of the road between Kastraki and Great Meteoron, about a ten-minute walk outside the village. Festooned across the face of the cave are lines of brightly colored scarves and kerchiefs. Every year on St. George's day, April 23 (or the first Friday after Easter, should April 23 fall during Lent that year), young men of the village make the often dangerous climb up to the chapel to replace these scarves with new ones. Some say the origins of this observance are unknown; others recount that back in the mists of time, someone whose leg was hurt bound it there with a pocket handkerchief and was miraculously cured; and others relate that these kerchiefs are hung by the young men as signals of love and serious intent to the lady of their choice.

Meanwhile, the rocks of the Meteora loom ever present, visible even at night from the glow of lights in the village, thrusting upward around Kastraki in breathtaking, otherworldly splendor. It is from here that you get a true sense of how they must have awed the first hermits—and called to them as well, with their echoes of some convulsive primeval grasping of the earth for the heavens.

As noted earlier, and as is visible close up, the rocks of the Meteora are conglomerates of stones, sand, and soil formed on the bottom of the great lake and river beds that once covered all of Thessaly. Water currents swirling around them seemed to have created their strange and distinctive shapes, which were then exposed and subjected to the smoothing effects of rain and wind when geological upheavals drained the lake some two million years ago.

How the monks managed to get themselves—much less their materials—up to the tops of these pillars in order to build their monasteries is, however, another question. A common tale is that Saint Athanasios, the founder of the original monastery of the Metamorphosis, or Transfiguration (now known as Great Meteoron), was carried up to its summit by an eagle. Some people smile, but this is about as easy to believe as any other theory, including one postulated on the rock-scaling abilities of 14th-century monks.

While details of the early history of the monastic settlements are scarce, it seems that the region initially attracted lone ascetics who settled in the rocks above the plain; according to tradition, the hermit Barnabas was the first to establish such a residence, in A.D. 985. Eventually a number of monks got together and formed a community at Doúpiani, just north of Kastraki. Later, Saint Athanasios came along and built his monastery as high as he could get it, some 1,780 feet above the madding crowd. (The word *metéora* is apparently a contraction of the Greek for "middle of the air"; once applied to the original monastery, it was then later applied to the entire complex of such skyscraping structures.)

It is tempting (although theologically a bit rocky, as it were) to speculate that part of the Orthodox monks' affinity for airy habitats, strikingly evident as well in Mount Athos (see Northern Greece), might be a reflection of their church's belief that man is capable of deification (*theosis*), of becoming "by grace what God is by nature... a 'second god,'" to quote Timothy Ware (now Bishop Kallistos of Diokleia) from his excellent study *The Orthodox Church*. These "monasteries of the air" can thus be thought of as symbolic way stations in upward striving, in the movement away from the mundane and the physical toward divinization in a universe permeated by the Holy Spirit, by "God's energies," writes Bishop Kallistos, "in the form of deifying grace and divine light."

These days the monasteries of the Meteora are more accessible. The world has built stairs and bridges and roads and almost literally raised the earth to meet them, so that now getting to the tops of these pillars has ceased to be the hair-raising enterprise it once was. As a result, the monasteries have virtually ceased to exist as such and have become museums instead, with only a very few nuns and monks there to act as guides and curators. Of the 24 monasteries that once functioned when the community was still reasonably isolated, only 5—Great Meteoron, Barlaam, Rousanou, Ayia Triada, and Ayios Stefanos—are still open. For an account of the way things used to be, including a description of being lowered from the monastery of the Great Meteoron in a wildly oscillating net, read Robert Curzon's 1849 *Visits to Monasteries in the Levant*.

Tours of the monasteries can begin from either the western or the eastern end, in both cases taking turns to the north off route E 87. This eastern approach leads up to the most easily accessible of the monasteries, the nunnery of Ayios Stefanos. From here a winding but ultimately circular route about 21 km (13 miles) in length leads you to within reach of all of the open monasteries and back down into Kalambaka, where the main route from Larissa can be rejoined. A tour on foot via the ancient stone walkways used to be possible, but these have now crumbled and are so overgrown as to be almost impassable. They are also, say the police, dangerously isolated should an accident occur. By way of the asphalt motorway, the ascent on foot from Kastraki to the monastery of the Great Meteoron takes about one and a half hours, while the entire journey via most of the other monasteries en route can be anywhere from four to six hours. There are no restaurants on the way, although most days there is a canteen truck parked outside the Great Meteoron—if the latter is open, which it may not be.

Here it must be noted that each monastery is closed one day a week (while being open the other six days on a regular basis mornings and late afternoons). Finding out on which day a particular monastery happens to be closed in that particular week is a bit of a task, since these closings often depend upon a logic that can best be described as other-worldly. You therefore should ask in Kalambaka at any of the tourist shops or the foreign newsstand on the second square. These people speak some English; they also sell maps and can tell you where to catch the local bus to Great Meteoron. Group tours can be joined in Kalambaka or virtually any of the major cities on the mainland, including Thessaloniki and Athens. Rock scaling is permitted; see the tourist police in Kalambaka for details. Unlike many other monasteries in this day and age, those of the Meteora still enforce rather strict dress regulations: No shorts allowed for either men or women, and no sleeveless dresses or "pantaloons" (presumably slacks) for women either. Fortunately, both the monasteries and some of the souvenir stands rent dresses, and long pants for men.

Each of the monasteries en route has its own special attraction. For the visitor with only a short amount of time (or, for that matter, with all the time in the world), the first choice is incontestably the first monastery to be established, that of the Transfiguration of Our Savior, better known as **Great Metéoron**. Its monastic privileges were guaranteed in 1362 by the Serbian emperor then in control of Thessaly, whose son, later the monk Ioasaph, became a member of the monastery and made it financially well off, a fact that its beautiful interior makes immediately obvious.

Of particular interest here are the **Refectory Museum**, a beautiful structure with displays of icons, manuscripts, and etchings, and the main church (*katholikón*), whose reconstruction was paid for by Ioasaph and whose inner narthex is covered with what can only be described as a Grand Guignol depiction of the variously hideous ways Orthodox saints were martyred. Recently cleaned, the frescoes have an interesting cheerfulness about them, as if to say (as Jesus allegedly said in a vision to Julian of Norwich) that no matter what happens here on earth, "all manner of things shall be well." The view from the terrace of the neighboring pinnacles and abandoned monasteries is spectacular. A shop opposite the Refectory Museum offers good-quality reproductions of prints and icons in the museum and monastery collections, as well as books on the Meteora. On the floor below in the old storage room is an interesting display featuring the monastery's kitchen utensils and the like. Also on this floor is the platform from which people and goods used to be winched to and from the dizzying heights. Today visitors must climb a flight of 115 steep, irregular stairs carved from the rock face.

Bárlaam (Várla-am), next in prominence as well as on the itinerary, was first occupied by a monk (Barlaam) during approximately the same period that Saint Athanasios and Ioasaph were establishing the Great Meteoron. Barlaam built a small church on the rock (still existing as a side chapel to the katholikon) that formed the basis for a monastery founded here in 1517. It, too, has a winching tower and a refectory turned museum. The katholikon's frescoes and iconostasis are worth seeing, as is an icon by Emmanuel Tsanes—but the greatest attraction of Barlaam is simply the monastery *in toto*.

The charming little nunnery of **Rousánou** is the wonderfully photogenic one that is on virtually all posters and book covers about the region. Established for monks in 1545, it was later abandoned and only recently turned into a convent. It has a cheerful ambience and a small church based on the design of that at Barlaam, its walls rich with excellent frescoes of the Cretan School (1560).

Ayia Triáda, the monastery of the Holy Trinity, is huddled on top of one of the area's narrowest pillars, which can be reached only by walking up a winding stairway of (depending on your source) 130 to 140 steps. Seriously damaged by a 1956 earthquake, Ayia Triada is now being extensively renovated and restored, somewhat on the order of a brand-new Swiss chalet.

The last monastery on the circuit (or the first if you are approaching from the direction of Larissa) is that of **Ayios Stéfanos**. Originally founded by monks in about 1400, it is now impeccably cared for by nuns and is one of the most popular stops in the Meteora, partly because it is so easily reached from the road. The monastery suffered a lot of damage in both World War II and the Greek Civil War. It was bombed by the Germans, and the portrait of its founder, the son of an Epirot emperor, was defaced by Communist guerillas in 1949. Its two principal treasures—a sacred relic, the head of Saint Charalambos, and an extremely beautiful hand-carved Byzantine iconostasis—were saved.

A sixth monastery, one not on the circuit and not open on any regular schedule, is that of **Ayios Nikólaos Anápafsas**, situated on a branch of the large rock that holds Great Meteoron. Although quite dilapidated-looking outside, it contains within its 16th-century basilica what are certainly the most beautiful frescoes in all Meteora, those of the Cretan master Theophanes, painted in 1527. Visiting is worth a try.

THE VALE OF TEMPE

During the drive from Larissa toward Thessaly's northern border and the Vale of Tempe, you begin to understand why **Mount Olympus** (as opposed to peaks almost as high and perhaps even more spectacular elsewhere in Greece, such as Mount Athos) might have been thought of as the home of the gods. Why not, for instance, the conically shaped Mount Ossa, just to the southeast of Olympus? Although at 6,488 feet not as high as Olympus (9,568 feet), it is much more prominent, and visible for miles in Thessaly, even in hazy weather. Perhaps the explanation lies in the shape of the Olympus range as seen from the south, as opposed to the shape of its summit, which is much more visible from the north. If the haze is not too thick and if there is snow across the top, the range resembles a magnificent flat-topped acropolis, its snow-covered crest appearing to hover in the haze, a place vast enough to hold as many gods and temples as the imagination could supply. (For climbing Mount Olympus, see Northern Greece, below.)

The Vale of Tempe (Tembi) was, before the carving out of a motorway on one side and a railway on the other, an extremely narrow gorge dividing Ossa from Olympus and, until Alexander hacked and chiseled his way around and above it, almost impassable if protected by an army. It is thus the natural gateway to and from the north. Here the Pinios river, so overhung with trees that it is almost invisible from the road, seeks its outlet in the Aegean just a few miles farther on. And here also multitudes of Greeks and tourists alike stop for a snack in the huge restaurant, the **Tempe**, just before the entrance to the gorge, or for an extremely refreshing visit to the little **church of Ayía Paraskeví** (renowned for the qualities of its holy water, particularly in curing eye diseases) on the other side of the river via a small but still (to those who are affected by such things) mightily swaying suspension bridge.

Alexander's circumvention of the gorge—one of the first instances of the brusque ingenuity that would cause him to slice through the Gordian knot rather than waste time trying to untie it—came shortly after his father's assassination. Having secured his rule in Macedonia, Alexander now had to do the same in Thessaly. When he and his troops found their way blocked by Thessalian soldiers and the gorge passable only in single file, he proceeded over Ossa by having his men cut steps in the mountain's granite face. Outflanking the surprised and impressed Thessalians, he was immediately accepted in Philip's place as the ruler of Thessaly, a signal honor for someone who was both an outsider and a 20-year-old "boy."

Being so green and well watered and in such proximity to the home of the Olympian gods, Tempe also blossoms with myth, particularly of the sylvan variety. It is here that Daphne, pursued by the infatuated god Apollo, appealed to her father, the river-god Peneus (i.e., Pinios), to save her virtue by working some metamorphosis that would render her less enticing. Whereupon, in Ovid's wonderful description, "a deep languor took hold on her limbs, her soft breast was enclosed in thin bark, her hair grew into leaves, her arms into branches, and her feet that were lately so swift were held fast by sluggish roots, while her face became the treetop. Nothing was left of her, except her shining loveliness" (*Metamorphoses*, Book One). She was turned into a laurel (*dáphni* in Greek), which Apollo, still loving her, honored by making it his sacred plant, with leaves forever green.

Other nymphs also haunt the glades, hence the numerous signs in and around the gorge pointing to the springs of Venus, Diana, and others. Poseidon, it was said, created the gorge with a blow of his trident, allowing the inland lake that covered the Thessalian plain to pour out via Tempe to the nearby Aegean sea—the sudden sight of which, to the traveller emerging from miles of seemingly interminable farmland, is a sparkling delight to the spirit and truly a gift of the gods.

GETTING AROUND

From Athens the drive to Volos along the national highway (E 92), the best in Greece, takes three and a half to four hours, with the natural entrance to Thessaly (but not its state-defined border), Thermopylae, a bit less than three hours nonstop. Larissa is another half an hour, Meteora an additional hour, and Tempe, the border with Macedonia, five and a half hours from Athens.

From Thessaloniki the drive to Tempe takes about one to one and a half hours, with the times to the rest of Thessaly corresponding in reverse to those above. There are buses (much faster and more dependable than trains) to Thessaly's various centers from Athens and Thessaloniki at least ten times a day. These are boarded at the Athens and Thessaloniki train stations. There are also at least eight trains a day. In summer tickets for buses and trains should be bought well in advance and can be purchased either at the train stations (different ticket windows) or at the National Railway outlets in the city centers.

There are no international airports in Thessaly. Connections with internal Olympic Airways flights are made at Athens or Thessaloniki. There are infrequent flights from Athens and Thessaloniki to Larissa but none to Volos.

Volos can also be reached from Thessaloniki either by a twice-weekly car ferry or by Flying Dolphin via the Sporades islands, the latter taking about four hours. There is also a Flying Dolphin link to the national highway at the Boeotian port of Ayios Konstantinos, opposite the northern straits of Evia.

Ships to and from the Sporades islands of Skiathos, Skopelos, and Alonnisos leave from Volos several times a day.

Many travel agencies in Athens and Thessaloniki offer guided tours lasting from one to nine days (a one-day trip from Thessaloniki to Meteora and back, for example, takes a good 12 hours, with only a single stop for lunch). The longer tours usually include sights outside of Thessaly, such as Dion and Pella in the north and Delphi, Thebes, Mycenae, and Epidaurus in the south.

Travel within Thessaly is accomplished by bus or the Thessalian railway, with regular service between the major cities and towns, including Kalambaka, Larissa, and Volos.

If you prefer to travel around Thessaly by car, the best rental agency is Theofanides, 137 Iasonas Street, Volos; Tel: (0421) 323-60 or 362-38.

ACCOMMODATIONS REFERENCE

▶ **Hotel Antoniadi.** Kalambaka, 422 00 Thessaly. Tel: (0432) 243-87.

▶ **Dimitroulia Brothers.** Horefto, 402 00 Pelion, Thessaly. Tel: (0426) 224-44.

▶ **Divani.** Kalambaka, 422 00 Thessaly. Tel : (0432) 233-30; Telex: 295319.

▶ **Erato.** Horefto, 402 00 Pelion, Thessaly. Tel: (0426) 224-45.

▶ **Hotel Galaxy.** 3 Ayiou Nikolaou Street, Volos, 382 21 Thessaly. Tel: (0421) 207-50/52.

▶ **Hotel Kastraki.** 148 Trikala Street, Kastraki, Kalambaka, 422 00 Thessaly. Tel: (0432) 222-86.

▶ **Katerina.** Horefto, 402 00 Pelion, Thessaly. Tel: (0426) 227-72.

▶ **Hotel Kypseli.** 1 Agiou Nikolaou Street, Volos, 382 21 Thessaly. Tel: (0421) 244-20 or 260-20.

▶ **Makrinitsa Guesthouses: Mousli, Sisilianou, Xiradaki.** Pelion, 402 00 Thessaly. Tel: (0421) 992-50.

▶ **Hotel Meteora.** 14 Ploutarchou, Kalambaka, 422 00 Thessaly. Tel: (0432) 223-67.

▶ **Park Hotel.** Deligiorgi 2, Volos, 382 21 Thessaly. Tel: (0421) 365-11.

▶ **Vizitsa Guesthouses: Yeroulanou, Katsanaki, Kyriakopoulou, Kontou.** Pelion, 402 00 Thessaly. Tel: (0423) 863-73.

▶ **Vlachos Kastraki.** Kastraki, Kalambaka, 422 00 Thessaly. Tel: (0432) 222-93, 231-34, or 237-44.

▶ **Xenia Hotel.** Plastira Street, Volos, 380 01 Thessaly. Tel: (0421) 248-25/27.

▶ **Ziogas Rooming House.** Kastraki, Kalambaka, 422 00 Thessaly. Tel: (0432) 247-57 or 240-37.

NORTHERN GREECE

By Tom Stone

In any other country in the world—France, Italy, or Spain, for instance—northern Greece would be the designated Riviera, famed not only for its superb beaches and blue-green sea but also for its snow-capped mountains, lakes, and ski resorts, and its wealth of history, culture, and archaeological treasures.

But in sunny, whitewashed Greece it is the image of the temple-bedecked, island-sprinkled south that holds sway in most travellers' minds. The north is perceived (even by Greeks) as a distant, shadowy, and somewhat savage place brooded over by the Balkans—boar- and bear-ridden terrain, rained upon, and *cold*.

All of which it is, yet in combination with its more Riviera-like endowments. And therein lies the north's appeal: It is a land of absorbing contrasts or, as Robin Lane Fox says in his excellent book *Alexander the Great*, "impossible" ones. The mountains of northern Greece are European, forested with pine, spruce, oak, juniper, and chestnut, while the lowlands are Mediterranean, a world of oregano, thyme, and olive trees.

Northern Greece is a world, too, of kaleidoscopic juxtapositions—of the stalagmites of Paleolithic cave dwellers and the columned glory that was Athenian Greece; of the rough splendor of the Macedonia of Philip II and Alexander and the arched and rotund grandeur that was Imperial Rome; of the golden-domed magnificence of Byzantium and the decaying, grass-tufted *hamáms* (baths) and minarets of the Ottoman occupations.

Northern Greece
0 miles 40
0 km 40
YUGOSLAVIA
BULGARIA
ALBANIA
TURKEY
TO ISTANBUL
MACEDONIA
THRACE
THESSALY
EPIRUS
PINDOS MOUNTAINS
Lakes of Prespa
Edessa
Thessaloniki
Axios R.
Naoussa
Mount Vermion
Veria
E90
Kastoria
Kozani
20
4
Aliakmon R.
Katerini
Mount Olympus
Konitsa
E87
Kalambaka
Ioannina
Larissa
Thermaic Gulf
Chalkidiki
Kassandra
Sithonia
Athos
E5s
Serres
Amphipolis
Philippi
Kavala
Nestos R.
Xanthi
Komotini
Alexandroupolis
Thasos
Samothrace
Thracian Sea
Limnos
N

Here the ground is soaked in blood, for the north has been the site of seemingly incessant battles, from those fought in Classical times between Athens and Sparta to the more modern carnage of the Balkan Wars (1912 to 1913), the Nazi invasion, and the Greek Civil War (1946 to 1949). Yet the region is also home to the incomparably peaceful peninsula of Mount Athos, a monastic republic that for more than 1,000 years has been one of the world's great spiritual centers.

While northern Greece's commercial and tourist routes follow the conducive north–south course that the Axios river valley cuts through the Balkans into Europe, its heart and soul lie to the east, in the holy city known to the Orthodox faithful as Constantinople (Istanbul to the rest of the world).

Thus, while paying due attention to the north and south as well as the Imperial Roman west, this section will proceed toward the east along the same path Alexander, his ancestors, and later the Romans followed: from the mountains of the Pindos range in the west, which harbored the pre-Dorian Makednoi tribe; down into the plains where the civilization of Philip II and the other Macedonian kings flourished; across the peninsula of Chalkidiki and past the ancient cities of Amphipolis and Philippi, which guarded the flanks of the timber- and gold-rich mountains of Pangaion; down to the port of Kavala and its mother island, Thasos; and into Thrace, whence came Alexander's fierce foot soldiers and archers and where today minarets coexist with tin-plated Orthodox spires. A mere four-hour drive beyond the border with Turkey lies Constantinople—*ee polee,* as the Greeks call it—"the city."

Thessaloniki's central location—literally on the pivot point connecting the length of western Macedonia with its dogleg east to Chalkidiki and the Thracian border—makes it a perfect base for visiting most of the rest of the area. From Thessaloniki it is possible to take leisurely day trips to virtually all of the important sites in northern Greece. You might easily even go as far south as Meteora in Thessaly or north to the gambling casinos in Sophia, Bulgaria; either of these round trips takes about 12 hours.

Within western Macedonia, day trips can be made to the mountain areas on the border with Epirus and Albania, to the beautiful lakeside locations of Prespa and Kastoria in the Pindos range, and, during winter, to the ski resorts of Seli and Tria Pigadia, perched on Mount Vermion above the vineyards of Naoussa.

Closer by—only an hour and a half by car—are the mighty

peaks and gorges of Mount Olympus in the south; the dramatic cataracts of Edessa in the north; and the Macedonian tombs and archaeological sites of Pella, Vergina, and Dion west and southwest of Thessaloniki.

To the east of the city, daylong excursions can be made to the sacred peninsula of Mount Athos, on the third finger of Chalkidiki; to the fortressed Ottoman port of Kavala, near the Thracian border, where the archaeological site of Philippi, city of both Alexander's father and of the apostle Paul, is just a 20-minute drive north; and to the sadly fire-scarred but still stunning paradise island of Thasos, only an hour away by ferry from Kavala's docks—about three and a half by car and boat from Thessaloniki.

And then there is the magnificent Riviera of Chalkidiki, just 45 minutes southeast from the center of the city on a new expressway. Looking like three fingers stretched lazily out into the Aegean, Chalkidiki's peninsulas offer wide sandy beaches and rocky forests that add up to some of the most magnificent seascape this side of California's Big Sur.

Thrace is just a bit too distant from Thessaloniki for day trips. And, as its excellent but scattered beaches are often inconveniently far from the main road and inland capitals of Xanthi and Komotini, Thrace is best suited for travellers with campers or cars. Nevertheless, the area's principal attraction, the remote and mysterious island of Samothrace, can be easily and comfortably reached from Thessaloniki in a matter of hours, even in time for lunch.

MAJOR INTEREST

Thessaloniki
Archaeological Museum (finds from Royal Tombs of Vergina)
The White Tower
Byzantine churches
Roman remains: Arch of Galerius, the Rotunda

Western Macedonia
Mount Olympus
Manor houses of Siatista and Kastoria
Lakes of Kastoria and Prespa
Pella, Dion, Vergina
Winter ski resorts of Seli and Tria Pigadia

Eastern Macedonia
Archaeological site of Philippi
Museums of Kavala

Archaeological site, museum, and beaches of Thasos
Mount Athos
Beaches of Chalkidiki and eastern coast

Thrace
Samothrace
Old quarters of Xanthi and Komotini
Post-Byzantine churches
Moslem presence
Beaches, camping

We will first focus on Thessaloniki, which was for many centuries northern Greece's only island of relative stability and continuity in a raging, shifting sea of occupying forces. Today it is still the vital heart (and capital) of Macedonia and Thrace as it at last begins to lead the area into the 20th century.

THESSALONIKI

From its founding in 316 B.C., seven years after the death of Alexander the Great, until its independence from the Ottoman Empire in 1912, Thessaloníki (also called Thessalónika or Salónica) has almost always played the role that great king seems to have imagined in his grand scheme for Macedonia: that of a crossroads and focal point between the cultures of East and West, through which would flow not only goods but ideas, and in which would coexist all manner of dichotomies.

Today, although its traffic with the East (and thus much of its true *raison d'être*) is virtually nonexistent, Thessaloniki still has a lively cosmopolitan air, possessing a patina it never lost from its past. And now the city is being given new life: As Greece prepares for full integration into the European Community, Thessaloniki is becoming the country's main commercial crossroads.

In addition, because the city has so long dealt with foreigners from both West and East, its spirit of enterprise is tempered by an inborn Levantine hospitality and an appreciation for the unusual that makes the visitor feel he or she is not so much a tourist as a person of interest, of substance and culture, from whom something other than money might be gleaned. In short, Thessaloniki is an extremely congenial place for visitors to stop, relax, and get their bearings, and it is an excellent base from which to make forays into the surrounding region.

Thessaloniki is an intriguing city, but one not as easy to know as its charm and hospitality might indicate. While all sights that deserve an obligatory visit can be seen within no more than a day or two, so much of the city's rich past has been eradicated by its successive occupiers (including the Greeks themselves) or destroyed by natural and man-made disasters, that a tour of today's Thessaloniki tends to raise more questions than it answers expectations.

For instance, the name. Why does it have so many different forms and spellings? Within these changes lies a virtual history of the city.

Upon founding the city, Cassander named it Thessaloniki, after his new bride, half-sister of Alexander and daughter of the polygamous Philip. Philip had named her after his victory (*niki*) in Thessaly, a conquest in which he had won her mother as a trophy. When the Romans subdued Macedonia in 168 B.C., the name was latinized and brought into general use; "Thessalonica" was how the New Testament referred to it in accounts of the apostle Paul's visits here in A.D. 49 and 56.

When the Ottomans took over in 1430 they called the city Selaïnik, after a contraction of Thessaloniki—"Saloniki"— often still used by the Greeks. This, in turn, was Westernized to "Salonica" (or "Salonika"). In 1912, after almost 500 years of Turkish rule, Salonica again became Thessaloniki when the city rejoined Greece. Most of the rest of the world still calls it Salonica.

And so the questions multiply. Why, visitors ask, does the city look so new? Where is everything—why no marble columns, no pediments? To foreigners, there doesn't seem to be anything "Greek" about the city. In fact, of the Hellenistic-Macedonian civilization that founded the city and built the original fortifications (and, incidentally, welcomed the first members of an important Jewish population), there remains little evidence, even in Thessaloniki's superb archaeological museum. What wasn't carried off by Roman conquerors was buried; remains are occasionally found when the foundations for new buildings are dug. More often than not, though, the finds are hastily covered over in the dark of night before archaeologists can demand interminable, if not permanent, delays in construction or certify the

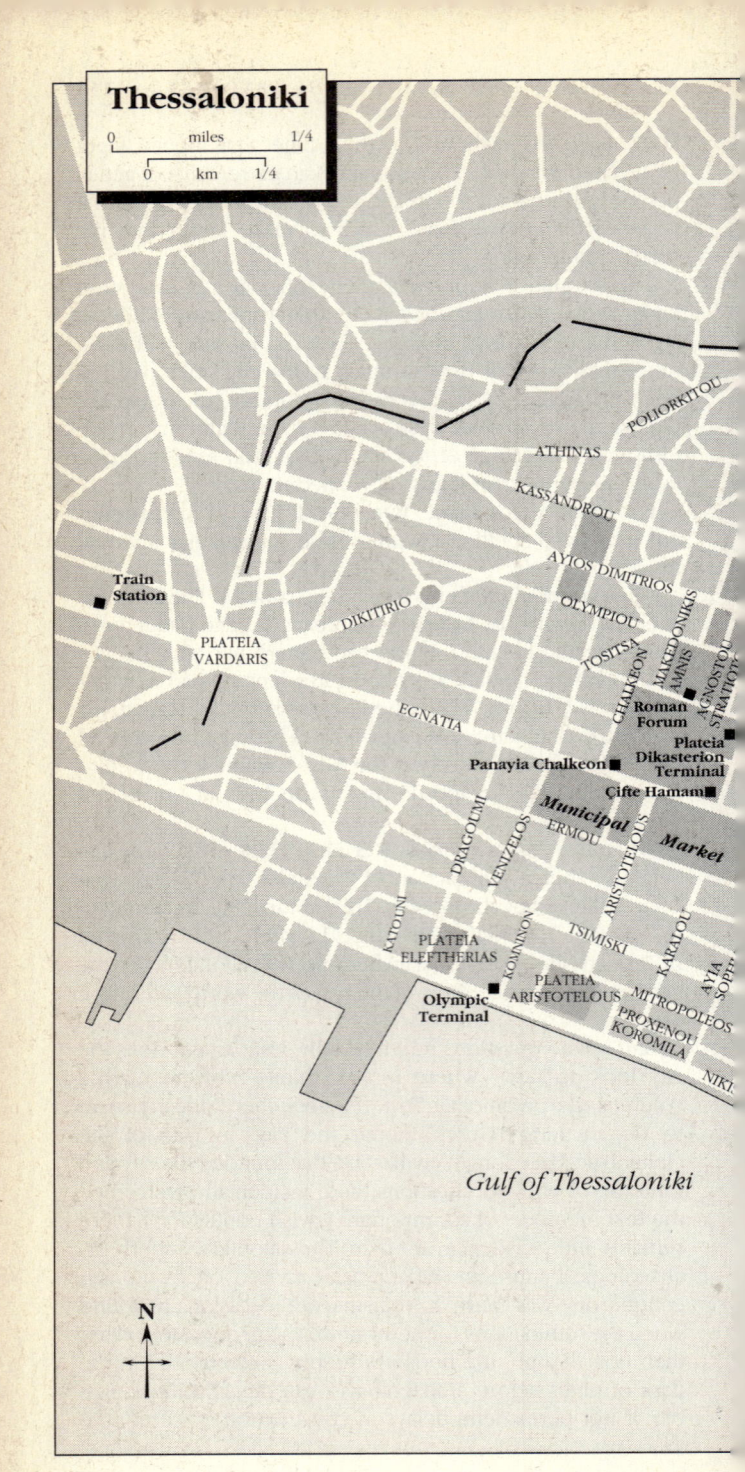

Thessaloniki

0 — miles — 1/4
0 — km — 1/4

Train Station

POLIORKITOU
ATHINAS
KASSANDROU
AYIOS DIMITRIOS
OLYMPIOU
TOSITSA
CHALKEON
MAKEDONIKIS AMNIS
AGNOSTOU STRATIOTOU

PLATEIA VARDARIS
DIKITIRIO

Roman Forum

EGNATIA

Panayia Chalkeon

Plateia Dikasterion Terminal

Çifte Hamam

DRAGOUMI
VENIZELOS
ERMOU

Municipal Market

ARISTOTELOUS
KARTOUNI
KOMNINON
TSIMISKI
KARAOLI
AYIA SOPHI

PLATEIA ELEFTHERIAS
PLATEIA ARISTOTELOUS

Olympic Terminal

MITROPOLEOS
PROXENOU
KOROMILA
NIKI

Gulf of Thessaloniki

N

Acropolis (Ta Kastra)

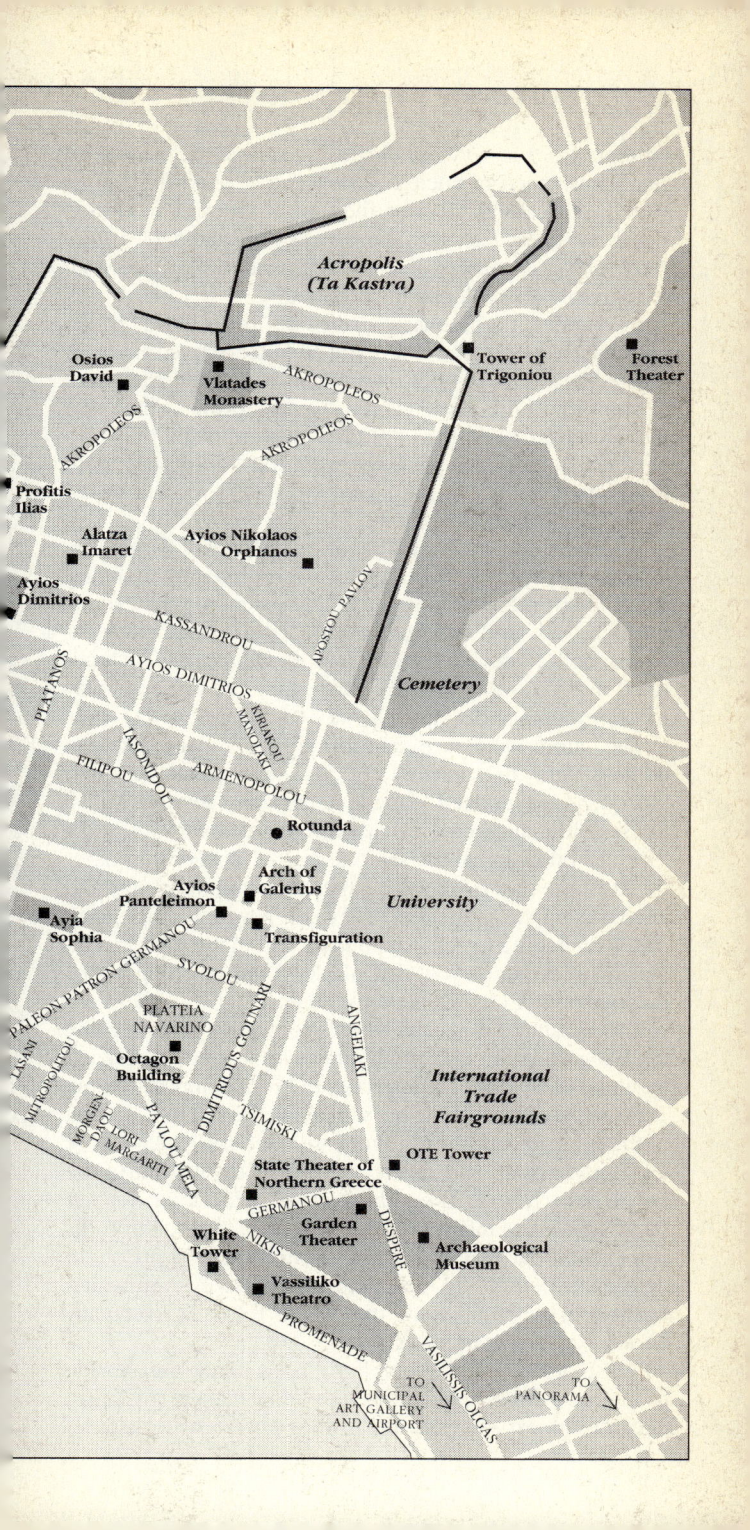

- Osios David
- Vlatades Monastery
- Tower of Trigoniou
- Forest Theater

AKROPOLEOS

- Profitis Ilias
- Alatza Imaret
- Ayios Nikolaos Orphanos
- Ayios Dimitrios

KASSANDROU

AYIOS DIMITRIOS

PLATANOS

IASONIDOU

FILIPOU

KIRIAKOU MAVOLAKI

ARMENOPOLOU

APOSTOLI PAVLOV

Cemetery

- Rotunda
- Ayios Panteleimon
- Arch of Galerius
- Transfiguration

University

- Ayia Sophia

PALEON PATRON GERMANOU

SVOLOU

LISANI

MITROPOLITOU

PLATEIA NAVARINO

- Octagon Building

PAVLOU MELA

MORGEN DAOU LORI MARGARITI

DIMITRIOUS GOUNARI

TSIMISKI

ANGELAKI

International Trade Fairgrounds

- OTE Tower
- State Theater of Northern Greece

GERMANOU

NIKIS

- White Tower
- Garden Theater
- Vassiliko Theatro
- Archaeological Museum

DESPERE

PROMENADE

VASILISSIS OLGAS

TO MUNICIPAL ART GALLERY AND AIRPORT

TO PANORAMA

basement of the new building as an official archaeological site. Thus much of ancient Greek Thessaloniki lies out of view in basements all over the city. The power to decide which of these sites can be viewed by qualified visitors (archaeologists, professors, etc.) rests with the Archaeological Service (Arkheologikí Ipiresía).

In contrast, the Roman remains are much more visible, particularly in the area where the attention-starved Galerius erected an arch and other monuments to himself. Elsewhere in the city is the great central Roman forum, which was discovered in 1962 when foundations were being dug for a new court building; plans to erect the courthouse were abandoned, and today the forum lies uncovered but below street level, barely noticeable.

When the Roman Empire devolved into that of Byzantium, temples were either converted into or replaced by churches. Intermittent refortification, including extending the protective sea walls and erecting towers, took care of other remains; both Roman and Hellenistic elements were incorporated into various structures, where they can be seen today incongruously or decoratively fitted into place.

The Ottomans, in turn, transformed the converted Roman edifices and the magnificent Byzantine churches into mosques and erected countless hamams, *imaréts* (almshouses), fountains, covered markets, private mansions, and a forest of minarets. At the same time, they covered up other traces of the past by crowding the city with immigrants and encouraging the settlement of as many Jews and other Europeans (including Greeks) as could fit within the walls, resulting in streets so narrow that planks could be slung across the tops of them for shade in the summer.

The Byzantine walls and towers, too, at last, had to come tumbling down. In 1866, with pirates no longer a threat and the need to facilitate commerce with Europe imperative, the Turks began demolishing the wall along the seafront, several of the great towers shortly afterward, then the lower part of the western wall, and finally, in 1889, what was left of the lower eastern wall. Along the seafront the only tower left standing was the infamous "Bloody Tower," where the Turks had carried out executions and still maintained a prison. In deference perhaps to European sensibilities, they whitewashed it, whereupon as the White Tower it eventually became the city's landmark.

Horse-drawn trams were introduced along the seaside promenade in 1893, and it was at this time that the city began in earnest to expand eastward, toward what today is Vasilíssis

Olgas Street, where many of the period's beautiful mansions are just now beginning to undergo restoration. One of the more impressive of these is the **Municipal Art Gallery**, at Vasilissis Olgas and 25 Mártio (the 25th of March) streets.

When the Greeks retook Thessaloniki from the Turks in 1912, they reconsecrated their churches and cleared the skyline of the hated minarets. But the real obliteration of the Turkish presence came five years later with the great 1917 fire that burned to the ground virtually the entire lower section of the city, destroying its crowded, colorful bazaars, elegant hotels and banks, beautiful Turkish mansions, and distinctive Jewish, Frankish, and Greek quarters.

Thus what the visitor largely sees today is the city that the French architect Ernest Hébrard, who was here on military duty in World War I, laid out with great and spacious refinement upon his pristine drawing board in the years that followed.

Modern Thessaloniki is, for all of its orderly planning, a refreshingly human city made for people, not cars (although cars have recently begun to befoul an urban terrain that in the early 1980s could be traversed from one end to the other in half an hour). Nevertheless, one gets a nagging sensation that this spaciousness is also a kind of emptiness, and that the real Thessaloniki can be perceived only in pieces and remnants, like left-over tesserae of a once brilliantly colored mosaic.

THE ESSENTIAL THESSALONIKI

The excellent paperback guide and map to the city by A. Papagiannopoulos, available in most bookstores in Thessaloniki, covers most of these pieces and remnants—which is to say, Roman, Byzantine, Turkish, and Neoclassical edifices—in exemplary fashion. With this in hand, it is entirely possible for you to see enough of Thessaloniki in a day or two to make a return visit eminently desirable. However, if you have neither the time nor the guidebook, there are three places, all within a five-minute walk of one another, that can encapsulate most of Thessaloniki's past and present for you within an hour. These places can also be starting points for a complete circuit of the city (which we will do in the following sections), although as overviews they are perhaps best saved until last or visited both before and after.

The three sites are, in no particular order, the White Tower, the Archaeological Museum, and the coffee shop of the Greek telecommunications tower. All are centrally located, just where the eastern park and promenade meet the city proper along the bay. At this junction stands the White Tower; a block to the northeast is the Archaeological Museum; and across the street from that, the coffee shop.

A visit to the **White Tower** (Lefkós Pýrgos) on the waterfront promenade is obligatory if only because, like the Empire State Building or the Tower of London, it is there. But it has recently been beautifully renovated and transformed into the repository of Thessaloniki's fine collection of Byzantine icons, frescoes, sculpted reliefs, glasswork, pottery, coins, and jewelry from all periods of the empire's 1,100-year presence in this, its second city and sometime co-capital.

The White Tower is flanked by two of the nation's finest theaters, the **State Theater of Northern Greece** (Kratikó Théatro), across the street, and the **Vassilikó Théatro**, to the east along the promenade. Together with the so-called **Garden Theater** (Théatro Kipou), on the way to the Archaeological Museum, and the **Forest Theater** (Théatro Dasous), on the hillside of the acropolis, they offer an extensive summertime program of concerts, dance, and theater pieces by Classical and popular Greek and foreign artists of the highest caliber. A schedule of events for all of these venues is often posted outside the State Theater. Information should also be available at hotels.

The **Archaeological Museum**, just inland from the White Tower, is the home of the strikingly impressive finds from the Royal Tombs of Vergina, which are now almost universally accepted as those of Alexander the Great's father, Philip II, and his family. Of particular interest here are the physical remains that seem best to confirm that the tomb was indeed Philip's: the pair of greaves (shin guards) and the skull (reconstructed) found in the most important tomb. It is known that Philip had a limp (one of the shin guards is shorter than the other) and had suffered a terrible arrow wound in his right eye, evidence of which is visible on the skull.

The museum also contains a superb collection of local finds from the Neolithic Age through the Roman occupation, including Roman sculptures, mosaics, and copies of Classical Greek works. On sale in the lobby is an excellent guide to the museum written by Professor Manolis Andronikos, the archaeologist who discovered Philip's tomb in 1977.

For a literal overview of the modern city you need only

walk across the street from the museum to the entrance of the International Trade Fair and ascend to the coffee shop at the top of the **OTE** (telecommunications) **Tower** (Pýrgos Otéh). This strange, spindly structure looks as if it has been transplanted from Seattle or some other foreign fairgrounds, so totally out of place does it seem in anyone's idea of even modern Greece. But from the air-conditioned comfort of the coffee shop–bar (breakfast, snacks, and sweets are served in addition to drinks) you will have an unmatched opportunity to sit in one place and be offered, through wide, tinted windows, the entire panorama of the city as the floor revolves 360 degrees, completing its circuit once every 30 minutes.

Toward the sea the tower offers, on the proverbial clear day (usually in winter, with a fresh north wind), a spectacular view of Mount Olympus rising majestically on the far side of the Thermaic Gulf some 60 miles to the south. To the east (left as you look seaward) along the curve of the bay are the suburbs of Kalamariá, Aretsoú, and Nea Krini, where the former king's palace is now a government ministry building. The beaches are polluted, but the fishing caïques still line up and the tavernas and restaurants, from basic to baroque, still flourish along the coast, serving everything from Chinese food and pizza to some of the best seafood in town. Also in this direction is the airport and the new superhighway to Chalkidiki.

Farther to the east is Mount Hortiátis, its peak capped by a radar tower courtesy of the United States but now no longer run by them. Below the summit—where the pashas used to collect and store ice for summertime sherbets—is the pedestrian-modern but wonderfully cool village of **Hortiátis**, abounding in tavernas.

Below Hortiatis is the burgeoning hilltop community of **Panórama**, home of the city's well-to-do and site of three very good hotels for visitors who want to get out of the heat and noise of the city. The **Hotel Nefeli** sits on the hillside just at the western entrance to the village from the city and has an excellent view of Thessaloniki from its upper floors. Inside the village, after the first right turn that takes you past the well-stocked Masoutis Supermarket and the local bakery, pharmacy, and record store/photography shop, is the **Hotel Pefka**, an older establishment without a view but quiet, comfortable, and less expensive than either the Nefeli or the well-appointed **Hotel Panorama**, on the road bearing to the right of the Pefka and up and around the top of the hill. Here is the best view of the city and the sunset, both from the hotel's rooms and from the spacious terrace of its coffee shop and restaurant.

Panorama is famous for its *trígona,* a cream-filled cone of sweetened filo pastry that does the soul good. (The best are made at **Tasos'** on the main road just past the Hotel Nefeli and at **Elenidis** at the far end of the village on the road to Hortiatis.) In the evening head for the lovely **Montagna** bar and restaurant on the road down to Thessaloniki from the village. Completely outdoors, it is very chic and romantic, the dimly lit decor bested by a starry summer night sky and intoxicatingly fresh, pine-scented air.

Panorama, as its name implies, offers superb views and is, in rush hour, about 20 minutes away by car and 45 minutes by local bus from the city center (number 57/58 runs east along Egnatia Street from Plateía Dikastírion terminal).

Also in this direction, just below and beyond the fairgrounds, are the Greek army base and the spacious university campus, part of the latter built on the site of the old Jewish cemetery. Above that and to the northwest is the park of Seih Sou, where the municipal zoo and the aforementioned summertime Forest Theater are located.

To the north-northwest, above the large Greek cemetery and the hospital of Evangelístrias, is Thessaloniki's **acropolis**, also called the Ano Polis (Upper City) or Ta Kastra (The Castles—plural because of the numerous castle-like towers that once stood here along with the castle of Eptapyrgíou, until 1988 a functioning, and abominable, prison). The large concrete structure on the hillside below the acropolis walls is an unfinished extension of the city's only monastery, **Vlatádes** (Moní Vlatádon), which is thought to be built upon the spot where the apostle Paul did his preaching. Around and below that is the extremely picturesque old **Turkish Quarter**, with winding streets in which are nestled several beautiful Byzantine churches and many lovely houses. The entire area is currently undergoing extensive restoration funded by both private money and the European Community. (See The Upper City, below, for more on Vlatades and the Turkish Quarter.)

The broad avenue that runs from the base of the OTE Tower westward past the Neoclassical YMCA building is not the famous Via Egnatia but its more elegant counterpart, tree-lined **Tsimiskí Street**. Tsimiski Street is so chic that when crocodile-label shirts and blouses were *de rigueur* among the fashionable crowd parading by, it was jokingly called O Nilos—the Nile.

Finally, there are the **International Trade Fairgrounds** themselves. Inaugurated in 1926 on land that was formerly part of the Turkish cemetery, the International Trade Fair continues a city tradition that dates back to the Middle Ages. In those days religious celebrations for Thessaloniki's patron saint, Ayios Dimítrios, took place from October 20 to 26 within the city walls, while commercial get-togethers involving merchants from all over the Byzantine Empire were organized on the plains of the Axios river west of the city. In modern times Saint Dimitrios's day is celebrated in a religious sense only on October 26, but the occasion is also marked by the Dimítria, an entire month of cultural events—including a film and music festival—preceded by the International Trade Fair in mid-September. The trade fair has taken quantum jumps in importance in recent years as Greece heads for full EC partnership in 1992. In the meantime, as Thessaloniki tries to swivel both its literal and spiritual orientation from the East to the West, the fairgrounds is the site of almost continual specialized trade exhibitions (of wine, furniture, farm equipment, and so on) throughout the year.

Of the many questions modern Thessaloniki poses to foreign visitors, one that must by now have risen in the reader's mind is, what were Jews doing in Thessaloniki, of all places, and what happened to them and their cemetery?

Exactly when the first Jews arrived is unknown—probably shortly after Cassander founded the port to handle the huge trade that developed with Alexander's eastern empires, parts of which were in the Levant. Thessaloniki's first Jews became totally Hellenized. When the Ottomans took over roughly 1,700 years later, these Jews fled with their fellow Greeks into the highlands and mountains for safety, deserting the crippled city and leaving it a virtual ghost town.

At about the same time, great numbers of other Jews were fleeing persecution in Germany, Hungary, Spain, and Portugal, and were looking for new places in which to settle. The sultan therefore let it be known that they would be most welcome in his newly acquired but moribund city.

By the turn of the 16th century Thessaloniki was thriving, as its Jews, particularly the Sephardic merchants, travelled throughout Europe reestablishing old ties and setting up a highly lucrative trading network between East and West while lending a definite Castillian character to the city. Thessaloniki's Jews also fostered the training of doctors, scientists, and scholars within their community, setting up schools and libraries and, all in all, undoubtedly showing the rather dispirited Jewish and Christian Greeks of the period that it was possible to both maintain one's identity and prosper under Turkish rule. Thus, the Jews became valued and honored members of Thessaloniki society and remained so long after the Ottomans left. (See the Institute for Balkan Studies' *History of Thessaloniki*, by A. E. Vacalopoulos, for a more thorough discussion of their contributions.)

But in 1941 the Nazis arrived, and in 1943 some 50,000 Thessaloniki Jews were shipped to concentration camps. Very few survived. Many of those who did simply could not bear to come back to a city full of ghosts. During the occupation, the Germans had dug up and desecrated the Jewish cemetery outside the eastern walls, and in 1949 ground was broken there to accommodate an expansion of the university. Gravestones of the old cemetery can still be seen lying on the lawns of the Polytechnic Building and even incorporated as parts of walkways and steps in the city. And so the number of Jews in Thessaloniki's total population, once above 50 percent (in the late 19th century), now numbers 1,080, a fraction of 1 percent.

THESSALONIKI BY DAY

When visiting Thessaloniki, keep in mind that the Greek working day is divided into two parts, the second half of which is sometimes nonexistent. Shopping hours are from about 9:00 A.M. to 1:30 or 2:00 P.M. and from about 5:00 to 8:00 P.M.; stores are closed in the afternoons and evenings on Mondays, Wednesdays, and Saturdays, except during July, when they are *never* open in the afternoon. Most churches lock up at about 3:00 P.M. Any tours of the city's places of interest—including its markets and shops—should be planned for the morning hours, one round devoted to the lower part of the city and the other to the upper part, reserving the museums, which usually stay open until 5:00 P.M., for the final, or a second, tour.

It is conceivable that by starting in the upper city—the area behind or just below the Byzantine fortifications—and working your way down, you could make a sustained dash through both the lower and upper halves of the city in a single morning, taking lunch much later, anywhere. The most sensible thing to do, however, if there is time, is to handle the lower and upper parts separately, and to begin with the lower part of the city, at its second most famous monument, the Arch of Galerius, on Egnatia Street near the northern end of the fairgrounds.

The Lower City

If Tsimiski Street is Thessaloniki's Fifth Avenue, then Egnatia is its Broadway, with the 42nd Street of Plateía Vardáris at its western end, a university along its upper length, and, in between, a host of discount clothing and electrical appliance shops. Egnatia Street may be just the kind of commercial thoroughfare the Romans had in mind when they began constructing it in about 130 B.C.

The original **Via Egnatia** crossed northern Greece from Thessaloniki to the Adriatic and connected it with Rome by boat and the Appian Way. Terminating in the east at Neapolis (modern Kavala in eastern Macedonia) when first built, the road was eventually extended to Byzantium and, with the decline of Rome in the fourth century A.D., became the main overland artery linking Thessaloniki to the heart of Constantinople.

The Egnatia that today runs alongside the old Roman forum and the Arch of Galerius is laid out on approximately the same route as the Roman one. It enters the city at Plateia Vardaris (just east of the modern train station and once the old western gate, the site of a triumphal arch honoring the 42 B.C. victory of Antony and Octavian over Brutus at Philippi), continues to the university, then meanders through the city, diminishing in width and importance until it emerges again on the eastern side as the asphalt motorway to Amphipolis, Kavala, and points east. Its recently opened modern counterpart—Nea (New) Egnatia—now extends from the university as a spacious freeway direct to the Chalkidiki seaside.

It was not until some 450 years after the Via Egnatia was built, however, that any truly massive construction of the sort we like to think of as Roman would occur—not until the rule of Galerius (A.D. 293 to 311), the eastern emperor of Diocletian's divided empire.

Galerius seems to have suffered from an inferiority complex that was aggravated by Diocletian. In order to claim the prize of co-emperorship of the East, Galerius was forced to divorce his first wife and marry Diocletian's daughter. Even after he became sole emperor (only because Diocletian had appointed him as his successor), Galerius apparently had a continual need to please his father-in-law and prove himself to the world. Consequently, he did up his capital city, Thessaloniki, in grand style (Diocletian's capital was Nicomedia, near a little town called Byzantium), and at the same time tried to outdo his father-in-law in persecuting the emerging Christians. As a result, Galerius gave Thessaloniki not only two of its most famous monuments, but also the martyrdom of its patron saint, Ayios Dimitrios.

The **Rotunda** was apparently the first of Galerius's monuments to go up, and may have been intended as his own mausoleum. But when Galerius died—in Bulgaria, near Sophia—his successor, Licinius, wouldn't hear of having the body transported back to Thessaloniki. So Galerius lies buried in the north in a place called Romulianum. Today the Rotunda is undergoing extensive restoration (expected to end in 1992) and is closed to the public. At the moment its interior is so honeycombed with scaffolding that it would be impossible to see the famous fourth-century mosaics of early Christian saints that have decorated the dome and recesses from the time the would-be mausoleum was converted to a Byzantine church, possibly around 379. There is, however, some recourse in Theocharis Pazaras's book *The Rotunda of St. George,* which features color photographs and detailed descriptions of the structure. Published by the Institute of Balkan Studies, it is available in some local bookstores.

Galerius had to try twice for the victory of 297 that allowed him to raise the **Triumphal Arch** (Apsída Galeríou, known to Thessalonians as *ee kamára,* "the arch") that stands below the Rotunda. The first time, in defending Rome's eastern border against the Persians, he was soundly defeated and subsequently treated with some contempt by his father-in-law. Heavy reinforcements brought him the necessary victory, although even then Diocletian didn't allow him to have the territory that came with his triumph—just the arch.

Originally the monument had two parallel rows of four pediments each (i.e., two small arches flanking one large one), of which there remain today only one of the large central arches and a smaller flanking one on its northern side. A dome rested above and across the two rows, supported by the large central arches. This was once an impressive passageway up to the Rotunda from the rest of Galerius's central city complex, which spread out toward the sea below and included a hippodrome, his palace, and an octagonal structure that may have been his throne room. Parts of these structures have been excavated and are open to public view in sunken areas along the wide promenade (Dimitríou Gounári Street) that extends from the Arch of Galerius down toward Tsimiski Street and the sea. (A marble arch from the Octagon Building, with a bust of Galerius on one side and a female figure representing the city of

Thessaloniki on the other, can be seen in the Archaeological Museum.)

The large square that opens to the west off Gounari Street is the deservedly popular **Plateía Navaríno**. Here, painted on the side of an apartment block, is a huge mural echoing the form of the Octagon Building. Among the square's other attractions is a fountain whose graceful, arching jet of water flows from the wonderfully impudent bronze statue of a young boy relieving himself. Tree- and awning-shaded cafés and restaurants (for good basic Greek fare, try **Ta Adelphia**—The Brothers—on the south side of the square just west of the Octagon Building) make Plateia Navarino the favorite hangout, midday and evening, of a multitude of Thessalonians, mostly young professionals from the worlds of both business and the arts.

Nearby are the two 14th-century Byzantine churches of **Ayios Panteleímon** and the **Transfiguration** (Metamorphosis), both on Egnatia Street a short distance west from the Arch of Galerius. Both of these are excellent examples of Macedonian church architecture, featuring a decorative mixture of brick and stonework and domes supported on raised drums that create a strong upward lift.

From Dimitriou Gounari Street walk east along the street that bisects it, Prínkipos Nikólaou. Along this street (also called Svolou) are a number of good clothing and shoe stores. The best shoe stores are found on the extension of the street that circles around to the north of our next stop, the magnificent church of Ayia Sophia, which sits in the middle of the square of the same name at the eastern end of Prinkipos Nikolaou Street.

Ayía Sophía (Holy Wisdom) was built in the eighth century or perhaps earlier. Some authorities contend that it was begun after the First Council of Nicaea (325), which declared Christ to be a manifestation of Divine Wisdom, while others believe that it was started about the same time as the great Ayia Sophia in Constantinople, during the reign of the emperor Justinian (525 to 563). However, some awkwardness in its dome construction indicates that at least that part of the church dates to a time when the technology was in a transitional phase, probably during the late eighth century. Noteworthy inside the church are the wonderful mosaics of the Ascension of Jesus in the main dome and, in the apse, the image of the Virgin Mary holding Jesus in her arms. She once held a cross instead, which is still partly visible; not until after the great Iconoclast controversy was resolved in 843 was it once again permissible to depict a human Jesus.

At the square of Ayia Sophias shops of all kinds spread out in every direction; the finest are south along Ayia Sophias Street to Tsimiski and then Mitropóleos, two blocks from the sea. On the corner of Ayia Sophias and Mitropoleos is an excellent coffee shop, **Family**, for a respite before you start exploring the stores in the area.

Along Tsimiski you'll find the most chic boutiques in town as well as the best confectionary shop, **Agapitos**, and the best store for foreign books, periodicals, and newspapers, **Molhos**, a Jewish family–run store that celebrated its 100th anniversary in 1988. For crystal, porcelain, and antiques, try **Decor**, 70 Tsimiski; for fur and leather goods, **Paschalis**, 36 Tsimiski; and for jewelry, **Vilidiris**, 31 Tsimiski. On and just off the street are many other boutiques as well as galleries featuring works by local and international artists, and some of the city's finest restaurants, bars, and *ouzeries* (discussed below).

At Komninon Street, a left turn (south) off Tsimiski leads down toward the Olympic Airways terminal and ticket office on the seafront, while a right turn leads up to the **flower market**, with its grass-tufted Turkish *hamám* the site of a battered old seafood taverna, **O Loutros**, which serves excellent barreled retsina and good deep-fried seafood, including mussels, whitebait, and cod. Close by is the **Municipal Market** (*modiáno*) with both open and covered stalls. Inside the Municipal Market, which sells all manner of foods and goods, are numerous small tavernas and ouzeries catering to the lusty eating and drinking habits of the marketeers and their customers and friends. This colorful crowd holds court from early morning until afternoon closing time or even far beyond, depending on how much cheer there has been that day and whether or not a passing *bouzoúki* player has been snared. The market, certainly as ancient as Thessaloniki itself, is a part of the old city that earthquakes, fires, and occupying forces have never managed to eradicate, and never will.

So it is here that one morning's tour of the city might end, with some lunch and a beer or retsina or barreled wine. There's no guarantee that afterward you will feel in fit enough shape to continue the task of peering into any more churches. Try **Thanasis's** taverna, in the corridor ending on the west side of the covered market halfway up the block from the flower market. This establishment is highly recommended on three counts: Thanasis himself, his clean and simple, tasty dishes, and his fascinating clientele.

It might interest those who have read the novel *Z* by

Vassilis Vassilikos, or have seen the Costa-Gavras film based on it, to know that it was in this immediate area that Grigoris Lambrakis, the leftist member of Parliament (played by Yves Montand in the film) was murdered by rightist thugs in May 1963. That act contributed to the downfall of the government of Constantine Caramanlis, and helped precipitate a series of events that would end in the 1967 coup of the colonels' junta. A new monument to Lambrakis has recently been completed on the site of the murder, at the corner of Ermoú and Venizélos streets, just about 30 yards from Thanasis's taverna.

Other luncheon places in the area come highly recommended, although they are perhaps just a bit more sedate, with little possibility of a customer suddenly leaping to his feet to sing his father's favorite love song, or of a gypsy and his bear marching in to the thud of a homemade drum. Among them are such ouzeries (restaurants that serve normal fare but also specialize in *mezédes,* or hors d'oeuvres, which traditionally accompany serious ouzo drinking) as **Aristotelous**, in a small alleyway off the east side of Aristotelous Avenue between Ermou and Tsimiski streets; **Totti's Ouzerie**, in the rather luxurious surroundings of the seaside Plateía Aristotélous; and the quiet, simple, and renowned but moderately priced **Olympos Naoussa**, two blocks down the seafront to the west of the Plateia Aristotelous, between the Olympic Airways terminal and Plateía Eleftherías.

For decades, since its founding in 1927, the Olympos Naoussa has been considered one of the premier restaurants in all of Greece. And this in spite of the fact that it makes no pretense whatsoever to fashion, is owned entirely by its waiters, refuses to open in the evenings (its hours are from 12:30 to 4:00 P.M.), and supplies its customers with a menu that, on the face of it (that part not given over to advertisements for automobile batteries and picnic coolers) seems to offer the same kind of fare to be found on ships to the islands or at a second-class hotel in Albania. Usually featured are such delicacies as fried eggs, spaghetti with meat sauce, and stewed beef with rice. But the quality of both the preparation and the ingredients is impeccable and the results so simple and quietly perfect as to be almost indescribable.

Around the corner from the Olympos Naoussa, on the side of the Plateia Eleftherias where the traffic heads up into the city, is the terminal for bus numbers 22 and 23, the only ones that make the tortuous route all the way up to the acropolis,

Ta Kastra (in the upper city). While it is possible to find taxis that will agree to go up there, they are at a premium. And although you can catch the bus somewhere en route, it is invariably packed with people by that time, most having gotten on at the market.

The Upper City

From the bus stop, just to the left of the big arch at Ta Kastra, a short tour of the mainly pedestrian but still pleasant upper city is recommended, if only for some refreshment in the tree-shaded square inside and for the fine view of the city from the Byzantine **Tower of Trigoníou** next to the square. This tower is at the eastern corner of the fortifications, about 100 yards long along the outside of the walls to the right of the big arch where the bus stops. Inside the arch next to the tower is the central *plateía,* where there is a pleasant café as well as tavernas specializing in grilled food. These are good but not the best: This honor has been firmly taken by **To Kastroperpatímata** (Castle Walk), which specializes in Cypriot cuisine, an excellent and slightly exotic change from basic Greek fare. It is located in the upper city's second square, the grassy area just inside the first arch at the top of the hill, and can be reached from the first square by following the main street a short distance around the inside of the city until it exits at the arch. To Kastroperpatimata is the first of two restaurants to the left of this arch, with sidewalk tables out under the trees during summer. It is a favorite both of the locals and of people in the know from the wealthier parts of Thessaloniki.

Through the arch and across the main road from the bus stop is the **Vlatádes Monastery** (Moní Vlatádon). Its pine- and cypress-shaded grounds inside the high surrounding walls offer a sudden and wonderfully refreshing sanctuary from the bustle outside. Worth visiting is its small central church, which contains a tiny chapel to the right of the apse; dedicated to Saints Peter and Paul, it is said to have been built on the spot where Paul preached to the Thessalonians on his first missionary journey to Greece in A.D. 49.

The most magical church in the upper city (and perhaps in all of Thessaloniki), Osios David (Blessed David), sits about 200 yards down the side of the hill from the Vlatades Monastery. The walk there is worth it not simply for the church but for the opportunity to pass through the narrow winding streets of the old **Turkish Quarter**. This area was considered prime real estate during the Ottoman era because of its cool, breeze-catching location and wonderful prospect of the Thermaic Gulf; it was high enough to be well above the riffraff of Greeks, Jews, and European businessmen below and yet within extremely convenient walking distance of the harbor. (As you look down at the sea from above it is impossible to believe, but nevertheless true, that a walk from the castle walls to the bay takes only 15 to 20 minutes.) The area, until recently the home of the poorest families in the city, is now being rehabilitated thanks to funds provided by the European Community and by young married Thessalonians who are beginning to restore these lovely Turkish dwellings.

To reach Osios David, head west along the outside of the upper city walls, following the direction the bus takes to its second stop. At that stop, next to a roisterous evening taverna, **Tzotzos's**, favored by locals and guitar-playing university students, are stairs descending to Poliorkítou Street, where you can get a glimpse of some of the restored Turkish houses. Just past these to the left, a stepped sidewalk leads down, bearing to the left past a small fountain and around to the gate and enclosed courtyard of the tiny **church of Osios David**.

Built around 500, it was later converted into a mosque by the Ottomans and is now completely missing its western side. Thus the entrance, which in Byzantine churches is always on the west, is located on the south side. But never mind; the church has a survivor's mien, an aura of quiet holiness that is palpable even from the street outside. The source of this radiance is most certainly the mosaic in the apse dome, which shows a beardless, somewhat orphic Christ as described in the vision of the prophet Ezekiel. The mosaic was hidden by a sheet of calfskin to save it from destruction during the ravages of the Iconoclasts in the eighth and ninth centuries, plastered over by the Turks, forgotten, and then rediscovered (so the story goes) in 1921 by an Orthodox monk from Egypt who was told, in a vision, to visit the church. He did so, and on March 25 (Greek Independence Day) an earthquake shattered the plaster and revealed the mosaic to him, whereupon he died.

Another 15 yards farther down the hill along the same cobblestone path leading from the Turkish houses above, other visions have been made manifest by the local, self-proclaimed "King of the Greeks," who has covered his bizarre "palace" (you cannot miss it) with sheets of tin inscribed with proclamations about the state of the nation and the world, from warnings of its imminent end to the dangers of pollutants in our foods. The neighbors tolerate these ravings with great good humor.

About 100 yards below this, to the left of the curve of Akropóleos Street, is a small plateia; the street on its northern side leads eastward to the early-14th-century **church of Ayios Nikólaos Orphanós**, notable for its superb frescoes and its mixture of Byzantine construction styles.

Return to the plateia off Akropoleos Street and walk one block down to the corner; turn right onto Athinas Street and walk three blocks to the **church of Profítis Ilías**. Built about 1360 on the site of the old Byzantine palace, it is notable for its cruciform-domed plan, one used in most of the churches of Mount Athos, and its good but damaged frescoes.

From here it is only three short blocks down to Kassándrou Street and the rear of the great church of Ayios Dimitrios. But before that, visit the Turkish **Alatza Imaret** to add a bit of Ottoman color to the Roman and Byzantine mosaic encountered so far. Set in the middle of a block of streets just off Kassandrou and the corner of Ayios Nikolaos, to the northeast of the church of Ayios Dimitrios, the Alatza Imaret is a beautiful and well-preserved example of its kind and is particularly worth seeing if it is open for a special exhibit. Originally its impressive, double-domed interior served as an almshouse. (It might also be of interest to those in the know about things Turkish that Mustafa Kemal, also called Atatürk—"Father of the Turks"—was born in Thessaloniki in 1881 and participated here in the 1906 formation of the Young Turks' movement against the Ottoman Sultan Abdul Hamid. The wood-framed house that was his birthplace [sometimes open to visitors] is on the grounds of the Turkish Consulate, on Apostolou Pavlou Street, between Kassandrou and Ayios Dimitrios, eight blocks east of the church of Ayios Dimitrios toward the university.)

Before entering the **church of Ayios Dimítrios**, pause to reflect—as befits the city's patron saint—on a tale or two about his deeds and importance to Thessaloniki.

The most memorable act of the ubiquitous emperor Galerius was his martyring of Saint Dimitrios. In 303 Galerius pushed his aging father-in-law, Diocletian, into issuing an edict prohibiting anyone from professing the Christian faith in public. The young Dimitrios, who had recently completed a very successful career in the military, was preaching Christianity in Thessaloniki's coppersmiths' district (still here, just to the west of the old forum and the 11th-century church of Panayia Chalkeon—Our Lady of the Coppersmiths). He was arrested and jailed in the old Roman baths, which can be seen today below the spot where his church now rises.

Meanwhile, Galerius was in the city sponsoring his favorite gladiator, one Lyaios, to throw out a challenge of single combat to all comers. A Christian friend of Dimitrios, Nestor, was moved to take up the challenge, and visited the jail to ask for Dimitrios's blessings. He then went to the stadium, apparently made Dimitrios's blessings known to the public, and fought and killed Lyaios. Predictably, Galerius had Nestor executed on the spot, and immediately afterward had Dimitrios speared to death in his cell, where, it was said, his fellow Christians then buried him.

The relics of Saint Dimitrios now lie in his magnificent, recently reconstructed (1926 to 1949) fifth-century church, all of which but the apse was burned to the ground in the great 1917 fire. When workers dug beneath the front of the apse to begin the task of rebuilding, they discovered rooms that appear to have been the baths in which the saint was martyred. The discovery there of a cross-shaped reliquary containing a phial of blood-soaked earth seemed to all but clinch the possibility.

Following a visit to Dimitrios's church, if you still have the energy, it is just a brief walk farther down the hill to Thessaloniki's **flea market** (*paliatzídika*), located on the short diagonal street of Tosítsa, just past the fenced-in and rather desultory grounds of the old Roman forum. Although the flea market is only a block long, you can find some interesting items in the dark corners of the dusty shops and spread out on the street by the itinerant junk collectors who arrive from time to time in their trucks. Also in the area are the metalwork shops where bronze and copper wares are turned out, mostly in the standard style found throughout Greece. But all are individually made and generally less expensive than items sold in a tourist shop. Nearby is the above-mentioned 11th-century **church of the Panayía Chalkéon**, while on the southeastern corner of the plateia, along Egnatia, is the old (and currently under renovation) **Çifte Hamám**, a bathhouse built by the city's Ottoman conqueror, Sultan Murad II, in 1444. Parts of old Roman buildings are visible below the bathhouse.

From here it is only a walk across the street back to the outdoor Municipal Market (discussed above).

THESSALONIKI BY NIGHT

The Eastern flavor that is an indelible part of Thessaloniki's character also enhances its cuisine, while the city's cosmopolitan heritage is reflected in its clubs, bars, and ever-changing round of fashionable discotheques.

Thus, Thessaloniki at night is very much worth the viewing, even if only to participate vicariously in its energy by walking among the crowds along the seaside promenade, between the White Tower and the Plateia Aristotelous, and up into the side streets in between, or to the Plateia Navarino and the pub-filled streets of its neighborhood.

In fact, a recent boom in quality as well as quantity has resulted in so many good places to dine, drink, and dance in Thessaloniki that to recommend any is to be certain to miss something of value. This problem is compounded in the summertime when, to compensate for the discos in the city that close for the season, many more open on the seaside highway to the airport, just before the turnoff for Nea Moudania and Chalkidiki.

That said, there are nevertheless a number of restaurants, tavernas, and ouzeries, from the most elite to the sawdust-on-the-floor variety, that must be pointed out, if only as starters.

RESTAURANTS

In the center of the city, the finest restaurants in terms of cuisine, decor, and clientele are the pricey but excellent Rayias, at 13 Nikis Street on the seafront promenade just off the Plateia Aristotelous, and the Bextsinar, at 11–13 Katoúni, near the northwest end of Plateia Eleftherias. The **Rayias** is minuscule but quietly elegant: a single room with about eight tables and a small bar; ash-gray carpeting on the floor, walls, and ceilings; wooden café chairs handpainted by a local folk artist; and 19th-century oil paintings. Its food is top-quality European and Levantine fare, prepared when ordered and featuring unusual dishes such as prunes wrapped in bacon and breaded avocado slices. Open every day but Sunday afternoons and evenings, it expands to its seaside sidewalk in summer. The more modestly priced **Bextsinar** has a similar simple elegance. It is housed in two medium-size rooms on the first and second floors of a renovated shop and storehouse in the city's former Turkish market; the decor consists of the natural beauty of the whitewashed walls and wooden beams of the house itself, while the menu features a variety of excellently fashioned Greek hors d'oeuvres and grilled fish and meat. It, too, expands to the sidewalk in summer.

For those who are drawn by the more vibrant atmosphere of elegant restaurants that are also unabashedly bars, there are three places that can be unequivocally recommended. The first is **Yuri's**, on the corner of Pavlou Mela and Paleon Patron Germanou streets, a beautifully designed and subtly lit establishment that serves excellent snacks, salads, spaghetti dishes, and other bar-type cuisine to the beat of contemporary rock for the well-to-do younger generation of Thessaloniki. A somewhat older, but not necessarily more sedate, crowd attends the **Mandragoras**, at 98 Mitropoleos Street, just up the diagonal of Pavlou Mela Street from the White Tower and easily spotted by its neon palm tree outside. Located on the second floor and overlooking a small square, Mandragoras is unquestionably the prototype of Yuri's, serving similar bar-type cuisine, but it is much larger and is wonderfully decorated with antique marionettes, blown-glass lamps, and the like. The music is softer and jazzier. Finally, there is an outdoor summer variation on these two, similar in style and atmosphere—the previously mentioned **Montagna**, situated in a pine grove on the main road leading up the hillside near the suburb of Panorama.

For those primarily interested in good food and various regional specialties at a reasonable price, the best in Thessaloniki, scattered in various areas throughout the city, are: the famous **Olympos Naoussa** (described above), at 5 Leofóros Nikis on the seafront, next to the Olympic Airways terminal, open only for lunch (it deserves a second mention here because of its no-frills perfection); **Ta Nissia**, at 13 Proxénou Koromíla—considered by many to be the best restaurant in the city—between Plateia Aristotelous and the White Tower, which offers basic, unadorned Greek cooking and two notable specialties, fried *gavros* (a kind of whitebait) and walnut pie; the **Rongotis**, on Plateia Eleftherias just around the corner from the Olympos Naoussa and two blocks from the Bextsinar, recommended for lunch (when it serves the area's businesspeople) and dinner and known for its tasty specialty, grilled cylindrical meatballs called *soutsoukákia,* which are best consumed on the cooler and quieter second floor.

Farther from the city center is the nicely informal **Prinkipo Nisia**, on the tree-lined streets and park of Plateia Kritis, up from the large amusement park on the water at the foot of 25 Martio Street; it specializes in very tasty dishes from Istanbul. Toward the airport about a mile beyond 25 Martio Street, in the area of Byzantion, is the **Krikelas**, at 32 Ethnikís Antístasis, which offers a huge variety of hors d'oeuvres and game specialties in a somewhat overblown, slightly tourist-oriented manner—but the food is excellent. And for fish lovers there is the **Kavos**, at 59 Nikifóros Plastíras Street in the suburb of **Aretsóu**, east along the coast (take a right turn off the airport road at Themistoklí Sofoúli, the first stoplight after 25 Martio) and past the promontory of Kivernio, the site of the old royal Greek summer palace. The Kavos is the best among the many seafood restaurants in this area; it's slightly more expensive than most but worth it, its spare, well-lit atmosphere emphasizing the fact that the clientele come here for the excellent fish, not the frills.

OUZERIES

These specialize in the great variety of hors d'oeuvres (*mezé* or *mezedákia,* or *orektiká*) that are traditionally partaken of while one is engaged in serious ouzo drinking. Ouzeries are a Thessaloniki tradition, offering in their way the most intriguing and tasty dishes in town, along with an extremely lively atmosphere. The best are on Proxenou Koromila and its extension, Lori Margaríti Street, just around the corner from the above-mentioned Mandragoras bar and restaurant. This area, one block behind the seaside location of the American Consulate, also has a plethora of drinking establishments that cater, for the most part, to the very youngest of legal imbibers, and thus the streets are often jam-packed with youths and their bikes during the witching hours.

The clientele of the ouzeries in the area are, however, young professionals, people in the arts, and other older and wiser types who value and appreciate the fact that these particular establishments boast chefs who have studied abroad and brought back a bit of *nouvelle cuisine* to lighten up the traditionally over-oiled specialties of times past. The best in this area are **Kapilio**, at 26 Proxenou Koromila, and **Aproopto**, at 11 Lori Margariti, although all of the rest are good, too.

Other ouzeries of special quality and interest are: **Totti**'s, on Plateia Aristotelous, the crème de la crème of ouzeries because of its elegant setting near the sea and its excellent and not too expensive dishes; the **Anapiros**, at 20 Svolou Street (also called Prinkipos Nikolaou), an earthier establishment with walls covered by Playboy centerfolds but with a generally respectable clientele; and, in the opening of an alleyway just on the opposite side of Svolou Street, **To Stenaki**, which has an outdoor eating area for summer and, at night, with its wrought-iron lanterns and wood-beamed interior, a romantic, almost French, atmosphere.

Last but not least is the very special **Navy Out**, off the road to the airport behind Agapitos, the suburban branch of the well-known Tsimiski Street *pâtisserie*. The Navy Out is actually a large caïque that floats on the sea near the ship-repair yards just beyond Finikas, a large low-rental housing project. This caïque-ouzeri—also known as *To pleío tis agápis* (The Love Boat)—has a limited number of tables, so go early. This area is also known for the phalanx of summer discotheques lined up between the main airport road and the seaside; their names often change, but the energy, class, and beauty of both the establishments and their clientele remain high, season after season.

TAVERNAS

These often have prepared dishes such as *moussaká* and *pastítsio*, are a bit rougher in atmosphere and decor, and are generally cheaper than the restaurants and ouzeries mentioned above, although the basic quality of the food, if not the inventiveness of its preparation, may be equal.

Of special interest among the city's many good tavernas are the previously mentioned **Kastroperpatimata**, inside the upper city walls and featuring Cypriot cuisine; **Thanasis's**, in the downtown covered market, serving such fare as charcoal-grilled patties, batter-fried cod, and hors d'oeuvres; and the **O Loutros Fish Taverna** on Komninon Street next to the flower market, a sawdust-and-retsina type of place, with huge barrels lining one wall and good deep-fried seafood.

Similar in sawdust, cuisine, and atmosphere but considerably livelier, particularly at night, is the **Limaniotis**. It is located on the customs dock near Plateia Eleftherias and has an interesting mixture of characters (a lot of them "slumming"), with retsina and occasional live bouzouki music being the great levelers. It is unquestionably authentic and the food excellent.

On the main road up to the suburb of Panorama are the renowned **Pylea Fish Tavernas**: the **Gramos**, on the tiny side street of Yiatroú Yiannoúdi, facing onto the high school basketball court, and the **Kerdilia**, on the unnamed square where the Pylea bus terminal is located. Just ask for the *psarotavérna* and you will be directed accordingly. The specialties at these places are a spicy mussel soup (*média soupa*) and fried fish of all kinds.

MUSIC

Mention must be made of two clubs in Thessaloniki that are unique in Greece and that underline the cosmopolitan nature of the city: the jazz-oriented **Mandato**, at 203 Vasilissis Olgas Street (Tel: 425-233), near the Municipal Art Gallery toward the eastern end of the harbor, and, in the same direction but closer to the city center, the extraordinary **Paralama**, off Vasilissis Olgas Street near the Radio City movie theater, at 54 Belissariou Street (Tel: 833-646). While the former offers good, basic jazz (often played by visiting U.S. musicians), the latter is the home of a superb Greek blues group, the Blues Wire, that specializes in black, Bible-belt blues of the Albert Collins–"Big Bill" Broonzy variety. It too is often the host of visiting U.S. blues singers. A thumping, low-down evening is guaranteed, but get there early (9:30 P.M.) because it is almost always packed. (Neither club is open, however, from June to September.)

Staying in Thessaloniki

In 1917 a devastating fire destroyed virtually all of Thessaloniki below and including the church of Ayios Dimitrios. In the process, all but one of the great turn-of-the-century hotels built to accommodate the then-flourishing trade of the Ottoman Empire in its final burst of energy was burned down. The sole survivor, the grand old Metropolitan, once renowned as the most elegant in the Ottoman east, suffered a tragic demise in the 1978 earthquake, and it is only recently that its wonderful seafront site, just across the street from the Olympic Airways Terminal, has been filled, not by a new hotel but by a luxury office-and-apartment building.

Although the city's two best hotels, the Macedonia Palace and the Electra Palace, offer high quality, neither these nor any of the other establishments built in Thessaloniki since the end of the Greek Civil War have aspired to anything near the elegance or the distinctiveness of the old places. Instead, the emphasis has been on the functional; hotels have been geared to service the transient businessperson, typically down from Bulgaria or Yugoslavia for a trade fair, with little concern for any of the features that make the best establishments into either second homes and/or unique experiences.

Thus, it is the location of the hotel rather than internal characteristics that recommends it. On this basis, many consider the **Macedonia Palace** to be the best. It is the city's only designated luxury hotel as well as its most modern, but its chief advantage is its enviable location on the eastern seafront promenade, which gives a wonderful view of the harbor and the city center, not to mention the sunset and, on a clear day, Mount Olympus in the distance.

About a kilometer (less than a mile) farther east and across the boulevard from the Macedonia Palace, with some of its rooms facing the sea, is the much less opulent **Queen Olga Hotel**, while in between the two and a block inland is the **Metropolitan Hotel**. The location of all three, while offering obvious advantages, suffers the drawback of being as much as a 20- to 30-minute walk from the city center.

Convenience is one reason many old-time visitors to Thessaloniki prefer the city's second-best hotel, the centrally located **Electra Palace**. Bang in the middle of the city's chic shopping and restaurant district and only two blocks from the Olympic bus terminal and ticket office, the hotel faces out on the spacious and café-lined seafront Plateia Aristotelous. Because it is older, the Electra Palace is more personable in atmosphere and service than the flashier but efficient Macedonia Palace. Its great drawback, though, is its location in the midst of a sea of noise, traffic, and city heat for most of the day and evening.

Also in the area, a block away from both the Electra Palace and the Olympic terminal, is the modest and very functional **Hotel City**, so squeezed in between office and department store buildings that, except for a tiny marquee out front, it is hardly visible.

Farther to the north on the other side of the main east–west boulevard of Egnatia is the clean and well-appointed **Hotel Olympia**, in the center of a five-block area that includes the Ministry of Northern Greece, the city's flea and copper markets, the Roman agora, and the important Byzantine churches of Ayios Dimitrios and Panayia Chalkeon.

The **ABC Hotel** also has an extremely convenient location. On the eastern end of Egnatia Street, it sits just across from the northern entrance to the International Trade Fairgrounds, half a block from the Roman Rotunda and Arch of Galerius, and three blocks from the Archaeological Museum. As with most of the other hotels, however, it is more than somewhat plain and subject to lots of street noise.

At the western end of Egnatia, when it becomes Monastiríou Street on the other side of Plateia Vardaris, is the newest of the first-class hotels, the **Capitol**. While conveniently close to the train station, it is also unfortunately just on the well-worked edge of the city's red-light and transvestite districts around Vardari, and is a bit far, too, from all the major tourist sites, shops, and better restaurants.

For visitors who have a car and don't mind being somewhat out of the center of things, highly recommended are the fresh air and peace and quiet enjoyed by the three hotels in the hilltop suburb village of Panorama—the **Hotel Pefka**, the **Hotel Nefeli**, and the **Hotel Panorama**, all a 20-minute drive east out of the city center. (See the text above for more on these hotels.)

WESTERN MACEDONIA

Western Macedonia, stretching from the Albanian border east toward Thessaloniki and from Epirus and Thessaly in the south to the Yugoslav border in the north, is Philip and Alexander country. It is a wild and often spectacularly beautiful region of lakes and mountains, wild boar, wolves, bears, and eagles. Olympus towers over the courtly, fertile plains where, at Dion, Pella, and Vergina, the Macedonian kings built their sacred shrines, palaces, and final resting places.

As if in response to the wildness of its landscape, western Macedonia has been a hotbed of human savagery, littered with battlefields and blood since before recorded time right up through the ravages of the Greek Civil War (1946 to 1949) to today's pollution of its lakes and burning of its forests by accident or arson.

From this region sprang the Dorian tribes, which, some say, swarmed over southern Greece in the 11th century B.C. and drove the remnants of a decaying Mycenaean civilization across the seas to Asia Minor, occupying virtually all of Greece but the heavily fortified Acropolis of Athens. Remaining behind in the north and moving down from the Pindos mountains and east into the foothills and plains were the Dorians' progenitors (says Herodotus) or perhaps brother tribe, the Makednoi, or Makedones. It was the Makednoi who, in the the fourth century B.C., populated the mighty, mountain-hardened war machines of Philip and Alexander, and then, in 316 B.C., established for themselves the great center of their civilization, Thessaloniki.

And it was back to the mountains and foothills of this

region that the Macedonians of the Middle Ages returned when, in the early 15th century, the Ottoman tidal wave engulfed their lowlands, and finally even Thessaloniki.

During this period, and later, in the 17th- and 18th-century heyday of trade between the Hapsburg Empire and Russia and other eastern European groups, the Macedonians created new kingdoms for themselves in their mountain hideaways. Some became roving warlords—the Robin Hood–like brigands known as *klephtes*—while others established themselves as middlemen between East and West. The latter group soon began building palaces, the fantastic manor houses that today can be seen at their most sumptuous in the village of Siatista and the lovely lakeside town of Kastoria.

Thus you can choose from equally enticing tours in western Macedonia: the one-day eastern lowland "Philip and Alexander" route covering Pella, Vergina, and Dion, with stops for a seaside swim or a visit to the refreshingly cool and charming towns of Edessa and Naoussa (the former famous for its waterfalls, the latter for its wine and forested parks); or a two- to three-day trip up into the western mountain ranges, back to the source as well as the succor of Macedonians from time immemorial. Here you will find the beautifully crafted (and relatively inexpensive) fur products of Kastoria and, if you have a car, the time, and the will, the opportunity for a swim and a lunch of freshwater fish at the mountain-ringed lakes of Prespa.

Last but not least there is Homer's "lightning-browned Olympus," which deserves to stand alone.

MOUNT OLYMPUS

So massive it catches every cloud that scuds across the Macedonian plain, Mount Olympus (Olymbos) receives 12 times the number of thunder-and-lightning storms that occur anywhere else in Greece. Small wonder, then, that the Macedonians chose it as the home for their Zeus-led gods, who replaced the dark, earthbound chthonic deities of the early (c. 2000 B.C.) Mycenaean Hellenes. Recent excavations in the foothills around the mountain range have brought to light settlements from the early Iron Age (tenth to seventh century B.C.), possibly of Macedonian origin; and other evidence shows that perhaps as early as the seventh century B.C. the Macedonians had established a sanctuary for the Olympian Zeus at Dion.

Western Macedonia

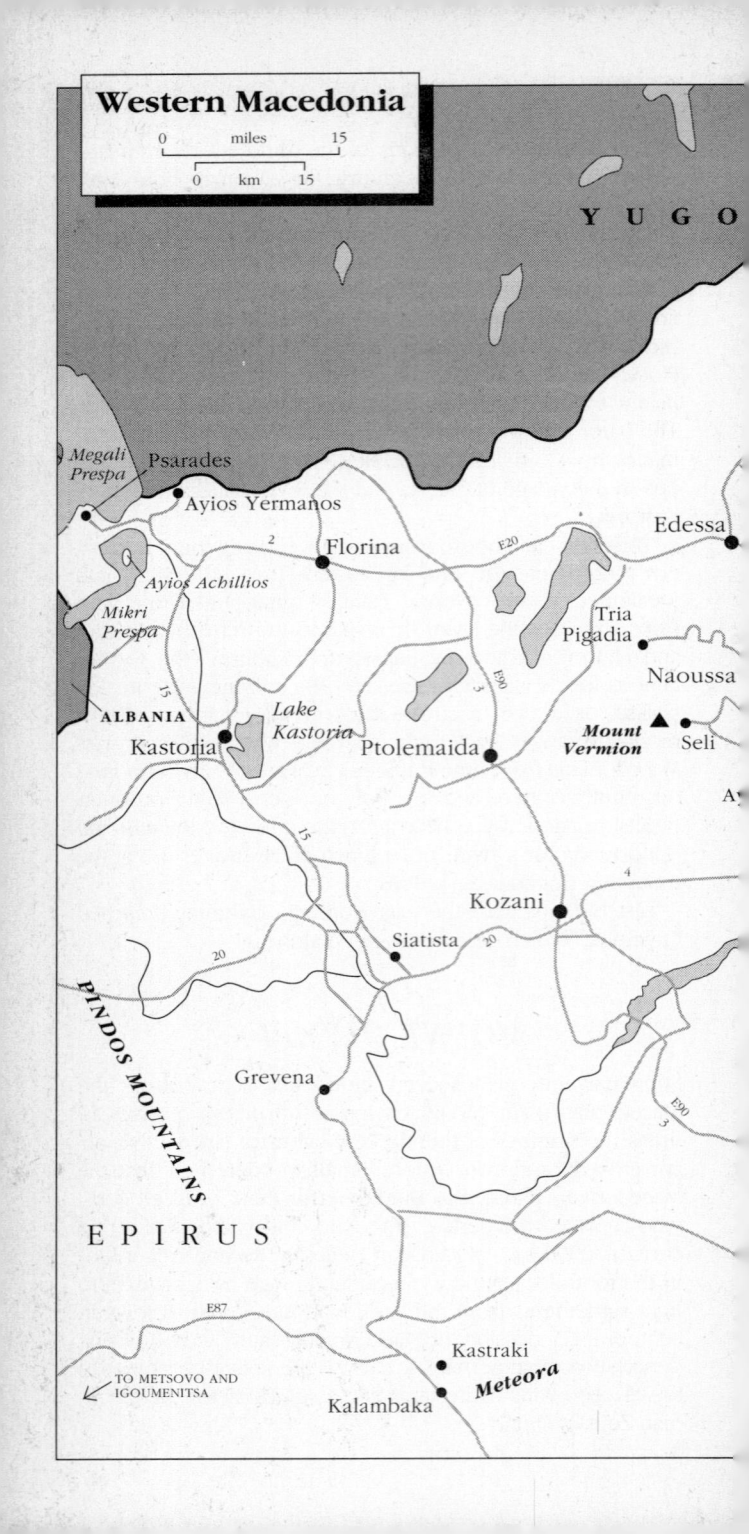

0 — miles — 15
0 — km — 15

YUGO

Megali Prespa
Psarades
Ayios Yermanos
Florina
Edessa
Ayios Achillios
Mikri Prespa
Tria Pigadia
Naoussa
ALBANIA
Lake Kastoria
Mount Vermion
Seli
Kastoria
Ptolemaida
Kozani
Siatista
PINDOS MOUNTAINS
Grevena
EPIRUS
Kastraki
Meteora
Kalambaka
TO METSOVO AND IGOUMENITSA

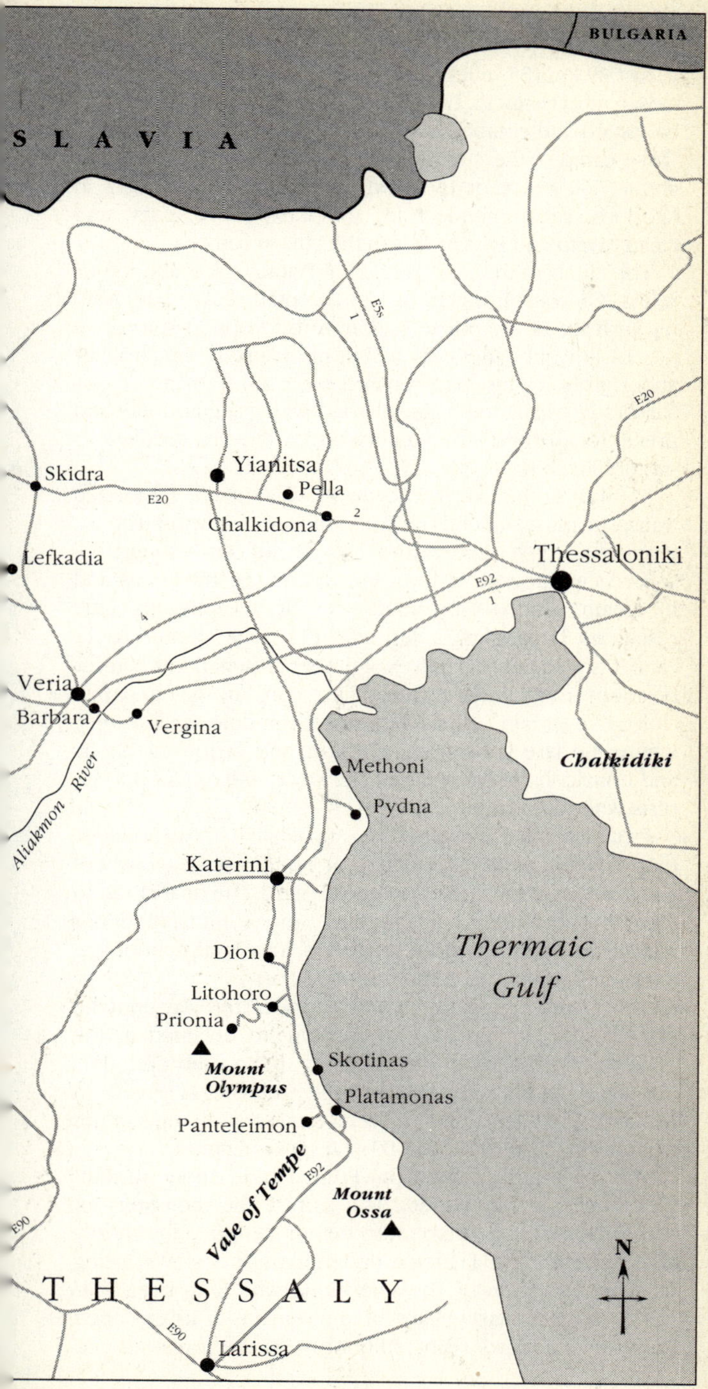

BULGARIA
SLAVIA
E5s
1
E20
Skidra
Yianitsa
Pella
E20
Chalkidona
2
Lefkadia
Thessaloniki
E92
1
4
Veria
Barbara
Vergina
Aliakmon River
Chalkidiki
Methoni
Pydna
Katerini
Thermaic Gulf
Dion
Litohoro
Prionia
Mount Olympus
Skotinas
Platamonas
Panteleimon
Vale of Tempe
E92
Mount Ossa
E90
N
THESSALY
E90
Larissa

Just 89 km (55 miles) southwest of Thessaloniki and even closer to Larissa (in Thessaly), Olympus can most sensibly be visited and climbed in a two-day period, starting from its "base camp"—the charming alpine village of **Litóhoro**—at about 7:00 A.M. (For those who wish to stay overnight in Litohoro, recommended are the inexpensive, cozy, and clean **Myrto** and **Park** hotels in the village center.)

The climb to the first "refuge" at Prionia takes about four hours. Or you can hitchhike, an accepted practice, by waiting in front of the police station. A third option is to drive the 18 km (11 miles) up to Prionia yourself, which takes about an hour. Just be prepared for a bone-jarring, nerve-shattering trip along a gravel road with no guardrails and precipitous drops. The scenery on the way is, needless to say, breathtaking.

So, too, is the safe harbor at **Priónia**, where motorized transport must be left. The site of a former sawmill (hence the name, which means "saws"), its magnificent setting, a 60-square-yard pocket of level ground amidst the pines and mountain peaks, is presided over by a captivating little restaurant built in 1972, just after the route opened up to cars. It is made of odd pieces of timber arranged in whatever positions caught the owner's fancy on any given day. A sluice-like stream courses beneath the middle of the eatery, where the fare is bean soup, bread, and various alcoholic and nonalcoholic beverages. (The key to the toilet opposite rests with the owner.)

From Prionia it is another two and a half to three hours by foot to an inn called Refuge A or Spilios Agapitos, where there are food and lodgings for the night. The final climb to the "Throne of Zeus" and the 9,571-foot summit of Mount Mýtikas (accomplished by dozens of local high-school students every year) takes another two hours.

The route is free from snow from about mid-May until the end of October. Specific details can be obtained at the Thessaloniki branch of the Hellenic Alpine Club (Tel: 031-278-288), the club at Litohoro (Tel: 0352-819-44), or from Kostas Zolotas, who runs the refuge midway up the summit from Prionia (Tel: 0352-818-00); he speaks English.

The drive back down from Prionia takes about 40 minutes. Highly recommended is a stop at the **monastery of Ayios Diónysos**, a five-minute detour to the right shortly after leaving Prionia. Blown up by Nazis, it is slowly being put together again by the sole monk who lives here. It is starkly and singularly beautiful, the remains of its exploded walls and windows rising stubbornly in the forest around the heart of the rebuilt church and altar. You may leave contributions in a plate at the altar to help the reconstruction. A few rooms are available for the night, rent-free.

Once back on flat and solid ground, at Litohoro you have a choice: a visit to the early-13th-century Crusaders' **castle of Platamonas**, overlooking the entrance to the Thermaic Gulf, and a swim at the nearby beaches of **Panteleímon** or **Skotinas** (which will be much needed after the climb up to the castle); or a trip to the wonderful museum and archaeological site of Dion, which we discuss below (see The Alexander Tour; a brief but excellent guide to the area, *Olympos, Katerini, and Dion,* with many good photographs, has been written by Sherry Marker, author of the Peloponnese chapter of this book).

THE MOUNTAIN ROUTE

A round-trip tour from Thessaloniki west over Mount Vermion and its foothills can be made comfortably and even leisurely by car in about 36 hours. This jaunt would include a short stop at Siatista, an overnight stay in Kastoria, lunch, possibly a swim in the lakes of Prespa, and the return to Thessaloniki via the Florina highway. The bus trip from Thessaloniki straight to Kastoria (there are several a day, but none from Kastoria to Prespa) is about 219 km (137 miles) and takes four to four and a half hours.

If you are going by car, you should set out from Thessaloniki early in the morning, as some of this scenery, particularly over Mount Vermion along route 4 between Veria and Kozani, is superb. The mountain road is new and wide, and the view across the Aliakmon river valley, some 3,000 feet below, is sensational, as is the curving, gliding drive down from the top of the road to the plains past Kozani.

The town of **Siátista**, about 25 km (15.5 miles) west of Kozani, is situated on an escarpment 4 km (2.5 miles) off the main route. The turnoff to the right is impossible to miss because of the immense cross that looms on the bluff above the road. Founded after the second Ottoman capture of Thessaloniki in 1430, Siatista eventually prospered as an east–west crossroads for trading caravans. At the same time, it developed—as did Kastoria, farther to the north—a thriving industry in the piecemeal fur business: Sable and marten hides brought from Russia were made into luxury items in Siatista, then traded to the West for better goods or sold for hard European cash.

By the mid-18th century these dealings had brought Siatista and Kastoria the kind of prosperity that resulted in wonderfully luxurious, ostentatious manor houses called *archontiká*. Although you can see similar houses elsewhere in northern Greece, most notably at Pelion, it is generally agreed that none are as sumptuous as Siatista's.

The principal features of these houses are thick stone lower floors, built that way for defensive purposes, and projecting upper stories that are usually constructed of lighter materials such as wood and plaster. The lower floors were used for storage and food preparation, while the upper floors were given over to creature comforts that are fantastic even by today's standards. Decorated principally in Ottoman-Baroque style, the rooms are lush, Oriental, and delicately limned. In each, paintings depicting the imagined landscapes of such far-off lands as Venice, Constantinople, and Frankfurt adorn the walls, ceilings, and woodwork—though it is obvious the painter never saw these places. Indeed, everything in the upper part of the house is designed to hover slightly above reality, somewhat like a magic carpet, ready at a moment's notice to whisk the occupant far, far away.

Three of these mansions have been preserved as museums, two in Siatista and one in Kastoria. In Siatista, keys for the two houses—the **Nerantzópoulos** and **Manoússi** mansions—and for the local Byzantine churches can be obtained from the Nerantzopoulos house, which is located on the right side of the main street in the lower part of town, near the charming square with its lovely clock and bell tower. If the curator is not there, you must ask around, as is usually the case. Just saying the names of the houses will do.

Lunch can be had at the **Archondiko** restaurant, just below the clock tower square on the road back to the main Kozani–Grevena route. It is the best in town, as is the hotel that houses it. Better, however, to push on to Kastoria, either by way of the Kozani–Grevena route or by continuing through Siatista and following its central road out of town until it joins route 15 going north to Kastoria.

Kastoria

In its time a virtual floating Roman and Byzantine fortress, the main town of Kastoria, a 44-km (27.5-mile) drive northwest of Siatista along the continual curves of route 15, sits on an irregularly shaped promontory that projects out into perhaps the loveliest lake in Greece.

Even though it is far from the beaches, boats, and bars of

the Aegean, Kastoria is one of those places that starts you thinking about what it would cost to buy a house here. Trees, mostly poplars and willows, hang over the lake in a continuous line; mountains and clouds are reflected in it; and ducks, swans, and occasionally flat-prowed fishing skiffs or sculls from the rowing club float on it—but that's about all. There are certainly very, very few tourists, if any.

Thus, as in Thessaloniki, the hotels are functional establishments geared to businesspeople (in this case, mostly fur buyers) and best recommended for their classifications and locations rather than any special characteristics. The best hotels are on the city's main streets and include the **Europa**, **Orestion**, and **Xenia du Lac**. The last, nestled on a hillock above the city center, has a view somewhat obscured by trees and a rather worn, varnished 1950s modern interior, dark and cozy. (Just opposite the Xenia's entrance is a new **Archaeological Museum** with an excellent display of Byzantine icons.) In contrast is the more modern, no-frills **Kastoria**, which has a wonderful location on the lakefront near the rowing club.

In addition to its archontika (the principal one known as the **Folk Museum**—*Laografikó Mouseío,* or *archontiko Nerantzis Aivazis*), which are located just behind the lakefront on the south side of the peninsula, there are numerous very fine Byzantine churches to be seen. Icons and frescoes also abound; Kastoria was the last bastion of the Macedonian school of religious painting to survive the 1453 fall of Constantinople.

Using a map to thread your way through the complicated warren of streets on the peninsula, you might consider the following itinerary, which covers special points of interest in the city starting from the north side.

First have a look at the outside of the impressive mansions of **Sapountzi** and **Tsiatsiapa** (and at the storks nesting on the chimneys), located just off the lakeside road of Leofóros Nikis. From there a short but steep walk leads up to the (possibly) 11th-century **church of Ayioi Anárgyri**, with its intricate brickwork and exterior frescoes of Saints Peter and Paul on either side of the doorway. Inside, blackened but visible frescoes include a depiction of the Pentecost, in which divine light is shown pouring down upon the heads of the Apostles. Another winding walk upward takes you to the unusually tall and narrow **church of Ayios Stéfanos**, perhaps built in the ninth century and notable for its brickwork but not for its frescoes, which are almost too blackened and badly desecrated by the Turks to be seen.

At the top of a rise on the other side of the peninsula is the delightful little **church of Panayía Kastriótissa** or **Koubelídiki**, which may date back to the mid-ninth century; while its dome strives to raise the church above the city, the exterior fresco of Salome dancing before Herod and the soon-to-be-beheaded John the Baptist brings it firmly back to earth. Below this to the south is the Plateía Omónia, where there is a wonderful old dark-wooded café and, as well, the 12th-century **church of Ayios Nikólaos Kasnitzi**, notable for its rustic but obviously deeply felt frescoes (possibly of 13th-century origin). Directly west from here is the **Plateía Emmanouíl**, the oldest square in the city and the center of the Greek quarter during the Turkish era.

From here it is a short walk to the Folk Museum, one block in from the lakefront road of Orestiádos. It is this road that will lead you, after a lovely half-hour walk along the lakeside, to your final destination, the **monastery of the Mavriótissa** (the Dark-Skinned Virgin Mary). The monastery was perhaps built by Alexios I Komnenos after his victory over the Normans in 1083. The name comes from the monastery's most prized icon, that of a dark-hued Virgin Mary, which is prominently displayed (and not all that dark) on the left-hand side of the iconostasis. Outside there is a charming café and restaurant, shaded in part by an immense plane tree and most certainly the best place in town for a relaxing lunch and refreshing view of Lake Kastoria.

An evening ouzo (or a meal of grilled foods) can be taken at the unnamed restaurant outside the monastery of the Mavriotissa or up at the top of the wooded acropolis at the lake end of the peninsula. Here there is an ouzeri, next to the church of Profítis Ilías, called **Tsardaki**, on the way to the city's new amphitheater, which offers an excellent view of the city. Another good spot is the rather low-key but popular ouzeri built on pilings over the lake; called **Ta Psaradika**, it's near the fish market and the Plateía of Makedonómachon (Macedonian War), which honors General James Van Fleet, a United States adviser to the Greek government forces in the Greek Civil War.

Fur items are sold at various shops all over town, from keychain tails to full-length mink coats, a newer specialty. It is worth shopping around, because quality and price can vary considerably. Some of the major dealers are **Tsoukas Brothers**, 1 Paparéska; **Xanthakou Brothers**, 28 Grammou; and **Likogiannis Furs**, 10 Eleventh of November Street.

The best restaurant in town is the **Klimataria** at 6 Orestion Street, just behind the lakefront near the Psaradika ouzeri. It serves ready-made Greek dishes of all kinds. Meanwhile, it must be said that the pubs, bars, and the city's disco can more than adequately supply an evening's entertainment. The young professionals of Kastoria seem to have a great fondness for getting together in these places throughout the long, cold winter—and the rather tedious summer, too. The best are to be found in the center, at the top of Leofóros Ayíou Athanasíou.

The Lakes of Prespa

On weekends, or whenever Kastorians have a free day, they like to drive a couple of hours or so north to their favorite beach across from, yes, Albania, for a swim in the Lakes of Prespa. The drive to Prespa is made memorable at its outset by the magnificent view the road affords of Lake Kastoria and the promontory of the city after just a few kilometers, once it starts to climb into the Pindos foothills. From there onward, the two-hour drive to Prespa becomes somewhat daunting, although not without considerable interest.

The road to Prespa is being transformed into a major artery. Already leveled, it has a layer of gravel along most of its 35-km (22-mile) length—which is to say that the ride is not all that bad but not all that smooth, either. It is, however, very beautiful. The road follows the deep basin of the Aliakmon river (the longest in Greece) as it flows on its circuitous way south almost to Thessaly and then northeast to the Thermaic Gulf at Thessaloniki. Even in spring there is a haunting autumnal quality to everything here; the occasional villages and houses, plastered with dusty red earth, rise out of the riverbank, resembling Etruscan dwellings.

It was here that some of the most vicious and decisive battles of many a war were fought, including those pitting Greeks against Turks and Bulgarians. Worst of all was the war of Greek against Greek, of Communists against Royalists and Republicans, from 1947 to 1949. The Communists were (and are) accused of forcibly separating hundreds of children from their families here and sending them across the Albanian border to be indoctrinated as future fighters for the Communist cause. The Grammos and Vitsi mountains surrounding Kastoria were the sites where, in 1949, the final bloody battles of the war took place, lasting the entire month of August and leaving more than 2,000 dead and many more wounded.

Fortunately, relief from the knowledge of this sad history is in sight. As the road climbs to the left out of the river basin, it reaches a saddle overlooking the beautiful Lakes of Prespa. These two bodies of water—Mikrí (Little) Prespa, shared by Albania and Greece, and Megáli (Big) Prespa, also touching the borders of Yugoslavia—constitute one of the last truly unspoiled places in Greece. The lakes are official sanctuaries for birds and unofficial ones for humans. It is significant that the residents of the area are extremely proud of their own and their country's efforts to keep the region pristine.

A narrow causeway divides the two lakes; you'll come to Little Prespa first, while Big Prespa is 9 km (5.5 miles) farther to the north. On the western end of this causeway are three small tavernas and a sailing club. There is also a long sandy beach facing Big Prespa, where those who are not put off by harmless, foot-long water snakes can go for a swim.

The best place to eat and relax (and perhaps even swim) is on the other side of the promontory at the end of the beach. A winding 6-km (4-mile) road leads over the promontory to the lovely little inlet and fishing village of **Psarádes**. Here you can gaze across the lake at the looming mountains of Albania and unwind at one of the three tavernas (try that of **Germanos Papadapoulos** at the far end) on some icy retsina and perhaps a perch (*perka*) just fished from the lake—a Chinese perch at that, the Albanians having stocked Prespa with fish acquired from their Communist allies.

There are 20 to 30 rooms available to rent in the village, and once a week there is a bus to and from the nearest major city, Florina, about 50 km (30 miles) to the east.

Over the hill on the other side of the inlet, about a 40-minute walk, is a beach with fine white stones. Here you not only can swim in the water but (the locals say) you also can drink it. Beyond the western end of the beach are a hermit's cave, some 170 steps down, and the 13th-century **church of the Metamorphosis**. Farther on is another, this from the 15th century, called the **church of Eléousas** (the Merciful Virgin Mary). There are also rock paintings from this period in these caves, made by the monks who inhabited them. This religious presence is another aspect of the area's reputation as a sanctuary. During the Byzantine Empire, both Prespa and Kastoria were centers of exile for various figures out of favor with the ruling secular and ecclesiastical powers.

Thus, on the little **isle of Ayios Achíllios**, which sits a few hundred yards out in the waters of Little Prespa, there are a monastery, a 16th-century church, and the ruins of a 10th-century basilica, this last with a beautiful mosaic of an egret on its floor. (To get to the isle, drive past the turnoff for

Psarades and continue around Little Prespa to a small quay easily visible from the lakeside road. With luck you will find a boat to take you across.)

On your way out of the area, stop to see the beautiful frescoes at the 10th-century **church of Ayios Yermanós** in the village of the same name, just a few kilometers straight on at the other end of the causeway.

The trip back to Thessaloniki is wonderfully scenic in places, particularly at the beginning, when you descend the 22 km (13 miles) from the Pisodérion Pass to Florina. But gradually civilization begins to intrude, and by the time you reach the outskirts of Thessaloniki, life on the road has become nothing but a traffic jam.

One bit of relief is **Edessa**, some 70 km (43 miles) on the E 20 east of Florina. Edessa is famous for its cataracts, and a stop-off here for some refreshments at one of the cafés overlooking the waterfall is a singular blessing. There are signs in English all over the town indicating "The Cataracts," but if you're in doubt about which direction to head in, turn left when the E 20 reaches the city's central plaza. By following the narrow canals, you will eventually reach the edge of the high bluff on which the city sits and where the cafés, park, and promenade overlook the plains and highway to the distant, invisible sea. (For a discussion of the archaeological site at the foot of these falls, see Pella, below.)

THE ALEXANDER TOUR

This tour takes in the three most important sites of ancient Macedonia: Pella, Dion, and Vergina. Alexander the Great was born at Pella in 356 B.C. His father, Philip, had taken important steps in forging links between the mountain and lowland network of baronies that formed his kingdom, making it a rule that the sons of the highland aristocracy should serve and be educated at Pella, where his son was growing up.

It was at Vergina (ancient Aigai, Pella's predecessor as capital of Macedonia) in 336 B.C. that Philip and Alexander and other members of the royal family gathered, along with delegations from the Greek city-states, for the wedding of Philip's daughter Cleopatra (not *that* one, but she too was of Macedonian descent) to the king of Epirus. On the way to the theater for the wedding games, Philip was assassinated; he was buried at Vergina. Alexander hurried back to Pella to consolidate his kingdom, and then, from the sacred place and military center of Dion, launched his campaign against the Persians.

Unfortunately, it is only in the eyes and trained imaginations of archaeologists that the sites live up to the story. Almost everything of value that was portable (including a lot of mosaics) was either looted by the Romans or has since been taken to museums for safekeeping, and certain areas—the Royal Tombs of Vergina, for example—are still off limits to the general public. Earthquake, fire, flood, and human spoilation have taken care of much of the rest.

The best way to visit the sites is with a guided tour (see Getting Around, below, for information), particularly because archaeologists have been reluctant to publish detailed guidebooks while so much excavation work is still in progress. Catalogues for sale in the associated museums (Thessaloniki for Vergina and on-site museums for Dion and Pella), however, will be of considerable help. In fact, to the nonspecialist the museums are infinitely more rewarding and fascinating (and more comfortable, too) than the scorching, virtually barren sites themselves.

This said, a brief visit is nonetheless in order.

Pella

Of the three sites, Pella is not only the easiest and quickest to get to but also the farthest from a beach and therefore, in summer, the first that should be visited on a day trip. Leave Thessaloniki on the Egnatia–Monasteriou road past the railway station and follow the road signs marked "Edessa." Pella is a 38-km (24-mile) drive northwest of the city on the standard two-lane asphalt highway, the E 20. You can also take the daily Thessaloniki–Edessa bus, which stops right on the corner of the main road where the archaeological site is located. On this corner is a sign indicating a turnoff to Pella on the right. That is the village, not the archaeological site. The site, to repeat, is on the main Thessaloniki–Edessa road right there at the corner, while the museum is on the road's left (south) side.

With most of its treasures gone (carted off to Rome after the subjugation of Macedonia in 168 B.C.) and its lagoon silted up, Pella was believed until recently to have been irrevocably lost, buried under silt and dirt. Then, in 1957, a farmer digging ground for a cellar chanced upon two columns of a colonnade, and thus Pella was "born again."

Since then, remains of the ancient city have been located along a swath extending up to the village of Pella, along the main Thessaloniki–Edessa road to the east and west, and across the road to the south. The site occupies perhaps as much as five square miles, but as of this writing neither the great palace of Archelaos nor the theater where Euripides' *Bacchae* may have been performed have been located. A large complex recently discovered on the acropolis west of the village, however, may yet prove to be the palace.

At the moment, only the small portion of the site that is on the corner of the E 20 would be of interest to the layman. Here are the foundations of three large buildings thought to have had some ceremonial or official function. Some of the original floor mosaics are still in place, but the best of these have been taken for display in the museum, which also includes what is believed to be a head of Alexander and some striking terra-cotta figurines. Particularly notable are those depicting the goddess Athena wearing a helmet with horns.

From Pella it is possible to return 8 km (5 miles) to Chalkidóna, turn right, and motor south to Veria (Beroia) and nearby Vergina on route 4. A much lovelier and more interesting route takes you to the tombs of Lefkadia and on possible side trips to the towns of Edessa and Naoussa.

Edessa, discussed above, is another 50 km (31 miles) west from Pella on the E 20 and might be a good place to stop for lunch at one of the cafés overlooking the waterfalls. An extensive archaeological site, below the cataracts and near the electricity station, was once believed to have been the Macedonian capital of Aigai. Although the remains below Edessa are of little archaeological importance, ongoing excavations nearby have recently brought to light a Roman graveyard consisting of some 40 tombs.

If you decide not to continue as far as Edessa, turn off the E 20 at the junction, skirting the town of Skidra, and travel the 20 km (12 miles) south toward Veria in order to visit the Macedonian tombs at Lefkadia and, as a refreshing side trip, the green and shady woods of Ayios Nikolaos at Naoussa.

Lefkadia and Naoussa

Arriving at Lefkádia from the north, you should not turn off at the sign for the village but continue straight on over the small bridge. Just on the right is a sign for the Macedonian Tomb of Lyson Kallikles, a site hidden in a farmer's field up a rough dirt road. The tomb is partially underground (you have to drop down through a hole in the ceiling as if you were a grave robber) and is locked. The key is farther up the road to Naoussa, past the Macedonian Tomb of Kinch (named after its Danish discoverer) on the left. About 100 yards beyond that, also on the left, is a sign saying "The Two Macedonian Tombs." This is the place you want.

Turn left and go down the road across a railroad track. There on the right is a large Quonset-type hut rising up out of an excavation in the ground. This is covering the first of the two tombs and sits next to the guardhouse. If the guard is not there, try the next tomb, about 200 yards down the road on the left.

This is the **Great Tomb**, the more beautiful of the two, and is the largest of its type ever discovered. It is, to say the least, with its ornamented and painted façade, extremely impressive.

If you can find the guard, and if he is in the mood, he will also open the other tombs. These are not, particularly after the Great Tomb, all that impressive, although the tomb next to the guardhouse is definitely worth a look.

More enticing than another tomb at this point, however, might be the picnic park of Ayios Nikolaos at Naoussa, with its bubbling brook, "one thousand trees" (the area is called just that: *Hília Dentra*), fresh rainbow trout, and the superb wines of Naoussa.

The turnoff for **Náoussa** is about another mile down the main road south toward Veria, and then 6 km (4 miles) to the west. Located in the foothills of Mount Vermion, Naoussa is a neighbor of the nearby ski resorts of Seli and Tria Pigadia, considered to be the best in northern Greece.

The park of **Ayios Nikólaos**, which can be found by following the signs through town, is very beautiful and extremely popular in the summertime, when a weekend visit could mean crowds. The park has a small hotel—the Hotel Vermion—plus several restaurants, the latter all specializing in brook trout home grown in enclosed pools watered by the river running through the site. Also to be sampled here are the wines.

The wines of Naoussa, especially those of the Boutari family, are considered to be of a quality approaching that of wines from France and California, a statement that would have been unthinkable ten years ago.

The Boutari clan (there are five brothers now running the family business) have done extensive research in European wine producing, blending, and aging methods and are now, along with the Naoussa Wine Producers' Cooperative (and estates of the Carras and Tsantalis families in Chalkidiki), producing vintage wines of wonderful quality and variety. For the very best, try the light, white Château Matsa and Santorini Vintage 1987, and the full-bodied reds of Naoussa 1986 and Grande Réserve Boutari 1983. There are also the considerably less expensive white Lac aux Roches, red and white Rotonda, and retsina, all of which are of a higher quality than most Greek table wines.

The drive to Vergina cuts through the foothill suburbs of Veria. Follow the road signs for Thessaloniki until you reach a wide turnoff. The road forks to the left for Thessaloniki but continues straight ahead for the lovely little village of Ayia Barbara (Várvara). Here, to the right, you'll find a very nice restaurant called **Ta Platania**, meaning "the plane trees," of which there are many shading the tables.

Vergina

The village and archaeological site of Vergína are about 6 km (4 miles) farther on, across the Aliakmon river. Signs in the village (named after an ancient, perhaps legendary queen of Beroia and settled in 1923 by population-exchange refugees from Turkey) point to a "Country Site, Platania," which is a picnic area under some plane trees along a small waterfall and brook just outside the village. There are also two signs for the archaeological site: one for the Royal Tombs (turnoff on the left) and the other for the Palace (straight through and out the other side of town).

The **Royal Tombs** are inside the village, fenced off and covered with corrugated roofing. They are inaccessible to the general public, for whom the only compensation is a nondescript café-restaurant and tourist shop on a corner opposite.

For eons a great tumulus mound stood within the enclosed area, seeming to indicate the presence of something important buried beneath it. But try as they might, neither archaeologists nor grave robbers were able to discover the true secret of the tumulus: The royal Macedonian tombs were hidden not in the center but near the edge, and were covered with the debris of broken tombstones from a later pillaging as if to indicate that there was nothing below left for the taking.

Professor Manolis Andronikos, discoverer of the Royal Tombs, speculates that one of Alexander's successors as king, Antigonos Gonatas (283 to 239 B.C.), the grandson of

Alexander's general of the same name, created this diversion to ward off potential robbers and protect both his own tomb and those of the family of the revered Philip.

In early November 1977, Professor Andronikos, on the final day of excavation before closing the site for winter, came across Philip's tomb. When entered through a small opening at the rear, the tomb was discovered to be untouched—the first of its kind found in such a state. In a few days' time the professor and his associates uncovered its stunning treasures, photographed them, and whisked them off to the Archaeological Museum of Thessaloniki, where they are today on display.

The road to the palace leads out of town, winding through rolling farmland that still covers the greater part of the town and vast royal burial grounds of ancient Aigai. On the way, the road passes the "Bella" tumulus (named for the man who owns the land), the site of three tombs also unearthed by Andronikos.

The **Palace**—or what is left of its foundations—stands on a low bluff overlooking the fields, with its back against the protecting and steeply rising foothills of the Piéria mountains. It was discovered by French archaeologists as long ago as 1861, but was hardly suspected of being of such importance until Andronikos uncovered the Royal Tombs in 1977. Today it offers little of interest to the layman except the wonderful view of the farmland and tumuli below, and of the theater (found by Andronikos only in 1982) near which Philip was assassinated. Its position below the palace is in perfect accordance with the facts that we have about his murder by one Pausanias, a bodyguard (not the Roman who wrote of his travels through Greece c. A.D. 160 to 180).

From Vergina, the fastest way to reach the sacred city of Dion is to turn right and drive east along the main road outside of town until it joins the Athens–Thessaloniki expressway. From there the trip south along the coast is an easy 50 km (31 miles). As you approach it, Mount Olympus rises with increasing majesty above the birthplace of the muses and the sanctuary of Zeus at Dion.

Dion

The turnoff for Dion, clearly marked, is to the right about 15 km (9 miles) south of the bypass of Kateríni. From there it is another 5 km (3 miles) through the village of Dio and around to the road on the right that leads out of its lovely circular plateia to the first intersection. A left turn takes you to the excellent museum and its cafés, shops, and restaurants. A right turn leads to the site, past the large Classical theater of ancient Dion, which in September 1990 inaugurated its first season of Classical works performed by the State Theater of Northern Greece.

The road divides the archaeological site into two unequal parts. On the left is the main entrance, where visitors buy tickets and view the part of the city thus far excavated. Be sure to see the superb and recently discovered mosaics of Dionysios at the eastern end of the main street. On the right a major roadway was unearthed in 1990; on it was found a magnificent Macedonian sword, leading to some hope that this might be the road to the as-yet-undiscovered Temple of Zeus, ancient Dion's main edifice. Excavation is continuing. Also on the right, a bit farther on alongside the road, are the **Sanctuaries of Asklepios and Demeter** and the **Sanctuary of Isis**. In the latter location, copies of the original statues (now in the museum) have been set in place, making this Hellenistic temple the most comprehensible (and striking) part of the entire complex. In the main area there is much to be excavated (recently found was a bath and altar to which barren women would come for prayers and therapy) and little of real interest to the layman, particularly under a scorching summer sun. What can be seen is primarily from the post-Hellenistic Roman and Roman-Christian eras up until the late fifth century A.D.

In the **museum**, however, you will find a well-presented collection of fascinating and beautiful finds from all periods, and on the second floor relief maps make clear the geographical layout of the entire area and nearby sites.

The site was first established in the fifth century B.C. by the Macedonian king Archelaos, who built a sanctuary to Zeus as well as a stadium and a theater where, much later, some of Euripides' plays were performed. In Philip's and Alexander's time Dion was a military center; Philip celebrated his capture and total destruction of Olynthos (an Athenian ally in Chalkidiki) here in 348 B.C., and Alexander gave sacrifice to the gods here before marching off to invade Persia. It may have been at Dion that Alexander, at about age 12, received and tamed the wonder horse Bucephalus. Later it was occupied by the Romans, and in A.D. 346 Dion was the site of a Christian bishopric. Recent and continuing excavations by Demetrius Pandermalis, a noted professor of archaeology at the University of Thessaloniki, have generated considerable interest, and much of value is certain to be uncovered in ensuing years.

From Dion, as mentioned above, you can visit various nearby beaches as well as the Crusaders' castle of Platamónas and, if you are heading south, the lovely Vale of Tempe (see Thessaly). At Platamonas, the large, new, air-conditioned **Platamon Beach Hotel**, on the sea but with a swimming pool, is recommended.

If you are going back to Thessaloniki, you might consider visiting two locations along the coast that have nothing of particular interest to see (except the lovely beaches, where the **Alkyon Hotel**, on the beach at Paralia (Seaside) Katerini, offers a nice respite from travelling), but are the sites of two battles that link the past and the future of things Macedonian.

The first in time (but the second along the road, about 45 km/28 miles south of Thessaloniki) is **Methóni**. Here, in a battle against the Athenians, Philip received a terrible arrow wound in his eye; just such an injury is evident in the skull found in the Vergina Royal Tombs (displayed in the Thessaloniki Archaeological Museum), compelling many to believe that the remains are indeed Philip's.

The second site is that of **Pydna**, 17 km (10.5 miles) north of Katerini and about 10 km (6 miles) south of Methoni. Here, in 168 B.C., the Romans decisively defeated the army of Perseus, the Macedonian king. Perseus escaped, however, fleeing toward the place where this account of northern Greece will eventually end: the remote, mysterious island sanctuary of Samothrace, which lies close to the edge of Asia at the easternmost limits of Greece.

EASTERN MACEDONIA

As western Macedonia was Philip and Alexander country, so the area east and southeast of Thessaloniki as far as Thrace is predominantly—and incongruously—that of Classical Greece, of Athens, and of Evia (Euboea). Indeed, along the coastal route (which is of most interest to the foreign visitor) the prevailing southern Aegean presence is felt down to the climate and vegetation (not to mention the beautiful beaches). It is as if the three fingers (to use an overworked but apt metaphor) of the hand that make up the peninsula of Chalkidiki were reaching down and drawing toward themselves the fragmented pieces of their southern kith and kin, the Aegean islands. So strong is this link between the two areas that the Sporades island of Skiathos, some 80 miles to the south, is so named because it is said to fall within the shadow (*skiá*) of the 6,685-foot peak of Mount Athos on Chalkidiki.

Conversely, Chalkidiki, Thessaloniki's virtual holiday suburb, is so named because, in the eighth and seventh centuries B.C., the Evian city of Chalkis (modern Chalkida), just 50 miles north of Athens, founded some 30 colonies on its shores, intermarrying with the indigenous tribes and establishing a southern connection. This, along with the colonizing influences of Athens prior to the Peloponnesian Wars, has resulted in a distinct difference between the character of the area's present-day inhabitants and that of their "northern" (which is to say, virtually next-door) neighbors in the rest of Macedonia. To anyone who has spent time living or travelling in Greece, the strong southern flavor of Chalkidiki, and particularly of Cycladic-seeded Thasos, is extremely striking.

CHALKIDIKI

If you imagine Chalkidikí as a three-fingered hand sticking out in the Aegean, Thessaloniki and its suburbs can be said to occupy the thumb in the northwest corner of the area. A spanking new four-lane highway running just parallel to the road to Thessaloniki's airport now connects the downtown area with Chalkidiki's first two fingers, Kassandra and Sithonia. You can get to Kassandra, only some 66 km (41 miles) away, in virtually no time at all—except, of course, during the massive traffic jams of Friday afternoons and Saturday and Sunday mornings. To join this route from downtown Thessaloniki, follow Egnatia Street and then Nea Egnatia east past the university and out through the suburbs. Because it is presumed that you know you are already in or going toward Chalkidiki, there are no signs (yet) to tell you so. If you are on the road to the airport, watch for the sign pointing left to Nea Moudanía and make the turn there. About 100 yards farther on is the new highway. A right turn onto this highway leads directly to the first finger, Kassandra, which you should reach in about 40 minutes following the

Eastern Macedonia

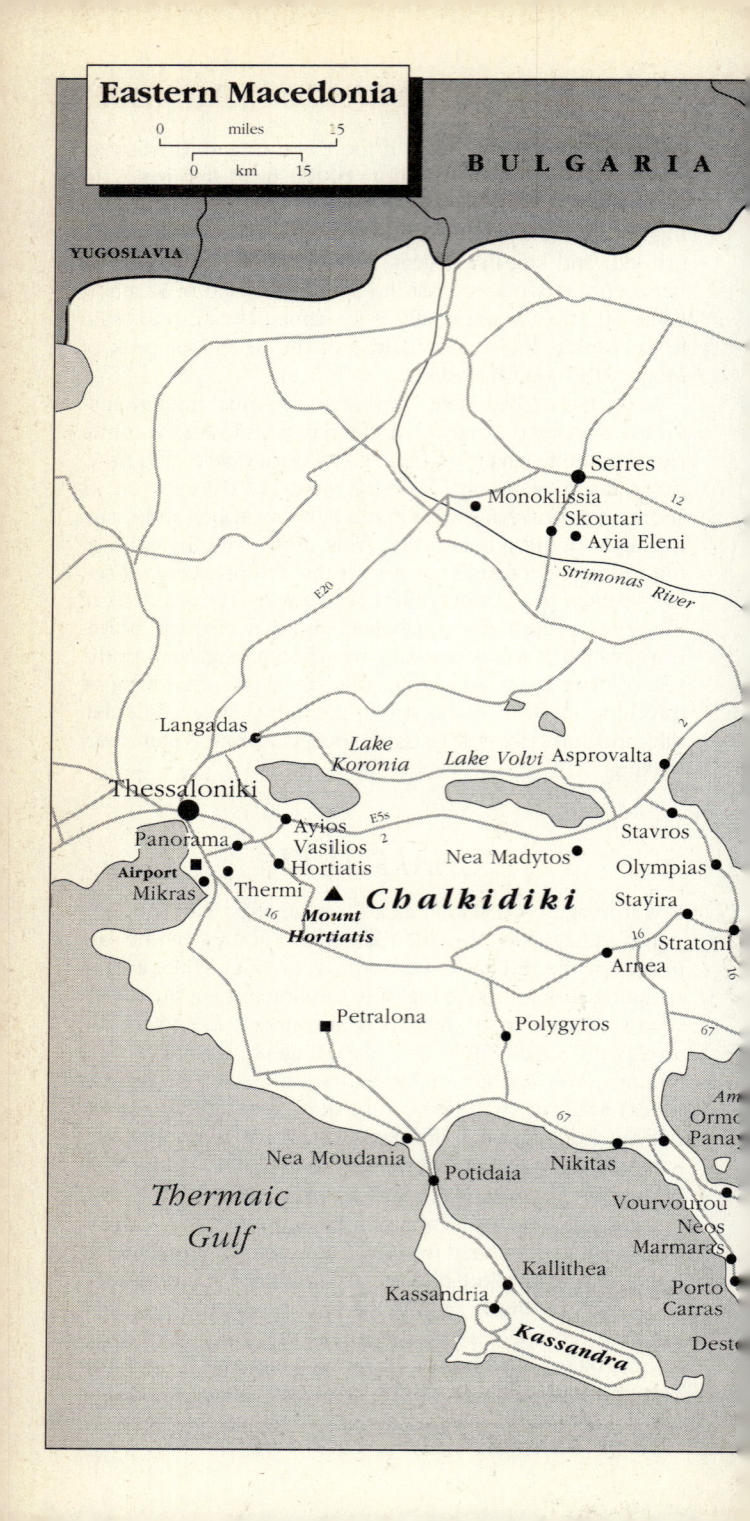

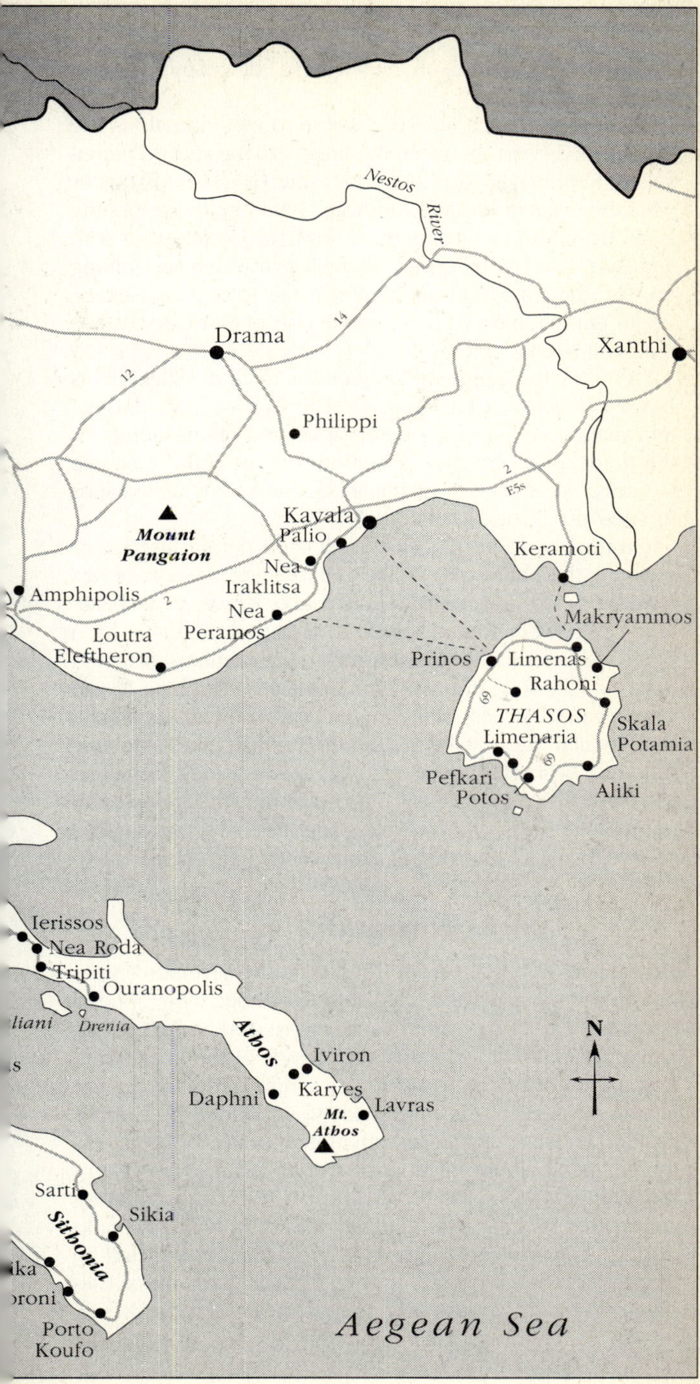
Nestos
River
14
Drama
Xanthi
12
Philippi
2
E5s
Kavala
Palio
Mount
Pangaion
Nea
Iraklitsa
Keramoti
Amphipolis
2
Nea
Peramos
Makryammos
Loutra
Eleftheron
Prinos
Limenas
Rahoni
THASOS
Skala
Potamia
Limenaria
Pefkari
Potos
Aliki
Ierissos
Nea Roda
Tripiti
Ouranopolis
Drenia
Athos
Iviron
Karyes
Daphni
Lavras
Mt.
Athos
N
Sarti
Sikia
Sithonia
Porto
Koufo
Aegean Sea

signs to Nea Moudania, on the northern edge of the entrance to the peninsula.

From this point it is also possible to continue along the beach-lined "web" between the fingers to the second peninsula of Sithonia, 38 km (24 miles) away. However, no matter what the maps may vaguely indicate, it is virtually impossible to go from Sithonia to the third finger of Mount Athos with any ease. This can be done only by backtracking and joining up with the comparatively narrow route 16 as it crosses the "palm" and then drops down to the port of Ouranopolis and the peninsula of Athos.

(A highly recommended guidebook to all of Chalkidiki is I. A. Papangelos's *Chalkidiki*. Overflowing with all kinds of information, area maps, photographs, and phone numbers, this guide, published in Thessaloniki as part of the Welcome Guidebook series, is available at bookstores and newsstands in Thessaloniki and Chalkidiki.)

On the way to Kassandra make a short detour just before reaching the peninsula—some 16 km/10 miles short of Nea Moudania—to visit the Paleolithic site of **Petrálona**. Its beautiful caves were first discovered in the early 1940s by a Greek shepherd who, to escape German bombers, scurried down a hole for safety. In 1960 a villager searching for an underground stream fell into the cave and discovered a skull, which has now been identified as that of a Paleolithic hominid, probably female, who lived here somewhere from 250,000 to 700,000 years ago. The cave has since been fitted out for sightseers, with walkways and life-size reproductions of cave dwellers squatting in dramatically lit grottoes.

Kassandra

Historically important from the fifth to the seventh century B.C., this peninsula was named after Cassander, who founded upon it a city of the same name, married Alexander's half-sister, Thessaloniki, and was a successor of the great ruler. Kassandra's principal port in Classical times, **Potidaia** (on the northwest neck of the peninsula) was founded by Corinth around 600 B.C.; Potidaia's attempted revolt from an enforced membership in Athens's Delian League was one of the main causes of the Peloponnesian War, Corinth having strong ties with Sparta. Potidaia was destroyed by Philip during his war with Olynthos, and was then resurrected by Cassander, who renamed it after himself. With the subsequent flourishing of the new port of Thessaloniki, however,

Kassandreia, as it had become known, gradually lost most of its former prominence. Now virtually nothing of interest remains to be seen in the area except the canal that was cut across the isthmus in 1937.

Today Kassándra is the most popular and populated resort area of Chalkidiki. It is a beautiful peninsula with glorious stretches of white sand punctuated with rocky, pine-crested promontories and studded with hotels, camping sites, shopping centers, discotheques, and various other gathering places frequented for the most part by the families of vacationing Thessaloniki, whose teenage scions run loose in hordes here during summer. Whatever, the quality of some of the hotels and beaches is excellent—particularly those of the twin **Athos Palace** and **Pallini Beach** hotels at Kallithéa, midway down the peninsula on the eastern coast. These sister hotels share a guard-posted roadway entrance and a long, beautiful beach of pure white sand. Among the best first-class hotels in Greece, they have, in addition to the beach, their own swimming pools, shopping concourse, movie theaters, tennis courts, seaside snack bars, and more. The hotels are so self-contained, however, that they tend to insulate the visitor from Greece itself. But if all you want is to be coddled in a luxurious environment at slightly less than luxury prices, then the Pallini and Athos hotels could not come more highly recommended.

The 38-km (23-mile) drive from Kassandra to Sithonia, Chalkidiki's second finger, follows a two-lane asphalt road and takes about half an hour, depending on how many mobile homes you encounter along the way. You may want to detour the 13 km (8 miles) north to **Polygyros** to take in the tiny **Archaeological Museum** there, which contains finds from all over Chalkidiki. Particularly interesting are objects from a sanctuary of Ammon Zeus (*ammo* means "sand"), an Egyptian-Libyan desert variation of the Greek deity, who inspired Alexander to make a significant pilgrimage there after he founded his eponymous city in the Nile delta. Also on display is a head of the ubiquitous Dionysus, whose influence is still to be found in certain aspects of Macedonian and Thracian life.

Between the fingers of Kassandra and Sithonia is a virtually unbroken line of lovely beaches and adjacent rooming houses, hotels, and camping sites. See, for example, the stunning seaside near the village of Nikítas. But some of the most beautiful parts of Chalkidiki (excluding Mount Athos) belong to the peninsula of Sithonia.

Sithonia

Sithonía's is a much more rugged and varied coastline than that of Kassandra, with isolated pockets of beaches, lagoons, and offshore islands. From Thessaloniki a leisurely drive around its coast road with stops for lunch, a swim, coffee, and sightseeing can be accomplished in 8 to 12 hours, round trip. If you have your own transport, this circular tour is best begun on the eastern side of the peninsula, so that as you head south you have the superb view of Mount Athos always in front or to the left across the bay. Otherwise, the local bus from Thessaloniki (boarded in the Thessaloniki suburb of Harilaou) to Sarti on the east coast of Sithonia travels, via Polygyros, all around the peninsula from west to east and back again. This wonderfully scenic journey takes about four hours one way. It does not, however, pass by one of the most beautiful areas of Sithonia, that of its northeastern corner. Here is the idyllic, islanded yachting harbor of **Ormos Panayías** and the attendant bay of Vourvouroú; a virtually private resort of families from Thessaloniki, it has only one small hotel, the clean and serviceable **Diaporos**, on the beach, and some houses with rooms for rent. (A separate bus from the Harilaou station in Thessaloniki services Vourvourou; the trip takes about three hours.)

Halfway down the peninsula from Vourvourou is the rather crazy little fishing village of **Sarti**. Settled by refugees from the 1923 population exchange with Turkey, Sarti is a haphazard collection of two-story homes and rooming and apartment houses built in various styles, from red-tiled, wood-balconied Macedonian to blue-and-white Rococo modern; it has, because and in spite of this, a definite, ineffable charm. It also has a long and marvelous beach that comes right up to the front steps and ramshackle flower gardens of its inhabitants, and a magnificent view (when the air is clear) of Mount Athos across the bay, silhouetted in the mornings by the rising sun. Because most of the rooming and apartment houses have neither names, addresses (being built on as yet unnamed streets), nor telephones, the only recourse is to deal through a local agent: **Sigma & Kappa Hellas**, 630 72 Sarti, Chalkidiki; Tel: (0375) 415-26. Most of the apartment houses cater to families with children; if you are one, ask the agent about the new **House Evi**, half a block from the beach but away from the noisier town center, with beds for two adults and bunks for two children. About half a mile south of town are the beachfront, tree-shaded grounds of **Sarti Beach**, a somewhat rough-and-ready camping site that also has rooms and bungalows for rent. For breakfast, lunch, or dinner in Sarti, try the breeze-refreshed **Ta Vrakakia** (The Rocks), right on the beach at its northern, rocky end. Grilled fish and meats as well as delicious ready-made foods such as *moussaká* make for a wonderful variety of both tastes and prices.

Another lovely place to stop for lunch or an evening ouzo and dinner is the beautiful bay of **Porto Koufo**, on the southwestern tip of the Sithonia peninsula. Its waters almost completely encircled by projecting, rocky headlands (called *koufó*—deaf—because the sound of the sea is so faint), the bay, now lined with concrete docks for caïques and yachts, was a submarine base during World War II, the somewhat spooky installations of which are still in place in a small cove around the northern headland.

North toward the grand resort complex of Porto Carras are several other beaches, all with camping sites and/or small hotels and rooming houses. Then begins the vast estate of the Carras family, which occupies both sides of the road for some 13 miles north. Here grapes are grown for some of Greece's best wines (under the name Domaine de Porto Carras). Try the red Bordeaux-like Château Carras and the Grand Vin Rouge, the white Carras Réserve and various Côtes de Méliton, and the Carras Rosé Spécial. (Some other excellent regional wines are those produced by the Tsantalis estate; among the best are the white Agiortikos and Makedonikos and the red Cava and Naoussa.)

Porto Carrás is one of the major resort areas of Greece; it is impossible to pass by without at least mentioning its two immense hotels—the **Meliton** and **Sithonia Beach**—and, on the yacht marina, the rooms and apartments of the considerably cozier **Village Inn**. There is also an 18-hole golf course, a concert hall, a large central beach, and numerous smaller ones in coves running south along the Carras estate.

Just north of Porto Carras is the lively and charming fishing village of **Neos Marmarás**, chock-full of tavernas, cafés, bars, and caïques bobbing in the harbor. There are no hotels, though, only rooming houses. This is where guests from Porto Carras and people renting houses in the area north of the village come for nights on the town.

The "Palm" of Chalkidiki

As mentioned earlier, when leaving Thessaloniki to join the new expressway to Kassandra it is possible to continue straight across the center of the palm to the third "finger" by turning left onto route 16, which eventually leads east to the Mount Athos ports of Ierissos and Ouranopolis. This is certainly the fastest way to reach the eastern areas of Chalkidiki and to see the countryside on the way. However, the *best* way to see the region is to approach it from the opposite direction, travelling east to west. This is because the "hand" as a whole—palm and fingers—is considerably higher on the eastern side than on the western. Thus, in going from east to west you're treated to a series of magnificent views from on high as the landscape, in a succession of plateau-like steps, drops from one level to the next. Graced by the sun setting in the west and low-lying clouds hanging over the plains, these panoramas offer an unforgettable experience.

Here is a possible itinerary for a day trip to the eastern part of Chalkidiki: Leave Thessaloniki from Plateia Vardaris, taking the E 20 north toward Serres. Turn right after 14 km (8 miles) onto the E 5s heading east toward Kavala. On the left (north) side are the lovely lakes of Koronia and Volvi.

Lake Koróni̇a, the first one you'll come to, is 9 miles long. On its shore is the stork-topped village of Ayios Vasílios. A right turn here eventually leads up to the hilltop towns of Hortiatis and Panorama (see above) and back down into Thessaloniki—a lovely drive—while a left turn leads to the lake and a very nice little taverna that serves fish from the lake. A short walk down to the lake's edge is recommended, if only to see the beautiful, gracefully curved black fishing skiffs.

Lake Volvi, 12 miles long, has a small picnic and camping area and café in the works. From a pier about three-quarters of the way along its length, opposite the inland village of Nea Mádytos, it is possible to swim in the lake. About 5 km (3 miles) farther east on the right is the unique and magical thatch-roofed **church of Ayía Marína**, built in 1869. Its surroundings are so verdant with plane trees and swards that it seems to be set in the English countryside, not the sun-dried landscape of Greece.

The turnoff for the eastern coast of Chalkidiki comes about another 5 km (3 miles) farther on, with signposts indicating the villages of **Stavrós** and **Olýmpias**. Both are wonderful, tree-canopied little fishing villages that as yet are not as tourist-ridden as they must inevitably become. The 14 km (9 miles) of coastline that separates them is spectacularly beautiful—rocky, clad in pine trees, and virtually uninhabited. Dirt paths lead down to the beaches.

Olympias is situated next to the promontory on which

ancient Stagira, the birthplace of Aristotle, was located. The relatively modern town of Stayira, nearby on the road back to Thessaloniki, has a lovely little park with a statue of Aristotle in it, but cannot legitimately claim him as its native son.

After Olympias you are again presented with absolutely stunning views down to the sea, but you should resist the temptation to follow the descent to the village of Stratóni. While beautiful from a distance, its coastline is marred by an immense mining structure wedged into the mountainside, invisible from above, but straddling the beach like some monster loosed from England's Industrial Age.

Instead, at the junction for Stratoni, either continue along the coast to Chalkidiki's third "finger" of Mount Athos—another 16 km (10 miles) to Ierissos and 32 km (20 miles) to Ouranopolis—or turn inland to take route 16 back the 100-km (62-mile) curving descent to Thessaloniki.

Ierissós is the sprawling, nondescript fishing village at which visitors to Mount Athos can choose to arrive after their stay on the peninsula. The smaller village of **Nea Roda**, 5 km (3 miles) farther south, is another possible disembarkation point. (But to go to Athos you must embark at Ouranopolis.) Both Ierissos and Nea Roda have good beaches, although, like others that belong to working fishing villages, they tend to be awash with litter.

Nea Roda is also known for its proximity to **Xerxes' Canal**, which the Persian king is said to have had dug across the isthmus in 480 B.C. to facilitate his second attempt to invade Greece, the first attempt having foundered on the rocks of Athos's headland. Today only a slight, sometimes marshy, and all-but-invisible depression remains in certain parts of the isthmus, which has risen some 46 feet since Xerxes' time.

Ouranopolis

Ouranópolis is notable for its turquoise sea and fine beaches, particularly along its 5-mile westward-facing coast and on the enchanting, tiny islands—**Amouliani** and **Drénia**—opposite. These islands are not to be missed. You reach them by an inexpensive 15-minute ride on a local caïque or by small outboard motorboats rented by the day. The larger island of Amouliani has a taverna on the western side of its gracefully curved beach of **Alykes**. The eight smaller Drenia islands enjoy a Carribean-like setting; the largest of them, **Gaïdorónisi**, boasts two thatch-covered bars on its longest beach that serve charcoal-grilled *souvlákia* and salads. The beaches on the other islands are of fine white sand and are superb for sunbathing and swimming.

Ouranopolis is also noted for the Byzantine **Tower of Profórion**, built on its point in the 12th century by Emperor Andronicus II. Once inhabited by monks of the Athos monastery of Vatopedi, the tower was abandoned in 1923 when the area, like many throughout northern Greece, was settled by refugees from Turkey during the exchange of populations that followed the Greco-Turkish War of 1920–1922. A Scottish-Australian couple, Joice and Sydney Loch, were engaged in helping Thessaloniki's noted American Farm School deal with the problems of these refugees. They eventually rented the tower and became near saints in the community, administering to the refugees' medical needs and encouraging them to channel their Anatolian rug-weaving skills into a cottage industry that was, until the recent boom in tourism, the mainstay of their economy. Sydney Loch died in 1954, but his wife stayed on in the tower until her death in 1982. Both are buried in the village cemetery on the hill above the port. The tower has recently been undergoing renovations, and the rug industry, featuring works incorporating motifs Sydney Loch borrowed from the Mount Athos monasteries, is still thriving. Sprouting in place of the former refugee shacks are numerous summer homes and apartments and room-renting complexes, as well as the usual restaurants and coffee and tourist shops.

Worth visiting among the shops is the **Akroathos**, on the seaside road south of the tower promontory. Owned by a husband-and-wife team of artist-jewelers, Akroathos offers a variety of handmade jewelry, icons, illuminated Byzantine manuscript pages copied on leather, and more. Next to it is the house of **Fani Mitropoulou**, who for 40 years has been producing the same style of rugs introduced by the Lochs and is now perhaps alone among the villagers in continuing to use the original techniques and natural dyes.

For an old-style taverna, try **Manthos**, a little farther down the seaside road to the south. It offers basic Greek cooking and less expensive varieties of fish, and is a great place to watch the sun go down behind the tower—as are, for that matter, the more costly restaurants along the sea on the tower's north side, which offer finer types of fish and meats, and breakfast as well.

Farther along the southern road toward the wall and gate that separate the world from the holy peninsula of Mount Athos is the **Skites** hotel and restaurant. Recently built, but with great respect for traditional decor as well as atmosphere, Skites is a small cluster of gardened rooms and apartments set, like the individual monastic living quarters for which it is named, in splendid (but not monk-like) isolation just above the sea about one kilometer (about half a mile) outside of town. Its restaurant is open to nonresidents and offers a limited and variable menu of homemade dishes that are just as inviting as the establishment itself.

Recommended within Ouranopolis is the first hotel built in the village, the **Xenia Hotel**, situated on the south side of the promontory away from the port's bustle. It was built in 1960, at the same time that the first and only road connecting the village with the mainland was gouged out of the coastal rocks. A very tastefully designed group of bungalows with a central dining-and-reception building, the Xenia is nestled in a grove of olive trees about 200 yards north of the village. Although isolated, it shares a continuous beach with Ouranopolis and looks westward toward the Amouliani islands.

To the north, some 7 km (4 miles) along the eastern line of beaches toward the produce dock of Tripití, is the luxurious family-style **Eagles' Palace**, a large, air-conditioned hotel-and-bungalow complex with a tennis court, piano bar, swimming pool, and a yacht for trips to the Amouliani and Drenia islands and the coast of Mount Athos. If these hotels are full, ask for assistance at the Bureau of General Tourism, organized by the townspeople. (For information on taking the caïque from here to Mount Athos—males only—see below.)

On the return trip to Thessaloniki, stops at the little park dedicated to Aristotle at **Stáyira** and at **Arnéa** provide pleasant breaks. On clear days Stayira affords an excellent view of Mount Athos and the peninsula; Arnea, known for its rather tourist-oriented handicrafts, has, in its central square (where the bus stops), a natural fountain that spouts from the trunk of a huge plane tree, where banged-up metal cups hang so you can quaff the deliciously cool, wood-filtered waters.

If you are returning late to Thessaloniki and need immediate sustenance, the little village of **Thermi**, which is on the right just before the junctions of the new expressway and the airport road (about 16 km/10 miles outside central Thessaloniki), is very popular for its *psistariá*—restaurants featuring charcoal-grilled foods and, in the case of Thermi, wild game in season. There is a line of these restaurants on a side road off the central circular plaza.

Mount Athos

Yes, it is true that chickens and certain other kinds of female animals are not allowed on the Athos peninsula; no, it is not true that the monks are long-bearded, lascivious old men lusting after the flesh of foreigners, innocent or otherwise. Such preconceptions should be left behind with all other baggage, which will only unnecessarily burden the visitor to this third and easternmost finger of Chalkidiki, where non-Greek males are allowed the privilege of spending four very full days of retreat on the promontory and its spectacular mountain.

Called Ayion Oros (Holy Mountain) by the Greeks, its impressive 6,670-foot summit once prompted Alexander the Great's architect to propose carving it into an immense statue of his leader, while it is still said that the Virgin Mary found the mountain's landscape so enchanting that she asked that it be made her special province.

It is amazing that not until the fifth to sixth century A.D. did any group of peoples claim the area as their own—and these were, in the beginning, only a few cave-dwelling hermits. In 885 a chrysobull (imperial decree) issued by the Byzantine emperor Basil I designated Athos (derived from the ancient, perhaps Pelasgian, name Akte) a place exclusively for monks and hermits. In 963 the first organized monastic community (*lavra*) of any significant size, called Great Lavra, was founded. In the 11th century another chrysobull, prompted partly by the incursions of wandering shepherds, prohibited entry to women, children, eunuchs, and every "smooth-faced person," meaning boys not yet old enough to have grown beards. The last of the peninsula's 20 monasteries were founded in the 14th century, although dependencies called *skites,* some as big as monasteries, were formed later.

Little has changed since then. There have been ups and downs in the number of resident monks and functioning monasteries, and in 1926 there was a formal union of the territory with Greece (although the peninsula's administration remains autonomous). Today Athos has its share of jeeps and trucks, as well as a creaking, clanking bus that travels to and from the administrative center at Karyés. There are also some virtually beardless boys sent by their families to attend secondary and ecclesiastical school in Karyes, from which they occasionally visit the monasteries. And nowadays visas are granted to young boys whose fathers wish to bring them along on a visit. (See below for details on how to arrange for a visa.)

Only men may visit Athos, women being restricted to gazing at it from the decks of cruise boats, which run organized tours along the peninsula's stunningly beautiful shores.

When visiting the area, it is possible to plan itineraries—for instance, a trip to the beautiful and treasure-filled **monastery of Great Lavra** seems imperative—but you should always be prepared to follow a different path at a moment's notice. The peninsula is rich with wonderful surprises, not to mention great physical beauty, and almost anywhere you go you will not be disappointed. As the monks say, nothing on Athos happens by chance, even a missed bus or a twisted ankle or a sudden storm diverting you from your course; the important thing is to pay attention not to expectations or preconceptions but to what actually *is*—because this is what is meant to be.

Getting Around on Mount Athos

Before visiting Mount Athos you must secure a place within the tightly restricted number of visitors (ten) allowed daily. This necessitates applying either in person or by mail weeks and sometimes months in advance. Applications can be made through either the Ministry of Foreign Affairs, Department of Ecclesiastical Affairs, 2 Zalokosta Street, Athens, 106 71 (Tel: 01-362-6894), or the Ministry of Macedonia and Thrace (formerly the Ministry of Northern Greece), Directorate of Political Affairs, Dikitourou Square, Room 218, Ayios Dimitrios Street, Thessaloniki, 541 23 (Tel: 031-270-092). Visas are issued only to males (and young boys accompanied by adult males), who should declare that the purpose of their visit is to make a religious pilgrimage to Athos.

Thessaloniki is the usual jumping-off point for a trip to Athos. Buses leave several times a day to the ferry port of Ouranopolis, where you then catch the mid-morning ferry for the port of Daphni on Athos's west coast. The trip from Thessaloniki to Ouranopolis takes about three hours.

Cruises along the spectacular coast of the promontory, where monasteries and churches cling to steep cliffs, can be booked either in Thessaloniki or Ouranopolis at various agencies. As noted above, on these women are most welcome.

Staying on Mount Athos

There is one rather ancient hotel in Karyes, but it is best to stay at a monastery. The rooms are usually quite clean, with three or more beds, occupied or not according to season. The rules state that visitors must move on after one night.

Payment for bed and meals is not required, according to an old rule of hospitality that applies to all of Greece—an "iron law," Lawrence Durrell calls it. This law is particularly applicable on Athos, since any visitor might be Christ resurrected and should therefore not be turned away. You can discreetly leave money in the church, in the sand beds of offertory candleholders, for instance. But it is *not* expected.

THESSALONIKI TO KAVALA

After following the previously described route E 5s past the lakes of Koronia and Volvi and the turnoff south to the eastern side of Chalkidiki, you now continue east to the coast, where you are again presented with yet another apparently endless stretch of beaches—actually about nine miles' worth. The best parts are in the lovely, refugee-built village of **Asprόvalta**, whose excellent beach and seaside road lined with tavernas and cafés must be visited to be believed—especially since it cannot be seen from the E 5s motorway.

At the mouth of the Strimónas river, where this stretch of beaches ends, a just-opened expanse of highway leads around the upcoming headland another 66 km (41 miles) to Kavala, thus avoiding the beautiful but somewhat heavily travelled interior route through the valleys of the Pangaion mountains and opening up some of the best virgin beach territory in the area. However, this new route also deprives you of the sudden, wonderful shock of coming upon the magnificent **Lion of Amphipolis** guarding the old iron bridge across the Strimonas. Reassembled and reerected in 1936, it apparently had been built originally in honor of Laomedon, a native of Amphipolis and the commander of Alexander's fleet during his siege of Tyre, and later the governor of Syria.

Amphípolis is some 3 km (2 miles) farther on, across the bridge and into the first large turn to the left, which leads up a narrow, winding asphalt road to the village. On the far, northwestern side of the village is the archaeological site. There is a marvelous view from here of the Strimonas meandering down to the sea, and some beautiful mosaics from later Byzantine churches—but little of ancient Amphipolis to see, although excavations are continuing.

First called "Nine Ways" because, recounts Herodotus, nine young boys and nine young girls were buried alive here by Xerxes in his march on Athens, Amphipolis was later colonized by Athens for its access to the famous gold mines of the Pangaion mountains and for its rich timber resources. The Spartans took it from the Athenian general Thucydides, who was consequently exiled for 20 years and left with nothing to do but write a history of the Peloponnesian Wars raging around him. Later, in an Athenian attempt to retake the city, both Cleon, the Athenian general, and Brasidas, the Spartan leader, were killed. Inevitably, Amphipolis was taken by Philip of Macedon, and its gold was used by him and by Alexander to finance their lavish expeditions. A museum is scheduled to open in the nearby village, which should make the detour much more worth the time and effort.

From Amphipolis you can either continue to Kavala on the old route through the scenic rolling farming valleys at the foothills of the Pangaion mountains or cut across to the newly opened seaside highway mentioned above. This latter route breezes past a virtually continuous line of sparsely inhabited beaches on its way to Kavala and takes about half an hour less than the inland route. Here in a 35-km (22-mile) stretch beginning with the ruins of a Crusader tower and ending at the beachside village of Nea Peramos, there are no hotels, rooming houses, or gas stations, and the few small tavernas between the road and the sea are open only in summer. Water is available at the hot-spring baths and hotels of **Loutrá Elefthéron**, 1 km (about half a mile) inland and signposted at the approximate center of this stretch. The beaches come in various shapes and sizes, rocky, pebbled, and sandy, and the water is an irresistible aquamarine.

The wide, curving bay at **Nea Péramos** spreads out in front of rich alluvial farmland famed for the quality of its white table grapes. It also lines the shores of several miles of superb sandy beach. The village itself is presently in the process of developing its tourist facilities and is constructing a large new hotel, the Thalia, on the best part of the beach. Scheduled for completion in 1991 or 1992, it has no phone number as yet available. At the opposite, eastern, end of the bay, a ferryboat now leaves three times a day—morning, midday, and evening—for the port of Prinos on the lovely island of Thasos (see below). In Thessaloniki, connecting buses for this ferry can be boarded at the Kavala terminal. This cuts half an hour off the trip to catch the ferry in Kavala, while adding a much pleasanter 20 minutes (and its small corresponding cost) to the voyage on the ferry.

Between Nea Peramos and Kavala, the procession of beaches continues through a virtually unbroken series of what should properly be considered suburbs of Kavala, and are thus dealt with in the section on that city that follows.

Kavala

Kavála is a bustling, picturesque seaport a little less than halfway between Thessaloniki and the Turkish border where old and new, East and West, and even Egypt come banging together in noisy but nevertheless congenial surroundings. It is the second-largest city in Macedonia (but doesn't seem to be) and its leading exporter of tobacco (which it doesn't seem to be either, so uncluttered is its harbor).

From here you can catch ferryboats to the islands of Thasos (one hour away) and Samothrace (four hours; see below for both), as well as to the northeastern Aegean islands of Lemnos, Lesvos, and Chios, and, depending on changing government routing regulations, maybe even to Samos, Patmos, and Rhodes.

Like Chalkidiki, Kavala has deeply rooted connections with the southern Greece of Classical times, and, like Thessaloniki, much of its history is reflected in the way its name has evolved. Founded in the seventh century B.C. as Neapolis (New City) by settlers from the Cycladic island of Paros who had recently colonized Thasos, it later became a member of Athens's Delian League (454 B.C.). In about 355 B.C. Philip of Macedon made it the harbor of his self-named city of Philippi, some nine miles to the northwest. The apostle Paul landed here on his way to Philippi from Asia and Samothrace in A.D. 49. Consequently, in the Byzantine era the port was called Christopoulos (City of Christ). In 1391 it was conquered and completely destroyed by the Ottoman Turks. Rebuilt several years later, the city was again renamed during the reign of Mehmet II (c. 1470), this time, for reasons unknown, Kavala.

Although reunited with Greece in 1912, Kavala has since been occupied three times by Bulgarian armies and remains a bone of contention (in Bulgarian minds anyway) in the so-called Macedonian Question. Since the collapse of the tottering Ottoman Empire the northern Balkan countries have been in a continually simmering dispute with Greece over racial, linguistic, and historical claims to Macedonia.

The most interesting areas of modern Kavala can be

visited in a couple of hours, i.e., while you're waiting to catch a ferry elsewhere. It takes about 20 minutes to walk up to the **Byzantine Castle** on the high promontory to the east of the port. From here there is an excellent view of both the harbor and the acropolis's aqueduct, built by Suleyman the Magnificent to carry water to the castle. On the way either up or down, you can stop at the **imaret** (on the right of the main street just after starting up the hill), a multi-domed almshouse for the poor, called "Tembel-Haneh," or "Lazy Man's House," by the locals. It is now in a bad state of disrepair and may be locked.

Unlocked and waiting for visitors (and their tips for a tour through it) is the **House of Mehmet Ali**. Ali was born here in 1769 of Albanian parents and later became pasha of Egypt. In 1827 his forces almost turned the tables against the Greek revolution in the Peloponnese until his fleet was caught and destroyed at the battle of Navarino. The dynasty Ali founded in Egypt ended with Nasser's revolution in 1952 and Farouk's abdication to his baby son, Faud II.

Kavala's **museum**, on the waterfront promenade at the western end of town just past the swimming pool, is one of the finest in northern Greece, housing the best collection of finds from Macedonian tombs that exists outside of Thessaloniki. There are also numerous Hellenistic and Roman finds from Amphipolis, Abdera, and Drama, as well as a large relief map showing the locations of sites in eastern Macedonia.

Lunch is recommended at any one of the three fish tavernas—**Vangelis**, **Panos-Zafira**, and **Ee Oraia Mytilini**—at the eastern end of the harbor, just past the colorful fish market and in the shadow of the castle promontory.

The best and most conveniently located hotels in the city center are the **Galaxy Hotel**, on the old port just before the market area, and the **Oceanis Hotel**, on Erythroú Stavrou Avenue one block behind the new marina. A few miles west of the city is the venerable **Hotel Lucy**, right on the promontory of the best beach in the area at Kalamitsa. All three are functional 1970s-modern with little to recommend them but their locations. Kavala's summertime swimming, dining, drinking, and dancing spots are around this area, which, farther along to the west, also has superb forested scenery as well as some very good clubs, restaurants, and resort hotels on the beaches of the communities of Palio and Nea Iraklítsa. Recommended are the **Batis Camping and Hotel**, a new, government-developed and beautifully designed resort complex at the base of a narrow, rocky inlet just outside the city; the **Tosca Beach Hotel**, the best in the area, a very attractive first-class establishment on a lovely beach in Palio, renting both rooms and bungalows; and, in the still-developing seaside village of Nea Iraklitsa on several miles of beautiful beach between Palio and Nea Peramos, the pleasant, serviceable **Hotel Egeo**, in the center of the tiny, one-street village and right on the beach.

Philippi

The road to Philíppi, which curves up out of the northwest end of Kavala and over a saddle between mountains, is virtually on top of the old Via Egnatia, the path that the apostle Paul and his entourage had to climb. From the top of this saddle looking north, you can see the acropolis of Philippi on the plain below, topped by a Byzantine tower, sitting beyond an airstrip paralleling a main north–south road. Philippi is on this road toward the city of Drama, about 15 km (9 miles) northwest of Kavala. Be careful not to take the turnoff to Philippi indicated by the sign: This goes to the village of Philippi only. The archaeological site is several hundred yards down the main road just past the road-stop village of Krinides, and is signposted as such at the entrance to its large parking lot.

The parking lot gives on to the ancient theater as well as a café-restaurant and rest rooms, while the main entrance to the complete site is a bit farther down the road. It is possible, however, to enter by the theater and walk around below it to the main areas.

Although Philippi is famous today as the site of battles in A.D. 42 between the assassins of Julius Caesar, Cassius, and Brutus and the pursuing Antony and Octavian, it had always been considered strategically important in guarding the approach from the east toward the gold-laden hills of Mount Pangaion and from the west to Kavala, Thasos, and the Bosphorus. No wonder Philip of Macedon proudly named it after himself. Later, the Roman construction of the Via Egnatia, which here ran east of the present road, and of the ancient city's acropolis, only heightened Philippi's importance.

In the first battle of Philippi, Antony defeated Cassius's forces, driving Cassius to commit suicide. Three weeks later, Brutus, who had previously beaten Octavian, was also defeated and committed suicide.

The apostle Paul's visit was no less significant. Here he made his first converts on European soil, the Lydians, and performed his first exorcism (on a woman), which eventually landed him in jail. He was later miraculously freed by an earthquake. After the collapse of the Roman Empire Philippi continued to thrive as an important site of Christian pilgrimage.

The ruins on the north side of the road, identified as **Basilica A** (c. 500), including a Roman crypt just below the basilica to the left, are popularly believed to have been the **prison of Saint Paul**, but this is by no means certain. **Basilica B**, on the opposite side of the main road, is of greater interest. Never completed or consecrated because its sanctuary dome collapsed during construction, the church is concrete evidence of the problems early architects faced in progressing from basilican to domed, cruciform structures. Unfortunately it is not known why the builders gave up on this church. The impressive pillars now stand majestically south of the **forum**, fissured high-rise dwellings for a multitude of sparrows and crows.

Fenced off to the east of the forum are the remains of an octagonal church, beneath which has been discovered a Macedonian tomb containing some gold items. Two other churches are thought to have existed on the same site, one from the fourth century, dedicated to Saint Paul.

The **museum** is farther along the road toward Drama, on the right below the acropolis. For the most part its holdings consist of architectural and sculptural remains from the Roman and early Christian eras. From here a path leads 1,020 feet up to the **acropolis**. The three large towers at the top are from the Byzantine era, built upon Macedonian walls. At the bottom of the hill and around it to the east, easily reached from Basilica A, are several **rock sanctuaries** dedicated to the Thracian god Bendis (Artemis), while on the path above, leading to the top, is a **Sanctuary to the Egyptian trinity**—Isis, Serapis, and Harpocrates.

The **theater** below was built at the time Philippi was founded and was remodeled during the Roman occupation. It underwent restoration for contemporary use from 1957 to 1959 and is now, in July and August, the scene of various theatrical and musical productions, often by the state theater company of Thessaloniki. The company gives summer performances throughout northern Greece, including at the ancient theater of the next destination, perhaps the most enchanting jewel in the entire Aegean—the emerald isle of Thasos.

Thasos

Slightly southeast of Kavala and only one hour away by ferryboat, the island of Thasos, with an excellent road encircling its 95 kilometers (59 miles), can be visited all the way around in a single day with stops for swimming, eating, and museum visiting, followed by the return trip to Kavala. However, so spectacular is this island, so breathtaking and varied in its beauty, that you are likely to feel that perhaps years of continual returns will never be enough.

Thasos might be called The Compleat Greek Island. It has everything other islands have only in part: A crystal-clear, turquoise-blue sea and incredibly beautiful beaches with fine white sand, some of them miles long, others, in isolated coves, only a few yards; a ruggedly mountainous, impossibly verdant landscape lush with all manner of trees and vegetation, from pine forests to olive groves; a magnificent Classical Greek archaeological site and equally magnificent museum; picturesque ports and lovely mountainside villages nestling in greenery so thick they are almost impossible to see from below; discos, nunneries, Byzantine churches, and monasteries; a superb resort complex complete with private bungalows, tennis courts, and a game preserve; beachside trailer parks; forest hiking; and one of the most polite and unfailingly cheerful indigenous populations this side of Mykonos.

All of this, of course, is not a well-kept secret. According to the latest figures from the Hotel Association of Thasos, there are 113 hotels and rooming houses on the island's 234 square miles, and in July and August Thasos is packed, a madhouse. But even then, such is the variety of the island and the seemingly numberless little coves, villages, and tavernas that it never *feels* that crowded. And in June it seems positively deserted, as if it had all been created just for you.

While the natural beauty of the island makes almost any hotel—even the most desultory—seem more than adequate, there are a few that stand out. In **Liménas**, the northern port and main town, the **Hotel Amfipolis**, one block from the harbor, has a great deal of quiet elegance, having been lovingly converted from an old Thasian mansion. It has a charming garden café and is—rare in Greece—fully air-conditioned. Flanking Limenas are two hotels inhabiting what can best be described as Caribbean-like settings. To the west, the reasonably priced **Glyfada Hotel** sits in its own miniature cove on a beach of pure white sand, a forest of pine trees embracing it on the landward side. And to the east of Limenas is the luxury resort of **Makryammos**, with private bungalows and tennis courts, whose setting, on a stunning beach surrounded by a lush game preserve, is perhaps the most beautiful on the island. Twelve kilometers (7.5 miles) farther east, far down the mountainside and nestled in the tree-shaded, southern corner of an immense and virtually undeveloped beach known as Chryssí Ammoudiá (Golden Sands) is the surprisingly luxurious **Miramare Hotel**. Hidden up a small ravine from the harbor of the little fishing village of Skala Potamia, it appears like a totally unexpected mirage, its glass and concrete walls reflecting and blending so perfectly with the rocky, leafy surroundings that it hardly seems to be there. Designed by a German architect and run by a Greek-German family, it is a haven of quiet, peaceful refinement, and reasonably priced, too.

On the opposite (south) side of Thasos are a small group of hotels at the lovely, tiny, pine-shaded beach of **Pefkári**. The best of these, the **Thasos Hotel**, is comfortable and serviceable and just off the beach. Between Pefkari and the equally lovely beach of Potos is the new, first-class **Alexander Beach Bungalows**. Set on a headland above the two beaches, it has its own swimming pool but is just a few steps above the Potos beach.

Buses ply the island's circular road and its inland branches all day long, and caïques from the ports of Limenaria and Prinos make day trips to various beaches all around the island; numerous car- and motorbike-rental agencies add to the ready transportation. There is also hitchhiking. And hiking. And mountain climbing. And camping.

It's best to begin at Limenas, which you can reach from only one point on the mainland: the small port at **Keramotí**, about 38 km (24 miles) east of Kavala, on the headland opposite Thasos. If you take the Kavala–Thasos or the Nea Peramos–Thasos ferry, it is necessary to disembark at the port of Prinos and then drive or take the waiting bus to Limenas, a distance of 16 km (10 miles). The big difference between the two methods of reaching Thasos is in the times (and corresponding prices) of the trips from Kavala or Nea Peramos and Keramoti. The trip from Keramoti takes half the time—35 minutes as opposed to about one hour—and costs about half the price.

Once you are in Limenas, a visit to the tourist police (at the harbor where the boat docks) is the first thing to do when looking for a room. Most of the hotels have complete lists of the accommodations available on the island. The president of the hotel association is also the proprietor of the very pleasant **Hotel Timoleon**, next to the tourist police. The island's intervillage bus stop is right here, too.

The **museum** and **ancient city** of Limenas are just behind the old harbor, about 100 yards to the east and around the corner from the tourist police station. The museum is small but rich in treasures. Of particular interest are the striking garden sculptures, the colossal *kouros,* and heads of Silenus and a youthful Dionysus.

The superb **ancient theater** is a 10-minute walk through a forested glade, up the hill to the left as you face the old harbor. Another 15 to 20 minutes farther on (and up) are the **temples of Athena and Pan** on the acropolis, with its superb view of Limenas and the island. Don't be surprised if you happen to run into a peacock or deer. They are wanderers from the nearby Makryammos game reserve.

For lunch or dinner at Limenas, try the **Syrtaki** restaurant on the wonderful, tree-shaded beach somewhat hidden beyond the point on the far western side of town, after the old harbor. Specializing in fish but serving a variety of dishes, it is a peaceful haven, particularly at sunset.

Be sure to purchase a small map and guidebook to Thasos as soon as you arrive, for only then are you able to get even an inkling of the wonderful possibilities at hand. If there can be but a single site to recommend for a visit, then let it be the idyllic little cove and beach at **Alikí** on the south side of the island. A trip there will also allow you to see much of the island's particularly beautiful eastern side, which is treasured now more than ever since two tragic fires of recent years destroyed large expanses of forest in the south and northwest. The second of these fires, which was set deliberately, consumed some 25,000 acres during a single windy week in August 1989.

After having explored eastern Macedonia's connections to the sunny south, experiencing a bit of the region's other, dark and chthonic, character is a good introduction to the mysteries of Thrace.

The Fire-Dancers of Northern Greece

This small group of religious devotees, part of a large number of refugees repopulated from Turkey to Greece in 1923, is renowned for a ceremony in which its members dance on white-hot coals. The ceremony, *pyrovassia,* or "fire-dancing," is formally called the *Anastenária;* its participants are known as the *anastenárides* (from the verb *anastenázo,* to breathe heavily or sigh or moan) because of the sounds they make upon reaching the ecstatic state necessary to proceed unharmed across the burning embers.

Certainly of pre-Christian origin, the present manifestation of the ritual originated in about 1250 in the eastern Thracian village of Kosti. According to local history, when the church of St. Constantine caught fire the villagers rushed in to save the icons of Saints Constantine and Eleni and emerged unharmed from the inferno, carrying the sacred pictures, which were not so much as singed. Today a three-day ceremony commemorates the event from May 20 to 22, during which celebrants dance with the sacred icons across burning coals and sacrifice a black bull or goat, feasting on the meat. The fire-dancing itself occurs at about 9:00 P.M. on May 21, the feast day of Saints Constantine and Eleni.

Where the ceremony takes place is another matter. In recent years Orthodox objections have managed to cancel the ritual where it is most popular, in the town of **Langadás**, 17.5 km (11 miles) northeast of Thessaloniki. This is not simply because of the pagan aspects of the ceremony but because of the carnival atmosphere the proceedings have lately generated—merry-go-rounds, bumper cars, and hot-dog stands set up in the streets to take advantage of the large crowds the fire-dancers, through no wish of their own, have drawn. Worse yet, television crews and home-movie makers breathe down the necks of the already harassed devotees as they prepare for their strenuous fiery ordeal. That the anastenarides manage to concentrate enough to succeed is perhaps more a miracle than the one that occurred at the event being commemorated.

Consequently, the rites are both under attack and in retreat, and it is difficult to know from one year to the next where they will be held. In 1990 the occasion was celebrated at the tiny village of **Ayía Eléni**, about 80 km (50 miles) northeast of Thessaloniki and 9 km (6 miles) directly south of the city of Serres, just east of the village of Skoutári. If you want to be sure to witness the proceedings, the only recourse you have is to go to both Langadas and Ayia Eleni early on May 21 (or, if possible, the day before) to check. Do not believe anyone who assures you, no matter how emphatically, that the Anastenaria will be held at Langadas; he or she is most certainly stating this only from past knowledge.

Also occurring in this area is another yearly, Dionysian-derived ritual from eastern Thrace called the *yinekokratía,* or "rule of the women." In this jolly affair, held each January 8 at the village of **Monoklissiá** (off the main E 20 highway from Thessaloniki, some 20 km/12 miles southwest of Serres), women take over the village for the day while the men stay home and (theoretically) cook and clean (and watch TV). In turn, there is much dancing and drinking among the women, both in the town square and at nearby cafés, the music supplied by a roving three-piece male band dressed in skirts and kerchiefs. The event lasts from about noon to well into the evening.

THRACE

Thrace extends from the north-south course of the river Nestos, about 40 km (25 miles) east of Kavala, to the north-south course of the river Evros at the border with Turkey, 178 km (110 miles) to the east. It has long been considered the "wilds" (as well as the "sticks") of Greece. In ancient times Thrace was home to fierce warrior tribes that the Greeks of the west and south thought barbarous because they tattooed themselves, offered human sacrifice, and, of all things, ate butter.

In modern times Thrace still harbors an "outlaw" element: that mysterious and fascinating group of nomadic shepherds, the Sarakatsáni, whom Patrick Leigh Fermor calls the Black Departers in his absorbing book on northern Greece, *Roumeli* (see the Bibliography). Fermor believes these nomads to be the direct, unalloyed descendants of the Dorians, whose geometric pottery designs are today mirrored in the weave of Sarakatsani textiles.

Because Thrace is reputed to be remote and somewhat inhospitable (not true at all), it is one of the last places in Greece whose great natural beauty has not yet been overrun by tourism—although the powers that be would like nothing more. To attract more visitors they are therefore currently refurbishing the region's coastline, albeit with very beautiful camping sites and other tastefully done, ecologically considerate projects.

In ancient times Thrace was renowned not only for its savagery but also for the mysterious religions of Dionysus and Orpheus, its bards, and its timber and gold from the Mount Pangaion range. Consequently, like much of eastern Macedonia, Thrace had its sprinkling of colonies from the south during Greece's Classical age.

When Alexander needed fearsome foot soldiers for his Asian campaign, he chose Thrace's gray-eyed, blond- and red-haired warriors. In A.D. 46 the Romans finally managed to subdue the area, later integrating it with the rest of northern Greece through the Via Egnatia to the Bosphorus.

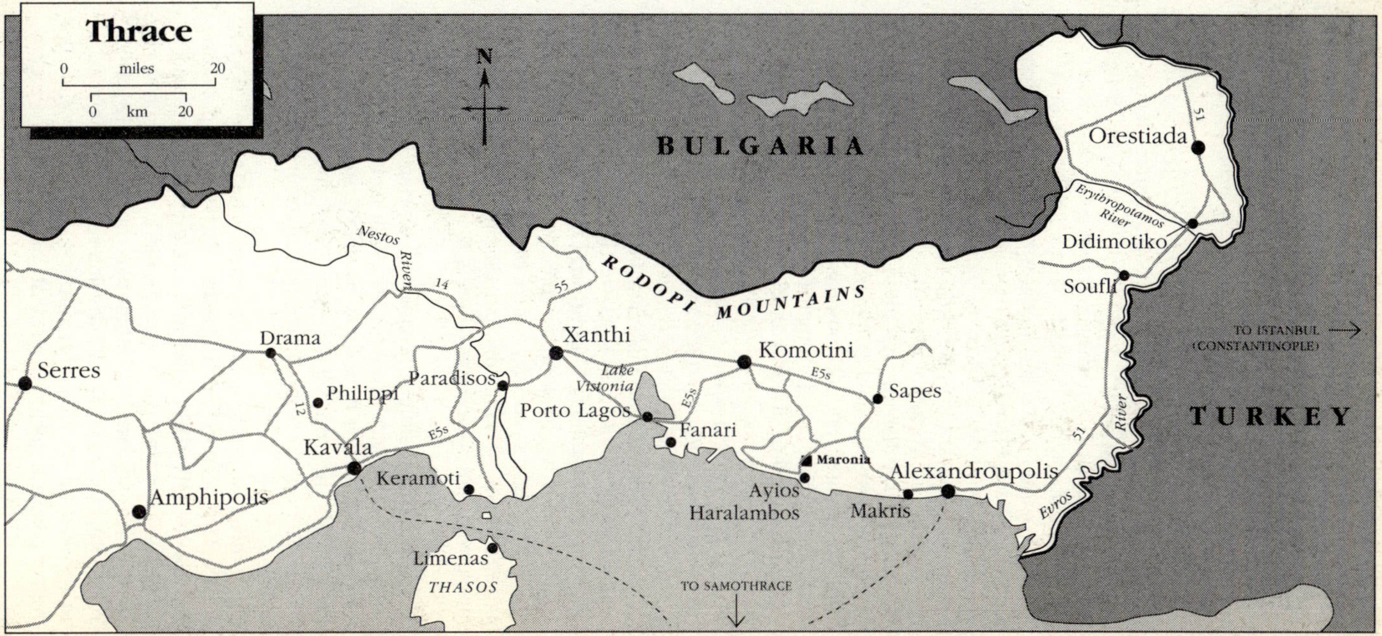
Thrace
0 miles 20
0 km 20
N
BULGARIA
TURKEY
RODOPI MOUNTAINS
Orestiada
Erythropotamos River
Didimotiko
Soufli
TO ISTANBUL (CONSTANTINOPLE)
Nestos River
14
55
51
Drama
Serres
Philippi
12
Paradisos
Xanthi
Lake Vistonia
Porto Lagos
Komotini
E5s
Sapes
Fanari
Maronia
Kavala
Keramoti
Amphipolis
Ayios Haralambos
Makris
Alexandroupolis
Evros
River
Limenas
THASOS
TO SAMOTHRACE

In 1919 western Thrace was officially joined to the rest of Greece following its occupation during the Balkan Wars (1912 to 1913) by Bulgaria, which still looks with longing at its former (if briefly possessed) port on the Aegean, the Turkish-named Dedeagatch, now Alexandroupolis.

The Greco-Turkish war of 1920 to 1922 resulted in an agreement that in 1923 effected a population exchange between Greece and Turkey; some 360,000 Turks and Bulgarians moved out and more than 1.2 million Greeks moved in, well over half of them settling in Thrace and Macedonia.

One provision of the agreement was that the patriarchate of the Orthodox Church could remain in Istanbul (as could any Greeks who wished to stay there), provided that any Turks who wanted to remain in Greece could do so—but only within the Thracian nomes of Xanthi and Komotini. Thus today's traveller through these regions is greeted with the pleasantly exotic sight of minarets rising in the midst of farmland villages, and of long-robed, kerchiefed Muslim women unexpectedly adorning the Thracian scene.

Now numbering about 120,000, these "Turks" are full Greek citizens who serve in the armed forces and are allowed to vote and serve in Parliament (one in fact did, following the elections of 1989 and 1990). They are officially known as Greek Muslims (*Ellinikí Mousoulmáni*), and to call them "Turkish" is to make a gaffe of considerable proportions. In fact, in January 1990 two Greek-Muslim political candidates were jailed for "disturbing Christian-Muslim relations" by referring to their constituency as "Turkish." The subsequent ugly street fights that broke out in Komotini between about 400 Muslims and Christians illustrated just how sensitive an issue it was—and is.

There are two possible approaches to touring Thrace. One option is to travel east from Kavala by car or bus to Alexandroupolis and return by ferry to Kavala via Samothrace. Or you can do the reverse: Take the ferry from Kavala to Alexandroupolis via Samothrace and then return overland to the west.

In either case, there is little of interest in Thrace's upper northeastern corner, which is chiefly rich farmland. Its uppermost city, **Orestiáda**, dates from the population exchange and is now a shiny new showcase for modern Greek prosperity. The pleasant town of **Didimótiko**, on the banks of the Erythropótamos river, is the most interesting in the area; it has an impressively situated acropolis with a set of twin walls (the town's name meaning just that) dating from the eighth to ninth century A.D. (and a charming café at the side), an immense mosque built by Murad I in the central plateia, and the ruins of the Roman settlement of **Plotinoupolis**, which Trajan founded and named after his wife, Plotina, on the hill of Ayia Petra to the south of the town, where a beautiful gold bust of Marcus Aurelius (now in Komotini's museum) was found.

Farther south is the desultory burg of **Souflí**, which has a few shops offering rather ordinary products of its well-known silk industry. Nearby are the forests of **Dadí**, which might make the detour worthwhile, praised as they are by hikers for their wild, unspoiled natural beauty.

The trick in managing the round trip from Kavala overland and by sea lies in coordinating your itinerary with the Samothrace–Kavala ferry runs. As of this writing, there is only one ferry a week from Kavala to Samothrace, on Saturdays at 10:00 A.M., and only one ferry a week back from Samothrace to Kavala, on Fridays at 2:00 P.M. Meanwhile, there are ferries once a day to and from Alexandroupolis, most of them leaving from Alexandroupolis at 10:00 A.M. and from Samothrace at 4:00 P.M. These times are never secure, however, and should be checked with the port authorities at Kavala; Tel: (051) 224-967 or 223-716.

Xanthi

A 56-km (35-mile) drive east on the E 5s from Kavala over the broad Nestos river (and through the lovely little village of **Parádisos**), Xanthi has a certain charm that makes it worth a stopover of an hour or two. Here you begin to glimpse the Muslim presence. The old quarter (on the north side of the new city as it begins to rise into the Rodópi mountains) is adorned with minarets and the grand 18th- and 19th-century mansions of the region's tobacco merchants, who were once so wealthy that they brought Sarah Bernhardt to the city— "direct from Paris"—to sing. Today the tobacco industry is still thriving, but not to the extent that it once was, the blond (*xanthó*) local tobacco losing favor to increasingly popular Virginia blends.

Take a walk through the cobblestoned streets of the old city up Mavromichali Street from the central square. After the beautiful façade of the Dimarxeion (City Hall), a former merchant's mansion, turn right and follow Orfeos Street as it continues through the old city. At the corner of the appropriately named Antika Street, a left turn leads past the **Folk Museum** and the 19th-century cathedral, upward to the heights overlooking the city. Here, at the beginning of the forested slopes of the Rodopi Mountains, is a summer theater and the **Xanthippi**, an excellent restaurant with a view.

Also excellent are the food and surroundings of **To Nisaki** (The Little Island), an outdoor restaurant (open from April 15 to September 15) nestled under two immense plane trees beside the Podonifi (Foot-Washing) river, which runs through the city center. This can be reached by following the above-mentioned Orfeos Street as it curves its way past the Folk Museum turnoff around and down to the banks of the river. Nearby, in the same tree-shaded park as To Nisaki, is the **Xenia** hotel, perhaps not the most modern in this city of commercial travellers, but unquestionably the quietest and most wonderfully situated.

On the E 5s southeast of Xanthi is the turnoff for ancient **Abdera**, where the atomist philosopher Democritus and the sophist Protagoras (of "Man is the measure of all things" fame) were born. It is not, however, enthusiastically recommended; the site consists of little more than the foundations of ancient buildings, which are hardly visible amid mounds of parched, unshaded grass.

An infinitely more appealing place to stop on the way to Komotini is the fishing village and pine-forested beach of **Porto Lagos**, 26 km (16 miles) southeast of Xanthi on the main E 5s road. It borders the lovely gulf and lake of **Vistónia** and has a yacht and caïque marina on a small inlet off the main road to the right. Beyond this is the pine forest and a camping site, with a large, well-appointed restaurant and a long, beautiful sandy beach. On weekends people from Xanthi come down in droves.

The road to Komotini leads over a causeway separating Lake Vistonia from the Gulf of Vistonia, where you are presented with the remarkable sight of a church that seems to float in the middle of the gulf. The church actually sits on an islet that is connected to the mainland by a narrow wooden bridge. This is the **monastery of Ayios Nikólaos**, where visitors are welcomed in a tiny, tree-shaded courtyard by a little old nun who would very much appreciate whatever contributions could be given for the upkeep of the church.

On the other side of the causeway is the turnoff south to the signposted village and camping area of **Fanári**. The village and, to the east, the camping site are at the beginning of a mile-long stretch of a wide, duned beach. In the village are numerous rooms to rent, plus the rather rococo **Bosphorus Hotel**, noted by visitors from Komotini for the quality of its kitchen, and the less expensive **Fanari Hotel**, favored for its hospitality. Also named Fanari is what must be one of the best mobile-home camping sites in all of Greece, a modern, tree-shaded park with every possible amenity situated on the best part of the wide, half-mile-long, white sandy beach.

Komotini

The city of Komotiní is the kind of place that makes you want to hang around for a while and get to know it better. Unfortunately, its hotels do not have the charm of the rest of the city; they are functional places designed with travelling salesmen in mind and subject to the city center's enormous traffic noise. A short distance from the center and thus somewhat less noisy are the new and personable **Anatolia Hotel** (the owner speaks English), north of the central park and with small signs pointing the way; and the older **Xenia**, about half a mile east on the main through street, with a rather sparse front lawn that sets it back off the road. Outside of the city, in an industrial zone about 3 km (2 miles) east on the national road toward Alexandroupolis, is the huge **Chris and Eve's**, which caters to bus-loads of Athenian tourists on their way to a tour of Istanbul.

A short walk from the Anatolia and Xenia hotels into the center of town is a beautiful park with outdoor cafés and a charming zoo. On the western corner of the park is an immense memorial "to the heroes," at which there is a military flag-lowering ceremony every evening, an indication, perhaps, of the constant pressure this city feels from the proximity of the Bulgarian border, only 25 km (15.5 miles) to the north.

Opposite this is the city's central square, on the left side of which is a lovely bar and café called the **Xanc**, fashioned out of an 1856 carriage house. Behind the buildings on the right (north) side, the **Turkish Market** area begins, complete with mosques, minarets, and Turkish copper-working and antiques shops. Highly recommended is the antiques shop of **Christos Karageorgiou**, at 11 Orfeos Street, for a wonderful selection of items. At night the area's central street, Serron, is converted into an outdoor dining area lined with ouzeries that serve a variety of delicious hors d'oeuvres and other dishes. Also try the taverna of **Moumin Mehmet Mouhsin**, opposite the clock tower at the market's eastern end. Here grilled foods are served with a delicacy that belies a "Turkish" hand at the helm.

A block and a half from the south side of the central square is the excellent **Folk Museum**, housed in a restored 18th-century mansion on Ayíou Georgíou Street.

At the west end of the market area, on Sofoúli Street near the corner of Venizélou, is the beautiful post-Byzantine **cathedral of the Virgin Mary**. Following Sofoúli Street south (i.e., to the left as you leave the church) leads you around to a small park in which is the excellent **Archaeological Museum**. The museum contains finds from all over the area, including the aforementioned bust of Marcus Aurelius, a phallic altar, various reliefs, sculptures, and grave finds from Abdera and Maronia, and displays a map of the region's archaeological sites.

The archaeological site of ancient **Maronia** is 30 km (18 miles) southeast of Komotiní. It can be easily reached in a 30-minute drive from the center of Komotiní by taking the signposted road at the corner of the park opposite the Archaeological Museum. Or you can take route E 5s east toward Alexandroúpolis and enjoy the Muslim-flavored countryside between Komotiní and Sápes, in which some of the villages are almost entirely Turkish in aspect. Then head to Maronia by making the first right turn after Sápes. From here it is 21 km (13 miles) down a sometimes rough but always interesting road to the striking seacoast site and the minuscule collection of hovels that is called Ayios Harálambos.

Ancient Maronia was an extremely important city from the eighth century B.C. until about 1400, when the Turks conquered mainland Greece. As is obvious from the wide dispersion of the excavations (including a Hellenistic theater far up on the hillside), Maronia was immense in Classical times and afterward. Though few and far between, these excavations extend right down to the high bluff that marks the edge of the sea. There, in the midst of a characteristic grove of gnarled olive trees, a simple, well-shaded fish taverna and café sits practically on top of a Classical excavation. Another taverna lies to the west, through the trees of **Ayios Harálambos**, and has a marvelous view of the bay and beach below.

Both the taverna at Maronia and the one at Ayios Haralambos sit on a promontory of sheer red-dirt cliffs, at the bottom of which a new harbor has recently been dredged and partially built by the government with the intention of making the area into a tourist attraction. At the moment, work has been stalled because of a lack of funds, but it will be interesting to see what happens to this naturally beautiful spot in the coming years.

On a promontory across the bay is the only hotel for miles: the well-equipped **King Maron Beach Hotel**, complete with tennis court, swimming pool, sauna, gym, disco, and miles of beautiful, unspoiled beach.

Continuing toward Alexandroupolis on the E 5s, here and there in the process of being widened into a superhighway, you'll come to the tiny village of **Makris**, on whose outskirts, at the top of a cliff overlooking the beach, is the entrance to what the locals have for centuries called the **Cave of Polyphemus** (*ee spiliá tou Polifímou*). Polyphemus was the Cyclops who attacked Odysseus and his men on their long voyage home from Troy to Ithaca.

If you are a spelunker, here are directions to the entrance. You'll need a light, as the cave is dark and deep, running as far back as the main road, some three miles. Rather than going down to the beach and climbing up (the directions that are usually given), the easiest way is to follow a path (turning off to the right at the second church on the left) that skirts the top edge of the cliff and leads to a point directly above the cave. Here some steps carved in stone lead down to the entrance.

On the headland above the cave, recent excavations seem to indicate that the area was once a site of some importance and may have been connected to ancient Maronia.

Alexandroupolis

Alexandroúpolis, southeast of Komotini, is named not after "the Great" but after the man who was king of the Hellenes, Alexander I, when Thrace was reunited to Greece in 1919. On the Aegean in the easternmost part of Thrace, the last possible place for a port before the border with Turkey, it has a lovely stretch of beach and parks to its western side, where you'll find nestled the city's best hotel, the first-rate **Motel Astir**, complete with bungalows and tennis courts, right on the beach. But except for a lighthouse that ends the promenade near the docks for Samothrace, and, close to the small plateia, half a block north of the promenade, the city's best taverna, the **Klimatoria**, which offers a stupendous variety of ready-made dishes, there is nothing of interest in the town's rather drab, concrete interior.

The docks for the ferryboat to Samothrace are some 200 yards below the first right turn at the end of the lighthouse promenade. Farther along the promenade street, past this turn, is the train station, clearly visible about 100 yards away. From here buses and trains depart for Thessaloniki and Istanbul.

Trains are not recommended for travelling anywhere in Greece, Turkey, or Yugoslavia because they take much too long and are always late. For example, the trip from Alexandroupolis to Istanbul by train is at least 12 hours, whereas by bus it may be only 6 hours, depending on the delays caused by officials at passport control on the Greek side of the border, where little is done to facilitate the travel of Greeks into the "hostile" territory of Turkey. By the time these buses reach Alexandroupolis, however, they are usually full of passengers from Athens, Thessaloniki, and points along the way. Therefore, if you wish to go to Istanbul, catch a plane from Athens or a bus from there or Thessaloniki.

Here we come literally to the end of the road but for our final stop, Samothrace, an important holy place long before Constantinople became the great religious center of the Greeks. Its lofty, 5,000-foot-plus Mount Fengari is the easternmost of a spectacular triumvirate of sacred summits that stand in a line across the entrance to northern Greece, forming what might be seen as some immense propylaeum: in the west, Olympus, home of the Dorian and Macedonian gods; in the center, Athos, home of the Christian Byzantine god; and in the east, Fengari, home of the dark chthonic gods of Anatolia.

Samothrace

About two hours by ferryboat from Alexandroupolis and four from Kavala, Samothrace (Samothráki) rises out of the Aegean in auspicious splendor long before the boat arrives, the peak of Fengári (Moon Mountain) often wreathed in clouds and the emerald-green coastal plain glowing in shafts of sunlight.

Arriving at the undistinguished little port of Kamariótissa therefore tends to be disappointing. There is a line of tiny buildings, cafés, a tourist agency—Niki Tours (English spoken; Tel: 0551-414-65)—an indoor kiosk where maps can be bought, some souvlaki stands, tavernas, trees, and two hotels. One of the hotels, the nondescript, single-story **Aeolos**, has a swimming pool that seems redundant on an island surrounded by the blue Aegean.

But one of the other disappointments of Samothrace is that it has no beaches, only rocks and stones to clamber over into the water. It is this almost absolute lack of the expected tourist amenities that makes many visitors want to catch the next boat out. But Samothrace was never a summer resort; its fascination lies in the dark and powerful "presence" manifested in its mountain, beneath which almost everything on the island that is man-made or man-oriented suffers by comparison. Except, that is, the ancient Sanctuary of the Great Gods, the cluster of edifices at the northeastern foot of the mountain where the ancient mysteries took place. This holds its own, and it is here that you should go as soon as you have found accommodations.

The hotel nearest the sanctuary and its museum, which are east along the northern coast road, some 7 km (4 miles) from the port, is at the almost nonexistent village of Paleopoli: the **Xenia**, a line of rooms and a restaurant nestled amid olive trees near the museum.

The best hotels on the island are, however, another 7 km along the road to the east, at the hot springs of **Loutra** ("Therma" on most maps). Sited in olive groves, these are the **Kaviros** and **Mariva** hotels, the former with rooms and a restaurant, the latter (as yet unfinished) with bungalows, and both with either arthritic Greeks seeking to ease their pains at the springs or adventurous, athletic ones eager to begin the four-hour ascent of Mount Fengari (more about this later).

Because ancient writers, Homer in particular, called the island the "Thracian Samos," it was believed that its early Greek settlers were from the island of Samos farther to the south. But recent inscription finds by the New York University archaeologists working on the island indicate that these Greeks, who came to the island about 700 B.C., were from northwestern Anatolia (as were the original non-Greek Thracian colonists) or nearby Lesvos.

The very first settlers arrived some 9,000 years ago in the Neolithic age. In fact, as the excellent N.Y.U. guide to the island (available in the sanctuary museum) points out, the Greeks believed that "the indigenous population of Samothrace had sprung from the earth earlier than any other people of Greece." This may well have been true, because the first significant migrations of peoples into Greece were from Anatolia during the Neolithic era. As the Dorians were attracted to Olympus, perhaps these Anatolian settlers were first attracted to Fengari as an impressive and thus obvious site for a sanctuary to their gods in this new land. Later, Homer would cite the mountaintop as the spot from which Poseidon watched the battle for Troy.

The Anatolians' cult centered on the Great Mother and

included the attendant gods and goddesses of the underworld as well as the powerful and demonic Kabeiri. Rites, often involving animal sacrifices, were similar to those of other mystery religions—but with two significant departures. First, initiation was available to persons of either sex and any age who wished to join; and second, there seems to have been a definite, almost Christian moral aspect to the rites, a purging of sin through confession that was required before one could be admitted to the innermost circle of initiates. It is interesting to note that the original, pre-Greek Thracian language continued to be used up until the first century B.C., much as Latin, with its mysterious intonations, was used in the Catholic church long after it had become incomprehensible to all but the special few, the priests.

During the Classical period and afterward, many notable figures were initiated on Samothrace, including Herodotus; Lysander, the king of Sparta; and Philip of Macedon and Olympias, Alexander the Great's father and mother, who were said to have fallen under each other's spell at the ceremonies.

The Romans also fell under the island's spell, with luminaries such as Hadrian visiting its shores. Even Saint Paul, on his way to Philippi for his first trip to Greece, stopped here in A.D. 49.

After its religious activities were curtailed by the Christian Roman Empire in the fourth century, the island declined rapidly, and since then has been somewhat of a backwater in the tides of history. Nonetheless, visitors from afar are today still compelled to explore its mysterious charms.

Since 1938 excavations of the **Sanctuary of the Great Gods** have been conducted by New York University's Institute of Fine Arts and are now being directed by James R. McCredie under the auspices of the American School in Athens. The university has published a superb book on its work and the history of the island; you can buy this guide, titled *Samothrace,* at the museum. It is indispensable for understanding the impressive finds displayed in the site **museum** and for grasping the impact of the site itself, although just a visit here is enough to intuit—in a spiritual sense—how initiates must have felt when they arrived. Here, among the twisted shapes of trees and rocks at the very foot of the mountain, with cloud-covered crags towering above you, the feeling you get is of absolute puniness. Reinforcing this sensation is the imposing nature of the site's man-made structures: the impressive size of the **Rotunda**, for example, at more than 65 feet in diameter, the largest of its kind in Greek architecture; the majestic, columned remains of the sanctuary building, the **Heiron**, set back against the mountain slopes; and, of course, the sight (in the mind's eye, at least) of the mighty *Winged Victory,* now in the Louvre. As a spot for introducing people to a power greater than themselves, there is no question that the site was, in every possible way, an inspired choice.

After visiting the excavations, a general tour of Samothrace becomes most worthwhile. A bus goes up to the picturesque capital town of **Hora,** from which you can take a taxi or even walk around the foothills of the mountain for views of the south side of the island, which is much more fertile and beautiful than the port side. A climb to the top of **Mount Fengári** is one of the main reasons many Greeks journey to the island. This can be tricky and even dangerous, however, particularly if there are clouds covering the summit; under good conditions, the ascent normally takes four hours from Loutra.

It is said that on a clear day, the visitor to the top of Fengari can become like a god. Besides taking in views of the islands of Imbros (a Turkish possession) and Limnos in the south, you can review virtually all the stops on your journey through this part of northern Greece: to the west Mount Athos on Chalkidiki, the island of Thasos, and the entire shoreline of Macedonia and Thrace in between; and to the north and east the city of Alexandroupolis and beyond to the Dardenelles and even the plain of Troy. Thus, to a Greek standing on this mountaintop, the view lacks only the holy city of Constantinople to be perfectly and satisfyingly complete.

GETTING AROUND

With Athens grudgingly giving up its cherished but somewhat impractical role as the gateway for everywhere else in Greece, Thessaloniki has been steadily able to increase the number of international flights entering and leaving its airport at Mikras, which is on the coast only 13 km (8 miles) southeast of the city center. Thus it is now possible to make connections with Thessaloniki to and from the United States via connecting flights at a number of European cities, including London, Paris, Amsterdam, Frankfurt, Zurich, Copenhagen, Stuttgart, and Brussels, among others.

In addition, Thessaloniki is the first major stop for trains and buses arriving from Europe. (The Yugoslav border is only 69 km/43 miles to the northwest.)

As a rule, in Greece buses are always better than trains in that they are invariably faster and usually arrive on time. On the other hand, there is the very nice advantage of being able to sleep on the night train from Thessaloniki to Athens. First-class, wood-paneled, Orient Express–style compartments, some now air-conditioned, for one to four people are relatively inexpensive, although limited in number; they should be reserved in advance. In addition, a daily express train (six hours one way) to and from Athens was inaugurated in the fall of 1989. The central ticket office for buying and reserving train and some bus tickets is in Thessaloniki at 18 Leoforos Aristotelous, just off Ermou Street; Tel: (031) 276-382.

There are two different bus organizations in Greece: OSE ("*oséh*"), a division of the railway lines, and KTEL ("*k'tél*"), which serves local communities. OSE buses provide express services between major cities, while KTEL buses connect the smaller areas. Sometimes buses have reserved seating, but not always, so to avoid the prospect of standing up in a hot, crowded bus for a few hours (or even minutes), get to the station very early. OSE buses leave and arrive at the local train stations, but KTEL bus stations are often drab, difficult-to-find ticket-windows on obscure little streets in the outlying areas of town, in the general direction the bus will be heading toward its next stop. In Thessaloniki, for example, the bus station for Chalkidiki is at 68 Karakasi Street near the corner of Papanastasiou and the 25th of March Street (25 Martio) in the southeastern suburb of Harilaou; the bus for Kavala, though, is at 59 Langáda Street, way over on the northwest side of the city, even though Kavala is farther east than Chalkidiki. (The main connecting highway for Kavala first leaves the city from the north and only later turns east.)

From Thessaloniki it is possible to catch numerous buses running throughout the day to various places as far west as the Igoumenitsa port for Corfu, as far south as Athens, and as far east as Istanbul. Anyone contemplating a trip to Istanbul should not try to leave by bus from anywhere east of Thessaloniki during the summer, Easter, or Christmas seasons, because buses are almost always fully booked from Thessaloniki.

The best place to go when looking for help in English to find out about bus stations and their schedules is the Greek National Tourist Organization (EOT—"*eh-ot*") office at 8 Aristotelous Square in Thessaloniki; Tel: (031) 271-888 or 222-935. Failing this, if you can find someone who speaks Greek, there are listings of all bus, train, and airline phone numbers (and some schedules) in the inside front page of the daily newspaper *Makedonías*.

Of great general help in making your way around Thessaloniki and environs is the *Welcome Guide,* a booklet chock-full of information, including the addresses and telephone numbers of various bus stations, ministries, museums, consulates, restaurants, discos, banks, shops, etc., that is sold with a very cumbersome map of the city and suburbs.

Taxis can be flagged down in Thessaloniki even when they seem fully occupied. Unlike the people in some other cities, the residents of Thessaloniki recognize that taxis are hard to come by, so people rarely object to being delayed and crowded by additional passengers. Some taxi drivers, however, do not like to go to the upper city. That is why taking the bus is often the easier choice.

There are domestic airplane flights from Thessaloniki daily or weekly to a limited number of cities and islands, including Crete, Samos, Rhodes, Limnos, and Lesvos (Mytilini). There are six to seven flights a day to and from Athens, from early in the morning until 11:00 P.M. (from Athens) and 12:50 A.M. (to Athens), the trip taking about 35 to 40 minutes. Buses for the airport (a 20-minute trip) leave from the central Olympic terminal and ticket office on the waterfront road at 7 Nikis Street, between Plateia Eleftherias and Komninon Street.

The number of ships plying to and from such a large port as Thessaloniki is surprisingly limited as well as highly subject to change. In recent years there has been an on-again, off-again weekly 30-hour run to Crete. As of this writing it is off again, but that means little. Fairly dependable service is available to Lesvos and Chios, but only in summer. Car/passenger ferries make twice-weekly trips to Skopelos, while Flying Dolphins run daily to Skiathos and Skopelos. Flying Dolphins sometimes also go to Nea Moudania, on the neck of the Kassandra peninsula of Chalkidiki.

Highly useful is the ship and car ferry reservation service provided by the **Polaris Travel Agency**, 22 Pavlou Mela (the diagonal street running between the White Tower and the church of Ayia Sophia) in Thessaloniki; Tel: (031) 278-613, 232-078, or 265-728. Here (and only here, in all of Thessaloniki) travellers can buy tickets and reserve places for themselves and their cars on ships and ferryboats that go to various points throughout almost all of Greece. This is of great help in avoiding much agony, for example, in the crowded madness that is the port of Piraeus (Athens) in summer, when there are too many people for too few ships.

Guided tours to various sites in and outside of Thessaloniki are offered by a few companies; the major one is **Doukas Tours**, 8 Venizelou Street, Thessaloniki, 546 24; Tel: (031) 269-984/87. Tours last from one to ten days and include a one-day "Alexander the Great" tour and a cruise around Mount Athos. Others go as far afield as Athens and Istanbul.

ACCOMMODATIONS REFERENCE

▶ **ABC Hotel.** 41 Agelaki Street, **Thessaloniki**, 546 21. Tel: (031) 265-421; Telex: 410056.

▶ **Aeolos. Kamariotissa**, 680 02 Samothrace. Tel: (0551) 415-95.

▶ **Alexander Beach Bungalows.** Potos, 640 04 Thasos. Tel: (0593) 517-66 or 513-22.

▶ **Alkyon. Paralia Katerinis**, 600 65. Tel: (0351) 616-13.

▶ **Amfipolis. Limenas**, 640 04 Thasos. Tel: (0593) 231-01/04; Telex: 452195.

▶ **Anatolia Hotel.** 53 Anchialou, **Komotini**, 691 00 Thrace. Tel: (0531) 201-32/34; Telex: 462114.

▶ **Motel Astir.** 280 Komotinis Street, **Alexandroupolis**, 681 00 Thrace. Tel: (0551) 264-48.

▶ **Athos Palace. Kallithea**, 630 77 Kassandra, Chalkidiki. Tel: (0374) 221-00/10; Telex: 418488.

▶ **Batis Camping and Hotel.** Bati, 653 02 Kavala. Tel: (051) 227-151.

▶ **Bosphorus. Fanari**, 670 63 Thrace. Tel: (0535) 312-16.

▶ **Bureau of General Tourism. Ouranopolis**, 630 75 Chalkidiki. Tel: (0377) 713-69. Private concern dealing with most hotels, apartments, rooming houses, etc., in the area.

▶ **Capitol.** 8 Monastiriou Street, **Thessaloniki**, 546 29. Tel: (031) 516-221/229; Telex: 412272.

▶ **Chris and Eve's. Komotini**, 691 00 Thrace. Tel: (0531) 289-46; Telex: 462112.

▶ **Hotel City.** 11 Komninon Street, **Thessaloniki**, 546 24. Tel: (031) 269-421.

▶ **Diaporos. Vourvourou**, 630 81 Sithonia. Tel: (0375) 913-13.

▶ **Eagle's Palace. Ouranopolis**, 630 75 Chalkidiki. Tel: (0377) 227-47/48; Fax: (0377) 313-83.

▶ **Hotel Egeo. Nea Iraklitsa**, 640 07 Kavala. Tel: (0592) 718-97.

▶ **Electra Palace.** 5A Aristotelous Square, **Thessaloniki**, 564 24. Tel: (031) 232-221/230; Telex: 412590.

NORTHERN GREECE 333

▶ **Europa.** 12 Leoforos Ayiou Athanasiou, **Kastoria**, 521 00. Tel: (0467) 238-26/28.

▶ **Fanari. Fanari**, 670 63 Thrace. Tel: (0535) 313-00/01.

▶ **Fanari Camping. Fanari**, 670 63 Thrace. Tel: (0535) 312-70.

▶ **Galaxy.** 27 Venizelou Street, **Kavala**, 653 02. Tel: (051) 224-811/812, 224-521, or 224-605; Telex: 452207; Cable: GALAXY.

▶ **Glyfada Hotel. Glyfada**, 640 04 Thasos. Tel: (0593) 221-64 or 299-20.

▶ **Kastoria.** 122 Leoforos Nikis, **Kastoria**, 521 00. Tel: (0467) 296-08 or 294-53.

▶ **Kaviros. Loutra**, 680 02 Samothrace. Tel: (0551) 415-77.

▶ **King Maron Beach. Platanitis**, 694 00 Thrace. Tel: (0533) 221-89.

▶ **Lucy. Kalamitsa**, 650 01 Kavala. Tel: (051) 832-600/605; Fax: (051) 832-501.

▶ **Macedonia Palace.** Alexander the Great Avenue, **Thessaloniki**, 546 40. Tel: (031) 837-520/529, 837-620/629, 837-720/729; Telex: 412162 MP GR; Cable: MACEPAL.

▶ **Makryammos. Limenas**, 640 04 Thasos. Tel: (0593) 221-01/02; Telex: 452107 IOSA GR.

▶ **Mariva. Loutra**, 680 02 Samothrace. Book through Niki Tours, Tel: (0551) 414-65.

▶ **Meliton Hotel. Neos Marmaras**, 630 81 Sithonia, Chalkidiki. Tel: (0375) 713-81; Telex: 412482 TOUR GR or 410704 TOUR GR; Fax: (0375) 712-29.

▶ **Metropolitan.** 65 Vasilissis Olgas Street, **Thessaloniki**, 546 42. Tel: (031) 824-221/228; Telex: 412380.

▶ **Miramare Hotel. Skala Potamia**, 640 04 Thasos. Tel: (0593) 610-40/43.

▶ **Hotel Myrto. Litohoro** (Mt. Olympus), 602 00. Tel: (0352) 813-98.

▶ **Nefeli.** 1 Komninon, **Panorama**, 552 36 Thessaloniki. Tel: (031) 942-002; Telex: 410356 SATG GR.

▶ **Oceanis.** 32 Leoforos Erythrou Stavrou, **Kavala**, 650 01. Tel: (051) 221-981/985.

▶ **Olympia.** 65 Olympou Street, **Thessaloniki**, 546 31. Tel: (031) 235-421/425 or 263-201/205; Telex: 418532 HOLY GR.

▶ **Orestion.** Plateia Davaki, **Kastoria**, 521 00. Tel: (0467) 222-57/58.

▶ **Pallini Beach. Kallithea**, 630 77 Kassandra, Chalkidiki. Tel: (0374) 224-80; Telex: 412148.

▶ **Panorama. Panorama**, 552 36 Thessaloniki. Tel: (031) 941-123/266.

- **Hotel Park.** Litohoro (Mt. Olympus), 602 00. Tel: (0352) 812-52.
- **Pefka.** Panorama, 552 36 Thessaloniki. Tel: (031) 941-790 or 941-153; Fax: (031) 941-035.
- **Platamon Beach. Platamonas,** 600 65. Tel: (0352) 412-12.
- **Porto Carras, Village Inn.** Neos **Marmaras,** 630 81 Sithonia, Chalkidiki. Tel: (0375) 713-81.
- **Queen Olga.** 44 Vasilissis Olgas Street, **Thessaloniki,** 546 41. Tel: (031) 824-621; Telex: 412290; Fax: (031) 830-550.
- **Sarti Beach.** Sarti, 630 81 Sithonia. Tel: (0375) 414-50.
- **Sithonia Beach Hotel.** Neos **Marmaras,** 630 81 Sithonia, Chalkidiki. Tel: (0375) 713-81; Telex: 412496.
- **Skites.** Ouranopolis, 630 75 Chalkidiki. Tel: (0377) 711-40/41.
- **Thasos.** Pefkari, 640 04 Thasos. Tel: (0593) 515-96.
- **Timoleon.** Limani Thasou, **Limenas,** 640 04 Thasos. Tel: (0593) 221-77/79.
- **Tosca Beach Hotel.** Palio, 655 00 Kavala. Tel: (051) 224-754.
- **Xenia.** 43 Sismanoglou Street, **Komotini,** 691 00 Thrace. Tel: (0531) 221-39.
- **Xenia.** Ouranopolis, 630 75 Chalkidiki. Tel: (0377) 712-02.
- **Xenia.** Paleopoli, 680 02 Samothrace. Tel: (0551) 412-30.
- **Xenia.** 9 Vasilissis Sofias, **Xanthi** 671 00. Tel: (0541) 241-35.
- **Xenia du Lac.** Plateia Deksaminis, **Kastoria,** 521 00. Tel: (0467) 225-65.

THE SPORADES

By Diana Farr Ladas

Diana Farr Ladas, a fan of Greece since 1963 and permanent resident since 1972, is a free-lance writer, translator, and editor. Author of a guidebook to Corfu and the Ionians, she has written a number of articles on aspects of Greek life and history and coedits the Chandris Hotels Magazine.

Scattered, as their name implies, like seeds in a stiff breeze, most of the northern Sporades islands—Skiathos, Skopelos, and Alonnisos, and the smaller outer islands—are an extension of Mount Pelion in Thessaly, and they look it. Their slopes are covered with dense pine forest interspersed with olive, cypress, plane, and fruit-bearing trees, and they are crisscrossed with springs and streams. Though the islands were inhabited long before antiquity, few vestiges of the distant past remain on them; centuries of plunder and a number of serious earthquakes have erased all but a few traces. The islands share a common history, having been conquered by anybody and everybody who coveted a base in the Aegean, from the Macedonians and Romans to the Venetians and the Turks.

Thanks to improved mobility in the form of airports and hydrofoils, the islands have recently become very popular with tourists, and each has its special appeal. Gentle **Skiáthos**, closest to the mainland and the most developed, is lively and sophisticated; **Skópelos**, just to the east, a "masculine" island, is steeper and better preserved; **Alónnisos**, still farther east and lacking many amenities, is rustic and wild. And **Skyros**, so far flung off the east coast of Evia (Euboea) that it seems to have no connection to the others, resembles one of the Cyclades: more rugged, less wooded, its traditions still thriving.

SKIATHOS

Though the name means "in the shadow of Athos," there is not a hint of anything dark or gloomy about Skiáthos. Its smallish perimeter is rimmed with an astounding 60 beaches, many of them literally golden, and its unpretentious town is a happy blend of cafés, tavernas, bars, and boutiques in careless juxtaposition to private houses festooned with bougainvillaea, jasmine, and myriad other colorful, sweet-smelling blooms.

MAJOR INTEREST

Sixty beaches, including Lalaria and Koukounaries
Kastro
Walks
Wining and dining
Kanapitsa's villas

Skiathos Town

There is only one town on the island, where most of the 4,000 inhabitants live. Also called Skiathos, it is built on two low-lying hills lining the port and occupies the site of the ancient settlement on the eastern coast. Though pleasant, it boasts no outstanding buildings; those were destroyed when the Germans set fire to them in reprisal for local resistance activity during World War II. Sad to say, not all recent construction is in the island tradition, but the place is so full of fun and charm that you tend to overlook the occasional concrete atrocity.

Life in the town is focused on the waterfront and the main drag, Papadiamánti Street, named after the island's most famous son, the 19th-century novelist Alexandros Papadiamantis (don't be misled by the street sign that reads Papadiamadi; Greeks observe no rules when transliterating their language). Papadiamantis's house lies to the right on

Skiathos and Skopelos

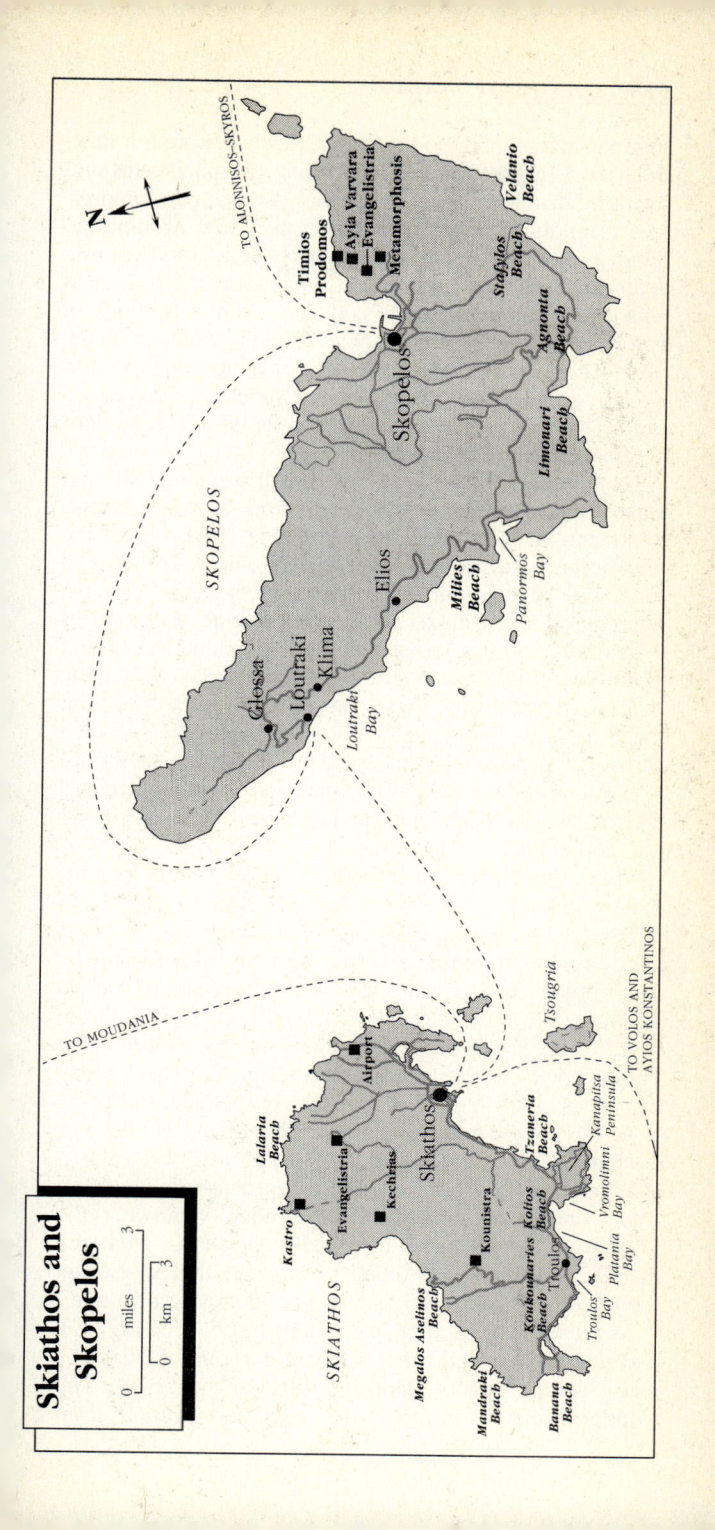

the first block going up the street. Newly restored, it functions as a simple museum containing personal items and furniture that belonged to the author. A much more impressive example of Skiathian architecture is the **Archipelago** antiques store opposite, which is as close to a folk-art museum as you'll find in the area. The rooms are decorated with old furniture, pottery, and tiles, with collections of embroidery, jewelry, and weapons tastefully arranged on the walls. The owners think of the shop as a museum, too, and encourage leisurely browsing. (Archipelago also has a branch on the waterfront, which sells attractive modern accessories and ceramics.)

Continuing up scruffy, busy Papadiamanti, you'll find smart boutiques, jewelry shops, travel agents, fast-food joints, and the occasional popular taverna. Here, too, are the telephone, post, and Olympic Airways offices. This part of town has become the "in" district of Skiathos with the opening on Evangelistria Street of **La Piscine**, a glamorous restaurant-bar-disco focused around a beautiful pool and open from 10:00 A.M. until the wee hours. For something more traditional, try **Elias's Taverna**, still a favorite with locals and foreigners alike. Though its tables are sprawled across an unspectacular courtyard into the street, the service is excellent and the food more imaginative than the standard taverna fare. Its shrimp and chicken casseroles are memorable (and eminently affordable).

Wandering through the back streets between Papadiamanti and the waterfront can be a great source of amusement—there are so many pubs, nightclubs, shops, and surprises to stumble upon. Most unexpected are the small hotels cut off from the street by wrought-iron gates opening onto quiet courtyards, tranquil oases amid all the bustle. The family-run **Hotel Ilion** and the **Bourtzi** and **Pothos** hotels belong to this genre, simply furnished, pleasant places to stay—in the mainstream but somehow not of it.

Activity on the waterfront, on the other hand, is endlessly fascinating. Fancy, floating gin palaces may be docked alongside dumpy excursion boats and spunky fishing caïques. The waterfront is bisected by a small promontory known as the **Bourtzi**, a fortified islet now indistinguishable from the mainland. Segments of Venetian wall surround an elegant though dilapidated Neoclassical school building and a café.

As you leave the Bourtzi, passing the ferry, Flying Dolphin, and motorbike-rental firms, you come to one of Skiathos's nicest antiques shops, **Morpho**, filled to the ceiling with wonderful objects, embroideries, rugs, and ceramics from all over northern Greece. Farther along the quay, try the **Carnayio Fish Taverna** and the **Limenakia**, both favorites with the locals for their seafood and delicious Greek fare.

The other (west) side of the waterfront is far more picturesque, a continuous stretch of cafés and tavernas distinguished from one another only by the color and style of their chairs and tables. These are the places from which to people-watch. With the exception of the wide range of tidbits available at the **Mezetzidiko** (don't miss the grilled octopus and fried cheese), eating here is likely to cost more than it should. Gourmet cravings are best satisfied in slightly less central neighborhoods.

If you continue to the end of the promontory and walk up the steps past the tavernas bearing right into the little church square, you'll come to another of Skiathos's fabulous antiques stores, the **Galerie Varsakis**. The owner, Harris Varsakis, has amassed an immense collection of *kilíms* (Anatolian rugs with no pile), embroideries, and handicrafts, among which he has hung his own inimitable, surrealistic visions of themes from Greek mythology. If you don't feel up to buying a whole rug or tapestry, you can pick a fragment, beautifully mounted on heavy paper and suitable for framing, for an unusual and evocative souvenir. The rotisserie next to the gallery is justifiably well known for its *souvlákia*.

For more elegant dining in the vicinity, proceed back toward the sea, where there is a collection of good eating places ranging from **Alexander's** taverna, which claims the finest *moussaká* on the island and makes an excellent stuffed and boned chicken breast as well, to the island's international restaurants. Here, names like **Le Bistro**, **Chez Julian**, **La Boheme**, and **Casablanca** are the rule. These are chic, charmingly decorated establishments catering to the select few. Go early so you can get a table on Le Bistro's tiny balcony. The menus are posted outside, so there need be no nasty surprises. If you'd prefer a pizza with your view, try **Kon Tiki**, next to Le Bistro; **Anemos**, near this Continental contingent, is noted for its fish. Much farther along at Plakes (where there are some flat rocks for sunbathing), is **Tarsanas**, a reconstituted shipbuilder's yard. Tarsanas has the most romantic location in town for a drink or dinner. Tables are placed on an enormous veranda overlooking the sea, far from the commotion in the port.

The area between Galerie Varsakis and Tarsanas is residential, picturesque, and free of traffic (most of the time; occasionally residents try to squeeze their cars through the narrow lanes that were intended for nothing wider than a loaded mule). A number of pretty pensions are tucked in among the private houses here, one being the small **Villa Orsa**, whose rooms have balconies overlooking the sea. The villa's minute, beautifully tended garden is set with marble tables.

Around the Island

The best way of getting around the island and visiting some of those 60 splendid beaches is to board one of the excursion boats lined up on the quay. There is a public bus that makes frequent runs from town southwest to Koukounaries, the most photographed beach in Greece—but it can get overcrowded. Motorbikes and cars may be rented, though the combination of narrow, potholed roads and heavy traffic can be disastrous for the inexperienced scooter driver.

Most of the beaches on the sheltered south coast as far as Koukounaries have been developed to some extent. This may take the form of a welcome taverna, a cluster of villas, or a hotel. Unfortunately, some of the hotels don't seem to fit in with their surroundings, but there are many delightful ones to choose from. The large, recently renovated **Nostos** hotel-bungalow complex overlooking Tzaneria beach about midway between Skiathos and Koukounaries is decorated with local handicrafts, slate floors, and traditionally styled furniture. Offering a pool, tennis court, water sports, taverna, and sea views from all the bungalows and most of the rooms, its one drawback is the set of stairs you have to climb up from the beach.

The **Kanapítsa Peninsula** (also known as Kalamáki) begins at **Tzaneriá** beach. This was the site picked in the early 1960s by English visitors who fell enough in love with the island to build houses here. If you'd prefer to live this kind of existence, you can rent a villa from **Mare Nostrum Holidays**, a firm specializing in providing privately owned houses in the Sporades to tourists when their owners are not in residence (see the Accommodations Reference, below). The **Plaza Hotel** at the eastern entrance to Kanapitsa is another pleasant alternative, with a restaurant, pool, roof garden, and watersports facilities. Its rooms are clean and quiet, looking onto the beach and pool or the surrounding pine woods. A walk on the dirt road encircling Kanapitsa will give you a glimpse of Skiathos at its best. You may want to pick up a copy of *Skiathos* (edited by Rita and Dietrich Harkort), an invaluable guide to the island, especially good on walks.

Vromolímni Bay on the west side of Kanapitsa is particularly scenic, and there's a good taverna on the beach. The bay takes its name from the nearby freshwater pond (*limni*). Near this point on the road, near Koliós, are two more popular tavernas, **Angelos's** and **Stathis's**. Stathis is renowned for his aggressive temperament, but his food is so exceptional that customers tend to ignore his tantrums. Unlike most tavernas, Stathis also offers desserts—and sumptuous breakfasts.

The next bays to the west, **Plataniá** and **Ayia Paraskeví**, have recently witnessed development on a grand scale, and one of the new hotels here is a contender for the prettiest on the island. Decoration at the **Atrium Hotel** was inspired by the monasteries of Mount Athos, and its rich earth colors blend nicely with the surroundings. At Ayia Paraskevi you can still enjoy the modest, family-run taverna next to the delightful little church, and the breezy, gleaming white **Arco Hotel** separated from the beach only by a stretch of lawn. **Troulos Bay** comes next, a more secluded beach with a nice taverna and a very special, cozy hotel, named after its location, with a pretty patio and lounge. Two steps from the beach and separated from it by a flower-filled garden, it is ideal for families with young children, but you needn't have children to be happy here.

Finally, you arrive at world-famous **Koukounariés**, half a mile of crescent beach backed with the thick pine wood to which it owes its name. Even when packed with people, its sand studded with umbrellas and its waters rent by waterskiers, it is still very attractive. But if you crave to strip, windsurf with more excitement, or picnic in more privacy, then head farther north for Banana, Mandraki, or Aselinos beaches. **Banána** is the nudist beach, **Mandráki** is where Xerxes lay in wait to ambush the Athenian fleet in 480 B.C., and **Megálos Asélinos** boasts a *bouzoúki* taverna, a campsite, and rollers when the wind is from the north. Most of the other beaches on the north side are inaccessible except by boat or by trekking long distances. **Tsougriá** island, just to the south of Skiathos town, is a favorite destination because of its fabulous beaches, but the most popular excursion is to **Lalária**, another famous and exquisite beach on the north coast. It consists not of sand but of beautifully rounded stones (which are pilfered every summer by tourists seeking paperweights and doorstops) and is adorned with a striking arch, hollowed out of the rock by the wind. The coast is punctuated with caves and grottoes along the way.

For a picture of Skiathos as something other than a tourist resort, leave the boat when it stops at **Kastro** and climb up to the old Medieval capital (1538 to 1829). To defend themselves against both Turks and marauding pirates the islanders founded this retreat on an impregnable rock, linked only to the hill opposite by a drawbridge. Once there were 30 churches and 300 houses perched here; three of the churches have been restored, and the main one has a lovely icon screen. It is easy to imagine the fear and misery the residents must have felt, battered by sea and wind, threatened by murderous buccaneers, clinging tenaciously to their rock and to life. The Kastro proved useful again during the last world war, providing a hideout for Allied soldiers—particularly New Zealanders—making their way across the Aegean to Turkey.

The view of the sheer cliffs and breathtaking colors of the sea is unforgettable. If you have the courage and it's not stiflingly hot, make the effort to walk from Kastro back to town (two and a half to three hours, not arduous). You will pass by monasteries, springs, pastures, and orchards and gain a totally different concept of the island. Needless to say, in spring the countryside is a dream.

On Skiathos monasteries are polka-dotted about the hills. The grandest and most imposing is **Evangelístria** to the north of the town. Protected against pirates by strong walls, it contains a lovely 18th-century church, a small museum, and an important library. The much smaller 17th-century monastery of **Kounístra**, now abandoned, lies between Troulos Bay and Aselinos. An enterprising layman has set up a refreshment stand within its walls, making it a popular destination for hikers. **Kechriás**, much more remote, is also abandoned. The compensations for walking here are the beauty of the surroundings and the delight you will feel at glimpsing its pink-and-blue cupola among the cypress trees. If you'd prefer the company of a local to lead you further into the exploration of Skiathos, get in touch with Leda Baldry, who organizes walks of all kinds, through Mare Nostrum Holidays (Tel: 0427-214-63/64; Fax: 217-93). But don't go at the height of summer. In fact, this island and all the Sporades are seriously overcrowded from mid-July to the end of August. The crush on the waterfront can be compared to the Tokyo subway at rush hour, so don't hazard it unless you have no alternative.

GETTING AROUND
Because of its popularity Skiathos is well served by both planes and boats. Olympic Airways schedules as many as eight flights per day from Athens at the height of the season.

There are also numerous charters from major European cities. (The airport is not far from town, though not close enough to be bothersome.) Flying Dolphins leave the mainland from both Volos (6 to 25 departures per week; one hour and 20 minutes) and Ayios Konstantinos (served by Flying Dolphin bus from Athens; 2 to 17 departures per week; one hour and 30 minutes). Ferryboats also leave from Volos (5 to 20 departures per week; three hours and 30 minutes) and from Ayios Konstantinos (3 to 7 departures per week; three hours and 30 minutes). These same hydrofoils and ferries serve Skopelos and Alonnisos, with less frequent connections to Skyros (hydrofoil 4 times per week in July and August; two hours and 45 minutes) and Moudania in Chalkidiki (2 to 4 times per week). Both types of ships dock right near the Bourtzi in Skiathos town.

SKOPELOS

Though Skópelos lies only a few nautical miles east of Skiathos, it is completely different in character—and far less commercialized. Living up to its name, which means "a huge rock piercing the sea," it has steeper mountains and more precipitous shores. Skopelos's easily accessible beaches can be numbered on two hands, but it has 360 churches and 40 monasteries scattered among its thick green forests; 123 of the churches are tucked away in the capital-port alone.

This does not mean that the 6,000 Skopeliots are more religious than their neighbors. In fact, most of the monasteries are deserted and many of the churches are unlocked only once a year on their feast day. But the island is noted for its architecture, and because Skopelos town, on the north coast, has suffered little earthquake damage and no wartime reprisals, it is still remarkably beautiful and unspoiled. White churches and white houses, roofed with either slate or red tiles, are wedged together in a semicircle rising straight up from the port. The ubiquitous overhanging balconies—enclosed with fancifully wrought iron, wood, or, alas, concrete—are embellished by flower pots and vines, while the doors and shutters are painted in a wide variety of colors. You can wander happily for hours up and down the maze-like stepped paths (most of which are immune even to motorbikes), being constantly surprised by the sudden appearance of a church, a luxuriant garden, or black-robed women engaged in gossip.

MAJOR INTEREST

Skopelos town
Churches and monasteries
Shopping
Milies beach

Skopelos Town

One of the best ways to start your explorations is to climb up the stairs on the extreme right of the port as you face inland, passing three exquisite churches, each older than the one before. The uppermost church, **Ayios Athanásios**, was founded in the 9th century. When you reach the top you are actually within the walls of the Venetian **Kastro**, erected in the 13th century by the Ghisi feudal lords who were subject to the Duchy of Naxos. The walls rest on polygonal masonry of the 5th century B.C., for here was the acropolis of ancient Skopelos, then known as Peparethos. Of more immediate interest, perhaps, is the presence of a delightful *ouzerí,* the **Anatoli**, to compensate for all that climbing.

Though you can easily lose yourself in the back streets as you wend your way down, there is no risk of getting really lost. As in Skiathos, all the essential places you need are located on or near the waterfront. You'll notice to the right as you get off the Flying Dolphin or ferry one of the locals' favorite tavernas, **Ta Kymata**, or Angelos's, as they call it. The cordial proprietor specializes in generous portions of Greek home cooking at congenial prices. Not far off to the left are two other landmarks, the **Platanos** jazz bar, good for both breakfasts and nightcaps, and the **Klimataria**, another taverna highly recommended by Skopeliots. Waterfront activity is livelier still under the mulberry trees a bit farther on. At this point the establishments become markedly less "traditional," with fast-food shops, cafés with neon lighting and bright plastic decors, and "gelaterias," but you'll be sure of getting a decent meal at **Spyro's** rotisserie, known for its spit-roasted chicken and other meats.

The side streets just off this part of the waterfront abound in beautiful shops, offering clothes and handicrafts of a distinction rarely found in tourist resorts. Look for **Plomisti** for amber beads, bags, paintings, and weavings; **Morko** for clothes, tie-dyes, antiques, and ceramics; **Frosso** for *kilíms* (Anatolian rugs); and **Daphni** for leather bags and sandals. But the real jewel among all the lovely shops in Skopelos is **Armoloi** (and its branch **To Allo**—The Other—just up the street). Assembled here are fabulous ceramics crafted by three gifted potters in their island studios, bags fashioned out of lovely fragments of old rugs, mirrors and trays painted in a naïf manner, and, upstairs, in their Anatolian corner, a wonderful collection of kilims, tapestries, and embroideries. The proprietors also run an elegant restaurant called **Selini**, located in a lovely garden on the other side of the harbor. Here you can dine on the best of Greek cuisine and find some respite from the waterfront bustle.

In close proximity to Armoloi are two of Skopelos's best pensions, Kyr Sotos, on the corner of the waterfront just before the shop, and Andromache, a short walk up the hill opposite the telephone office. Casual **Kyr Sotos**, run by Neil, an Englishman, and his Skopeliot wife, Alexandra, consists of 12 rooms, a small lounge, courtyards, and two roof terraces in what was once Alexandra's family home. Kyr Sotos has also published a useful guide to the island's walks. **Andromache** is another family mansion, converted with care and taste and decorated with tiles and mirrors from Armoloi. It, too, has a roof terrace and is open all year. Its owners, Machi and Yiorgos Drossos, are the local Flying Dolphin agents and run the **Madro Travel** agency; they are a mine of information about the island.

Other attractive places to stay are the Elli, Aperitton, and, as of 1990, Dionysos, new hotels on the road that runs through the uppermost part of the town. The 25-room **Elli**, built in traditional style, has a lovely patio and a swimming pool, a welcome addition in a town that has no decent beach. **Aperitton**, which opened in 1989, is dazzlingly whitewashed and has a chic blue trim; it also has a restaurant and a swimming pool. The 50-room **Dionysos**, in traditional style like its neighbors, has a pool as well. With the construction of these three beautiful hotels, Skopelos town has acquired an element of discreet elegance that actually adds to its appeal.

Quite the other direction, on the other side of the harbor from Skopelos town, is Skopelos's most luxurious hotel, the 60-room **Prince Stafylos**, which also has a swimming pool, a garden, and a restaurant. From a distance, its long slate roof is the only thing visible above the trees. Its interiors, too, are traditionally furnished, though a bit heavy for the summer.

Just beyond it is **Skopelos Village**, an appealing cluster of 37 studios and maisonettes, each with an individual lawn or balcony facing the sea or pool.

If you continue past Skopelos Village and the scant remains of an ancient *asklepieion* (hospital) armed with the *Sotos Walking Guide,* you can negotiate the paths up to some of the island's most impressive **monasteries**: Evangelístria, Metamorphosis, Ayia Varvára, and the Tímios Pródromos. Though the first and last are the only ones still inhabited, the others are worth viewing from the outside. The following sign is posted outside the Prodromos nunnery: "Please no entry with no good dressing"; in other words, women should not wear shorts or sleeveless blouses.

Around the Island

Of course Skopelos has beaches, too. These are best reached by excursion boat from the port or by bus. The first stop going clockwise around the island is **Stáfylos** beach, a very pretty cove on the south coast that tends to get crowded. Stafylos is named after the legendary Minoan prince whose reputed tomb was excavated in the vicinity in the 1920s. Skopelos was colonized by Cretans after the fall of Knossos, and Stafylos was one of the Argonauts who set off from Volos (Iolkos then) to help Jason find the Golden Fleece. A short walk from Stafylos over the headland will take you to **Velánio**, where nudism is officially permitted.

Next comes **Agnónta**, a tiny horseshoe-shaped port rimmed with tavernas where you can be sure of getting fresh fish. Though the setting is delightful, the beach is very stony and the sea fills up with yachts, so at the height of the season it's better to think of it as a romantic place to have lunch or dinner (try **Pavlos's**). The beach is littered with shards, though no ancient site is visible. They may have come from the amphoras of Skopelos wine that the island used to export in vast quantities to Rome. Small boats ferry bathers to the lovely cove of **Limonári** around the point.

The broad bay of **Pánormos** follows. Panormos was the site of the second of Skopelos's three ancient cities, and sections of the old wall can still be seen to the right above the **Panormos Beach Hotel**. The owner of this immaculate and well-tended place has spent even more on the grounds than on the building; visitors will enjoy his 600 rosebushes just as much as the view of the bay from their tranquil rooms.

Miliés, considered the island's finest, is the next beach. One of its three silvery crescents lined with trees has a taverna.

The next section of Skopelos is strange indeed. This is the only part that has been affected by the chthonic rumblings that shake the region from time to time. As you drive by you will notice an unsightly modern settlement on the coast at Eliós. This was built in a hurry to house the residents of the hill village of Klima when their houses started to slide down the mountain after the earthquake of 1965. Though there is nothing to commemorate it, Elios is where Skopelos's patron saint, the bishop Reginus, had a premonition of his fate and cried out for mercy (*eleós*) when he landed in the fourth century. He is believed to have delivered the island from the bane of a fearsome dragon that had its lair at Panormos, but he was later martyred by fanatic followers of Julian the Apostate, who were determined to stamp out Christianity.

Klima is now inhabited by a handful of elderly men and women who refused to be relocated. A great many of the houses, untouched since the quake, are for sale. Foreigners are buying, but the locals are not lured by the prospect of property that is inching its way down the hill to the coast.

From Klima it's only a short distance northwest to **Glossa**, Skopelos's second town, a pleasant place perched more securely on the hillside that has made few concessions to tourism. The bay of **Loutráki** directly below it is a secure harbor, amply endowed with tavernas, where the hydrofoils dock comfortably even when the main port is flecked with whitecaps.

A dirt road just before Glossa leads to the picturesque **church of Ayios Yanni Kastrí**, built on a rock at the edge of the sea. Though the road is negotiable by car or motorbike, it also makes a lovely walk in spring, past some of the plum orchards for which Skopelos is famous, to the musical accompaniment of nightingales. There are streams to drink from and a beach to plunge from at the end... after you have struggled up the steps carved in rock to the quaint little church.

Travelling around this peaceful island, it is hard to believe that its history was so fraught with peril, inconceivable that the notorious Barbarossa murdered every one of its inhabitants in 1538. Much more apparent is the prosperity of the 18th and 19th centuries, when Skopeliot merchants traded with Romania and Odessa and supplied almost as many ships to the Greek Navy in 1821 as Spetses and Hydra.

GETTING AROUND

Visitors to Skopelos may wish to take advantage of the airport facilities at Skiathos. Both the island's ports—Glossa and Skopelos town—are served by the same boats as Skiathos. Flying Dolphins leave the mainland from both Volos (6 to 25 departures per week; two hours and 15 minutes) and Ayios Konstantinos (served by Flying Dolphin bus from Athens; 2 to 17 departures per week; two hours to Glossa; two hours and 30 minutes to Skopelos town). Ferryboats also serve both destinations from Volos (5 to 20 departures per week; five hours) and Ayios Konstantinos (3 to 7 departures per week; five hours). Glossa is 30 minutes from Skiathos, Skopelos another 30 minutes from Glossa. Skopelos is only about 40 minutes from Alonnisos by hydrofoil and one hour and 40 minutes from Skyros (departures 4 times per week). Dolphins also "fly" to Moudania in Chalkidiki 2 to 4 times per week. These short distances make it easy to island-hop.

To get around the island itself, you can rent a car or scooter or take the convenient public bus, and you can use caïques to reach the most popular beaches.

ALONNISOS

Before the days of airports and Flying Dolphins, Alónnisos was a remote outpost patronized by fishing caïques, dedicated spear fishermen, and the occasional camper. Now, though lacking fine hotels, boutiques, public transport, and paved roads, it is gaining in the popularity polls. More and more people flock to this funky place, attracted by its splendid beaches, relaxed atmosphere, and delightful population. Nature is at its best in Alonnisos; what man hath wrought is another story.

After suffering over the centuries the same slings and arrows of outrageous fortune as its larger neighbors, the people of Alonnisos led a quiet, uncomplicated existence from the Greek revolution until 1950, when the wheel of fate turned against them once more. First, their prosperous vineyards withered overnight, struck by phylloxera. Then, in 1965, the earth gave a mighty heave and destroyed their hilltop capital, Hora, or Alonnisos town. The inhabitants

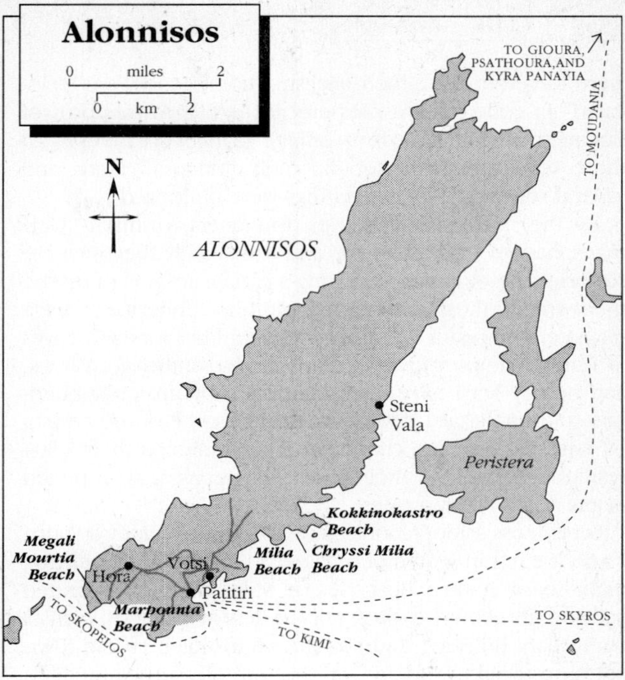
Alonnisos
0 miles 2
0 km 2
N
ALONNISOS
TO GIOURA, PSATHOURA, AND KYRA PANAYIA
TO MOUDANIA
Steni Vala
Peristera
Kokkinokastro Beach
Milia Beach
Chryssi Milia Beach
Megali Mourtia Beach
Hora
Votsi
Patitiri
Marpounta Beach
TO SKOPELOS
TO KIMI
TO SKYROS

Skyros
0 miles 5
0 km 5
N
Airport
MERI
Gyrismata
Molos
Magazia
Horio
Atsitsa
Aspous
Achilli Beach
Ayios Fokas Beach
Ayios Panteleimon
Pefkos Beach
Ayios Fokas
TO ALONNISOS
Linaria
Kalamitsa
Kalamitsa Bay
VOUNO
Caves
Kolymbada Beach
Treis Boukes
Renes Beach
Glyfada Beach
TO KIMI

were forced to leave their ancestral homes and were "relocated" in concrete eyesores erected by the Army Corps of Engineers. To add insult to injury, loans were refused to those who wanted to rebuild their homes in Hora, and several relatively sound dwellings were bulldozed.

By the mid-1970s, however, foreigners, primarily Germans, had spotted a bargain, and it is mainly they who are restoring the old town, incurring a certain amount of resentment among those who parted with their inheritance for a pittance. The result is that the delightful harbors and coves of Patitiri, the port town on the island's southeastern coast, and nearby Votsi have been blemished by unsightly buildings and haphazard development, and some of the areas a bit farther inland are charmless indeed, though their 1,500 residents have done their best to compensate with potted plants and flowering vines.

Scruffiness aside, Alonnisos can promise a happy sojourn if you are not in search of organized recreation, scintillating nightlife, or culture. Boat trips or walks along pine-scented paths to gorgeous beaches, sails to deserted islands, picnics on verdant hillsides, and the chance to watch an old town being restored to life are some of the pleasures Alonnisos offers.

MAJOR INTEREST

Hora
Superb beaches
Offshore islands
Simple pleasures

Patitiri

Most of Patitiri's amenities are immediately apparent upon arrival at the dock. On the waterfront just to your right is **Ikos Travel**, the Flying Dolphin office cum travel agency, where Panos Athanassiou will help you with accommodations and answer any other questions. On this side of the port, up the hill, are two of the island's nicest hotels and one of its best tavernas. The **Liadromia Hotel**, recognizable by its attractive roof garden, combines traditional decor with friendly service and a pleasant view. Directly in back of it is the 31-room **Paradise Hotel**—comfortable, clean rooms surrounding a spacious patio looking out over the pine trees to the sea. **Dzimakos's** taverna lies at the far end of this section of waterfront (that is, a few steps on—Patitiri is very small).

The other side is occupied by an assortment of tavernas, restaurants, and cafés overlooked by the **Galaxy Hotel**, a 100-bed establishment run as a hobby by a very congenial family whose serious business is the Delphi restaurant in Athens. All three hotels exemplify what is most appealing about Alonnisos—kindness, humor, and hospitality.

Around the Island

A visit to **Hora**, above Patitiri and just under a mile from town by footpath or just over two miles by road, is a must. Not only are the views from it among the best you'll enjoy on any island, but it is gratifying to watch the old town coming back to life. Though restored dwellings are juxtaposed with ruins, there is a feeling of optimism to offset the melancholy. A lot of care is going into the restoration, and already there are tavernas to make the climb up the hill worth your while (Alonnisos has only one taxi and not enough motorbikes to go around). Up here you have to make the choice between good views and good food, for, as is so often the case, the establishments with the best vantage points tend to neglect cuisine. **Aloni** has the most spectacular location, **Nikos** has no view at all, and **Paraport** is a good compromise. **Astrofengia** is where you can satisfy your craving for steak *au poivre vert* or Stroganoff.

Patitiri is the departure point for the excursion boats serving the various beaches around the island—**Megáli Mourtiá, Miliá, Chryssí Miliá, Kokkinókastro** (the last framed by eroded red cliffs, the site of both a ruined Medieval castle and the ancient settlement of Ikos), to name a few—**Stení Vala**, a fishermen's haven rapidly becoming "resortified," and the **offshore islands**.

For the most part deserted except for the lone shepherd or monk, these offshore islands are a yachting paradise, with protected bays, grottoes, derelict monasteries, and quiet beaches. **Gioúra** is believed to be where the Cyclops had his lair; **Psathoúra** conceals a sunken city—perhaps ancient Alonnisos—to lure snorkelers off its shores; **Kyrá Panayiá** and **Peristéra** are riddled with private coves.

There are more beaches on Alonnisos's southwest coast, though few on the steep windswept north. One of those in the southwest, **Marpoúnta**, boasts a bungalow complex with recreation facilities, bar, taverna, pool, and tennis courts, built on a small promontory overlooking two lovely beaches.

As with all the islands there are rooms available in private houses, even up in Hora. But don't dream of island-hopping without reservations in July or August.

GETTING AROUND

More remote than Skiathos and Skopelos, Alonnisos has benefited from the expanded airport at Skiathos and the quick service provided by hydrofoils. It lies at the end of the Flying Dolphin and ferry lines (see Getting Around for Skiathos and Skopelos) and is about three hours on the hydrofoil (counting stops) from Ayios Konstantinos or Volos and six hours on the ferry. There are also two Flying Dolphin departures per week for Skyros and two to four per week for Moudania in Chalkidiki.

There are no cars for rent on Alonnisos, and not very many roads. A few scooters are available for hire; caïques are a popular and convenient way of beach-sampling. Caïques also make day trips to the neighboring uninhabited islands of Psathoura, Gioura, Kyra Panayia, Peristera, and more.

SKYROS

Off by itself in the middle of the Aegean, Skyros could not be more different from the rest of the Sporades. It has the dazzling white Cubist architecture of the Cyclades, but many of its customs and crafts are found nowhere else in Greece, and its isolation has kept it free of extravagant tourist development.

MAJOR INTEREST

Horio, the old capital
The Kastro
Pottery and other crafts
Lobsters
Carnival
The Faltaits Folklore Museum

The largest of the Sporades, Skyros consists of two halves linked by an isthmus: Vounó, rocky and mountainous, and Meri (a corruption of *ímeros,* meaning "tame"), fertile and fairly green. Because most of the southern portion (Vouno) is virtually inaccessible except by boat, and because there are so few roads in the north, you can really see everything that *is* accessible in two days. But why rush? The island should be savored.

The boats dock at Linariá, a cluster of modern buildings packed around a tiny port in the middle of the west coast. There's no real reason to linger here, except to gorge yourself on the excellent fish served at the unprepossessing-looking restaurant, **I Kali Kardia**, on the right as you disembark. The boat will be met by Skyros's two buses, which make the 15-minute journey across the island to Skyros's only village, Skyros, also known as To Horió (The Village), or to Magazia and Molos on the beach beneath it.

Horio is perched on the crest of a steep rock that rises dramatically from the plain, a smaller version of Acrocorinth. This has been a favored location since earliest times; bastions of Cyclopean walls are still visible halfway up the hill, and the Byzantine castle at the summit rests on ancient foundations. Initially invisible from the sea, the fortress village could ready its defense against attackers and pirates and command a panoramic view of the sea routes. Little went on that the Skyrians did not know about.

Legend and history are still very much alive on this rock, where King Lykomedes had his palace in the Heroic Age. Here Thetis hid her son, Achilles, dressed as a girl, among the queen's ladies-in-waiting, hoping to save him from dying in Troy. Here Theseus, banished from Athens, sought to regain his forefathers' throne, but Lykomedes resented the intrusion and shoved him over the cliff. When Kimon of Athens gained control over the island in 470 B.C. he found the hero's bones and had them enshrined in the Theseion in the Agora. The Athenians, having reduced the local inhabitants to slavery, ruled the island for most of antiquity. Debate still rages over the marble lion embedded in the archway above the entrance to the castle: Is it the Lion of Saint Mark, as many used to believe, or the symbol of Athenian supremacy?

Horio

Be prepared to be disappointed at your first sight of Horió. The buildings on the fringes have no particular charm, and all the utilitarian services—supermarkets, the school, OTE (telecommunications), taxi stand—are concentrated at the main square. But a few steps up the hill (nicknamed Sisyphos Hill), and you're in the midst of a traditional island village. Not even motorbikes can negotiate the narrow, convoluted streets. Though there are some concessions to tourism—pubs, gelaterias, souvenir shops—these are all on a small scale and confined to the main street, Agorá (Market) Street, one of the few that has a name. Here the souvenir shops are not peddling just the ubiquitous tee-shirts and kitsch, they are giving you the opportunity to get a good look at the ceramics and carpentry work that adorn even the humblest Skyrian house. Everywhere you wander, through the labyrinthine lanes, up steps, under archways, you won't be able to resist the temptation to peer through doorways and windows for a glimpse of the interiors. Every dwelling is a veritable museum, the walls festooned with faïence and porcelain plates from Asia Minor, Delft, China, and England, with copper disks and utensils, and with delicate embroideries. The furniture will invariably include the diminutive Skyrian chairs, whose backs are carved with intricate symbolic patterns. Despite their size they are intended for adult posteriors.

For centuries only a handful of aristocratic families had access to these treasures, acquired through a symbiotic relationship with the pirates based in Treis Boukes on the southern part of the island. But during the 19th century these families began to sell them off to the middle class, who had long coveted them. In time a household's social status was measured in terms of these valuables. Around 1920 some enterprising potters decided to make this wealth accessible to all and started copying the priceless antique china. And that is why, in both the homes and the shops, you see so many European and Oriental look-alikes alongside traditional Skyrian motifs.

There are two landmarks in Skyros town—the Kastro and To Brook—and most streets seem to lead to one or the other. The **Kastro** is, of course, the old acropolis, where the Byzantines erected their fortress and which was later improved by the Venetians in the 14th and 15th centuries. Within the walls of the castle are the monastery of St. George of Skyros, founded in 962, a Byzantine cistern, a Venetian reservoir (also used as a prison), and from every side a glorious view. To the east you can see the beaches at Magazia and Molos stretched beside the open Aegean, to the west the pale patchwork of flat gray rooftops outlined in white, like a painting by Juan Gris.

To Brook, on the other hand, is a footnote to more recent history. Here, on the northern outskirts of town a stone's throw from a splendid Cyclopean bastion, stands a bland, banal statue dedicated to Rupert Brooke and eternal poetry. Few monuments could be so unevocative of the tragic young romanticist who died in Skyros of septicaemia while on his way to fight at Gallipoli in 1915. (His actual grave is at Treis Boukes on the other side of the island; see below.)

Flanking the statue are the town's two museums, the **Archaeological Museum** to the south and the **Faltaits Historical and Folklore Museum** to the north. The former contains finds from various eras and sites on Skyros, ranging from Mycenaean through Roman, Byzantine, and Frankish times, and one part of it is fitted out like a typical Skyrian house. The Faltaits Museum is a private collection amassed over the centuries by one of the island's oldest and most powerful families. Housed in the family mansion, the collection includes all manner of objects, ranging from ancient cannonballs to costumes, pottery from the world over, exquisite embroideries, carved wooden icons, weapons, and an extraordinary treasury of rare books, the oldest dated 1503. The founder, Manos Faltaits, is devoting much energy and imagination to keeping this history alive by researching every aspect of the island's folk tradition and promoting Skyrian crafts in the museum's workshop.

Because Skyros has as yet very few hotels, the cottage industry known as *domátia,* or renting rooms in private homes, is particularly widespread on the island. Many of the houses down by the beach have been built expressly for the purpose of accommodating summer visitors. Apart from the cheerful, tasteful **Nefeli Hotel** on the road leading up to the town, which opened in 1989 and has 12 comfortable rooms, all with balconies, your only option if you want to stay in Horio is to live with the locals. It is prudent to see a few rooms before you decide, because though many make up in charm what they may lack in comfort, some are pretty claustrophobic, with quaint plumbing (seatless loo and a shower on the balcony). By the shore at nearby **Magaziá** and **Molos** the rooms tend to be larger, the plumbing more conventional—but they may lack "atmosphere." On the other hand, you can go for a swim before breakfast. Check with Lefteris Trakos at **Skyros Travel** when you've made up your mind which you prefer, and he'll try to match you with the right place (see Accommodations Reference, below). A luxurious hotel complex with pool may change the seaside accommodation picture within the next year or so. This ambitious project is currently under construction at Gyrismata, north of Molos.

Eating out in Horio also presents a limited range of options, with most of them—on Agora Street, anyway—consisting of *souvlákia*. But try **Glaros**, at the start of the main square, or **Kabanera** (follow the signs for "fish restaurant" or ask directions) for good, traditional Greek cooking—lots of stews and vegetable dishes. Both are recommended by the locals. If you want good service and better food, it's advisable to eat early (between 8:00 and 9:00 P.M.). **Psarotaverna**, on a vine-covered terrace just beyond Kabanera, serves fish. For a change of pace and locale, turn left instead of right on reaching town and look for signs for **Kristina's** restaurant. Opened in 1989, it offers the peace of a pretty, flower-filled courtyard and a selection of Greek and international dishes skillfully prepared by the Australian proprietress.

By the sea there are several more fish restaurants to choose from, but **Stephanos's** location at Magazia near the Xenia Hotel is preferred (if you can cope with the proprietor's rudeness). If you decide against eating here, step across the street into **Stamatis Ftoulis's** pottery workshop and watch him and his assistants applying their intricate designs, one color at a time. For pleasanter service and an even more romantic setting, **Anna's**, in the *mylos* (mill) a bit farther north at Molos overlooking the small fishing port, is where to go. You don't pay a premium for her beautifully cooked fish and lobsters. Unlike so many of the islands, Skyros usually has an ample supply of fish, and it is not uncommon to see people wandering around clutching lobsters by their antennae or to see octopus hung on a clothesline to dry.

The beach area and Horio are linked by roads and by sloping footpaths whose resemblance to Golgotha varies tremendously according to how much sun you've had and how much to eat and drink. You always seem to be at the wrong end of the walk.

Around the Island

The beach beneath Horio is large, sandy, and beautiful, big enough to accommodate even a nudist section. The unsightly boulders rising out of the sea in front of the Xenia Hotel are intended to protect the waterfront from winter waves. Hopefully with time they will settle and weather. To explore the rest of the island, you either have to rent a motorbike in town or place yourself once again in the hands of Skyros Travel, whose bus crosses over to the east coast and whose caïque makes trips from Linaria to the lovely coves of Ayios Fokas and Pefkos in the northern half and

Treis Boukes, Renes, Glyfada, and the sea caves in the south. The dirt road to Treis Boukes and beyond has been leveled and is now passable by motorbike and car.

An asphalt road leads out of Molos toward the airport and the giant airbase, which has cordoned off a considerable chunk of the north part of the island. It's worth following the road parallel to it just to get an idea of its size and to see that they've at least chosen the most exposed beaches. The east side of the island is far more wooded than the rest, with pines predominating. The coast here is rocky, stunning to look at but not so inviting to swim from. Most people head for **Atsítsa** on the west coast. With its offshore islets, tree-studded coves, and intriguing 19th-century iron-mine installations, it's a delightful place to spend the day (the best swimming is over past the taverna). A center for "holistic health and fitness holidays" has its headquarters and bungalows here. Offering a wide range of activities from aerobics to yoga (not to mention juggling, dreamwork, and stress management), the **Atsitsa Centre** is affiliated with the Skyros Centre in Horio and the Skyros Institute (for more information, write 1 Fawley Road, London NW6 1SL, England).

Ayios Fokás, 6 km (4 miles) down a passable dirt road (bear right at the fork), is worth the trip just to sit at **Kyria Kali's** taverna, though there are three very pleasant beaches here as well. Kali's days are filled with baking bread, brewing wine, making cheese, and growing the vegetables she feeds her family and delighted visitors. Her husband catches the fish and her young daughter helps serve. It is one of those magic places in Greece that are fast disappearing.

If you persevere down the main dirt road, you eventually come to the humble chapel of Ayios Panteleímon, from which there is a fantastic view of the cove of Pefkos, Linaria, and the huge bay of Kalamitsa beyond. **Pefkos** has a lovely beach and a couple of tavernas. It is more accessible from Linaria than from Horio.

The road from Horio to Kalamitsa starts just after Aspoús, which is south of town on the isthmus between the two parts of the island. Try **Oscar's** taverna on the beach at Aspous; he specializes in homemade pitas (vegetable or cheese pies), imaginative appetizers, and fish, all presented in an attractive surrounding. The first beach you come to on the way to Kalamitsa is called Achilli—the hero is said to have set sail for Troy from here. After passing a few farmhouses and goats you will arrive at the massive bay of **Kalamítsa**. By going all the way around to the south you'll reach the wonderful beach of **Kolymbáda**, a white crescent against a turquoise sea. Though this part of the island is stark and barren, streams of pink oleander cascading down the hills make it strangely beautiful.

Among these rugged hills is where Skyros's much diminished herds of indigenous Shetland-type ponies range; only wild animals feel comfortable on this part of the island. Though the road is improved, it is still easier to take a caïque from Linaria to **Treis Boukes**—so named for the three entries to this natural harbor—where Rupert Brooke admirers can make a pilgrimage to his marble tomb before a swim. The caïque may also stop at the sandy beaches of **Renes** and **Glyfáda**—the latter on one of the islets fronting Treis Boukes—and in calm waters go around the tip of the island to the **sea caves** on the east coast.

Finally, if there is any chance of your being in Greece at **Carnival** time, don't miss the fascinating festivities in Skyros. Some of the men put on masks made out of a baby goat and coats of goat hide, belted with dozens of sheep and goat bells. Accompanied by an entourage consisting of a *korélla*, a young man dressed up like a bride, a *frangos*, a comic European figure, and his lady, the *yeros* (old man) makes his way through town, shaking his bells provocatively while the rest of the troupe jest and taunt the other *yeri* and their counterparts. An incredible amount of wine is drunk in the final three weeks before Lent, and the spectacle—with its overtones of fertility rites and Dionysiac frenzy—is like no other in Greece. (Read Joy Coulentianou's *The Goat Dancers of Skyros* for a fascinating look at the customs associated with this unique celebration.)

GETTING AROUND

Skyros is not as easy to get to as the other northern Sporades. Unless you take the small plane from Athens (daily in July and August, twice per week the rest of the year), the trip involves three hours on two ferries and two bus rides (up Attica and across Evia), a total of about five hours. It is possible to hop on the Flying Dolphin from Skiathos and Skopelos (four times per week; two hours and 45 minutes and one hour and 40 minutes, respectively) and Alonnisos (twice per week; around two hours). Island-hoppers will, however, be able to link up with many of the Cyclades via a steamer that starts in Thessaloniki and stops at Tinos, Mykonos, and other islands on its way to Crete. Schedules are posted in prominent spots around town.

There are no cars for rent in Skyros, but motorbikes can

be hired. Skyros Travel runs excursions by bus to points on the west coast and by caïque to beaches in the southern part of the island.

ACCOMMODATIONS REFERENCE

Skiathos

▶ **Arco Hotel. Ayia Paraskevi Bay**, Mossialos SA-Arcotel Enterprises, P.O. Box 65, 370 02 Skiathos. Tel: (0427) 493-77/87 or 217-09; Telex: 282433.

▶ **Atrium Hotel. Platania**, 370 02 Skiathos. Tel: (0427) 493-45; Fax: (0427) 493-76.

▶ **Bourtzi Hotel. Skiathos Town**, 370 02 Skiathos. Tel: (0427) 213-04.

▶ **Hotel Ilion.** Papadiamanti and Syngrou streets, **Skiathos Town**, 370 02 Skiathos. Tel: (0427) 211-93.

▶ **Nostos Hotel. Tzaneria Beach**, 370 02 Skiathos. Tel: (0427) 225-20/23; Telex: 282215 NOST GR; Fax: (0427) 225-25. Or contact: Ionian Hotels, 5 Ipitou Street, Athens, 105 57. Tel: (01) 322-5684.

▶ **Plaza Hotel. Kanapitsa Bay** P.O. Box 12, 370 02 Skiathos. Tel: (0427) 219-71/74; Fax: (0427) 221-09; or 72 Iasonos Street, Vouliagmeni, 166 71. Tel: (01) 896-1101; Fax: (01) 896-3829.

▶ **Pothos Hotel. Skiathos Town**, 370 02 Skiathos. Tel: (0427) 226-94.

▶ **Troulos Bay. Troulos**, 370 02 Skiathos. Tel: (0427) 493-75; Telex: 282264; Fax: (0427) 217-91.

▶ **Villa Orsa.** c/o Alex Mitzelou, P.O. Box 3, **Skiathos Town**, 370 02 Skiathos. Tel: (0427) 223-00.

▶ **Villa rentals-Travel agents.** Mare Nostrum Holidays, 21 Papadiamanti Street, P.O. Box 16, **Skiathos Town**, 370 02 Skiathos. Tel: (0427) 214-63/64; Fax: (0427) 217-93; Telex: 282208.

Skopelos

▶ **Andromache Guesthouse. Skopelos Town**, 370 03 Skopelos. Book through Madro Travel (see below).

▶ **Aperitton.** P.O. Box 210, **Skopelos Town**, 370 03 Skopelos. Tel: (0424) 222-56.

▶ **Dionysos. Skopelos Town**, 370 03 Skopelos. Tel: (0424) 232-10/15.

▶ **Elli. Skopelos Town**, 370 03 Skopelos. Tel: (0424) 229-43. Winter address: 25 Delta Dalezeou, Volos, 382 21; Tel: (0421) 307-59 or 333-96.

▶ **Kyr Sotos. Skopelos Town**, 370 03 Skopelos. Tel: (0424) 225-49.

▶ **Panormos Beach Hotel.** c/o Tassos Falcos, 370 03 Skopelos. Tel: (0424) 227-11.

▶ **Prince Stafylos. Skopelos Town**, 370 03 Skopelos. Tel: (0424) 227-75 or 227-44; Telex: 282229 SKOP.

▶ **Skopelos Village. Skopelos Town**, 370 03 Skopelos. Tel: (0424) 225-17; Fax: (0424) 229-58. Bookings from April. In winter they may be reached by Telex: 410930.

▶ **Travel Agents.** Yiorgos and Machi Drossos, **Madro Travel, Skopelos Town**, 370 03 Skopelos. Tel: (0424) 229-40, 221-45, or 223-00; Telex: 282224 MADR GR; Fax: (0424) 229-41.

Alonnisos

▶ **Galaxy Hotel. Patitiri**, 370 05 Alonnisos. Tel: (0424) 652-51/54. In Athens: 13 Nikis Street, Athens, 105 57. Tel: (01) 323-4869.

▶ **Liadromia Hotel.** c/o Ikos Travel, **Patitiri**, 370 05 Alonnisos. Tel: (0424) 655-21.

▶ **Marpounta Village Club.** 370 05 Alonnisos. Tel: (0424) 652-12/19. In Athens: 9 Valaoritou Street, 106 71, Athens. Tel: (01) 360-7759; Telex: 282322.

▶ **Paradise Hotel.** Kostas Efstathiou, **Patitiri**, 370 05 Alonnisos. Tel: (0424) 652-13 or 651-60; Fax: (0424) 651-61.

▶ **Travel Agent.** Panos Athanassiou, **Ikos Travel**, 370 05 Alonnisos. Tel: (0424) 653-20/21; Telex: 0282330 IKOS GR; Fax: (0424) 653-21.

Skyros

▶ **Nefeli Hotel. Skyros Town**, 340 07 Skyros. Tel: (0222) 919-64.

▶ **Travel Agent.** Lefteris Trakos, **Skyros Travel**, 340 07 Skyros. Tel: (0222) 911-23 or 916-00; Telex: 272178 SKTR GR. Rooms, tickets, excursions.

THE IONIAN ISLANDS

By John Chapple and Diana Farr Ladas

The Ionian islands are the remnants of a long, submerged mountain range lying between Italy and the Greek mainland that once stretched from Trieste down to Crete. (The Ionian islands are so-called because they are in the Ionian Sea, off the west coast of Greece, not from any connection with ancient Ionia, which was in what is today the west coast of Asia Minor.) Although the Greeks call them the Eptánisa, or Seven Islands, this is really a misnomer; there are at least 17 inhabited islands and countless deserted islets in this archipelago. Traditionally, the 7 major Ionian islands, proceeding from north to south, are Corfu, Paxi, Lefkada, Ithaca, Kefallonia, Zakynthos, and Kythira.

Most of the islands were prosperous in antiquity. Homer lists several of their city-states as having sent ships and men to Troy. But their prosperity and advantageous location in the midst of the heavily travelled sea-lanes between the West and the Levant and Egypt did not always work to their benefit. Time and again they were pawns in the power games played by the Romans, Saracens, Normans, Byzantines, and freebooting buccaneers. Centuries of plunder combined with a few disastrous earthquakes have destroyed virtually all traces of ancient glory. Some ruined walls, columnless temple bases, and fragmented statues are all that remain. Classicists may be disappointed, but admirers of Medieval fortifications will be pleased with the stalwart castles so prominent on all the islands but Ithaca.

Lush, fertile, gentle, and sophisticated, the Ionian islands often seem to be more Italian than Greek. Though this may

Ionian Islands
0 miles 30
0 km 30
TO ITALY
ALBANIA
Corfu
Igoumenitsa
CORFU
EPIRUS
Parga
Gaios
PAXI
ANTIPAXI
Preveza
Ionian Sea
Ayios Nikolaos
Lefkada
LEFKADA
Nydri
Vassiliki
Fiskardo
Frikes
TO ASTAKOS
KEFALLONIA
Vathy
Ayia Evfymia
ITHACA
Sami
Argostoli
TO PATRAS
Poros
TO KYLLINI
Pessada
N
Skinari
TO KYLLINI
KYTHIRA
Ayia Pelagia
Hora
Zakynthos
ZAKYNTHOS
TO KYTHIRA

be partly due to similarities in landscape, it is also a consequence of six centuries of occupation by a succession of Frankish feudal lords followed by the Venetians. (Only Lefkada suffered the Turks for any considerable length of time.) The Venetian influence, by far the strongest, is most obvious in Ionian architecture, though Ionian culture and achievements in the arts, literature, and education also reflect this heritage. All the islands are dotted with Italianesque basilicas and bell towers; the icons inside them are painted in a more realistic style than their counterparts on the Greek mainland or in the Aegean; and the local dialects are filled with Italian words.

The impact of the French and English is not as obvious. Nevertheless, exposure to the ideals of the French Revolution and to the freedom of the press permitted under the English fostered the fervor for union with Greece. There is no question that the Ionians under the British were far in advance of their mainland compatriots. Corfu had a university well before Athens did; the ships plying the Adriatic with Zakynthian currants and Corfiot olive oil brought the latest news and the latest Paris fashions. At the same time, the British were building roads, schools, waterworks, and hospitals, raising the standard of living while ruling with their customary discipline. But political awareness continued to grow. Unionists fomented increasing discontent, and, after some time, England's Greek protectorates became more irritating than they were worth. With unprecedented, bloodless generosity, England handed over the islands to the new Greek state in 1864.

In the years that followed, the Ionian islands suffered an economic decline under Athens-centered policies. Trade with Liverpool, Paris, and Venice dried up, and increasing numbers of people left for Athens or for America, Canada, and Australia. Now the islands are experiencing renewed prosperity as their popularity with tourists increases. Indeed, in some of the newly developed areas of Corfu and, to a lesser extent, Zakynthos, it sometimes strikes the observer that the islands are undergoing yet another foreign occupation. But such depredations are by no means the rule, and these lovely, gracious islands are rewarding to explore. Choose **Corfu** for its delightful 18th-century town, lush landscape—Paleokastritsa is still gorgeous—and varied nightlife; **Lefkáda** for its serene lagoons and rustic style; **Ithaca** for its almost total lack of development and unique atmosphere; **Kefalloniá** for its magnificent beaches and feisty population; **Zákynthos** for its gentle beauty and increasingly sophisticated pleasures; and **Kýthira** for its castles and adventurous appeal. Tourism will continue to expand, but the Greekness of these islands, which has persisted throughout the centuries, will no doubt survive the challenges and threats.

CORFU

Corfu (Kérkyra), off the coast of Albania, is the flagship of the Ionian islands, the greenest and the most developed. Nearly 100,000 people live on this, the northernmost island of the Ionian Sea, and approximately 500,000 tourists visit each year. The latter are lured by the charm of what may be Greece's most beautiful town in combination with the incredible variety of the island's landscape, which ranges from the lush, lagoon-like coves on the east coast to the dramatic cliffs and broad, golden beaches on the west, with olive-carpeted hills and two highish mountains in between.

While development, both tacky and sophisticated, has sprung up on both coasts to accommodate visitors, the interior has remained surprisingly unchanged. Old women in traditional costume may still be seen in the narrow streets of many mountain villages, and the riotous vegetation soon camouflages even the most flagrant architectural mistakes. Though an English breakfast may be easier to find than a genuine Corfiot specialty, Corfu can be much more than its resorts, unless all you want from it is sun, sea, and a swinging nightlife.

MAJOR INTEREST

Corfu town: Italian influence
Gorgon in Archaeological Museum
Luxuriantly beautiful landscape
Civilized atmosphere
Day trip to islands of Paxi and Antipaxi

Corfu has been inhabited since the Upper and Middle Paleolithic periods (ca. 70,000 to 40,000 B.C.). Although there are indications of Mycenaean settlement on the Ionian islands of Kefallonia, Ithaca, Lefkada, and Zakynthos, there is no archaeological evidence on Corfu dating to the 13th or 12th

Corfu

0 miles 5
0 km 5

- *Sidari Beach*
- Roda
- **Mount Pantokrator**
- Kassiopi
- Ayios Stefanos
- Kouloura
- Kalami
- Lakones
- Skripero
- Paleokastritsa
- Sgoumbros
- Ipsous
- Dassia
- Nisaki
- Ermones
- Kontokali
- *Myrdiotissa*
- Corfu
- *Glyfada Beach*
- *Ayios Gordis Beach*
- Perania
- Kanoni
- Kinopiastes
- *Pontikonisi*
- Gastouri
- Lake Korissia
- Perivoli
- Lefkimmi
- Neohori

N

centuries B.C. identifying the ancient Phaeacians described by Homer. (The Corfiots themselves, however, have no doubt that their island was the land of the Phaeacians, where Odysseus reached shore on the last stage of his long journey home to Ithaca.) One theory argues that the name Kerkyra derives from the Semitic word for a fast Phoenician boat (*kerkouros*) and that the seafaring Phaeacians were actually Phoenicians.

In 734 B.C. Corinth founded the colony of Corcyra. Except for one short period, Corfu remained under Corinthian control until the tyranny of Corinth fell in 582 B.C. It was at approximately this time that the **Temple of Artemis**, from which the extraordinary archaic Gorgon pediment now in Corfu's Archaeological Museum has been reconstructed, was built on the Paleopolis peninsula (no remains are visible on the site). Corcyra was too remote to take much part in Greece's Golden Age. Nonetheless, the Peloponnesian War (431–404 B.C.) was kindled by Athenian ships helping Corcyra against Corinth.

The island came under Roman hegemony in 229 B.C. In the following century Corfu, luckily, supported Caesar against Pompey but, unluckily, supported Antony and Cleopatra against Octavian (later Augustus) at the battle of Actium (31 B.C.). After the battle Corfu's monuments were razed in punishment. Nothing much seems to have happened on Corfu during the remaining, apparently prosperous, years of the *Pax Romana,* although the emperor Nero stopped at Kassiopi in A.D. 66 on his way to Athens and gave a song recital.

After Roman hegemony faded, other powers dominated and then lost power in the Ionian. Here and there Corfu played small but sometimes pivotal roles, but it was the 411-year rule by Venice (1386 to 1797) that really set the island's character. And therein lies the source of the island's charm. Virtually all of the rest of Greece experienced what Corfu did not: the counterbalancing effect of Ottoman rule. After the Venetians, the French controlled the island from 1797 until 1799, the Russians and Ottomans cooperated to support the extraordinary Septinsular Republic from 1799 to 1807, and the French controlled the island again from 1807 until Waterloo in 1815. Thereafter the English ruled Corfu until 1864, when the island became part of Greece.

Corfu Town

The town of Corfu, in the center of the island's east coast, is built on a large peninsula shaped roughly like a shoe. The peninsula of Paleópolis to the south forms the toe of this shoe, and the smaller peninsula to the northeast occupied by the **Old Fort** (walled at least by the mid-15th century) forms the heel. As your boat nears the peninsula with the Old Fort you can see the two fortified hills that give Corfu its western name (*korifí* in Greek means "peak"). Little remains of the Medieval Venetian town of Corfu that stood on this peninsula. A plan is being considered to use the Old Fort for the Ionian University; at present it forms the backdrop for the summer sound-and-light show.

In the late Middle Ages the town began to grow beyond the Old Fort, but an open area, an esplanade, was kept for a clear field of fire in case of invasion. This esplanade (known as the *plateía* or the *spianáda*) is now an important part of the town's structure and lifestyle. It is dotted with statues and relics from the days of Venice and England, but you will also see evidence of a foreign influence that has remained very much alive. The Italian love of music has stayed with the islanders, who support 16 bands on the island and have produced many fine musicians. Greece's oldest band, the Corfu Philharmonic, plays from its wrought-iron bandstand in the esplanade.

At the northern end of the esplanade is the **Palace of St. Michael and St. George**, a Regency building with a Doric colonnade. It was built by the British between 1818 and 1823 to provide a home for the Lord High Commissioner, to house the Ionian senate, and to serve as headquarters for the Order of St. Michael and St. George, established to reward service in Malta and the Ionian islands. The building was used by the Greek royal family as a summer home until 1913, and today it houses archives, the local offices of the Greek Archaeological Service, and quite a good collection of Oriental art.

The road through the arch of St. George leads along the waterfront lined with 18th- and 19th-century houses to the **Old Port**, where the ferryboats from mainland Igoumenitsa dock. The so-called **New Fort** (1577 to 1588) looms above, adding a stern note to the cheerfully hectic harbor. From the Old Port you have a fine view of the uninhabited island of Vidos, which the French fortified in 1801.

The two handsome apartment buildings with arcades facing the esplanade were begun by the French, inspired by the rue de Rivoli in Paris, although construction was finished under the British. The two buildings are known as the **Listón**, adding the Greek genitive plural to the English word "list" to mean the list of people with sufficiently high social standing to walk under the arcades. Under Venetian rule the aristocracy had been an exclusive caste, whose names were registered in the so-called Golden Book (*Libro d'Oro*). You can get a clear idea of the conglomerate nature of Corfiot life by sitting at one of the Liston cafés drinking ginger beer and watching the Greeks play cricket in the esplanade. In the southwest corner of the esplanade is the 19th-century statue of Ioannis Kapodistrias, the first president of independent Greece, who was born on Corfu in 1776.

Venturing past the Liston façade into any of the narrow streets leading into the heart of the old city (where cars are not allowed) will take you into a fascinating mixture of tourist shops, 17th-century town houses, elegant churches, and secluded piazzas. Chic fur, gold, and clothing boutiques are sandwiched between gaudy displays of kitschy beachware, bottles of sugary *kum-kwat* liqueur, and aromatic cheese pies. Of the locally made handicrafts, articles in genuine olive wood (not walnut or some other lesser tree) are a good buy at the **Olive Wood Mini-Shop** on Philellínon Street between the cathedral and St. Spyridon's church, while the hand-embroidered blouses, bedspreads, and table linen sold at the handicrafts shop around the corner are other lasting souvenirs of the island.

Take time to wander away from the main shopping streets and you'll come to residential areas where the tall 17th- and 18th-century buildings, usually festooned during the day with laundry hung out to dry, seem to have been transplanted from Italy. In one of the oldest neighborhoods, **Campiello**, there is a lovely Venetian well head that has given its name to a romantic square and bistro, an inviting place to have a bite or drink away from the crowds. Wander some more and you'll find brilliant blue jacaranda trees flowering and small boys kicking a ball around with not a tourist in sight.

One block behind the Liston runs Guilford Street, named after the eccentric fifth earl of Guilford, who established Greece's first university, the Ionian Academy, in 1824. Lord Guilford went about "dressed up like Plato, with a gold band round his mad pate and flowery drapery of a purple hue." The street runs along one side of the **Town Hall**, begun in 1663 for merchants. The Catholic **cathedral**, to the south, was built in 1658 and is an unusually understated, dignified monument. At the other, higher end of this pleasantly "landscaped," sloping square is the 17th-century building that was originally the Catholic archbishop's residence. It now houses a branch of the Bank of Greece, but it was used for law courts for more than a century until it was bombed in 1943. Both the cathedral and the residence were carefully restored after the war.

The **Archaeological Museum** is south of the esplanade, past the Corfu Palace Hotel one block inland. Even if your interest in archaeological remains is minimal, don't miss the Gorgon from Paleopolis's sixth-century B.C. Temple of Artemis here. There is nothing else in Greece like this sculpture; the archaic pediments from the Acropolis in Athens pale in comparison. The Gorgon, flanked by attendant beasts, in this case panthers, seems to be a Corinthian invention, but it is not known what she represented. She is a charming, enigmatic monster.

A lovely way to understand something of what life on Corfu was like for the British during the 19th century is to visit the **British Cemetery**, an oasis in time. Approximately 250 yards south of Theotóki Square (also called Sarókko) on the western side of Corfu town at the northern end of Alexándras Avenue, it is a veritable botanical garden in spring, with numerous wildflowers, especially orchids, in bloom among the graves. The cemetery lies near Corfu's only intact ancient monument, the massive circular tomb dedicated to Menecrates, a Corfiot consul who died around 600 B.C. It is incongruously situated within the grounds of the local police station.

There are more than 700 churches on the island (39 in Corfu town alone), mostly Italianate in architectural style. The remains of the island's patron saint, Ayios Spyrídon, are kept in the **church of Ayios Spyrídon** (1596), a few blocks west from the northern end of the Liston. Saint Spyridon was a Cypriot bishop who attended the First Ecumenical Council in Nicaea in 325 and who lived a long and virtuous life on his native island. His remains were exhumed and taken to Constantinople when Cyprus was captured by the Arabs in the seventh century. Before the Ottomans took Constantinople in 1453 his remains were removed again, this time with the remains of Saint Theodora, and brought to Corfu. Saint Spyridon is credited with saving Corfu from a famine, two plagues, and an Ottoman siege. His casket is removed from its chapel behind the marble iconostasis and carried in procession around town four times a year: on Palm Sunday, at Easter, on August 11, and once in November. He is held in such reverence that more than half the men of Corfu are named after him.

Two early Christian churches, the **basilica of Paleopolis** and the **church of Saints Jason and Sosipater**, are on the

Paleopolis peninsula. Only the outer walls of the basilica are now standing, incorporating an ancient architrave and columns. The church of Saints Jason and Sosipater may date to as early as 1000.

From Kanóni, on the tip of the Paleopolis peninsula, you can look down on the little island of Pontikonísi, just south of the monastery of Vlachérna, also on a small island but joined to the mainland by a narrow causeway. Pontikonisi is also known as Nisí ton Nekrón, the Island of the Dead, for it is believed to be the unfortunate ship Poseidon turned to stone because it had taken Odysseus to Ithaca. (Poseidon was angry with Odysseus for blinding his son, the Cyclops Polyphemos.)

Dining and Staying Around Corfu Town

Corfu's cuisine, like her architecture, is heavily influenced by Italy. One of the favorite places—among Corfiots and visitors alike—to try local specialties is **Yiannis**, near the church of Saints Jason and Sosipater. Go early (reservations are not taken) and choose from the dishes simmering on the range. These may include *bourdétto,* a stew of scorpion fish boiled in water and oil with onions and an abundance of hot pepper; *sofritto,* sliced veal sautéed with parsley and much garlic; *pastitsáda,* a rich spaghetti dish where the pasta is cooked in its sauce rather than in water; and *osso bucco,* thick slices of veal shank with a juicy portion of marrow bone. You can find other Corfiot specialties in town—candied kumquats, *freskaménta* (prickly pears, or Frankish figs), and *tsi-tsi biéra* (ginger beer).

Restaurants frequented more by locals than foreigners are the **Porto Corfu** pizzeria, at the south end of Moustoxýdou Street, and **O Tsounas**, an excellent, reasonably priced fish taverna in the quaint old district of Mandoúki, north of the New Port. For lunch try the **Yacht Club**, on the quay between the citadel and the Corfu Palace hotel, and enjoy the wonderful view of the Old Fort along with your fish or salad.

The most famous restaurant on the island—and justifiably so—is **Tripa**, in the village of Kinopiástes, in the hills about a 15-minute drive south from Corfu town. The waiters and waitresses perform Greek dances and then encourage the customers to dance as well. Often such packaging of Greece is kitschy, but here it is tastefully done with a light touch. Tourists come in buses, but Corfiots eat here as well. For a basic fee of 5,000 drachmas per person you are served a continual series of very good dishes, far more than you can eat.

If you are going to stay in Corfu town, the **Corfu Palace** represents one of the last truly great luxury hotels of the old school in Europe. Swiss-owned, it is attractive and distinguished, with a lovely garden surrounded by a segment of old city wall, and both indoor and outdoor pools. This must be considered a monument to the fast-fading art of gracious living. On a less grand scale, there are at least two charming hotels in converted mansions dating from the last century: the **Bella Venezia** near Town Hall Square and the **Calypso** across the street from the Archaeological Museum. Accommodation can also be arranged in private houses in town and smart villas in the countryside (see Accommodations Reference, below).

For a more rural setting within easy reach of town, a good choice would be the **Aiolos Beach** hotel and bungalows at Pérama, 8 km (5 miles) south of Corfu town, with its own stretch of beach and bungalows set on a low slope among trees. One word of caution: The hotels in Kanoni just outside town are too close to the airport for comfort.

Around the Island

Much of Corfu's almost 230 square miles is extravagantly beautiful. Much of it is also planted with olive trees, between three and four million of them covering every available inch of ground. The density of these trees is not fortuitous; it is owing to a combination of Venetian insistence on a one-crop economy and Corfiot cupidity. Some decades after the Venetians took control of the island, they lost their olive groves in Koroni on the Peloponnese to the Turks, and in their desire for oil they ran a crash program in olive cultivation, offering the locals the irresistible incentive of 12 gold pieces for every hundred trees planted. The result is that almost two-thirds of Corfu is an olive grove.

These tall, gnarled trees cast their dark shade everywhere except the higher slopes of Mount Pantokrator in the north and the flatter country below the Ai Deka mountain range in the south, which is planted with wheat and vines. Being so devoted to agriculture and less dramatically beautiful, the south has only started reaching out for tourism relatively recently. Unfortunately development has had little regard for tradition here. Nevertheless, **Lefkímmi**, Corfu's second-largest town, is of interest for its lack of similarity with the capital, and the marshes around **Lake Korissiá** and the salt pans (Alikés) attract flocks of bird watchers.

The island's most famous sights and beaches are, with a few exceptions, to the north of the capital. Do rent a car and explore on your own. The roads are sinuous and narrow—too narrow to accommodate two-way traffic with safety, so proceed with caution whatever your choice of transport. A drive up the east coast will take you past the packed resort areas of Dassiá and Ipsoús to Nisáki, where development starts to thin out and the road starts to climb. Here among the olive trees you'll glimpse the façades of old mansions, painted in yellow, brick red, or *vieux rose,* and down by the sea an occasional glistening cove.

Roads do go down to the water at frequent intervals, with some of the prettiest and least spoiled destinations being Kalami, Kouloura, and Ayios Stefanos. At **Kalámi**, about 32 km (20 miles) from Corfu town, the **White House**, where Lawrence Durrell wrote *Prospero's Cell* about Corfu (one of the author's friends maintained that Corfu is the island of Shakespeare's *The Tempest*), is now a taverna. **Kouloúra**, the next town up the coast, seems suspended in a time warp, a tiny bay with an old mansion and a few other houses. For an idea of what Greek seaside villages used to be like, **Ayios Stéfanos** may be as close as you'll come to finding out. This little horseshoe-shaped cove about 5 km (3 miles) from Kouloura is dotted with gaily painted fishing caïques and sports two pleasant tavernas, the **Eucalyptus** and the **Cochili**. It is also the closest point to Albania. The road continues on to **Kassiópi**, with its ruined 13th-century Angevin castle on the headland. It bears little resemblance to the quiet fishing port about which Durrell wrote so eloquently. (Boats from Corfu town and other points along the coast also make the trip to Kassiopi.)

The wide sandy beaches of the north coast resemble parts of the United States New Jersey shore, except for **Sidári**, where the wind and waves have created fascinating shapes and tunnels in the soft limestone cliffs. The most glorious beaches are on the west coast, from Ayios Yiórgios south to Ayios Gordis. High cliffs covered with a tangle of vegetation tower over gem-like bays and extended stretches of sand. One of the best places to view this lovely sight is from the Byzantine **castle of Angelókastro**, beyond the famous double bays of **Paleokastrítsa**. And the best place to see Paleokastritsa is from the **Bella Vista** café outside the village of Lákones in the mountains above it. From there the hotels hardly show. Next comes the beach of Ermónes, overlooked by the **Ermones Beach Hotel**, attractively set into the wooded mountainside. Guests here have it easy, with a lovely pool-terrace and a cable car to carry them down to the uncrowded beach and back. Both rooms and lounges are spacious and airy. The hotel is also conveniently close to the Ermones Golf Club.

Between Ermones and the popular beach of Glyfada the coast conceals the miniature cove of **Myrdiótissa** (no hotels, difficult access), where nudists sunbathe among the rocks. The long expanse of sand at **Glyfáda** is home to two large resort hotels, the **Grand** and the **Glyfada Beach**, both well run if impersonal places with all the amenities, just a few steps from the water. You can try everything from fresh fish (at the two tavernas down the beach) to paragliding at Glyfada.

About 20 minutes south of Corfu town, near the village of Gastoúri, is the **casino** housed in the incongruous **Achilleion**, the palace completed in 1892 for the empress Elisabeth of Austria. Though the grounds are beautiful, the palace itself (a museum by day) has been called a monument to bad taste and is filled with Germanic kitsch installed by Kaiser Wilhelm II, who bought it in 1907. After World War I the Achilleion became the property of the Greek state. At the **Bella Vista** just down the road you can have a pleasant lunch or dinner while enjoying one of the most delightful views on the island.

Finally, a word about alternative living and shopping on the road to Paleokastritsa. At the **Tsavros** junction where the roads to Kassiopi and Paleokastritsa meet, about 12 km (7 miles) northwest of Corfu town, you'll find one of the best bakeries on the island and a fine supermarket, with piquant Corfu salami and the richest, thickest yogurt imaginable. There is also an olive-wood workshop, where the prices compare favorably with those in town.

Continuing on toward Paleokastritsa, at **Sgoumbros** there's a delightful bungalow complex, the **Casa Lucia**, which has nine tranquil cottages converted from the buildings of an old estate. These have retained their traditional appearance and are set amidst a lovely flower garden planted around a swimming pool. A short walk westward will bring you to the **Studio Gallery**, where prints by local artists capture the essence of Corfu, and a pottery shop whose wares are far more imaginative than the mass-produced things found elsewhere. *The Corfu Book of Walks—The Road to Old Corfu,* by Hilary Whitton Paipetis, is also on sale at the Studio Gallery, should you wish to discover more of the island on your own. At Skriperó, farther down the road, is Nikos Sakalis's **Leather Workshop**, where bags and other items can be made to order.

No matter where you stay, if you have time take the day trip from the Old Fort to **Paxí**. Its diminutive capital, Gaios, sits at the end of a fjord-like harbor presided over by a stately 19th-century mansion and the remains of a Venetian castle. Like Corfu, the island is virtually one large olive grove, while the limestone cliffs and caves on its north coast are among the most impressive sights to be seen in Greece. **Antípaxi**, its barely populated neighbor, has one of the most idyllic beaches in the Ionian.

GETTING AROUND

You can reach Corfu by charter or regular commercial flight from many European cities. From Athens four or five flights make the 50-minute trip each day during the summer and two during the winter. There is one flight a week from Thessaloniki.

Throughout the year regular ferryboats come in from Brindisi and Ancona; during the high season they also come in from Bari, Otranto, and Dubrovnik. From Patras, on the Peloponnese, two or three ferryboats leave for the 12-hour trip to Corfu each day during the summer. At the height of summer international ferries call at Sami (Kefallonia) twice a week. The most travelled route is by ferryboat from Igoumenitsa; during the summer the boats leave approximately every hour and a half. The trip takes 2 hours.

Up to five buses leave each day from Athens for the 11-hour trip to Corfu via Igoumenitsa. For information about buses, call (01) 512-9443 in Athens.

You can travel throughout Corfu by public bus. For information about buses serving the nearby suburbs of Corfu town, call (0661) 315-95. Buses going farther afield leave from Theotoki Square on the western side of Corfu town at the northern end of Alexandras Avenue. For information call (0661) 398-62. It is highly recommended, however, that you rent a car. Motorcycles can be rented as well.

There are also excursions by boat to Parga on the mainland or the nearby island of Paxi. For information ask any travel agency, the shipping offices on the quay some 30 yards to the left of where the ferryboats from Igoumenitsa land, or the port authority (Tel: 0661-326-55).

—*John Chapple with Diana Farr Ladas*

LEFKADA

Lefkáda, also known as Lefkás, is a large, green, mountainous island, deeply incised on the south and east by several bays and blessed by a thin line of beautiful beaches along most of its northern and western coasts. The capital of the island, also called Lefkada, is in the north, with a busy harbor before the northern, narrow stretch of the Lefkada Canal that separates the island from the mainland. Many of the island's vineyards, olive trees, and settlements are along the protected eastern shore down to Nydri, near the spectacular enclosed bay of Vlychos. This is a busy, productive island, only recently awakening to tourism; here you'll find a mixture of the basic and the luxurious.

MAJOR INTEREST

Lefkada town: Italianate churches
Unspoiled beaches on north and west coasts
Island of Meganisi
Fishing village of Vasiliki
Sappho's Leap

Lefkada may have been linked to the mainland in the remote past, but a canal was cut in the seventh century B.C. The present channel, dredged in 1905, put **Fort Santa Maura** on the mainland side. The fort was built at the beginning of the 14th century by John Orsini, who had acquired Lefkada by marrying the daughter of the Despot of Epirus. Much of what is visible of the fort today are Ottoman and Venetian additions.

Many foreign powers have ruled Lefkada, and all have left their mark, both architecturally and linguistically: Franks (1300 to 1479), Ottomans (1479 to 1684), Venetians (1684 to 1797), French (1797 to 1798), Russians and Turks (1798 to 1800), Septinsular Republic (1800 to 1807), French again (1807 to 1810), and British (1810 to 1864).

Today the island of Lefkada is connected to the mainland by a floating drawbridge; the town is down the causeway to the south. The wall now housing the lighthouse immediately to the north was built during the English rule of the Ionian islands. You can see the remains of the Turkish causeway parallel to the modern causeway running south to town.

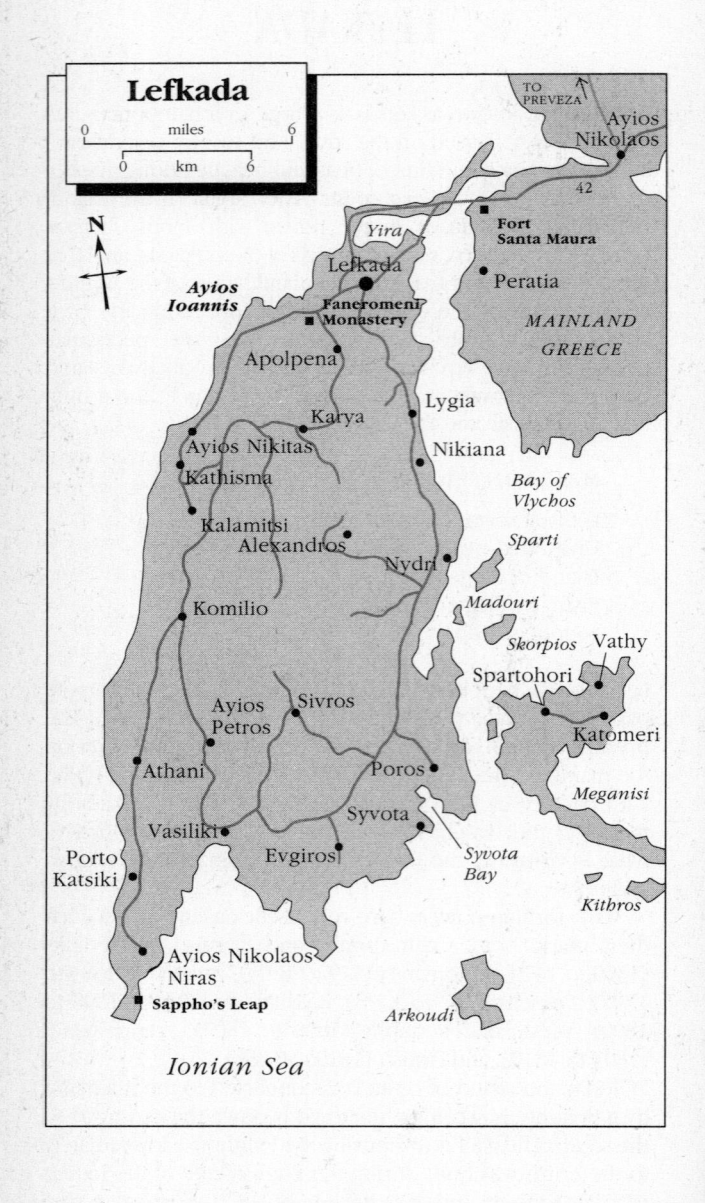

Lefkada

miles 0–6
km 0–6

N

TO PREVEZA

Ayios Nikolaos

42

Fort Santa Maura

Yira

Lefkada

Peratia

Ayios Ioannis

Faneromeni Monastery

MAINLAND GREECE

Apolpena

Karya

Lygia

Ayios Nikitas

Nikiana

Kathisma

Bay of Vlychos

Kalamitsi

Alexandros

Sparti

Nydri

Madouri

Komilio

Skorpios

Vathy

Spartohori

Ayios Petros

Sivros

Katomeri

Athani

Poros

Meganisi

Vasiliki

Syvota

Porto Katsiki

Evgiros

Syvota Bay

Kithros

Ayios Nikolaos Niras

Sappho's Leap

Arkoudi

Ionian Sea

Lefkada Town

Despite earthquake damage, most recently in 1948, the town has a distinct late-Medieval appearance, although the busy artery of the main street (known as the Market, or Agorá) is becoming increasingly dotted with new storefronts. The upper floors of many of the houses are covered in sheet metal, often painted in pastel colors, to keep out the rain and humidity. This gives the town a rather ramshackle appearance that has its own quaint charm. There are 34 extraordinary churches on the island, 19 of them in town, all built within a few years after 1684 when the Venetians expelled the Ottomans. Their simple, elegant stone façades are Italianate, with no resemblance to the typical Greek Orthodox church, and their icons and frescoes are Renaissance in style rather than Byzantine. The oldest, **Ayios Spyrídon**, on a corner of the main square, was built in 1685. All of the churches suffered from earthquake damage in the 18th and 19th centuries and were reconstructed in their present form after 1830. **Ayios Menás**, at the far end of the main street near the open market, was built in 1704 where a large plane tree had been uprooted by an earthquake. An icon to the saint was found miraculously in the tree's roots.

The most comfortable hotels in Lefkada town, all near the canal, are the light and airy **Xenia**, the more upmarket **Lefkas**, and the **Niricos**, with its lobby decorated with photos of old Lefkada. These hotels are all relatively new and offer clean, unadorned rooms with balconies. Of the many restaurants the **Agrambeli**, next to the Lefkas Hotel, aspires to be the most elegant. The **Adriatica**, on the northern edge of town on the road to the Faneromeni Monastery (see below), and the **Romantica**, in town (a short way to the right off the main street after the police station), are good, middle-of-the-road restaurants with pleasant gardens. The Adriatica uses garlic plentifully in many dishes, sometimes when you least expect it. More casual is the unpretentious **Regantos's**, which has tables on the street a couple of blocks down from the square. If you are coming from the sea, turn right down the road entering the square at its near edge. For good home cooking (albeit heavily salted), particularly at lunch, go to **Eftychia's**, opposite the small fountain on the main road before reaching the square. Eftychia's is not the restaurant on the road, but the one immediately behind it, with tables under awnings in the alley. Wherever you eat, if you are feeling adventurous, try the local dark red wine, Madonna, or the white, Taol.

Lefkada is well known for its locally produced salami (ask for *aéros*), which is quite good but has more fat and pepper than most other salamis. *Mandoláto* is a locally produced sweet, much like nougat, which you will find at stands along Market Street. You might like to take home some of the delicate embroidery made by the island women. Several stores along Market Street sell this fine work, but the widest selection is in a store about two-thirds of the way down Market Street from the port toward the church of Ayios Menas on the left side of the road. In the window is the improbable sign, in English: **Cooperative Artisanal of Lefkada.**

Overall, Lefkada town is a genuine Greek market town, filled with shoppers by day and strollers at sunset. Its low, unassuming buildings and wide streets hardly give the impression of an island capital. It is peaceful and pleasant enough, but most visitors just give it a cursory look before rushing on to more picturesque spots.

The Northwest

You need to be mobile on Lefkada. If you don't have a car, rent a small jeep, motorcycle, or bicycle in the capital or Nydri. The Yira, the round saltwater lagoon bordered on the north and west by sand dunes, is directly ahead as you come over the pontoon drawbridge. Lefkada's incomparable beaches begin at the lighthouse, and, because the road circles the lagoon, you can easily get to an unoccupied section of beach. The remains of several windmills are on the western edge of the Yira. The prevailing wind that drove these windmills still blows, so the northern coast is not much developed. Past the windmills on the beach of Ayios Ioánnis (named after a small Angevin chapel built in 1331 where the mountain cuts the beach) there is, however, one small restaurant run by an affable Greek returnee from Australia. Many of his customers are avid windsurfers, who come here for the strong wind.

The 17th-century **Faneroméni Monastery**, 3 km (2 miles) behind and above town, provides a lovely view of the canal. You reach it not from the Yira, but by following signs to the monastery from the north side of Lefkada town. After the monastery the road soon opens to give a commanding view of the startling expanse of white sand along the western coast toward **Ayios Nikítas**, 14 km (9 miles) southwest of Lefkada town. Several miles of open beach are accessible here as the road drops down near sea level. The village of

Ayios Nikitas was an untouched Medieval fishing village until ten years ago when the road brought in large numbers of tourists, then discotheques and fast food. The paved road continues past Ayios Nikitas to **Káthisma**, another once-remote, increasingly popular, beautiful stretch of sand beach, the far end of which is used for nude bathing. Two attractive hotels have opened in Ayios Nikitas, the **Odyssey**, with 28 rooms, each with a balcony, and the **Ayios Nikitas**, tastefully arranged around a pleasant courtyard. The latter is more discreetly in tune with its surroundings, but the former is planning a pool for the future.

Inland

The highland is dotted with villages, many with houses dating to Medieval times. Virtually all the workable slopes are terraced, a task that seems to have been undertaken centuries ago. The largest inland village is **Karyá**, in the mountains 14.5 km (9 miles) southwest of Lefkada town, famous for embroidery. All over the island you will see Lefkada women wearing the traditional black, dark-brown, red, green, or blue costume, but here you will see more. You can buy the traditional embroidery in individual houses in Karya and in several stores in Lefkada town.

The East Coast

The east coast of Lefkada south to Nydri is gentler terrain, filled with olive trees. **Lygiá**, 5 km (3 miles) from town, is a snug fishing harbor with a few local restaurants. **Nikiána**, 5 km farther on, has a fine hotel with bungalows, **Porto Galíni**, on the beach. Its apartments (each with a kitchenette) are arranged with consideration for privacy and are set amidst a luxuriant garden. The spare cubist lines of the complex complement the lush backdrop and compensate for its relative priciness. There are many restaurants in the area, but go to the family-run **Breath of Zorba**, which has tables on the water. If you go for dinner, get there by 9:00 to choose your table.

Nydrí, 17 km (10.5 miles) south of Lefkada town, is the big draw for this coast—it's now a bustling tourist town as well as a yacht haven. The setting is lovely, with the little white chapel beneath the Dörpfeld monument across the entrance to the large bay of Vlychós. (The German archaeologist Wilhelm Dörpfeld is held in high esteem on the island because he believed Lefkada was Homer's Ithaca.) Along the quay, which is packed with restaurants and cafés, look for the one with the blue-and-white awning near the north end. Called simply "taverna-restaurant," it specializes in fresh fish. But if you'd like a change from the boisterous crowds, try the **Olive Tree** outside town on the road to Vlychos for a peaceful, more traditionally Greek evening meal.

A boat trip from Nydri around the Onassis island, Skórpios, and the smaller island of Madoúri is a pleasant excursion. The cypress trees thrusting through the dense foliage on the rounded hills above the lagoon are reminiscent of—though even more romantic than—the Italian Riviera.

On no account miss the island of **Meganísi**, easily reached by boat from Nydri. Its three villages, Spartohori, Vathy, and Katomeri, are all equally picturesque and unspoiled, equipped with tavernas and rooms, but only one hotel. The **Meganisi**, new in 1990, is a friendly family-run place situated between the port of Spartohori and the inland village of Katomeri. For a small island (despite its name), Meganisi contains extraordinary contrasts. Its east coast is indented by tranquil, olive-rimmed coves, while limestone cliffs towering over turquoise waters make the west coast simply stunning.

South and West

Below the village of **Poros**, 10 km (6 miles) south of Nydri, is a well-protected bay with an adequate restaurant (it has no name, but it's the only one there) looking down over the bay, as well as rooms to rent, camping facilities, and a shaded, pebbly beach. The neighboring bay, **Sývota**, is curved and dramatically narrow, with a small fishing village. Try to have dinner at one of the tavernas in this enclosed harbor. By day its sleepy waters are not inviting.

The small fishing port of **Vasilikí** is in the southwest part of the island, 38 km (23.5 miles) from Lefkada town on a large, beautiful bay protected by the long sharp arm of Sappho's Leap. There are a handful of unpretentious restaurants along the quay, all specializing in innovative variations on souvlaki. Vasiliki is a good place to hop on an excursion boat bound for Meganisi or Sappho's Leap.

Far and away the most dramatic sight on the island is **Sappho's Leap**, on the tip of the long mountainous peninsula pointing south. If you'd rather drive, turn off the mountain road at Komilió north of Vasiliki and follow signs to Atháni, the last village on the peninsula. The pavement soon stops, but the road is perfectly passable if you are careful of motorcycles barreling around turns. The mountain drops steeply down to the sea here. At a few places the walk down to the water takes you to beaches well worth the climb down, although perhaps not the climb up. At Porto Katsíki (Goat Port) a dirt road has just been bulldozed down to the beautiful beach, but many cars will be there before you.

Sappho's Leap has a modern lighthouse built approximately where a temple of Apollo once stood. The white 200-foot cliffs here gave the island its name (Lefkó means "white"), and you can, carefully, get right to the edge—the poet Sappho is supposed to have leaped to her death here. Later in antiquity, apparently, the leap was made as a trial or sacrifice, with the performers tied to live birds to slow their fall.

GETTING AROUND

You can reach Lefkada by flying from Athens to Preveza and then taking the 20-minute bus or taxi ride to Lefkada town. There are up to nine flights a week and the trip takes one hour and 15 minutes. Book your flight with Olympic Airways; in Athens, Tel: (01) 961-6161; in Preveza, Tel: (0682) 283-43. Don't cut your return connections closely because the flights often are delayed. Twice a week in summer Olympic has a flight linking Zakynthos and Corfu, with stops at Argostoli and Preveza.

Three or four buses make the six-hour trip each day from Athens to Lefkada; in Athens, Tel: (01) 513-3583.

Trips by boat down to Meganisi, Ithaca, and Kefallonia can easily be arranged from Lefkada town and Nydri. Ferryboats to Ithaca (Frikes) and Kefallonia (Fiskardo) leave from both Nydri and Vasiliki in season. For information call Dana Travel, Tel: (0645) 246-50, or the port authority, Tel: (0645) 223-22.

Public bus service runs to most of the villages on Lefkada from the bus station on the harbor road past the Phoenix movie theater; Tel: (0645) 223-64. You would be far better off, however, to rent a car, motorcycle, or bicycle. Several rental agencies are in Lefkada town on the short stretch of road between the Lefkas and Xenia hotels, and another car rental agency is 50 yards past the Xenia Hotel by the quay. You can also rent cars and motorcycles in Nydri.

—*John Chapple with Diana Farr Ladas*

KEFALLONIA

The largest of the Ionian islands, Kefalloniá lies 53 nautical miles off the coast of the Peloponnese, opposite Patras and between Ithaca and Zakynthos. Among the Greeks, its inhabitants have the reputation for being a bit mad. This may be sour grapes, because it is certain that they are among the wittiest, cleverest, most cultivated and successful groups of people in the country. A high percentage of university professors, politicians, and shipowners are Kefallonian. Many, however, have had to seek their fortunes abroad, because the island, though large, is mountainous and demanding, and there is not enough water to make farming profitable.

For many years the islanders resisted tourism, but now it is viewed as one way to keep the population at home prosperous. Resorts are developing at Lassi (near Argostoli, the capital), Lixouri, and Poros, but much of Kefallonia has retained its traditional rhythm. For Kefallonia, like Zakynthos and Ithaca, the greatest change was wrought by the massive earthquake of 1953, which flattened most of the island's buildings. When they were reconstructed little time or thought was given to aesthetics. So you don't visit the island to admire the architecture or antiquities, but to enjoy its natural wonders and lively people.

And natural wonders abound: the highest mountain in the Ionian, huge caves, a submerged lake, a "bottomless" lake, and beautiful beaches of all kinds and descriptions. Before the earthquake there were even stranger geological phenomena: a massive boulder, Kounopetra, that rocked on its bed, and "swallow holes" where water flowed "backward," from the sea into the land, fast enough to power a flour mill. Now the water just trickles, but scientists have established that it travels through subterranean channels to discharge into Melissani, the underground lake on the other side of the island.

MAJOR INTEREST

Natural wonders: caves, mountains, underground lakes
Beaches, especially Myrtos
White wine
Coryialenios Historical and Cultural Museum in Argostoli

Assos and Fiskardo
Venetian castles
Lush Livatho valley

Most seaborne visitors arrive at Sami, a one-street village whose inhabitants seem to do little else but watch ferryboats dock, unload, and depart. Sami is on the east coast close to Karavómilos, the entrance to Lake Melissáni, where a feisty boatman speaking delightfully fractured English rows you around the underground lake, pointing out fanciful resemblances in the stalactites and the changing blues of the water. Spelunkers will want to compare it with the Drogaráti cave off the Sami–Argostoli road.

Argostoli

For those who want to explore the whole island, Argostóli, on a lagoon on the southwest coast, makes the best base. Though you might be dismayed at first by the funky commotion on its main street—a typically Greek mixture of chaotic traffic, open-air markets, and scruffy cafés—the place grows on you. By night its tree-lined back streets, spacious *plateías* (squares), and garden tavernas seem romantic and welcoming. In or around Valliánou Square are some of the town's liveliest and best restaurants: the Kefalos, with good, cheap home cooking; the Kalyva (Cabin), with a more genteel version of the same; and the Gondola, a trendier establishment with tasty pizzas and steaks. But don't overlook Patsoura's beyond the square, opposite the Xenia Hotel. Also called Perivolaki (Little Garden), it's a good place to sample the Kefallonian specialty, *kreatópita* (meat pie with rice topped with tomato sauce). Wine lovers will want to try Robola, the best wine in the Ionian and one of the finest whites in Greece. It can be purchased, bottled or from the barrel, at the Cava next to the bus terminal. The Calliga vineyards, which produce a pricier version of Robola, can be visited on weekdays.

Accommodation in Argostoli is of excellent quality and includes the sparklingly clean 44-room Mouikis Hotel, with its fabulous view of the lagoon; the friendly, casual Cephalonia Star, near the ferry landing; and, also on the waterfront, the Olga, an elegant example of Postmodern Neoclassical design, both chic and comfortable. A pleasant alternative, particularly for families, is Mouikis Village, a complex of 28 apartments around a pool, not far from the airport. Laid out to evoke a traditional village, it also offers a panorama of the coast.

Kefallonia and Ithaca

0 — miles — 5
0 — km — 5

KEFALLONIA

Fiskardo

Assos

Myrtos Beach

Myrtos Bay

Potami

Lixouri

Argostoli Bay

Havriata

Lepeda Beach

Argostoli

Ayios Yerasimos

Xi Beach

Platy Yialos
Makry Yialos

LASSI

Kounopetra Beach

Peratata

Kourkoumelata   Metaxata   Pe
Domata   Spart
Airport   Kalligata

N

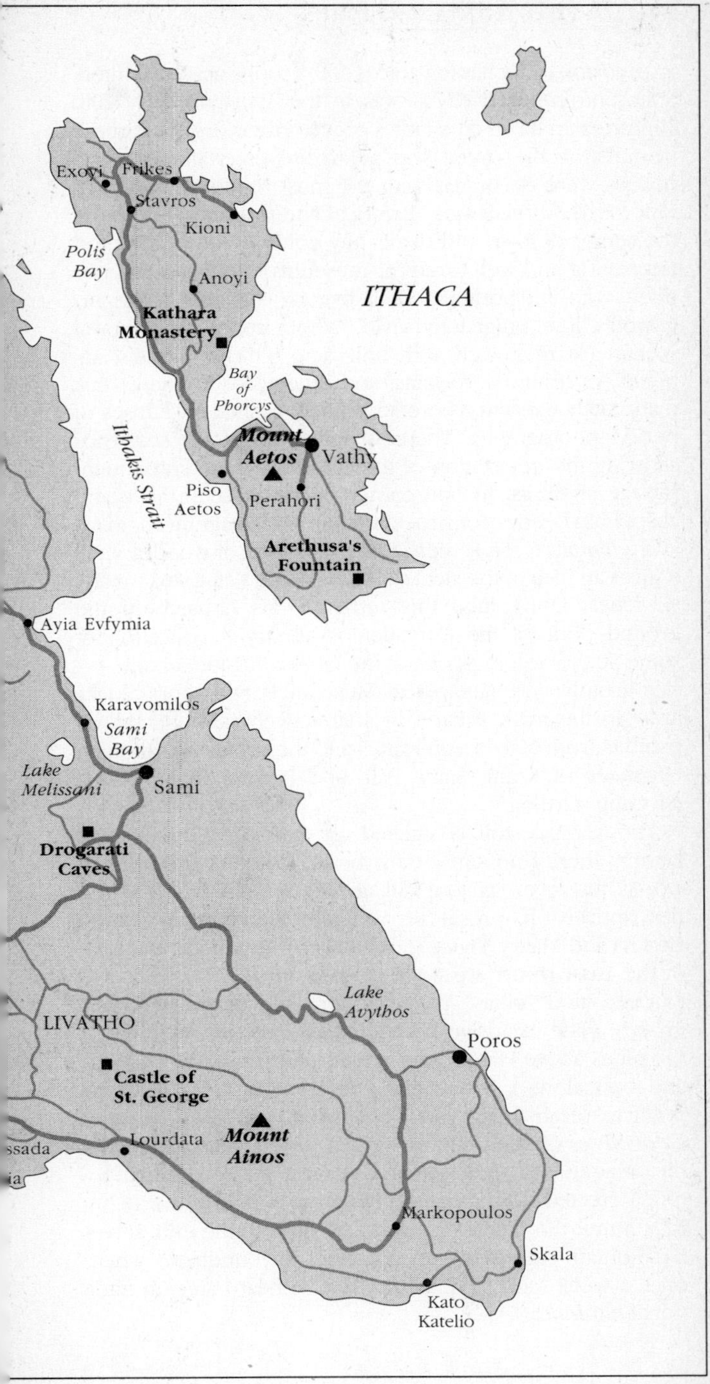

ITHACA
Exoyi
Frikes
Stavros
Kioni
Polis Bay
Anoyi
Kathara Monastery
Bay of Phorcys
Ithakis Strait
Mount Aetos
Vathy
Piso Aetos
Perahori
Arethusa's Fountain
Ayia Evfymia
Karavomilos
Sami Bay
Lake Melissani
Sami
Drogarati Caves
Lake Avythos
Poros
LIVATHO
Castle of St. George
Mount Ainos
Lourdata
Markopoulos
Skala
Kato Katelio

Argostoli today has few traces of the sophisticated, fashionable, and cultured city it was in the 19th and early 20th centuries. In those days ladies ordered their dresses directly from Paris, the opera was a favorite entertainment, and houses were decorated with the most refined furniture. A visit to the **Coryialenios Historical and Cultural Museum** in the center of town will dispel any doubts. One of the most interesting and well-cared-for museums in the country, it is filled with memorabilia of a bygone age that make Argostoli's loss poignantly vivid. Whole rooms and typical scenes are re-created with dolls and life-size models, antiques, portraits, porcelains, and other accoutrements that made daily existence here so refined, against backdrops of period photographs. There is also a horrifying sequence showing the devastation of the earthquake and subsequent salvage attempts. In one corner of the museum an island chapel has been reconstructed intact. With magnificent icons and a *templo* (icon screen) that is a marvel of woodcarving, it gives an idea of the riches hidden inside Kefallonia's many churches. Don't miss this museum; it's housed on the ground floor of the Coryialenios Library, a collection of some 50,000 volumes, one of the largest outside Athens.

Argostoli's **Archaeological Museum** is two short blocks away in the main square. It is attractively laid out, but its exhibits from Mycenaean tombs and the ancient Kefallonian city-states of Krani, Sami, Pali, and Pronni don't contain anything startling.

Though Argostoli is situated on the edge of a pleasant lagoon, there's no sign of any beach in the vicinity. Not to worry; just over its low hill are some splendid beaches, descriptively if prosaically named **Platý Yialós** (Wide Beach) and **Makrý Yialós** (Long Beach). They form the core of the **Lassi** resort area, where there are fancy hotels, restaurants, and "villas" patronized mostly by package-tour groups. (The exclusive **White Rocks**, discreetly set among the pines above Platy Yialos, has tastefully appointed rooms and bungalows.) If you take the short drive around the point to reach them, you'll pass what's left of the famous *katavóthres* (swallow holes) near a rusted water mill and a picturesque old lighthouse, a replica of the original rotunda erected during the British protectorate in the 1820s. In summer the **Thalassomylos**, next door to the mill, serves Kefallonian specialties in pleasant surroundings, where once a week local troubadours can be heard singing traditional *kantádes*.

Lixouri

A 25-minute ferry ride from Argostoli brings you across the lagoon to Lixoúri (ancient Pali), whose inhabitants are reputed to be the wittiest of all the Kefallonians. Once lively and cosmopolitan, Lixouri today is sleepy, even though resort hotels catering to package tours are springing up on its outskirts. Instead of heading straight for the long, red sandy beaches that line the southern coast of this peninsula, take time to visit the **Iakovátos Mansion**. This is one of the few houses that did not collapse in 1953, and it gives you the chance to see what a stately Kefallonian home was like. Stained-glass windows and Venetian-inspired paintings on the ceilings complement the family's icon collection and library. Some performances of the island's annual choral festival are held in the Iakovatos garden every September.

Now, what about those beaches? Just take the road south out of Lixouri, looking for branch roads that lead down to the sea. Watch for such names as **Lépeda**, **Havriata** (Nice Church), **Potámi**, **Kounópetra**, and especially **Xi**, a two-mile crescent of red sand.

The Heart of Kefallonia

Southeast of Argostoli, the region known as **Livathó**—lush, green, sprinkled with delightful villages—is one of the most prosperous areas on the island. Each village has its landmark or story: **Metaxáta** is where Byron stayed before making the ill-considered decision to leave for Mesolongi in central Greece; **Kalligáta** is where the wine-making Calliga family hails from, and both Kalligata and **Domáta** are renowned for their church interiors; **Kourkoumeláta**, with its squeaky-clean Neoclassical cultural center, is the model of an affluent suburb reconstructed through the efforts of a wealthy Greek industrialist. **Lourdáta**, a bit to the east on the coast, is a popular beach, barely visible but well posted amid the tangle of greenery. The local taverna proprietors grow their own vegetables in this natural greenhouse. If you'd like to stay in the Livatho district, there's a new family-run hotel, the **Lara**, with 26 rooms looking onto a peaceful olive grove. **Peratáta** boasts the lovely **monastery of Ayios Andréas** with its wonderful 17th-century frescoes uncovered by the earthquake. The church is very proud of its prize relic—the sole of Saint Andrew's right foot.

The chief monument in Livatho is the impressive **Castle of**

St. George, built around the 13th century and entirely rebuilt by the Venetians when they finally gained control of the island in 1500. The ruined buildings of the Medieval capital adorn the hill below it. The castle is in remarkably good condition, with all its external walls preserved. Coats of arms of leading families decorate the massive bastions, one of which conceals a tunnel leading to a secret exit.

The road southeast from Livatho clings to the side of Mount Ainos, offering lovely views of the fertile valley and passing through a chain of tiny villages. One of these is **Markópoulos**, undistinguished except for the phenomenon of its little snakes. Every summer, a few weeks before the feast of the Assumption of the Virgin, harmless reptiles bearing a mark resembling the sign of the cross on their heads begin to appear around the main church. On August 15 they make a beeline for the Virgin's icon in the church and then vanish abruptly. Miraculous or not, they are thought to bring good luck. It is said that 1953—the year of the earthquake—was a snakeless year.

The road branches off to descend to the fishing village of **Kato Kateliό**, on a pretty crescent beach, and **Skala**, a burgeoning resort catering to British holiday packages on the southeast coast, bordering a stretch of golden sand that goes on almost as far as the eye can see. Mosaics from a Roman villa, brought to light after the earthquake, can be seen under a shed near the beach. The main road continues north to **Poros**, where the boats from Kyllini (on the Peloponnese) dock. This is where you would go to make connections for another ferry to Zakynthos (though if you have your own wheels, the new link that alternates between Argostoli and Pessada in Livatho and Skinari on Zakynthos is far quicker—not more than an hour and a half). You can also get to Poros from Skala over an acceptable dirt road that passes some temptingly isolated coves for private swimming. Poros, too, is showing signs of eclectic development, as Greeks in particular discover this well-shaded village and its clean beaches. Tragically, some of the splendid forest between Poros and Markopoulos was destroyed by fire in 1988.

If you venture north to Sami along the eastern flank of Mount Ainos you'll see some violently beautiful scenery—thick stands of tall cypresses jutting from tumbled rocks and rugged boulders—to make up for the poor condition of the first four miles of the road. You also pass the "bottomless" **Lake Avythos**. Originally there were two such deep lakes, but in experimenting with the water source the scientists and engineers succeeded in making the smaller one dry up.

Another route out of Argostoli (eventually heading northeast) crosses the lagoon over a bridge completed by British engineers in 1813 and passes a quaint pyramid commemorating the event. Overlooking these landmarks, a bit farther along the road, are some Hellenistic walls marking the boundaries of ancient Krani. The road passes vineyards that produce the island's Robola wine and leads on to the Omála valley and the **monastery of Ayios Yerásimos**. Kefallonia's patron saint was born on the Greek mainland in the 16th century and lived several years as a monk in the Holy Land and in Zakynthos before he took over this monastery. Ayios Yerasimos is greatly revered by the locals, who celebrate his feast days (August 16 and October 20) with stately processions similar to ones in Corfu and Zakynthos. Of relatively recent construction, the monastery itself is of no interest architecturally.

The ascent of **Mount Aínos** (signposted) proceeds from this route, and it is here that the towering, cedar-like firs unique to the island, *Abies cephalonica,* are most common. When the Venetians were in command of the Ionian, the mountain was so thickly forested that they christened it Monte Negro (Black Mountain). Several centuries, countless galleon masts, and several fires later, the forest is much diminished but still impressive. There is that lovely sense of quiet that huge trees produce, and the view from the summit is worth the detour.

Fiskardo and the Erissos Peninsula

Some would say this is saving the best for last. This northern section of the island is so different from the rest: mountainous, virtually treeless, and blessedly untouched by the earthquake. Here are two of Kefallonia's most attractive villages, **Assos** and **Fiskárdo**, and one of the most strikingly beautiful beaches in Greece, **Myrtos**. The area is filled with startling contrasts: the miniature, tree-lined port of Assos beneath the vast Venetian fortress on the crest of the stark hill; the dizzying view from the corniche of Myrtos's blindingly white sands merging with a turquoise sea; the pale façades and tiled roofs of Fiskardo's delightful old houses protruding through the dark green of the surrounding cypress wood.

Formerly a simple fishing port, Fiskardo fills up faster with yachts and sailing flotillas than with caïques nowadays; besides being so picturesque, it is the only safe anchorage on this coast. Its name is a corruption derived from Robert Guiscard, the Norman adventurer who died here 19 years after the battle of Hastings.

As for accommodation on this peninsula, if you are besotted by views, choose the **Kavos Pension** in Assos. Overlooking Myrtos Bay and the white cliffs of Pali, it is also charmingly decorated with carved furniture and handwoven textiles from Crete. Both tavernas in Assos serve good food. In Fiskardo the six-room **Panormos** is still the only official hotel, but visitors will be more than pleased with the guesthouses converted from private homes by the GNTO or with the apartments provided by the Greek Islands Club. The carefully restored seven-room **Fiscardona**, for example, has been embellished with traditional furniture, and the **Filoxenia** is even lovelier. Fiskardo also boasts two of the nicest shops in the Ionian: **To Katoi**, with original clothes, ceramics, glass, and boat paintings; and **Maistrali**, for imaginatively displayed, very reasonably priced local handicrafts. When hungry, try **Dendrinos** by the port or **Nicola's** garden, run by a zany guy whose humor is in as much demand as his cuisine.

Be warned: These are small places (Fiskardo has a permanent population of 100) that lose much of their charm in the August tourist crush. Fiskardo on the first of August looks as if it's being invaded from the sea, as fleets of rubber boats with enormous outboards plane over the waters from Bari loaded with Italians, who literally take over the village for the month. If you avoid the height of summer, you won't be disappointed.

GETTING AROUND

You can get to Kefallonia by air from Athens (Olympic Airways has daily flights year round and several a day in summer, and there are charters from various European cities) or by boat from Italy or Patras and Kyllini on the Peloponnese. The Patras ferry goes on to Vathy, Ithaca's main port. At the height of summer some of the Italy-bound ferries stop at Sami, and then proceed to Paxi and Corfu. Smaller ferries link Fiskardo with Frikes on Ithaca and Nydri and Vasiliki on Lefkada, and Pessada and Argostoli with northern Zakynthos.

For getting around on the island, cars and motorbikes can be rented in Argostoli, though Kefallonia is too big to be thoroughly explored by moped. There are several public bus routes, but their schedules may not always suit yours. Organized excursions to the main attractions are also available.

—*Diana Farr Ladas*

ITHACA

Lying midway between Lefkada and Kefallonia, Ithaca (Itháki) resonates with echoes of Odysseus. On every road and pathway are signs directing you to the Cave of the Nymphs, Arethusa's Fountain, Homer's School, and even to Laertes' goats. The trouble is that no archaeological evidence exists to prove that Homer's hero ever had a palace here. Schliemann mistakenly thought he had found it on the top of Mount Aetos (but in fact the structure dates only from around 700 B.C.), and later generations have not been much more successful. Nevertheless, one of the great pleasures to be had on a visit to Ithaca is tracking down the wily king. Whether or not you find any trace of him, the reward lies in the search (as the poet Cavafy so wisely wrote).

To those in pursuit of high living—chic boutiques, discos, and the like—Ithaca may appear to be little more than two steep rocks linked by a vertiginous narrow ridge in the middle of the sea. They'll understand why Odysseus left home for so long and was in no hurry to get back. But for sailors, hikers, and people looking for something different, Ithaca seems a paradise. Its tourists are definitely not run-of-the-mill, and the herd instinct does not manifest itself here.

MAJOR INTEREST

Search for Odysseus
Hiking and sailing
Views: Exoyi and Kathara

Ithaca is too small to accommodate large numbers of people, and those who do come must endure a four-and-a-half-hour ferry ride from Patras via Kefallonia, or try to make connections on the smaller boats linking the island with Nydri (Lefkada) or Ayia Evfymia and Fiskardo (Kefallonia). There are two adequate but noisy hotels in Vathy, the **Mentor** and the **Odysseas**, which is why most visitors stay in rooms rented in private homes. As usual the prettiest houses and apartments are available through the Greek Islands Club, though Frikes now has a clean and comfortable hotel, the **Nostos**, and the eight apartments at the **Hotel Kioni** are delightful with their bougainvillaea-bedecked balconies right on the waterfront.

Vathy

As the ferry approaches Ithaca it passes a seemingly endless succession of tantalizingly inaccessible coves and beaches interspersed along an inhospitable rocky shoreline. At last, around the umpteenth bend, Vathý (also called Itháki or Thiáki) appears in the distance. It's aptly named, placed as it is at the end of the *deep* bay on the east coast. Surrounded by wooded mountains and shaped like a large horseshoe, Vathy is pleasant to look at. Its low houses were badly damaged in that ruinous 1953 earthquake, but many of them were reconstructed using the original stones, and there are few eyesores. It's important to remember that Ithaca has always been extremely poor, and that a large percentage of its population has had to take to the sea, or even emigrate, to make a living.

A large sign on the **Lazaretto** (former quarantine station), an islet in the middle of the bay, sets a welcoming tone: "Every traveller is a citizen of Ithaca." They of all people appreciate what it's like to sail into a new place. While Byron used to swim out to this islet, you might prefer the beach on the right arm of the horseshoe, where there are congenial tavernas situated under the trees—try **Gregory's**.

Vathy, which has a population of 2,000, can be taken in at a glance. Its quay is also its main square, around which all village life revolves. Though it may seem empty and bleak by day, wait till night, when the cafés and tavernas move their tables onto the waterfront, the lights go on, and the promenade starts. Then it becomes very festive. The locals recommend the **Trechandiri** one street in and **To Kandouni** on the port. Ithaca is far more culture-oriented than you might expect of a small, remote island. Vathy has a decent **Archaeological Museum**, a cultural center where lectures on the Homeric tradition (among others) are frequently given, and it sponsors two festivals (funding permitting) each summer—a drama competition, and a series of pop-music concerts. It also has one of the best handicraft shops in the Ionian. Located near the ferry landing, **Nitsa's Women's Cooperative** is stocked with wonderful embroideries, sweaters, blouses, and other enticing items, all made locally.

Around the Island

If you make Vathy your base you can easily get around to the rest of the island by boat or bus (Ithaca is only 38 square miles in area). The road linking the southern and northern sections is excellent. Sights in the southern half include **Perahóri**, a village in the mountains above Vathy—no Homeric associations here, but it's near the deserted Medieval capital (an easy walk), which is worth exploring; **Arethusa's Fountain**, where Odysseus hid with Eumaios the swineherd until his son Telemachus arrived to help him oust Penelope's suitors (more evocative if you've brought the *Odyssey* along, but a great walk nevertheless); and the unspectacular **Cave of the Nymphs**, where Odysseus is supposed to have hidden the 13 tripods given him by the Phaeacians (Corfiots) as a farewell gift. Dexiá Bay, dubbed **Bay of Phorcys**, the first cove as you head west from Vathy, is supposed to be where he stepped ashore. He would have had to lug those heavy things a long way up the hill, and archaeologists have recently discovered another cave on the sea near Polis (see below) that seems a more likely spot—and they found 12 tripods in it!

As the road north crosses **Mount Aetós**, one fork descends to the minuscule, little-used port of Piso Aetos and passes some of the walls of the seventh/eighth-century B.C. acropolis that Schliemann thought was the Mycenaean palace. One of the locals' favorite spots, the **Kathará Monastery**, lies up a mountain opposite the bay of Vathy. Sooner or later everyone makes this pilgrimage, not because of the monastery but because of the magnificent view. If it's wonderful churches you're after, continue on to the village of **Anóyi** (Above the Earth), whose Medieval church has a truly memorable icon screen. A few miles farther on, the road arrives at **Stavrós**, pleasant but undistinguished, the biggest village in the northern portion. Its shady main square is a good place to stop for a bite or a drink. If you have only a day or two on the island, take this road to Stavros and return by the main road above the coast, one of the most exciting corniches in Greece. It's almost as good as being airborne.

Below Stavros and facing Kefallonia (west) lies the bay of **Polis** (City), a strange name for a spot where there is no trace of any urban life. But ancient place names always have meaning, and archaeologists are still searching. It is off this bay that the other Cave of the Nymphs was discovered (not worth a visit). The tripods and other finds related to cult worship unearthed here are on display in a makeshift museum not far from Stavros. If you find the exhibit disappointing, make your way up to **Exóyi** (Out of the Earth). The view from the chapel at the end of the road past the village is absolutely out of this world.

The northeast coast of the island is picturesque rather than dramatic. The shores are perfect for swimming: quiet and unspoiled, indented with lacy coves and rimmed with cypress trees and pines. The main attractions over here are the two delightful fishing villages of **Kióni** and **Frikes**. Consisting of little more than a cluster of houses around a tiny port, a handful of tavernas, and more cypresses, they have been discovered but not at all destroyed by tranquillity-seeking vacationers. For some, Ithaca has indeed supplied the "enchanting voyage" promised by Cavafy.

GETTING AROUND

There are daily ferries from Patras (sometimes twice a day in summer; four and a half hours) and from Astakos on the mainland (two hours); you can also hop from Frikes to Nydri on Lefkada and to Sami and Ayia Evfymia on Kefallonia.

Though buses and boats connect Vathy with Stavros, Frikes, and Kioni, you may want to rent your own car, motorboat, or scooter in Vathy. Sailing yachts can be rented from agencies in Nydri or Corfu well ahead of the season, or you can join a flotilla holiday group in Great Britain.

As for walking, it is what you want it to be, from leisurely strolls to beaches to arduous hikes up Mount Aetos. Some paths are well marked, some you will find by asking locals or following faded signs. Martin Young (see Bibliography) has some directions to the better-known sites.

—*Diana Farr Ladas*

ZAKYNTHOS

Lying just ten miles off the west coast of the Peloponnese, Zákynthos (Zante) is somewhat isolated from the other Ionians and has few links with them. In the past you could only get there by ferry from Kyllini on the Peloponnese, and since there was no other reason to go to Kyllini, this fertile, fragrant island remained virtually unvisited by foreigners. Charter flights and package tours have changed this, and some areas of Zakynthos seem to have sprung up overnight to accommodate the flood. But it is a large and beautiful island with much to delight the traveller.

Zakynthos was so highly prized by the Venetians during their centuries of rule (1484 to 1797) that they made up a jingle to praise it: *Zante, fior' di levante* (Zakynthos, flower

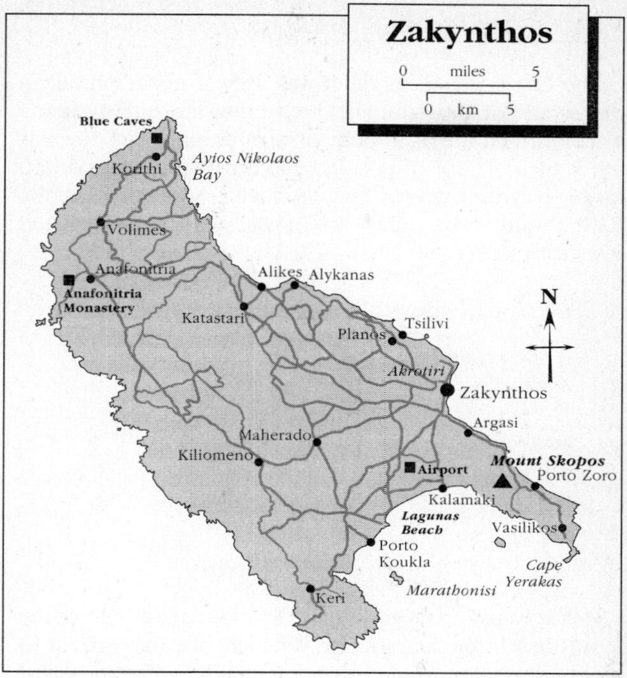
Zakynthos
0 miles 5
0 km 5
Blue Caves
Korithi
Ayios Nikolaos Bay
Volimes
Anafonitria
Anafonitria Monastery
Alikes
Alykanas
Katastari
Tsilivi
Planos
Akrotiri
Zakynthos
N
Argasi
Maherado
Kiliomeno
Airport
Mount Skopos
Porto Zoro
Kalamaki
Lagunas Beach
Vasilikos
Porto Koukla
Cape Yerakas
Marathonisi
Keri

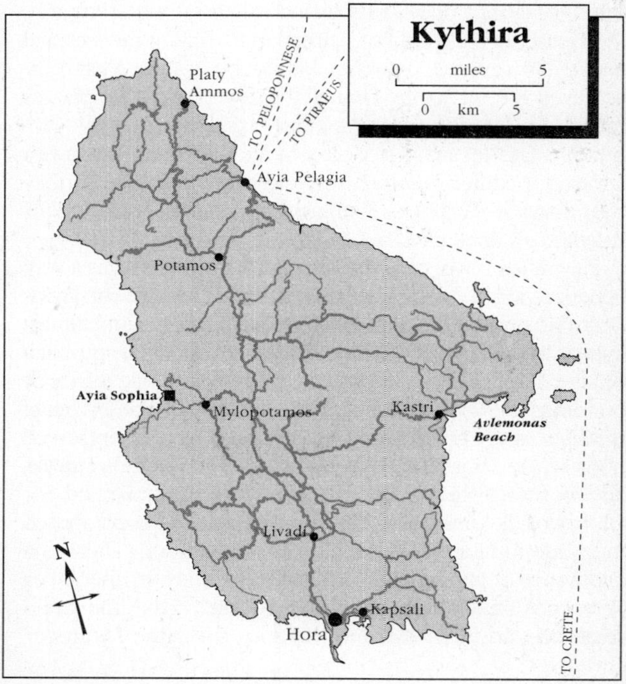
Kythira
0 miles 5
0 km 5
Platy Ammos
TO PELOPONNESE
TO PIRAEUS
Ayia Pelagia
Potamos
Ayia Sophia
Mylopotamos
Kastri
Avlemonas Beach
Livadi
N
Kapsali
Hora
TO CRETE

of the East). Architecturally it was a jewel, geographically a temperate paradise—and not just a pretty face either. Zante's artists formed the main body of what came to be known as the Ionian School of post-Byzantine painting; it produced more than its share of famous poets—Solomos, Foscolo, Kalvos—and playwrights; and music echoed through the town's arcades.

> **MAJOR INTEREST**
>
> Post-Byzantine museum in Zakynthos town
> Sea turtles
> The Blue Caves and Keri Caves
> *Kantádes* with your supper
> Church interiors
> Beaches on the way to Cape Yerakas

Zakynthos Town

Two forces have shaped the face of modern Zakynthos: the more than three centuries of Venetian rule that helped to mold its architecture and its culture, and the earthquake of 1953 and the fire that swiftly ensued, which seemed to reduce this heritage to a pile of rubble. In a valiant effort to recapture their past, the Zakynthians painstakingly rebuilt their capital and their revered churches, stone by stone. What they achieved is remarkable. Though the town's two main piazzas may seem like the set for a mega-production by day—the building façades are so perfect—by late afternoon, filled with strollers, peddlers, motorbikes, and happy commotion, they bear no trace of artifice. In August, they form the backdrop for Zakynthos's annual festival.

Zakynthos town, on the east coast of the island, has a very Venetian air to it; the campanile and **basilica of Ayios Dionýsios**, named after the island's patron saint, almost appear to float on the left side of the harbor as you approach on the ferry. This 20th-century church was one of three buildings in town that survived the earthquake; its chief treasure is an ornate sarcophagus holding the preserved body of the saint. The ferry docks close to **Solomós Square**, an enormous piazza just off the waterfront, named for Dionysios Solomos, the 19th-century poet who composed the "Ode to Liberty," Greece's national anthem. (There is a Dionysios in almost every Zakynthian family, as there is a Yerasimos on Kefallonia and a Spyros on Corfu.) You'll find references to these two most famous sons (the Dionysioi, poet and saint) all around the island. Here in Solomos Square are the poet's statue and a statue of Liberty, plus a bust of Ugo Foscolo, who became one of Italy's best-known poets. The square is lined with impressive buildings; the beautifully restored, honey-colored stone 14th-century **church of Ayios Nikólaos tou Molou** stands out (on the quay) on the right. On the same side is the public library–cultural center, which faces the town hall. The **Museum of Post-Byzantine Art** occupies the whole side of the square opposite the sea.

This museum is a must, particularly if you aren't able to visit any of Zakynthos's marvelous churches. It contains some remarkable examples of carved, gilded icon screens, or *templos,* an art form perfected in the Ionian. Fanciful beasts, especially lions and dragons, vines and bunches of grapes, and angels are common motifs. The angels in this museum are notably voluptuous, more reminiscent of mermaids than of divine spirits. Templos separate the public part of the Orthodox church from the altar and are decorated with icons arranged in a specific hierarchy. In many island churches modern reproductions often hang next to superb 17th- and 18th-century paintings. Here at least you will see some of the masters of the Ionian School formed by the meeting of Cretan refugee artists coming face to face with the Renaissance as personified by Italian masters such as Tintoretto and the Carracci. The resulting icons have more fluid lines, humanistic sentiments, and perspective depth. Look for such names as Tzanes, Poulakis, Lombardos, and Damaskinos—all from Crete—and for paintings by the native Zakynthians Koutouzis, Kandounis, and the Doxaras family. In the museum you can trace the development of Ionian post-Byzantine art up to the 19th century, with its hints of sentimentality.

St. Mark's Square (Ayíou Markou), just two blocks away, is much more intimate and more commercial than Solomos. Pizzerias, restaurants, and boutiques keep lively company with the serene forms of the **Solomós Museum** and the Catholic church. The former contains the sarcophagi of Solomos and Andreas Kalvos, along with literary memorabilia. A comfortable, inexpensive hotel in this area is the **Diana**, with its cool lounge, while **Strada Marina**, on the waterfront, is the town's swankiest, with a swimming pool and roof garden. Another good choice is the quiet, ivy-covered, family-run **Hotel Bitzaro**, closer to the National Tourist Organization beach and the exquisite **church of Our Lady of the Angels**, named for the charming angels decorating its façade. Most of the rooms in these hotels have balconies with fine views of the sea. At the **Arekia** taverna in this neighborhood the patrons are likely to start singing traditional Zantiot *kantádes* as the evening gets going. And the food is tasty, too; try the soufflé or such Zakynthiot specialties as *saltsa,* a rich beef and tomato stew, or rabbit *stifádo* (with pearl onions), washed down with the local Verdea wine. Be warned that Zantiot dishes are likely to be liberally infused with garlic. Other restaurants worth trying in town are **Oraia Ellas** for reasonably priced home cooking, in a courtyard on Ayios Ioánnis Logothéton Street, and the **Village Inn**, a block south of the Strada Marina, for excellent but expensive French cuisine.

Beginning at St. Mark's Square is Zakynthos's main shopping street, lined with arcades. In among the grocers and clothing stores, keep an eye out for the pottery shop at number 18, where some of the prettiest ceramics in the Ionian are on sale, and for the embroideries and handmade linens at number 54. The tourist shops are strung along the waterfront. You can't help spotting an incredible array of bottles and scent jars among the tee shirts and kitsch. Zakynthos is famous for its liqueurs and perfume essences, not to mention its nougat, *mandoláto* (give some to your favorite dentist). Look out for the **Women's Cooperative** at the far end of the *paralía*. It's stocked with sweaters, rugs, and embroideries of all kinds—from hankies to tablecloths—made by island women, many of them from the northern village of Volimes (see below), the second-largest settlement.

Before heading for Zakynthos's many and varied beaches, go up to **Bókhali**, the district directly above the town. This is where the Medieval population lived within the fortification walls of the **Kastro** until the Venetians made it safe to venture closer to the sea. Built by the Tocco lords from Naples in the 14th or 15th century, the castle was strengthened by Venice, and a benign Lion of Saint Mark still adorns the entrance gate. Not surprisingly, this is also the site of the ancient acropolis, of which there is not a trace. If you walk around the walls of this large enclosure you'll see the island's fertile interior plain thick with vines and kitchen gardens, the green slopes of Mount Skopos opposite the harbor, and in the distance to the south the hotels lining Laganas beach.

Other landmarks near Bokhali are **Lofos Strani**, where Solomos composed his famous ode, and **Akrotíri**, a thickly wooded headland where imposing villas and good restaurants can be spied among the trees. One of the latter, **To**

Akrotiri, is in a cool, rustic setting where a rich variety of grilled meats and imaginative *mezedákia* (appetizers) is served by good-humored waiters. At Stavros, the junction between Bokhali and Akrotiri, the newly renovated **Lina Hotel** offers a lovely view of the port and the island's interior, plus a swimming pool set amidst a splendid flower garden. It is only a few steps from the **Quartetto di Zante**, where the locals go to hear *kantades*.

Around the Island

Zakynthos is well organized for exploring. You can choose between public buses or tour buses, rented cars or motor-bikes, depending on your preferences and pocketbooks.

The closest beach to town heading north toward Akrotiri is the National Tourist Organization bathing pavilion; the most famous beach, **Laganás**, lies in the opposite direction on the southeast coast past the airport. Though Laganas is Zakynthos's most popular beach and the hardest hit by tourism, its charms pale when compared to some other places on the island. Ironically, it is also one of the favorite breeding spots of the sea turtle *caretta caretta,* an endangered species. Squads of volunteers are active on summer nights trying to track the turtles and transfer their eggs to a safer hatchery, away from the umbrellas and lounging chairs. At Laganas, amid the high-rise hotels and blistering sunbathers, look for the **Driftwood Bar**, where you can get imaginative snacks and join a scuba-diving expedition to the **caves at Kerí** around the point. The large **Zante Beach Hotel and Bungalows** near the canal has two swimming pools, an expanse of lawn, and all the amenities you would expect from a high-class resort hotel.

Though the Blue Caves in the north of Zakynthos have received more publicity (more on these below), the island's west coast is lined with spectacular, stark white limestone cliffs. Boats are available at Laganas and Keri harbor to take you to visit the grottoes and the miniature beaches at their fringes. For an even more amazing view of this scene, go by road to the village of **Kerí**, follow the path to the lighthouse, and look down. Even the locals never tire of the sight, especially at sunset. Keri was not touched by the earthquake, so it provides a glimpse of what island architecture was like before 1953. Above Keri harbor (Límni Keríou) is one of the most spectacularly situated hotels in the Ionian, the **Villa Meltemi**. The sensitively designed 11-room complex looks out over the huge bay of Laganas, the white cliffs of Marathónisi, and the green slopes of Mount Skopos.

For a more complete image of pre-earthquake Zakynthos, take the dirt (or, to be more precise, chalk) road from Keri up the hilly west side of the island. Paved after Kilioméno, it passes some charming, utterly unspoiled villages and wonderful churches amid the pine woods, then joins the main road to **Anafonítria**. This monastery was founded in 1429 by the Tocco family, lords of Naples, and is venerated as the place where Ayios Dionysios earned his claim to sainthood. Here, while abbot, he gave sanctuary to his brother's murderer.

Just before Anafonitria is the turn for the village of **Volímes**, where most of the island's handicrafts are made. You'll see them displayed on clotheslines at the entrance to town. The **church of Ayia Paraskeví** here is one of the oldest (12th century) and prettiest on Zakynthos. Its blue ceiling decorated with Old Testament scenes and the sweeping lines and delicate gilding of its templo will probably be more appealing to Western tastes than the intricately carved templo in **Ayia Mavra** at **Maherádo**, to the south in the heart of the island. This ornate church is the one most highly esteemed by the locals.

From Volimes it's not far to Koríthi and Ayios Nikolaos Bay in the northernmost reaches of the island, where there are a few simple tavernas and boats waiting to carry sightseers to the famous **Blue Caves**. Make an appointment with a fisherman to take you there between 11:00 A.M. and noon, when the sun splashes incredible blue reflections all over the cavern walls. You could spend the night at the small (20 rooms, but there's also a pool) **La Grotta Hotel** after arriving on the late ferry from Pessada and feast on the local specialty, lobster, at Ayios Nikólaos Bay. (Excursion boats also make the trip to the caves from Zakynthos town.)

Unfortunately, the road down the hilly northern section of the east coast ranges from poor to nonexistent, so you have to turn inland on your return south. As the road starts to descend you find yourself overlooking the salt flats that give the budding seaside resort town of **Alikés** its name. There are several hotels and restaurants catering to package tours here at the start of its long white beach, but nothing like the development at Laganas. **Alykanás**, a tiny fishing port slightly to the east of Alikes, has a more "Greek" feel to it.

This eastern portion of the island consists mostly of gentle hills and fertile valleys that still produce the currants the English doted on for centuries. The area is sprinkled with farms and villages where tourism is barely noticed. On the coast, at **Tsiliví** and **Planos**, hotels, tavernas, and "villas" are mushrooming, but development is camouflaged by the lush surroundings. Tsilivi is especially popular with the Greeks, who feel a bit alienated by the heavily English scene at Laganas. At Planos, just south of Tsilivi, look out for **Avgoustis's** taverna, where the fish is hauled in on the owner's own caïque. Planos also boasts one of the island's most luxurious hotels, the **Caravel**, affiliated with the Athens hotel of the same name. It is ideally situated on a little cove—you can almost tumble out of bed right into the sea. Its rooms are arranged in a sawtooth design for greater privacy, and the public rooms are attractive without being unduly opulent.

Another favorite destination for both tourists and turtles is the string of beaches on the peninsula that juts eastward just below Zakynthos town, topped by Mount Skopós, Zakynthos's highest mountain. On the way out of town toward Argasi you pass two typically Zakynthian stone churches and **Karavomilos**, one of the island's best fish restaurants, a bit classier than a taverna and more expensive because of its specialty. Though blessed by flowering vines and sweet-scented shrubbery, Argási itself has been overly anglicized; the names of its pubs and restaurants—Carissimo, Piccadilly, Tootsie's Bar, and the Magic Mushroom, to list a few—give you an idea of what to expect. But farther out along the cape, in among the thick pine woods, olive groves, and cow pastures, one lovely beach follows another. **Porto Zoro**, about midway along the north coast, is not only a delightful cove, but it also has a fabulous taverna, **O Adelfos tou Kosta**. Kosta's brother, Yannis, is another owner who loves to entertain his customers with *kantades*. With water sports at **Ayios Nikólaos Bay** (not to be confused with the northern version), woods, and roaming peacocks at **Mavrántzis Bay**, and more wooded coves at **Vasilikós**, this peninsula offers a wide range of choices. At the tip, **Cape Yérakas**, surrounded by beautiful, banded red-and-white cliffs, are the nicest beach and another splendidly sited turtle hatchery, where only turtles may spend the night. But just 300 yards away, the **Liuba Cottages**, ten pastel-colored apartments near an olive grove, provide a quiet, private alternative to the development of Laganas and Argasi.

GETTING AROUND

There are daily Olympic Airways flights from Athens (some from Kefallonia) and charter flights from some European cities. Ferryboats (five to seven in summer; three off-season) run from Kyllini on the Peloponnese. Interisland connections are via Kefallonia: five flights a week and by ferry between Pessada and Argostoli on Kefallonia and Ayios Nikolaos Bay (Skinari) in the north of Zakynthos. Twice a week an Olympic flight island-hops from Zakynthos to Corfu, stopping at Argostoli and Preveza on the way.

—*Diana Farr Ladas*

KYTHIRA

Kýthira (formerly also known by its Italian name, Cerigo) is the seventh Ionian island, the one nobody ever remembers. This is hardly surprising, since Kythira, lying off the southeast leg of the Peloponnese and some 35 miles northwest of Crete, is a good 180 miles southeast of Zakynthos, the southernmost of the main group. In fact, its inclusion among the Ionian islands is a historical accident. Like the others it was a Venetian colony and part of the package ceded to England by the Congress of Vienna. But it has virtually nothing in common with its siblings; geographically, it represents one of the last surviving fragments of the land bridge between Africa and Europe, and it is administered today from Piraeus.

Physically, Kythira consists mainly of a high, barren plateau with an alluvial valley halfway down the east coast that ends in the beach at Avlemonas. There are none of those lush green areas found in the other Ionian islands. Instead there are gulleys, ravines, and windswept moors, making the scenery more dramatic than romantic. It's hard to envisage the island as the birthplace of the goddess of love unless we remember that Aphrodite means "born of the sea foam." And of that there is plenty, because Kythira is located on the cusp between the Ionian, Cretan, and Aegean seas and is subjected to sudden and often violent changes of weather.

Sightseeing in Kythira is a matter of individual initiative and intuition—no organized tours exist. This, of course, is why people go to Kythira—to get away from all that. The search for adventure does involve some risk, however. Kythira's season is short—from the end of June to the end of August. If you go before or after, you'll find few tavernas open; if you go at the peak time, you may not find a place to stay. The island's population booms during the summer with the return of many of its native sons and daughters from Australia.

MAJOR INTEREST

Free-lance exploring
Hora and the Kastro
Kapsali
Mylopotamos and Kato Hora

Kythira has two ports: Kapsali to the south, Ayia Pelagia to the north. Most travellers land at **Ayía Pelagía**, a small, ramshackle resort with an adequate pension (the 15-bed **Kytheria**), rooms, tavernas, and a few pretty beaches, such as **Platý Ammos**. But the rest of the island is far more picturesque, with traditional Ionian architecture left over from the British occupation, Venetian remnants here and there, and mountains dotted with monasteries. Kythira's population of 4,000 or less is scattered among a number of villages, of which the largest is **Potamós**, a market town about a 15-minute drive southwest of Ayia Pelagia. On Sundays there is an open-air bazaar attended by farmers and peddlers of all sorts, providing a glimpse of a lifestyle that hasn't changed for centuries.

On the south side of the island lies **Hora** (a.k.a. Kythira town) and its port, **Kapsáli**, 3 km (2 miles) below. Tiny Hora, the capital, has none of the zip associated with a main town, but it has a charm of its own, thanks to the small Neoclassical buildings around the *plateía* and its imposing Venetian **Kastro**. Originally built by the Venieri feudal lords (who claimed descent from Venus) in the early 14th century, the castle was reinforced by the Venetians when they took over in 1503. Both the view from it of Kapsali and the Avgó (Egg) islet offshore and the sight of it from below are exciting and evocative of ages past. Kapsali is the tourist center of the island; its beach is lined with tavernas and rooms to rent. The beach is ordinary but it has the advantage of being accessible.

For accommodations, try the eight-room **Kaity Pension**, tastefully decorated in blue and white, in an alley off the main square in Hora, or get in touch with the **Greek Islands Club**, which has a virtual monopoly on all the nicest rooms in Hora and Kapsali. Halfway up the hill from Kapsali, the lovely **Raikos Hotel**, new in 1990, has 25 comfortable rooms and a pool with a view of the Kastro. **Zorba's** family-run taverna is a good choice for eating out in Hora. As for Kapsali, one caveat: Avoid the places that "put on airs"—they don't measure up. But do by all means head for **Antonis O Magos** (the Magician), next to the Ionian Shipping Agency, for good fish and a friendly, casual ambience; **Artena**, noted for having the grumpiest owner, the least plastic, and the best food; and the **Ouzeri**, on the main back street, whose atmosphere is more memorable than its *mezé*. And believe it or not, the **"Bikini Red" Pub** serves classical music with its cocktails from 7:00 to 9:00 P.M.

Around the Island

To see the rest of the island, a car or scooter (the latter may be rented in Hora) is virtually essential, as public transport is very erratic and taxis will not want to risk their tires on the more "interesting" roads. Though six cars are theoretically up for hire, these are booked from year to year by regular visitors. One must is a visit to the lovely inland village of **Mylopótamos**, roughly equidistant from Potamos and Hora, with its charming fountain, shaded square, and churches. Less than a mile away is **Kato Hora**, the site of a Venetian mini-fortress complete with arched gateway, sculpted lion, and several tiny stone-tiled churches. Just before the entrance to the fortress stands another anomaly, an impeccably constructed English school, Gothic windows and all, erected in 1825. (There are other such incongruities on the island, including a magnificent bridge going nowhere near Livádi just north of Hora.) Finally, the **cave of Ayia Sophía**, with Byzantine wall paintings and several chambers of stalactites and stalagmites, may be explored just outside Mylopotamos. Ask at the café in the *plateía* for the guide and key.

The beach on the east coast at **Avlémonas**, the island's largest—too big ever to get crowded—is worth a trip. There are a few simple tavernas in the tiny fishing port nearby. And if you get tired of sunbathing you can always look for shards at **Kastrí** (Paleopolis) on the southwest end of the bay. This is where the Minoan acropolis of Skandia, one of the Cretan empire's earliest colonies (2000 B.C.), once stood.

GETTING AROUND

The volatile seas and weather of Kythira can play havoc with travel plans, as both getting here and leaving are outside human control. Thus, the daily Olympic Airways flight (14-

seater) may be abruptly canceled because of high winds or fog, and the Flying Dolphin (five hours, four times weekly) is equally subject to the caprice of weather. (The hydrofoil stops at Nafplion, Porto Heli, and Monemvasia, and sometimes at Kyparissi, Yerakas, and Leonidion, picturesque villages on the Peloponnese, before arriving at Ayia Pelagia.) A surer but slower alternative is the twice-weekly steamer from Piraeus (10 to 12 hours), which also stops at Gytheion (the port of Sparta) after Ayia Pelagia and before going on to Kapsali, Antikythira, and Crete (Kastelli). Finally, you can drive to Neapolis in southeast Laconia in the Peloponnese and hop onto a small ferry there (one hour).

—*Diana Farr Ladas*

ACCOMMODATIONS REFERENCE
The Greek Islands Club has lovely apartments and villas all over the Ionian from Paxi to Kythira. Contact them at: 66 High Street, Walton-on-Thames, Surrey KT12 1BU, England. Tel: (0932) 220-477; Telex: 928561.

Corfu
For information regarding accommodation in a stately town house on Corfu, write C. Lamvranos, 5 Moustoxydi Street, Corfu Town, 491 00 Corfu. Tel: (0661) 256-53. A good travel agent to contact is **Corfu Villas Travel,** *at 43 Cadogan Street, Chelsea, London SW3 2PR. Tel: (071) 581-0851; Telex: 919773 (Corvilt); or 7 Donzelot Street, Corfu Town, 491 00 Corfu. Tel: (0661) 240-09.*

- ▶ **Aiolos Beach.** Perama, 491 00 Corfu. Tel: (0661) 331-32.
- ▶ **Bella Venezia.** 4 Zambelist Street, **Corfu Town,** 491 00 Corfu. Tel: (0661) 422-90 or 465-00.
- ▶ **Calypso.** 4 Vraila Street, **Corfu Town,** 491 00 Corfu. Tel: (0661) 307-23.
- ▶ **Casa Lucia.** Sgoumbros, 491 00 Corfu. Tel: (0661) 914-19.
- ▶ **Corfu Palace Hotel.** 2 Dimokratias Avenue, **Corfu Town,** 491 00 Corfu. Tel: (0661) 394-85/87.
- ▶ **Ermones Beach Hotel.** Ermones, 491 00 Corfu. Tel: (0661) 942-41/42; Telex: 332-162.
- ▶ **Glyfada Beach Hotel** (Ioannis Mexas). Glyfada, 491 00 Corfu. Tel: (0661) 942-57/58.
- ▶ **Grand Hotel.** Glyfada, 491 00 Corfu. Tel: (0661) 942-01/04.

Lefkada

▶ **Ayios Nikitas.** Ayios Nikitas, 311 00 Lefkada. Tel: (0645) 994-60/61.
▶ **Lefkas Hotel.** Lefkada Town, 311 00 Lefkada. Tel: (0645) 239-16/18.
▶ **Meganisi Hotel.** Meganisi, c/o Dana Travel, Lefkada Town, 311 00 Lefkada. Tel: (0645) 246-50.
▶ **Niricos Hotel.** Lefkada Town, 311 00 Lefkada. Tel: (0645) 241-32/33.
▶ **Odyssey Hotel.** Ayios Nikitas, 311 00 Lefkada. Tel: (0645) 993-66 or contact Dana Travel, (0645) 246-50.
▶ **Porto Galini Hotel.** Lygia, 311 00 Lefkada. Tel: (0645) 924-31/33.
▶ **Xenia Hotel.** Lefkada Town, 311 00 Lefkada. Tel: (0645) 247-62/63.

Kefallonia

▶ **Cephalonia Star.** 50 Paralia Metaxa, **Argostoli**, 281 00 Kefallonia. Tel: (0671) 231-80.
▶ **Filoxenia Guesthouse.** Fiskardo, 281 00 Kefallonia. Tel: (0674) 514-87.
▶ **Fiscardona Guesthouse.** Fiskardo, 281 00 Kefallonia. Tel: (0674) 514-84 or (01) 802-1838.
▶ **Kavos Pension.** Assos, 281 00 Kefallonia. Tel: (0674) 513-76; in winter, 4 Iktinou Street, Herakleion, 713 05 Crete. Tel: (081) 253-015.
▶ **Lara Hotel.** Lourdata, 281 00 Kefallonia. Tel: (0671) 311-56/57; in winter, contact Errikos Benetatos, 13 Konstantinopoleos Street, Ano Pefki, 151 21. Tel: (01) 806-3743.
▶ **Mouikis Hotel.** 3 Vironos Street, **Argostoli**, 281 00 Kefallonia. Tel: (0671) 230-32.
▶ **Mouikis Village.** Lakithra, 281 00 Kefallonia. Tel: (0671) 230-32.
▶ **Olga Hotel.** 82 Paralia Metaxa, **Argostoli**, 281 00 Kefallonia. Tel: (0671) 249-81/84; Fax: (0671) 249-85.
▶ **Panormos.** Fiskardo, 281 00 Kefallonia. Tel: (0674) 513-40.
▶ **White Rocks Hotel and Bungalows.** Platy Yialos, **Argostoli**, 281 00 Kefallonia. Tel: (0671) 283-33.

Ithaca

▶ **Hotel Kioni.** Kioni, 283 00 Ithaca. Tel: (0674) 313-62 and 317-89 (Katherine Ventouras), or contact the Greek Islands Club.
▶ **Mentor Hotel.** Vathy, 283 00 Ithaca. Tel: (0674) 324-33.
▶ **Nostos Hotel.** Frikes, 283 00 Ithaca. Tel: (0674) 316-44.

▶ **Odysseas Hotel. Vathy**, 283 00 Ithaca. Tel: (0674) 323-81.
▶ **Rooms in Kioni.** Mimis (Dimitris) Soukis, **Kioni**, 283 00 Ithaca. Tel: (0674) 312-03.
▶ **Rooms in Vathy.** Polyctor Tours, **Vathy**, 283 00 Ithaca. Tel: (0674) 331-20.

Zakynthos
▶ **Hotel Bitzaro.** 46 D. Roma Street, **Zakynthos Town**, 291 00 Zakynthos. Tel: (0695) 236-44.
▶ **Caravel. Planos**, 291 00 Zakynthos. Tel: (0695) 252-61/63.
▶ **Diana.** 11 Kapodistriou and Mitropoleos, **Zakynthos Town**, 291 00 Zakynthos. Tel: (0695) 285-47.
▶ **La Grotta Hotel. Volimes**, 291 00 Zakynthos. Tel: (0695) 312-24.
▶ **Lina Hotel. Stavros-Psilomatos**, 291 00 Zakynthos. Tel: (0695) 285-31 or 224-59.
▶ **Liuba Cottages. Vasilikos**, 291 00 Zakynthos. Tel: (0695) 353-72.
▶ **Villa Meltemi. Limni Keriou**, 291 00 Zakynthos. Tel: (0695) 333-07/66; in winter, contact Athanasios Plagiarinos, 10 Poseidonos Street, Paleo Phaleron, Athens, 175 61.
▶ **Strada Marina.** 16 K. Lomvardou Street, **Zakynthos Town**, 291 00 Zakynthos. Tel: (0695) 227-61.
▶ **Zante Beach Hotel and Bungalows. Laganas**, 291 00 Zakynthos. Tel: (0695) 511-30; in Athens, 95 Demokratous Street, Athens, 115 21; Tel: (01) 724-5500.

Kythira
▶ **Kaity Pension.** 28 Livanou Street, **Hora**, 801 00 Kythira. Tel: (0735) 313-18.
▶ **Kytheria Pension. Ayia Pelagia**, 801 00 Kythira. Tel: (0735) 333-21.
▶ **Raikos Hotel. Kapsali**, 801 00 Kythira. Tel: (0735) 337-66 or 336-29; in winter, Mrs. Raikou, 8 Chrys. Smyrnis Street, Kato Pefki, 151 22.

ARGO-SARONIC GULF ISLANDS

By John Chapple

The Argo-Saronic Gulf islands are havens from the Athenian metropolis, easily accessible by the Flying Dolphin hydrofoil from Athens's port of Piraeus. The nearest to the mainland, and usually within sight of Athens (except when the weather is particularly muggy), is mountainous **Aégina**. Beyond Aegina is the small island of **Poros**, with its white houses crowded right next to the channel separating it from the Peloponnese. **Hydra** is farther yet, a rock-mountain of an island with one of the loveliest harbors in the Aegean. And finally there is **Spetses**, with the gentlest, greenest landscape of these islands. During the summer months all of the Argo-Saronic Gulf islands are crowded, for they are the weekend playgrounds for many Athenians—some people even commute to Piraeus from Aegina every day.

AEGINA

Aégina (Aíyina) is the nearest island escape from the Athens metropolitan area. It is a mountainous island, but most of the slopes are not steep, and the north and east coasts slide gently to the sea. Here you can enjoy a taste of Greece's ancient, Medieval, and modern history as well as eat in seaside fish tavernas and swim off gentle sand beaches.

MAJOR INTEREST

Archaeological site of Kolona
Omorfi Ekklesia (frescoes)
Medieval church of the Faneromeni
Abandoned Medieval town of Paleohora
Sanctuary of Aphaia
Fishing village of Perdika
Offshore island of Moni: swimming

In Greek mythology, Aegina was one of the daughters of the river Asopos. Zeus was smitten with her and hid her on the island from Hera, his jealous wife. Aegina's father was told of her abduction by the king of Corinth, Sisyphus, who for his treachery was forced to forever roll a heavy stone up a steep hill in Hades. Aegina gave birth to a son, Aiakos, who asked his father for companions; Zeus obliged by turning some ants into humans, the Myrmidons.

When the oracle at Delphi was consulted about a drought, the oracle replied that Zeus would listen only to Aiakos, who prayed to Zeus from the top of Mount Oros, the highest mountain on Aegina. The rains came, and the people built a sanctuary to Zeus on the mountain. Today local fishermen maintain that it will rain whenever Mount Oros is covered in cloud.

Aegina Town

Aegina town, on the west coast of the island, is a harbor town that has not yet decided between its 19th-century past and the advantages of modern concrete. So many ferry boats and Flying Dolphins come in from the Athens-Piraeus urban conglomeration that it is almost an extension, yet it maintains its island ways for all its urban bustle. Notice the 19th-century buildings built when Aegina was the capital of newly independent Greece.

Most of the town's enterprises are right on the waterfront, facing the moored yachts and caïques: restaurants, tourist shops, travel agencies, bakeries, banks, grocery stores, the magazine and paperback bookstore, and the fish market. Down from the boat landing, near the large church of the Panayítsa, there are often small vegetable stands; several

The Argo-Saronic Gulf Islands

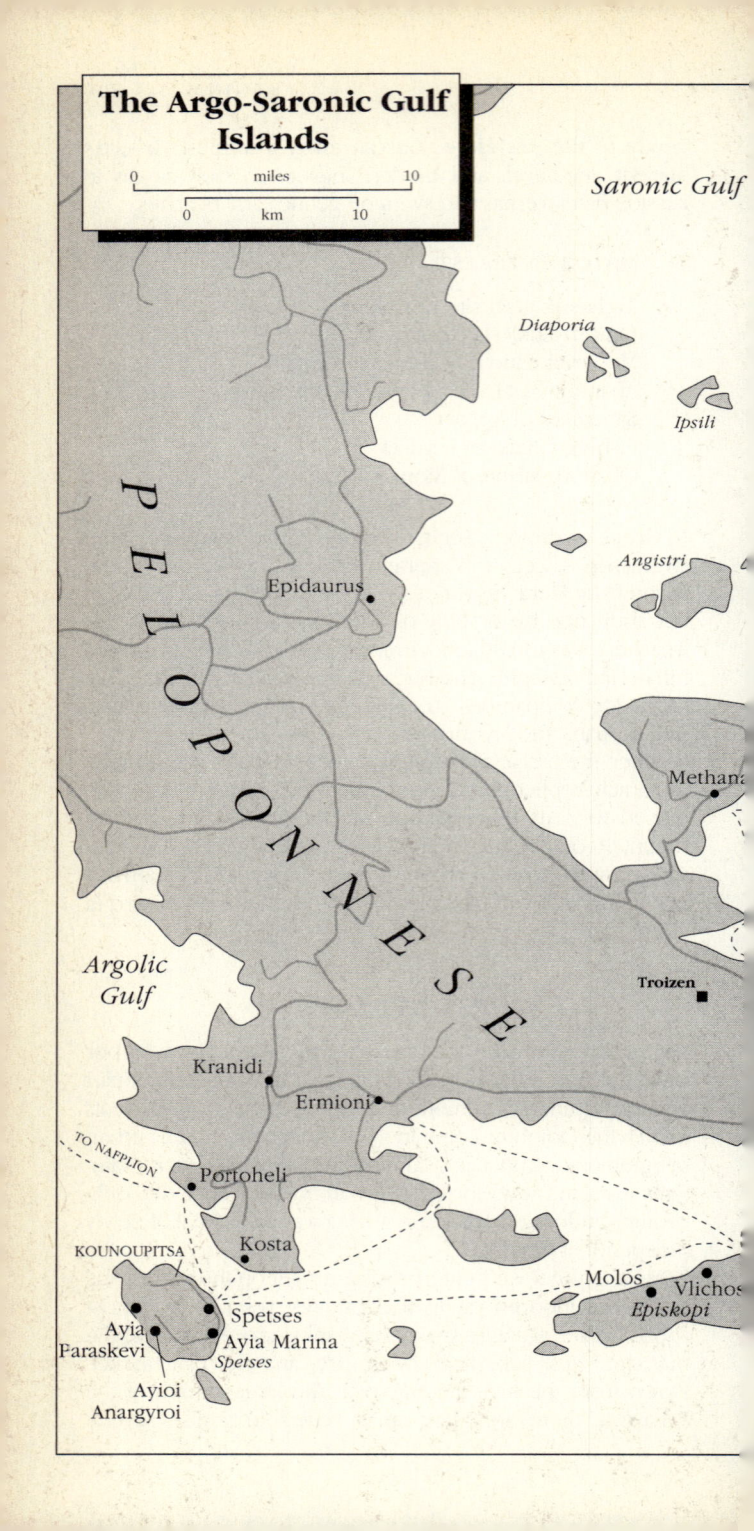

0 miles 10
0 km 10

Saronic Gulf

Diaporia

Ipsili

PELOPONNESE

Epidaurus

Angistri

Methana

Argolic Gulf

Troizen

Kranidi

Ermioni

TO NAFPLION

Portoheli

Kosta

KOUNOUPITSA

Molos • Vlichos
Episkopi

Ayia Paraskevi

Spetses
Ayia Marina
Spetses

Ayioi Anargyroi

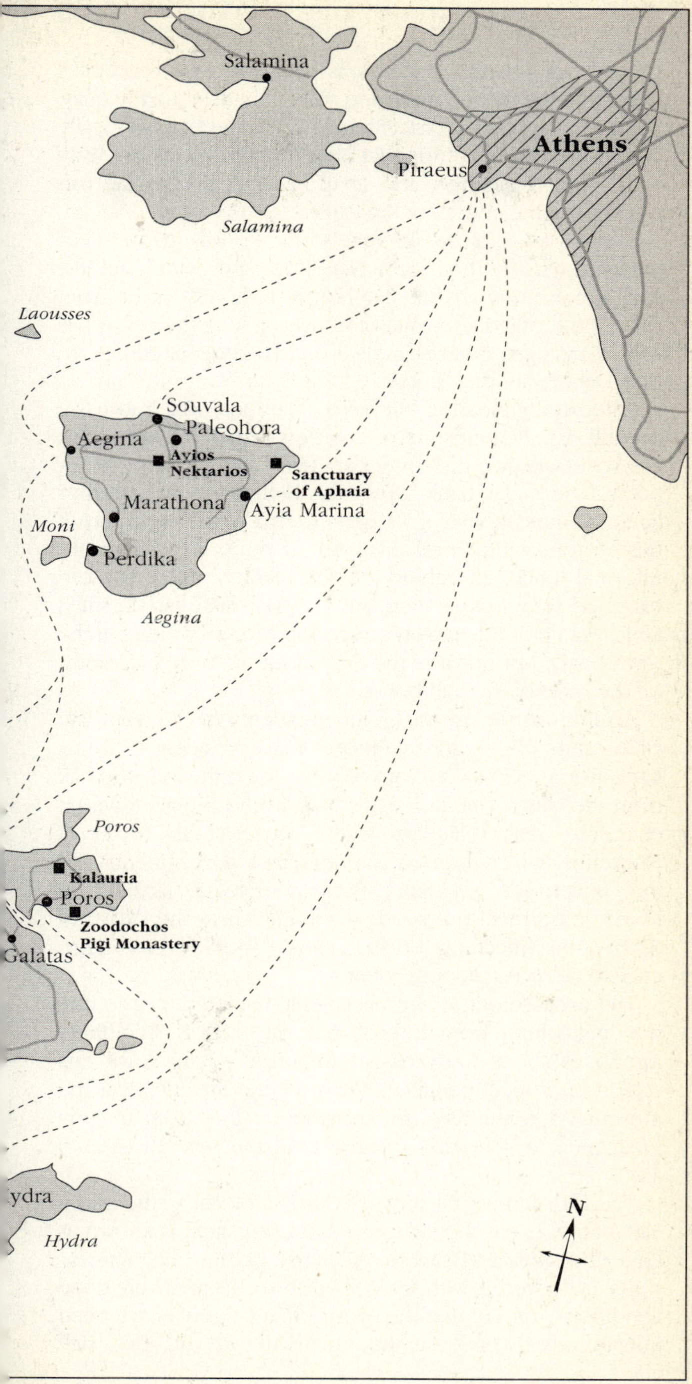

Salamina
Athens
Piraeus
Salamina
Laousses
Souvala
Paleohora
Aegina
Ayios
Nektarios
Sanctuary
of Aphaia
Marathona
Ayia Marina
Moni
Perdika
Aegina
Poros
Kalauria
Poros
Zoodochos
Pigi Monastery
Galatas
ydra
Hydra
N

caïques act as grocery stores as well, bringing vegetables over from the Peloponnese and selling them along the quay. Aegina has extensive pistachio orchards, and bags of locally grown pistachios are for sale all along the waterfront. Buy your fresh bread from the small bakery between the fish market and the church of the Panayitsa.

The most comfortable hotels on the island are near Aegina town. The first is the **Nafsika**, a family-run hotel just past Kolona toward the lighthouse, only 400 yards from town. Built of stone on the bluff overlooking the sea, it has rooms arranged in a rectangle around a large garden court. The **Danae**, another hotel 100 yards farther on, is not so architecturally pleasing but has a small pool and also has a friendly family atmosphere. The best restaurant in town is the **Vostitsano**, on the street parallel to the quay, one block behind the Ionian bank. Open only in the evening, it tries to keep the atmosphere of a Greek taverna of the early part of this century, wine barrels included. If you prefer a far more informal lunch, go behind the fish market, where you can eat grilled octopus, prawns, and various small fish on small tables set up in the narrow street. You can swim either at the town beach just north of the main dock or, more pleasantly, off the rocks at the lighthouse.

Aegina was the capital of independent Greece from late 1826 until 1828, and Greece's first president, Ioannis Kapodistrias, was sworn into office in the cathedral, set back from the waterfront. Some 50 yards from the twin-towered church of Ayios Nikólaos is the square, pink **Tower of Markéllos**, which housed Kapodistrias's government until the governor's residence was completed farther up Kyverníou Street. The residence is known as the Palace of Barbayannis (meaning "Uncle Ioannis"), an affectionate reference to Greece's first president.

The archaeological site of **Kolóna**, named after the one standing column from the sixth-century B.C. Doric **Temple of Apollo**, is about 300 yards north of the Aegina town bus station on a small peninsula. As you enter the site, near the museum, note the reconstructed mosaic floor from an early synagogue, which stood nearby until the seventh century A.D.

The 13th-century basilica of Ayíoi Theódoroi, to the northeast of town near the village of Ayíoi Asómatoi, is known as **Omorfi Ekklesía** (Beautiful Church) because its interior walls are covered with frescoes that are in relatively good condition—except that the eyes of many figures have been gouged out. If you know the way it will take you about half an hour to walk there. The church is kept locked, however, and can be unlocked only by an official from the archaeological museum at Kolona (Tel: 222-48) after the museum closes. Arrange with the official ahead of time, and take him to the site by taxi or horse carriage.

Another 13th-century church, **Faneroméni**, is about 400 yards up the road to Ayia Marina from the old prison on the southern edge of town. According to tradition, the church kept falling down every night while being built until the builders miraculously discovered an icon of the Virgin Mary in a small cave. The underground chapels were finished but other construction was stopped, leaving the church as it stands.

Farther along this road, about 6 km (3.5 miles) east of town, is the **monastery of Ayios Nektários**, in which 22 nuns live. It was built between 1904 and 1910 by the bishop of Pentápolis, who lived here until he died in 1920. The bishop, canonized Ayios Nektarios in 1961, is the newest Greek Orthodox saint, and an increasingly popular one.

Paleohora

On the rocky slopes across the small valley from the monastery of Ayios Nektarios are 38 churches, all that remain of Paleohóra, the old town built by the islanders after Aegina town was sacked in 896 by Arab raiders based on Crete. When Kheir el-Din Barbarossa made his butcherous raids throughout Greece in 1537 he did as much damage as he could to the town, and it was briefly occupied by the Venetians in 1654 during the lengthy fighting between the Venetians and the Ottomans. In the early 19th century the townspeople began moving back to Aegina town, eventually leaving Paleohora deserted.

The small road to both the monastery of Ayios Nektarios and Paleohora branches to the left from the main Aegina town–Ayia Marina road. It heads up a ridge, leaving Paleohora on the right before dropping down to Souvála. Before the road reaches the top of the ridge there is a turn to the right, with parking for a few cars under some pine trees. A path continues to Paleohora, where you can wander among the abandoned Medieval churches, many containing frescoes. The few locked churches will be opened upon request by a caretaker from the Greek Archaeological Service, who is on the site every morning except Tuesdays.

Across the main road from the monastery of Ayios Nektarios and Paleohora, and higher than both, is the **monas-**

tery of **Panayía Chrysoleóntissa**, built early in the 17th century. The nuns who live here welcome anyone who makes the hour's climb (you can also spend the night). Most of the year the monastery is quiet, but many people climb to it on August 15, the feast day of the Virgin Mary.

The Sanctuary of Aphaia

Aphaia, meaning "invisible," was a Cretan-Mycenaean deity who fell into the sea while fleeing King Minos. Some fishermen rescued her and brought her to Aegina, but as soon as they reached the island one of the fishermen pressed his advances. Aphaia fled again, and this time she disappeared. Her pre-Hellenic cult eventually merged with that of Athena.

The Sanctuary of Aphaia stands 325 yards above the port of Ayia Marina, just south of the island's northeastern corner. Lines drawn from it to the Parthenon in Athens and the Temple of Poseidon in Sounion form an equilateral triangle.

Two temples, one dating from the seventh century and one from the sixth century B.C., were built on the site before the present temple was erected in approximately 490 B.C. The fifth-century Doric temple had beautiful Archaic pedimental sculptures, most of which are now in the Munich Glyptothek. Some fragments from the original eastern pediment, including heads of warriors, are in the National Archaeological Museum in Athens. This temple, on a lovely site, is one of the finest examples of Archaic architecture.

Ayia Marina

This little port town below the Sanctuary of Aphaia has become a thriving tourist center; buses make the 30-minute trip from Aegina town to Ayía Marína every half hour in the summer. Ayia Marina has more than 40 hotels, all of them relatively recent concrete structures. The sea here is cleaner than on the other side of the island, however, so if you want to stay here consider either the **Apollo** or the **Argo** hotel, in that order. The Apollo is the larger and more comfortable of the two, with high ceilings and, therefore, cool rooms. Both have fine views down over the bay. **Soto's Grotto**, on the rocks beside the Apollo hotel, is a good place for an informal lunch. Soto's serves fine omelettes and excellent sandwiches, and the *galeos,* a member of the shark family, is delicious.

Incongruous though it may be in such a setting, the **Bonsai** Japanese restaurant has excellent food. Take the Ayia

Marina road all the way down past where it turns right to run parallel to the water, then take the first left leading down to the beach; the Bonsai is on the left. Tables are set on a veranda beneath grape vines. The meat, fish, and vegetable dishes are cooked smartly in light oil by your table. If you want to go to the opposite cultural extreme, try the **Honey Tree**, a real country taverna a short way out of town off the road to Aegina. Two other good tavernas are **Takis** and **Costas**, 2 km (about a mile) west of Ayia Marina in the village of **Alones**. For swimming around Ayia Marina, base yourself at the small jetty or at the sandy bay just to the south.

Perdika

Pérdika is a small fishing village on the island's southwestern point, its harbor a haven for caïques and small yachts. The waterfront is lined with fish restaurants, any one of which is a pleasure—far nicer than the restaurants in Aegina town. The **Moondy Bay Hotel** at Marathóna, approximately 4 km (2.5 miles) north of Perdika, is a good bungalow hotel on what amounts to its own quiet bay, with a full complement of sailboats and windsurfers available for rent. Staying here and eating your meals in Perdika is a good strategy.

The best place to swim in Aegina is not on Aegina itself, but on **Moní**, the little island just offshore from Perdika. Small boats leave frequently for the ten-minute trip from Perdika to Moni, where you can either swim off the gentle sand beach or cross the headland to swim off the rocks.

GETTING AROUND

Regular ferry boats leave throughout the day from Piraeus for the 90-minute trip to Aegina. Smaller boats, designated "Express," make the journey in about 75 minutes. Some of these boats go to Souvala as well as Aegina town, and some go to Ayia Marina. During the summer the hydrofoils, known as Flying Dolphins, leave from the main Piraeus harbor for Aegina town and take only 35 minutes. For information about the Flying Dolphins, call the main office in Piraeus between 8:00 A.M. and 7:00 P.M. at (01) 452-7107. On Aegina, check with the Flying Dolphin ticket stand by the main pier in Aegina town for connections to other islands.

You can get around on the island by taxi, bus, or moped. The few taxis are most likely to be found waiting near the piers for passengers disembarking from the ferries or the Flying Dolphins. The bus service throughout the island is good; the bus station is on the northern edge of Aegina town, just to the left as you come off the dock. There are several places where you can rent mopeds, but the most convenient is next to the second *períptero* as you walk to your right from the Flying Dolphin pier along the quay.

POROS

Poros really is two islands. The small island on which the white town is crowded, right above the waterfront, is separated from the main body of the island by a small canal that runs past the Naval School. The town is a busy place, accentuated by the coming and going of ferry boats and Flying Dolphins. The town's great appeal is its collection of white buildings rising directly up from the water; from the ferry's upper deck you seem to be just out of reach from somebody's third floor. Much of the main body of the island is covered with pine trees, and there are beaches along the coast both to the east and west. There are ancient remains on both the island and the Peloponnese opposite, and many buildings from the early 19th century as well. Poros town runs along the waterfront, with pleasant small stores and restaurants.

MAJOR INTEREST

Sanctuary of Poseidon
Damalas, on the mainland, for ancient Troizen

The area around Poros is rich in both myth and history. One of the early mythological kings, Saron, gave his name to the Saronic Gulf by drowning in its waters, and Troizen, who lent his name to the city of Troizen and peninsula of Troizenia on the Peloponnese just across the straits, was the son of Pelops, whose land we know as Pelops's Island, or the Peloponnese. Plutarch reports Theseus's father as Aegeus, the king of Athens, and tells the story of his being raised in Troizen. When Theseus was 16 years old his mother told him his father was Aegeus, who had left sandals and a sword for the boy under a large rock. Theseus easily lifted the rock to retrieve the tokens before setting off on his adventurous trip to Athens. The modern inhabitants of Troizen (today called Damalas), about 8 km (5 miles) from Galatas directly across from Poros town, have identified the stone Theseus lifted and set it on a concrete base. Aegeus gave his name to the Aegean Sea by jumping to his death at Sounion when Theseus failed to raise white sails to signal to his father that his journey to kill the Minotaur in Crete had been triumphant.

Poros means "passage," or "ford," and it came to be associated with a Medieval settlement of farmers who lived on the island for safety and crossed over the straits to work the fertile fields of Troizen. Herdsmen brought cheese and milk to the nearest point on the mainland across from the island, which came to be known as Galatas (Milkman). (There is a more famous Galatas over another "poros," or strait, the Bosphorus, in what is now Istanbul.)

After the Ottoman fleet was destroyed at Navarino on October 20, 1827, the English, French, and Russian ambassadors to the Ottoman Empire met at Poros to formulate what is known as the Protocols of Poros, which led to Greece's becoming a kingdom in 1832. In 1831 the Hydriots raised a short-lived but dramatic uprising against the government of Kapodistrias by capturing the ships in the Poros harbor, the government's arsenal, and Fort Heideck, the small island fort controlling the southern approach to the harbor. When Kapodistrias called in Russian ships, the Hydriot admiral Miaoulis defiantly blew up the two ships he controlled before escaping with his men to Hydra.

Poros Town

Poros town, with its whitewashed houses rising up a hill topped by a clock tower, is as pleasant as it is picturesque. Virtually all of the island's business takes place along the waterfront, extending from the Naval School to the north down to where the ferry boats and Flying Dolphins dock and then on down toward the small lighthouse at the island's southern tip. There is a constant flow of people, bicycles, cars, and boats along the extended waterfront. If you want to stay in town the **Seven Brothers Hotel**, right behind the main square where the ferries dock, is a clean, family-run establishment with a good restaurant on the ground floor. The **Poros Hotel** is about a mile northwest of town (to the west [left] after the Naval School). It is one of the cement-box constructions built so often in Greece, but it is quiet, well set into the land, and right on the water. The **Pavlou Hotel**, a few hundred yards farther on and with its own swimming pool, is another good choice.

If you walk southeast along the quay from where the ferries dock you'll see several *ouzeries,* Greek bars serving ouzo with *mezé* (appetizers, notably delicious grilled octopus), along with wine and other drinks. There are also many restaurants in this area. You can get a perfectly good meal at any one of them, but the best-known place for your evening meal is **The Sailor**, about 100 yards away. Another spot for fish, slightly inland, is **The Dolphin**. To reach it, go down the narrow street by the post office, and then turn left up the stairs. They have as good fresh fish as you can find on the island. The third restaurant to keep in mind is the **Zazas**, at the other end of town, immediately before the Naval School. The Zazas is open for both lunch and dinner and has a good selection of meat dishes, notably a fine beef stroganoff.

Excursions

The beach beneath the 18th-century monastery of Zoodóchos Pigí—northeast of town, approximately 20 minutes by bus or boat—is a good place to swim. The water is clean and there are three tavernas near the beach. You can also swim at **Neórion Bay**, northwest of town (the water is cleaner and the swimming more private the farther from town you go). A boat can be hired to take you to one of the small bays near the eastern lighthouse and pick you up for the return journey. The ruins in the last bay before Cape Neda are of an early-19th-century Russian naval station. If you wish, you can rent a small boat to pilot yourself for the day.

Ruins of the ancient city of **Kalauria** and the **Sanctuary of Poseidon** are in the center of the island, 5 km (3 miles) northeast of the modern town. The ancient Greek orator Demosthenes took refuge in the Sanctuary of Poseidon after the Athenian revolt against Macedonian rule following the death of Alexander the Great, but the Athenians were obliged to surrender him to Antipater. When he was found by an Athenian supporter of the Macedonians he swallowed poison, stepping outside the temple before he died so as not to defile the sanctuary. The ancient town was abandoned after Slav raids in the third and sixth centuries. Very few ruins remain, for much of the ancient building material was used in constructing the monastery of the Panayia on Hydra in the 19th century.

There is little of interest in Galatás, on the Peloponnese immediately across the straits from Poros town, but if you continue 8 km (5 miles) to the west, 15 minutes by bus, you can visit the extensive ruins of the ancient city of **Troizen**, including the lower walls of several sanctuaries, the **Temple of Hippolytus** (the ill-fated son of Theseus and stepson of Phaedra), and the **Asklepieion** (Hospital). Immediately to the west of ancient Troizen is the **Devil's Gorge**, up an unpaved road that turns past an ancient tower toward the mountain. The road becomes a footpath and passes over a narrow bridge high above the gorge. A face, presumably of the devil, is carved into the steep rock sides below the bridge.

You may wish to go swimming at **Alíki** and **Artemos** along the coast south of Galatas, below the extensive lemon forest. For information and assistance about any of these excursions, visit Greek Island Tours in Poros town (Tel: 0298-242-55). Their office is to the left of the ferry boat and Flying Dolphin landing area, before the telephone exchange (OTE). You may also want to talk with them about finding accommodations, for they will know what hotels have space, and they represent several studio apartments.

GETTING AROUND

Regular ferry boats leave from the main harbor in Piraeus and take two and a half hours to reach Poros. The Flying Dolphins, which leave from the Zea harbor in Piraeus, take an hour and 15 minutes. For information about the Flying Dolphins, call the main office in Piraeus between 8:00 A.M. and 7:00 P.M. at (01) 452-7107. Once you are on Poros, visit the Flying Dolphin ticket stand opposite the quay where the Flying Dolphins dock for information about moving on to another island.

Boats approaching Poros from the north squeeze through a narrow channel and turn south into the protected water between the island and the peninsula of Troizenia, continuing on to dock by the town's main street. If you are on one of the steamers you will not miss this view, but if you are on a Flying Dolphin, when you near the island be sure you're in a spot on the vessel from which you can see.

Once on Poros, you will get around by the buses that leave from the town's central square, by taxi, or by small boat. These boats are for hire along the quay, and they regularly cross to Galatas. Buses leave from Galatas to Troizen, and there are some, but not many, taxis. You can also negotiate with the boat operators to take you to Neorion or the monastery beach on Poros to swim.

HYDRA

Hydra (Ydra) is a long, thin, dry rock, 14 miles long and only about 4 miles wide. Its beautiful harbor is one of the gems of the Aegean, ringed by tiers of 19th-century buildings, many of them impressive mansions built by shipping wealth. Although there are many shops, mostly along the waterfront, good sense has been used in tastefully restoring many of the old houses and in maintaining the island's traditional appearance.

MAJOR INTEREST

Harbor
Archontiká, 19th-century mansions
Monastery of the Panayia

Hydra Town

The history of the island is dominated by one short period in the late 18th and early 19th centuries when Hydriot captains were occupied in international shipping, gaining the seafaring expertise and money that they used against the Ottomans during the Greek War of Independence. The captains built the large gray mansions known as *archontiká,* all constructed in the early years of the 19th century, designed by Italian architects and built by itinerant Greek workmen from the central Peloponnese, Epirus, Pelion, and Tinos. These mansions dominate the harbor, from the Tsamádos house (now the National Merchant Marine Academy) to the east of the harbor through the Tombázis (School of Fine Arts), Voúlgaris, Koundouriótis, and Votsis houses to the west. The **monastery of the Panayía**, with its clock tower, was built in the 1760s and 1770s, incorporating much ancient building material from the Sanctuary of Poseidon on the nearby island of Poros.

Hydra town forms three sides of a rough rectangle around the harbor, with the sea to the north. The ships and Flying Dolphins land on the east side, and the Flying Dolphin ticket office is just up the road from the harbor in the southeast corner.

If you plan to stay on the island, make reservations at the small **Orloff Guest House**, managed by Irene Tragea, approximately 80 yards up the road from the harbor's southwest corner. The term "guesthouse" is apt, for staying here is like visiting hospitable friends in a tastefully restored old island mansion. The rooms are air-conditioned and have fresh flowers, and, most unusual for Greece, the windows have screens. A complete Continental breakfast is served in the enclosed garden, lined with honeysuckle and bougainvillaea. The **Miranda Guest House** is also a restored island mansion, not quite as attractive as the Orloff but a good second choice. To reach it, turn up the road just before and parallel to the road leading to the Orloff Guest House.

In general, the better dining spots are away from the harbor, although the **Archontiko** restaurant near the center of the southern side of the harbor rectangle has fresh fish and good service. There are several comfortable restaurants up from the southeast corner of the harbor. Take the left fork approximately 30 yards after the Flying Dolphin ticket agency. Soon you will see the **Loulaki Bar**, popular with the social set. Past it, on the right, is the **Three Brothers** taverna, which serves standard, good, Greek fare throughout the week. Beyond the Three Brothers is **The Garden** restaurant, locally known for serving good meat. Another reliable taverna, the **Kseri Elia**, also known by the owner's name, Doukos, can be reached by walking down the narrow street immediately outside the wall of The Garden restaurant (as you leave The Garden, go to the left). Turn right on the first road and then left again as soon as possible; the Kseri Elia will be straight ahead. All these restaurants and tavernas have tables in shaded gardens. The **Remezzo**, up from the southwest corner of the harbor and near the Orloff Guest House, is another Greek taverna well worth trying. At Vlichós, 2.5 km (1.5 miles) down the coast to the southwest, there are two more delightful tavernas, **Kyria Maria** and, right on the water's edge with a marvelous view of the sunset, **Eliovasilema**.

You can swim almost anywhere along the shore, but the most pleasant places are at the farthest hamlets of **Palamidás** and **Molos**, down the coast to the southwest, where the sandy beaches are usually less crowded. Arrange with one of the caïques or boat taxis to take you down and pick you up (no cars or motorbikes are permitted on the island).

You'll probably spend your time on Hydra near the shore, but there are six monasteries on the mountain and a small, hidden, fertile valley known as **Episkopí** above Molos. The monasteries, which date from the 18th and 19th centuries, are unusual only in that they are on an island so close to the mainstream of modern life yet remain so far removed. You can reach them only by walking or on a mule. It takes an hour to reach the nearest, **Ayía Matróna**, which is now occupied by a small group of nuns. If you're curious and would like more information, pick up a copy of Catherine Vanderpool's *Hydra,* a concise, thorough guide to the island.

GETTING AROUND

Regular ferry boats make the three hour and 15 minute trip from Piraeus to Hydra twice each day during the summer. The Flying Dolphins, which leave from the Zea harbor in Piraeus, take only an hour and 50 minutes, and make 11 trips each day. For information about the Flying Dolphins, call the main office in Piraeus between 8:00 A.M. and 7:00 P.M. at (01) 452-7107.

No cars or motorcycles are permitted on the island, but you can easily get around by taking a caïque or a water taxi. The small caïques, which are slower and far less expensive than the water taxis, leave from the center of the southern side of the harbor. The water taxis depart from the southeast corner. See the Flying Dolphin office just up from the southeast corner of the harbor about moving on to another island.

SPETSES

Spetses, the greenest of the Argo-Saronic Gulf islands, is farthest from Athens. It has gentler slopes and more beaches than either Poros or Hydra and a cleaner sea than Aegina. Here, as on Hydra, successful 19th-century ship captains built large mansions, but the great houses seem less dominating on these more congenial hills. The town is open and relaxed, with comfortable, although not luxurious, hotels and enough restaurants, tavernas, and beaches for a pleasant and varied stay.

MAJOR INTEREST

Dapia harbor area
The Old Harbor

Spetses Town

The **Dápia**—the small harbor in the center of Spetses town guarded by aging cannon next to the pier where the Flying Dolphins dock—is the town's congenial, bustling heart, with cafés, restaurants, hotels, the Flying Dolphin office, and the all-important central kiosk. There are more than 20 hotels and rooming houses on the island, most of them in Spetses town. The **Possidonion Hotel**, on the northwest side of the Dapia, is an imposing Belle Epoque structure whose rooms do not quite match the quality of its impressive façade. The **Spetses** and **Kasteli** hotels, although not as architecturally interesting, provide more comfortable accommodation. Both are on the island's northwest coast, the Spetses Hotel half a mile from Dapia and the Kasteli hotel another 200 yards farther on, immediately after the Anargyrios and Koryialenios School.

Restaurants are grouped in or near the Dapia (including at Clock Tower Square, inland just a few blocks south of the Dapia), in the Old Harbor (see below), and along the northwestern shore from the Possidonion Hotel toward the school. Of the restaurants in town, don't miss **Lazaros's**, up the hill past the police station from Clock Tower Square. Lazaros's is an old-fashioned family taverna, with wine barrels, old Greek music on the jukebox, and a consistent refusal to adopt things modern and plastic—and the food is good, too.

The Old Harbor

The Old Harbor is 1.5 km (about a mile) southeast of the Dapia, to the right as you face the sea. To get there you can take a horse-drawn carriage from the small square adjacent to the Dapia and ride in style. If you choose to walk, take the right fork at the kiosk past the town beach and go straight up the hill past the **monastery of Ayios Nikólaos**. The monastery was built in the 17th century, although extensive repairs have since been made; the white-marble campanile was built in 1905. The Spetses flag was flown from this campanile in 1821 to show that the island had joined the erupting Greek War of Independence against the Ottomans.

The Old Harbor still provides safe anchorage for large sailing boats, and many 19th-century mansions, most of them with pebble mosaics, overlook the harbor from the slopes. There are several pleasant waterfront restaurants, of which by far the best—and most expensive—is **Trehandiri**, at the beginning of the harbor as you enter from the Dapia.

The road continues past the **Ligeri** restaurant, open only in the evening, to the **Sioras** restaurant, with tables on a wooden platform over the water. Sioras has fresh fish and delicious cooked dishes. **Vassilis's** café, adjacent to the Sioras restaurant, has a small, tasty selection of dishes that can be ordered with an ouzo. The **Mourayio** restaurant, on the left before the first of the remaining shipyards for which Spetses once was famous, has aspirations. Fifty yards inland from the first shipyard is the small 19th-century **church of the Evangelístria**, which partly covers a small 6th-century basilica.

Past the **Il Padrino** bar the road rises over a small peninsula to more shipyards and the inner harbor, which is packed with boats and cocktail bars. Occasionally you will see the bare ribs of a caïque under construction.

The slopes of the lighthouse headland are dotted with villas, and there are two ruined windmills there. Between these windmills are the ruins of another fifth- or sixth-century Christian basilica.

Northwest of Spetses Town

The road that leads northwest from Spetses town passes by the Possidonion Hotel to a pleasant stretch of coast known as **Kounoupítsa**. Of the several 19th-century houses here, note **Bouboulina's** house, past the town hall. Bouboulina was the famous woman admiral who, among other exploits during the Greek War of Independence, blockaded the Turkish garrison in Nafplion. The coast here is dotted with bars and restaurants all the way down to the Anargyrios and Koryialenios School. This enjoyable proliferation has been encouraged by the many English tourists who visit the island. The **Patralis** restaurant, 50 yards before the Spetses Hotel, has tables right over the water and a deserved reputation for serving well-prepared fresh fish. Between the Spetses and Kasteli hotels is the Anargyrios and Koryialenios School, which functions only as a conference center, a far cry from the days when John Fowles taught here and dreamed up *The Magus,* which was set on Spetses.

Around the Island

For swimming, take one of the several large caïques that leave the Dapia in the morning with groups for **Zogeriá**, **Ayía Paraskeví**, and **Ayioi Anárgyroi**, all of which have fine sand beaches. (Ayia Paraskevi tends to be the least crowded, but Ayioi Anargyroi, on the west coast of the island, has two summer tavernas. If the weather is calm, you can take a water taxi to one of them, **Tasos's**, for a lovely dining experience.) You can reach **Ayia Marína**, on the east coast, by an easy 30-minute walk or by bus from town. If you want to swim without any crowds, arrange with a water taxi in the Dapia to take you to and pick you up from any stretch of coast you like. If you rent a motorbike you can get around the island on your own and, if you're lucky, find an unoccupied cove.

GETTING AROUND

You can reach the village of Kosta on the Peloponnese across from Spetses by bus and then take a water taxi to the island, but going by ship is easier. The ferry boats take approximately five hours to make the journey that the Flying Dolphins, leaving from Zea harbor in Piraeus, make in two hours and 15 minutes. For information about the Flying Dolphins, call the main office in Piraeus between 8:00 A.M. and 7:00 P.M. at (01) 452-7107. Arrange your travel to any other island or back to Piraeus with the Flying Dolphin office in the Dapia.

During the day buses leave from the town beach southeast of the Dapia for Ayioi Anargyroi and stop at Ayia Marina on the way. There is one automobile taxi, which is difficult to find, but there are many horse-drawn carriages. The carriages for the Old Harbor wait in the small square near the pier on the southeast side of the Dapia; those that head up the northwest coast road toward the Spetses and Kasteli hotels wait below the Possidonion Hotel. Caïques leaving from the Dapia make regular trips to several beaches. The water taxis, based in the Dapia harbor, are considerably more expensive, but you can arrange with them to go virtually anywhere you wish around the island or on the opposite coast.

ACCOMMODATIONS REFERENCE

Aegina

▶ **Apollo Hotel.** Ayia Marina, 180 10 Aegina. Tel: (0297) 322-71/74.

▶ **Argo Hotel.** Ayia Marina, 180 10 Aegina. Tel: (0297) 322-66.

▶ **Danae Hotel.** Aegina Town, 180 10 Aegina. Tel: (0297) 224-24/25.

- ▶ **Moondy Bay Hotel.** Perdika, 180 10 Aegina. Tel: (0297) 251-47.
- ▶ **Nafsika Bungalows. Aegina Town**, 180 10 Aegina. Tel: (0297) 224-77; Fax: (0297) 223-33.

Poros
- ▶ **Pavlou Hotel.** 180 20 Poros. Tel. (0298) 227-34.
- ▶ **Poros Hotel.** 180 20 Poros. Tel: (0298) 222-16.
- ▶ **Seven Brothers Hotel.** 180 20 Poros. Tel: (0298) 234-12.

Hydra
- ▶ **Miranda Guest House.** 180 40 Hydra. Tel: (0298) 522-30.
- ▶ **Orloff Guest House.** 180 40 Hydra. Tel: (0298) 525-64.

Spetses
- ▶ **Kasteli Hotel.** 180 50 Spetses. Tel: (0298) 723-11.
- ▶ **Possidonion Hotel.** 180 50 Spetses. Tel: (0298) 722-08.
- ▶ **Spetses Hotel.** 180 50 Spetses. Tel: (0298) 726-02; Fax: (0298) 724-94.

THE CYCLADES

*By Jeffrey Carson
and Elizabeth Boleman Herring*

Jeffrey Carson has lived on the island of Paros since 1970 and teaches art history at the Aegean Center for the Arts. The author of four books, he is also an art-book reviewer and occasional tour leader in Greece. Elizabeth Boleman Herring is editor of The Southeastern Review: A Quarterly Journal of the Humanities in the Southeastern Mediterranean. *She is also a professor of journalism at Southeastern College in Athens and the author of four books.*

It is hard to articulate precisely why these islands have so captured our imagination; though beautiful, there is nothing voluptuous about them. Dry, mountainous, and rough-coasted, the Cyclades are a granite and limestone archipelago in the Aegean Sea east of the Peloponnese. The soil is rocky and the sea-lanes treacherous (T. S. Eliot called the Cyclades "anfractuous"). Yet anyone with an interest in Greek mythology and art or the historical and intellectual origins of Western Civilization, or who simply loves the Aegean and sunlight in clear water, is irresistibly drawn to these islands. Even summer crowds cannot conceal that Mykonos has the prettiest village in Greece, Naxos the most splendid landscape, Santorini the most majestic bay.

It is a traveller's truism that the most appealing places tend to be developed for tourism first, and so it is with the Cyclades. Though some of our choices, such as Milos and Andros, are rather untouristy, and no member of the archipelago is unworthy of a visit, we discuss those islands

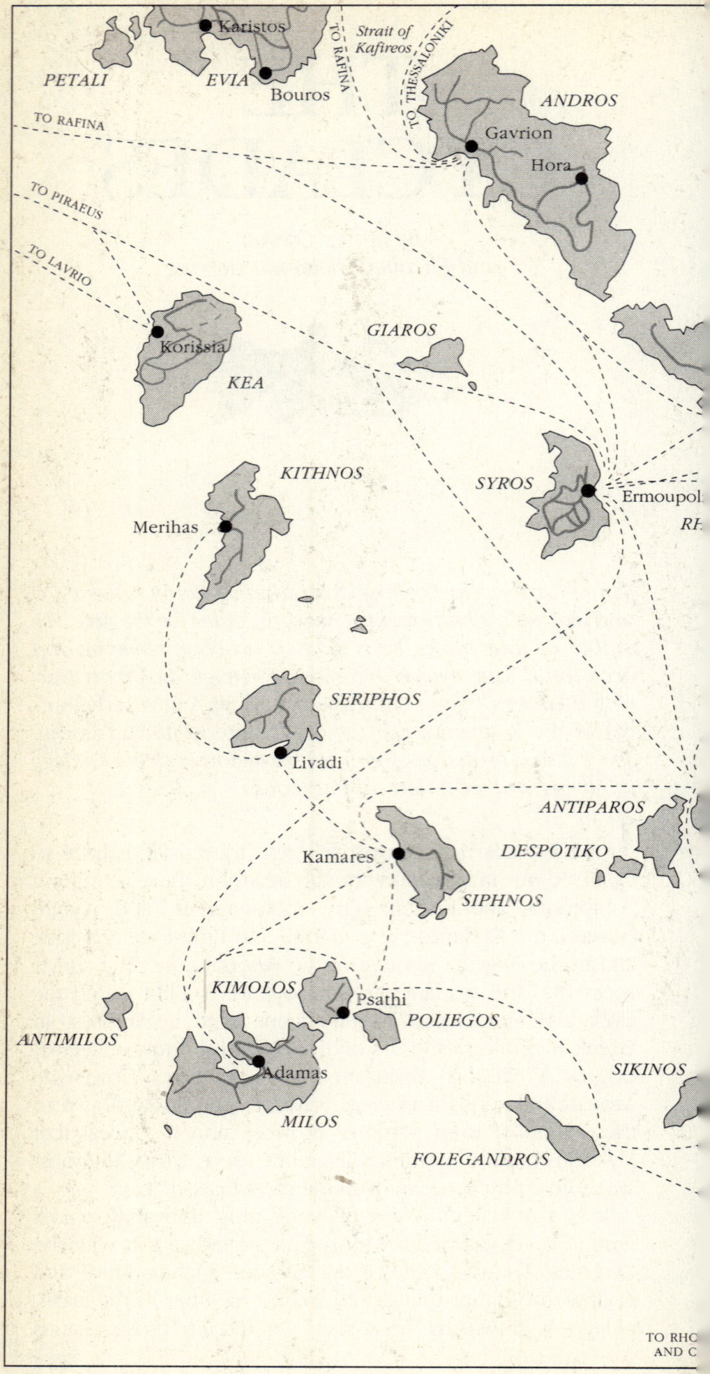
Karistos
PETALI
EVIA
Bouros
TO RAFINA
Strait of Kafireos
TO THESSALONIKI
ANDROS
Gavrion
Hora
TO RAFINA
TO PIRAEUS
TO LAVRIO
Korissia
KEA
GIAROS
KITHNOS
SYROS
Ermoupol
Merihas
SERIPHOS
Livadi
ANTIPAROS
DESPOTIKO
Kamares
SIPHNOS
KIMOLOS
Psathi
POLIEGOS
ANTIMILOS
Adamas
MILOS
SIKINOS
FOLEGANDROS
TO RHO
AND C

The Cyclades

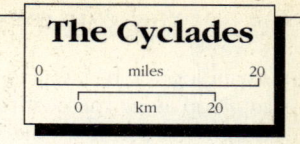

Aegean Sea

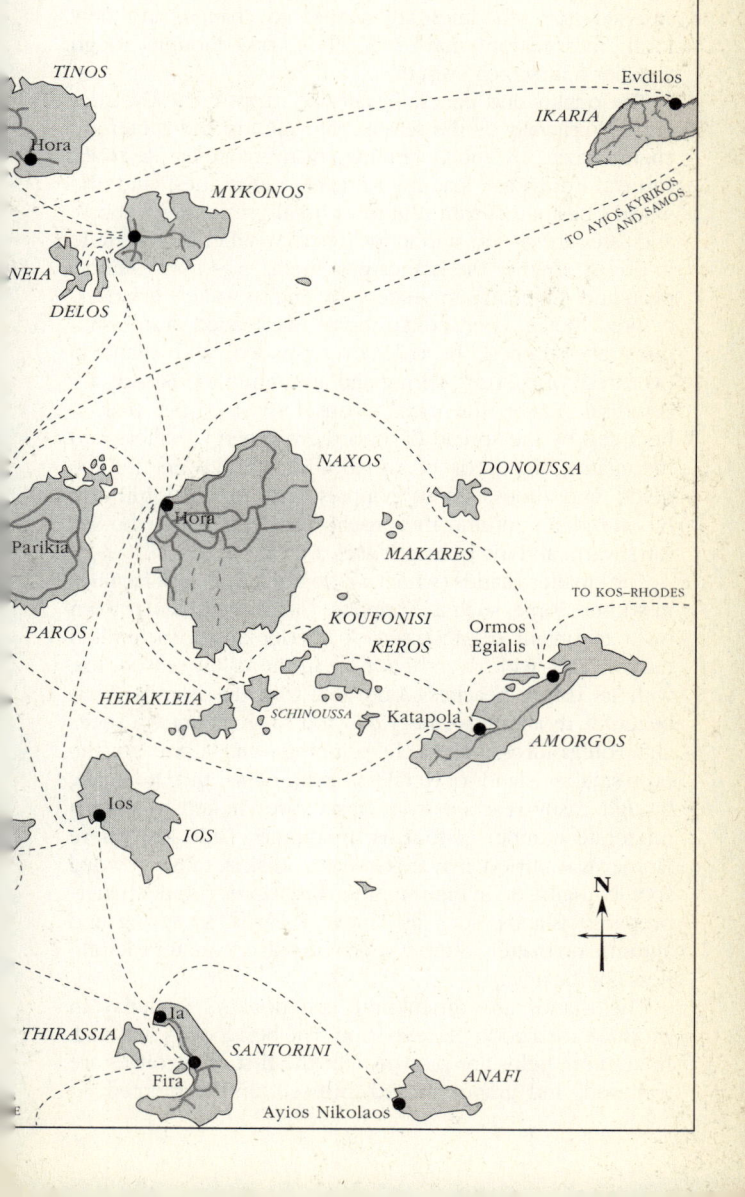

TINOS
Hora
MYKONOS
Evdilos
IKARIA
TO AYIOS KYRIKOS AND SAMOS
NEIA
DELOS
NAXOS
DONOUSSA
Parikia
Hora
MAKARES
PAROS
KOUFONISI
KEROS
TO KOS–RHODES
Ormos Egialis
HERAKLEIA
SCHINOUSSA
Katapola
AMORGOS
Ios
IOS
N
THIRASSIA
Ia
SANTORINI
ANAFI
Fira
Ayios Nikolaos

outstanding for beauty and interest. It is good strategy to island-hop along the boat routes: Syros–Paros–Naxos–Ios–Amorgos–Santorini is one possibility; Kythnos–Seriphos–Siphnos–Milos–Folegandros is another. In season innumerable ferries, steamers, and small caïques crisscross the Cyclades in a bewildering pattern, making boat information confusing, but an intricate itinerary feasible. It must be stressed that schedules are subject to change, and only local information may be relied on—though rough weather may scotch even that.

The quality and general aspect of a trip to the Cyclades depend crucially on the season. Late autumn and winter are characterized by much farming, many name-day festivals, carnival festivities leading to Lent's austerities, and the world's best citrus fruit. But most hotels, restaurants, shops, and cafés are closed, and in inclement weather there is little to do. In summer the islands give themselves over to European and Athenian sun-seekers: By August waiters are overworked, hotels overbooked, boats overloaded, water supplies overstrained, beaches overcrowded, and islanders overtired. In contrast, spring and autumn in the islands are paradisal. Easter, the most joyous festival of the year, is heralded by the spread of a northern green to valleys and mountains; hundreds of varieties of wildflowers fill the fields, and thousands of poppies turn terraced hillsides blood-red. In autumn the beaches are empty, but the sea stays warm and the pomegranates are ripe.

The smaller islands (which we do not cover) lack facilities in winter. Some, such as **Sériphos**, with its spectacular town on a mountain of Medusa-rock overlooking a yacht-filled harbor; **Kea**, with rivers that flow in the driest season; **Ios**, with its dainty beaches; **Amorgós**, with the islands' most beautiful monastery—the Hozoviótissa, built into a sheer cliff; **Folégandros**, with its cliff-gripping white village; and the even smaller islands of **Herákleia**, **Schinoússa**, and **Donoússa**, though easily reached from Naxos, are choked by even a moderate number of tourists in summer. Little Ios, where Homer was buried, may be Greece's noisiest, most crowded spot in August. So in high summer and winter visit the better-prepared islands, such as Tinos or Paros. In spring and autumn, no matter where you go you will encounter friendliness and beauty.

The islands are agricultural, and donkeys loaded with produce are a good place to shop. The best food is seasonal. In autumn, fields are plowed after the first rains, olives are gathered, and grapes picked, pressed, and fermented. In winter trees and vines are pruned and walls rebuilt. In spring vegetables are planted. In early summer grain is reaped, winnowed, and stacked. In May and June, when the seas are calmest, fishing boats sail for weeks at a time, often selling their catch in Piraeus. (In all Greek restaurants, fresh fish is sold by the kilo, according to category; you should choose the fish yourself.) Farmers' cheese is richest in winter, when the animals graze on grass. A shortfall of rain since 1986, however, has made farming more precarious.

Tourism, though, has made the islands rich; rich, but not luxurious. There are few quality hotels and even fewer elegant restaurants; most attempts at the latter are inauthentic rip-offs. Consequently, our recommendations, except where indicated, tend toward practical, pleasant places, and to fresh, simple food.

The word Cyclades derives from "circle" (or "cycle"), and the islands circle the ancient religious center of Delos, itself too barren for more mundane use. Although as early as 8000 B.C. Melian obsidian lured visitors, villages did not appear in the Cyclades for another 4,000 years. The earliest examples excavated were on Kea and Saliagos in the Antiparos strait. After 3000 B.C. the islands suddenly bloomed. Rich burials unearthed on the islets of Keros, near Naxos, revealed the production of fine sculpture, pottery, and jewelry. The cultural blossoming continued during the subsequent Minoan and Mycenaean epochs, as the ruins on Santorini and Milos attest. The islands were colonized during Greece's Dark Ages (1100 to 900 B.C.) and reemerged in the Geometric and Archaic periods as centers of Ionian civilization, rich in poetry, sculpture, architecture, and philosophy. The Persian ascendancy (500 B.C.) suppressed this golden age, though the islands, first under Persia, then Classical Athens, then Macedonia, and finally Ptolemaic Egypt, stayed prosperous until the Roman age. The Byzantines evinced scant interest in the archipelago, and plagues, invasions, and rampant piracy caused severe depopulation. The Cyclades became an independent Venetian protectorate in 1207, with the capital at Naxos, and despite struggles with piracy the islands grew slowly more prosperous—even after the 16th-century Turkish conquest. Traces of this rich past are everywhere: strewn in fields, built into houses, found in the little local museums, and embodied in the spirit and traditions of the people.

ANDROS

Andros, the northernmost of the Cyclades, is a Janus-faced island: Sun-bleached and typically Cycladic (barren, rocky) to the north (where it is separated from southern Evia by the Strait of Kafiréos, or Doro Passage), the island is a watershed to the southeast, where springs keep its valleys and hillside villages full of flowers year round. Some geologists maintain that this abundance of water has its source in the Evian mountains, reaching Andros through seabed aquifers. Whatever its origins, the water of Andros, especially that bottled at Sariza, both still and sparkling, is as famous throughout Greece as Perrier and Badoit are in France. Tourists of another era came to Sariza to "take the waters"; today's visitors are just as likely to come to Andros for the salt variety lapping the island's numerous and uncrowded beaches and coves.

MAJOR INTEREST

Patrician Hora: Modern art and archaeological museums
"Private" beaches dotting the west coast
More than 70 beautiful villages, many "undiscovered"
Byzantine churches and monasteries
Verdant countryside
Mineral springs
Nightingales
Unusual schist walls and dovecotes

Once sacred to Dionysus, Andros was inhabited at least as early as the Mycenaean period (1500 to 1100 B.C.), though the most impressive ancient finds on the island date from the ninth century B.C. and the late Geometric period (900 to 700 B.C.), when Zagorá, on a windswept southern headland, was the island's architecturally impressive capital. From 600 B.C. to A.D. 330, Paleopolis succeeded Zagora, following which, until A.D. 1202, Andros was an important Byzantine center of learning. Emperor Leo V (The Wise) completed his education at the island's philosophical school. The Crusaders did not do well by Andros, but the Venetians did, from A.D. 1207 until 1536. Under Ottoman domination, on and off from A.D. 1416, the island was invaded, in turn, by the

Andros

0 miles 4
0 km 4

Felos Beach
Vasamia
Gavrion
Tower of Ayios Petros
Batsi
Paleopolis
Apikia
Stenies
Stavropeda
Menites
Yialyia Beach
Messaria
Hora
Monastery of Panachrantos
Sinetia
Zagora
Vourni
Kochylou
Korthion

N

Tinos

Genoese, the Albanians, and the Russians, and was finally united with the modern state of Greece in the 19th-century War of Independence.

As paradoxical as the island's geography is the makeup of the modern tourist population. The island, especially Hora, the capital town, is home away from home to many of Greece's wealthiest shipowners and businessmen. They build palatial homes here and raise thoroughbred horses in the nearby countryside. This Greek "ship set," their offspring, and Athenian friends invade for a short holiday stay between June and August. But another group is already in evidence: the package tourists.

As early as April, organized and relentless foreign groups, primarily British, flood specific areas of Andros—not, of course, those enclaves frequented by the rich and famous. The two sets pass on the serpentine coast road, but do not mingle.

Strangely enough, few other types of visitors have been attracted to the island, and therein lies the challenge. Discerning travellers may still find on Andros—well away from the package-infested areas such as Batsi—unspoiled villages and "private" beaches. But because of the resident aristocracy's unwillingness to allow building in their well-manicured backyards, as it were, Andros is not as accessible as its Cycladic neighbors to the south. Bus connections are inadequate, information on archaeological sites is sketchy, coach tours are few. On Andros, settle in at one of a handful of excellent new hotels and then set out, by rented car and then on foot, to explore. Of the Cyclades, 373-square-mile Andros, smaller only than Naxos, is a big island to make one's own.

The West Coast

Unfortunately, on Andros all ferries dock at **Gávrion** on the northwest coast. In summer the port town is as stark and dusty as a de Chirico, as though Andros were trying to discourage all comers. There are three important tasks to accomplish in Gavrion before leaving, however: Acquire a map; rent a car, if you have not brought your own; and book tickets on a steamer out, if you failed to do so in Athens or Rafina. Tickets for the *Bari Express* may be purchased on the harbor at George Batis's office. Look for Ventouris Lines banners; Tel: (0282) 714-89 or 710-40.

The one good restaurant in town is located, oddly enough, at the camping ground behind the port. Spread out around a lighted swimming pool, this taverna is a pleasant surprise. (Andros is not a gastronomic paradise.) The café-ouzerie **En Gavrio** serves breakfast, drinks, and homemade sweets all day. Look for this little oasis of marble-topped tables on the waterfront.

Buses bound for Batsi (to the south), Hora, Korthion (both on the east coast), and other villages leave from a stop near the dock, and their schedules are tied in to those of the ferries. (If you're bound for Hora the same day you disembark, you may well have to sprint to catch the bus.) Cars may be rented in Batsi and Hora as well as in Gavrion; visitors arriving at night may prefer to tackle the coast road in daylight hours, remembering to honk horns before blind curves.

An indication of Andros's willingness to entertain the idea of quality tourism is the plush new **Hotel Andros Holiday**, situated just south of Gavrion on a private stretch of headland. There is no comparison between this jewel and the pedestrian waterfront hotels. With its pool, restaurant, tennis courts, and lively bar, the hotel may be the one good reason to stay in Gavrion. By taxi, moped, or car, the fine beach at **Felós** is about a 4.5-km (3-mile) drive northwest via the village of Vasamiá. Other beaches farther north may be explored, but there are no amenities on this undeveloped stretch of coastline, which is being settled by Athenian householders.

The **Tower of Ayios Petros**, 3 km (2 miles) east of Gavrion, is one of the island's unique, if inscrutable, sites. This 65-foot freestanding tower, part of which may date from the 14th century B.C., is an archaeological enigma. What the structure was used for is unknown.

To reach the resort of **Batsí**, turn right out of Gavrion and proceed south on the coast road. The 8-km (5-mile) drive will take you past accessible beaches and rocks to the fine sandy beaches around the headland, before the amphitheatrically situated town of Batsi proper. Batsi is a fishing village that just grew. Busy as it is in season, the holiday atmosphere may be attractive to some travellers. There are numerous adequate hotels and bungalows on the road from Gavrion and on the headland overlooking the town. On a hillside to the left, before you enter the village, are the new, luxurious **Epaminondas Holiday Apartments**, an elegant retreat near the beaches but well out of the fray. Families and couples like Epaminondas; each apartment has its own kitchen and bathroom. Restaurants in Batsi are, for the most part, disappointing. Three establishments "up the steps" from the waterfront are a bit better than average: **Ta Del-**

phinia, **O ti Kalo**, and **Stamatis**, the last being the best bet for service and value.

Nine kilometers (5.5 miles) farther south on the coast road is the tree-shaded village of **Paleópolis**. Stop in here at Mr. and Mrs. Giannias's **The Beautiful Paleopolis** for a memorable meal (lunch or dinner). Open all year, this roadside restaurant is a good place to sample Andros's renowned *froutália,* an oversized omelette containing local sausage, potatoes, cheese, and mint.

Present-day Paleopolis is situated atop a steep hill that runs down to the sea where the ancient capital site was located, part of it now underwater. You can descend the 1,039 steps to the beach, but if you are interested in antiquities you will find little of interest either here or at the site of Zagora farther south, which in any case is closed to visitors. Both sites' rich finds are now housed in the Archaeological Museum in Hora (see below), including the famous *Hermes of Andros* and late Geometric period finds from Zagora.

Inland

Fifteen kilometers (9 miles) south of Batsi at Stavrópeda are the main crossroads of the island. Here you may turn left and proceed to Hora through rolling pastoral countryside dotted with villages and Medieval dovecotes, or bear right for Korthion. Hora, or Andros town, is a 12-km (7.5-mile) drive from Stavropeda. After the drama of the precipitous coast road, the drive inland exhibits the other, more bucolic, face of Andros.

Off the main road to Hora are the lush villages of Menites and, farther north, Apikia. **Ménites**, where springs gush out of the hill through the mouths of marble lions, is a cool, green grotto. The road dead-ends beneath enormous trees and the **church of the Virgin Koúmoulos** (Plentiful). The **Oasis of Walnuts** restaurant here is worth the little trek. Nightingales, nesting in spring, sing in the trees; tables are set out on a terrace overlooking the brook; the froutalia, whole rooster, and chicken-stuffed tomatoes are fortifying.

Apíkia, 2.5 km (1.5 miles) north of Menites, another hillside village, is the source of Andros's famous Sáriza water. A deluxe hotel built in island style, the **Hotel Pighi Sarisa**, is located almost atop the spring itself, and visitors will find the restaurant, balconies with superb views, pool, live music, and bar good incentives for staying. (The mineral water, whose name derives from an ancient word for "arrow," was so called because it could "break stones"; even today Sariza is recommended to those with kidney ailments.)

From Messariá, on the Stavropeda–Hora road, or via Sinetia and Vourni, you can get to the **monastery of Panachrántos**, one of several noteworthy Byzantine sites on the island. This tenth-century edifice commands a stunning view of the valley and Hora below and is home to the relics of Saint Panteleimon, whose name day is celebrated on July 27. Bishop Evthokimos Frangoulakis, a friendly holy man from Milos, is likely to be serving lunch to package tourists brought up by coach from Batsi.

Hora

Hora itself, in the middle of the island's east coast, is the most interesting destination on Andros. Here are the ruins of the Venetian fort of **Mesa Kastro**, the **Maritime Museum**, and, adjacent, Michael Tombros's bland but monumental statue to the Unknown Sailor. The maze of streets that form **Kato Kastro**, the Medieval city, and the 18th- and 19th-century mansions of the **Riva District** are all situated on a narrow, rocky peninsula between the twin anchorages of Paraporti and Imborio bays. Both bays have fine, if somewhat exposed, beaches.

Here, too, are the beautifully organized **Archaeological Museum of Andros** (look for the *Hermes of Andros,* a second-century marble copy of a Praxiteles original) and the spectacular **Museum of Modern Art**, both established by Basil and Elise Goulandris of Andros's famous shipping family. The latter museum, divided into two buildings, is an international treasure. The collection includes works by important Greek artists of the 20th century; several rooms are devoted to the sculpture of Michael Tombros (1889 to 1976), whose powerful work should not be missed. (The Goulandrises sponsor important temporary exhibitions in their museum during summer; the last two shows featured Kandinsky and Balthus. Check in Athens for dates.)

The entire town of Hora is a creation of the shipping families, a very private place funded by private fortunes. This is not a small city devoted to the tourist trade, but rather a real-life Greek town complete with a daily routine of its own that seems to date from a half-century ago. In Hora it is still possible, at **Constantine Laskaris's** shop on the main street, George Embirikos (named after another shipowner, of course), to purchase 14 varieties of traditional Greek "spoon sweets," or heavy preserves, including quince and candied eggplant. Here, too, are walnuts in honey, *kaltsoúnia* (mincemeat confections), and *amýgdala* (crushed almond cakes).

There is, as yet, no luxury accommodation in Hora, but the state-run **Xenia**, with balconies overlooking the sea, is serviceable. The modest but newly renovated **Hotel Egli** is in the heart of town, next to the Church of the Virgin, and the place to rent a car. Bungalows and rooms are springing up at **Imbório**, the beach "suburb" below Hora, where the **Naftikos Omilos Androu** (sailing club) is open May through September. The club, with its swimming, windsurfing, and sailing facilities, features a restaurant and cafeteria, cabins, and showers, and is open to nonmembers from 3:00 P.M. on.

The East Coast

The village of **Steniés** and its nearby beach of **Yialyiá** are about 6 km (4 miles) north of Hora. Certainly the most beautiful village on the island, and perhaps the wealthiest, Stenies is a botanist's dream. Poinsettias, cherry and pomegranate trees, and a profusion of snapdragons make Stenies an aromatic oasis. When you walk into this village (it is closed to wheeled traffic) you will find a pleasant place to sip coffee under an 18th-century plane tree in the little square. The swimming cove at Yialyia, where there is a fish taverna of the same name, is a good spot to spend the afternoon.

You may now choose to head south through the villages of Sinetiá and Kochýlou to reach **Kórthion**, a seaside town 30 km (18.5 miles) from Hora. The terrain on this southern half of the island is mountainous and rocky; the famous stone field walls made of local schist; Andriot dovecotes are much in evidence.

On the water in Korthion, the spotless, family-run **Hotel Korthion** is open from May through October, and Messrs. Nikolaos Skordos, Nikolaos Voulgaris, and Christos Skordos all run tavernas here. Very busy in season, Korthion's beaches—for bathing and fishing—are accessible by foot or caïque.

GETTING AROUND

Andros has no airport, but getting there by hydrofoil from Piraeus or by ferryboat from the mainland port of Rafina is relatively easy. In summer, buses leave for Rafina from Mavromateon Street, adjacent to Areos Park in the center of Athens, on an average of every 20 minutes, from 6:00 A.M. until 9:00 P.M. It's wise to give the Rafina Port Authority (Tel:

0294-233-00) a call to check the ferry schedule before setting out. There are several departures daily in high season and at least one per day in winter. The two-and-a-half-hour voyage on such vessels as the *Bari Express* is pleasant. Meals and cabins are available, and passenger fares are reasonable. The only catch involves taking your car over: Those travelling in rental or private vehicles should book ferry space to and from Andros in advance through one of the Rafina ferryboat offices. Phone numbers are available from Athens travel agents, but you will find it easiest to have the travel agent arrange the booking for you; the ferry companies' phones seem to be permanently engaged, and the clerks often don't speak English. Some ships continue on to Tinos, Syros, and Mykonos, Andros's closest inhabited Cycladic company.

—*Elizabeth Boleman Herring*

TINOS

Amid Andros, Mykonos, and Syros, Tinos rises from the sea like a dragon: writhing, spiny, and mystical. Outside of Greece it is the least known of the big Cyclades, probably because its main town, Tinos, or Hora, on the southwest coast, lacks charm; there are few good beaches; and the north wind howls steadily (ancient mariners used to sacrifice to Poseidon when circling the island). A place of pilgrimage, it is perhaps the best known in Greece: All Orthodox want to worship here at least once.

MAJOR INTEREST

Church of Panayia Evangelistria
Mountain villages and landscape
Dovecotes

Hora

The Orthodox church kept Hellenism alive during the Turkish occupation. In 1822, one year after the revolution began, a nun, Sister Pelagia (canonized in 1971), was visited in a dream and vision by the Virgin, who told her where to dig up a miraculous icon of the Annunciation. The Tenians,

Tinos and Mykonos

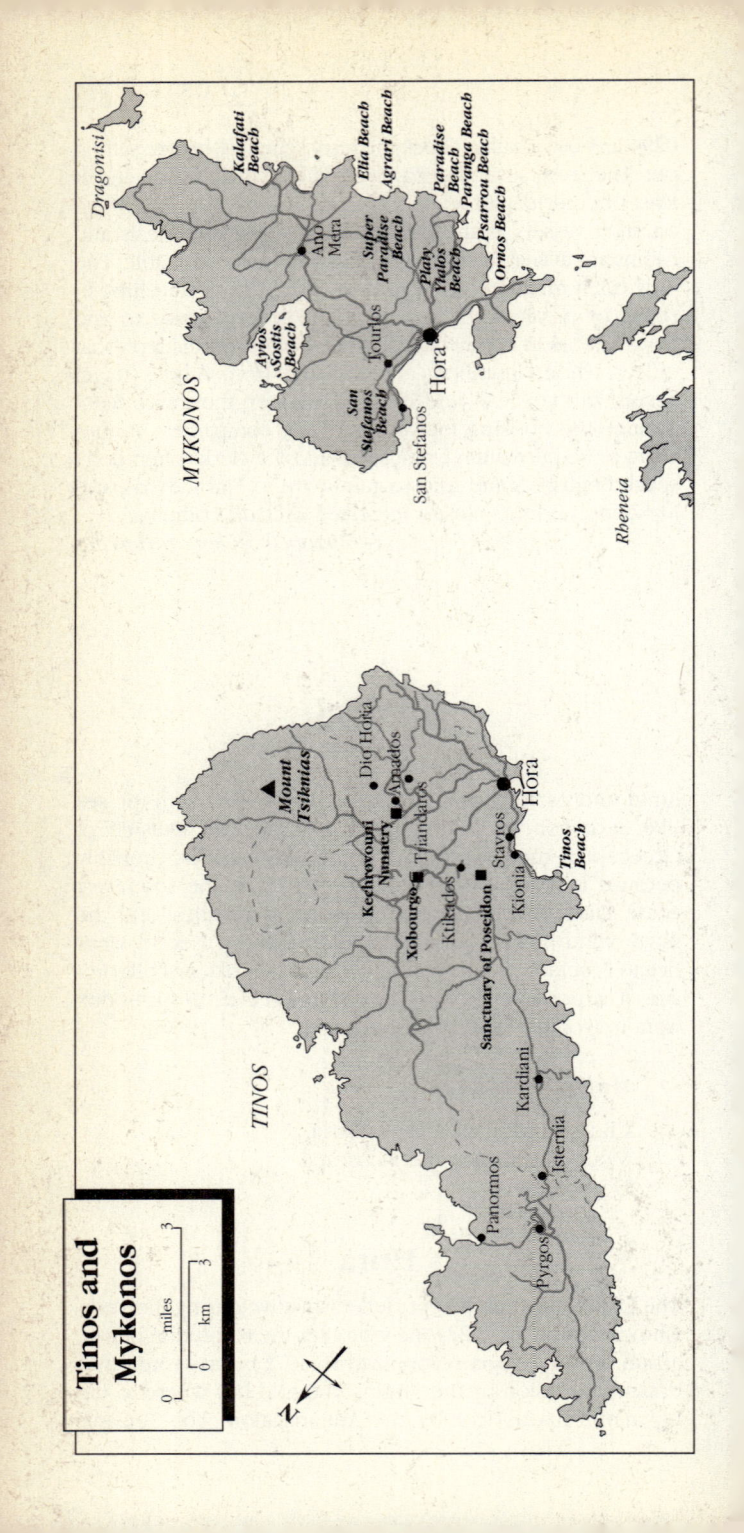

supported by a fledgling government aware of its patriotic potential, built a church in Hora—**Panayía Evangelístria** (Our Lady of the Annunciation; completed in 1831)—to house the icon. The icon started healing the sick immediately, and it continues to do so.

The infirm sometimes delegate a young female relative to visit the icon and beseech the Virgin on their behalf. As she sees the Evangelistria upon disembarking, she must fall to her knees and crawl to the church up the central lane of the wide new street, an arduous task, with vehicles speeding indifferently about her. The nonpilgrim might stroll up the parallel market street, lined with shops and hucksters hawking huge candles, amulets, phylacteries, holy-water containers, cheap crockery, trinkets, sweets—a lively spectacle. Hora's quay is all raucous restaurants, overlit cafés, and block-like hotels, with the old sleepy town behind.

The Tenians went all out for this church of the Virgin Annunciate, even though it was built at a time when Greece was poverty-stricken. Entering the great courtyard paved with pebble mosaic, you ascend a wide staircase to the church and its complex of cells, offices, health station, chapels, and seven museums. The huge quantity of marble came from Tinos's own quarries, from Delos, from Poseidon's temple north of Hora at Kionia, and from Paros. The interior of the three-aisle church dazzles with countless *ex-voti* of silver, gold, and tin, many in the form of sailing ships, gifts from those grateful for their cures. The silver tree to the right of the entrance was donated by a once-blind man who, upon miraculously regaining his sight, first saw an orange tree. Gold candelabra, oil lamps, and jewels reflect the glow of offertory beeswax candles. You must nearly always wait on line to kiss the icon, enshrined in the left aisle. Covered with jewels, gold, and pearls as it is, precious little of it can be seen.

On the lower level the Evresis (Finding) chapel celebrates the icon's unearthing on this spot on January 30, 1823. To its right a chapel commemorates the loss of the ship *Elli*, torpedoed by an Italian submarine on Dormition Day, 1940.

The arcaded inner courtyard, paved in marble, contains 120 cells, a treasury, and displays of documents and relics of Tinos's artistic and religious traditions. Pilgrims camp in the porticoes, as their ancestors did in ancient temples to Asklepios, keeping vigil for several days, sleeping and eating little. Ethiopians make the pilgrimage in spring, and in August thousands of gypsies arrive in their glittering finery. On the church's two feast days, March 25 (Evangelistria, or

Annunciation) and August 15 (Dormition), the icon is paraded through Hora, and a throng of thousands works itself into a state of religious ecstasy.

On the main street back to the quay, the **Archaeological Museum**'s collection of local objects includes a sun dial made in the first century B.C. by Andronicus of Cyrrhus, who also designed Athens's Tower of the Winds, and some gigantic eighth-century B.C. vases found in the ancient town of Tinos on Xobourgo (see below). Hora itself dates back only to the fifth century B.C., when Tinos joined Athens against the invading Persians.

The big restaurants, with their hundreds of tables facing the bay, cater to the religious holiday-makers. But a couple of restaurants still retain the flavor of old times. To find them, walk into the shopping street opposite the round dais on the waterfront and turn right into the first alleyway, George Gaphou Street. There you will find three restaurants in a row with tables outside: an old-fashioned tripe soup kitchen and two tavernas. The first taverna, **Michaeli's**, features rabbit stew and beef stew with baby onions. The second, **Pigada**, specializes in moussaka and macaroni.

In summer, when the harbor reeks with sewage, you might stay at the **Argo**, an unpretentious hotel away from the crush of religious Athenians, on Ayiali Point, just out of town to the east, facing the mile-long pebble beach of Ayios Fokas.

Kionia

The coast road to the northwest out of Hora immediately passes the little fish-market square where the local pelican hangs out. After 1.5 km (1 mile) it passes **Stavros**, where, tucked under the seacliff church, **Markos's Café** serves from a cave-like room; below, a popular beach stretches to the long jetty built during the Classical era. And in another kilometer you pass the extensive, untended **Sanctuary of Poseidon** and his sea-nymph wife, Amphitrite, which occupies the Kiónia meadow between sea and mountain. Only fourth-century foundations can be discerned, but the sanctuary is actually older. Pliny says that in ancient times Poseidon rid infested Tinos of serpents. Nereid and dolphin sculptures found here are in the Hora museum. The shrine, like today's Virgin of Tinos, attracted many pilgrims, since Tinian Poseidon was a healer as well as a threat to sailors. This tradition continued to Roman times; an Augustan verse reads, "to think Delos is abandoned, and Tenos yet thriving!"

On the hill above, the lovely village of **Ktikádos** has

yielded Geometric graves. The primitive painter Panayiotis Kontiras and his son run the pleasant **Tsambia** restaurant here, its terrace cooled by Poseidon's sea breeze. Kontiras often paints scenes of his home village; when the mood strikes, he may sell a painting.

After another half a kilometer on the coast road you reach **Tinos** beach, the island's best because it is partially sheltered. The elaborate **Tinos Beach Hotel**, a resort in itself, has a big saltwater pool, which, on account of the relentless wind, is for once not superfluous. The **Alonia Hotel** on the east road out of Hora is better run, however, and has a spring-fed pool. It is in a verdant area next to a seasonal river, and old villas and dovecotes dot the half-mile walk to the sea.

Around the Island

To reach the villages decorating the terraced mountain behind the Alonia Hotel, white amid their green orchards, follow the signs north to "Monastery" or to "Dio Horia." As the good road winds upward, you will see many of the beautiful dovecotes for which Tinos is famous. These fantastic buildings have two stories: The lower serves as a storeroom, while the upper is decorated with many thin schist slabs patterned to resemble embroidery. The finials are schematized doves. Pigeons love them, and Tenians do, too. Some of the island's 1,300 dovecotes, outnumbering the 800 churches, are new.

After 9 km (6 miles) you reach **Kechrovoúni Nunnery**, also a place of pilgrimage. You can visit the cell where Saint Pelagia had her dream (her embalmed head is in the wooden chest). Almost a walled village, the convent gleams with donations. Outside a nun sells, among knickknacks, apotropaic garlic; Tinos's strong garlic was recommended by Aristophanes.

One kilometer farther on, by the radar tower, is the village of **Arnados** (no sign), 1,600 feet above the sea. Most of Arnados's streets are gated and tunnel-vaulted for protection from sun, wind, and pirates—they stay as cool as a Medieval cloister. One and a half kilometers (1 mile) farther along, the double hamlet of **Dio Horia** rises up its cliff. In front of its public fountain-house (these are peculiar to Tinos), a marble plaque dates the planting of the huge plane tree here to 1885.

From Dio Horia the road circles widely to reach the lower village of **Triandáros**, whose one outdoor restaurant is pleasant and popular with Greeks; 34 of the houses here have been lovingly restored by their new German owners, who do not mind the wind-driven mist that often veils the town. The Tenian marble sculptor Ioannis Kyparinis has his workshop here and offers small sculptures for sale; he specializes in iconostases and bell towers, such as the three-story tower in Dio Horia.

Past the Arnados turnoff the road runs along the mountain, with high peaks all around. Mount Tsiknias, to the east, rises 2,391 feet. The dragon-spines on its ridge are huge boulders, two of which mark the grave of the sons of the god Boreas (North Wind), who were killed by Herakles.

The road branches to many villages—Tinos has 48. One leads west to the towering rock of **Xoboúrgo**, 2,100 feet high. This scary, windblown place, home to crows and yellow lichens, was Tinos's main town in the Archaic era, and then again under the Venetians. In 1207 the doge awarded Tinos and Mykonos to the Ghisi family, who held them until 1310; then the Venetians ruled them directly, but Tinos held out alone until 1714, when the Venetian governor fled, later to be imprisoned in Venice for desertion. Tinos's heroism left the island depopulated and impoverished until the icon revived its fortunes.

The West Coast

The route north from Hora toward Pyrgos follows Tinos's long west coast and affords continuous stupendous views of the sea, especially west toward Syros, ten miles away. The prettiest of the villages, which seem to hang from cliffs overlooking the foamy coast, are **Kardianí** (21 km/13 miles from Hora), which was inhabited before 2000 B.C., and **Istérnia**, or Cisterns (24 km/15 miles), with its gardens and marble square. Look for the marble plaques set over doors that illustrate the resident's name and even profession—a truck for a truck driver, for example. A paved road winds down to Isternia's small bay, far below, where there is a beach and a good fish taverna, the **Mprotolog**.

After Isternia the road climbs over the watershed and past a row of ruined windmills that used to grind Black Sea corn for all the Cyclades to the east-facing village of **Pyrgos** (32 km/20 miles from Hora) overlooking the safe harbor of Panormos. The parking lot and bus stop of Pyrgos (Tower) are directly opposite the **Kardamites Museum**, which is located in the house of Tinos's renowned sculptor, Iannoulis Chalepas (1851 to 1938). Tinos is a sculptors' island; the Pyrgos sculpture school, in the town's highest building, still trains master masons, whose carved door frames, lintels, balconies, fountains, and elaborate fanlights decorate all the villages, especially Pyrgos, where so many sculptors were born. The cemetery behind the big church is filled with their work. The marble-paved street next to the Chalepas museum leads into town. Turn right at its end into the market street, which leads you past Lambros Diamantopoulos's marble workshop and into the charming main square. Here the **Platanos** café, under a skyscraping plane tree and surrounded by marble buildings, offers excellent sweets.

About 50 yards down from the bus stop, Markos and Dorothea Mavromaras's **Vinia** restaurant—the best on Tinos—serves Greek dishes, such as chicken pie, in a garden. Continue down the road 4 km (2.5 miles) to **Pánormos**, whence ships used to export green Tinos marble. Along the Panormos quay are several fish tavernas and a popular beach with a fallen-in sea cave.

GETTING AROUND

Tinos is served by ferries from Piraeus and Rafina every day. The Piraeus route via Syros takes five to seven hours, that from Rafina via Andros four to six hours, depending on season, weather, and additional stops. In summer there are daily ferries among Tinos, Andros, Syros, and Mykonos. There are also frequent connections with Naxos, Paros, Ios, and Santorini. Boats to Tinos bulge with pilgrims around Easter and August 15, so advance tickets are recommended, if you can get them.

Buses go everywhere on Tinos. Schedules are posted at the main stop, near the boat dock in Hora, where taxis also wait. Cars and motorbikes are for rent; though the roads are good, they are very steep.

—*Jeffrey Carson*

MYKONOS

Among such treasures in the Mýkonos Museum as the seventh-century B.C. amphora with reliefs depicting the capture of Troy (complete with a warrior-filled Trojan horse) is a lovely third-millennium B.C. mirror. Some anonymous

Mykonian woman (a woman, for the object bears a distinctive delta sign) filled this shallow bowl with water and then, like Narcissus, looked into it to see her reflection.

It is an apt metaphor for today's Mykonos, possibly the Mediterranean's busiest resort in season. The island is a mirror, and depending upon your point of view, you will see in it an idyllic Cycladic beauty or a modern-age harlot. Both images are there for the viewing. In practical terms this island would appear to have little to recommend it: A rocky mass of indefinite shape anchored in the heart of the Cyclades, it is bare, almost treeless. By some unique, intangible magic, its scattered pearl-white villages and khaki-colored hinterland combine with the cobalt sea that laps its bays and inlets to produce a Calypso-like aura of seduction. Visitors are drawn again and again to its sparse shores.

Named for a grandson of Delos-born Apollo, the island has been occupied, in turn, by Carians from Asia Minor, Egyptians, Phoenicians, Cretans, Carians again, and then Ionians, Persians, and Romans. It was always, it seems, a popular place.

The Byzantine Empire was next to lay claim, followed by the Venetians until the island was seized by Barbarossa in 1537. (The main town, Hora, may be pretty, but its architecture was designed to discourage a frontal assault by pirates. The backs of the houses "front" onto the seaport, thus forming a protective barrier.)

In 1615 the Commune of Mykonos was established, and the Turks, who followed on the heels of the pirates, granted Mykonos a measure of autonomy. For four years in the 18th century Mykonos was ruled by the Russians. Pre-revolutionary Mykonos became a formidable naval power, with a fleet of 22 ships, and the island's most noteworthy heroine, Mando Mavroyeni (1796 to 1848), was responsible for turning back a Turkish insurgency in October 1822. A marble bust of Mavroyeni ornaments the main square in Hora.

Since the 1940s Mykonos's invaders have come primarily from the north and west, bearing easels, then sleeping bags, and now matching Louis Vuittons and hard currency. Scattered around the 53-square-mile island are some of the Aegean's loveliest beaches; in Hora are gourmet restaurants, bars and clubs of every stripe, and a thousand ways to overuse any number of credit cards. The campers of the 1960s have been replaced by the camp of the 1980s: Though Mykonos's reputation as *the* gay summer retreat of the Mediterranean has been toned down in recent years, the City

Bar's 1:30 A.M. drag show is still one of the main attractions of the wee hours.

MAJOR INTEREST

Beautiful beaches and international ambience
Cubistic Cycladic architecture
Luxury accommodations and dining
Endless nightlife
Sun, sea, and shopping
Cycladic "gateway" to Delos

Hora and Environs

Hora, the island's capital, located on the west coast, is a labyrinth of streets easy to get lost in—or to lose someone in, a reminder that this was the best security against centuries of sudden pirate raids. It is a whitewashed maze whose streets (three-foot-wide alleys, really) were arbitrarily named by the junta. The only way to locate anything but the sea (which is always downhill) is to ask—and ask again. Around the helter-skelter center is a circle of broader streets, which, together with the waterfront, provide the favorite evening promenade where everybody literally bumps into everybody else. One of the chief charms of Mykonos and its capital is its human scale; here there is no privacy—everything is seen, heard, known.

Hora can be a noisy place to stay, but there are numerous hotels on the fringes of the town where life is less frenetic. Visitors lodging in town avoid long hikes home and taxi lines, as most of the best restaurants and bars are in Hora. However, most of the outlying luxury hotels are quite willing to collect and deposit guests in town at all hours, if these transfers are requested in advance.

In town, at the site of the Tria Pigádia (Three Wells; custom has it that if you drink from all three wells, good luck will be yours), the family-run **Hotel Kouneni** is quiet and central, with a pleasant garden. The **Leto Hotel**, with a view of the port, is an old, traditional hotel with a garden; it's located on the port near the Ano Mera bus stop. Near town, the **Despotiko**, with superb views, a pool, and a garden; **Vienoula's Garden Hotel**, a ten-minute walk from both Hora and the sea, quiet, with balconies overlooking the garden; the small, no-frills **Belou Hotel**, with a restaurant and bar; and the **Mykonos Beach Hotel**, with great sea views from each bungalow balcony at Megali Ammos, are all comfortable and reasonable, by Mykonian standards. (The Mykonos Hoteliers' Association publishes a glossy brochure available at the harbor travel agents' offices and accommodation agencies.)

On the road north to San Stefanos beach just one kilometer (about half a mile) from Hora is the luxurious **Cavo Tagoo** ("Pour les happy few," as the brochure aptly states), with its pool, restaurant, and view of the sea and port. Cavo Tagoo has won awards for its architecture, and, after the Santa Marina, is the jet set's hotel of choice. In San Stefanos proper, 2.5 km (1.5 miles) north of Hora, above the beach, is the quiet, elegant **Hotel Princess of Mykonos**, which also has its own saltwater pool and a beautiful view of Hora's "string of pearls" night harbor.

At Ornos beach, 3 km (2 miles) south of Hora, are the stunning **Santa Marina** villas and apartments, a complex that features its own heliport and absolutely anything else your heart desires—air-conditioning, tennis, sauna—24 hours a day. There are also several swimming pools, and the two restaurants here maintain their own fishing caïque. This is the furthest cry on the island from the official campsite on Paradise beach. A few minutes from the Ornos bus stop is **Bistrot Bohème**, a Greek taverna (despite its name) and just the place for hungry Santa Marinans who don't want to change for dinner.

The best beaches are, of course, those that are accessible only to motorcyclists (read dirt bikers), snorkelers, or visitors who arrive with their own Zodiacs. Mykonos's long, sandy strands have been "discovered" for over a quarter-century now, but the best places to start are still the beaches at the termini of the regularly scheduled island buses and caïques.

Beach buses depart from two terminals. The Elia beach/Ano Mera village/Kalafati beach and Tourlos/San Stefanos terminal is located just in front of the Leto Hotel to the north of Hora on the waterfront road. To the south of town, near "the crossroads," is the terminal for the Ornos/Platy Yialos and Psarrou beach buses. From Platy Yialos you can catch a caïque for Paradise, Super Paradise, Agrari, and Elia. Alternatively, it's a 15-minute walk to Paránga (or Ayía Anna), the first nudist beach beyond Platy Yialos, 25 to Paradise, and about 30 minutes to Super Paradise from Platy Yialos. **Ornós, Platý Yialós, Psarroú,** and **San Stéfanos** still qualify as "family"—read "just" topless—beaches, at least most of the time. **Paradise, Super Paradise, Agrári, Eliá,** and **Ayios Sostis** (this last reachable only by sturdy four-wheel drive vehicles) are for nudists. This is not a hard-and-fast rule, though, as nudism is sanctioned on most Mykonos beaches, or at the far ends of most beaches.

There are caïque connections to all beaches with amenities, either from the old pier near the tourist police and OTE (telecommunications) offices in Hora, where boats depart for Delos, or from Psarrou and Platy Yialos. It is also possible, through local agents and hotels, to rent cars, jeeps, and mopeds, though Mykonos's gravel-strewn and sinuous roads are hazardous for two-wheeled transport.

Satisfying if less sybaritic are Hora's excellent museums, notably the Mykonos, or **Archaeological Museum**, which houses Mykonian, Delian, and Rheneian antiquities and is located on the road to the yacht marina; the **Aegean Maritime Museum**, at Tria Pigadia, privately endowed and a model museum (don't miss the old island lighthouse in the back garden); **Lena's House**, a lovingly preserved Mykonian home of the 19th century; and the **Mykonos Folk Museum**, a former sea captain's house full of 18th- and 19th-century Mykonian memorabilia.

Wandering about Hora, by day or night, and getting lost is one of the great delights of visiting Mykonos. On a labyrinthine ramble, keep in mind that the harbor and sea are always downhill: There's no Cretan Minotaur chasing you here, so just enjoy the whitewashed stairs, chapels, and alleyways of this town that has been maintained as an informal, modern museum of Cycladic architecture. Seek out the four adjoining chapels known as **"The Gossippers,"** located in the center of town. Another cluster of churches, the **Paraportianí**, near the harbor, is actually four churches sharing a single, Sphinx-like roof. Whitewashed Paraportiani, which may date from the 15th century, is as singlular and beautiful a structure as you are likely to find in the modern world. At dusk, against Mykonos's pink summer sky, this creation of anonymous builders has inspired myriad painters and photographers.

At around 7:30 P.M. in summer you'll want to find a window seat in one of the island's two "classical music bars," the **Montparnasse** and the **Kastro Bar**, both on the water between the area known as **Little Venice** and Paraportiani, both with views of the sunset. The **Minotaur Bar**, also classy and quiet, is tucked away near one of Hora's best restaurants, **Katrin's**. Situated in the Ayios Yerasimos area, Katrin's has a French menu of flown-in filets and other non-Greek delicacies. At Tria Pigadia is the **Astra Bar**, New Age and glossy, designed by the Greek jeweler Minas. **Pierros**, at the harbor end of Matoyiánni Street, is the island's most notorious night spot, primarily gay. The **City Bar** (on Iglési, behind the Paraportianí), like Pierros mobbed in summer, charges a cover at the door for its early-morning drag show, something everyone should see at least once during a stay on the island. For Greek dancing, the **Mykonos Bar** nearby on Katsóni remains the place to go. In summer, the **Anemo Théatro** (Wind Theater) stages dramatic and musical performances. (Ask at Opsis Gallery—see below—for details.)

Antonini's Restaurant, at the taxi square on the waterfront, has been a favorite for lunch and early dinner (traditional Greek food) since 1955. **Kounelas Fish Taverna**, off the waterfront, is also an old standby. **Phillipi's**, **Edem**, and **El Greco** are all recommended for Greek and international cuisine.

The **Sesame Kitchen**, adjacent to the Maritime Museum, and **Lotus** (on Matoyianni Street) restaurants are favored by the island's foreign residents, who enjoy their innovative cookery. **Dolce Vita**, up from the elementary school, is a superb Italian restaurant. **La Taverna Italiana**, less pricey, has great pizza, and nearby **L'Angolo Bar**, a chic espresso bar, has the only real coffee in town.

Just out of town are two little-known restaurants. At Tourlos, just 2 km (1 mile) north of Hora, homey **Mathew's** has good Greek food and a view of Hora's night harbor. On the way to distant Kalafáti beach, 13 km (8 miles) due east of Hora, is the **Osteria del Pesce da Lú** a small Italian restaurant worth the trip (Tel: 714-97 to book a table with Bruno).

Shopping in Hora, after the beaches and nightlife, is another of Mykonos's great attractions. **Lalaounis** and **Zolotas**, Greece's famous jewelers, have gold stores on the island. **Theodore Rousounnellos**, on Matoyianni Street, carries Cartier and Rolex along with his own opulent jewelry; **Y. Voulgaris**, on the harbor, features original creations as well. And though **Vienoula Kousathana** died several years ago, her shop is still the best place to find a warm wool sweater for Mykonos's notoriously chilly and windy evenings. **Anna Gelou's White Shop** stocks lace, embroideries, and sweaters—all white, of course. Jeweler to the locals, **Yiannis Michaelidis** features lovely traditional Cycladic earrings in gold with seed pearls. The **Opsis Art Gallery**, with regular exhibitions of internationally known artists (as well as such locals as Couteau, Pipikios, and Kristensen), is a must, as is Bo Patrick's **Little Venice Gallery** of photography. **Trussardi**, the exclusive Italian fashion chain, has a shop on Matoyianni

Street. For gifts and toys shop at **Katoi-i** and **Nostalgia**. There are five banks in town if you run out of legal tender.

Around the Island

There is literally a vacation for everyone on Mykonos. Hikers will find the walk from Platy Yialos to Elia on the south coast a stimulating, sometimes taxing journey, crisscrossing from the coast to the hinterland. In spring and summer, throughout the Cyclades, keep an eye out for the small black snakes known as pit vipers. Swimmers should also be alert to the fact that the Aegean is visited in some years by jellyfish, whose sting is very painful, especially for those eschewing bathing suits. But don't panic: Snakebites and jellyfish stings are actually rare occurrences in Greece. Windsurfers, water-skiers, and snorkelers will want to stay at a favorite beach all day. While dancers get their fill of the very latest amplified rock music in Hora, if you seek quiet you may retire inland to the village of **Ano Merá**, 8 km (5 miles) east of Hora. At **Maria Stavrokopoulou's Café** (the sign reads "Vaggelis") on the village square near the 16th-century monastery of Our Lady of Tourlianí, sample Mykonos's traditional specialties, *kopanistí* cheese, *loukániko* (sausage), and grilled octopus with ouzo. Around the corner at **O Takis**, enjoy *loukoumádes* (Greek doughnuts) and other sweets. From Ano Mera you can go on quiet walks through rural Mykonos, encountering a number of isolated churches where saint's-day feasts are still celebrated. Check with the locals or your hotel for dates of these public festivals.

Excursions to the islands of Delos, nearby all-but-uninhabited **Rhéneia**, and **Dragonísi**, home to the shy and endangered monk seal, may be arranged through your hotel or a travel agent, or at the main port in Hora.

GETTING AROUND

Reaching Mykonos is relatively easy. There are charters from virtually every northern European capital in season, and Olympic Airways' trusty little Skyvans and small jets set down from Athens, Rhodes, Kos, Crete, and Santorini up to 12 times daily. (Pick up a current schedule of Olympic flights at the airline's office on Athens's Syntagma Square; the Mykonos winter schedule is much leaner.) The rich, famous, and impatient arrive by private helicopter and jet or by yacht. Ship and car-ferry connections from Piraeus, Rafina, Andros, Syros, Tinos, Paros, Naxos, Ios, Santorini, Ikaria,

Samos, Amorgos, Astypalaia, and Crete are also frequent in summer. Schedules may be checked in Athens, but it's best to book both flights and car space on ships well in advance. The Delia (Tel: 0289-223-22, 224-22, or 236-50; Fax: 0289-244-00) and Sea and Sky (Tel: 0289-228-53; Fax: 0289-245-82) travel agencies on the waterfront in Hora are well equipped to answer all travel and accommodation queries on the island. At Sea and Sky ask Takis for his indispensable blue map of Hora.

From the airport, an Olympic Airways bus will drop passengers at the airline's office in town, an awkward place to end up with lots of luggage as taxi queues in summer can run to 40 impatient people. It's best to make hotel reservations in advance from Athens and arrange, simultaneously, for the hotel shuttle to meet your plane or ship.

—*Elizabeth Boleman Herring*

DELOS

Delos is an isle with a glorious past but no true present. In stark contrast to hedonistic, populous Mykonos, the nearest point of debarkation for Delos-bound visitors, it is both uninhabited and commercially unsullied; there are no shops, accommodations, discos, or restaurants. Apollo's birthplace is an arid, sun-starched museum alfresco, strewn with precious but shattered marble. It takes imagination, and an archaeologist's guidebook to the site, to appreciate that life once burgeoned on this tiny strip of land at the heart of the Cyclades. (*Delos: Monuments and Museum,* by Photini Zaphiropoulou, ephor of antiquities, is a helpful companion on Delos. The artists' sketches of the site during its zenith are especially enlightening.)

MAJOR INTEREST

Vast "museum" alfresco
Panoramic view of the Cyclades from Mount Kynthos
The "birthplace" of Apollo

Southwest of Mykonos by 2.5 nautical miles, a half hour by motorized caïque, Delos is a long, narrow lozenge of land, two square miles in size. **Mount Kynthos,** more properly a hill, rises in the center of the island to a height of 368 feet, and from this vantage point, once honeycombed with sanctuaries and temples to a plethora of gods, visitors have a good view, on clear, breezy days, of Delos's neighbors: Mykonos, Tinos, Syros, Rheneia, and, sometimes, other Cycladic islands.

Best visited in the spring, when winter rains have brought out poppies, lilies, and delicious wild asparagus, by July Delos has baked to a dusty, lizard-enlivened desert of schist and granite, frosted with marble antiquities.

In the hot summer months the intense *meltémi* winds can make the tricky crossing from Mykonos an unpleasant experience for the queasy. In whatever season, canny travellers will take along windbreakers, sunscreen, hats, thermoses of water or juice, and lunch, preferably packed and bagged at Mykonos's L'Angolo Bar.

Inquire at the Mykonos Harbor Authority (Tel: 0289-222-18) for morning departure times, and be at the *old pier* early. Tickets may be purchased from harborside travel and shipping agents (Sea and Sky, for example); caïques usually leave at around 9:00 A.M. (except Mondays and holidays) for a three-and-a-half-hour stay on Delos. Guided tours may be joined, and private excursions arranged. There is a reasonable entrance fee to the site.

Serious students of Greek history and archaeology may require several days to explore Delos thoroughly. It is physically impossible to cover all the important areas in the course of one trip, and the caïques do not wait for stragglers.

Delos was once called Ortygia, or Quail Island, for good reason. Zeus, that notorious womanizer, was as resourceful as he was amorous. The father of the gods metamorphosed himself and his mistress, Leto, daughter of the Titans Coeus and Phoebe, into quails for a very important tryst: Their union resulted in the birth of Apollo and Artemis.

Hera, Zeus's vengeful spouse, was undeceived by the feathers, however, and dispatched the deadly serpent Python to hound pregnant Leto "that she should not be delivered in any place where the sun shone." Hera had not counted on peripatetic undersea islets, it seems.

Fortunately, as Pindar recounts in his famous hymn, at the time of Hera's wrath the sun did not shine on Delos, an unstable and soggy islet that "was blown by all the winds over the billowed sea." But as soon as Leto, in the throes of labor, set foot on Delos, four pillars "shod in adamant" sprang up from the seabed and held the skittery little rock in place. Formerly known as "A-delos," or "the invisible," the island underwent a name change after the birth of the god of light to Delos, or "clearly seen."

As Leto had promised that wherever her luminous child first saw light he would remain and bestow great good fortune, tiny Delos thereafter remained stationary above the waves.

Inhabited since the third millennium B.C., most probably by the Carians from Asia Minor, who built huts on the high ground of Mount Kynthos, Delos first came into prominence during the Mycenaean period (1500 to 1100 B.C.). The Ionians followed in the wake of these settlers, and Delos became an Ionian religious center in the first millennium B.C.

Both Homer's *Odyssey* and the *Hymn to Apollo*, which celebrated the great Delian Festival held here, bear out the fact that by 700 B.C. Delos was a sacred site. Not to be outdone by the locals, other powers, such as Naxos, Paros, and Samos, erected holy buildings and votive offerings on Delos. Athens, Delos's most determined rival for political and religious supremacy, carried out the first religious ceremony of purification on the island in 543 B.C.

Following Persian invasions and the defeat of the Asians, the first Athenian League was formed in 478 B.C. The headquarters of this embryonic United Nations was at holy Delos, where the league's incomparably rich treasury was housed until its removal to the Athenian Acropolis in 454 B.C. A second purification of Delos was imposed by the finicky Athenians in 426–425 B.C., when Delians were forbidden to die or give birth on their island, and all graves were summarily removed to nearby, now desolate, Rheneia. Delos then entered a new period of political, commercial, and religious dominance. Athens's General Nicias showed up with a huge bronze palm tree (Apollo was said to have been born under a palm), and the Delian Games were revived at this time. Plutarch later recorded the toppling of the tree in a storm.

The island's greatest period began in 315 B.C., however, when Alexander the Great's general, Ptolemy I of Egypt, ruled the Aegean, and Delos was granted self-government. During this period Delos's reputation garnered it offerings from all over the then-civilized world, and rich shrines to many foreign gods—Serapis, Isis, Anubis, Atargatis—and even a synagogue, were erected.

The Romans came next, in 250 B.C.; they later made Delos a slave market and commercial center. However, most of the island's beautiful private homes, with their exquisite mosaic floors, date from this period—Aegean echoes of Pompeii and Herculaneum.

Mithridates, king of Pontus (an ancient kingdom on the south shore of the Black Sea), dealt the Romans and Delos a crushing blow in 88 B.C. Pausanias, the famous travel writer, numbered the dead at 20,000. In 69 B.C. pirates finished the work Mithridates had begun.

Thereafter, Rome fortified the vulnerable settlement, and Athens once again took up the reins of power, but Delos's heyday had passed. Invasion after invasion followed. By the end of the fifth century A.D. Delos's name had reverted, aptly, to A-delos. Under the Turks, in 1566, the once-holy isle became a pirates' lair and a source of marble for whitewash and metal for ammunition.

Today visitors may appreciate the islet's former grandeur; the industrious French, followed by the Greeks, have since 1837 conducted thorough excavations of the site. A **museum** (not always open to the public) on the island houses Archaic and Classical marbles, pottery, Hellenistic sculpture, grave stelai from Rheneia, and artifacts documenting the Delians' everyday life.

With guidebook in hand, seek out the great phalloi on their plinths, offerings to Dionysus; the **Terrace of the Lions**, the leonine features now softened by the elements; the third-century B.C. **theater**; the **sanctuary district**; the famous **mosaic floors**; the **Temple of Isis**; and the **Sacred Cave**. A sense of the mystery of the place still prevails: This island was a sacred shrine of pilgrimage for over a thousand years.

Don't become too engrossed in your maps and reading materials: The caïques depart for Mykonos—and the 20th century—on schedule.

—*Elizabeth Boleman Herring*

SYROS

The name Syros (Syra) may come from the Phoenician words for "happy" or "rock" or, perhaps, both, as Syros has always been a fortunate, if arid, outcropping.

Homer was the first to sing the island's praises, in Book 15 of the *Odyssey*. Markos Vamvakaris, one of Greece's most

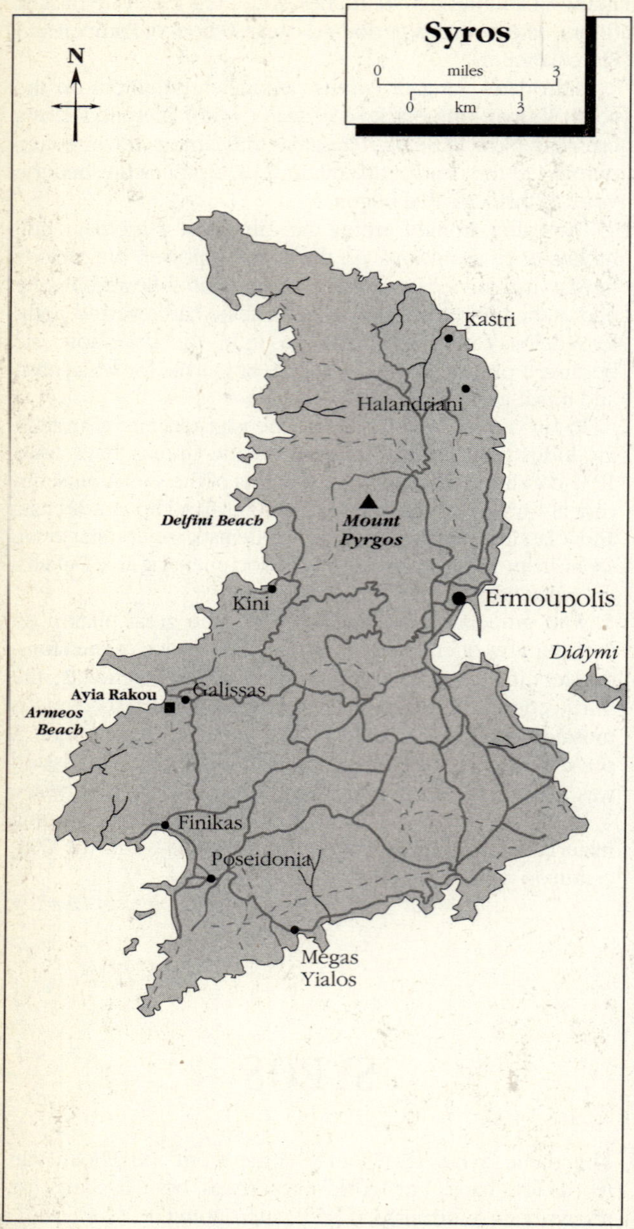

Syros
0 miles 3
0 km 3
N
Kastri
Halandriani
Delfini Beach
Mount Pyrgos
Kini
Ermoupolis
Didymi
Ayia Rakou
Galissas
Armeos Beach
Finikas
Poseidonia
Megas Yialos

famous balladeers, wrote a song celebrating the beauty of its women of Venetian or French descent, the "Frangosyriani." Herman Melville, writing in 1856–1857, gave the men equal time: "Lithe fellows tall, with gold-shot eyes, Sunning themselves as leopards may."

You may be put off at first by the mercantile and merchant-marine bustle of modern Ermoupolis, the port and capital city. But if you are adventurous another Syros awaits you at the top of the island's twin conical hills and in the inland and coastal villages. With its airport still unfinished and its beach settlements largely undeveloped, Syros has much to attract you if you prefer to seek your vacation spots down less-frequented paths.

(Those especially interested in architecture would do well to pick up a copy of Anastasios Kartas's *Syros,* available in Athens at the Compendium Bookshop at 28 Nikis Street.)

Near the center of the Cyclades, due east of Kythnos and west of Mykonos, rocky Syros covers an area of 52 square miles, the modest 1,450-foot peak of Pyrgos rising northwest of the capital. To the southeast and southwest of the deep harbor at Ermoupolis, in the middle of the east coast, sheltered bays enclose sandy swimming beaches, while pebbled coves accommodating nudists and other less-gregarious types are a short walk away over scrub-covered headlands.

MAJOR INTEREST

Medieval town of Ano Syros
Neoclassical mansions in Ermoupolis
"Undiscovered" coves and beaches
Capuchin and Jesuit monasteries
Turkish delight

Ermoupolis

Ermoúpolis spills like multicolored lava from the twin colonial hills of Ano Syros and Vrontádo, topped respectively by a Roman Catholic and a Greek Orthodox cathedral. Approached from the sea Ermoúpolis is stunningly beautiful. Capital not only of the island but of the entire Cycladic island group, Ermoúpolis was the main port of Greece for half a century after its conception in 1822, during the War of Independence.

During this struggle refugees fleeing from the Turkish massacres on the islands of Chios and Psara chose the site of the ancient "town of Hermes" (god of travellers) on which to raise their new city and crowned it with the cathedral church of the Anástasis (Resurrection) on Vrontado.

The island has a rich history stretching back almost unbroken to the Neolithic era. Dwellings and a prehistoric acropolis at **Kastri** to the north and Early Cycladic finds at **Halandrianí** (just south of Kastri) indicate an advanced early civilization on Syros. The **Archaeological Museum** of Syros, which contains artifacts dating from the third millennium B.C. as well as Hellenistic finds, is one of the oldest in Greece. (Don't miss the black-figure vase depicting Odysseus's escape from the Cyclops's cave, and a clay "water mirror" incorrectly identified in the catalog as a frying pan.) Founded in 1834–1835, the small museum is located up the steps to the left of the **Municipal Palace** of Ermoupolis. Call before visiting, as the two-man staff is hard pressed to maintain regular hours; Tel: 284-87.

The palace itself, which today houses the capital's administrative offices—as well as two 19th-century fire engines in the entryway—is a good example of Syros's illustrious, if more recent, past. Designed by the chosen architect of Greece's first monarchs, Ernst Ziller, the impressive structure is located on Ermoupolis's equally impressive **Miaoúlis Square**, two blocks behind the port. Here a band shell, with nine sculpted Muses, several 19th-century ocher-hued kiosks, and a statue of Admiral Andreas Miaoulis ornament a vast expanse of marble pavement. Young men and women execute a courtly *volta*—shopping for suitable marriage prospects—of a weekend evening. The volta, like much else on Syros, harks back to a gentler, more patrician era.

Rising above Ermoupolis is **Ano Syros**, where Venetians and the inhabitants of the island erected a walled town in the Middle Ages, immuring themselves against pirate incursions. The upper town preserves its original character, and from the Roman Catholic bishopric and the church of St. George on down the hill, this lofty retreat maintains its 13th-century integrity.

Ten minutes—straight up—by taxi from the port, Ano Syros is best visited in the early morning or late evening in summer. Ask your driver to let you off at the monastery, and then proceed up to the highest point in town, where a bronze bust of Pherekidis commemorates that imaginative sixth-century B.C. philosopher, believed to have been a teacher of Pythagoras.

The **bishopric**, where bishops have presided since the time of Irinaios, in A.D. 343, is downhill from the monastery and up a flight of ocher stairs. Downhill again is the **Jesuit**

Monastery, founded in 1744, and the adjacent church of the Virgin of Carmel. Four Jesuit fathers now inhabit this monastery; the adjacent guesthouse of Sister Mary accommodates some six pilgrims.

Still farther downhill is the **Capuchin Monastery**, home for the past 40 years to Father Dimitrios Freris, an authority on all things Syrian—and spiritual. Only visitors on official religious business are allowed to enjoy a sojourn in Father Dimitrios's jasmine-scented garden overlooking Ermoupolis, and a discussion—in Greek, Italian, or French—of the visitor's choosing. Asked if he has ever felt lonely during his four decades of monastic life, the monk is likely to answer: "He who dances alone may leap as much as he wishes." Beloved by Catholic and Greek Orthodox alike, this lively Capuchin is evidence of the goodwill between the two branches of Christianity on Syros. Once all Catholic, Syros is now two-thirds Orthodox, but relations remain cordial and the Venetian-French influence has given the island's culture and architecture a distinctive flavor.

Money has poured into Syros since the days of the Duchy of Naxos. Greece's first high school (Eleftherios Venizelos attended) and Greece's first shipyard were established on Syros. Syros also boasts the **Apollon Theatre**, a small-scale version of La Scala (situated behind Ermoupolis's main square), and streets full of two- and three-story mansions with graceful wrought-iron fanlights washed in pastels. In the **church of the Assumption** (in the center of town, next to the Hotel Europe) is an icon of the same name executed by one of Crete's most famous sons, El Greco.

Following the War of Independence, Syros, along with Nafplion, was proposed as a site for the fledgling nation's first capital. Waves of rich immigrants from Smyrna (today's Izmir), Chios, Hydra, Psara, and Crete made the island a cultural and commercial hub. Today there is still a whiff of this old-money perfume in the air, though the harborfront is more redolent of *loukoúmi,* Turkish delight.

Since before World War II, manufacturers in Ermoupolis have been turning out vast quantities of this confection flavored with pergamon (a citrus fruit), rose, pistachio, or mastic (resin from trees grown only on Chios). Seven bonafide loukoumi producers still maintain shops on the island—notably, the **Livadaras** brothers and the firm of **G. Passaris**. Taking a box of this sweet, gummy candy home is sure proof of having been to Syros. It is refreshing with a cup of Greek coffee and a chaser of ice water. (Nougat, in pancake form, pressed between leaves of flour-paste filo, is another Syrian treat; visit the Passaris shop at 25–27 Thimáton Sperhíou Street in Ermoupolis to see the confectioners at work.)

Two very special Neoclassical villas in Ermoupolis offer fine accommodation. The **Hotel Homer** is a 150-year-old mansion tucked away on one of the capital's quiet, narrow lanes, with views of the town and port and rooms decorated in 19th-century Cycladic style. The **Hotel Vourlis**, built in 1886, was awarded the Europa Nostra Award in 1985 and features rooms decorated with 19th-century heirlooms. Also comfortable are the stately, recently renovated **Hotel Hermes**, on Kanáris Square, and the **Europe Hotel**, located in Ermoupolis's first public building, built in 1823—and renovated since, of course. Suites and apartments at such places as the posh new **Sea Colors** may be booked through the TeamWork Holidays office on the waterfront at 10 Akti P. Ralli. These rather exclusive apartments with kitchenettes are housed in a newly renovated Neoclassical-style house. Located in the center of town just five minutes from the port, each is fully equipped with kitchen, refrigerator, bathroom, and balcony. Take note: Water is scarce on Syros, so hotels routinely mix saline with their fresh water—quite a shock when you've just lathered your hair and the shampoo won't rinse out. Bring along saltwater soap, sold at yacht supply stores.

Dining in Ermoupolis, as elsewhere on the island, is nothing special. Breakfasts of many stripes are served on the quayside at places like **Corto** and **Tramps**. The **Eliana**, on Miaoulis Square, is probably the town's best restaurant, a friendly place to sit and watch the passing crowd while enjoying excellent local food. The **Silivani**, a family taverna opposite the lively **Piano Bar**, also on the square, is a favorite with locals. The **Pantheon**, on the square, serves pizza and other light fare, while **Ta Yannena**, on the waterfront off Kanaris Square, serves grilled meats and seafood; it can be noisy in summer. The **Medusa**, up little Androu Street, serves traditional Greek foods. Try to sample Syros's smoky San Michali cheese and local wines, especially the Vatis label whites and barrel wines from the village of Vissas.

After hours there is the aforementioned Piano Bar and, about five minutes out of town on the Vari road, the **Neraïda**, a bouzouki club.

In Ano Syros enjoy meatballs, *loukániko* (Greek sausage), and *louza* (spicy salt pork) at **Lilis** restaurant and bouzouki at **Rachamos**.

Around the Island

From the harborfront in Ermoupolis a fleet of ancient but stalwart faded-aqua buses plies the routes to outlying villages and beaches in addition to Ano Syros. Blue bus schedules are posted everywhere on the island, but it's wise to check at the milk bar across from the alfresco depot for actual departure times, which tend to change depending on any number of factors.

There are five major bus routes, and departures are frequent, though the last daily bus back from the beach may leave a bit too early for some bathers. Gray taxis are omnipresent and reasonable. Renting mopeds is ill-advised: Bus drivers sound their horns mightily at blind curves; other drivers may not. To visit the inland agricultural villages, with their distinctive Cycladic architecture, you really need to arrive with a rental car or rent one on the island through TeamWork Holidays.

At the end of its own express bus route is **Kini**, 9 km (5.5 miles) west of Ermoupolis, a long horseshoe bay with two beaches. The **Kelepouris** taverna here is a good place to watch the sun sink behind Kythnos. Around the headland to the right (north), a half-hour walk or ten minutes by caïque, is **Delfíni**, a nudist beach with a lone taverna and the occasional jellyfish, depending on wind direction. After dark visit **Dakrotsides** on the beach at Kini for authentic—not dressed up for the tourist trade—bouzouki.

To the southwest, 8 km (5 miles) from Ermoupolis, **Galissás** is Syros's most "northern European" beach resort; it is undergoing development and offers modern amenities plus camping grounds and pubs. The **Maistrali Café/Bar and Hotel** is a good place for breakfast. The **Françoise Hotel** caters to package tours, but it is the only hotel near a truly beautiful beach: Over the headland past the little chapel of Ayia Rakou is the small, pebbly nudist beach called **Armeos**, where the water is clean and the view uncluttered. Here, tamarisk trees soften Syros's stark topography.

There are three other adequate beach resorts providing basic services on the southern bus route: **Hotel Olympia** in Fínikas; **Possidonion Hotel** in Poseidonía (or Dellagrázia); and **Hotel Alexandra** in Megas Yialós. All are crowded in season, primarily with Athenian families, and all have tavernas. Visitors electing to stay at one of these resorts will have to round bluffs on foot or by caïque to reach more secluded bathing spots. Wear sturdy shoes—that reptile in the path is probably a lizard, but it could be a pit viper—

wear head gear, and take along water. There is little shade afforded by Syros's monkey puzzle and agave trees.

GETTING AROUND

A four-and-a-half-hour ferryboat trip from Piraeus in good weather, Syros may be socked in for days at a time when the *meltémi* blows or during winter storms. The summer crossing is pleasanter if you take the trouble to book ahead—preferably first class—on air-conditioned vessels such as the *Panayía Tínou*. Cabins are available on some ships, and these should also be booked in advance through a travel agent. Make reservations for cars and campers well in advance, too, and purchase return space upon debarkation in high season.

Syros, with its busy port, has good connections with all the other Cycladic islands as well as with Piraeus and Rafina. The Gaviotis travel agencies (24 Aktí Papágou or 52–54 Aktí P. Ralli) on the harbor supply information regarding all steamship lines and sell tickets for all ferries. Other offices may decline to inform travellers about ships listed with rival companies. There are daily ferries from Piraeus from early April through October; crossings are every other day in winter. Elias and George Gaviotis will also arrange excursions to neighboring Mykonos, Tinos, and Delos in season and boat rentals to less crowded and thus more attractive beaches on Syros proper.

TeamWork Holidays, at 10 Akti P. Ralli, also on the waterfront, is a good place to arrange for accommodation in Ermoupolis or at one of the beach resorts (Tel: 0281-234-00 or 228-66; Fax: 0281-235-08).

—*Elizabeth Boleman Herring*

NAXOS

When Mykonos got too crowded, purists headed for Paros, sweetly similar. When Paros suffered the same fate, they crossed the six-mile strait to Naxos, tartly dissimilar. Now Naxos is equally crowded, although, as is always true in the Mediterranean, only near the sea. Since Naxos, by far the largest of the Cyclades, is composed mostly of mountains,

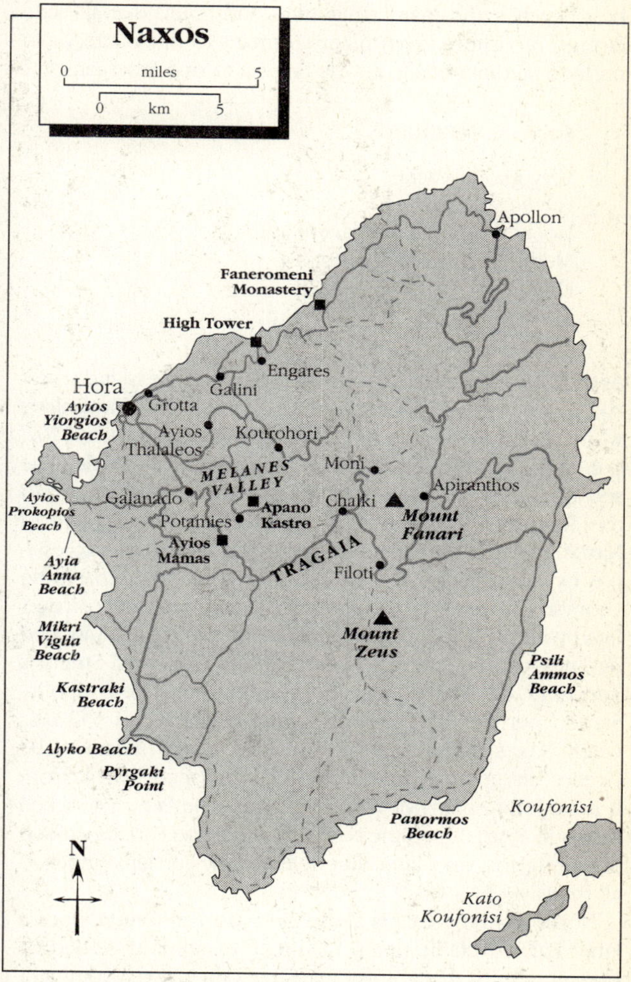
Naxos
0 miles 5
0 km 5
Apollon
Faneromeni Monastery
High Tower
Engares
Hora
Galini
Grotta
Ayios Yiorgios Beach
Ayios Thalaleos
Kourohori
Moni
Melanes Valley
Apiranthos
Ayios Prokopios Beach
Galanado
Apano Kastro
Chalki
Mount Fanari
Potamies
Ayios Mamas
Ayia Anna Beach
Tragaia
Filoti
Mikri Viglia Beach
Mount Zeus
Psili Ammos Beach
Kastraki Beach
Alyko Beach
Pyrgaki Point
Panormos Beach
Koufonisi
N
Kato Koufonisi

isolated villages, and fertile valleys, even in season it is easy to escape the hectic town. A continent in miniature, Naxos especially beckons the hiker, the Medieval-history buff, and the lover of Byzantine art—130 churches with wall paintings have been investigated so far. It has some of the Cyclades' best beaches and many restaurants and hotels that attract a farrago of visitors, from hiker Germans to biker Italians to nudist Scandinavians to rowdy English to rich Athenians.

MAJOR INTEREST

Very good beaches
Fertile valleys
Isolated mountain villages
Medieval ruins and churches
Hiking
Medieval Kastro

As the boat approaches the docks at Hora on the island's west coast, you will see two holy places. One is the immaculate white chapel on an islet built into the Venetian dock in 1707, but now separate, dedicated to the Virgin of Myrtle. The second is the great 21½-foot-high gateway (called Portara) to the Temple of Apollo, which has become the emblem of Naxos. The Naxians call this temple, on a second islet accessible by a causeway, the **Palátia**. It was thought that here Dionysos, whose symbols appear on Naxos's ancient coinage, lived with his bride Ariadne, the Cretan princess abandoned by Theseus. (For the whole story listen to Richard Strauss's *Adriadne auf Naxos*.) But the building belongs to Apollo. Started perhaps by Lygdamis, tyrant of Naxos, in 530 B.C., when Naxos dominated the Cyclades, it was meant to be Greece's largest temple, but was left unfinished. Marble from it is built into many of Naxos's houses. The Persians sacked Naxos in 490 B.C., and the Naxians (unlike the Parians) joined the Athenians, who, after they defeated the Persians, annexed all the islands.

North from the Palatia along the coast lies **Grotta**, once a large Early Cycladic (after 3200 B.C.) community settled by Jews in the 16th century A.D. The other two prominent monuments on Hora's quay are the Catholic **church of Saint Anthony** (near the Palatia), built in 1440 by the dowager Duchess Crispo, and the modern bronze statue of Minister of Finance Petros Protopapadakis, whom the Naxians consider a hero, although he was shot for high treason in 1922.

Hora

The town of Naxos, where 3,000 of the island's 14,000 people live, feels like three or four towns jammed together: the port, with its bustle and dilapidation, cafés and tourist services; the *borgo* (market area), with its narrow winding alleys, better shops, and old restaurants; new Ayios Yiórgios, which looks like a Piraeus suburb but is full of shops and eateries popular with the Greeks; and the crowning Kastro (Castle), a serene, preserved Venetian hilltown. Though the town is officially called Naxos, most maps and residents call it Hora. And while not fresh and pretty, Hora is not dull; in fact, there may be more to explore here than in any other town in the Cyclades.

Start your tour in the main square, rather toward the northern end of the waterfront near a shop that sells the sweet citron liquor distilled from Naxos lemons. Take the main street to the right (back to the sea), past **Mathiassos's** sweetshop, which makes its own triple-thick yogurt, up to the **church of Profitis Ilías**, built by the same Duchess Crispo. Inside are two excellent icons by Angelos of Crete, who taught Domenikos Theotokopoulos, known elsewhere as El Greco. Continuing up through the maze of alleys and forking left, the street enters the only preserved gate of the **Kastro**'s original seven, built by the conquering Venetians in 1207, when they also rebuilt the ancient sea mole in the harbor below to enhance their sea power. The wood of the original door, for all its worn, rough appearance, feels as soft as velvet. Inside, the Kastro is quiet and noble, unchanged for half a millennium.

In 1204 the Fourth Crusade, instead of freeing Jerusalem, conquered Byzantine Constantinople, the wealthiest city in the western world. The Cyclades, rich spoils, went to the seafaring Venetians, and the doge's nephew, Marco Sanudo, established his rule in Naxos. When Venice refused to grant him independence in 1210, Sanudo allied himself with Henry of Flanders, the Latin emperor, and became duke of the Archipelago, superior in rank to all the other Aegean barons. The Sanudi held sway from their capital at Naxos until 1383, when the Crispi (who now live on Paros) assumed power by assassination.

All over the Cyclades families bear Italian names. Here on Naxos's Kastro the names on the doors of the fine old houses—and the coats of arms over them—belong to descendants of the Venetians who ruled for nearly 400 years and who were until recently the landed, rich aristocracy. The Barozzi, who ruled Santorini; the Della Rocca, who ruled Athens; the Sommaripa, who ruled Paros—all are still here and attend mass at the 13th-century Catholic cathedral on the Kastro's uppermost square. The marble slabs in the church floor—the earliest date from 1619—entomb their ancestors. Near the church are the massive Ursuline Convent, once renowned but recently closed; stately gardens and mansions; and the French School, built in 1627, which now houses the Archaeological Museum. The school's most famous alumnus, Nikos Kazantzakis, later wrote *Zorba the Greek* and *The Last Temptation of Christ*; in his autobiography, *Report to Greco,* he praises highly the education he received here. The five-story building, part of the Venetian fortification wall and including two of its towers, is one of the Kastro's handsomest. (For fascinating accounts of Naxos covering the period of 1687 to 1885, see *Naxos, Old Travel Descriptions,* edited by Christian Ucke.)

The **Archaeological Museum** of Naxos rivals the museum on Delos for the best collection of antiquities in the islands. Most important are the Cycladic (3000 to 2000 B.C.) marble goddesses (if that is what they are) with folded arms and prominent breasts, belly, and pubes; they were meant to lie on their backs, not to stand upright, as displayed. Although Naxos seems to have suffered the general depopulation of Greece's Dark Ages (1100 to 850 B.C.), the ensuing Geometric period (850 to 700) contributed many fine objects, including giant amphorae with meander and cross designs. The Geometric cemetery above the village of Chalki (see below), marked by a seven-foot monolith, provided small pots with linear designs. A colorful mosaic floor depicts a half-nude nereid riding a sea monster, watched by deer and peacocks.

On the north side of the Kastro, above the Orthodox cathedral, are two quiet (rare in Naxos) hotels, both with splendid views: the **Panorama**, with the wider view, and the **Anixi**, with a lovely garden. A rich relation to these is the nearby **Chateau Zevgoli**, Naxos's prettiest hotel, whose manager, Despina Kitini, keeps the decor authentically Cycladic. Since so many places in the Kastro have panoramic views, you may want to eat there; try the **Oniro Roof Garden** or the **Castro**, on the high square by the statue. The oldest restaurant (1908) in the busy borgo below is **Lukullus**, whose owner, Vasilis, has recently fixed it up. The museum deskman also runs the most interesting shop in the borgo, **Loom**, stocked with expensive old objects.

AROUND THE ISLAND

Naxos's inland scenery, with its dramatic mountains, suddenly revealed valleys, distant villages, and rich gardens, surpasses that of the other islands. There are two main routes to take by vehicle to get an idea of this richness: to the Melanes Valley just east of Hora, and to Apollon through the central mountains and back along the north coast road.

The Melanes Valley

The road to Melanes leaves Hora to the south, passes through a few flat miles of potato fields (potatoes are Naxos's chief export), and ascends (northward) to the village of Ayios Thalaléos. Then the villages of Melanes come into view. The first one, **Kourohóri**, claims the Della Rocca Tower. As you continue on into the mountains, 12 km (7.5 miles) from Hora a crude sign directs you down into a green orchard. A *kouros,* a 26-foot-tall unfinished statue of a nude youth from circa 550 B.C., reposes in a lush garden amid olive and lemon trees, vines, and running water. His broken thigh probably demanded abandonment of the unwieldy slab of stone. There is a similar kouros in some fields above. The owners of the garden, who discovered the kouros in 1943, serve snacks and cold drinks under trees; the garden remains cool even in summer.

Potamies

The longest, fullest excursion on Naxos is to Apollon on the northeast coast; the bus takes three hours, crossing the island's massif and providing at least a glimpse of many villages. Soon after leaving Hora you pass through Galanado to the southeast, and then right away past the Bellonia Tower, which watches over the coastal plain. As the road ascends you see the sandy beaches of the southeast coast: **Pánormos** and **Psilí Ammos** are both suitable for swimming and are accessible by boat or car (the road to Panormos, however, is poor). Then you reach a pass with the most spectacular view in the Cyclades: the Potamiés (Rivers) Valley. The gray church in the orange grove below, **Ayios Mamas**, was built in the ninth century; it fell into disuse after the Venetians made it Catholic. The road winds about Mount Profítis Ilías, passing, on a bleak crag, Apáno Kastro, fortified by Marco Sanudo II after 1262, obviously to keep control over Naxos's central, fertile valleys; 400 feet to the southeast lies the aforementioned **Geometric Cemetery**.

Tragaia

The immense paradisal olive grove beyond Potamies is called the Tragaía; scattered within it are 12 little villages and many Byzantine churches. Arcadian walks here are numberless. In **Chalkí**, right by the bus stop, stands the recently restored **church of the First-Enthroned Virgin**, whose inscription dates it from 1052, but with parts of the church 500 years older. Usually open from 10:00 A.M. to 1:00 P.M., it contains many beautiful and historically important wall paintings; some of these, such as the Apostles in the bema, are pre-Iconoclastic (before 726). The Annunciation over the sanctuary is a masterpiece. The 17th-century **Grazia Tower**, the best preserved on Naxos, with the Barozzi coat of arms, overlooks the church.

Just past Chalki on the main road, a paved road to the north leads to the village of **Moní**, where there are restaurants and cafés with spectacular views over the Tragaia. Halfway to Moni, on the right, is the cemetery and church called the **Drosiani**, or Dewy Virgin; if it's closed, ring the bell and the priest's wife will unlock it (a small donation is not inappropriate). The roughly built church, parts of which date from the sixth century, contains impressive, if damaged, wall paintings of great antiquity. The iconography of the dome painting, with two facing busts of Christ as a youth and as a mature man in roundels, is unique. The painting of the Virgin in the north conch (seventh century) has an especially haunting, ovoid face. Two other small churches near Chalki—**Ayios Yiorgos Diasoritis** and **Ayios Ioannis Keramí**—also contain splendid old wall paintings. Chalki's reluctant priest keeps the keys.

The views between Chalki and Filoti to the south refresh you with the flashing pale green of olive trees as the road winds around Mount Zeus (Zas), at 3,295 feet the Cyclades' highest mountain. The ancient Naxians believed that Zeus was born in a great cave halfway up. (While the more accepted place for the birth of Zeus is Mount Ida on Crete, this cave of Zeus was a place for prehistoric cult worship.) The cave is one of Greece's largest. To walk there, leave the main road above Filoti and climb Mount Zeus's northwest slope, passing through a grove of olive trees with a marble cistern. You will see the cave's mouth at the head of a big gorge (8 km/5 miles), and just before the cave, a spring with cold water. Don't forget a flashlight, even though it may disturb the bats in the huge main chamber.

Except for Hora, now some 19 km (12 miles) west, **Filóti** is the largest village on Naxos; it has restaurants, groceries, and cafés under plane trees—and a chronic water shortage, which does not inhibit the three-day festival of the Dormition starting August 14.

Apiranthos

North of Filoti the road rises rapidly along the northwest flank of Mount Zeus and doubles back high above the town. From here you get the best view of the Tragaia. The road now passes the radar station next to a chapel dedicated to St. John the Theologian and emerges on the other side of Zeus with a long view to the northeast. Nine kilometers (5.5 miles) north of Filoti is Apíranthos. The streets of this high mountain village are paved in marble, and many of the old gray-stone houses, built by the Crispi in the 14th century, have marble doorways. Sometimes very old men in the traditional costume of wide pants and vest can be seen drinking at the café, with its vast mountain vista. The folk of Apiranthos came from Crete, and they speak with an accent; they also produce some of the best musicians on an island renowned for music. With strangers their manner is reserved. The little **museum** of Apiranthos, a labor of love of the Apiranthian mathematician Michael Bardiani, displays some unique marble plaques primitively decorated with, it is thought, magical scenes of everyday life: the hunt, grazing animals, and sea journeys. Most of the plaques are from the Protocycladic period. If you have time to kill while waiting for the bus, a visit to the **Geological Museum**, on the second floor of the school, is of local interest.

Apollon

North of Apiranthos, as the road skirts Mount Fanári, the landscape is forbidding—until the windy Stavros Pass, where breathtaking views open to the west and east toward Amorgos. As the road descends toward Apollon its hairpin turns go through several remote villages, whose men work Greece's only emery mine. An abrasive now exported to Germany, emery was used to polish marble in ancient times.

A little fishing village, Apóllon (49 km/30 miles northeast of Hora) is touristy in summer, with tavernas, the pretty, simple, Cycladic **Hotel Adonis** by the sea, a well set up campsite, and a little beach, usually pounded by waves. Since there's not much choice at Apollon, the Adonis hotel's clientele is mixed. Apollon also claims its own rough-hewn bearded kouros on a hillside above the village. Thirty-five feet long and weighing 30 tons, it was abandoned about 600 B.C. Perhaps it suggested the town's divine appellation.

The North Coast

The northern coast road back (no bus) is rough but much shorter than the inland route. Ten kilometers (6 miles) southwest of Apollon you pass the Cocco family tower, built in 1770 to dominate northern Naxos. After another 13 km (8 miles) you pass the abandoned **Faneroméni Monastery**, built in 1606, very prepossessing in this lonely spot. From the village of Engarés the road becomes paved again and passes through Galíni (Tranquillity). From here a turnoff leads to the High Tower, which dominates its valley. This tower was built in 1660, also by the Cocco family. In the 17th century the Orthodox Cocco and Catholic Barozzi clans feuded after a Cocco insulted a Barozzi's wife, who was daughter of the French consul. Barozzi murdered and mutilated his enemy, whose kinsmen in turn murdered the French consul. The Barozzi daughter called upon her husband, the Maltese privateer Raimond de Modène, to besiege the High Tower, but the Cocco held out. Twenty years later the clans resolved the vendetta with a marriage.

The Turks, contrary to their fierce reputation, left Naxos and the islands alone, only collecting taxes here. But 2 km (about a mile) before Hora there is one monument to their long domination (1566 to 1821), the little, domed **Aga's Fountain**, built in 1759. The Ottoman calligraphy on it means "The renowned Aga, Voivode of Naxos, built the fountain with great care in the hope that its water will make passers-by tolerant and forgiving."

Western Beaches

The road south from Hora down the west side of Naxos leads to fine beaches, all protected from the north wind. The first, before the peninsula, Ayios Yiórgios, is overdeveloped; the second, **Ayia Anna**, attracts nudists; then comes **Ayios Prokópios**, beautiful despite many new villas; **Mikrí Víglia**, where expensive bungalows are for rent; **Kastráki**, also with villas to rent; and **Alyko**: all long, sandy, out of the north wind, and with superb views of Paros. Each beach has a taverna. Then comes **Pyrgáki Point**, where there is a large, isolated resort overlooking the long beach. Despite such development these beaches are often uncrowded. Lord Byron liked to swim, too, and Naxos was his favorite island, where he wanted to settle forever.

GETTING AROUND

In summer three or four ferries a day from Piraeus and Rafina (near Athens) stop at Naxos; fewer make the trip off-season. The voyage takes seven to nine hours, depending on season, weather, and stops (boats always stop first on Paros, sometimes on Syros). Naxos has boat connections with 15 islands: daily connections with Syros, Paros, Ios, and Santorini, regular connections with Donoussa, Schinoussa, Herakleia, Koufonisi, Ikaria, Samos, Amorgos, Mykonos, Folegandros, Anafi, Sikinos, and with Rafina on the mainland. Advance tickets are recommended for Easter and August 15, when schedules temporarily change.

Buses go to nearly all Naxos's many villages. The schedule is posted at the main stop on the quay near the boat dock. Beach routes are jammed in summer. Many cars and motorbikes are for rent; since Naxos is the biggest and most mountainous of the Cyclades, choose with care. Many taxis wait on the quay.

—*Jeffrey Carson*

PAROS

Paros was the favorite island of Nobel Prize–winning poet George Seferis, and Archilochus, the creator of iambic verse, wrote the first signed love poem here in the seventh century B.C. Paros has been praised for poetic reasons: charming villages, cafés by the sea, blond beaches, harmonious landscapes, a sense of history. But resources are not overstrained (except in mid-August), and the popular ideal of what a "Greek island" should be is authentically realized here. Consequently, Paros's popularity has risen dramatically in the last decade.

Writers have frequently praised Parian marble, perhaps the world's best. The stone, in Classical times the most expensive, is more translucent than that of Carrara. The

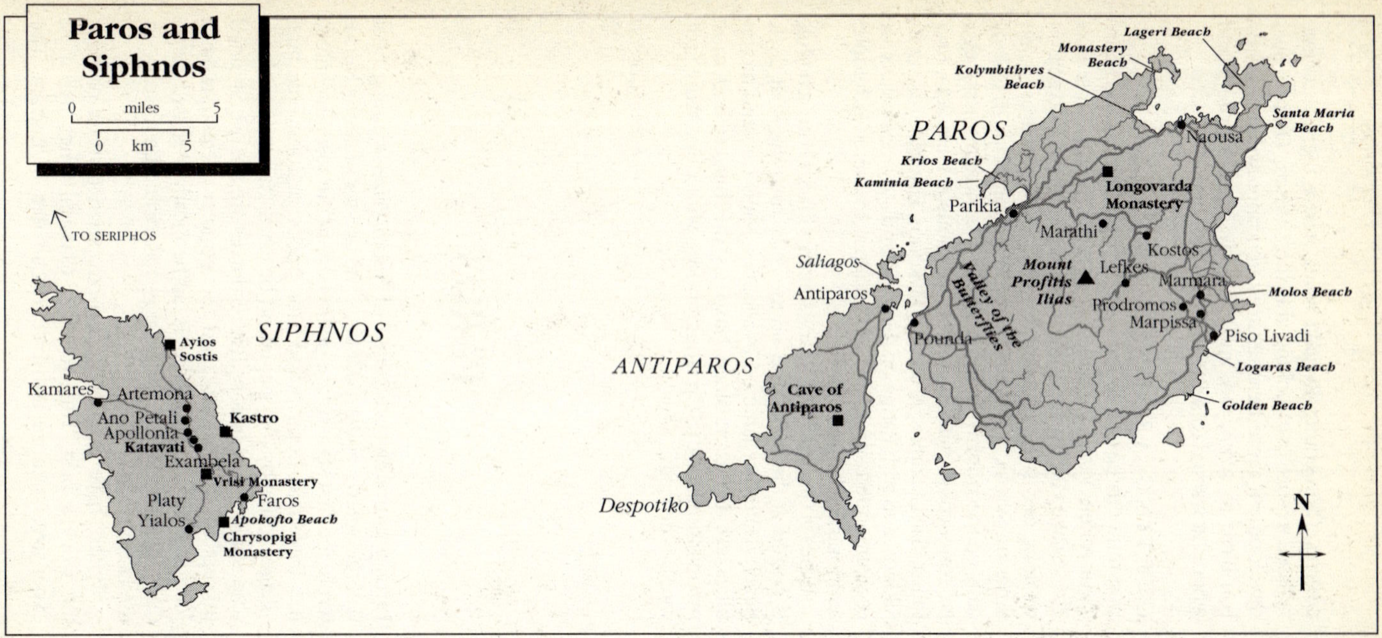

Paros and Siphnos
0 miles 5
0 km 5
TO SERIPHOS
SIPHNOS
Ayios Sostis
Kamares
Artemona
Ano Petali
Apollonia
Katavati
Kastro
Exambela
Vrisi Monastery
Faros
Platy Yialos
Apokofto Beach
Chrysopigi Monastery
ANTIPAROS
Despotiko
Cave of Antiparos
Antiparos
Saliagos
PAROS
Krios Beach
Kaminia Beach
Parikia
Kolymbithres Beach
Monastery Beach
Lageri Beach
Santa Maria Beach
Naousa
Longovarda Monastery
Marathi
Kostos
Lefkes
Mount Profitis Ilias
Valley of the Butterflies
Pounda
Marmara
Prodromos
Marpissa
Molos Beach
Piso Livadi
Logaras Beach
Golden Beach
N

Venus de Milo, the Hermes of Praxiteles, the tomb of Napoleon, and many fragments built into houses and walls here possess an unequaled sheen. The deep tunnels of Marathi's ancient quarries (see below), once worked by thousands of slaves, are strewn with chunks of it, allowing you to see why ancient builders preferred it for roof-tiles—to let the light glow through.

Because of its marble Paros assumed cultural importance in the Cycladic Age (3000 to 2000 B.C.). Beautiful statuettes and vases were exported around the Aegean in boats no bigger than the many caïques that bring in fish every morning. Later Paros became a center of Ionian civilization. The Parian sculptor Skopas worked with the famed marble in the fourth century B.C., and the late Isamu Noguchi visited the quarries to get some stone in more recent times.

MAJOR INTEREST

Charming villages
White-sand beaches
Undeveloped landscapes
Ancient marble quarries
Church of a Hundred Doors
Day trip to island of Antiparos

Paros today is small enough to feel insular—sea vistas are the rule—yet large enough to absorb younger travellers here for the vigorous (overly vigorous in August) nightlife, families looking for an affordable beach holiday, and the many Europeans who have built luxurious villas. Paros also has a variety of accommodations ranging from upper middle class (but not luxury) to camping. Though only a few restaurants remain open all year, from May to October there are dozens to choose among.

Paros has three main towns—the port and capital Parikia on the west coast, the fishing village of Naousa to the north, and the farming mountain town of Lefkes—as well as a sprinkling of little villages.

Parikia

Parikía, along with Mykonos, may be the Cyclades' prettiest port town; Seferis said it was visual music.

From the dock, caïques take bathers to the beaches of **Krios** and **Kaminia** across the bay; because they are pretty, sandy, and protected from the prevailing north wind, they are very popular. On the hill above them are the ruins of the Archaic **Delion**; not much is left of Apollo's temple, but the splendid view toward Delos is a reminder of the god's power.

The two main streets, the waterfront, and the market converge at the windmill by the dock, now a tourist information center. Starting here and walking into the market, you traverse a large square with new shops, cafés, travel offices, taxi stands, and the somewhat-parched town gardens. As you continue the town becomes quite charming. At the first crossroads is the **Yria** pottery studio, whose owners, Stelios and Monique Ghikas, have been much praised for their designs based on ancient and Byzantine models. (You can also visit their busy workshop right above the road to the village of Kostos.) Turn left here and you pass more shops, the house where Greek revolutionary heroine Mando Mavroyeni ended her life forgotten and neglected, and some stately town houses with marble balconies and gardens where the descendants of the old aristocracy still live. Finally you reach the **Church of a Hundred Doors**, Greece's oldest church in continual use.

The church is officially called the Dormition of the Virgin; the Parians call it the Panayía (All Holy Virgin); history books call it Katapoliani (Below the Town); and guidebooks call it the Church of a Hundred Doors, a misleading name. No one knows its exact age; it was built in the sixth century, probably during the reign of Justinian, perhaps by a Parian disciple of the architect of Istanbul's St. Sophia. It is certainly beautiful enough. According to legend, Saint Helen, the mother of the first Christian emperor, Constantine, vowed to establish a church on Paros, where she had weathered a storm, should she find the wood of the True Cross. She did, and Justinian fulfilled her vow.

The whitewashed cloister was built to protect monks in the 17th century, when pirates such as Hugues Creveliers (Byron's Corsair) operated from Paros. Today it encloses a lovely courtyard resplendent with flowers, old marbles, and church bells hanging in a gnarled cypress—the bell tower fell down in an earthquake in 1783. In September the Santorini Music Festival presents classical music concerts in this heavenly spot.

Entering the church (in modest dress), you are immediately struck by a sense of the mysterious and by the clear proportions of the sanctuary. The columns are pre-Christian, but the marble capitals are elegant Byzantine work, as are the marble screen and iconostasis. Nicholas Mavroyenis, a

Parian who became a high government official under the sultan, donated the silver reliefs over the three large icons in 1788, as well as the three elaborately carved marble fountains in the market. Saint Theoktisti's tiny footprint is sunk in the stone under the wooden floor-screen. She was kidnapped from Lesvos by Arab pirates, perhaps in the ninth century, and escaped on Paros. It is said that when a visiting hunter cut off her hand for a relic after she died, his boat's sails filled but the boat did not move. He restored the hand. Her cenotaph is here, as well as one of her wee bones.

At the back of the church a door leads into what is really the separate **church of Ayios Nikólaos**, older than the main church. It has an austere double row of Classical Doric columns, a 1611 iconostasis, and a marble bishop's throne. The spirit of early Christianity finds its true home here. Next to the church stands the old baptistry (c. 1000), whose marble font has a famous frieze of Greek crosses; it was closed for years, but baptisms are now sometimes performed here. There are scant traces of a mosaic floor and many fragments from the Roman-period buildings that preceded it. The church celebrates the day of Dormition on August 15, Paros's most crowded day.

After leaving the church, return to the first crossroads, start down the market street, and you will see to your left, over an archway, two folk statues that the Parians claim once marked the entrance to a house of ill repute. A bit farther on to the right, stairs climb to the 13th-century **Kastro** on the ancient acropolis that rises between the market and the waterfront. The Kastro's fortification wall is constructed of remains from the two or three Classical temples that once covered the hill (ancient Paros was famous for its architecture). The marbles were reconstructed into a fort by the Venetians, who conquered Paros in 1207. The island was then ruled from Naxos, first by the Sanudi and then by the still-resident Crispi, until the Turks took over in 1566. A stone-paved road began at the fort and traversed the island (see Lefkes, below) to another fort on the Kefalos hill, overlooking Marpissa and beautiful Molos beach. On the Kastro's high point stands the arcaded church of Saints Constantine and Helen, whose blue dome is first glimpsed from the ferry. Next to it are the foundations of an Archaic (c. 500 B.C.) temple to Apollo. During the Persian invasion of Greece in 490 B.C., the Parians deliberately delayed sending their ships to join the battle. When the victorious Athenian general Miltiades attempted to punish the prudent Parians, who were holed up behind the acropolis (now Kastro) walls, he broke his thigh leaping the wall, abandoned the siege, was impeached, and died of gangrene.

Farther along on the left past the steps to the Kastro is **Kostas Akalestos's Parikia Tours**; in addition to the usual travel arrangements, Kostas rents villas and bungalows. A little farther along is the unpretentious, friendly **Dina Hotel**, with a cool garden, frequently patronized by returning visitors who don't care for frills. Bear right at the split and you'll pass the old Neoclassical building that houses the **Aegean Center for the Arts**, whose gallery and art school attract many artists to Paros. Artists on extended stays often exhibit at this American college, poets give readings, and there are lectures.

Just past the Aegean Center the market rejoins the newly widened waterfront street. To the right (toward the dock) is where the famous Paros nightlife centers, to be avoided by the post-pubescent and sober. To the left a row of cafés and eateries faces the evening parade and sunset. If the prevailing north wind is too blustery, a quiet place in town for an aperitif is the **Apollon Café**, with its garden under fruitful pear trees; its building used to house Paros's olive press. And in summer the quietest restaurant in town is Alfons Weber's **Tamarisko**, which also has a secluded garden. Beyond the cafés the waterfront road climbs past a small jetty to St. Anna's hill, with a windmill and the two most comfortable hotels on Paros, the **Xenia** and the **Pandrosos**, where better-off visitors stay. Their seaside rooms have magnificent views of Parikia Bay and the sunset. The stairs down the cliff lead to a sea cave once haunted by nymphs and now dedicated to Saint John.

The **Archaeological Museum**, between the church and the new high school, contains half of the famous Parian Chronicle (the other half is in the Ashmolean Museum at Oxford), a chronological account of the main events of Greek history, from 1582 to 264 B.C., carved on a lucent slab of Parian marble. (Some of the dates are correct, some are not.) Objects added most recently to the small collection are from the excavations near Naousa. The large mosaic showing Herakles hunting was found in the Church of a Hundred Doors.

The **Valley of the Butterflies**, 6.5 km (4 miles) from Parikia on Paros's western slopes, is in a beautiful area of lush vegetation, not far from the convent of Christ of the Woods (Tou Dasous). It makes a lovely walk, taking about one and a half hours one way.

Naousa

The first paved road on Paros leads to Náousa, 10 km (6 miles) northeast of Parikia. On the way it passes (right after the fork) a little ruin called **Three Churches**—remains of three 17th-century churches made from one 7th-century church, which in turn was constructed of marbles from the 4th-century B.C. heroön of Archilochus. Then in the mountains to the right you pass **Longovárda Monastery**, established in 1683. The present abbot, Father Hierotheos, used to paint icons before assuming (by democratic vote) leadership. Visitors (men only) are received courteously, but they are not encouraged.

Just 20 years ago Naousa was a sleepy fishing village; today it attracts sophisticates from all over Europe. Boutiques and bars are everywhere. The center of all this nightlife is the enclosed little fishermen's harbor and wharf, whose brightly colored boats jostle gunwale to gunwale. The half-submerged Venetian ruin that forms part of the breakwater was rebuilt by the Russians (under Count Orlov), who used Naousa as a base in their campaign against the Turks from 1700 to 1774. Too picturesque for its own good, such a port would charge admission in North America. It is *the* place on Paros to sit for drinks; those in the know order *souma,* the clear, local firewater. (Try **Kargas** *ouzerí* out by the church, where the seafood is prepared over charcoal.) Fishing activities proceed as always; the fishermen disdain the tourists as a point of honor.

Probably the best restaurant in Naousa for a regular Greek meal is the **Minoa**, on a square on the long through-street up toward the big church. And across the street from it is the **Laloula**, which serves good Continental cuisine in a garden out of the crush. Nearby is Naousa's fanciest restaurant, **Christos**, in a quiet courtyard with old, whitewashed walls and excellent Greek food.

From the harbor, caïques take bathers to four beaches around Naousa's capacious harbor. **Kolymbíthres**, the most developed, has much-photographed, wind-eroded rocks; **Monastery** is for nudists; **Lageri** and **Santa Maria** are less crowded, long and sandy, and frequented by windsurfers.

Lefkes and the Lower Villages

The mountain road to Lefkes (10 km/6 miles east of Parikia) passes the turnoff to the ancient marble quarries at **Maráthi**, where three ancient tunnels still bore deep into the marble mountain, skirts the pretty village of **Kostos**, and traverses Paros's richest olive groves. Lefkes (which means "poplars") is representative of a common phenomenon in Greece: a cool, green mountain village with few tourists because it is inconvenient to the sea. In Turkish times, when ports were subject to pirate raids, Lefkes was the island's capital, with fine houses and 3,000 inhabitants. The **Hotel Xenia** here, splendidly situated, is comfortable, spacious, and well run, perfect for in-season visitors who hate noise and disdain the "in" scene. The terrace restaurant overlooks the valley and serves, albeit slowly, excellent snails, rabbit, pigeon, and fritters.

From Lefkes you can take an excellent road that climbs **Mount Profítis Ilías**, 2,500 feet high and capped by a radio tower and two churches, for a panoramic if windy view of Paros and the islands. The road down from Lefkes leads to the Lower Villages, as does the stone-paved way on the valley's right side, the Byzantine highway that once crossed the island. Walking this takes about an hour and concludes at the walled village of **Pródromos**. Parians favor **Yannis Roussos's** restaurant just outside Prodromos's wall for Sunday lunch; chickpeas are the specialty.

Of the other Lower Villages, **Márpissa** and **Mármara** (whence a dirt road goes to splendid **Molos** beach and a couple of fish restaurants) are quiet and pretty, but **Piso Livádi**, a fishing village with a beach, gets lively in summer. A mile past it is popular **Logaras** beach, and past that is **Golden** beach, the most extensive stretch of sand on Paros. If you're in an exploring mood, a drive around Paros will take you past many unfrequented beaches.

ANTÍPAROS

Antíparos means "across from Paros," and the island's fortunes have always depended upon her big sister. In fact, underwater ruins show that a causeway once joined them.

There are two ways to get to Antiparos. One is by caïque from Parikia, a beautiful 40-minute ride along Paros's gentle western coast. The islet in the strait to the west is **Sáliagos** (Snail), important archaeologically because the earliest traces of Protocycladic village life—from before 4500 B.C.—have been excavated here, including house foundations, obsidian tools, and female figurines. The next verdant islet, Revmatonisi, belongs to the Goulandris family, who established Athens's Cycladic museum. The other way to get to Antiparos, better in rough weather, is to go by bus from Parikia to Pounda (7 km/4 miles) and then take the new six-car ferry, a ten-minute ride.

The port of Antiparos has one main street and two centers of activity: the quay area and the main square, a block in. To the right of the square are houses and the castle's 15th-century wall. At the other end of the quay from the ferry dock a dirt road takes you, after ten minutes on foot, to an idyllic sandy beach; you can wade across to the islet opposite, Fira, where sheep and goats graze. A crowded campsite abuts the beach, popular with young nudists.

In the 19th century the most famous tourist sight in the Aegean was the **Cave of Antiparos**. In August it still attracts over 500 visitors a day. Antiparos's one bus drives the 9 km (5.5 miles) and climbs the 538 feet to the grotto. Four hundred steps descend into huge chambers, pass beneath enormous pipe-organ stalactites, and skirt immense stalagmites. In 1673 the French ambassador celebrated Christmas Mass here with 500 guests, who stayed three days. The huge stalagmite known since then as the Altar Table has a commemorative inscription on its base.

GETTING AROUND

Paros is a hub for Aegean sea travel; more boats (often 30 a day) stop at Paros every day than at any other island. The trip takes from five to seven hours, depending on season, stops, weather, size of boat, and departure from Piraeus or Rafina (shorter). Paros also has scheduled boat connections with 20 other islands and with Thessaloniki. Daily connections (in summer) are with Syros, Naxos, Ios, Santorini, Mykonos, and Delos. Regular connections are with Thessaloniki, Skiathos, Skopelos, Schinoussa, Donoussa, Herakleia, Koufonisi, Rhodes, Kos, Crete, Siphnos, Tinos, Anafi, Sikinos, Folegandros, Ikaria, and Samos. A new boat service was initiated in 1990 linking Ancona, Piraeus, Paros, Samos, and the Turkish port of Kuşadası. At Easter and on August 15 schedules go haywire and the boats are mobbed; advance tickets are recommended. Contact Parikia Tours, Tel: (0284) 224-70; Fax: (0284) 224-50.

Depending on the season there are two to six daily flights between Paros and Athens. The flight takes 30 to 40 minutes; there are also two flights a week to Rhodes and two to Crete. Seats must be booked in advance. Low clouds and south winds cancel flights, big north winds cancel boats.

Buses go from Parikia to all main towns on Paros. The

schedule is posted at the main stop to the north of the boat dock along the quay. Buses are jammed in summer. There are many cars and motorbikes for rent, most of which work. Taxis wait in the main squares of Parikia and Naousa.

—*Jeffrey Carson*

SIPHNOS

Siphnos is a *kore*—one of those elegantly draped young female figures the Archaic islanders liked to carve. Her beauty is graceful and modest. Unlike her parched neighbor Seriphos, just 12 miles northwest, Siphnos is well watered and fertile, a garden island. But to passing boats she appears formidable, for her sweetness is guarded by steep cliffs, broken suddenly by only a few deep-cut bays with safe anchorage. The main towns of Siphnos, Apollonia and Artemona, lie in the center, and the popular beaches are in the south; the rugged north, where the ancient silver mines were, is sparsely inhabited and reachable only by foot or caïque. Because Siphnos is small (2,000 people) and relatively undeveloped (though ministers and ambassadors have houses here), her 30,000 tourists yearly overwhelm resources in August: The beaches are clogged and the buses packed.

MAJOR INTEREST

Beautiful villages
Charming landscape
Siphnian pottery

The most protected of Siphnos's anchorages is the port of **Kamáres**, a small white town on a bay on the west coast with high cliffs on either side, a good beach with dripping tamarisk trees, and a narrow green valley whose road takes you to the interior.

Little Kamares contains as many shops, restaurants, hotels, and bars as the much larger capital, Apollonia. A couple of potters' studios still function, and there is a mining establishment at the north end, in one of whose shafts nymphs were once worshiped. But Kamares is a hectic tourist port, with new Athenian villas, and you'll want to move on. The old

fishermen who still reside here whisper about nereids—
and they don't mean the scantily clad tourists lunching at the
beachside fish tavernas.

The bus ride from Kamares up (southeast) to Apollonia
(5.5 km/3 miles) provides a sweet initiation into Siphnos's
enchanting landscape. You will see two-story dovecotes;
delicate chapels hugging the hillside; a Hellenistic watchtower (Siphnos has remains of more than 40); ruined windmills; and very narrow terraces with golden wheat, glinting
olive trees, or low grape vines buttressed by elegant stone
walls that prevent them from washing into the ravines below
during winter storms. Siphnos appears to have suffered less
than some of the other Cyclades from the shortage of rain
since 1986. In spring the hillsides are so yellow with Spanish
broom they are hard to look at in bright sunlight.

Apollonia

Apollonía, capital of Siphnos since 1836, seems a gentle,
disheveled sprawl on the high undulation of the island's
middle. Actually, there are six villages here. The bus stops at
the lively main square, the busy central crossroads for all
Siphnos. The big building with a terrace houses the **Folklore
Museum**, full of traditional pottery, weavings, embroideries
(another Siphnos specialty), and vestments.

The best way to see the villages is on foot. From the main
square next to Lakis's café, a street winds upward to traverse
the prettiest sections. On the right (east) side of the street,
through an archway, gleams the **church of the Heaven-
Bearing Virgin**. The marble carvings around the door give the
date 1767, but the church itself is older; the relief overhead
depicts Saint George and the Dragon. The marble column by
the courtyard well is from the seventh-century B.C. temple to
Apollo, Apollonia's namesake.

Now the road crosses into **Ano Petáli**, quiet and pristine,
tucked between its larger neighbors. The islanders' scrupu-
lous dedication to whitewash makes the villages of Siphnos
seem daintier than those of the other Cyclades. The flag-
stones here are carefully delineated with very thin white
lines, reapplied weekly; this is much more time-consuming
than the thicker lines preferred elsewhere.

Artemona

The flagstone street then descends slightly to cross a stone
bridge over the seasonal Marinou river. Artemóna, named

after Apollo's virginal sister, is the most beautiful village in Siphnos. The walls of the **church of the Virgin of the Troughs**, on the rock outcropping to your left, were frescoed in the primitive style by a local monk 150 years ago. Marble tombstones are set into the floor.

Next you come to a small square named for Nicholas Chrysogelos, a local teacher who led a contingent in the 1821 revolution and who later became Greece's first minister of education. His marble bust reigns over the tiny town hall and substantial houses. Soon the same street reaches Artemona's capacious main square, where the bus turns to go back down to Apollonia. The 18th-century church here, with its ghostly white stairway, is dedicated, like the square, to Saints Constantine and Helen. Right next to the church is an excellent taverna, the **Manganas**, which features local dishes such as a salad made of dried capers with vinegar, oil, and onions. (A few caper shrubs, distinguished by showy white flowers with feathery blue stamens, cling to the embankment wall of the car road between Artemona and Apollonia near a couple of chic bars and restaurants.) Near Manganas is the comfortable hotel **Artemon**, with a garden restaurant.

The stone-paved street continues to wind through Artemona. The large Neoclassical houses on both sides of the street, with gardens of trees, vines, and flowers in front of them, belong to families of shipowners who became wealthy a hundred years ago. The quiet coexistence of elegant edifices and small houses, many with the characteristic Siphnian chimney caps of multispouted inverted pots, all united by fresh whitewash, gives Artemona its graceful appearance. Past these houses, the pretty building with the tiled roof is the **Artemona Xenon**, a diminutive guesthouse in a large cool courtyard of lemon trees and a noble cypress; despite, or maybe because of, its utter simplicity—bare white rooms, few facilities, and many songbirds—it is the most charming place to stay in Siphnos.

The street now comes to Artemona's multidomed chief church, the **Kochi**. In its courtyard, where Artemis's temple once stood, the Siphnian Cultural Society presents readings and concerts in summer. Just past Kochi, turning left down a narrow lane, you reach, on the right after about 30 yards, a little two-story house marked by a plaque as the place where poet John Gryparis (1871 to 1942), indifferent to the world's praise (but not, gossip the Siphnians, to his bossy wife's), wrote mournful sonnets. In May, perfumed Easter lilies bloom on every porch, and as you stand here it is easy to see where Gryparis got his inspiration. Just to the right past his house is the **Liotrivi** (Olive Press) restaurant, set in a large garden. The best restaurant on Siphnos, it features excellent hors d'oeuvres such as spiced chick-pea balls.

Ayios Sostis

In the Archaic era, Siphnos grew rich from its silver mines. Walkers from Apollonia can reach the ancient mines at Ayios Sostis on the northeast coast in a couple of hours (you cannot drive there). Siphnos shared in the Neolithic Cycladic culture from before 3000 B.C., and in the second millennium B.C. the Cretans founded a town here called Minoa. But it was not until the sixth century B.C. that the mines made Siphnos important. All citizens shared in the wealth, and the main square was paved with expensive Parian marble. But then the Siphnians substituted a gilt ball for one of gold as their annual contribution to Delian Apollo, and trouble set in. The sea flooded the mines as a punishment for this sin. Then the Samians embezzled money and used it to buy Hydra. Not long after, the mines ran out of metal, and Siphnos has never again been especially prosperous. When the Turks tried to reopen the mines 2,000 years later, the Siphnians, fearing enslavement as miners, hired some Frankish corsairs to sink the sultan's ships.

Exambela and Vrisi

From Apollonia three paved roads lead to three coastal villages. The road south to Platy Yialos passes through the villages of Katavati and Exámbela. Exambela is especially pretty and white, with flowers by every stoop. In Turkish times (from 1617 to 1830) Exambela was considered a hot night spot, renowned for its songs. The ruined Neoclassical buildings were schools, and at the edge of the village are the ruins of a Hellenistic watchtower. On the Hill of St. Andrew to the southwest lies an ancient acropolis, but not much is left. Objects from 3000 to 400 B.C. keep turning up, but little of Siphnos's ancient splendor has survived to our time. A bit farther along, whitewashed steps climb to the **Vrisi** (Wellspring) **Monastery**, cared for by the Lambrinos family. A deep, vaulted gateway opens into the courtyard and church, whose arcaded porch employs Classical Doric columns from an earlier temple. A couple of rooms are occupied by a museum of religious arts. The Vrisi's flowing water is considered the best on Siphnos.

Platy Yialos

The southernmost of the coastal towns reached from Apollonia is Platý Yialós (Broad Beach), 10 km (6 miles) away, the most popular beach on Siphnos. The comfortable, island-style **Hotel Platyialos**, with its seaview restaurant, is at the far end of the beach. There are many less-expensive places to stay and eat, however. Platy Yialos is one of several beaches where potters used to make the island's chief export, cooking pots. Some of the houses here are actually large, converted kilns. One workshop on the beach still operates regularly, producing traditional ware for export and sale on the primitive premises. The master potter is young Frangiskos Lemonis, whose family has worked at the wheel for generations. Siphnos was famous for pottery 2,000 years ago, and the potters of the island used to wander all over Greece plying their trade; the tradition has mostly dissipated.

Chrysopigi

Between the beaches of Platy Yialos and Faros, a touristic fishing hamlet, lie **Chrysopigí** (Golden Wellspring) **Monastery** (8 km/5 miles southeast of Apollonia) and the long sandy beach of **Apókofto**, where there is a taverna. The Siphnians think of the monastery, built in 1650, as paradise, and the simple rooms it rents are booked way in advance. (The rooms have no electricity or running water, the farm family that runs it does not speak English, the gates are locked before midnight, and there is no public transportation.) The church sits on a rocky headland, with water lapping all about it. The chief icon here, which fishermen discovered gleaming in the waves, saved Siphnos in 1675 from plague and in 1928 from locusts. The gap in the entranceway, through which the sea whistles and hisses, was cut by another miracle. One dawn some local maidens who came to tend the church found seven pirates asleep. When the brigands awakened and pursued them with impure intentions, the maidens prayed to the Virgin. Aristomenes Provelengios, who often wrote in a cell here, described what took place: "Suddenly a great quake shook the cape and cut it from the shore . . . the women fell to their knees and glorified the Virgin for her grace."

Kastro

Kastro (Castle), 3.5 km (2 miles) east of Apollonia, is an acropolis overlooking a little bay. Herodotus knew it when it was already a thousand years old. Before 1833 Kastro was the capital city, with a population of 2,000; it was built on the site of ancient Siphnos. Today, though picturesque, it feels forlorn, and only 30 families remain all year. Most of the buildings are from the 14th century, many in ruins. The Da Corogna family wrested Kastro from Naxos's control in 1307, and it did not fall to the Turks until 1617. There are five gates and a few through-streets, with many alleys passing under arches from one house to another on a higher level. Kastro's **Virgin of Mercy**, once the island's main church, was last restored in 1635, the date on the marble lintel. The **Dormition of the Virgin**, 1593, is elaborately inlaid in Siphnian style. The marble holy table, a Classical altar, is adorned with Dionysian bulls' heads and swags such as have been found all over the islands. In the middle of the town, in a Venetian building, the **Archaeological Museum** displays a collection of smaller objects from pre-Christian times. The Classical sarcophagi now in the main street were recently brought up from the flowing riverlet below, where they had been used to water cows; the graceful Archaic torso of a *kore* that once reposed there has vanished.

GETTING AROUND

In summer six ferries a week from Piraeus call at Siphnos; in winter, two. The trip takes four to seven hours, depending on season, size of boat, weather, and stops. These ferries also regularly call at Kythnos, Seriphos, Milos, and Kimolos. There are also frequent connections with Santorini, Paros, Syros, and Folegandros. Around Easter and August 15, advance tickets are recommended.

Buses serve all the villages that have roads; in summer they are impossibly packed. Schedules are posted at the Kamares stop and at the main crossroads in Apollonia. Taxis are available in both towns. Cars and motorbikes are for rent; as the season progresses, constant use wears them down.

—*Jeffrey Carson*

MILOS

Lawrence Durrell wrote that Milos is dull—but then he was never here. From the boat, Milos (Apple) resembles a crab whose claws protect the biggest and best bay in the Cyclades. During World War I the Anglo-French fleet claimed safe anchorage here, and in World War II the Germans occupied it.

Before entering the Bay of Milos, you first sail by Kimolos on the left; then on your right the islet Erimomilos (Desert-Milos) rears 2,100 feet above the sea like a B-movie dinosaur-island. In fact the chamois, a rare wild goat protected by law, grazes its precipitous cliffs. Entering the majestic bay, you pass, on the left, some weirdly shaped rocks, which the Melians insist resemble rampant bears, jutting 35 feet from the sea. To the right the highest peak, Profítis Ilías (2,465 feet), dominates the green western "claw." To the left, high on the mountain, gleam three villages, and below them ancient Melos descends to the little fishermen's port of Klima, a single row of houses with colorful doors.

Mining operations have scarred the mountains. Milos today mines perlite (Greece is third in world exports), bentonite, kaolin, and other minerals. Because of the mines Milos is different from the other Cyclades, which supported farmers and fishermen who had enough to eat but lacked cash and so grabbed at tourism. The Melians were miners with salaries; tourism is only now being developed, and the Melians aren't all that happy about it.

MAJOR INTEREST

Relatively undeveloped for tourism
Hot springs
Beautiful coast with strange geological formations
Day trip to the island of Kimolos

Adamas

The port of Adamás was founded by Cretans fleeing the Turks in 1853, though early Christian tombs have been uncovered here. With its narrow quayside, restaurants, cafés, and fishermen, Adamas has become the liveliest town on Milos, where business is done and amusements pursued. It

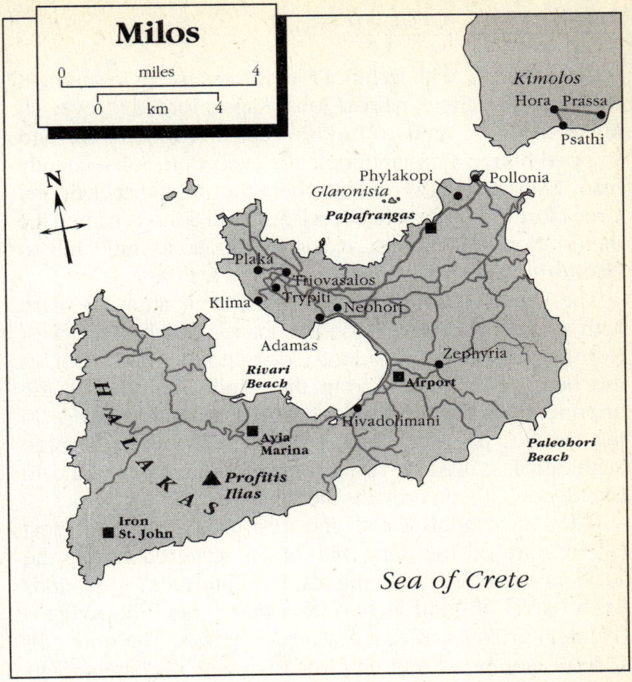

Milos
0 miles 4
0 km 4
N
Kimolos
Hora
Prassa
Psathi
Phylakopi
Pollonia
Glaronisia
Papafrangas
Plaka
Triovasalos
Trypiti
Klima
Nehori
Adamas
Zephyria
Rivari Beach
Airport
Hivadolimani
HALAKAS
Ayia Marina
Profitis Ilias
Paleobori Beach
Iron St. John
Sea of Crete

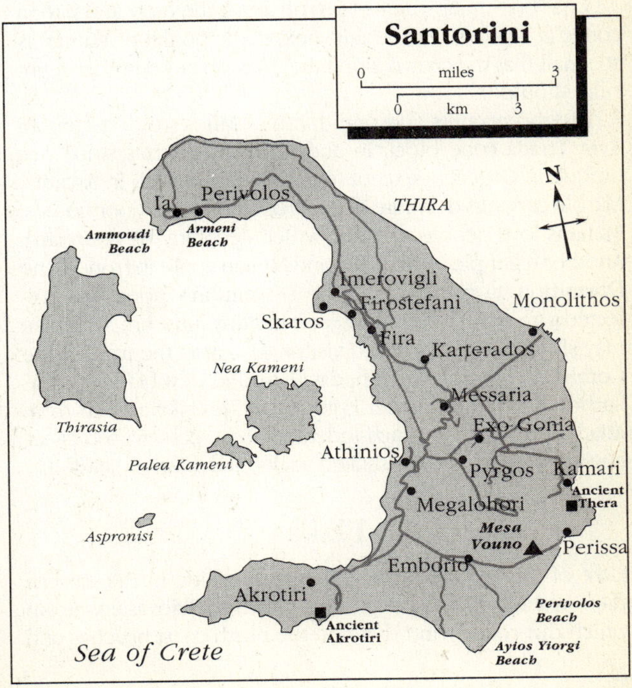

Santorini
0 miles 3
0 km 3
N
THIRA
Ia
Perivolos
Ammoudi Beach
Armeni Beach
Imerovigli
Firostefani
Skaros
Fira
Monolithos
Karterados
Nea Kameni
Messaria
Exo Gonia
Thirasia
Athinios
Pyrgos
Kamari
Palea Kameni
Ancient Thera
Megalohori
Mesa Vouno
Perissa
Aspronisi
Emborio
Akrotiri
Perivolos Beach
Ancient Akrotiri
Sea of Crete
Ayios Yiorgi Beach

is the only town with facilities for visitors, except in summer. A Greek buccaneer named John Kapsis lorded it over all Milos in 1677, until a Turkish captain nabbed him and shipped him to Constantinople for execution. Subsequently many Melians fled to London, where they built that city's first Greek Orthodox church. (Greek Street in Soho is named for them.) Now Adamas has expanded about its little hill to **Neohóri** (Newtown) along the beach to the east.

The **Venus Village** hotel complex, a large, attractive place with a resort atmosphere on the shaded beach to the west (turning left on disembarking), does not need its pool, as the beach is sheltered from the wind. Behind it is the unpretentious **Delfini Hotel**, on whose verdant terrace visiting families pass the heat of the day. Its owner, George Mathioudakis, used to run a freight caïque from island to island; now his son captains the boat.

Milos is unsophisticated, and fresh fish is plentiful. Most tavernas are on the quay, with tables scattered among the strollers a few yards from the sea. The **Phloisbos** (Surfsound) has a barrel of good local retsina on tap, and the **Kynigos** (Hunter) grills its fish on a charcoal brazier. The only full-scale restaurant, a hundred yards east along the bay, belongs to the **Trapsetelli** brothers. The Melians traditionally come to Adamas on Sunday nights to stroll along the quay and have a coffee at **Yanko's** seaside café, next to the bus stop. Adamas is so small that the crowd along the quay on any summer night rubs shoulders.

The three vaults and one dome of Milos's oldest church, **Ayía Triáda** (one block in and up from the bus stop), are unique in Greece—except for one other church in Arcadia. Marble carvings decorate bell tower, lintels, and door frames. Melians love pebble mosaics, which decorate the courtyard. Another example is the eagle and Melian apple in front of the **Dormition** atop the town. The Dormition's priest has collected a group of religious objects in a tiny museum, which he may show to the interested visitor. Also atop the town is the **Corali** hotel, simply furnished with a good view of the Adamas harbor. When the weather is good, caïques take tourists from Adamas around the much-indented coast, past twisted islets, huge sea caves, color-streaked rocks, and bizarre landfalls.

Plaka

Most of the island's 4,500 inhabitants reside in the eastern claw. Leaving Adamas you climb north to Triovásalos, from which dirt roads wind down to the north coast beaches and fishing hamlets. After 4.5 km (3 miles) you reach Plaka, the capital of Milos and its prettiest village, with old houses on lanes too narrow for cars. The village was constructed about 1800. Louis Brest, the French consul and virtual ruler of Milos, built the Catholic **Virgin of the Rosary**, a block past Plaka's one café, in 1823, using stones from Zephyria's ruined church (see below). The old marbles in the neighboring courtyard belong to the adjacent Virgin of Corfu church. Next door, an old mansion houses the **Folklore Museum**, with its authentic displays of well-to-do family life in days gone by.

At the bottom of the town, the **Archaeological Museum** looks rather more impressive than its collection warrants. It displays small objects (the big ones are in Athens) from all periods of pre-Christian Milos. The prize piece is the Lady of Phylakopi, a terra-cotta statuette in Minoan style from about 1350 B.C. that rather resembles a lampstand.

From the Plaka bus stop, the street to the north, mostly stairs, climbs up to **Kastro**, a ruined Medieval town built on top of an ancient one, hugging a basalt cone. Once-fine homes, some now being restored, formed the outer fortification wall. The big church a little below the summit, with a superb bay view, is the **Mariner Virgin**, built in 1728. The marble door lintel displays the escutcheon of the Crispi family, who wrested Milos from the ruling Sanudi in 1363. At the top are old walls and new reservoirs.

Ancient Melos

A short distance south of Plaka is the mountain village of **Trypití**. Not far from the church of Ayios Nikólaos, whose bell tower houses a large clock, a little café serves coffee and fresh snacks on a small terrace overlooking the Vale of Klima and the bay. A road to the south leads to these places. From Kastro to Klima, ancient Melos sloped to its harbor. A road sign points out the path that leads to some of the Classical city's remains. Past the polygonal masonry of the East Gate, a plaque marks the spot where the *Venus de Milo* (known to Greek sculpture buffs as *Aphrodite of Melos*) was unearthed in the 1820s. Passing some column drums, pedestals, a Byzantine marble font, and the great Black Wall (as the islanders call it), you enter the ancient theater, with seven rows of marble seats still intact, and marbles from the stage building strewn about.

About 300 years after the fall of Phylakopi on the north coast (see below), circa 1200 B.C., the Melians built their city here, and it lasted until Byzantine times. These ancient Melians had tribal connections with Dorian Sparta, and not, like most of the other Cyclades, with Ionian Athens, which may explain why Melos produced few poets, sculptors, or philosophers. Still, it was one of the four islands to resist the Persians in 480 B.C. But in 416 B.C., during the Peloponnesian Wars, the Melians also resisted the Athenians, who coveted the harbor. Athens then sent a delegation of persuasion. Thucydides' *Melian Dialogue* chillingly recounts the classic example of the might-makes-right argument. Despite offers of compromise, the Athenians besieged the city, massacred the men, and sold the women and children into slavery. Recolonized, Melos never fully recovered, though it was still exporting sulfur, alum, and pumice in Roman times.

Christianity got an early start here. A sign on the road to Klima, just below the ancient East Gate, points the way to the extensive first-century **catacombs**, whose 291 tombs have all been plundered. The 600 feet of vaulted tunnels are the oldest known place of Christian worship in Greece. **Klima** (Vine) lies on the ancient port, and in an olive grove to the north is a Roman mosaic. Klima itself is tiny—a colorful row of houses and garages for caïques, some cut into the cliff. Many such cliff caves are in use all over Milos.

Zephyria

Zephyría, in the flat center of Milos just east of the airport, has a strange history. It was built after A.D. 500, when ancient Melos and Kastro were abandoned. In 1383 the ruling Crispi made their capital here and the town flourished, partly as a trading center for pirates, with a population of 5,000. But in 1793 the people of Zephyria mysteriously sickened, possibly of noxious fumes from nearby marshes and sulfurous rocks. The survivors briefly reestablished Kastro, then built Plaka at Kastro's foot. This is why so many of Zephyria's valuables are in other Melian churches, though many old marbles remain *in situ*.

From Zephyria a partially paved road crosses the low southern mountains to the island's most popular beach, **Paleohóri**, on the south coast. There are rooms available on the beach and two tavernas (bus in summer). A long sandy stretch with rocks streaked yellow, red, and green, its waters are warmed by hot springs beneficial to arthritics. Sometimes vapor clouds boil up from the sea. Hot water spouts (the ancient *thermae*) bubble up all over Milos, even in the quayside cliff at Adamas, where the cave is now barred over.

Halakas

The coast road around the bay makes for a beautiful ride in wild country. Past the airport turnoff, after the saltworks, you pass one of Milos's best beaches, **Hivadolimáni**, opposite a lagoon once used as a vivarium. Now the road climbs into Halakas, the mountainous, green, western claw of Milos. Twelve kilometers (7.5 miles) southwest of Adamas is **Ayía Marína**, once an important monastery. The church, whose elaborate lintel bears the date 1616, abuts well-watered gardens with many pistachio trees that belong to the Papageorge and Deliyannis families. Below, a dirt road winds to the beautiful lagoon and beaches of **Rivari**, where caïques from Adamas call in summer.

A long ride of 14 km (9 miles) west from Ayia Marina, through rough countryside, ends at the deserted **church of Iron St. John**, affiliated with the monastery of St. John on Patmos. The festival here on September 25 is the most popular on Milos. All Melians can (and will) tell you the legend of this place: When pirates attacked during a festival, the faithful prayed to the saint, who turned the wooden door to iron. A determined pirate climbed to the dome and tried to fire his pistol through a hole, but it exploded and fell to the floor below, along with his severed hand.

Phylakopi

Ten kilometers (6 miles) to the northeast along the northern coast road from Adamas is Phylakopí, marked by a small sign. Phylakopi, on a hillock between the road and the sea, will please admirers of Minoan civilization, or anyone who enjoys imagining where ancient towns rose and thrived. Phylakopi got its start about 2600 B.C. and had close ties with Minoan Crete, including a similar script. Its houses, now a jumble, were once adorned with works of art. Some of the art is now in the Plaka museum and some—such as the much-reproduced fresco of flying fish—is in Athens. The sea has risen since ancient times, and Phylakopi's port is now underwater. What looks like bits of smoky glass strewn everywhere is obsidian, used for sharp Stone Age tools—ancient Melos was the eastern Mediterranean's chief source of obsidian from 7000 B.C. on.

The coast just above Phylakopi's parking lot provides a good view of the huge sea cave of **Papafrángas**, with strange rocks and caves on either side. A caïque from nearby Pollonia will bring you here; it also circles the islets called

Glaronisia (Gull Islands), noted for their extraordinary prismatic lava formations.

Most visitors like **Pollonía**, a pretty little fishing village on a beach about half a mile east of Phylakopi, with a couple of tavernas and rooms to let (daily caïque to Kimolos).

KIMOLOS

Volcanic Kímolos, half a mile from Pollonia, looms over the village. Though only five miles across, Kimolos is big enough for the Milos steamer to call twice a week. Only 20 minutes by caïque from Pollonia, it makes a pleasant half-day excursion into an older Greece. Captain Avgoustis chugs over from Kimolos every morning to bring workers for the mines; he returns about 7:15 A.M. with the schoolteacher. Passing the long shaded beach of **Alikí**, you see a quarry where islanders cut blocks of tufa stone, which explains the four-square neatness of the local architecture. The uphill walk from the harbor, **Psathi**, to the main village of **Kimolos**, or Hora—no buses or taxis here—takes 20 minutes. There is one interesting church near the main square: **St. John Chrysostom** was built in the 14th century and is now being repaired. The alleys and arcaded passageways of Psathi are noisy with chickens and donkeys; otherwise it is as quiet as the past—though there are a restaurant and café and a bakery that has first-rate cheese pies. The roofs of the houses are still made of a combination of bamboo, seaweed, and soil; plowing and winnowing are done in the same way they have been done for thousands of years, as no big machines have been imported to the island. Above the town are the haunted ruins of the 14th-century **Kastro** and a line of windmills, one of which still grinds.

The hot springs at the beach of **Prassa** are, unfortunately, radioactive, but there is a good reason to make the 15-minute walk to the north from Psathi. Off the coast here lie the sunken remains of the ancient city that J. T. Bent saw and wrote about in his 1885 account of his travels. You need a facemask to see them, a five-minute swim from the beach.

Though only 900 people live on Kimolos, in summer the figure triples, when islanders resident in Athens return home. The Milos caïque returns to Pollonia at 1:00 P.M.

GETTING AROUND

Two to seven ferries from Piraeus call weekly at Milos, depending on the season. The trip takes five to eight hours, depending on weather, season, and stops. These ferries usually also stop at Kythnos, Seriphos, Siphnos, and Kimolos. There are less-frequent connections with Ios, Santorini, Syros, Sikinos, and Folegandros. Again depending on the season, there are two to seven weekly flights from Athens; the trip takes 30 to 40 minutes. Reservations are required. Fog and strong southerly winds cancel flights.

Buses leave the main square of Adamas, 100 yards west from the boat dock along the quay, for all the towns, according to the posted schedule. At the same place a sign lists taxi fares to all destinations on Milos. There are motorbikes and a few cars for rent.

—*Jeffrey Carson*

SANTORINI

Santoríni (Thira), which is actually a cluster of islands on the windy southern periphery of the Cyclades, 128 nautical miles southeast of Piraeus and 70 miles north of Crete, invites simile and metaphor. There are few places that will affect you in such a way—the Grand Canyon, Taormina's Greek theater with Mount Etna looming above it, and the ice field beneath the Jungfraujoch being others.

To stand atop the cliff of Santorini's caldera at dusk and gaze out over the still-active volcano in the bay at the sun settling into the sea behind Thirasia is to experience a 17th-century cartographer's vision of land's end: A bottomless abyss yawns and unnamed creatures lie in wait.

Not for nothing have some scholars named Santorini the site of the lost civilization of Atlantis; not for nothing is it called Greece's black pearl. If it is not the most beautiful of the Greek islands—and it may well be—Santorini is certainly the most awe inspiring. Robert Liddell, writing about the place in 1954, described its visual impact as "Light and line. The light as beautiful as anywhere in the Aegean ... the line ... at least as fantastic." But Liddell noted, too, uneasily, that "in some lights, Thera is like nothing so much as a vast lower jaw, with a good many teeth missing: there is something dental, even gingival about its appearance. It is the model of a monster's jaw made by an infernal dentist."

As it has always elicited this somewhat divided response, descriptions of it reflecting terror and euphoria in equal measure, it is no surprise that the island still goes by two names: Santorini, after the island's patron saint, the martyr Irini of Thessaloniki who died here in exile in A.D. 304; and Thira, after the colonizer, King Theras of Sparta, son of Autesion. Two names, two faces, but a dramatic apparition on anyone's horizon. To experience Santorini's impact fully you must arrive by ship, preferably on a warm night very late in summer.

MAJOR INTEREST

Stunningly beautiful volcanic caldera
Ancient Akrotiri
Ancient Thera
Unique, barrel-vault Cycladic architecture
Endless black beaches
Unspoiled towns and villages
Singular Santorinian wines

As you approach the island from the north, Santorini seems at first to be just another vine-and-chapel-dotted Cycladic isle. Then, as you round the cape between Thirasia and Thira, your head flies back in astonishment. Even the most jaded travellers sit back on their proverbial heels.

The western coast of Santorini consists of precipitous cliffs that loom above the gawking tourist on the steamer's deck, curving around the giant bay like a jagged crescent moon. You and the deceptively innocent-looking star-shaped crater are the only inhabitants of the great sea-filled caldera, formed when the volcano blew its top in the second millennium B.C.

What's left of the island once called Stróngyle (the Round One) and Kallíste (the Fairest One) was perhaps best named by the Turks, who called it Degelmenlik, or "We are not coming back!"

Today Santorini is a geologically unstable cluster of five islands: Thira, Thirasía, Paleá Kaméni (which surfaced in 196 B.C.), Nea Kaméni (A.D. 1711–1712), and tiny Aspronísi (the only part of the original island left). And since it is still 80 degrees Celsius (176 degrees Fahrenheit) out there in the center—and you can take a peek into the cone if you dare—you get the distinct feeling it's not all over yet. When the boat puts in at Ia, on the northern tip of the island; the main town of Fira, on the west coast, facing the caldera; or, most often, the port at Athiníos, just south of Fira, you are only too glad to put a little distance between yourself and the volcano.

Fourteen lovely villages, each with a distinctively different flavor, dot the crescent-shaped island, with Ia on the northern periphery of the caldera and Akrotiri 30 km (18.5 miles) to the south. Fira, the largest village and the capital, is located midway on the cliff face across from the crater.

Akrotiri

Dangerous as this island has always been, set at the uncertain juncture of two vast tectonic plates, it has been attracting visitors—colonists, crusaders, pirates, and tourists—for some 5,000 years. Thira was inhabited as early as the third millennium B.C.; the oldest pottery finds on the island belong to the second phase of Early Cycladic civilization (c. 3200 to 2000 B.C.). The internationally famous excavations at Akrotíri on Thira's south coast have revealed evidence of a high level of sophisticated civilization during the island's next major period, the Middle Cycladic (2000 to 1500 B.C.).

Begun by Professor Spyridon Marinatos in 1967 and carried on after his death at the site by his colleague, Dr. Christos Doumas, the Akrotiri dig has yielded an array of Bronze Age treasures. (Dr. Marinatos's grave is located within the Akrotiri dig, forever crowned by a laurel wreath; guides will point it out to you.) The picture that has emerged of Aegean life in the 20th century B.C. is a startling one. Doumas believes Akrotirians were essentially the merchant marines of Minoan Crete; they plied their trade over perhaps the entire Mediterranean in great ships some 98 feet long and manned by 20 to 40 oarsmen.

Their capital on Thira's coast, directly to the north of Crete, is a sort of fossilized portrait of what life was like throughout the entire Aegean at that time. Buried by thick deposits of ash in the monstrous eruption of circa 1500 B.C., the city was beautifully preserved. Two- and three-story dwellings face onto an elegant little triangular square. Indoor plumbing was connected to a public drainage system beneath the city streets. Frescoes adorned the walls of every residence. The dress, the pastimes, the flora and fauna, the great fleets and distant ports of call observed by those Bronze Age Onassises and Niarchoses—all have been immortalized on the walls of Akrotiri.

Though the frescoes and many of the site's rich finds are still on loan to the Archaeological Museum in Athens (don't miss them on the second floor), Dr. Doumas looks forward to their return to Thira, when the construction of a new museum in the island's capital, Fira, is completed. The site itself, where the dig is still in progress and yielding new buildings, frescoes, and artifacts, is open to the public and well worth a visit. (Tour operators organize tours, with guides, out of Fira.) A bus trip to Akrotiri and a caïque ride to a stunning red-pebbled beach (named, appropriately, Red beach) enable the resourceful traveller to view the dig and enjoy a swim in one trip. Be sure to purchase a plastic bag of tiny, delicious indigenous tomatoes and yellow Thiran *fava* (split peas) at the entrance to Akrotiri.

The flourishing life of Akrotiri ended dramatically with the great eruption. According to Doumas, minor tremors preceded major quakes, forewarning Thira's inhabitants, who quickly evacuated. Therefore no victims—or any gold—have been found. The buildings at Akrotiri suffered considerable damage in the quakes, and there is some evidence that at least a few residents may have returned and were undertaking repairs when disaster struck again. Still, even they may have had time to board their vessels and flee to neighboring islands. (Ios, Sikinos, Folegandros, Anafi, and Crete are all visible from Thira on rare, perfectly clear days.)

The final cataclysm began with a fine rain of pumice that covered the entire circular island—and Bronze Age life ended on Santorini. A following paroxysm brought forth coarser pumice, which reaches a thickness of a foot and a half in the area of the excavation. Elegant Akrotiri was now buried, like Pompeii and Herculaneum, but preserved for posterity.

In the final explosion, the whole cone of the volcano disappeared, blown sky-high. The volcano's shell, hollowed out after the ejection of cubic miles of matter, collapsed, the sea rushed in, and the present, peaceful-looking lagoon was born. There would be other eruptions, and many other earthquakes, but the giant was beheaded.

No one rebuilt Akrotiri, but Santorini was to foster yet another major civilization, on higher ground to the northeast.

Ancient Thera

Travellers today can reach the site of Ancient Thera (about midway between Fira and Akrotiri) by a tortuous cobbled road straight up the face of the 1,210-foot-high promontory of Mesa Vounó, above black-sand Kamari beach (see below). The ancient city itself occupies an acropolis on the spine of the mountain and has the appearance of a compact narrow ship in a sea of air, sheer drops on all sides. Clearly, these people, like the great Garbo, wished to be alone.

Archaic tombs show that ancient Thera existed before the ninth century B.C. Most of the monuments, however, belong to the era of the Ptolemies (300 to 145 B.C.)—the Egyptians maintained a garrison here to keep an eye on the Aegean.

Doumas's *Santorini: A Guide to the Island and Its Archaeological Treasures* is a useful aid to making sense of the site, as most of the structures have been leveled over the years, the limestone blocks hauled away to build Christian churches or converted into whitewash.

The agora, Roman baths, and theater are still recognizable, and the **Terrace of the Festivals**, dating from the sixth century B.C., has some interesting features. This terrace was the religious center of the oldest Doric cults, and on it were celebrated the *gymnopaidiai*, or dances of naked youths, in honor of the Carneian Apollo. Even today visitors can see graffiti immortalizing the long-dead dancing boys scratched into the rock by their admirers. Such inscriptions as "Laquididas is fine" and "Eumelos is the best dancer" illustrate some of the earliest known Greek alphabetic writing. A helpful guard will show you where to look.

The Dorian society of Ancient Thera was isolationist and conservative, protected atop its rocky fortress; but then, as now, the terrible pressure of drought was the island's foremost foe. It was a long dry period that forced the inhabitants of ancient Thera into an uncharacteristic act: colonization.

Grinus, a Theran king, was ordered by the Delphic oracle to found a colony in Libya, so the story goes. Not knowing where this Libya was, he did nothing, and seven years of drought ensued. The Therans sent another embassy to Delphi and were reminded of their negligence. Thus they were spurred, around 630 B.C., into founding Cyrene, which became a city greatly renowned for its arts and letters. It was a Cyrenean poet who "continued" Homer's *Odyssey*, describing the last adventures of Odysseus. In fact, he foreshadowed Virgil in that he gave Odysseus a son, Arcesilaus, and connected the royal line of Cyrene with the wily Ithacan.

Skaros

From 1207 to 1335 Santorini was held by the Barozzi as a fief of Marco Sanudo, though the Barozzi of Santorini spent less time in their castle of Skaros than on their Cretan plantations. Then, during the reign of Duke William II, the volcano that had been quiet for over 700 years spoke up again, and in 1457 there occurred "the birth of a memorable monster," another outcropping in the ghastly bay. The event was commemorated in what William Miller terms "a set of detestable Latin hexameters inscribed on a slab of marble at the castle of Skaros and addressed to Francesco Crispo... who was at that time baron of Santorin." Contemporary visitors, shod in cleats and accompanied by a guide, may visit what's left of the "Latin" fortress rock of Skaros (the Venetian Medieval capital), several miles hard hiking out of Fira.

Today the 46 square miles of Santorini are occupied by post-Akrotiri Greeks and the Catholic descendants of the Venetians and their converts.

Fira

Shipowner Nomikos's cable car from Firá down to the tiny seaport of Skala Fira, where cruise ships call, has taken a sizable chunk out of the famous Santorini donkey owners' earnings; the donkeys used to be the only sensible means of getting up and down Fira's 588 steps to the sea.

Once you are up in town, it takes a little time to decipher Fira's maze of cobbled streets—there are only a handful, however—but because cars are prohibited here you must get your bearings on foot. Fira is best visited in the spring (for Orthodox Easter in the cathedral) or fall, when weather conditions are less reliable but tourist hordes are less in evidence. This is a noisy place in high season, June through August, when you may decide to find lodging in Firostefani, Ia, Imerovigli, or Kamari, and simply drive to Fira to shop or enjoy the nightlife.

For those who demand a room with a view, with price no consideration, the old, elegant, high-ceilinged **Atlantis Hotel** is situated on the lip of the cliff in Fira. In town and near all services is the family-run **Pelican Hotel**, with its central garden and cozy breakfast room, open all year and fully heated for spring and winter guests.

Fira's restaurants are many and varied. The **Kastro**, near the cable cars, serves filet and prawns, with a view of the bay; the **Selene Restaurant/Bar**, below the Atlantis Hotel and the cathedral, is "Athens chic"; nearby is **Nikolaos Dakotros's** taverna, over a quarter-century old and reliable, off-season, for Greek fare; and next to the pharmacy (across from the Pelican Hotel) is the **Garden Restaurant Delfi**, open from 8:00 A.M. until late at night, serving breakfast and light meals. Discos in Fira come and go, mercifully, but the **Kira Fira Jazzbar** endures, with big-band music and blues. **Every Day**, one door down from Kira Fira, has breakfast, sweets, and excellent coffee (plus rock and roll). **Franco's Bar**, on the cliff edge, is quiet, with classical music and tall drinks.

Shopping in Fira is rewarding, but selectivity is crucial. Gold stores have proliferated in the last decade, and Fira at night seems to have been touched by King Midas with all ten digits. **Greco Gold**, on Ypapántis Street, features the work of former Elsa Peretti associate Minas. The art gallery **Palia Fabrika** has a case of Athens jeweler Fanourakis's delicate gold floral and gem creations, along with paintings by Christophoros Assimis (who executed the cathedral paintings) and ceramics by Eleni Assimis. The art gallery **Zoi** features the work of naïve painter-under-glass Antonios of Santorini, and the **Golden Odyssey** is known for meticulously worked 22-karat reproductions of Archaic and Classical jewelry. The last three shops are on the nameless main road parallel to the cliff.

For those interested in local crafts, carpenter **Stylianos D. Damigos** ships island furniture worldwide, and tinsmith **Anargyros Kafieris** (Fanopios) fashions lamps, wedding wreath boxes, and pistachio boxes, and all sorts of other fast-vanishing staples of last century's marketplace. Ask a local for directions to their shops.

For a respite from the rigors of shopping, step into the cool entranceway of the Dominican Convent, which adjoins the **church of the Virgin of Rodários**, to listen to the singing of the cloistered nuns, praying 24 hours a day for peace on earth.

Bellonias Tours, operating out of Fira, arranges many interesting island excursions, among them trips to the various wineries for evenings of wine-tasting or even grape-stomping in season. The best bottled bets are, among white varieties, Santorini, from the Santo Cooperative, and Boutari's Santorini. The red Roussos Caldera is fine, as are the white, rosé, and red wines of Atlantis. (**Renos Prekas**, an old-timer in Fira, has a tiny, barrel-filled corner shop where local vintages may be sampled, bottles filled, and wine lore learned.)

Around the Island

It is easy to get to outlying villages and beaches by car; you may stay in Firostefani, swim at Perivolos, catch the sunset in Ia, dine in Fira, and dance at Kamari all in the same day.

Firostefáni, one kilometer (about half a mile) north of

Fira, is a quiet retreat from the capital. Easter is especially lovely here at the church of Ayios Yerásimos. The **Aktaion**, near the church, is an authentic island *kafeneío*, patronized by retired seamen. Between Fira and Firostefani, on the main road, is the **Pergola Restaurant**, noted for Santorini specialties such as "false meatballs" and chick-pea salad, along with more sophisticated fare and excellent *tsigouthiá*, a Greek version of white lightning.

In **Imerovígli**, 2 km (about a mile) north of Fira, seek out the **Fish Tavern Scarus** and the **Altana Apartments Traditional Settlement**, built in the attractive local style of architecture, on a quiet beach. On the square in this village, **Eleni Kathourou**'s fine little restaurant hasn't changed in her lifetime.

The drive north is dramatic: precipitous cliffs to the east, with the isle of Anáfi visible on a clear day. Ia, at road's end, is a burgeoning resort with several fine hotels. The **Atlantis Villas** and the new **Oia's Sunset** are both apartment complexes with pools. The Atlantis's rooms are actually cut out of the cliff face. Oia's Sunset is a cleverly honeycombed Cycladic maze of flatlets with kitchenettes. Lodgings are rented out by **EOT** (the Greek National Tourist Organization) in traditional Ian houses called *skaftá*, Santorinian cave dwellings; these are quite comfortable and are located in Ia's most scenic neighborhood. Ia's mansions, which fell in the 1956 quake, are being reconstructed, their ocher walls studded with bits of red limestone. Some of the caldera-side dwellings have been made into the **Armenaki Villas**, luxurious personalized retreats with a matchless view. The **Maritime Museum** in Ia is worth a visit, and if you are feeling intrepid you might hike down to the little beaches of **Arméni** and **Ammoudi**. Contact Karvounis Tours in Ia for more information on beaches, lodgings, and transport here.

About 8 km (5 miles) south of Fira are the villages of **Exo Goniá** and **Pyrgos**. Exo Gonia is noted for the **church of Ayios Harálambos**, its interior murals by artist Christophoros Assimis, and Pyrgos for the extant Medieval castle within the city walls. Pyrgos is also the site of special Easter celebrations in the square, where you can sit on the terrace at **Café Candouni**. (The nearest place for lunch—and good service—is **Mario's** restaurant in Messaria.) In Karterádos, about halfway between Fira and Pyrgos, is the **Damigos Tennis Club and Pool**, a traditionally decorated apartment complex; nearby Messariá boasts the immense, modern, and rather exclusive **Santorini Image Hotel and Bungalows**, complete with an Olympic-size pool.

Above Pyrgos the paved road climbs to the 18th-century **monastery of Profítis Ilías**, open to visitors on rare occasions such as its Feast Day, July 20, when islanders and visitors alike are specially invited for soup and folk dancing. From Pyrgos turn left for the beach at Kamari or right for Akrotiri and Perissa beach.

Kamári, 8 km (5 miles) southeast of Fira, is a booming seaside resort, its black sand packed with bodies in high season. Here, the air-conditioned (heated in winter) **Bellonia Villas**, with a fresh-water pool and kitchenettes; **Roussos Hotel**, also with a swimming pool; and **Kamari Hotel**, with kitchenettes and balconies, are all highly recommended. The **Christos Apartments**, also with kitchenettes, have small bathtubs, spacious verandas, and, downstairs, a restaurant/bar. (They will also pick up visitors from the airport or docks.) The **Sphinx Restaurant/Bar** is a lively, lovely place for lunch, dinner, and dancing. **Camile Stefani** is Santorini's best restaurant, relocated from Fira to Kamari. It specializes in Greek food with a French twist and has its own wine label.

En route to Perissa it is worth detouring, preferably on foot, through **Megalohóri**, a picturesque village little-touched by tourism, and **Embório**, where a *goulas* (Medieval fortress) survives largely intact.

Périssa, 15 km (9 miles) southeast of Fira, is an unattractive beach settlement, but if you turn off to the right after Emborio you'll find less-crowded space on the black sands of **Perívolos**. There are several marked and unmarked turnings for the area called Ayios Yiórgis or Perivolos, where the sea is deep, clean, and inviting.

GETTING AROUND

Both reaching Santorini and getting off the island can be daunting, especially in high season. The airport near Monolithos receives charter flights from northern Europe in season, and there are at least two Olympic Airways connections per day from Athens year round. In summer, flights from neighboring islands and those farther afield are scheduled. However, reservations must be made well in advance, and flights may be delayed or canceled in strong spring and summer winds, which sometimes alter even the steamer schedule, though boat connections are more reliable.

Car and passenger service from Piraeus is regular, and connections to Anafi, Crete, Ios, Milos, Mykonos, Naxos, Paros, Rhodes, and Syros are available in season. A call to Bellonias Tours (Tel: 0286-222-21, 224-69, or 236-04) in Fira, or Karvounis Tours (Tel: 0286-712-90/92/09; Fax: 0286-712-91) in Ia from abroad or from Athens may take many snags out of a trip to Santorini. When in Greece, it is always better to deal with someone *in situ,* as reliable information on weather, connections, and accommodation is often hard to come by in Athens. Despite the length of the sea journey—between 12 and 15 hours from Piraeus—you should opt for travelling by boat to appreciate fully the visual impact of arrival at Santorini. Arkadia Lines' *Poseidon* makes the trip in 8 hours.

Boats put in at Ia, Fira, or, most often, Athinios; a regular bus connects Athinios with the main town of Fira. Those arriving by plane will find an Olympic Airways shuttle bus waiting near the luggage carts and very reasonable taxi service to hotels and towns.

The bus schedule in season is frenetic, and getting around by motorcycle unspeakably hazardous. Car rental is reasonable and may be arranged through most hotel receptionists—rental companies will pick up visitors and take them to their cars—but gas stations are few and far between and sometimes on strike. (Toula, at Budget in Fira, is helpful. Budget is the only company that rents minibuses for groups, and rates are very reasonable.)

—*Elizabeth Boleman Herring*

ACCOMMODATIONS REFERENCE

Andros
- Hotel Andros Holiday. Gavrion, 845 00 Andros. Tel: (0282) 710-98; in U.S., (718) 956-7646; Fax: (0282) 710-97.
- Hotel Egli. Hora, 845 00 Andros. Tel: (0282) 223-03 or 222-62.
- Epaminondas Holiday Apartments. Batsi, 845 00 Andros. Tel: (0282) 211-77; in Athens, Tel: (01) 801-8121 or 647-2083.
- Hotel Korthion. Korthion, 845 02 Andros. Tel: (0282) 612-18.
- Hotel Pighi Sarisa. Apikia, 845 00 Andros. Tel: (0282) 237-99 or 238-99; Fax: (0282) 224-76.
- Hotel Xenia. Hora, 845 00 Andros. Tel: (0282) 222-70.

Tinos
- Alonia. Hora, 842 00 Tinos. Tel: (0283) 235-41/44.
- Argo. 842 00 Tinos. Tel: (0283) 225-88.
- Tinos Beach. 842 00 Tinos. Tel: (0283) 226-26/28.

Mykonos

- Belou Hotel. Megali Ammos, 846 00 Mykonos. Tel: (0289) 225-89.
- Cavo Tagoo Hotel. 846 00 Mykonos. Tel: (0289) 236-92/94; Telex: 293338 AGEA GR; in Athens, Tel: (01) 643-0233; Telex: 224621 AECO GR.
- Despotiko Hotel. 846 00 Mykonos. Tel: (0289) 220-09 or 234-62.
- Hotel Kouneni. Hora, 846 00 Mykonos. Tel: (0289) 223-01 or 234-63.
- Leto Hotel. Hora, 846 00 Mykonos. Tel: (0289) 222-07 or 229-18.
- Mykonos Beach Hotel. Megali Ammos, 846 00 Mykonos. Tel: (0289) 225-72/73.
- Paradise Beach Camping. 846 00 Mykonos. Tel: (0289) 221-29 or 225-07.
- Hotel Princess of Mykonos. San Stefanos, 846 00 Mykonos. Tel: (0289) 230-31 or 238-06; Fax: (0289) 230-31.
- Santa Marina. Ornos Bay, 846 00 Mykonos. Tel: (0289) 232-20; Fax: (0289) 234-12.
- Vienoula's Garden Hotel. Vrisi, 846 00 Mykonos. Tel: (0289) 242-14, 243-25, or 229-83.

Syros

- Hotel Alexandra. Megas Yialos, 841 00 Syros. Tel: (0281) 425-40 or 426-10.
- Capuchin Monastery and Guesthouse. Ano Syros, 841 00 Syros. Tel: (0281) 225-76.
- Europe Hotel. Ermoupolis, 841 00 Syros. Tel: (0281) 287-71/72.
- Françoise Hotel. Galissas, 841 00 Syros. Tel: (0281) 420-00.
- Hotel Hermes. Ermoupolis, 841 00 Syros. Tel: (0281) 230-11/12 or 280-11.
- Hotel Homer. Ermoupolis, 841 00 Syros. Tel: (0281) 249-10; Fax: (Athens) (01) 671-1280.
- Jesuit Monastery and Guesthouse. Ano Syros, 841 00 Syros. Tel: (0281) 223-43.
- Hotel Olympia. Finikas, 841 00 Syros. Tel: (0281) 422-12 or 423-35.
- Possidonion Hotel/Bungalows. Poseidonia, 841 00 Syros. Tel: (0281) 421-00 or 423-32/00.
- Sea Colors. 6 Athinas, Ermoupolis, 841 00 Syros. Tel: (0281) 234-00 or 228-66 (TeamWork Holidays).
- Hotel Vourlis. Ermoupolis, 841 00 Syros. Tel: (0281) 284-40; Telex: 293206 MIT GR; Fax: (0281) 285-13.

Naxos
- ► **Adonis.** Apollon, 843 00 Naxos. Tel: (0285) 813-60.
- ► **Anixi.** 133 Amphitrites, **Kastro**, 843 00 Naxos. Tel: (0285) 221-12.
- ► **Chateau Zevgoli.** 843 00 Naxos. Tel: (0285) 229-93.
- ► **Panorama.** Amphitrites, **Kastro**, 843 00 Naxos. Tel: (0285) 223-30.

Paros
- ► **Dina.** Parikia, 844 00 Paros. Tel: (0284) 213-25.
- ► **Pandrosos.** Parikia, 844 00 Paros. Tel: (0284) 229-03.
- ► **Xenia.** Lefkes, 844 00 Paros. Tel: (0284) 416-46.
- ► **Xenia.** Parikia, 844 00 Paros. Tel: (0284) 213-94.

Siphnos
- ► **Artemon Hotel.** Artemona, 840 03 Siphnos. Tel: (0284) 313-03.
- ► **Artemona Xenon.** Artemona, 840 03 Siphnos. Tel: (0284) 315-87.
- ► **Hotel Platyialos.** Platy Yialos, 840 03 Siphnos. Tel: (0284) 312-24; Fax: (0284) 313-25. In winter contact Simone Kartali, 6 Julius Petichaki Street, Rethymno, 840 03 Crete; Fax: (0831) 210-42.

Milos
- ► **Corali.** Adamas, 848 00 Milos. Tel: (0287) 222-04.
- ► **Delfini.** Adamas, 848 00 Milos. Tel: (0287) 220-01.
- ► **Venus Village.** 848 00 Milos. Tel: (0287) 220-30; Telex: 293165.

Santorini
- ► **Altana Apartments Traditional Settlement.** Imerovigli, 847 00 Santorini. Tel: (0286) 232-40/04.
- ► **Armenaki Villas.** Ia, 847 02 Santorini. Tel: (0286) 712-92/90; Fax: (0286) 712-92.
- ► **Atlantis Hotel.** Fira, 847 00 Santorini. Tel: (0286) 222-32, 221-11, or 228-21; Telex: 293113.
- ► **Atlantis Villas.** Ia, 847 02 Santorini. Tel: (0286) 712-14.
- ► **Bellonia Villas.** Kamari, 847 00 Santorini. Tel: (0286) 311-38.
- ► **Christos Apartments.** Kamari, 847 00 Santorini. Tel: (0286) 319-45; Fax: (0286) 311-45.
- ► **Damigos Tennis Club and Pool.** Karterados, 847 00 Santorini. Tel: (0286) 221-22 or 230-13; Fax: (0286) 236-98.
- ► **EOT Traditional Houses.** Ia, 847 02 Santorini. Tel:

(0286) 712-34. In Athens, contact EOT, Tel: (01) 322-2545 or 322-3111.

▶ **Kamari Hotel. Kamari,** 847 00 Santorini. Tel: (0286) 312-43/16.

▶ **Oia's Sunset. Ia,** 847 02 Santorini. Tel: (0286) 714-90/20; Fax: (0286) 714-21.

▶ **Pelican Hotel. Fira,** 847 00 Santorini. Tel: (0286) 231-13/14; Telex: 293143.

▶ **Roussos Hotel. Kamari,** 847 00 Santorini. Tel: (0286) 312-55.

▶ **Santorini Image Hotel and Bungalows. Messaria,** 847 00 Santorini. Tel: (0286) 318-74/75.

CRETE

By Nikos Stavroulakis

A native of Crete, Nikos Stavroulakis returns there frequently. He is the director of the Jewish Museum of Greece and teaches Byzantine and Ottoman history at a college in Athens.

Nearly equidistant from three continents and surrounded by the Sea of Crete and the Libyan Sea, Crete has a history and traditions decidedly different from those of mainland Greece. Only in 1913 was it formally annexed to the Greek state, and for the first time in centuries the fortunes of the island are being determined by the mainland. Improvements in communications, demographic changes, economic advancement, and tourism all have had their effects in drawing Crete into the general matrix of modern times. Nonetheless, the traveller will find that Crete has a culture with an integrity of its own, one not dependent on the major events of ancient, Medieval, or contemporary Greece. This uniqueness can make Crete an especially exciting place to visit in conjunction with a trip to mainland Greece, as it provides an alternative "Greek experience."

The rich embroideries of the island, its architecture, music, cuisine, customs, and the people themselves continue to show signs of influences—Anatolian, Greek, Arab, Egyptian, Venetian, Ottoman—that reveal the history of the Great Island, as it is still called in Greek. Cretans are sensitive and proud of a character that is their own, and discovering Crete in its villages and people adds new perspective to the generally accepted view of Greece and the Greeks.

MAJOR INTEREST

An "alternative" Greek experience
Minoan sites: Knossos, Phaistos, Ayia Triada, Mallia
Varied terrain: Mountains, gorges, beaches
More than 600 Byzantine churches

Herakleion
Archaeological Museum
Venetian Renaissance architecture: Loggia
Byzantine churches

Lasithi Plateau: 10,000 windmills and Diktian Cave

Resorts on Cretan Sea at Elounda and Ayios Nikolaos

Ierapetra and beaches on southern coast

Rethymno
Veneto-Ottoman quarter
Archaeological Museum
Excursion to Arkadi Monastery

Amari Valley

Hora Sphakion and Imvrou Ravine

Chania
Archaeological Museum
Kastelli
Venetian and Ottoman monuments

Samarian Gorge

Crete should not be visited casually. It is a large island—nearly 161 miles long by about 35 miles at its widest and 7.5 miles at its narrowest—formed by a ridge of mountains that are geologically linked to the islands of Kythira (off the southern Peloponnese) and Karpathos (midway between Crete and Rhodes), and to Turkey. This ridge drops precipitously into the Libyan Sea, so that if you approach the island from its southern, African, side it appears as a great barrier. Ierapetra is the only town of any importance on the southern coast, and its proximity to Africa and its comparative isolation from the rest of Crete give it a distinctly African atmosphere—Libya being only 155 miles to the south. The northern coast is quite different: The mountains slope more gently toward the Sea of Crete, and great sandy stretches of beaches, small coves, and natural harbors articulate the contours of the coast.

The mountainous ridge of Crete is not continuous but is broken up into a number of massive peaks: In the west are the White Mountains (Lefká Ori), which at the summit reach 8,050 feet, so called because of the heavy snows that collect there in the winter and last until as late as May; Mount Ida (Psilorítis) rises in the center to a height of 8,060 feet; and to the east are the mountains of Lasíthi (7,050 feet) and the Thripte (4,850 feet). Piercing the ridge from north to south are a number of valleys, ravines, and gorges. There are few plains; those of Omalos and Messara, however, are capable of sustaining a sizable cultivation of crops.

The "pockets" formed by the mountains, valleys, and plains have always separated the people of Crete into defined areas. These divisions make the Cretans basically a mountain people despite the existence of important and historically rich cities and towns. From late Minoan times (1500 B.C.) and the arrival of the Greek-speaking invaders from the north through the last world war and the German occupation, the mountains have provided refuge in crises. Despite living on an island, the Cretans do not take easily to the sea.

At one time the mountains of Crete were covered by great forests of cedars and cypresses. These have all but vanished, though a few varieties can still be found on small islands lying off the coast. The commonly heard story that the Ottomans destroyed the forests is not true; the deforestation had been going on long before their arrival, thanks to the combined efforts of goats, charcoal burners, and ship builders.

The island's geographic link with Anatolia and its subsequent isolation have resulted in flora and fauna unique to Crete. More than 150 varieties of native wildflowers can be found, including rare orchids and irises. Spring is an especially beautiful time to visit. Beginning in March and continuing well into June the island is covered with a carpet of blossoms and wild herbs, including wild dill, parsley, artichokes, and edible greens that form part of the traditional Cretan diet. Migrations of birds make Crete a bird watcher's paradise. The island boasts a number of species of wild cats, badgers, and an especially nasty large spider, the *rogalida,* which happily is seldom seen because it burrows deep in the ground. The most typical of all of these creatures is the Cretan ibex (*kri-kri*). Now almost extinct, this proud, stubborn highlander with great arching horns has had an almost totemic influence on the traditional Cretan character.

The Cretans are a complex people. In the view of mainland

Greeks, the islanders fall into two categories: very good and very bad. While simplistic, this generalization captures the contrariness typical of the Cretan character. As might be expected of people who have experienced many foreigners, they are not xenophobic toward non-Cretans. They magnanimously ignore foreign manners and attitudes, though they can be highly suspicious of Cretans from other parts of the island.

Cretan Food and Drink

The opportunity to enjoy authentic Cretan food is going to be limited unless you are invited to a wedding, a baptism, or someone's home. In eating in restaurants you will be exposed to the "classic" and, alas, ubiquitous, Greek menu of Greek salad, *souvlákia, pástitsio, moussaká* and a number of other preparations that are certainly not native to Crete or representative of Cretan cooking. These and certain other foods, such as feta cheese, gyro, and souvlakia in pita, have become part of the standard expectation of tourists, and the demand has been met so successfully that Cretan specialties seldom appear in restaurants.

The traditional Cretan diet depends on a wide variety of seasonal wild greens, many of which are peculiar to the island, wild artichokes, and pickled bulbs. Cretan cheeses are justifiably famous, especially *graviéra, mezýthra, anthótiri,* and milk products (mostly from goat or sheep milk) in the form of butters and staka, made from ewe's butter. Cheeses are incorporated in meat dishes, appear alone, or are made into delicious small pies known as *kaltsoúnia,* in which the cheese (usually mezythra) is mixed with mint, onions, spinach, or other greens, and occasionally even chili peppers.

Staple meats are goat, young lamb, suckling pig, and hare or rabbit as well as chicken. These are either grilled, roasted, combined in stews, or boiled together to make broths, including the liquid in which rice is boiled. Cretan *stifádo* is quite delicious and calls for hare, great quantities of onions, tomatoes, potatoes accentuated with ginger, coriander, cinnamon, cloves, and orange juice as well as peel. A similar combination of spices is used for cooking snails, another Cretan favorite, which is also exported.

Rice, usually short grained, and spaghetti are widely eaten. One especially festive *piláfi* (rice dish) that appears at every wedding as a symbol of richness is prepared by parboiling the rice in meat broth. When it is two-thirds cooked it is drained and then quickly plunged into hot, melted butter or staka and cooked until tender. It is ferociously and perhaps even mortally rich—but delicious.

Cretans are usually avid fish eaters if they come from coastal regions. Until very recent times the seas abounded with a great variety of fish, some "native" (if from the Cretan Sea) and others "foreign" (if from the Libyan Sea). The use of dynamite, overfishing, foreign fishing boats (e.g., from Malta), and recent pollution have had their effects on the seas, as has the Aswan Dam, which also changed much of the ecological balance of the seas south of Crete. Nonetheless you can still find bream of many varieties, red mullet, moray eel, swordfish, and even shark. If you are a real fish eater then you should certainly try sea urchins, in which the very essence of the sea seems to have been distilled. They are eaten raw and can be highly addictive.

Cretans enjoy a wide variety of sweets, including pastries and fruits and nuts in syrups. Some pastries call for doughs that are made up of flour, *tsikoudiá* (Cretan raki), and/or orange juice. Some are deep fried, covered with ground nuts, honey, and cinnamon. A deliciously famous Sphakiot "pie" is made of tsikoudia-laced dough that is covered with butter, pressed with cheese, and then fried to be eaten hot and smothered with honey.

Cretan wines are justifiably famous and do not include *retsína,* a dubious intruder from the mainland (though now produced in Crete, usually from inferior wines). According to some authorities the Malvasia vines were brought to Crete from the Morea (the Peloponnese) by the Venetians, especially to the area around Herakleion, which still turns out some of the finest wines on the island. Kissamo Kastelli produces very elegant white wines, and those from Chania and Rethymno, when of considerable age, can have a nutty flavor and bouquet not far from Sherry. (They can also be quite strong.) Most Cretan families will have their own barrels or have access to shops that do. These are carefully labeled and cared for according to age, though vintage is usually ignored. In ordering wines you have your choice in many restaurants of taking a commercially bottled wine or asking for house wine. The latter in most cases is the best— but, alas, not always available.

The national drink of the Cretan, however, is not wine but tsikoudia. This bears no resemblance to ouzo and is always drunk neat from small glasses. It is made according to a number of different recipes and can be based on mulberries or the remnants left over after pressing grapes. It is very strong and quite fiery and is not sold commercially, but very commonly offered as a welcome and again at the end of a meal. In many mountain villages a good shot of tsikoudia starts not only one's day but also can be used to start the fire. On holidays it is an affront not to accept a glass, even in the mornings, should it be offered.

History

The earliest people to settle on Crete appear to have arrived in the sixth millennium B.C. during the Neolithic period. Archaeological evidence suggests that they came from Anatolia, though there is evidence of settlers from North Africa as well. Out of the interaction of these peoples Minoan civilization developed, reaching its peak during the period 2200–1500 B.C. (although around 1700 the Minoan palaces were destroyed, probably by an earthquake). We know remarkably little about the Minoans. They left few writings, and what survives is in a language that we still cannot understand, set down in an alphabet that has not been deciphered. The Minoans are one of the great mystery peoples of antiquity. Their later influence on Greek mythology is apparent in the legends of King Minos, the creative and convoluted sexual interests of his wife Pasiphaë, the labyrinth, and Daedalus. What was known of the Minoans until the early part of this century came mainly from these legends, all of which had been reworked by the Greeks and hence came to us in somewhat distorted versions.

The British archaeologist Sir Arthur Evans, after appropriating the archaeological site at Knossos, devoted his life to excavating the Great Palace and to establishing the main lines of Minoan chronology. The silence of the Minoans, plus the impressive ruins that have been identified all over the island, have made them popular in certain spheres of academia. It is evident that they had a wide-ranging international trade and that they exerted a powerful influence on mainland Greece and, especially, on the Cycladic islands. From the surviving frescoes it appears that men wore codpieces and women left their bosoms bare. Both sexes wore their hair long. Archaeologists also indicate that they were preoccupied with plumbing. Whatever they were, the Minoans certainly were interesting and apparently life-loving.

Sites of Minoan palaces, towns, and villages are found all around Crete. Many insignificant modern villages are now built over ruins that indicate places of importance in Minoan or later in Greek times. Visiting these sites is not only difficult but also requires a good deal of time—but most are well worth it if only for the opportunities they afford for long walks into the mountains and valleys.

Minoan civilization came to a dramatic end in the course of the 15th century B.C. (although for reasons not entirely understood, civilization at Knossos outlasted other Minoan cities by about 70 years). Its demise was probably caused by a combination of earthquakes, volcanic eruptions, and the arrival of the earliest Greek-speaking invaders. Like good Cretans, many Minoans took to the hills and became known as Eteocretans; those who remained on the lowlands became slaves of the Greeks.

From this time until the Roman occupation in the first century B.C. the island was, for all practical purposes, without a history. One of Crete's stalwart sons, Epiminides, is credited with the famous quip "All Cretans are liars"—which Saint Paul appears to have taken at face value, though, since Epiminides himself was a Cretan, the paradox provided problems for others. The Dorian Greek conquerors' legal experiments in ruling the enslaved Cretan populations eventually brought Crete into the pattern of Sparta's rigorous system of law and social organization. Crete also succumbed to the endemic political sickness of the Greeks and entered into a long period of interurban warfare.

In 67 B.C. Crete was subjected to the Pax Romana after an especially harsh war that won for its victor, Metellus, the added appellation of Creticus. Gortys, south of Herakleion above the rich plains of Messara, became the capital of a new province that linked the island with Libya (Cyrenaica). By A.D. 33 Jews had settled on Crete; they are mentioned in the Acts of the Apostles as being present at Pentecost. The Romans brought peace to the island, and many of their cities, such as Aptera (near Chania) and Gortys, have extensive and impressive remains.

Between the fifth and seventh centuries Crete entered into a period of prosperity under the early Christian (Byzantine) emperors. The remains of some 40 great basilicas bear witness to strong influences from the Syro-Palestinian coast. There may well have been an influx of immigrants fleeing to the island from Syria, Cyprus, and eastern Anatolia in the wake of the Islamic conquest of these regions between 632 and 700. By the early part of the eighth century the Byzantine Empire was in difficult straits, and Islam began to exert an interesting ideological influence on the empire as well. In 823 an Andalusian Arab fleet sailed into Souda Bay (near today's Chania) on what its sailors thought was a raid. Its leader literally burnt his boats behind him by ordering some 40 ships to be destroyed and then turned his men to the conquest of the island, which was achieved within a remarkably short period. This Arab emirate set itself up at what is now Herakleion. An enormous moat (*handaq*) was built around the fortifications, and it is the corruption of *handaq* into Candia that gave Crete its Medieval name.

By 961 the Byzantines were in the process of expansion, and under Nicephorus Phocas, who later became emperor, they set out to reconquer the island. After they catapulted the heads of Muslim captives into the city, Rabdh al-Handaq (Herakleion's proper name in Arabic) fell. There are accounts of incredible riches carried off to Constantinople, followed by a century of aggressive missionary activity waged to bring the Cretans once again into the Christian fold. Churches were built, and many of these, especially those of the 13th century, can be found in what are now out-of-the-way villages. The island's population was also revitalized during the succeeding years by the official Byzantine policy of resettling Slavs, Armenians, and Anatolian Greeks. The influence of these peoples and their cultures has had a decided impact on Cretan music, songs, dances, and poetry.

Venice acquired Crete in a rather roundabout way in 1204. For more than half a century the island had been neglected because of Byzantine concerns with the Seljuk Turkish conquest of Anatolia, and later the Crusades. The deposed emperor Alexis IV passed Crete on to Boniface of Montferrat, who in turn sold it to the Venetians for 1,000 silver marks.

Until the 15th century the Venetians exploited the island mercilessly; in the process, it was colonized and feudalized. They also alienated the Orthodox population by attempting to force a union with the Catholic church and proscribing the activities of native bishops. The Cretan response was open rebellion until, after the revolt of 1363, the island was given an independent status, and its own nobility was awarded equal standing with the Venetians. It was mainly after this period that many of the finest Venetian buildings in Crete were erected, either in old towns such as Herakleion or newer, refounded, ones such as Chania. Villages also received their share of fine structures in the form of manor houses of a hybrid Creto-Venetian architecture.

Catholicism and Orthodoxy reached a modus vivendi, and the "native" Venetians became thoroughly Cretan in their love of the island. Thanks to the interaction of the populations,

Crete began to create its own Creto-Venetian culture and to absorb influences from the West. Poets, playwrights, musicians, and painters produced for a rich patronage, and the result was the Cretan Renaissance.

The last century of Byzantine history was hardly culturally stagnant; many of Crete's new arrivals were painters who brought techniques that were to reach maturity in what is now called the Cretan School, the last phase of Byzantine art. Characteristic of the Cretan School was its dependency on the styles and iconography of Constantinopolitan art that developed during the 14th and early 15th centuries. Especially at Mystra, in the Peloponnese, there was a revival of art and poetry that was in full swing when the Ottomans took Constantinople in 1453. For this reason Mystra appears to have attracted painters from Thessaloniki and Constantinople, who later fled (after 1459) to Venetian-held Crete. Native Cretan painters appear to have been following very conservative traditions in fresco painting or were working in the Italianate manner for Venetian patrons until the arrival of an influx of these painters from the Peloponnese, which acted as a catalyst for the creation of a new style.

Three painters of the 16th century, all native Cretans and quite possibly trained in the same atelier, stand out distinctly: Theophanes Strelitsas, Michael Damaskinos, and Domenikos Theotokopoulos, or El Greco. Theophanes was a monk, and as early as 1527 was working at the Meteora (Thessaly) where he decorated the jewel-like chapel of St. Nicholas. He later worked on Mount Athos, and his paintings, conservative and dependent on the main stream of Byzantine art, were to evolve into the Athonite School. Damaskinos and Theotokopoulos were roughly contemporaries who studied in Herakleion (Candia at that time) and reached maturity on the island. Damaskinos remained all of his life representative of the Creto-Venetian society in which he matured. Active in Venice, where he worked for the Cretan community there in decorating the church of St. George, he returned to Crete in 1582 and was to influence Cretan icon painting for several generations through such painters as Tsanes, Poulakis, and Kournaros, all active in the Ionian islands and Venice. Theotokopoulos was quite different, as he deliberately chose what most Cretans fear the most: exile from Crete. From Venice, where he studied and worked until 1576, he moved on to Rome and then Spain, where he remained for the rest of his life. Despite the high degree of "westernization" that characterizes his paintings, his use of glimmering veils of light and intricate iconographies is all attributable to his Cretan-Byzantine origins. It is claimed that El Greco was born at Fodela, not far to the west of Herakleion. There is a monument to him there but nothing else.

The cultural flow was not one way. Cretans travelled easily into the West; a press was established in Venice, and Cretan professors taught in the universities of Venice and Florence. Native Cretans Hortatzis and Vitzentzos Kornaros produced two of the greatest pieces of literature in Medieval Greek—respectively, the *Erophili* and the *Erotokritos*.

In 1669 Candia was taken by the Ottomans after a 22-year siege. This occupation began at an unfortunate time. The Turkish Empire had passed its zenith (the period of Suleyman and Selim) and was already showing signs of the debilitating illness that was to make it the "Sick Man of Europe." In order to repopulate certain regions it was necessary to bring Turks into the island. The burdens of taxes and perhaps even religious conviction caused a large number of Cretans to convert to Islam. Despite modern revisionist attempts to make these conversions appear forced, the fact is that many Cretans quite comfortably accepted Islam in a form that was distinctly Cretan. Ottoman remains on the island are more quaint than architecturally significant.

By the 18th century the Cretans were in revolt again, though, apart from an uprising in 1770, it was not until 1821 that open rebellion took place, followed by growing hostility between the Christian and Muslim communities that resulted in riots, massacres, and flight. By 1896 the population was pretty much divided between urban Muslims and village Christians; this split led to a crisis that caused an allied fleet to occupy the island in 1898. Crete then enjoyed a period of autonomy, with its own postage stamps, currency, and customs, until 1913, when it was formally annexed to Greece. The final chapter in the story was the forced deportation in 1923 and again in 1930 of more than 30,000 Cretan Muslims to Turkey, where the community still survives today as *Giritli*, Cretan to the heart. Many speak a dialect of Cretan now lost on the island because of the influence of mainland Greece.

The last foreign occupation of Crete was under the Germans in World War II. Systematic bombing of Chania, Rethymno, and Herakleion destroyed many of the most important Venetian buildings. The villages put up a strong resistance with almost no arms, and in retaliation the Germans executed entire populations and leveled their villages.

Today Crete is entering a new period dominated by mainland politics, tourism, and the European Community. Much of its old life has vanished, and its economy is being adjusted to suit the needs of European stomachs and pocketbooks. It is once again in the process of change.

Getting beneath the surface of Crete is not easy. The usual visit to Knossos (just south of Herakleion) and a few other Minoan sites, plus a day or so at one of the beach resorts, will provide you with little that is genuinely Cretan.

Crete has four main urban centers along the northern coast: Herakleion, Crete's administrative center and the gateway to Knossos and other Minoan sites, in the middle of the coast; Ayios Nikolaos, a resort town east of Herakleion; Rethymno, about 80 km (50 miles) west of Herakleion; and Chania, still farther to the west. These towns are connected by a fine national highway that makes travel between them not only convenient but quick. From each of these cities it is possible to cut to the southern coast by means of subsidiary roads running between or along the flanks of the mountains. Most of the Minoan sites are in the east, and the later Greek, Roman, Byzantine, Venetian, and Ottoman sites are in the central and western parts of the island. Granted a rented car and a comfortable ten days—or, better still, two weeks—day trips can be planned out of the main towns to take you into the heart of the island. Walking shoes are advisable on such journeys, as many of the finer Byzantine churches are located not in villages but in outlying areas. Don't be put off by not knowing Greek; the Cretan is quick enough to figure out why you have ended up in his village. For women planning trips to monasteries and churches, it is best to wear skirts and some covering for the arms; headscarves needn't be worn.

HERAKLEION

Fortunately Herakleion (Irákleion) has changed since the 19th century, when Edward Lear noted that it was "mealy-ruiny, earthquaky, odious." Since then it has become the administrative capital of the island, the main center for commerce, and—since the discovery of nearby Knossos—the main tourist stopover; few find it attractive enough to make it more than this. Though it is a harsh, crowded city, Herakleion contains many surprises and represents an aspect of modern Crete that cannot be ignored. It provides easy access to Knossos and Phaistos and has *the* major museum dedicated

Eastern Crete
0 miles 10
0 km 10
Sea of Crete
Dia
Panormos
Rethymno
Perama
Fodela
Herakleion
Chersonisos
Milatos
Mt. Ida
Linoperamata
Gouves
Mallia
Elounda
Kournas
Axos
Tilisos
Knossos
Mohos
Gonies
Neapolis
Bay of Mirabello
Vai
Anoyeia
Gonies
Potamies
Lagou
Siteia
Moni Toplu
Idean Cave
Archanes
Mirtia
Aydou
LASITHI PLATEAU
Ayios Nikolaos
Amari
Mount Junctus
Diktian Cave
Lato
Moni Vrondisi
Psychro
Ayios Yeorgios
Kritsa
Moni Preveli
Frangokastelo
Kamares
Prinias
Moni Valsamonero
Zaros
Ayia Varvara
DIKTI MTS.
Gournia
Lithines
Etia
Ziros
Kato Zakros
Ayia Galini
LASITHI MTS.
THRIPTE MTS.
Makriyialos
Gortys
Ayia Triada
Phaistos
Arvi
Myrtos
Ierapetra
N
Komos
Kamilari
Matala
Pitsidia
Koufonisi
Chrisi
Kali Limenes
Libyan Sea

solely to Minoan archaeology. Even if you are planning to spend some time in the western or southwestern part of Crete, it is feasible (should you feel that Lear had a point) to stay to the east of Herakleion at Elounda or farther east (about an hour away by car) at Ayios Nikolaos (see below for more on both). From these less frenetic but slightly glitzy resort areas you can visit Herakleion and the sites in its vicinity.

Staying in Herakleion itself presents few problems, as there are a good number of fine hotels in town as well as on the sea. The best in-town hotels, all centrally located and with good restaurants, facilities, and services, are the Astoria, Esperia, and Galaxias. While commanding no sea views, the **Astoria** has a swimming pool and tennis courts. The **Galaxias**, too, has a swimming pool, while the **Esperia** is a smallish pension. The **Xenia Hotel** is reliable and located in town, just off the sea, but its kitchen is rather mediocre. In addition, there are a number of other seafront hotels to choose from just outside of town, away from the bustle of Herakleion. The **Apollonia Beach**, just west of Herakleion in Linoperamata, and the **Creta Sun Hotel**, 35 km (22 miles) east of Herakleion in Gouves Pediádos, both have excellent bathing facilities and good atmosphere. The Creta Sun is a self-contained resort complex with water sports, a swimming pool, and a tennis court. Another nice hotel in the area is the **Knossos Beach**, just out of Herakleion at Kókkino Hani. These last three hotels have good to excellent restaurants offering local and international cuisines.

Herakleion has had a difficult history. It began as a Minoan seaport and got its present name after the Roman conquest of the island, when it continued to function as the port for Knossos. Only after the Arab conquest in the early ninth century did it become really important, as the emirate was established here. Shortly after the Arabs took the town they constructed an enormous moat (*al-handaq,* in Arabic) and Herakleion entered Medieval history as Rabdh al-Handaq. From here Arab corsairs raided southern Greece and western Anatolia at a time when the fortunes of the Byzantine Empire were at their lowest. Greece was being invaded by the Slavs, and eastern Christendom showed signs of being ideologically weakened by the successes of Islam. All of the churches built in Crete before the ninth century were destroyed during this period, and Nicephorus Phocas, while preparing for the reconquest of the island, called it "accursed Crete," referring to a willing apostasy on the part of the people in accepting Islam. Handaq was retaken in 961, and the Byzantines immediately set about taking control of the island. Traditionally they are credited with establishing 12 noble families in order to create a uniform administration, the center of which was Kastro, as Handaq then became known. From it missionaries went out to reconvert the island, but apart from this little is known of the period from 961 until the arrival of the Venetians in the early 13th century.

In 1204, when the Fourth Crusade succeeded in taking Constantinople, Crete was purchased by the Venetians. Handaq became known as Candia and, as the official residence of the duke, gave its name to the entire island.

Until the fall of the island to the Ottomans in the late 17th century, the Venetians did much building in Herakleion, and the city is marked by many fine monuments that reflect the strong influence of early and later Renaissance art and architecture. In the center of Venizelos Square, just northeast of the center of town, is the **Morosini Fountain**, a composite made up of a 17th-century retaining tank with lively scenes of marine mythology. Above it, supporting the fountain head, are an impressive group of lions, probably dating from the 14th century (Duke Morosini was the uncle of the last Venetian defender of Crete). Not far from the fountain is the ducal **church of St. Mark**, which was the burial place for the representatives of the *serenissima* and which under the Ottomans became a mosque (Defterdar Djamii). Today it houses the **Cretan Historical Society** and also hosts some fine temporary exhibits.

Adjacent to St. Mark's is the 17th-century **Loggia**, also built by Morosini, which was the center for Venetian administration. One of the most remarkable Venetian Renaissance buildings in Crete, it was deemed worthy of being reconstructed down to its last detail in Rome as the Venetian pavilion in 1911. Behind the Loggia is the **church of St. Titus**, the patron saint of Crete and a convert of Saint Paul. The original structure dated from the tenth century; from it missionaries went forth into Crete and brought the island back to Orthodoxy. St. Titus became a Roman Catholic cathedral under Venice and was converted to an Islamic mosque under the Ottomans. Today it is once again Orthodox, and the head of the saint (having survived all this turmoil) is its most treasured relic.

Travelling straight on (north) you'll reach the port, site of the **Kastro**, where the arsenals and repair sheds of the Venetians were located. There is a fine Lion of Saint Mark on the face of the castle. This is a pleasant place to walk in the evenings, with reliable tavernas in the area and, on occasion, good musical concerts and dancing. To the west and east of the harbor the great Venetian walls spread out in a circle cut by several gates—some with fine carvings. To the west, next to the Koum Kapi harbor, is the **Historical and Ethnographic Museum**, which has an interesting collection of artifacts covering the Medieval and modern periods. The museum also has a fine collection of Cretan textiles, including embroideries that are typically Cretan in their compact and dense patterns of flowers, figures, and symbols derived from a common repertoire found throughout the Near East.

In St. Catherine's Square, southwest of Venizelos Square, is the **church of Ayía Aikateríni** (St. Catherine), a former dependency of the great monastery of that name on Mount Sinai. It has an elegant, simple façade pierced by a large oculus typical of churches built in the 15th century in Crete under Venetian influence. Purists have occasionally been severe in their assessment of Renaissance influences from the West in Crete without taking into account that the impact was softened by a strong and creative Byzantine tradition. It is fitting that this dependency of the great monastery on Mount Sinai, where the finest collection of Byzantine icons in the world is found, should have its own excellent collection, plus a large number of wall paintings from churches on the island. Many of its icons are signed (a rare occurrence) and date from the 16th to 18th centuries. Some of the finest icons in St. Catherine's are by Michael Damaskinos. Next to Ayia Aikaterini is a small church dedicated to the **Ayioi Deka**—the ten saints martyred under the emperor Decius for their profession of Christianity.

The heart of modern Herakleion is its **market**, located on 1866 Street, not far from the Morosini Fountain. In addition to selling spices, herbs, and masses of fruits and vegetables, vendors offer typical and well-made baskets—some for drying cheese—as well as festive Cretan breads, preserved in some mysterious way and covered with delicate flowers of dough.

At the southern end of the market is a small square that is the site of the **Valide Mosque**, dedicated to Turhan Valide, the mother of Sultan Mehmet IV, as well as the **Bembo Fountain**, constructed in 1588 and adorned with a headless statue from Ierapetra. Evans Street, which runs off the square, leads to the **New Gate**, where summer concerts are held. Not far from here an ascent can be made to the top of one of the bastions where the **tomb of Nikos Kazantzakis** is located. The film version of his *Zorba the Greek* was made in Chania and Akrotiri.

When shopping in Herakleion keep in mind that it is a tourist center. It would appear that the merchants use sheer quantity in an attempt to get customers to buy something. Yet don't be too critical of Minoan reproductions when you see them by the hundreds on the shelves. There they may appear as simply the imitations that they are; isolated and in other settings, individual pieces can be striking. Many of the vases decorated with naturalistic motifs, taken from finds made at Knossos, work especially well in modern decor. Pieces of Kamares ware, more colorful and sophisticated in terms of abstraction and simplification of organic forms, are works of art in themselves despite being copies. Many jewelry shops offer fine copies of Minoan goldwork, which utilize techniques of granulation and casting that duplicate those of antiquity. In the best examples, pendants, earrings, and gold seal rings are copies of the originals that you'll see in the Archaeological Museum. Shops also sell local pottery as well as handwoven woolens.

The best area to shop in Herakleion is along 25th Augoústou and Dikaiosínis streets. On the former, just opposite the Loggia, is a small and very select shop called **Eva Grim**. Though expensive, many of the embroideries and coverlets are very fine and characteristic of native crafts now all but dead. Along Dikaiosinis Street are a great number of shops featuring fine gold work, icons, and good-quality copies of Minoan ceramics and pottery. If hunger has set in, head north of Dikaiosinis to Daedalou Street, where you'll find at number 8 a delightful new restaurant with the air of a traditional taverna. **Klemataria** serves regular fare—well prepared—as well as grills, salads, and an excellent house wine (Tel: 246-483).

Actually, eating in Herakleion can be problematic. Most of the old seafront tavernas at the end of 25th Augoustou Street near the Kastro have been forced out of business by car-rental shops and tourist offices. What remains on the seafront now must contend with a main thoroughfare for cars and trucks that make the area noisy, dusty, and generally inadvisable as a choice for either lunch or dinner. You may, however, try the **Glass House**, which is located on Venizélou Street and is not so bad in the evenings. **Maxim**, located on Minótavros Street, which runs along the eastern flank of El Greco Park, is reliable; **Caprice** and **Knossos**, though quite old, are good for lunch (both are found on Nikiphóros Phoká Square).

The Archaeological Museum

Herakleion's Archaeological Museum, west of the market on Xanthoudídou Street, warrants a visit that can easily take half a day, if not more. It is quite simply the world's richest repository of the remnants of Minoan civilization. Its collections, originally drawn from the finds of Sir Arthur Evans at Knossos, have been enriched in the course of the last 50 years with finds from other sites throughout the island. The museum is arranged chronologically, covering the Neolithic (c. 6000 B.C.) to Minoan periods (3000 to 1500 B.C.), down to Greek and Roman times (1100 B.C. to the first century A.D.). The famous Ayia Triada sarcophagus, with scenes of ritual oblations depicted in fresco work, as well as the Phaistos disk, which bears an inscription in an undeciphered alphabet, are two of the great Old Palace treasures to be seen here.

Gold jewelry utilizing sophisticated techniques, snake goddesses, personal adornments, and household artifacts are evidence of the rich and complex lives of the Minoans. The ceramic collections cover the entire period from 6000 B.C. until after the dissolution of Minoan civilization and well into the Dorian period. Perhaps in no other sphere of creativity did the Minoans leave such a mark of their particular genius in creating a balance of form and decoration. Important insight into the complex world of the Minoans—which is otherwise mute—is to be found in the fascinating collections.

A perfect spot to rest and digest the wonders of the museum is the **Pizzeria Napoli** at 7 Eleftheriou Square, with a garden, a relaxed atmosphere, and, despite the name, good Greek as well as international cuisine. It is efficiently run and the pizzas are excellent.

SOUTH OF HERAKLEION

Herakleion, Ayios Nikolaos, and Elounda (see below) make convenient bases for day trips to Knossos, Phaistos, and the southern coast. Visiting Knossos is an incredible experience despite the masses of tours that invade the Great Palace all year. How Minoan sites in general are approached is a matter of personal taste, but there is a decided choice to be made in regard to which to visit first: Knossos or Phaistos. Sir Arthur Evans, the discoverer and excavator of Knossos, has come under a great deal of criticism, especially regarding his techniques and views of how to handle an archaeological site. A pioneer and a man of genius and wealth, Evans had a prodigious ego. As he excavated Knossos he reconstructed or reinforced certain areas using concrete. If at Knossos you can detect King Minos and the hand of the legendary Daedalus (who in antiquity was credited with having built the labyrinth, along with Pasiphaë's cow and wings for his ill-fated son), that of Evans is evident as well. The other palace, that of Phaistos (see below), while equally—or nearly—as grand as Knossos, was excavated by the Italians well into our century with disciplined accuracy for detail. It is austere, down to the bare evidence, but is situated on a site that commands one of the most breathtaking views in Crete.

Knossos

A visit to the Great Palace of Knossós (5 km/3 miles south of Herakleion) requires at least a day, as the site is enormous and rambles in various directions—perhaps indicating the origins of the legends of the great labyrinth. Because the site was inhabited from Neolithic times (c. 6000 B.C.) to the fifth century A.D. (a bishop of Knossos is noted as having attended the Council of Ephesus in 431), it is almost impossible for a layperson to disentangle the various levels without a good site guidebook, many of which are in print (see the Bibliography). The usual approach to the site is through what was apparently a ceremonial corridor that opened at one end to a magnificent view and that contained paintings of offering bearers. The originals of these and other paintings are in the Herakleion Archaeological Museum. The processional route leads into the great central court, on three sides of which the palace structures extended and descended on various levels. It is in the reconstruction of these structures that Evans has been attacked by contemporary archaeologists.

The question of accuracy and how much of Evans's own *Zeitgeist* entered into the interpretation of what he found and reconstructed at Knossos is still controversial. By comparison the sites at Phaistos, Mallia, and Kato Zakro are barren, excavated in accordance with the discipline of modern archaeology. What remains is what is to be found, and it requires considerable knowledge and, even more important, imagination in order to create in the mind's eye the walls, stairways, and superstructures that surrounded the great, now-barren courtyards. At Knossos Evans has left "clues," visual aids that, once grasped, allow you to get some sense of the magnitude of the structure along its vertical as opposed to horizontal axis. Narrow-footed columns support roofs and line stairwells. Inner rooms off small sanctuaries, dark and sinister, retain some mystery that is lost in the full light of the sun. Grooves cut in piers leading to small, cut receptacles at their bases become more feasibly spots where blood libations were poured to appease the bull god who periodically rocked the island in his throes. Stairs take you down into the very bowels of the palace where, according to Evans, the queen had her suite. Cool light filters down into an exquisite room decorated with flying dolphins. It is as if you have descended to the bottom of the sea. Once you have grasped visually some of the effects that were created by the use of light wells, air shafts, and water-drainage systems, it makes wandering through the other more "purely" excavated sites more rewarding and exciting.

If it is difficult to unravel the structure of the palace itself, it is no less difficult to unravel the legends surrounding the great king Minos. Hidden in the depths of this maze, the Palace of the Labrys (Axe, or Labyrinth), was the Minotaur, the monster son of Pasiphaë, Minos's queen. He was born under quite strange circumstances, as his mother had developed a passion for a sacred bull sent by the god Poseidon. Failing to arouse his interest she had Daedalus create for her a brazen cow in which she seduced him. From this union was born the Minotaur, who from shame was hidden in the depths of the palace where his appetite for human flesh was met with tribute children brought from cities under the sway of Crete. It is into the great maze of Knossos that legend has Theseus grope while holding the thread of Ariadne. It is in the great courtyard of the palace that bull-baiting acrobatics were carried out, depicted vividly on some of the remaining wall paintings. Were these innocent games twisted and embellished by time and ignorance into the strange story of the Minotaur, or does Knossos still hide a sinister tale that will never be told? The Minoans have hidden their secrets well, and the monstrous horns of the bull rising high on the present walls of the palace seem to guard them.

If you go to Knossos first, you can then continue south along the road about another 20 km (12 miles) to Mirtiá, a small village with a well-organized museum in honor of the writer Nikos Kazantzakis.

A major day trip from Herakleion could also be made to **Archánes**, 11 km (7 miles) south of Knossos on the main road. Archanes is famous for its wine, and there are some important Minoan sites in the village. In fact the first unmolested royal tomb was found here, as well as two other *tholos* (round tombs). Just outside of Archanes (you will have to ask once you leave the village) is a small, 14th-century Byzantine church, the **Asómatos**, with fine frescoes dating from 1315. While in Archanes you can look to the western horizon and find the profile of Zeus on Mount Juctus—which is where one legend has it that the god was born and died. It would seem that the Greeks associated their own sky god Zeus with a chief male deity of the Minoans, a vegetation god who underwent death in the autumn and resurrection in the spring. The death of the god appears to have given rise to the legend that Zeus died in Crete.

To Phaistos

The journey from Herakleion down through the plain to the southern coast of Crete provides a subtle introduction to the beauties of the Cretan landscape as well as to the vastness of its history. After getting onto the Phaistos road in Herakleion, you will be driving through vineyards that produce some of Crete's best Malvasia wines. In the 15th century it was from these vineyards (the vines appear to have been brought from the Peloponnese) that cuttings were taken off to Madeira, introducing viticulture to that island. The Victorian song "Have some Madeira, m' dear" and, more sadly, the "malmsey-butt in the next room" in which the young duke of Clarence was drowned in Shakespeare's *Richard III,* owe their inspiration to these vineyards, as Cretan malmsey was one of the island's main exports during the Middle Ages.

At **Ayía Varvára** (30 km/18.5 miles south of Herakleion) you can cut right to get deeper into the foothills of Mount Ida by taking either the turn to Priniás (a sharp right) or the road to Kamáres and Zaros. Along the latter road are two monasteries—**Moní Vrondísi** and **Moní Valsamónero**—that are worth a stop. The former, originally constructed c. 1400, has been rebuilt substantially since it was destroyed during the Cretan rebellion in 1866. (It was here that Michael Korakas proclaimed the freedom of eastern Crete from the Ottomans.) There is a lovely late-16th/early-17th–century fountain with figures of Adam and Eve—alas, headless. Moni Valsamonero has paintings dating from the 14th century and was, from Venetian times until well into the Ottoman period, a center for intellectual life in Crete.

At the termination of this road is the **Kamares Cave**, where a horde of polychrome Minoan pottery was discovered. (In itself the cave is not especially exciting, and the rich finds of Kamares pottery are now on display in the Herakleion Archaeological Museum.) Climbing **Mount Ida** requires a guide, as it is about five hours of rough hiking to reach the **Idaean Cave**, where one legend says that the infant Zeus was born, and another five hours to reach the summit. (You can also drive to the cave from Anoyeia; see below under To Rethymno.)

After Kamares take the road back to Ayia Varvara and then cut south to **Gortys**, the capital of Crete and Cyrenaica (Libya) during Roman times and prominent until it was destroyed by the Arabs in the ninth century. It has not been excavated thoroughly, and much of it lies beneath the fields, from which jut up odd capitals, fragments of statues, and the imposing ruin of **St. Titus's Church**, one of the few that was not razed entirely during the emirate. North of St. Titus is a well-marked path leading to a Roman **theater** that was reconstructed under the emperor Trajan in A.D. 100. Into its curved back wall are set the fifth-century B.C. stone blocks on which the famous **Law Code of Gortys** is inscribed. Apart from its legal interest, the Law Code is one of the few surviving examples of ox-plow script, in which long pronouncements were written in antiquity. After you've read along for 20 or 30 feet, the text, rather than making you go back to your starting point for the beginning of a new line, conveniently turns about and works its way backward. From Gortys the descent to the Libyan Sea begins—Africa is not far in the distance—and the terrain takes on a much different character, opening into the great plain of Messara, of vital importance to the Romans for growing grain.

The road to Phaistos (63 km/39 miles southwest of Herakleion) is well marked; a visit to the site as well as that of nearby Ayia Triada is feasible in an afternoon trip from Herakleion.

Phaistos is as ancient as Knossos but was very likely a dependency of it. Dominating the Messaran Plain beneath it, the palace was every bit as sumptuous as the one at Knossos. Destroyed during the earthquake of 1700 B.C., Phaistos was rebuilt and, after the arrival of the Greeks, was an independent state until it was destroyed again in about the second century B.C. The excavation of the site has simply laid bare its bones; no reconstruction has been done here as at Knossos. The elevation of the palace is not apparent, and the view out over the plain has an indescribable serenity.

From Phaistos you can take a footpath that rambles through clumps of wild sage, oregano, and thyme down to

Ayia Triada, a later site than Phaistos that was probably destroyed by fire.

Ayía Triáda (the Holy Trinity) is the modern and quite Christian name for an ancient and very distinctly Minoan site. The excavations here have not revealed the traces of cramped urban dwellings that were to be found around the palace at Knossos or Phaistos. The compact plan, including storage rooms, an archival room, and small sanctuaries (without "public" areas in the form of courtyards or even sunken libation areas), has led some experts to conclude that this was a private palace. The present ruins date from the middle of the 16th century B.C., though evidence has been found of earlier buildings dating back to the early part of the third millennium B.C. From the site you can look down across the valley to the Libyan Sea, and it is possible to sense the close connection that this site had to it. Ayia Triada is beautifully located and elegantly poised, taking advantage of the splendid southern location and the sea.

Most accounts of the small palace claim that it was a summer palace, which makes no sense at all if you have ever been caught in the summer heat that can come burning in from Libya. If anything this was a winter palace, exposed to the southern, low sun and protected from the harsh northern winds. Included in the rich finds here is the famous sarcophagus in the Herakleion Archaeological Museum.

The Southern Coast

The southern coast is not far from Phaistos, and after reaching sea level the road divides for either the northern road to Ayia Galini (west of Phaistos), the middle road to Komos and Matala (southwest), or the road south to Kali Liménes, identified as the port where Saint Paul was shipwrecked. This region can be very hot and dry in August, and its potential as an attractive destination for tourists is being developed at a rapid pace. There are some small Byzantine churches located in a few of the villages as well as an interesting Minoan site at Pitsidia, on the way from Phaistos to Matala (see below).

Ayía Galíni has a questionable beach, but it is "in" with lobster-red tourists and very popular (read, crowded). The **Greenwich Village** is a good fish restaurant here with a garden and terrace, off the beaten taverna track. There are a number of comfortable hotels, including the **Acteon**, which has good views. The town of **Mátala**, on the coast south of Ayia Galini, has attracted the off-beat pseudo-hippy crowd for a number of years but recently seems to be taking second place to the small village of **Pitsídia**, about 3 km (2 miles) to the northeast off the Phaistos road. (If you must visit Matala you can check out the **Marinero**, an all-night jazz bar.) In Pitsidia's village square is a small hotel called **Petros**, which has rooms with trellises, balconies, and kitchens. There is a good beach convenient to Matala and Pitsidia at **Komos**, where a number of new hotels are being built. Farther east there are more stretches of quiet or deserted beaches. The **Oasis Hotel** near Kamilári, north of Pitsidia, has a garden and a restaurant; if you have a car, this is a good choice—it is quite idyllic.

EASTERN CRETE

Southeastern Crete is dominated by **Mount Dikti**; there are two ways around it. The route around its western flank begins at Chersonisos (26 km/16 miles east of Herakleion) and continues more or less straight down to the sea at Arvi or Myrtos. This itinerary takes you through rich mountainous countryside and interesting villages, many of them the sites of small churches dating from the 13th century. Just before Arvi there is a banana grove, densely green and tropical, and **Arvi** itself has a fine beach. The other, more circuitous and difficult route along the eastern flank (which also brings you eventually to Arvi and Myrtos) goes through the Lasithi Plateau, and is the more impressive choice.

Lasithi Plateau

You can make a trip to the Lasíthi Plateau (2,625 feet up in the Dikti mountains), with its 10,000 windmills and the Diktian Cave, by taking the winding Mohós road south out of Chersonisos. You will find, just before Potamiés, a fine small church, the **Panayía Gouvernítissa**, an abandoned monastery originally founded in the ninth century, destroyed during the Arab Emirate, and refounded after the Byzantine recapture of the island. It has some excellent frescoes as well as an intact figure of Christ Pantokrator (Universal Ruler) in its dome. Farther on at Avdoú, 6 km (4 miles) south of Mohos, there are several other interesting churches: Ayios Antónios, Ayios Yeórgios, the Annunciation (Evangelismós), and Ayios Konstantínos—all from the 14th and 15th centuries. (Be sure to take a flashlight.)

Leaving Avdou continue on the route to Goniés, where

the ascent to the Lasithi Plateau begins. Plan to stop at Krásion, where there is a very ancient plane tree, before continuing on to the monastery at Kerá, also known as the **Kardiótissa**, one of the most important frescoed churches in Crete. The only recently uncovered paintings date from the 14th century. This monastery had in its possession one of the most famous of the wonder-working images of the Virgin Mary attributed to the hand of Saint Luke, but it was stolen by the Venetians in the 15th century and taken to Rome (where it is still kept in the church of San Alphonso), eventually to become the prototype of all images of Our Lady of Perpetual Help in the West. Not far out of Kera the road winds up and past Karfí, the Spike Peak, appropriately named after its shape. This peak appears to have been an important stronghold of the Eteocretans who fled from the Greek-speaking invaders of Crete into the mountains.

Just before reaching the highest point of this journey it is a good idea to stop at Seli for a magnificent view over the Cretan Sea as far as Santorini. Not far from here you will see some of the famous windmills of Lasithi and just beyond, at Lagou, you enter plain.

The Plain of Lasithi is surrounded by several high peaks and appears to have been a natural fortress for descendants of the Minoans (Eteocretans). Even prior to that time, however, it was heavily inhabited, and human remains have been found dating back to 7000 B.C. at Tsermiádou in the Trapéza cave. So isolated has this area been even into the present age that its inhabitants are purported to be descendants of stock dating back to Minoan times. Today there are about 20 villages on the plain. The last of any interest is **Ayios Yeórgios**, about 2.5 km (1.5 miles) after Mesa Lasíthi on the road marked for the Diktian Cave; its **Folk Museum** is well worth a visit. Built in a typical and authentic farmhouse, the museum shows every aspect of Lasithian village life.

From here the 3-km (2-mile) journey west to the village of Psychró and the Diktian Cave is easy. You must leave your car at the village and walk the half mile to the site. A visit to the cave itself requires a steep climb down and up again; strenuous, but thrilling, too. The cave was sacred in antiquity as one of two places in Crete where Zeus was said to have been born, the other being Mount Ida. The **Diktian Cave** of Psychro evokes much of the mystery and strange events that surrounded the birth of Zeus and for that reason is the more probable of the places claiming this honor. Once inside the grotto it is not difficult to imagine Gaia, Mother Earth, hiding her grandson in its depths while her daughter Rhea fed stones wrapped like swaddled infants to her husband, Kronos. Here Zeus was said to have been nursed by dryads and nymphs and fed with honey and fruits from the plain and milk from the sacred goat, Amaltheia. At the entrance to the cave stood guard the Kouretes, holy youths who clashed their swords and shields while dancing in order to mask the cries of the infant Zeus. It is said that the *syrtó,* one of the most Cretan of Cretan dances, descends from the dance of the Kouretes. Deep in the heart of the cave there is a sacred pool and initiation area surrounded by a strange aura cast by the muted light that filters in from the entrance.

After leaving Psychro it is best to return by the route you have thus far taken. At Mesa Lasíthi take the right turn that leads up to Neapolis, where you join the national highway; from here you are about 15 km (9 miles) from Ayios Nikolaos.

To Ayios Nikolaos

Most of the excavated Minoan sites and luxurious resort hotels in eastern Crete are along its northern coast. The main national highway leads directly out of Herakleion to Ayios Nikolaos, skirting the coastline on its way; along and off this course are a number of interesting archaeological sites. As the distance is not far (80 km/50 miles), you can combine sightseeing, bathing (there are a number of fine beaches), and perhaps even a picnic. Fourteen kilometers (9 miles) east of Herakleion take the turnoff at Hanion tou Kokkini (also known as Kókkini Hani) to the site of a Middle Minoan villa dating from about 1550 B.C. In the course of excavating the area, Evans was convinced that he had discovered a subsidiary palace of Knossos. Opinions still differ. The site was in any case quite rich in votive offerings as well as a number of fine frescoes that are now in the Herakleion Museum.

Two kilometers (about a mile) eastward on the main highway there is a turnoff marked for Gouves that leads to **Skoteinó**, an ancient Minoan cave sanctuary. Today a Christian church marks the entrance and attests to its continued use as a sacred spot for centuries, going back through the Roman, Hellenistic, and Classical periods and into Minoan antiquity. From finds that were made in the cave it appears to have been dedicated to the Cretan mother goddess.

Along the stretch from Gouves to Chersónisos there are a number of excellent hotels and beaches. In antiquity Chersonisos functioned as the port for the ancient city of **Lyttos**, the site of which is located about 20 km (12.5 miles) inland and is known today as Ksidas. A rival to Knossos, Lyttos itself was very famous, and, at one time, very powerful. It is credited with being the city in which Lycurgus, the lawgiver of Sparta, studied the constitutions of the Cretans and eventually wrote that of Sparta. Certainly the origins of Lyttos are very ancient: A legend has it that Rhea, pregnant with Zeus, was hidden here by her parents from Kronos.

Take time for a drive through the countryside before returning to Chersonisos. Not much of the ancient port town remains other than a few Roman and Byzantine ruins—including those of a basilica that undoubtedly was destroyed in the ninth century during the Arab takeover of the island. Today **Chersónisos** is best known for its fine beaches, resorts, and several fine hotels, including the **Ikaros Village**, **Kernos Beach**, and **Sirens Beach**; all are excellent, with reputable restaurants and occasionally good evening entertainment. The **Creta Maris**, with excellent facilities in its sprawling complex and a fine kitchen, is the most outstanding hotel here.

From Chersonisos you can cut east to **Mallia** some 5 km (3 miles) away, and beyond that to an ancient Minoan site of great interest (it is well marked). The ancient name of this site is unknown; the word Mallia provides no clues as it is a corruption of the Venetian Villa de Maglia. Like Knossos and Phaistos the site is beautifully located. Its chronology links it with the former two great palaces, and its history has been traced back into Neolithic times. It was destroyed c. 1700 B.C., rebuilt shortly after, and then destroyed and abandoned in 1450 B.C.

Not far east of Mallia (5 km/3 miles) at Sísion, the highway takes a sharp southern turn inland through a ravine to Vrahásion and then directly to Ayios Nikolaos. If you have the time a short side trip can be made to **Mílatos** from Vrahasion (which has a famous monastery dedicated to Saint George). Milatos is mentioned in Homer's *Iliad*, and its port was very active in antiquity. It is also credited with being the mother city of Miletus in Asia Minor, one of the greatest of all the Ionian cities, the city where Thales and many other pre-Socratic philosophers taught. Today there is little to see of the ancient town, but it is a lovely excursion with some good small tavernas and fish restaurants along the shore.

Ayios Nikolaos and Elounda

Ayios Nikólaos, about 45 km (28 miles) east of Herakleion on the Bay of Mirabello, is rightly much publicized. It is compact, picturesque, and very comfortable, with evening spots for all-night entertainment (such as the trendy **Yachting Club**, which draws locals and tourists alike), outrageously expensive harborside restaurants (savvy travellers will instead go to **Itanos Taverna** on Venizelos Square, with good food at reasonable prices), and fine hotels—also expensive. It is not a good place to shop, as the prices are inflated.

In the midst of contemporary tourist clutter, it is difficult to pick out remnants of the Venetian structures that made up the harbor, but the **Archaeological Museum** is well worth a visit. Its collections include finds from all over eastern Crete and also many artifacts that were formerly kept in Herakleion. The ceramics, stone vases, and cult objects are perhaps less enthusiastically publicized, but in many instances are more striking and *sui generis* then those found elsewhere. Close scrutiny and an open mind reveal clear influences of the Cyclades, Egypt, and Anatolia on many of the artifacts. The gold work is magnificent and fine examples of the most sophisticated technique of all—granulation—are in evidence. In this process minute globules of gold are arranged in a pattern and then annealed to the gold surface to create a beautiful texture.

If you decide to stay here, there are a few modest hotels that are clean, reliable—and quiet. Try the **Pension Istron** on the harbor. On a grander scale, there are some excellent hotels that command magnificent views of the sea. The **Coral Hotel** is a well-organized complex with water sports, tennis courts, evening entertainment, and a good restaurant. Even more impressive is the vast and elegant **Hermes**, with resort-type amenities and good shops.

There are also some extremely luxurious hotels in **Eloúnda**, about 11 km (7 miles) north of Ayios Nikolaos. The **Elounda Beach** and the **Elounda Mare** are both on the sea, with bungalows that have their own swimming pools. Both also offer evening entertainment, and access to good beaches and water sports. The Elounda Beach, which has the simulated atmosphere of a traditional Cretan village, has an excellent restaurant. Also at Elounda is the **Astir Palace**, a lavish hotel with bungalows and rooms, plus water sports and tennis.

South of Ayios Nikolaos

Not far from Ayios Nikolaos, about 11 km (7 miles) to the southwest, is **Kritsá**, famous in Crete for its woven textiles. There are a couple of tavernas of little note, so you should plan on having a light lunch. Also here is one of the finest churches in Crete, the **Panayía Kyrá**. The church's paintings constitute an important clue to the complicated character of Medieval Byzantine art in Crete. Three distinct periods are represented here. The oldest section, in the nave, dates from the 13th century and is iconographically typical of the Monastic, or Oriental, School introduced into the island by monks fleeing the Seljuk Turkish conquest of Anatolia in the 11th and 12th centuries. The iconography is very ancient and characteristic of an Oriental Christian tradition in painting that developed independently of Constantinople. The figures are squat, strongly delineated, and explicit in depicting gospel narratives and theology. Even in these 13th-century paintings certain distinctively Cretan innovations can be discerned, in the use of dark undercoatings and very sharp white highlights.

Paintings of the 14th century are found in a later side chapel. They are dependent on an alternative tradition that developed out of Constantinople, Macedonia, and Mystra. The painting in these works is much livelier; the figures are developed in terms of mass and volume, with genre elements and a clear intention to depict not only the historical milieu but also inner, psychological states of mind. This intent represents a significant break with Medieval hieratic Byzantine art, a tradition in which explicit theological issues or dogmas determine the manner in which a scene is depicted. The last period represented at Kyra—painting attributed to the 16th century—is also in the nave. In iconography and style these works are more akin to the Monastic School, though in a more developed Cretan style.

Leaving Kritsa, you can walk the 3 km (2 miles) north to **Lato**, a city that dates from the seventh century B.C. The walk takes you through typical eastern Cretan mountain landscape. The excavations at Lato have never been completed, hence the remains appear somewhat romantically scattered across a considerable area. There are the remains of the agora, a theater area, and some broken columns—but not much more. The site is evocative and exquisitely beautiful in late afternoons when you can look out across the Bay of Mirabello on the one side and the Plain of Kritsa on the other.

A number of other fine excursions can be made quite easily out of Ayios Nikolaos to Minoan or other ancient ruins, or to fine beaches. The landscape here is rich and varied, marked by twisted, folding mountains. Twenty kilometers (12.5 miles) southeast is **Gourniá**, the Pompeii of Crete: a complete Minoan settlement with some of the buildings almost intact. Passing Gournia the road continues south to the Libyan Sea and **Ierápetra**, the largest town on the southern coast and a good place to stay. The light and atmosphere are decidedly African here, and the pace is less frenetic than at Ayios Nikolaos and Elounda. There are some Ottoman buildings—two mosques and a *medresse* (religious school)—and many fine beaches and good fish restaurants. The **Petra Mare** hotel here is very well situated and is air-conditioned. It has a good beach and provisions for water sports. The **Ferma Beach**, also on a good beach and air-conditioned, has both rooms and private bungalows and a tennis court.

East of Ayios Nikolaos

The eastern end of Crete is arid and has less of the monumental grandeur of the central and western parts of the island. Its most important Minoan site is at Kato Zakros on the eastern tip of the island, best reached by staying at Siteia on the northern coast. It makes sense to visit the monastery of Moni Toplu and perhaps the palm groves of Vai from Siteia as well.

Siteía, 73 km (45 miles) east of Ayios Nikolaos, is a very modern town despite being built over one of the most ancient sites in Crete. It is well laid out and takes full advantage of an excellent seafront. Here you will find none of the winding little streets that make for quaintness. Nonetheless Siteia has its own charms and is a very pleasant place to stay if you are planning to take excursions to the far eastern end of the island. Its modernity is due to the fact that it was abandoned from 1651 until 1870 after the Venetians deliberately destroyed it in order to keep it from falling intact into the hands of the Ottomans. In 1870, when the provincial organization of Crete was reorganized, Siteia was rebuilt, and what ancient and Medieval remnants had survived were buried under it. The seafront is lined with good coffee shops and a number of restaurants. Siteia leatherwork in the form of boots and bags is quite good. Occasionally you can find hand-beaten copper goat bells in different sizes, and, consequently, with different pitches.

Siteia has a good, if sparse, **Archaeological Museum**, and limited accommodations. Two well-equipped and reliable hotels with bungalows are the **Sanguin** and the **Siteia Beach**.

The monastery of **Moní Toplú**, about 20 km (12.5 miles) northeast of Siteia, has a single great treasure and an interesting belfry. The former is an icon painted in 1770 by Ioannis Kornaros, a member of the family that produced the great

Kornaros who wrote the *Erotokritos* in the Middle Ages. This is the only painting attributed to Ioannis that has survived. Its theme is the phrase "Holy Art Thou O Lord," and a huge cast of characters from the Old and New Testaments appears in it—all contrived in Cretan landscapes and towns. It is a painting worth the visit, but don't expect too much of the drive.

From Moni Toplu it is a short drive north to **Vái** and the date palm groves that were planted by neither the Phoenicians nor the Arabs (as reported in the brochures). These are, instead, survivors of an indigenous species that has now all but died out in Crete. The beaches along the coast have a tropical flavor, but the sea here has little vitality.

South of Vai is **Kato Zakros**, a large Minoan palace that is of great importance as it was archaeologically plundered only in the 20th century. Recent excavations indicate that the site, its ancient name unknown, can be ranked with the palaces at Knossos, Phaistos, and Mallia, whose chronology it follows. It was destroyed in 1450 B.C., never to be reinhabited. For this reason, and because it was never pilfered, it has been an especially rich source of information regarding the daily life and customs of the Minoans. One of its unique features is a large, circular cistern set obliquely off-axis in a large room off what are believed to be the royal quarters.

Returning to Siteia you can take the road that goes south and west to Lithínes, from which the southern coast is accessible. This is Eteocretan land. All along the route are Minoan sites and villas. At **Ziros** (about midway between Kato Zakros and Lithines) there are frescoed churches, and **Etiá**, a bit farther west, has a Venetian tower house that belonged to the Dei Mezei family, replete with *machicoulis* for pouring hot oil on uninvited visitors. This building is one of the finest examples of such Venetian country dwellings that has survived, and the village itself, with many old, intact buildings of the Venetian period, is very interesting to walk through. The road from Lithines descends to Makriyialós and the coast; turn right here and you can follow the shore back to Ierapetra. The beaches along the way are superb and marked by villages and occasional tavernas.

WEST TO RETHYMNO

The usual and quickest approach to Rethymno is from Herakleion, which is 78 km (48 miles) to its east, along the national highway. If you are in the southeast—at Ierapetra,

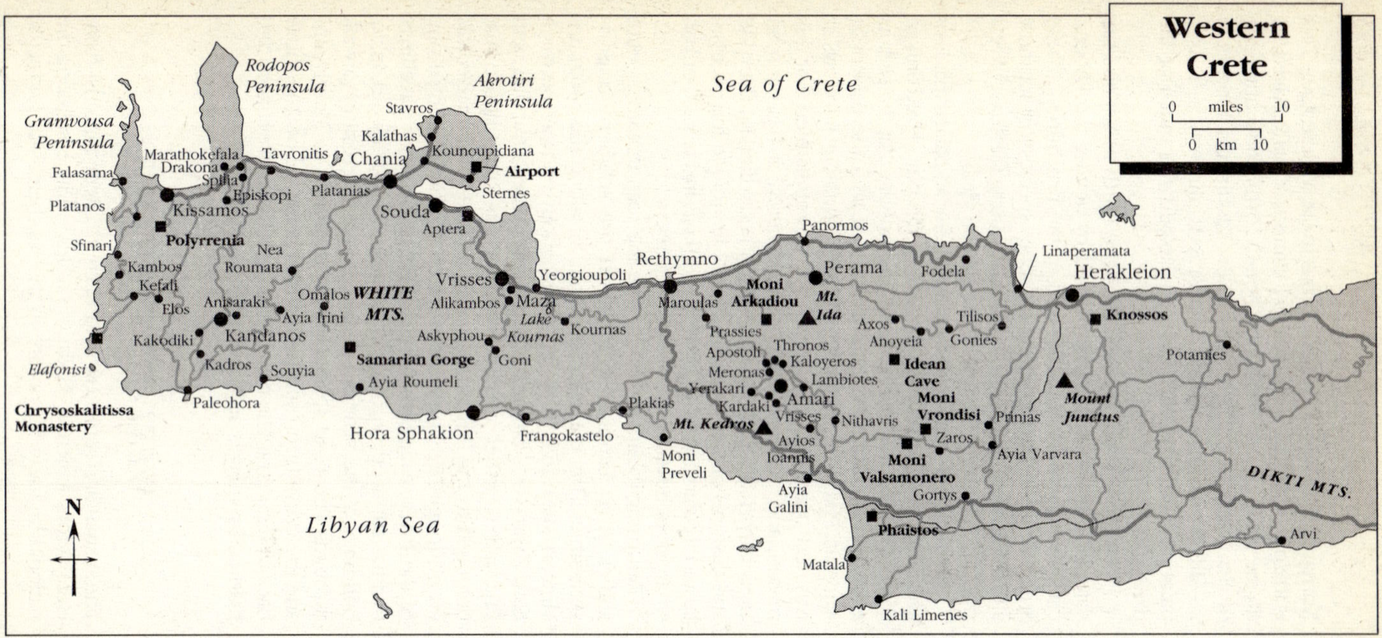
Western
Crete
0 miles 10
0 km 10
Sea of Crete
Libyan Sea
Gramvousa Peninsula
Rodopos Peninsula
Akrotiri Peninsula
Falasarna
Platanos
Sfinari
Kambos
Kefali
Elos
Kakodiki
Kadros
Elafonisi
Chrysoskalitissa Monastery
Paleohora
Marathokefala
Drakona
Spilia
Episkopi
Kissamos
Polyrrenia
Nea Roumata
Anisaraki
Kandanos
Souyia
Tavronitis
Platanias
Stavros
Kalathas
Chania
Kounoupidiana
Airport
Sternes
Souda
Aptera
Omalos
Ayia Irini
WHITE MTS.
Samarian Gorge
Ayia Roumeli
Hora Sphakion
Vrisses
Alikambos
Maza
Lake Kournas
Kournas
Askyphou
Goni
Yeorgioupoli
Frangokastelo
Rethymno
Maroulas
Prassies
Moni Arkadiou
Panormos
Perama
Mt. Ida
Thronos
Apostoli
Kaloyeros
Meronas
Lambiotes
Yerakari
Amari
Kardaki
Vrisses
Nithavris
Mt. Kedros
Ayios Ioannis
Plakias
Moni Preveli
Ayia Galini
Fodela
Axos
Anoyeia
Idean Cave
Tilisos
Gonies
Moni Vrondisi
Zaros
Moni Valsamonero
Gortys
Prinias
Ayia Varvara
Phaistos
Matala
Kali Limenes
Linaperamata
Herakleion
Knossos
Mount Junctus
Potamies
DIKTI MTS.
Arvi
N

for example—you should return to Herakleion to go to Rethymno: There is no southern coastal road from there, and the road that runs up through the mountains is difficult. Rethymno is accessible, however, from Ayia Galini on the southern coast, a two-and-a-half-hour drive.

So, leave Herakleion by the old national highway marked for **Tílisos**, the site of several Minoan villas that yielded some of the bronzes, including great cauldrons, now in the Herakleion Archaeological Museum. The area surrounding Tilisos is a rugged, barren, and forbidding landscape, gradually rising and leading west into the Sklavókambos valley. The route then ascends to Goniés, a mountain village set dramatically against the peaks of Mount Ida. Your main destination will be Anoyeia, another mountain village, but just before you reach it a sign indicates a turnoff to the left that leads to the **Idaean Cave** where, according to one legend, Zeus was born. (An alternative account says he was born in the Diktian Cave.) The cave is quite magnificent and has an atmosphere unlike that of Mount Dikti, with sacred areas for initiations and a sanctuary. (This approach to the Idaean Cave can be made by car and is much easier than the one mentioned earlier, in the section To Phaistos, from Kamares.)

Anóyeia, the largest mountain village in Crete, is well set up for tourists, but it has few hotels of any size. The food is good—any one restaurant is as reliable as another here—and the village is known for its woven textiles and for a summer festival that features Cretan dancing and singing, all authentic. Anoyeia has been rebuilt since the last world war, as it suffered an "action" under the Germans; it was all but razed and many of the villagers were killed.

Out of Anoyeia the road leads west to **Axós**, which in Byzantine times boasted 46 churches. From Axos you can reach the **Sedóni Cave**, one of the eeriest in Crete, with delicate, fairyland-like stalactites and stalagmites. A local story says that a young girl was once lured into the cave by Nereids (sea nymphs) and entranced away into death, to be found eight days later with a beatific smile on her face. The cave is well marked and lit.

From Axos the road takes you up to Pérama, from which you should continue north until you meet the national highway along the northern coast at Pánormos. A pleasant detour can be made at Platanies to the village of **Maroulás**, 5 km (3 miles) south of the main highway, one of the best-preserved Venetian hill villages in Crete, with fine old stone houses and a tower marking its peak.

RETHYMNO

Once in Réthymno, 23 km (14 miles) west along the national highway from Panormos, you enter a different part of Crete, with decidedly richer vegetation and a slightly wilder atmosphere. There are also fewer excavated Minoan sites, not because there were no Minoans here but because many of the great Minoan sites are now buried beneath towns such as Rethymno and Chania—or have simply not yet been discovered.

From a distance Rethymno has a strange profile, marked with minarets, its Fortezza (Venetian fortress), and a subtle decline into the sea. In Venetian times it was noted for its poets, writers, and painters. One of Rethymno's sons, the writer Pantelis Prevalakis, creates in his *Tale of a Town* a vivid impression of the place during the early part of this century. He describes the last years of an age when Rethymno still looked to Constantinople and its markets were filled with delicate perfumes, attars, spices, and goods from Alexandria destined for Constantinople's harems and the seraglio of the sultan. The Rethymniots still have a character that is less frenetic than that of the Chaniots to the west and yet different as well from that of eastern Cretans. Rethymno's geography is not marked by extremes, and access to the Libyan Sea to the south is not difficult.

The layout of Rethymno has been exploited rather mercilessly in the past few years. The harbor area to the west and against the Fortezza meets with a wide beach in the town itself. Along this stretch, fast-food eateries and many tourist shops have been built, behind which, on Arkadíou Street, most of these shops have deceptively hidden alternative entrances. It is unfortunate that most of the old Venetian fronts are almost unrecognizeable now. That is not to say you should neglect Rethymno: The western part of the town is quiet and has many notable buildings. There are, as well, a number of quite small and unnamed tavernas along the west harbor area. There is a **Loggia** on Neárchou Street that is every bit as fine as, though smaller than, that in Herakleion; it now houses the **Archaeological Museum**. Not far from here, at the corner of Paleológos and Thessaloníkis streets, is the **Arimondi Fountain**, which dates from the early 17th century—a fine late-Renaissance work. There are a number of churches that belonged to Catholic religious orders, most of which were converted into mosques and which now serve quite different purposes: St. Francis (Franciscan), Our

Lady of the Angels (Dominican), and the great **church of St. Mary** (Augustinian), which as a mosque was known as Neradje Djami and still retains its fine minaret—and so is easy to find. To the east of the town is **Kara Musa Djami**, built over the ruins of the old church of St. Barbara, and at the southern extreme of the Old Town is a mosque known as the **Valide**, erected most likely by Rabia Gülnüş herself as a gift to her hometown—where a good number of the inhabitants had already converted to Islam.

More than 600 Venetian houses mark the western part of Rethymno. Many have been restored and have had Ottoman face-lifts with the interesting addition of wooden extensions or superstructures with lattices, behind which Muslim women could sit looking out into the streets from the seclusion of the harem. Nicephorus Phocas, Tsoúderou, and Arkadíou streets and the small lanes running off them still have some of the finest Venetian façades to be found in Crete, most dating from the 15th and 16th centuries.

Dominating Rethymno is the 16th-century **Fortezza**, now more or less a ruin, with cisterns and a small mosque shorn of its minaret. Not far from the Fortezza is an old *hamám* (Turkish bath), now unused but possibly the one in which an old woman, abandoned after the forced expatriation of the Rethymniot Muslims in 1923, revealed that she was Madame Hortense, the courtesan of Chania made famous by Kazantzakis. Her pathetic end was a far cry from the days when, in 1897, she complained that her entertainments for the allied admirals in Souda had kept her "naked for nine hours out of ten."

Rethymno has a tradition of good food, but avoid the restaurants in the larger hotels in favor of the good tavernas along the waterfront, especially on the far west side. **Tassos's**, in the harbor area, is dependable, and the **Samaria**, next to it, has good seafood. But the **Cava d'Oro**, on the old harbor toward the end, is truly first class. Their carefully chosen fresh fish and fresh squid are matched by the quality of their wide selection of meats (this can be rare in Greece); the atmosphere is also very good. Don't miss the *kakaviá* (Cretan fish soup). There is a quaint and unpretentious vegetarian restaurant called **Our House** near the Kriti Hotel (not to be confused with the Kriti Beach Hotel), and at the **Gounaki** on Koronaíou Street you can spend an evening sampling local dishes and listening to authentic Cretan music. For more music and dinner, try **Avli** in the Old Town at 22 Xanthoudídou Street. Open for dinner only, it can be crowded; for reservations, call 243-56. Near Plátanos Square, **Ta Agrimia** is a very good, untouristy restaurant with a simple ambience and an excellent house wine. The **Kompos**, just outside town, is a favorite restaurant for Rethymniots. To get there, take the Chania road out of Rethymno; when you get to a little ocher-colored church (Ayios Nikólaos), take the small road that cuts up a steep hill to the restaurant.

Near the Rethymna Beach hotel you'll find more attractive choices. Right next to the hotel is **Siroccos**, beautifully located on one of Rethymno's best beaches; their excellent seafood, fine selection of wines, and lovely courtyard offering a splendid vista of the sea are not to be missed. If reliable and traditional is what you're after, **Taverna Maria**, just off the road above the hotel, serves lunch and dinner (it is well marked); Tel: 714-55. And across the road from the Rethymna Beach is the new **China Town**, serving delectable duck, sweet-and-sour prawns, and incredible desserts—especially the fried bananas swimming in ginger sauce. On New Beach Road, another excellent choice for fresh and well-prepared seafood is **Porto Marino**; Tel: 216-52. And **Marinos**, for fish and only fish in very simply prepared fashion (no extravagant sauces), is also located on New Beach Road.

Shopping in Rethymno includes all of the predictable souvenirs as well as some local, especially Rethymniot, products. On Souliou Street is the icon-painting studio of **Andreas Theodorakis**, not far from the **Herb Shop** at number 58. All along Nicephorus Street are knife merchants as well as a number of shops that sell baskets and local handicrafts. (Knives and guns are almost a fetish with Cretans. No woman would have been without her silver-sheathed and ivory-handled blade for defending her honor. Most of the blades on traditional knives are engraved with couplets or aphorisms, and the handles are set with chains and sequins.)

Stelle's, at 242 Arkadiou, has a good selection of inexpensive but well-chosen jewelry; at number 196, **The Golden Fleece** sells excellent-priced leather goods of high quality, including clothes for both men and women. You can be fitted and have your purchase in a day or so; the styles are varied and contemporary. Also for leather, **Nikos Notonakis** on the seafront at 3 Eleftheriou Venizelou Square (near the old harbor) carries traditional Cretan leather goods: bags, boots, and the like.

Accommodations in Rethymno are quite modest, as the town—enclosed as it is by the sea and old land walls, and limited by restrictions set by archaeological authorities—has discouraged large tourist complexes. The dependable

Xenia Hotel is located at the east end of the seafront with easy access to a good beach, but its kitchen is mediocre at best. Also in town is the **Kriti Beach**, which is conveniently located for using Rethymno as a base. It is a small, modest hotel with access to the beach and parking facilities, an advantage if you are spending some time in Rethymno. Just outside the town are several new complexes with excellent facilities for water sports, good beaches, and well-catered restaurants. The quiet, peaceful **Rethymna Beach**, with both rooms and bungalows, is about 8 km (5 miles) west of Rethymno on the Herakleion highway. Similar in style is **El Greco**, at Kambos Pygis, just outside of Rethymno, with a reliable if unimaginative kitchen, a pool and tennis court, and access to a good beach. The **Creta Star Hotel** commands a fine beach and has facilities for water sports, a good restaurant, and evening entertainment occasionally featuring Cretan music.

AROUND RETHYMNO

A pleasant morning trip about 25 km (15.5 miles) southeast takes you up to the **Arkádi Monastery**, the symbol of Cretan resistance to the Turks. Here, during the insurrection of 1866, the abbot Gabriel and an estimated 964 insurgent monks, women, children, and villagers, confronted by the army of Mustafa Pasha, blew themselves up by igniting the powder magazines, an event that finally brought home to Europeans the intensity of the problem of Cretan independence. The Baroque façade of the church is one of the most beautiful in Crete.

The more ambitious excursions out of Rethymno are a day trip southeast through the Amari Valley, with its Medieval churches, or a longer excursion to Moni Preveli on the south coast, out of which the road continues west to Frangokastelo and Hora Sphakion and then back up through the Imvrou Ravine to Chania. (For the second excursion see To Chania, The Southern Route, below.) Quite apart from the scenery and wild undulating mountains, this part of Crete is rich in Byzantine churches and chapels that contain frescoes dating from the 13th to 17th centuries.

Also ambitious but very rewarding, especially for those who enjoy touring by sea, is a cruise originating in Rethymno (7:20 A.M.) that continues on to Chania (another possible point of origin) and ultimately to **Gramvoúsa** at the far western end of the island. This uninhabited peninsula jutting out into the sea is a haven for wildlife of all sorts, and has beautiful beaches and clear seas. Contact Rethymniaki Shipping Line, Tel: (0831) 292-21, or any travel agent.

The Amari Valley

The Amári Valley route is breathtaking, passing along the western flank of Mount Ida and the eastern flank of Mount Kedros. If you are interested in seeing the churches, it is best to obtain a good road map and do some homework, as they are often slightly off the beaten path. Be prepared for some frustration, as many will not meet expectations—perhaps only a fragment survives, and in some cases the paintings have been calcified. Even if this should be the case you will have walked through groves of olives and walnut trees or vineyards that make up the living profile of Crete.

From Rethymno go 11 km (7 miles) southeast to Prassies, just south of which the Amari Valley begins. **Prassiés** itself has some very fine Venetian buildings and deserves a good visit. From Ayia Fotiní, about 20 km (12.5 miles) southeast of Prassies, the Amari Valley opens out majestically with Mount Ida to the left (east) and Mount Kedros to the right. Some 40 villages are scattered throughout the valley; the route is circular, returning to either Ayia Fotini or nearby Apóstoli.

Some of the most important churches here are found in many villages just off the main road, such as **Thronos**, which has a fine mosaic floor from a 6th-century or earlier basilica on top of which a 14th-century church was constructed; **Kalóyeros**, with several churches from the 14th to 16th centuries; **Monastiráki**, 13th century; **Amári**, St. Anne, 1225, one of the earliest; **Lambiótes**, 13th century; **Vizári**, the ruins of a 7th-century basilica. At Níthavris the road turns to the northwest and goes along the eastern flank of Mount Kedros. The afternoon views over the valley toward Mount Ida are incredibly varied, with tones of green, olive, violet, and mauve. As you climb, the vegetation becomes dense. **Ayios Ioánnis**, west of Nithavris, is worth a look, after which you could stop for a while at **Vrisses**, where there are great walnut trees and water fountains. At **Kardáki**, the **church of the Archangel Michael** has an extraordinary apsidal painting of the Pantokrator, Christ as Ruler of All, flanked on either side by the Annunciation. Dated to the 13th century, the decoration and iconographic layout are very similar to those in another church, **Ayios Isídoros**, in the village of Tselenianá. These two churches are almost miniatures of the great cathedral of

Monreale in Sicily. There are equally interesting churches at Yerákari, Méronas, and finally back at Apostoli.

As for lunching along the way, it's best to pack your own; taverna hours en route are most unpredictable.

TO CHANIA
The Northern Route

Two main routes lead from Rethymno to Chania and the west of the island. The northern route follows the national highway along the sea coast; this trip is very quick (an hour) and passes a beautiful and more or less abandoned four-mile length of beach, just before the village of Yeorgioúpoli (22 km/13 miles from Rethymno) and not far from Lake Kournas. It will undoubtedly be given up to hotel development in the very near future, but at the moment it is still open sea and sand.

At Yeorgioupoli turn left to **Lake Kournás**, an interesting detour and, as Lear noted in his diary, "very fine and Cumberlandish." The water is cold, refreshing, and a pleasant change from the sea. The village of Kournas, above the lake, has some old and neglected Venetian houses and a church containing 13th-century frescoes. These have only very recently been cleaned and show peculiarities that date them earlier than those at Amari. The elongated and carefully poised figures are stylistically related to similar images found in churches in the northern Greek town of Kastoria (see Northern Greece).

Returning to the main highway, you begin to ascend the side of the southern ridge of Souda Bay, one of the largest natural harbors in the Mediterranean. Rising in the distance behind is the massive hulk of the White Mountains (Lefka Ori), which mark the western spine of Crete.

High up on the Chania road, 18 km (11 miles) east of Chania, is the barren and ruin-strewn ancient site of **Aptera**, with a lone and isolated Turkish bastion dominating a view over Souda Bay and the distant Akrotiri peninsula. (From this point on, it is best to refrain from taking photographs; the area from Aptera to the town of Souda is considered a strategic zone.) After Souda the road runs directly to Chania.

The Southern Route

A more leisurely way to get to Chania—a comfortable day's journey—is to take the above-mentioned road from Rethymno down to Moni Preveli on the south coast. **Moní Préveli** is not very old—in its present state—but is beautifully situated, and from it you can drive west slightly inland from the sea. There are a number of so-so beaches, as the shore is very irregular; these are rockier and less sandy than the north coast beaches.

The best place to stay on the south coast (which until quite recently had few facilities for tourists), and perhaps one of the finest accommodations on the island, is the **Kalypso Cretan Village** at Plakiás, about 10 km (6 miles) west of Preveli. The Kalypso is a luxurious, self-contained resort with all the usual amenities—a good base if you want to enjoy the countryside and the sea. From here it is approximately 30 km (18.5 miles) farther to **Frangokástelo**, a small village of houses typical to this rocky region of Crete, with narrow doors and small courtyards. The main attraction is the squat Venetian fortress, one of the finest remaining buildings of its type on Crete.

This road continues on until **Hora Sphakíon**. Alive with tourism as the town is, it is impossible to imagine even remotely the days (not long ago) when ships from Libya and Alexandria stopped here to unload spices, textiles, perfumes, and the like, which were then transferred up the ravine by camel or donkey to Chania and Rethymno. Out of these towns Cretan goods would be loaded on ships for Istanbul, Izmir, and Rhodes. A century—and the EC—have changed all of this. Today Hora Sphakion is a bustle of tourists who have been "disgorged" from the Samarian Gorge (see below), then taken by bus to Chania and Rethymno, and later exported back to Leeds, Oslo, and Düsseldorf. It is worth strolling about in Hora Sphakion, however, to see the houses peculiar to this region of Crete, where the direct influence of the Venetians is not so apparent and a tradition of building indigenous to the island has been maintained.

Hora Sphakion is the gateway to one of the least accessible parts of Crete, an area credited with many stories of near-mythical exploits on the part of its very proud and aloof inhabitants. It is claimed that Sphakia has never been conquered by anyone—which may be the case, but it's mostly by default, as there have been few attempts. Sphakia also reportedly hosts vampires and myriad other supernatural beings that haunt and molest both the living and the dead. It is a natural fortress. Pavlos Lassithiotakis, a contemporary Cretan writer, describes the region thus: "I know of no other place where one has the peculiar sensation when one walks the steep slopes and terrible gorges and finds oneself at the center: the sensation of being in a stronghold."

The Sphakiots are dour, tough highlanders. The women tend to stay indoors and the men, a few of the older ones still in traditional dress, spend their time in the coffee shops. That women work and men protect them is still considered to be a noble division of labor.

North of Sphakia the ascent is breathtaking and forbidding; it winds into the canyon-like walls of the **Imvrou Ravine** and up to the vibrant green Askyphou Plateau. The village of **Askýphou** has a few rooms for rent and some good places serving truly local Sphakiot food. Don't be deceived by appearances: The ambience may be dubious, but the food will be well prepared and authentic. **Goní**, near Askyphou, is an almost untouched village with fine old houses in the Sphakiot tradition.

Farther north still, at **Alíkambos**, is a small church painted by Ioannis Pagomenos (there are two others in the vicinity, at Maza and Komitádes). Pagomenos was an itinerant lay painter of the early to mid-14th century who signed his works; there are at least ten attributable to his hand. His paintings, while incorporating the traditional squat, almost doll-like figures of the Monastic School, have a vitality and energy that stem from his strong sense of line. He incorporates genre and folk elements edged with wit and a lightness surprising in the hieratic art form in which he worked.

Vrisses, just off the main highway (not to be confused with the Vrisses in the Amari Valley), is in a milder atmosphere. Gushing springs, giant walnut trees, plane trees, small fountains, and some good coffee shops make it an ideal place to sit and relax after a hard drive. From Vrisses you get on to the national road for Chania, passing through Aptera and Souda Bay (see above, To Chania, The Northern Route).

CHANIA

Chaniá, 59 km (37 miles) west of Rethymno, is full of contradictions. On one side it is dominated by the White Mountains and on the other by the sea. As a seaport it was once of great importance; ships from England, France, Russia, and Turkey filled its ports or docked securely in nearby Souda Bay. The old Chaniots were cosmopolitan, possessing the vigor and quickness of people who live in ports. They were also known for their chic. Those were the days of town and country, when villagers descended to sell their wares and then made their way back to the farms. "Town" vanished rather quickly after union with Greece in 1913, the combined result of centralization, the expatriation of the mostly urban Muslim population to Turkey, and the departure of wealthier families for mainland Greece or elsewhere. "Country" filled the gap, which meant that the old port, Venetian churches, arsenals, and Ottoman mosques were ignored, and the old houses neglected or reinhabited by refugees arriving from Asia Minor.

Chania asserts its own pace and character on its inhabitants. People fall in love with this town, which has a vitality that is catching. Chania's climate can be extreme: In the winter it is attacked by vicious and violent storms that bring the sea frothing up from the harbors and send the inhabitants into seclusion; in the summer the heat is almost African. In the spring torrents of rain make Chania and the west of Crete a paradise of every possible hue of green.

Chania has two main parts—the old and the new. The New Town, which embraces the Old Town, is rapidly spreading willy-nilly in every direction. Its physical incursion into the Old Town has been prevented by some remnants of the old walls as well as, more efficiently, by archaeological zoning restrictions. The Old Town itself has two parts, both enclosed by the 16th-century walls erected by the Venetians. The "oldest" part of the Old Town is located to the east and extends up to the Kastelli (Citadel) and beyond it into the Koum Kapi and Splantzia quarters. The old Venetian harbor (the inner harbor) with its arsenals and rector's palace are in this section. The "newer" part of the Old Town is dominated by the outer harbor and comprises a number of quarters (roughly all in what was known until very recent times as the Kolombo), such as the Ovraiki (Jewish Quarter), the Renieri, and the Top Hana. Both of the latter were important Muslim quarters until the 1920s. Remnants of the walls (torn down in this century)—or the course they once followed—still determine the main streets and thoroughfares of the "new" part of the Old Town.

The ancient name of Chania was Kydonia. Its history goes back to Minoan times; the ruins of Kydonia lie buried beneath the present town and hint at being as extensive as those at Knossos and Phaistos. Well into Roman times Kydonia was, with Gortys, one of the most important cities in Crete. During this period the Kastelli served as the acropolis; after the Arab occupation that building was refortified and Kydonia was renamed al-Hannim and given the nickname Badh al-Djobu (the "Cheese House").

Little is known about the history of Chania after the Byzantine reconquest in the tenth century, and the absence of any Byzantine buildings from this period until the Venetian takeover is puzzling. The Venetians' purchase of Crete in 1204 did not automatically give them Chania; it was only in 1252 that it was subdued, at which time it was named La Canea. The Kastelli was then given major fortifications that incorporated a great amount of material from the ancient Roman city; within them palazzi, a rector's palace, a cathedral, and a central archive, as well as great arsenals and repair sheds, were built. Most of these buildings lasted well into this century but, sadly, were strafed and bombed to smithereens by the Germans in World War II.

In 1537 Greek-turned-Turk Barbarossa, admiral of the Ottoman fleet, savagely raided the Cretan coasts. The Venetians extended the fortifications by building great walls, bastions, and a moat that permitted the protected expansion of the city into what is now the outer harbor. A mole was extended to guard this, and, at its tip, a fine lighthouse was built just across from one of the sea bastions. This "new" quarter is one of the most fascinating parts of Chania to wander through.

The native Cretans in Chania never took well to the Venetians, and in 1645, after a suspiciously short siege, the Ottomans gained the city. It is recorded in Ottoman accounts that the Chaniots gave them access, and for that reason the town was neither pillaged nor sacked. In fact it was given special privileges and was to become the Ottoman administrative center for Crete until the end of the 19th century, when the honor was given to Herakleion. This transference of importance has remained a bitter source of contention between the two cities.

The New Town

The New Town of Chania is dominated by the **covered market**—an enormous cruciform structure dating from the early part of this century. Into its specialized wings flow local produce and imports. In one wing, joints of meat, chickens, rabbits, sausages, and innards line both sides; the opposite wing has great marble slabs dripping with eels, swordfish, sea bass, octopus, and squid. Vegetable, fruit, spice, and coffee shops are jumbled together in the other two wings. Herbs, mountain and medicinal teas, wild sage, and Cretan dittany (an herb unique to Crete and mentioned by Virgil) can still be bought. Dittany and labdanum (also to be found in the market) were formerly used in the preparation of perfumes, though today dittany is primarily used in infusions. It is found wild only in almost inaccessible mountains, which undoubtedly has added to claims that it is a cure-all. Cretan saffron, thyme, and oregano make good purchases, as does Cretan honey.

Near the bazaar is a small minaret marking the site of a mosque that was set aside for the use of Abyssinian workers. These people were mostly expatriated from Crete in 1927, and their descendants still live in a number of villages in Turkey where they speak the old Chaniot Cretan dialect.

The Outer Harbor

The main thoroughfare that leads north to the old city is Hálidon Street, lined with tourist-oriented shops selling jewelry, "Greek art," and knickknacks. Some of the jewelry is locally handcrafted, and some of the icons are authentically painted using old techniques, though too often they are artificially aged.

A little more than halfway down Halidon is the **Metropolitan Church of Chania**, with a bronze statue of Patriarch Athenagoras in its court. The Orthodox church of Crete is within the jurisdiction of the Patriarchate of Constantinople and is independent of the Greek Orthodox church of the mainland. Its priests and hierarchy are progressive and well trained; many have completed their theological studies in Germany or have served as bishops in Europe.

A bit farther on, to the left, is the **Archaeological Museum**, housed in the former Venetian church of St. Francis. Under the Ottomans it was converted to Islam as the Yusuf Pasha Djami. Only the base of its minaret remains. There are remains of a fine fountain in the side court and a very pleasant and quiet café. The museum has a rich collection of Minoan, Greek, and Roman finds from western Crete.

Halidon Street opens into a large square, and to the left stretches the outer harbor and its shops, cafés, and bars, including **Faka**, in the harbor area behind the old arsenal. Open for lunch and dinner, Faka features mainland, Cretan, and international cuisines, accompanied by an excellent house wine; Tel: 412-40. Behind the waterfront were formerly two main quarters, the **Ovraikí** and the **Top Hana**. The first was the Jewish Quarter—very old and famous for its rabbis. The old synagogue, called **Etz Hayyim**, can still be seen in a small dead-end street called Párodos Kondyláki, just off Kondylaki Street. The building was originally the

16th-century Venetian church of St. Catherine, given to the Jewish community of Chania by the Ottomans in the late 17th century. It has now been abandoned by Jew as well as Christian under circumstances that are especially sad. The last Jews of Crete resided in Chania in 1944, in which year they were arrested by the Germans and subsequently drowned off the island of Milos.

The winding streets to the west of the Ovraiki are now filled with pensions, little bars, and buildings with quite impressive Venetian façades. There is a fine new pension at 9 Theophánous Street, the **Casa Delphino**, which is quiet and sumptuous, built in a renovated Veneto-Ottoman *konak* (town house). (Most of the buildings in this part of Chania have Venetian substructures dating from the 16th century with Ottoman upper stories, often of wood.) The rooms at the Casa Delphino are equipped with kitchenettes, baths, and well-designed sitting areas. The pension has no restaurant or pool, but its location in the center of Chania's most picturesque quarter is a definite advantage. Another good choice in the area (on Theotokopoúlou) is the quiet, well-run **Xenia Hotel**, a member of the reliable, if conservative, Xenia chain. Its kitchen is unambitious, its views over the sea and old city are exquisite, and it has a modest pool.

The waterfront can be a bit of a meat market, but it is full of life and bustle, and the hotels here are noisy, but their views open magnificently to the sea. In this part of the Old Town, also known as the Kolombo, many native residents still speak a dialect that is distinctly their own. The western end is marked by the **Naval Museum** in what was the Firká, or Turkish military center.

Running up from the museum is Angélou Street, which is quiet and has attracted some small shops of interest. The **Meltemi** (next to the museum), sheltered from the sun, has good coffee, fresh orange juice, hard drinks, and a fine view of the east harbor. It attracts local young people and has good music. Next door a shop called **Tagastiri** offers high-quality ceramics made by local craftsmen. Diagonally across the street is the **Top Hanas**, which has the best collection of Cretan woven and embroidered textiles to be found on the island. Many of these items are from Selinos (in southwestern Crete; see below) and Sphakia, traditionally famous for weavings; here you can actually enjoy your bargaining. Next to Top Hanas, **Carmela's** has good buys in jewelry, finely crafted ceramics, and small paintings by a local artist. The ceramics are elegant and painstakingly crafted using burnishing and firing that revive ancient techniques. If you are in

Chania in the fall or winter, **Faggotto**, diagonally across from Carmela's, is a great evening spot: Small and laid back, it offers first-rate recorded jazz as well as classical music. If you are visiting in winter, you can enjoy a pleasant evening of Vivaldi in this Venetian basement boîte while a Chaniot storm rages outdoors.

You can reach the sea from the top of Angelou Street by turning right on Theotokopoulou Street, which also has some good shops. **Vasilikaki** sells locally made ceramics as well as others from the eastern end of the island. There is a well-preserved and very typical Ottoman wooden house on the corner, and after that, set in to the right, is the small **church of San Salvadore**, which once served the Venetian neighborhood. It was later used as a mosque and is now being turned into a museum—probably for Cretan icons.

Nea Hora

A 15-minute walk west along the road skirting the sea takes you to Nea Hora, with a small marina and a beach much frequented by Chaniots as well as visitors. There are a number of restaurants and fast-food bars. By far the best seafood restaurant in Nea Hora is the **Akrogialli**, with a peculiar character all its own, much appreciated by the Cretan families who frequent the spot. (Here you can enjoy an excellent fish soup.) Many of the fish served in this area are caught in local waters, but some are referred to as "foreign," meaning that they have come from far out in the Libyan Sea and farther west. Bream of various varieties are usually available, such as *lithrini* (pandora or red bream), *sargo* (black bream), and *melanoúri* (saddled bream); grilled on charcoal they are delicious. Seasonally you can find *barboúnia* (red mullet) as well as a variant called *koutsomoura*. Charcoal-grilled octopus, cuttlefish, and deep-fried *kalamári* are seasonal, as are crisply fried *marídes* (picarel). On occasion moray eel can be found, as can sea urchins—the latter being a decidedly acquired taste.

Kastelli and Inner Harbor

Dominating the Kastélli region and inner harbor is the **mosque of Hasan Pasha**. Its prayer hall is the old Venetian customhouse, and its great bubble of a dome surrounded by bubblets is Ottoman. Hasan Pasha has only recently lost its minaret and, sadly, the little graveyard (between the mosque and the Plaza Hotel) that held the remains of *Hadjis* (those who had made the pilgrimage to Mecca). What is now the Plaza Hotel was the Qur'anic School, and the old bronze spigots of the *shadirvan,* where the faithful used to wash prior to prayer, now provide a splashy, watery backdrop to café conversation. A good place to eat is the **Kavouria**, located in the northern end of the building and adjacent to the mosque. One of the oldest restaurants in the harbor, the Kavouria serves authentic Cretan food; especially good are the local mushrooms (seasonal) and snail stews.

Walk past the mosque into the inner, or work, harbor. Here are vast Venetian arsenals into which galleons were drawn to be caulked in the winter months when the sea was churning. The Rector's Palace is a sad hulk; at one time it must have been magnificent. At the end of this esplanade the street narrows until it is possible to get onto the mole and walk along it to the lighthouse. Shipbuilders are always at work on some new caïque here, incongruously next to a Piraeus-type bouzouki club obscenely lit at night and belching out Athenian imports. A walk along the mole allows a panoramic view of Chania, the mountains, and the sea. The lighthouse was recently renovated; its base structure and shaft are Venetian, and the upper portion was added under Mehmet Ali when Crete was ruled from Egypt by the great pasha in the early 19th century.

Just past the massive front of the Rector's Palace is a small square at the back of which is an excellent restaurant called the **Karnagio**. It offers a wide variety of local specialties in the form of cheese pies (made with *mezýthra,* a famous Cretan cheese, as well as *staka,* made from fresh ewe's butter), and on occasion wild artichokes and other greens peculiar to Crete. Karnagio also caters to European tastes, with a good selection of meats. Mutton is never eaten in Crete, by the way, young lamb and goat being preferred. Cretan veal, on the other hand, is fairly mature and bears no resemblance to that of Italy or France.

The **Kastélli** (Citadel) itself is easily reached from a number of different directions. If you are on Halidon Street where it ends at the junction of the two harbors, there is a street that leads up onto the Kastelli to the right. Another route is from the inner harbor, where a stone staircase leads to the top, following the west flank of the Rector's Palace. Most of the Kastelli is today in ruins, its great palazzi broken open revealing arches and structural details once masked by beautiful fronts. The bombing of this part of Chania can still be felt in all of its savagery. Here and there, in the pits and empty lots, several Minoan buildings have been unearthed as well as tablets in Linear B (an alphabet adapted to express a very primitive Greek). Undoubtedly such Minoan buildings are to be found everywhere under the Kastelli. The far eastern side of the Kastelli (just before the stairs that lead down to the inner harbor) retains the Gothic ribs and part of the Dominican cloister of the church of St. Nicholas.

To the right, and dominating much of Chania before the football stadium night lights outshone it, is the minaret of Sultan Ibrahim Djami, in front of which is the small church of San Rocco. The quarter around the former mosque, known as the **Splantzia**, is a maze of tiny, convoluted streets with houses that almost touch each other at roof level. Nearby at 19 Sifaka Street is the **Pafsilipou Taverna**, which specializes not only in Cretan fare but in well-loved Chaniot dishes, including cheese pies with honey and a fine selection of vegetables and stews (especially the hare).

Beyond Splantzia lie the eastern city walls and a quarter known as **Koum Kapí**, or Sand Gate. Beyond Koum Kapi a century ago was a settlement of more than 1,500 Bengazi Arabs living in tents and small huts, their camels wandering aimlessly about. They were brought to the island after an insurrection in Libya, no doubt to cool their heels.

Hotels are good and quite dependable in Chania. In addition to those mentioned above, there is the **Doma**, on the road into Chania from the airport. It has a great view and is quietly and demurely out of the main tourist area. **Porto Veneziano** is located at the far eastern end of the old harbor, and, while somewhat nondescript, is a good, quiet hotel. Its kitchen is not highly recommended, but there are a number of small restaurants (including the above-mentioned Karnagio) nearby on the waterfront.

Akrotiri

Akrotíri is a large, somewhat barren peninsula that juts out into the sea east of Chania (the airport is located on its southeastern side). As the well-marked road from Chania ascends the peninsula it passes **Halepa**, a fashionable neighborhood with many fine Neoclassical houses. In the early part of this century it was an important Christian suburb. At a crossing marked Kounoupidianá, or Venizelos Graves, the road to the left takes you first to the tombs of Eleftherios Venizelos and his son, Sophocles. Venizelos was a remarkable statesman who, after leading Crete into Greece, led Greece into World War I and indirectly into the Smyrna disaster. The site is austere and quiet, with a grand view over Chania and the sea. Scattered about are the fragments of a giant statue of Elefthería (Liberty) that was shattered to pieces by a bolt of lightning.

The village of Kounoupidiana has some Venetian barns and small Cretan houses. Its road splits at one point to either **Stavrós** or **Kalathas**, both of which have good beaches with bungalows, pensions, and some good restaurants, though none worth singling out.

The alternative route—to the airport—crosses the isthmus and then skirts Souda Bay. About 6 km (4 miles) outside of Chania, a left turn off the main road leading up a small hill will bring you to a restaurant called **Nykterida** (it is well marked on the main road). It has good food—many of its specialties are versions of local food—and the view is stupendous. You can follow the road to the airport to the point where it cuts off from the Sternes road.

Sternes has an intriguing collection of Byzantine and Venetian buildings that suggest that it may have been important as an administrative center after Nicephorus Phocas retook the island in the late tenth century. The airport turn leads to the **monastery of Ayía Triáda** and farther on to that of **Gouvernéto**. Both are architecturally interesting, especially the former, which has a clean and majestic Doric façade in good 17th-century Renaissance style. The Gouverneto is to the north, its church set in an enclosure with Venetian elements nicely worked into the simple façade. A not-too-long walk leads to the **cave of the Panayía Arkoudiótissa** (the Bear Virgin). Excavations have revealed that in antiquity this cave was a center for the worship of a Minoan bear or mother goddess, whom the Greeks later associated with Artemis under the name of the Arkoudiotissa; in time she became associated with the Virgin. Farther on is the **cave of St. John the Hermit**, a local saint who is associated with two caves—one near Kissamos, where he spent his early years, and this one, where he is buried. Continuing on from here a path leads down to a rocky beach.

WESTERN CRETE

From Chania to the west and south the landscape is cut with mountains and ravines through which buzzards, hawks, and eagles fly. The valleys are covered with ancient olive trees, and orange and lemon groves stretch out in every direction.

Packaged and homogenized tourism has taken over most of the beaches and obscured the sea along the coast west of Chania until Plataniás, about 10 km (6 miles) away. However, some inlets have not yet been seized and still have good beaches—some sandy, others rock-strewn, with good vigorous waves and strong undertow. (Don't expect the U.S. Pacific coast, however.) The **Crete Chandris** is an excellent hotel/bungalow complex with a pool, beach, evening entertainment, and a fine restaurant, at Máleme, about 15 km (9 miles) west of Chania on the Kissamos road. If you are planning to visit the western part of the island and the south through the region called Selinos, and the area around the town of Kandanos (see below), this is a good place to stay as a base for making day trips.

The Samarian Gorge

The gorge, or *farángi,* a steep, cavernous ravine that slices through the White Mountains down to the Libyan Sea, is best done as an excursion from Chania. It can be wild and treacherous, with torrents of water periodically rushing through it in the early spring, making passage not only difficult but possibly fatal. In the summer months there is only a trickle of water but a torrent of tourists who hike the 11 miles to the sea. "Doing" the gorge is much less the feat than it once was; because many people walk through it today, it no longer has the lonely and desolate atmosphere that formerly gave it a peculiar quality. Nevertheless, the scenery is incomparable, and there is always the off chance that you'll spot a kri-kri (this is a national preserve where the animals are allowed to do as they please). For many visitors it is a highlight of a Cretan vacation, and, quite apart from the certificate granted for making this literal rite of passage, it is well worth doing. Take along a good pair of walking shoes as well as drinking water. The passage takes about five hours.

It is probably best to take an organized tour for this trip unless you wish to walk back to your car—which can be done. The 37-km (23-mile) road from Chania south to Omalós takes you up high into the White Mountains and the vast and rich Omalos Plain. From there you reach Xylóskalo, the entrance to the ravine. The guided tour, after passing through the gorge, exits at Ayía Roúmeli and from there goes by boat to either Hora Sphakion or Paleohora, where you pick up the bus to go back to Chania.

South of Chania

Just out of Chania is a turnoff marked for Perivólia that is the beginning of the road south leading to the villages of Nea Roúmata and Ayía Iríni. At Ayia Irini, 42 km (26 miles) south of Chania, the road enters the **Iríni Ravine** and descends through magnificent, though harsh, mountain country to **Soúyia** on the coast, where there are fine beaches. Should you wish to stay at Souyia there are rooms available in private houses and a very small hotel, the **Pikilasos**. Check with the Tourist Association in Chania for making reservations (Tel: 0821-264-26). An alternative drive to the southern coast leads to **Paleohóra**, which is rapidly becoming a Nordic haven and highly commercialized.

Of course, you needn't end up on the southern coast. The route to Paleohora leads through **Sélinos**, a region known for vendettas, its inhabitants stubborn, proud, and foxy, with a tendency to blue eyes. They rose en masse against the movement of the Germans into this region in 1941, and several villages were singled out for special action, their men and women shot and the villages leveled. In light of their resistance to the Nazis, it is odd that the Veneto-Cretan inhabitants of nearby Kandanos almost immediately converted to Islam with the coming of the Turks, many of its young men becoming Janissaries. (The town of Kandanos is in the prefecture of Selinos; Kandanos, Selinos's principal town, and the surrounding area are usually referred to as Kandanos.)

Staying in **Kándanos** for a few days and exploring the surrounding area and its churches will get you into the heart of the region. Accommodations will be simple, possibly in private houses. The village is rebuilt, as it was destroyed in World War II, but the surrounding giant olive trees still provide a sense of its age with their great twisting and writhing trunks. Some of the nearby villages are actually aggregates of neighborhoods or family compounds, as at **Kakodíki**, where vendettas dissolved the village nucleus. The magnificent churches in this region represent every period of Cretan fresco painting from the 14th to the 17th centuries. **Tseleniatá** has an exceptional church, **Ayios Isídoros**, as well as another with paintings by Ioannis Pagomenos, who was very active in this area. Several of his churches survive, for example, at Kandanos and nearby Kadros and Anisaráki.

Return to the northern coast via the road that exits at Tavronítis. To the west the main highway skirts the coast and the uninhabited Rodopós Peninsula. A short cutoff, just before the peninsula, is marked for the **monastery of Goniás**, which played an important part in the Cretan uprising of 1866 and was destroyed as a consequence. Rebuilt, it commands a majestic view over the sea and has a good collection of icons by native Cretan masters of the 17th and 18th centuries.

Spiliá, Drakóna, and Episkopí, all south and just off the Kissamos road, boast 14th-century frescoed churches. Just before the village of Spilia is a turnoff to Marathokefála, and a short walk from there leads to the original **cave of St. John the Hermit**. The **church of Ayios Stéfanos** at Drakona is believed to date from the 9th century, and that at Episkopi, the **Rotunda** (the church of the Archangel Michael), dates possibly from the 11th century, with a dome unlike that of any other church in Crete.

Kissamos and the West Coast

Kíssamos (Kastelli) has two names—one derived from its Venetian *kastelli* (fortress). It is beautifully situated close to the sea and can be quite dusty; consequently it has magnificent sunsets. This agriculturally rich area is famous in Crete for its vineyards and wines. Accommodations are limited (stay at the Crete Chandris in Maleme, discussed above), though there are some good seafood restaurants. Kissamos offers a number of Venetian remnants and a small archaeological museum that is inexplicably closed most of the time.

In antiquity Kissamos was the port for the inland city of **Polyrrenia**, the site of which is easily reached some 8 km (5 miles) to the south. Once one of the most important cities in Crete, its ruins lie scattered over a wide and unexcavated area that extends up a hillside. The terrain is beautiful and idyllic; it should not be bypassed.

Two good centrally located restaurants in Kissamos are the **Makedonos** and the **Papakis**. Both serve local specialties, such as stews and cheese pies, as well as grills. The best seafood restaurant is **Stimadourakis Fish Restaurant**, just west of town.

The westernmost part of Crete is easily accessible from Kissamos, with detours into areas of archaeological and natural interest. The road to Falasarna, on the sea 16 km (10 miles) west of Kissamos, skirts the Gramvoúsa Peninsula, which is uninhabited and cut by rocky shores and small inlets. An asphalt road cuts northwest at Plátanos and ends at **Falasárna**. This ancient Hellenistic emporium served ships arriving from the west, especially during the Roman period. Today the site is archaeologically important if somewhat difficult to comprehend; the ruins, including the walls and part of the acropolis, remain, though its once-teeming harbor is now located 150 feet inland. (In late antiquity Crete tilted, lifting the western end of the island some 28 feet above sea level.) The impressive beach is rock-strewn and occasionally the victim of oil spills. **Stathis's** is a dependable hotel here.

From Falasarna the road south begins to wind upward to Sfinári and Kambos, after which the deserted coast can be reached easily by detours. Just past Kambos several small roads run off to the right, leading to the western coast and the sea. As the main road continues south from Kambos it begins to descend to the Libyan Sea and the **monastery of the Chrysoskalítissa**, the Virgin of the Golden Stair. Just past the village of Kefáli, take a sharp right turn onto a minor road leading southwest to the convent, home to a small community of nuns. An interesting legend surrounds the 90 steps that lead up to a small chapel and cave dedicated to the Virgin: It is said that one of the steps is of solid gold, although only a person who has never committed a sin will be able to discover which it is. Needless to say, there are still 90 steps.

South of the monastery the road ends at **Elafonísi**—a small island with beautiful and usually barren sand beaches that can be reached by walking through the shallow water.

From here double back on the main road about 11 km (6.5 miles) to Kefali and take the inland route to the north coast. This road leads up the mountains to the town of Elos, site of the annual October Chestnut Festival, down into a valley, and then into the **Topólia Ravine** and the **Kissamos Valley**—a beautiful drive. On reaching the main road at Kaloudianá turn right to return to Chania.

GETTING AROUND

Crete does not have an entirely predictable or even uniform climate, and as a rule there are only two proper seasons: winter and summer. Winter storms can be quite vicious, and it is not uncommon for planes to be grounded (or not arrive) for a day or so. In weather of this sort ships do not take to the sea, and one can (given the luxury of time) feel quite deliciously cut off from the rest of the world. The winter months begin in early November preceded by variable weather, and, most often, the snows begin to fall on the mountain ranges in December and January. Good rainwear is worth having as well as warm pullovers and light jackets. Summer usually begins slowly in April and reaches a crescendo of some intensity in August. Without a doubt the best times to visit Crete are in the months of April to July and from September until late October (you can count on good swimming during these months). As this is not peak tourist season you should check well in advance for accommodations; many of the better hotels close down over the winter months.

When planning a trip to Crete, keep in mind that at certain times of the year there is exceptionally heavy booking. For several days before and after both Greek Easter and the Feast of the Assumption (August 15) reservations must be made well in advance. Eastern Orthodoxy celebrates Easter according to the old Julian calendar; thus its relation to Latin Easter is variable. During the latter period there is a rise in foreign tourism and during the former an increase in domestic travel as people celebrate the holidays with their families. Holy Week is filled with impressive ceremonies and vigils of great antiquity and majesty. Many of the hymns, ceremonies, and rituals retain a sense of the grandeur of ancient Byzantium. Easter is also an ideal time to suffer what minor inconveniences might be involved in order to stay, if possible, in a Cretan village. Many traditional customs reappear, and Cretan hospitality to visitors cannot be surpassed.

The Feast of the Epiphany on January 6 is celebrated in all of the seaports of Crete with the Blessing of the Sea and its denizens. The high point of the ceremonies is carried out on the seaside when a cross is thrown into the newly blessed waters and young men dive to retrieve it.

Traditional Cretan weddings tend to be almost public; if you have a chance to attend one, it is an experience never to be forgotten.

There are several islands located off the coasts of Crete, such as **Dia**, north of Herakleion, and **Koufonísi**, **Chrisi**, and **Gavdos**, all isolated out in the Libyan Sea. These are stark and forbidding, seldom visited and all but uninhabited. They are all worth a visit, but staying is difficult as there are no accommodations of note. Details should be obtained on Crete.

Crete is well connected with mainland Greece by air services operating out of Chania and Herakleion. Rethymno has no airport; its needs are served by direct bus service to and from the Chania and Herakleion airports. From late spring and summer until late fall there are several flights a day to Athens (about 45 minutes). Both Chania and

Herakleion handle international charter flights that arrive daily from European cities. During the summer Herakleion has flights to and from Rhodes as well as a weekly flight to Cyprus. Lasithi province (Siteia) is served by flights to Rhodes, Karpathos, and Kasos.

There is a highly efficient ferryboat service from the mainland to Chania and Herakleion, with several boats leaving daily from Piraeus. The boats serve the needs of both tourists and natives as well as providing transport of goods to and from the island. The trip takes approximately 11 hours; some ships leave in the evening and arrive in the early morning, and there is also a daytime service.

Other services by boat are erratic and should be checked with a travel agent. A service out of Kissamos connects the island with Gytheion and Piraeus twice a week. Ferries from Ayios Nikolaos and Siteia go to Rhodes and Karpathos, and to Piraeus via Santorini.

Internally the island has good roads and an efficient bus service. The roads in Crete do not have route numbers or means of identification other than the names of towns and villages. If you travel by car you should obtain a good road map; not all are reliable.

Streets are irregularly marked—and occasionally not marked at all—or are known by local names. In looking for a hotel or restaurant, it is best to simply ask the way if you discover that the street named in your notes is located neither by a street sign nor on your map.

ACCOMMODATIONS REFERENCE

Hotels in Crete are generally open during the active tourist months (March/April through October/November). During the winter months, many are closed. It is best to call hotels in the mornings, between 8:00 and 9:00 A.M.

▶ **Acteon.** Ayia Galini, 740 56 Crete. Tel: (0832) 912-08.
▶ **Apolloria Beach.** Linoperamata, Herakleion, 712 01 Crete. Tel: (081) 821-64 or 821-602; Telex: 262224.
▶ **Astir Palace.** Elounda, 720 53 Crete. Tel: (0841) 415-80; Telex: 262215.
▶ **Astoria.** 5 Eleftherias Square, **Herakleion**, 712 01 Crete. Tel: (081) 229-002. Telex: 262152.
▶ **Casa Delphino.** 9 Theophanous Street, **Chania**, 731 01 Crete. Tel: (0821) 426-13; Telex: 291261.
▶ **Coral Hotel.** Akti Koundourou, **Ayios Nikolaos**, 721 00 Crete. Tel: (0841) 283-63/67; Telex: 262165.

▶ **Creta Maris. Chersonisos**, 700 14 Crete. Tel: (0897) 221-15; Telex: 262233.
▶ **Creta Star Hotel. Rethymno**, 741 00 Crete. Tel: (0831) 718-12; Telex: 291186.
▶ **Creta Sun Hotel. Gouves Pediados**, Herakleion, 712 01 Crete. Tel: (0897) 412-41/46; Telex: 262171.
▶ **Crete Chandris. Maleme**, 731 35 Crete. Tel: (0821) 622-21/25; Telex: 291100.
▶ **Doma**. 124 Eleftheria Venizelou Street, **Chania**, 731 00 Crete. Tel: (0821) 217-72.
▶ **Elounda Beach. Elounda**, 720 53 Crete. Tel: (0841) 414-12/13; Telex: 262192.
▶ **Elounda Mare. Elounda**, 720 53 Crete. Tel: (0841) 415-12 or 401-02/03; Fax: (0841) 413-07.
▶ **Esperia**. 22 Idomenous Street, **Herakleion**, 712 02 Crete. Tel: (081) 228-512.
▶ **Ferma Beach. Ierapetra**, 722 00 Crete. Tel: (0842) 613-41.
▶ **Galaxias**. 67 Dimokratias Street, **Herakleion**, 713 06 Crete. Tel: (081) 238-812.
▶ **El Greco. Kambos Pygis**, Rethymno, 741 00 Crete. Tel: (0831) 711-02.
▶ **Hermes**. Akti Koundourou, **Ayios Nikolaos**, 721 00 Crete. Tel: (0841) 282-53/56; Telex: 262430.
▶ **Ikaros Village. Mallia**, 700 07 Crete. Tel: (0897) 312-67/69; Telex: 262191.
▶ **Pension Istron. Ayios Nikolaos**, 721 00 Crete. Tel: (0841) 237-63.
▶ **Kalypso Cretan Village. Plakias**, 740 60 Crete. Tel: (0832) 312-96 or (0831) 233-92 (Rethymno office).
▶ **Kernos Beach. Mallia**, 700 07 Crete. Tel: (0897) 314-21/25; Telex: 262255.
▶ **Knossos Beach Hotel. Kokkino Hani**, Herakleion, 710 01 Crete. Tel: (081) 761-310; Telex: 262206.
▶ **Kriti Beach**. 18 Papanastassiou Street, **Rethymno**, 741 00 Crete. Tel: (0831) 274-01.
▶ **Oasis Hotel. Kamilari**, 722 00 Crete. Tel: (0892) 422-17.
▶ **Petra Mare. Ierapetra**, 722 00 Crete. Tel: (0842) 233-41/49.
▶ **Petros. Pitsidia**, 722 00 Crete. Tel: (0892) 423-86.
▶ **Pikilasos. Souyia**, 731 01 Crete. Tel: (0823) 513-52.
▶ **Porto Veneziano. Chania**, 731 00 Crete. Tel: (0821) 293-11/13.
▶ **Rethymna Beach. Rethymno**, 741 00 Crete. Tel: (0831) 294-91/95; Telex: 291112.

► **Sanguin Hotel.** Makriyialos, **Siteia**, 723 00 Crete. Tel: (0843) 516-21/24.
► **Sirens Beach.** **Mallia**, 700 07 Crete. Tel: (0897) 313-21/25; Telex: 262194.
► **Siteia Beach.** K. Karamanli Street, **Siteia**, 723 00 Crete. Tel: (0843) 288-21/24.
► **Stathis's** Falasarna, 712 02 Crete. Tel: (0822) 414-80.
► **Xenia Hotel.** 2 Theotokopoulou Street, **Chania**, 731 00 Crete. Tel: (0821) 245-61/62.
► **Xenia Hotel.** Soph. Venizelou Street, **Herakleion**, 712 02 Crete. Tel: (081) 284-00/04.
► **Xenia Hotel.** 30 Psarou Street, **Rethymno**, 741 00 Crete. Tel: (0831) 291-11/12.

THE DODECANESE

By Beryl Biggins and Tom Stone

Beryl Biggins has lived in Athens for seven years and has written guides to the Dodecanese, Athens, Istanbul, and Anatolia. Tom Stone, who contributed the section here on Patmos, also wrote the chapters in this guidebook on Thessaly and Northern Greece.

Variety is one of the charms of the Greek islands, and the Dodecanese (Dodekánisa, Twelve Islands, sometimes rather confusingly called the Southern Sporades) are no exception. The 14 islands that now officially constitute the group are so varied in character that they are almost custom-made for island-hopping.

From earliest times these islands were essential links in the Mediterranean trade routes. **Rhodes**, the largest, situated off the southwest "corner" of the Anatolian mainland (now part of Turkey), was the gateway to Egypt and the Middle East. Its strategic position and fertility combined to ensure its conquest and reconquest throughout history. Wide golden beaches stretching almost the entire length of the island, an idyllic climate, ancient sites, and a Medieval walled city built by the Crusaders ensure its popularity today.

Tiny Megisti, far over to the east, virtually off the map of Greece, faces Kaş on Turkey's southern coast. Better known as **Kastellórizo** (Red Fortress), it was formerly the single link between Rhodes and Cyprus, and was prosperous out of all proportion to its size until the days of steam allowed traders to pass it by. Now luxury yachts fill the safe harbor, and its beautiful houses are being restored. To the southwest of

Rhodes, halfway to Crete, are **Kasos** and **Kárpathos**, surrounded by stormy seas. Mountainous and beautiful, both these islands are prosperous, with or without a tourist trade (Karpathos is the larger and has fine beaches). The much smaller **Chalkí**, off the west coast of Rhodes, having lost its historical role in the sponge-fishing industry, almost expired before being rescued by UNESCO. It is perhaps best done as a day trip from Rhodes.

The remaining islands are strung along the coast of Turkey north of Rhodes. The beautiful horseshoe-shaped harbor and Neoclassical mansions of **Symi** are some of the most-photographed in Greece, both by professional photographers and by the thousands of tourists who throng the streets of the town, mostly as day-trippers. Although Symi's neighbor to the west, **Tilos**, is not easily accessible, its inhabitants moved a whole village from the mountains to the sea to make a new resort. Boatloads of tourists arrive daily at the next island to the north, **Nísyros**, to visit its volcano. Quiet, but still emitting sulfurous fumes, the volcano is ringed by attractive villages perched on the rim of the island and surrounded by almond trees.

Next in size and popularity after Rhodes is **Kos**, with its glorious beaches and pretty mountain villages. There are extensive Roman remains, but the island is best known for the shrine to Asklepios, god of healing; the ancient hospital/medical school that was attached to it; and Hippocrates, the father of modern medicine.

Lonely **Astypálaia**, southwest of Kos, is almost part of the Cycladic group and shares much of its architecture. Quiet and pastoral, it is fast becoming more accessible from Kos and Kalymnos and is attracting many European package-tour groups. **Kálymnos**, former island of sponge fishers, is mountainous, with fertile valleys and beautiful seascapes. Its inaccessible northern coast almost touches **Leros**, whose rolling green hills are a paradise for walkers. The last in the chain is monastic **Patmos**, where Saint John wrote his Revelation. Patmos lost its austerity in the Middle Ages and is now attracting an artistic crowd.

These fascinating islands have seen many new faces and many changes of fortune. Their ships have been engaged in almost every Greek conflict since the Trojan War—to which they sent several fleets. They were heavily fortified in the Middle Ages by the Crusaders, who lost them to Suleyman the Magnificent. It was under the Turks that the islands banded together to negotiate great concessions for their powerful ships and first became known as the Twelve Islands (the group did not then include Rhodes and Kos, which were powerful in their own right). Prosperous though these islands were under Turkish rule, their stout ships were in the forefront of the fight for Greek independence. Ironically, they gained their freedom in 1821 only to be handed back by the Western powers in exchange for Evia; they suffered terrible repercussions in consequence.

"Liberated" by Italy in 1912, the islands soon became part of Mussolini's dream of "Mare Nostra"—more of a nightmare for the unwilling inhabitants, who lost their schools and struggled to keep their own language alive. With the Italian armistice in 1943 the islands again became a battleground, the Germans temporarily driving out the Allied forces until the final liberation.

When the Dodecanese were finally reunited with Greece in 1947, the beautiful Classical houses lay in ruins, and there was no money for reconstruction. Emigration might have been the final blow, but Greeks have a habit of returning—and bringing hard-earned cash.

Vacationers fall in love with these islands, and they too return. In spite of so many centuries of uninvited guests, the islanders welcome visitors with genuine warmth and hospitality. Many tour operators arrange two-island vacations; the English Twelve Islands tour company even offers to arrange for clients to be "castaways" on uninhabited islands with tent, food, inflatable boat, first-aid kit, and two-way radio. (Contact them at Angel Way, Essex RM1 1AB, England; Tel: 0708-75-26-53; Fax: 0708-76-89-18.)

Both Rhodes and Kos have regular ferry services to the Turkish mainland. This can be a great asset to the latter-day Odysseus whose travels stretch out far longer in time than originally planned. When the three-month visa-free stay in Greece has flown by too quickly, a short trip to Turkey qualifies you for reentry and another 13 weeks of carefree wandering.

RHODES

Rhodes (Rodos), capital of the Dodecanese, is a favorite playground for northern European sunseekers, who flock to the beaches and crowd into the restaurants, bars, and discos

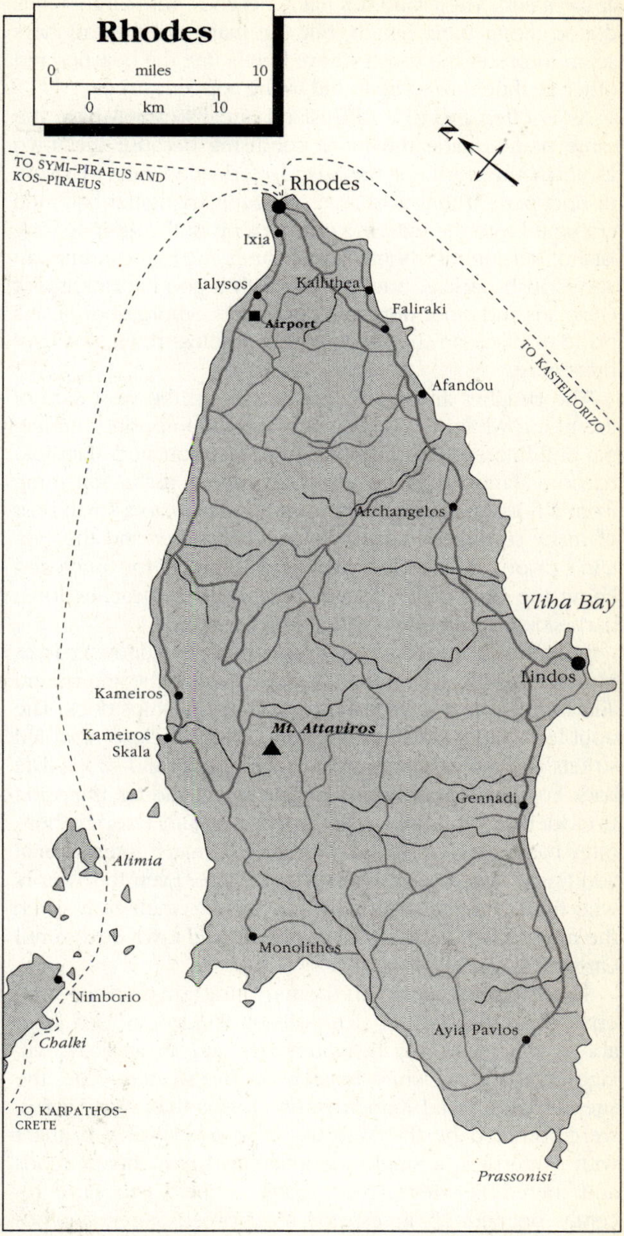

Rhodes
0
miles
10
0
km
10
N
TO SYMI–PIRAEUS AND
KOS–PIRAEUS
Rhodes
Ixia
Ialysos
Kallithea
Airport
Faliraki
TO KASTELLORIZO
Afandou
Archangelos
Vliha Bay
Lindos
Kameiros
Kameiros
Skala
Mt. Attaviros
Gennadi
Alimia
Monolithos
Nimborio
Chalki
Ayia Pavlos
TO KARPATHOS–
CRETE
Prassonisi

at day's end. The island has many beaches, with large hotels dotted along their length, but the majority of vacationers seem to prefer the town, where hotels line the beaches and other facilities are to be found in the adjacent streets.

As is often the case, the island and its capital have the same name, made the more confusing because the town itself, in the north of the island, is divided into two very distinct parts. The tourist area, a roughly triangular half mile crammed into the extreme northern tip of the 48-mile-long island, is a summer-home away from home for Scandinavian and British package vacationers, with a good sprinkling of Germans and other northern Europeans. Smorgasbord takes pride of place on the menus of the endless rows of restaurants here.

The beaches and hotels are mainly on the west side of the point, while on the east side are the imposing municipal buildings, relics of the Italian occupation, and Mandraki harbor. Mandraki is the place to hire a yacht—anything from a floating palace, with or without crew, to a small boat of many summers, usually lovingly cared for and the captain's pride and joy. He will do the shopping for lunch and know the best places to fish and the best beaches for a barbecue, and the price will not be exorbitant.

Immediately to the south of Mandraki the old town curves around the big commercial harbor, where the interisland and international ferries and the big cruise ships dock. The double-moated walls of the old town enclose cobbled streets and alleys where most of the houses and shops date back to the Turkish era and before, including imposing Crusader-era buildings. The restaurants and tavernas here offer basically Greek food, though with many international additions. The pace of life is slower here: Even the visitors who fill the town in the mornings seem to melt away when the museums close at 3:00 P.M., and the old town dozes until early evening.

The island of Rhodes has other attractions: on the eastern coast, the ancient acropolis of Lindos, poised high above two incredibly beautiful bays and an attractive village of sparkling white houses; on the western side, the sites of Ialysos and Kameiros, two towns that, with Lindos, were founded by the Minoans; a wooded valley brilliant with butterflies; a single mountain with switchback roads and incredible views. New roads in the south have recently opened up access to more broad sandy beaches and also to little villages that offer delightful possibilities for exploration.

MAJOR INTEREST

Medieval Crusader city
Palace of the Grand Masters
Ancient sites of Lindos, Ialysos, and Kameiros
Long sandy beaches

RHODES TOWN
The Old Town

The deep harbor of Rhodes town, where a port was created by the inhabitants of the three ancient cities of Lindos, Ialysos, and Kameiros, is now filled daily with ferries from all over the Aegean, along with busy cargo vessels and cruise ships discharging passengers into tour buses. From here your first view is of the great walls of the Medieval city built by the Crusaders.

Left in ruins by the Turks and restored by the Italians, who were in occupation from 1912 to 1943, the old town with its cobbled streets seems utterly remote from the modern town only a few minutes' walk to the north.

The busy bazaar area offers goods and refreshments of many kinds, but in the twisting alleys by the southern walls there are no modern shops. The young women sit outside their street doors making lace or embroidering fine linens for their hope chests or for sale. It's a spooky place to walk around at night when the streets are empty, lit by an occasional dim lamp, but it's quite safe.

The Knights Hospitalers took Rhodes from the Saracens in 1309 after retreating from Jerusalem, Acre, and Cyprus. The knights were organized according to their origins and distinguished by language—nations as such were hardly known. Each tongue was responsible for patrolling and maintaining a section of the great moated walls that stood against waves of invaders for two centuries. They built their lodges side by side in the northern section, creating the only straight road in the old town, Ippóton, which presents a somber frontage. The courtyards and gardens are hidden from view. Look for the Inn of France, restored and opened to the public by the French Institute, which uses it as a gallery.

At the head of Ippoton and open to visitors every day (except Mondays) from 8:30 A.M. to 3:00 P.M. is the **Palace of the Grand Masters**, rebuilt by Mussolini for use by himself and King Victor Emmanuel III. Although Mussolini removed many art treasures from the island, he spread many others lavishly throughout this building. The arcaded courtyard is lined with statues in Roman style, ancient mosaics from Kos are set into marble floors, and modern facilities are cunningly disguised.

The ramparts of the city walls can be toured twice a week, on Mondays and Saturdays, in the early afternoon (times keep changing; check locally). The massive fortifications can only be seen properly from the ramparts, the best vantage point in the town for photographs. At the foot of Ippoton is the **Archaeological Museum** in the old Hospital of the Knights. The museum contains the famous *Aphrodite of Rhodes,* as well as finds from the ancient sites of the island. The international goldsmith **Lalaounis** uses the bare stone walls of a small, vaulted building near the museum to provide a dramatic setting for his shop's exquisite jewelry.

Restaurants are crowded into Orpheos Street, outside the palace. An old favorite tucked away down a quiet lane has now acquired three parrots, which try desperately to be heard above the Greek music that is played fortissimo to lure potential customers. A few yards away in Ippodamos, past the mosque of Suleyman, is the pleasant courtyard of the restaurant **Symposium**, where gentler music is played. **Restaurant Fay** is set back from the same street, in a garden with a fountain and goldfish pool; the tables are laid under apricot and pomegranate trees. Incidentally, Rhodes produces beautiful wines. Try the dry white Lindos, recommended in Johnson's *World Atlas of Wine,* the red Chevalier du Rhodes, and the local C.A.I.R. "Champagne."

Parallel to Ippoton is Sokrátous Street, the center of the **bazaar** area, where hundreds of little shops, from elegant goldsmiths to simple "supermarkets," cater to all the visitors' needs. You may buy fur coats of good quality and great variety at incredibly low prices; exquisite laces and embroideries, many of which are made by residents in the old town itself; ceramics of all kinds (deer are the local emblem), including decorative perfume containers; paintings; clothing and accessories; museum copies of ancient jewelry and artifacts; and wines and spirits.

For the last 40 years the Dodecanese have enjoyed special duty-free status, so alcoholic drinks have been sold at duty-free-shop prices. This happy concession has fallen victim to EC regulations and is only partly compensated by a 30 percent reduction on the VAT (value-added tax) current in other parts of Greece.

Halfway up Sokratous, on the left, is a building set at an odd angle, its upper floor extending over the street and supported by a single pillar. Here, just off the main thoroughfare, is **Asteros**, a tiny shop where souvenir hunters may buy a hubble-bubble (water pipe) or kitchen utensils collected by the coppersmith from the islands during the winter.

Just behind the Asteros, on Menekléous Street, the **Captain's Garden** offers Greek and international dishes. Plátonos Street, parallel to Sokratous, is much quieter. For handmade treasures, **Loom** on Platonos has a wonderful selection of items of outstanding quality, including laces and silks.

At the other end of Platonos, in Plateía Ippokrátous where the seahorse fountain stands, is the **Castellania** building, where the Medieval traders' court met on the upper floor to hear disputes. Hidden away on the opposite side of this square behind the tavernas and bars is the tiny **Mediterranea Bourse**, where an Italian trio designs and makes purses and bags of all kinds from tough and colorful canvas. (Ask Miriam to demonstrate the secure, leather-strapped document belt that converts into a roomy shoulder bag.) Woven bags have now been added to the stock, as well as soaps, cosmetics, and oils made from natural ingredients. Mr. **Chatzigeorgalis** on nearby Pythagora will tailor your shirts to measure in two days. Also on Pythagora, in an alley to the left, a few yards from the square, is the **Makedonia Grill House**, with simple Greek food and a lively atmosphere.

To the southeast is the old **Jewish Quarter**, where the Square of the Jewish Martyrs commemorates the massacres of the last war. The synagogue has been lovingly restored by a survivor in memory of his lost family.

Many pensions provide accommodation in the old town. Just off the square on Demosthénous Street is the **Fantasia Pension**, with private bathrooms, kitchen facilities, a pleasant courtyard, and a delightful welcome. Tucked away to the far south, only 100 yards from the port, is the tiny **Kava d'Oro Hotel** (turn right inside the gate from the ferry port and follow the signs). Great care has been taken to preserve these original buildings situated in the shadow of the city walls; their arched ceilings and rustic furnishings give the rooms a country air.

The New Town

Along the waterfront outside the old town are the imposing administrative buildings and the **cathedral** overlooking **Mandráki harbor**, where the **Colossus of Rhodes** is believed to have stood. After the death of Alexander the Great Rhodes remained loyal to his general, Ptolemy of Egypt, who was born on the island. The Macedonian Poliorkitis the Besieger attacked the city with an enormous force in 305 B.C., using floating forts and siege towers of a size previously unknown. A year later he withdrew, defeated, leaving his siege engines behind. It was the sale of these that provided the islanders with the means, in 293 B.C., to erect an enormous statue of the sun god Helios in thanks for their deliverance. One of the Seven Wonders of the World, it was short-lived, toppled by an earthquake some 60 years later.

The harbor, now watched over by the symbolic Deer of Rhodes, is filled with yachts and tour boats that leave daily for local beaches and for many of the nearby islands. A hydrofoil also serves Kos on a regular basis—and other islands, too, if there is sufficient demand. There are also trips to Marmaris in Turkey, but if you've arrived in Rhodes on a charter flight, be aware that if you visit Turkey during your stay the Greek authorities may not allow you to board your return flight, but insist on your returning by scheduled flight via Athens.

Swimming and water sports are catered to everywhere in Rhodes. Beginning scuba divers and those wishing to take qualifying courses for the British Sub-Aqua Club can enroll here with the Waterhoppers, divers belonging to the Professional Association of Diving Instructors. Dive boats leave for Kallithea (discussed below) each morning. Those who like to keep the water underneath them may hire a boat by the month, day, or even hour—or dine on the **Kontiki**, a floating restaurant. On the quay is the restaurant **Neo Rion**, where a band plays nightly.

Just in from Mandraki is the **New Market**, where butchers and poulterers are slowly being replaced by tourist shops. Many of the tavernas that used to be part of the tradition now believe they must ape foreign restaurants, eroding the very atmosphere that draws the visitor to their tables. However, **Adam's Greek Kitchen** has resisted such change and has kept its atmosphere intact. In the center of the market, the odd, circular fish market is an interesting place to visit on weekday mornings.

By the side of the New Market, in Alexándrou Papágou Street, is the taxi rank, to the right of which are the **Rhodes Tourist Office**, the departure points for island buses, and a sound-and-light show. Follow the same street to reach the **Oasis** café-restaurant, which has its own swimming pool, sunbathing platform, and fountains. Unfortunately, a candle-lit evening meal by the pool may be completely ruined by the nearby disco using a sound system better suited to crowd control at a football match.

The new town is skirted by wide sandy beaches, which are liable to be crowded because the area is lined with hotels and filled with discos, bars, and restaurants. Menus here cater to Scandinavian and English tourists.

Rhodes has hotels of every size and classification, but the town streets are noisy and can be suffocatingly hot in summer. For a luxury hotel go a little farther down the coast to **Ixia**. The beautiful gardens of the **Miramare Beach Hotel** here extend alongside the beach, and the air-conditioned apartments are attractively situated among the trees. Across the road under a small cliff, the **Rodos Palace** and **Olympic Palace**, both popular convention centers with swimming pools, each stand in extensive gardens; their first-class restaurants are open to the public. Excellent Greek food is available as well at the taverna **Tzaki**, on the main road through Ixia. Many hotels are fully booked for most of the year, so it makes sense to enlist the help of an agency such as Triton Tours, which also organizes tours to various parts of the island. They are at 25 Plastíra Street; Tel: (0241) 216-90.

The East Coast

The 53-km (33-mile) journey south from Rhodes town to Lindos can be pleasant, but the road runs inland, and the many idyllic beaches that line this coast are not visible from the road. On arrival in Lindos the tour buses often have to wait in line to let their passengers off. The local bus takes two hours and fills before leaving town, continuing to pick up passengers along the way. Anyone not used to this method of travel is liable to need a week's rest before climbing the acropolis hill, even on a donkey. It's much pleasanter to take one of the boats that go daily from Mandraki harbor.

Beautiful **Kallithéa**, formerly a spa, is a well-known spot on this coast, with a tiny sandy cove and lots of rocks from which to bathe, about 12 km (7.5 miles) out of Rhodes town. **Faliráki** beach, immediately to the south, has many large hotels, including the luxurious **Sunwing**, whose rooms command magnificent views. The hotel is now a base for the Sandhoppers diving school and offers all water-sports, tennis, volleyball, and miniature golf. Another first-class hotel right on the beach is the **Faliraki Beach Hotel**, with a delightful poolside taverna, a hairdresser, and room service.

Faliraki is fast becoming the water-sports capital of the island, with scuba diving, water scooters, waterskiing, paraskiing, windsurfing, and water slides for the kids. Still farther south, out of sight to the east of the Lindos road, are more beaches, including a wide golden stretch at **Afándou**. On the shore of Vliha Bay, 3 km (2 miles) north of Lindos, are two beautifully placed hotels, the GNTO-run **Steps of Lindos Hotel**, with tiers of apartments set into the cliffs, village-style furnishings, and an Olympic-size swimming pool; and the **Lindos Bay**, also with a pool. Both hotels have good water-sports facilities, tennis, very good restaurants, and, of course, transport facilities.

The origins of **Lindos**, one of the greatest of the ancient cities of Rhodes, were lost in myth long before Saint Paul arrived to preach to the Lindians. Athena's temple had supplanted that of Aphrodite—to be supplanted in its turn by that of the Virgin. The Crusaders raised impressive walls, which command magnificent views over the twin bays and rugged coastline. The walls consumed much of the marble from the earlier temples, but at their foot the deep relief carving of the **Trireme of Timocharis** still stands. This elegant ship was originally surmounted by a statue of Timocharis himself. Variously described as captain and priest, he was possibly both; many of the ancient peoples were led to war by their priests, and no distinction existed between soldiers and sailors.

Perched high above the present village, the towering walls are approached by a steep path and a long flight of steps. Two marble plaques from 99 B.C., found on the site, record the names of priests and visitors, including Herakles; Cadmus; Danaos with his 50 daughters; Agamemnon and Helen on their return from Troy; Artaphernes, King of Persia; and Alexander the Great. Many of the bases of the statues, donated by wealthy visitors, remain, the statues themselves believed to have been removed by Cassius to Rome. Immediately inside the gatehouse-fortress are the remains of a Hellenistic **stoa** from which a stairway leads through the **propylaea** (gateway) to the highest point, the site of the **temple of the Lindian Athena**, tucked into a narrow corner. Down below the walls at this point can be seen traces of an ancient **theater**.

The village at the foot of the acropolis has long been popular with the English, many of whom are resident, thus ensuring that your tea comes with milk and toast with butter. The town's 16th-century flat-roofed villas, most of which are block-booked by tour agencies, have Gothic windows and traditional black-and-white patterned courtyards. The Byzantine **church of Our Lady**, near the entrance to the village, has magnificent examples of this mosaic flooring and well-preserved murals that represent the story of the gospels, including an early picture-strip painted by Gregory of Syme (Symi), completed in 1779.

Below the church and to the right, the **Rustic Taverna** offers an imaginative menu and a comprehensive view from the roof garden. The Lindos shops sell lace (though it can be rather expensive here) and local pottery, a good buy. Flower motifs, traditional in Lindos, and deer motifs, the special symbol of Rhodes, adorn much of the pottery. The ceramics may come from Archángelos (on the coast between Lindos and Rhodes town), which is also famous for its weaving.

The beaches south of Lindos are just as fine as those in the north and are far less crowded. The two beaches at Lindos itself are not special.

The West Coast

The other ancient cities of Rhodes, Ialysos and Kameiros, are both on the west side of the island. A tour could include a visit to the **Valley of Butterflies** in Petaloúdes, 7 km (4 miles) inland along the left turnoff, immediately south of the airport. In high summer the strikingly marked Jersey tiger moths are attracted by the mulberry trees. Unfortunately, increasing numbers of tourists are fast reducing their numbers.

The site of ancient **Ialysos** stands inland of the modern town of that name on a tree-lined hill at Filérimos, just 15 km (9 miles) south of Rhodes town. The site was favored by the Crusaders, who used the remains of earlier buildings for a monastery. They also built a double church, which is now used by both Orthodox Greeks and Catholics. Its pulpit stands outside in the monastery garden.

Kameiros, just off the coast road some 36 km (23 miles) south of Rhodes town, was never fortified and has not been occupied since the ancient inhabitants left over a thousand years ago. The reason they left is a mystery. The temple base and the huge water cistern remain, as do the foundations of hundreds of tiny houses on a gentle wooded slope overlooking the sea.

To the south the road passes **Kameiros Skala**—a tiny port for boats travelling to nearby Chalki—before climbing the slopes of pine-covered **Attáviros**, the island's only mountain. Here the landscape changes dramatically. The road climbs and twists past cultivated terraces and isolated vineyards, with the sea on one side and sheer crags on the other. An isolated bell tower stands, though there appears to be no one to summon but the bees.

The bus from Rhodes town takes this route on the way to **Monólithos**, where a ruined fortress stands on the single pinnacle of rock from which it takes its name. The bus waits two hours, but this is not time enough to descend the hill and climb up to the castle, so personal transport is needed. An alternative is to stay at the nearby **Thomas Hotel**, which offers comfortable self-catering apartments and is a good base for touring the southern part of the island.

The open seas to the west are never calm; bathing is better on the other side of the island. The contrast can be seen from the lighthouse at the very tip of the island, where a spit of land connects with Prassónisi (Green Island).

GETTING AROUND

Ferries link Rhodes and Piraeus by three routes: via Kos, Kalymnos, Leros, and Patmos (daily in season); via Symi, Tilos, Nisyros, Kos, Kalymnos, Astypalaia, and Paros; and via Chalki, Karpathos, Kasos, Siteia (Crete), and Santorini. There is also a ferry to Kastellorizo. Current ferry information can be obtained from the City of Rhodes Tourist Organization on Rimini Square near the New Market.

Excursion boats ply to Symi, Nisyros, Kos, and Chalki (from Kameiros Skala). There is hydrofoil service daily to Kos, weekly to Chalki, and to other islands according to demand.

International ferries connect Rhodes with Marmaris, Turkey; Limassol, Cyprus; Haifa, Israel; and Alexandria, Egypt. Rhodes is a port of entry for Greece.

There are flights to Athens, Thessaloniki, Kastellorizo, Kos, Karpathos, Kasos, Siteia and Herakleion (Crete), and to Santorini, Lesvos, and Paros, as well as charter flights from northern Europe.

—*Beryl Biggins*

KASTELLORIZO

Here is an island that is quite literally "off the map." Seventy miles east of Rhodes, with a small but safe harbor, Kastellórizo (Red Fortress), or **Megísti**, was once a vital port for Mediterranean shipping on the way to Cyprus and the Middle East. But that was before the advent of steam. Now the tiny, arid, rocky island, just off Kaş on the Turkish coast, is virtually unknown outside of Greece.

MAJOR INTEREST

Getting away in a quiet way
Charming yacht harbor
Blue Grotto

Although out of sight, the island is far from out of mind to the Greek state. The old Classical name of Megisti has officially been revived (though no one on the island ever uses it). It means "largest"—which it is, in relation to the group of even smaller islands that surround it. The last one of these smaller islands to be inhabited became deserted in 1985, when the last inhabitant, known as the Lady of Ro, died at the age of 104. Having lived on the island alone for many years, steadfastly refusing to leave her solitary home, she was much admired. She kept the Greek flag flying daily over the years in defiance of Italian and German invaders and the Turks across the water. On her death she was given a state funeral.

Kastellorizans welcome visitors, some of whom are the returning children or grandchildren of islanders who emigrated, perhaps even in the last century. They may be on a first visit to the ancestral island, but they are not strangers, having retained contact with relatives over the intervening years. The family house may still be standing, though not necessarily habitable.

At first sight it is not easy to see that some of those tall, balconied Neoclassical houses are derelict. Only as the boat nears the harbor is it evident that neat houses, with gaily painted doors and window frames, stand next to others that are empty shells. This is rapidly changing; everywhere these lovely houses are being restored. They have been passed on as dowry through several generations, and owners who are not at present able to restore are usually not willing to sell.

Houses, restaurants, tavernas, and *ouzeries* line the road skirting the harbor, with boats moored a yard or two from the front door. Other houses are wedged in, two to five deep, on a narrow shelf of land that takes a sudden upturn and becomes a mountain. A jagged line rises almost vertically above the houses to the mountaintop. This is the stepped path that leads to the little **church of Ayios Yiórgios of the Mountain**, every step painstakingly whitewashed and gleaming brilliantly in the sunshine.

There are no beaches on the island; swimming is from the terrace of the **Hotel Megisti**, a single, low, modern building on the right-hand side of the bay, whose wide terrace is ideal for sunning and for watching the world go by. The hotel is owned by the islanders, and the obliging manager will give up his room and sleep in his office when the need arises.

The small, gray structure just across the bay from the hotel is the **Castle of the Knights**, built by Juan Fernando Heredia, the eighth Grand Master of the Knights of Saint John. The original structure was destroyed by Arabs and rebuilt by Neapolitans in the 15th century.

Part of Kastellorizo town—the only town on the island—was completely destroyed during World War II. There is little trace of the hundreds of houses that once completely covered the hill below the castle. The **Archaeological Museum** is housed in a villa there. The small harbor of Mandráki beyond the hill is overlooked by only a few buildings. One of them, a domed structure looking rather like a little subterranean church, covers something much older than the castle: one of the underground cisterns that dot the island, which have been in use since prehistoric times.

On the saddle between the harbors by the church of Ayios Yiórgios Santrape stands the much more magnificent **cathedral of Saints Konstantínos and Eléni**, whose columns are from the ancient Temple of Apollo at Patara in Lycia, Turkey. Many islanders return for the great feast of the saints on May 21.

On the subject of feasting: The food in Kastellorizo is exceptionally good. At **Savva's** restaurant on the right-hand side of the town square a simple meal of *pastítsio* and green beans cooked in sauce can prove to be a memorable experience. The fish, always freshly caught, is superb. (The island exports quantities of swordfish to restaurants in Rhodes.)

Eating, talking to the islanders, or just puttering around town, you will find this is a relaxing place to stay. Everyone knows everyone else. For a little variety it is easy to arrange a boat trip to the adjacent island of **Ayios Yiórgios** for swimming. More exciting perhaps is an early-morning excursion to the **Blue Grotto** (called "Fokiali"—Seal Refuge—by the locals) on Kastellorizo. The entrance is low but inside it's loftier than the grotto at Capri. It takes over an hour to reach by boat (local fishermen will take you in boats that hold three people), and the red rocks appear insurmountable at any point. It becomes apparent that the whole island is a fortress—Kastellorizo.

GETTING AROUND
A small airstrip provides connections to Rhodes three times weekly, but the sea brings most visitors, either by yacht or on one of the three ferries that arrive each week from Rhodes. Dolphins can often be seen leaping in the wake of the ship.
—*Beryl Biggins*

KASOS, KARPATHOS, CHALKI

To the west of Rhodes lie Chalki, tight by its western flank, and Karpathos and Kasos, halfway to Crete. Again, three islands with quite different characters. Kasos has very few visitors and is a quiet retreat, while the wild, mountainous, pine-clad Karpathos is fast developing into a popular tourist center. Despite their proximity, strong winds and heavy seas ensure that there is relatively little contact between the two; little Chalki attracts a few short-term visitors and is sometimes teamed with Rhodes or Symi for two-island package vacations. Efforts by the National Tourist Board to develop the two smaller islands by offering free ferry tickets from Rhodes have been abandoned, and the ferry service to Kasos and Chalki has now been reduced to once weekly, weather permitting. Chalki has its own early-morning ferry to Kameiros Skala on Rhodes, and there is a Sunday hydrofoil from Rhodes town. Both Karpathos and Kasos have air connections with Rhodes and with Siteia, in Crete. Karpathos airport now accommodates charter flights.

The ferry connecting the three islands with Crete and Piraeus leaves Rhodes late at night. If you are visiting all three, it is easier to start in Kasos, taking the ferry back to Karpathos and Chalki during daylight hours.

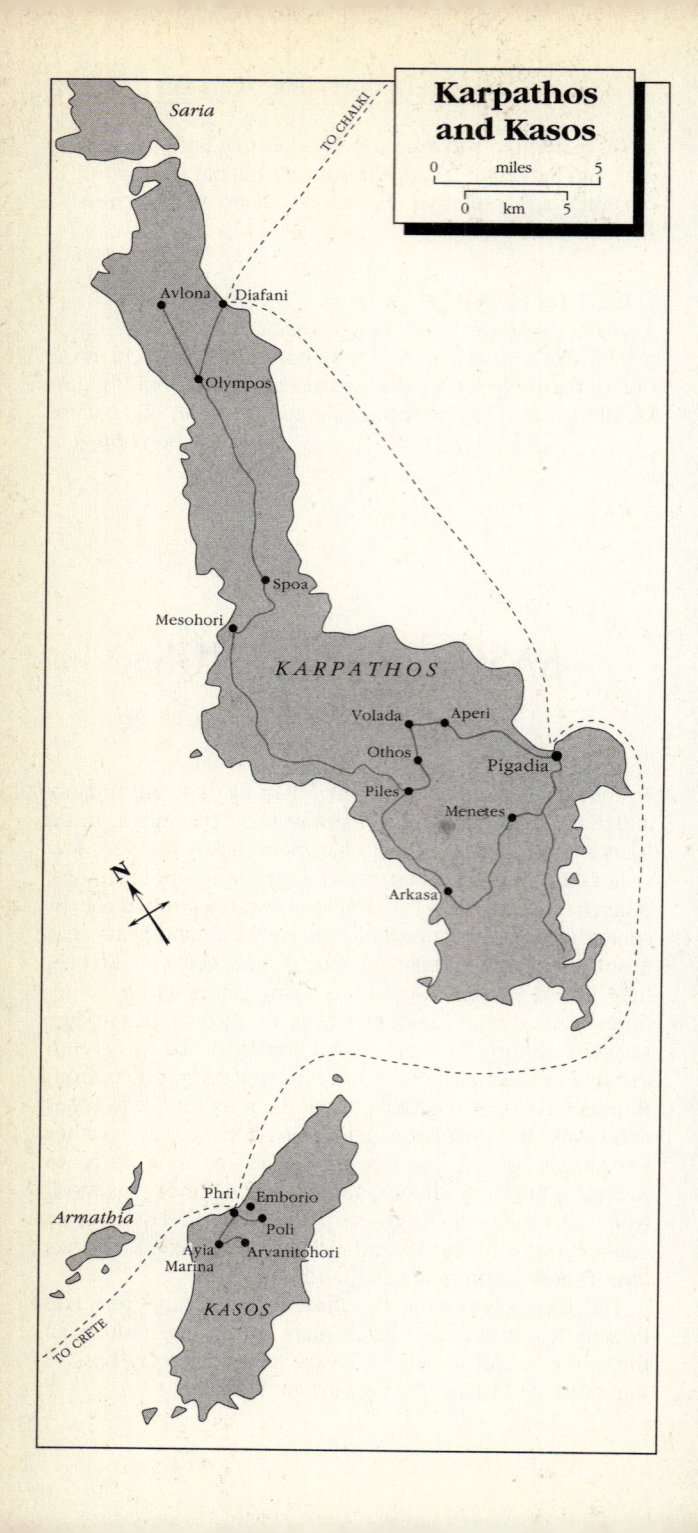

Karpathos and Kasos

KASOS

The Phoenicians called it "the island of sea foam," while the local brochure describes it as "the tranquil island." Both are right. Constant winds bring the waves crashing onto the rocks and often make ferry transfers tricky—and sometimes impossible—at the little port of **Phri**, on the northern coast. Although Karpathos is clearly visible to the northeast, very few boats make the trip, and only on the calmest of summer days. But amid its wild seas the island is quiet, with a pleasant lifestyle and, as yet, few tourists. So few, in fact, that they are known to everyone in the little port.

MAJOR INTEREST

Peaceful and remote atmosphere

The island has not always been tranquil. It was at the mercy of pirates and attackers throughout history. In 1418 it was laid waste and resettled, with Astypalaia, by Albanians. In 1547 it was conquered by the Turks, who offered some protection in return for a twice-yearly tax, but in 1579 it was again in ruins and remained so for 20 years. By 1622 the island was sufficiently recovered to sever its connection with the Karpathian archbishopric and establish its own patriarch, and by 1670 the population numbered 5,000.

During the Orloff Revolution (1768 to 1774) the island was occupied by Russians in conflict with Greece, but then reverted to Turkish domination. The Kasiots, though paying taxes to the Turks, retained self-rule and maintained their church, schools, and customs. In 1822, at the time of the Greek War of Independence, the population numbered 11,000, and the island owned a well-armed fleet of 100 merchant vessels (which also engaged in raiding other islands and the North African coast, as was the custom of the day). The Turkish governor of Egypt, who wanted to subdue Crete, saw Kasos as a danger to his plans and on May 17, 1824, his fleet besieged the island with 45 ships and 4,000 Albanians. The island withstood the siege for three weeks before the Albanians managed to get a foothold on the island, whereupon they marched from village to village butchering the women and children and looting and burning the houses.

Around the Island

The small **Hotel Anagenessis** in Phri serves a good breakfast, and the rooms (en suite) overlook the sea. On the ground floor are a shop and a travel agency owned by the hotel proprietor, M. E. Manoussos. He and his wife are very well informed on island history. They are also helpful with transport and can give detailed information on which roads to take where. They also have apartments to rent in the village.

On the road to Emborio, the **Ekaterini Markou Apartments** also offer very pleasant rooms in a modern single-story house with two spacious self-contained apartments. These can be rented complete or as three separate bedrooms sharing the bathroom and a kitchen with facilities for preparing light meals—a great asset to the spring visitor, as until late May there is only one taverna open in the town.

The harbor at the hamlet of **Emborió**, a ten-minute walk from Phri, is more sheltered, but it is too small to accommodate the large ferries that now ply this route and is only used by fishing boats and yachts. It's worth walking down to Emborio to see if the fish taverna there is operating. The fishermen and their families are often to be found mending nets in the evenings.

The other villages on the island cluster in the hills above Phri. All are served by the island's single bus, which carries the shoppers, the schoolchildren, the bread (the housewives run out to collect it from the driver), and the occasional lamb sitting docilely on its owner's knee. There are a couple of taxis, too, but any of the villages would make a pleasant walk from the port. The gardens are gay with flowers, and the views across the island and coast and over to Karpathos are magnificent.

Ayía Marína, high above the port, overlooks the cliff-edge airstrip. There is no taverna in this pleasant agricultural village, but Greek coffee is available, and possibly a light snack. Close by at **Kathistres** is the **cave of Ellinikokámara**, which is enclosed by a Hellenic wall; near the airport is **Selai cave**, with stalactites and stalagmites.

The old inland capital of **Poli** has a small fortress, from which the mountain road leads to the deserted **monastery of Ayia Mamas**. More interesting to visit, however, is the **monastery of Ayios Yiórgios**, in the mountains to the south—a thrilling, if sometimes nerve-racking, journey along a wide, unsurfaced road through the mountains. The caretaker will almost certainly offer you Greek coffee. (Incidentally, don't be surprised if your host does not drink with you. This is not part of the tradition of Greek hospitality; guests are offered refreshments, not asked to share them.)

Combine the visit with swimming at the pebble beach at **Khélathros**, a fertile valley with a few fig trees for shade. The tourist agency can arrange transport for the trip or for a boat to the nearby island of **Armathía**, which has a good sandy beach. You will need to take refreshments to both places, as you will be alone there until the driver or boatman comes to collect you at a prearranged time.

The village of **Arvanitóhori** was founded by Albanian refugees at some point in the island's checkered history. (Ask if the **Kasiotikó Spiti** [Kasiot House] is open. If not, you may well be invited into a resident's home for coffee.) More often than not it was the Kasiots who were the refugees or who simply left to find work. Many labored on the construction of the Suez Canal and stayed on to become canal pilots. When the Panama Canal was built, many pilots left for the other side of the Atlantic. Kasiots can still be found in Egypt, Panama, and the United States, as well as in the world's merchant fleets. One retired sea captain who lives in Phri is rather suspicious of visitors, having seen the way some tourists behave on some of the more popular islands. "We don't need tourists," he says, "but we like people from other countries to visit us." A nice distinction.

KARPATHOS

Just northeast of Kasos and sharing the same stormy seas, the much larger island of Kárpathos is gaining in popularity every year. The island is rugged in every sense, with a heavily inletted coastline and pine-dotted mountains that rise toward the north, dividing the island effectively in two. The northern mountains are all but impassable; the north is usually reached by the ferry—which calls at Pigadia in the south and anchors off tiny Diafani in the north when the weather is not too rough—or by local boats small enough to tie up in Diafani. Both ports are on the more sheltered east coast. The airport, south of Pigadia, has been extended to accommodate charter flights from Europe as well as the twice-daily flights from Rhodes.

MAJOR INTEREST

Wild mountains with beautiful villages
Sandy beaches and coves
Dorian village of Olympos

Pigadia

Pigádia (or Karpathos town), the island's capital, has expanded upward and outward from the harbor and now has a good selection of hotels and pensions; the harborside tavernas have become full-fledged restaurants and the menus more international. The new development is being carried out in a more sensitive way than was some of the earlier building in the town, and the island can easily cope with the new arrivals without losing its character.

Karpathians abroad, including Telly Savalas, keep their family connections. Though they may spend half the year in America, where their families are equally at home, this does not mean that the Karpathian traditions have been lost. The islanders are very proud of their heritage. Anyone who is lucky enough to see an island wedding—in which the whole village accompanies the groom to claim his bride and wild tunes are played on *lyra* (with bow), *laoúto* (plucked), and *tsamboúna* (goatskin bagpipes)—may begin to understand their independent character.

Hotels on the island are above average, and prices are a little higher than in most of the Dodecanese. The **Romantica**, facing Vronti beach on the northern outskirts of Pigadia, has studio apartments set in a garden behind the hotel. It's very popular with British tourists and is the only Greek island hotel selected by the British Consumer Association for inclusion in their worldwide Hotels Guide. (At the other end of the beach stand the marble remnants of a fifth-century church, **Ayia Fotiní**.) **Vronti** beach is long and sandy, but nonswimmers beware: There are patches of slippery weed under the water. Another hotel of elevated standards, the **Seven Stars**, situated high on the hill, has magnificent views over the bay.

Pigadia also has many pensions to choose from, such as the **Kanaki**, with private baths, and the simpler **Neohori**, tucked in among private houses at the top of the town and benefiting from the view. Information sheets on hotels and pensions are distributed by Possi Travel and Karpathos Travel. Stop in at the latter for leaflets giving the current bus schedules.

In the evening life centers around the harbor, where the restaurants on the edge of the attractive bay offer plenty of choices—a pleasant place to while away the time. In town, just past the Olympic Airways and OTE offices, is the friendly **El Greco**, where the atmosphere is quiet and the owner will remember your preferences.

A short bus or caïque ride to the south of Pigadia is **Amópi** beach, a broad half-moon of sand skirted by trees. There are a few small tavernas and pensions, too. A white church stands on a hillock at the end of the bay. Caïques also call at isolated sandy coves to the north of town, which are accessible only from the sea.

The Villages

The grandeur of the Karpathian mountains is softened by small fertile valleys and a scattering of pine trees. The villages above Pigadia seem to hang in the sky at night like clustered stars—they are the first thing visible from the night ferry. Surrounded by orchards of apricots, figs, and pomegranates, and bright with flowers, their charm does not diminish on closer acquaintance. **Othos**, **Apéri**, **Voláda**, and **Pilés** can be visited by taking one of the local buses, leaving time for a stroll around Piles before returning to Pigadia. Even on the hottest day the wind blows, the trees rustle, and the sea far below is flecked with white. Piles is noted for honey, which can be bought in a little old-fashioned village shop. The snack bar at the entrance to the village serves simple but good local food. In Othos a traditional house has been made into a **folk museum**.

To the southwest of Pigadia another surfaced road climbs up to **Menetés**, standing on a high mountain shelf with a sheer drop below. The road then winds through the lonely mountains to the western coast, where **Arkasa**, an interesting village to explore, straggles around a deep gully. (A nearby peninsula to the southwest has the remains of Mycenaean walls.) The long-established **Petalouda** taverna in Arkasa serves excellent food, especially fish. Kasos is visible across the water and can be reached from here by local boat on calm weekends in the summer. There is only one bus daily, so return to Pigadia must be by taxi, with fares set by fixed tariff.

North of Arkasa a hook of land protects **Lefkos** beach, at the foot of the mountains, from the more open seas of the west. With three sheltered sandy beaches, scattered pines, and a taverna surrounded with flowers, remote Lefkos is very beautiful indeed.

Motorbikes can be rented, but the remaining roads are hazardous with loose stones, sweeping curves, and strong winds that are sometimes channeled by the landscape into dangerous and sudden gusts. The only neighbors are goats, and these isolated roads are no place to have an accident—or even to run out of fuel.

Olympos Village

Above the village of Spoa the hazardous mountain road is little used; the northern part of the island is best reached by boat from Pigadia to **Diafáni**, a tiny port on the east coast. The twice-weekly ferry also carries passengers (and the occasional goat), who will find on arrival that the water is shallow; the boat anchors offshore and waits for a small caïque to bring out those who wish to embark. Exchanges are often made with the small boat pitching and tossing as people and goods are passed across a three-foot-wide gap in frantic haste. Sometimes the whole procedure is abandoned and would-be arrivals are taken on to the next port of call.

The local boat from Pigadia is met by a tiny bus that ferries the passengers in relays up to the village of Olympos, which spills in dramatic swaths down the ridges of Mount Profitis Ilias.

The people of Olympos are believed to be directly descended from the Dorians, and still use Dorian words. The women wear traditional dresses made from material woven on their own looms. These are white mid-calf tunics with high necks edged by a strip of neat embroidery. At festival times these elegant tunics are exchanged for flowered skirts, worn with blouses that are almost invisible under a stomacher of gold chains and coins. These costumes are handed down, with the family house, to generation after generation of elder daughters upon marriage. The finery comes out for weddings and the Festival of Saint John the Baptist (August 29), when everyone moves over to the nearby village of **Vurgunda**, a stiff two-hour walk to the north, for a celebration lasting for three days (Icelanders in the Westman Islands have the same tradition at midsummer).

The quality of the dresses is equaled by that of the intricately stitched boots of soft goatskin made by a local shoemaker. It's possible to order a pair made to measure, but they will be costly. There's a long waiting list—you will receive them long after you've forgotten you ordered them. They are worth waiting for, however.

Olympos is large and surprisingly prosperous. Little disturbed by the weekly influx of tourists, life here goes on pretty much as it always has. The houses are comfortable and well furnished in the traditional style, with a few additions. Wood-fed communal outdoor ovens are often supplemented by the most modern electric equipment installed in bright kitchens with cool marble floors.

CHALKI

Chalkí, the last port of call for the ferry *Olympia* on its journey to Rhodes, lies close to the larger island's western shore. While Chalki is slowly being resuscitated by UNESCO, it does not offer enough to the tourist to merit an extended stay, but might make a pleasant side trip from Rhodes. As the sponge trade dwindled many Chalkiots emigrated and, as at Kastellorizo, the houses fell into disuse. But the harbor is more open here and the architecture is quite different. The rectangular façades are horizontal rather than vertical and devoid of trim, giving the houses a forbidding appearance from a distance.

Closer inspection reveals that the uniformity is an illusion and that the little port of **Nimborió**, or Skala, is busy with renewal. The quay is being expanded, and there are numerous craft moored in front of a half-dozen tavernas. Many of the Chalkiot houses were restored by UNESCO, which designated Chalki "the Isle of Peace and Friendship" and holds youth conferences on the island.

There is no other village on the island; inland **Horió** has long been deserted. A road donated by Chalkiot divers in Florida, named Tarpon Springs Boulevard, leads to a nearby strip of sandy beach with sun beds, umbrellas, and a pleasant taverna. When finished the road will reach the **monastery of John the Baptist** to allow islanders to drive to the annual festival around August 29. It takes two hours to walk, but this is not really walking country. Nor is it driving country; this is the island's only road.

Chalki's one hotel, **Xenonas Halki**, owned by the municipality, is an imaginative conversion of a sponge-cleaning factory. The approach is through a small boatyard, which presents something of an obstacle course. Reached by a rough flight of steps and crossed by two great wooden beams and a taut rope or two, this is no place to be at night without a good flashlight.

Boats run to the uninhabited island of **Alimía**, which has a sandy beach and a ruined Crusader castle. Two local boats make the trip to Kameiros Skala (Rhodes) at 5:00 A.M. weekdays and on Sunday afternoons. The Sunday boat does not connect with public transport on Rhodes, thus necessitating a taxi ride of more than 30 miles to Rhodes town.

GETTING AROUND
In summer, a weekly ferry from Rhodes to Piraeus calls at Chalki, Karpathos (Diafani and Pigadia), Kasos, Crete (Siteia),

and Santorini; and one calls at Karpathos (Pigadia) and Crete (Herakleion), Santorini, and Paros. There are also weekly ferries in the opposite direction. Ferries calling at Diafani anchor offshore and transfer is made by caïque. Heavy weather can sometimes prevent stops at Kasos, Diafani, or Chalki, and all ferries are subject to change of time or date, so confirmation should be made as near as possible to sailing time.

Almost all ferries calling at Pigadia also anchor off Diafani, weather permitting, to transfer passengers by small boat. Not even the largest ferries call at Chalki in bad weather. The 5:00 A.M. daily caïque from Chalki to Kameiros Skala (Rhodes) links up with the morning bus to Rhodes town (except on Sundays), which arrives at about 8:30 A.M. It sails only if the captain knows the night before that there are passengers. Tickets can be purchased from a grocery shop in Nimborio (Chalki); not for people prone to seasickness.

Olympic Airways flights link Karpathos and Kasos to Rhodes (for Athens), Siteia (Crete), and each other. Flights are more frequent in summer.

—*Beryl Biggins*

SYMI, TILOS, NISYROS

To the north of Rhodes, between it and Kos, are the islands of Symi, Tilos, and Nisyros, all connected by the same ferry route from Piraeus and also served by interisland ferries in season. These three are different enough to offer a three-island vacation of great variety. The small, modern village that has recently sprung up around the quay at Tilos contrasts strongly with the picture-book prettiness of Symi's houses, arrayed up the hillside around the deeply curved harbor. Each of these two islands has just one more tiny village apart from its port, while Nisyros is ringed by a handful of lovely hamlets set in the fertile soil, which has its origins in the still-simmering volcano.

SYMI

Tucked away between two long peninsulas of the Turkish coast north of Rhodes, Symi is popular with day-trippers. In addition to the once-weekly Piraeus–Rhodes service, an interisland ferry, and an occasional hydrofoil, several boats run daily from Rhodes. These usually visit the 18th-century monastery of Panormitis, in the southwest, as well as the main port of **Yialós**, in a deep and well-sheltered bay in the northeast. No modern construction has been allowed to spoil the town's original charm. The Neoclassical red-roofed houses climb steeply up the heights flanking the horseshoe-shaped harbor. They appear on thousands of postcards and brochures as well as in the motion picture *Pascali's Island,* which was filmed in 1988 in Symi and Rhodes.

MAJOR INTEREST

Picture-book charm
Fine architecture
Good walking
Deserted beaches, accessible only by sea

Many of the 19th-century sea captains' mansions in Yialos have recently been restored and converted into hotels and pensions, some of a higher class than those found on the other small islands. The *Pascali's Island* people stayed at the prettily restored **Aliki**, on the waterfront of the second bay, just behind the clock tower. The elegant **Dorian Hotel**, another fine old mansion, stands immediately behind it in a quiet, paved road. No bigger than the Aliki, the Dorian has several annexes, including the magnificent but decrepit-seeming mansion next door, which looks down on its neighbors from the top of innumerable flights of steps. The Dorian has not been restored, but small modern bathrooms have been added to each of the rooms, which lead off a huge central hall. Breakfast is served on the balcony, with breathtaking views. At the rear of a public square to the right of the harbor (turn left at the back of the square), is the **Grace Hotel**, with its shady courtyard. Small and in keeping with its surroundings, with cool, comfortable rooms, this is a pleasant alternative for the weary-footed who do not want to climb a hundred steps to get to bed, as you must at some of the other local accommodations. There are less expensive rooms at the delightful **Villa Marina**, white with blue trim,

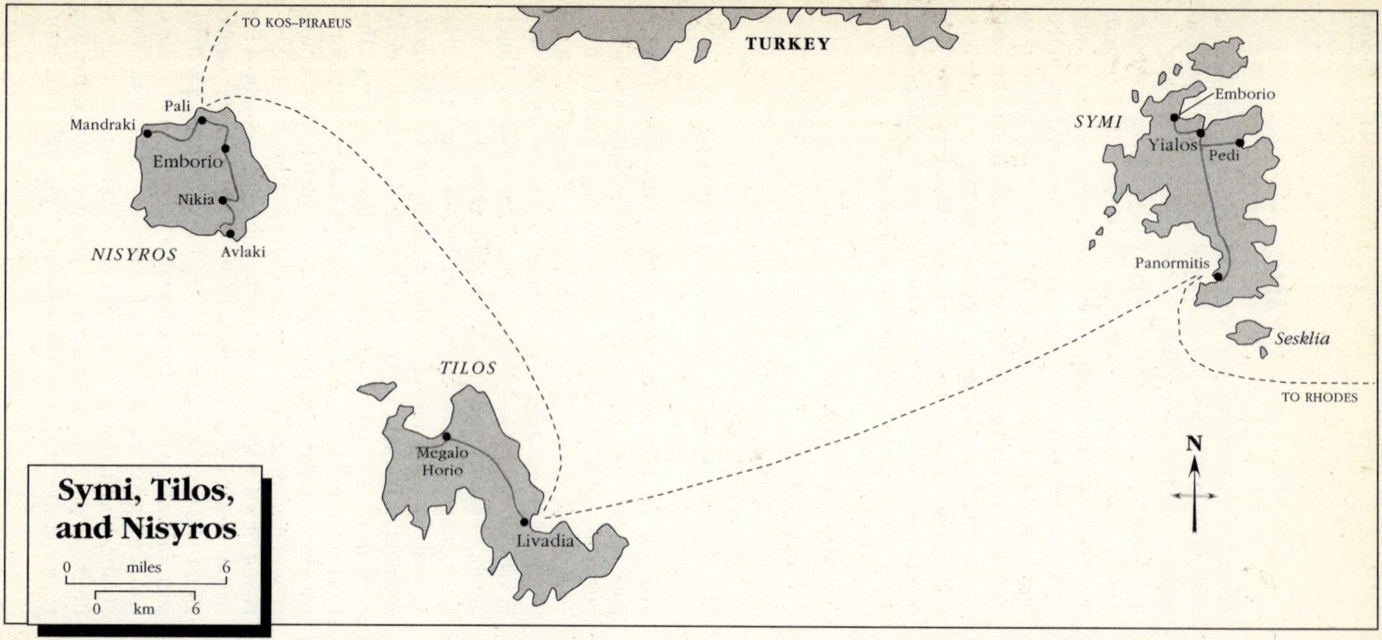
Symi, Tilos, and Nisyros
0 miles 6
0 km 6
TO KOS–PIRAEUS
TURKEY
Pali
Mandraki
Emborio
Nikia
Avlaki
NISYROS
TILOS
Megalo Horio
Livadia
SYMI
Emborio
Yialos
Pedi
Panormitis
Sesklia
TO RHODES
N

higher up the hill, and at many other small hotels and pensions. Swimming is from **Nos** beach, around another small headland past the boatyard.

Symiots built boats for the Trojan War, for the Crusaders, and later for the Turks. The advent of steamships severely reduced this lucrative trade, which came to a halt when wood from Turkey, grown on land owned by the islanders, was lost to them under the Italian occupation. The island suffered. Many of the elegant houses were abandoned until tourists began to arrive. It has now been a long time since any houses have stood empty on Symi.

The island caters to countless day trippers from Rhodes, who rarely stray far from the waterfront. Herbs are for sale everywhere, often encased in little pillows that are hand-painted—some with great skill, some merely with enthusiasm. Another Symiot specialty is delicious, sticky *frangósiko,* a sort of Turkish delight made from wild prickly pear.

The harbor is surrounded by restaurants, tavernas, and snack bars patronized by visitors but also by the fishermen who dry their nets in front of the souvenir shops. The Germans signed the surrender of the Dodecanese at the restaurant **Les Katerinettes**, on the harbor. This event is commemorated annually on May 8: Greek naval vessels put into the harbor and the town celebrates in a big way. (Les Katerinettes is among the best restaurants on the island, and George, the owner, also lets the beautiful old rooms above the restaurant.)

The port is really two towns: Higher up the hill it is seamlessly joined to **Horió**, the island's capital. Because of its endless steps, the connecting road ("Kali Strata") is still accessible only to donkey and foot traffic. Many a weary tourist pauses halfway up the road at **Jean and It** for refreshment. Jean, from Birmingham, England, has made the island her home for many years and welcomes both travellers and islanders who patronize her quiet, friendly bar. A house on the high side of town has been converted into a **museum** that displays costumes and other items of local interest. Despite the signs, it isn't easy to find.

The old **Kastro** is also a challenge to find because, once "up top," it is difficult to retain a sense of direction. One way to find the castle is to walk through the children's play area, just below Jean's bar, to the concrete road (which eventually changes to paving). At that point the castle is visible, as is the zigzag path that leads up to it. Crowning a small peak, the castle has been added to by all and sundry through the ages. Only the old wall remains, surrounding the church of the

Panayía, but the views are stunning. Near the windmills in Horio is the **Hotel Village**, composed of four small houses set on several levels round a courtyard. Again, this is a new hotel designed totally in keeping with its surrounding, one that offers comfort and a homey atmosphere.

A single road along the waterfront has been extended outside the town to reach Horio; it then trails gently down to the little port of **Pedi**, about 5 km (3 miles) to the east. An hourly minibus connects Pedi with Horio and Yialos, but it is a pleasant walk from Horio along a tree-lined road. The reasonably priced, two-story **Pedi Beach Hotel** here, with air-conditioning and its own sunbathing terraces, is very popular with families; the bay is quiet and safe for children. There are one or two tavernas and even a little snack bar offering Mystery Fudge Green Tomato Cake, made by a retired chemist who takes his recipes very seriously and prides himself on their unvarying quality. Small, sandy **Ayios Nikolaos** beach can be reached on foot along the hillside from Pedi, or by caïque.

Emborió, a dark-sand beach north of Yialos, can also be reached on foot. Pedi and Emborio are where Symiots spend the summer, as the sun's rays seem to concentrate in Yialos, making it too hot for comfort.

In spring or autumn it is possible to make the walk, partly through pine woods, to the aforementioned **monastery of Panormítis**, spreading along the sandy shore of a well-concealed bay in the southwest. The monks have simple rooms for the use of visitors, and there are shops and a museum as well as a single taverna near the monastery with good food and moderate prices. In August many Greek families combine a visit to the monastery with a vacation. There is no charge for the rooms, but a donation is naturally expected. The church contains numerous votive offerings from sailors.

Many of the island's beaches can be reached only by boat. The peninsula of **Ayios Emilianos** is a popular boat trip, as is the fertile island of **Sesklia**, near which the Athenians beat the Spartans in battle—but the Spartans returned next day with reinforcements and sank the Athenian fleet. The Athenians who escaped were said to have swum to Sesklia and there founded a colony. The Spartans annexed Symi and built a memorial on the hill above the windmills, the foundations of which are still visible.

TILOS

Tilos, southwest of Symi, has for long been little disturbed by visitors. It is now becoming more accessible, with interisland boats supplementing the ferries.

MAJOR INTEREST

Peace and quiet
No motorbikes and few other vehicles
Bones of (small) woolly mammoths
Deserted village of Mikro Horio

Tilos's port, **Livádia**, is a pleasant little village with a nice pebble beach, though it is too new to have much atmosphere. The inhabitants of Mikro Horio, on the mountain, moved here *en bloc* relatively recently, bringing their furniture and the roof tiles from their old houses.

There are several good tavernas in Livadia, including the **Blue Sky** bar by the quay, a good place to get information and to watch the to-ing and fro-ing on the quay when a boat comes in. Livadia has various accommodations. The **Irini Hotel**, in a small garden, offers room and breakfast. Unfortunately, breakfast is not served until 9:00 A.M., which is rather late for serious walkers who want to avoid the midday heat. The popular alternative is one of the simple, clean rooms in private houses by the long pebble beach. They provide good breakfasts as well as insect screens over the windows, often necessary.

The deserted village of **Mikró Horió** is a pleasant hour's walk west from Livadia, with the occasional tree for shade and wheeling hawks for company. The well-built stone houses are still standing, without roofs. In among the empty streets and gray walls the church stands brightly painted and well cared for. It is surrounded by railings to keep out marauding goats, but the cool porch is a good place for a picnic.

On the return journey the old road, still well maintained, is clearly visible. This makes an interesting alternative return route; from its heights old cave houses used by Germans during World War II outside Livadia can be seen.

The capital, **Megálo Horió**, in the northwest of the island, is even smaller than Livadia. A small **museum** housing the bones of woolly mammoths found on the island and a Venetian castle standing on the crag above it are its only claims to distinction. About a 45-minute walk away are the sandy beaches of **Ayios Antónios** and **Eristos**. The tavernas at Eristos offer fresh vegetables and locally caught fish. A bus runs daily from Livadia to Megalo Horio and the beaches. The island is very quiet and mercifully free of motorbikes. Except during the Feast of Saint Panteleímon, celebrated at the monastery in the far west of the island from July 25 to 27, a quiet stay is almost guaranteed.

NISYROS

An attractive, fertile island, Nísyros is best known for its semi-active volcano. Served by the same ferries as Symi and almost as popular, Nisyros draws its day visitors from Kos. The trip, in small caïques, is exhilarating for those who love a lively sea.

MAJOR INTEREST

Volcano
Picturesque coast and countryside, ideal for
    walking

This is a roughly circular island, about five miles in diameter. Legend has it that Nisyros is a lump of rock torn from Kos by the sea god Poseidon, who threw it at the giant Polyvotis, pinning him down. The giant has been trying to free himself ever since, and in 1522 succeeded in blowing out the center of the island. He made a weaker attempt in 1888.

Nisyros is prosperous and not dependent upon tourism. The quarrying of pumice provides a steady income, and the island is fringed with vineyards and fruit trees. If you are travelling in winter, don't miss the sight of the almond trees in blossom in February. Almonds are the basis of the nonalcoholic drink *soumáda,* a must for anyone who loves marzipan. The tavernas here serve good local wine.

From the quay, the main town of **Mandráki** (in the northwest corner of the island) is reached by an attractive promenade built over the black volcanic rocks that line the shore. Many of the island's small hotels are situated near the quay; more are being built all the time—mostly rectangular blocks with tiny balconies. The attractive **Porfyris**, which has its own swimming pool, looks out over a citrus grove to the sea. Just a little above it is the modest pension **Ipapandi**, built in the village style and delightfully situated. The **Romantzo**

Hotel, near the harbor, rents simple rooms and serves simple food and delicious fresh-squeezed lemonade.

Mandraki is squeezed in between rocks and sea, where the upward slope becomes gentler, though the roads are steep. The brightly painted houses are separated by a maze of little alleyways that run at all angles and seem to dictate the shapes of the houses, rather than the other way around. Balconies almost meet overhead. There are rooms to let in some of these intriguing houses; ask at the tourist office or in the square near the war memorial.

The shops are decorated with pictures showing their wares. The whole has a slightly toy-town air, enhanced, atop a small but steep hill, by the crumbling walls of the Venetian **Kastro**, which enclose the 19th-century **monastery of Panayía Spilíani**, open to visitors each morning from 10:00 A.M. (the few monks usually keep out of sight). It is possible to scramble down the other side of the hill onto a black-sand and pebble beach. In a small corner on the town side of the monastery is the **Dilino** (Sunset) **Restaurant**, whose specialty, lobster, can be enjoyed at sundown when the setting sun outlines the monastery and cliff with hazy color.

Within easy walking distance to the southwest of Mandraki is the **Paleokastro**, a small fortress whose massive, tightly fitting stones can only be of Mycenaean origin. Slightly farther away in the same direction is the **Evangelístria Monastery**, where the people of Mandraki celebrate Easter in style with food and wine for all.

Transport is one of the difficulties here, as the buses only run to Polybates, the island's volcano; the exception is a morning bus to **Nikia**, a pretty village in the south of the island. Many of the motorbikes for rent in the village are beat-up wrecks; the responsibility for insurance is with the renter.

After leaving the port the road divides to Pali village and Porfýris beach on the coast or to Emborio, whose scattered houses are mostly uninhabited, and Nikia village, farther south and suspended above the volcano with views of the other islands and Turkey. Beyond is **Avláki**, a delightful tree-lined beach. **Pali**, with its sheltered harbor, has a wide, white sandy beach, on the far side of which is a huge stone spa hotel, unfinished and apparently abandoned. Most of the new buildings in Pali, which now outnumber the old, are of the rectangular concrete variety. **Lies**, beyond Pali, has sand of a strange brownish color.

Excursion boats from Kos are met by buses headed for the volcano, **Polybates**. These take the road to the left, which climbs up the rim of the island above villages clinging to the shore among the rocks below and passes through the hamlet of Emborio at the crest of the rise before descending. Hardly a trace of green relieves the hard, pumice-colored ground of the central plateau. Fumes rise from holes in the floor of the small central crater, leaving a constant faint whiff of sulfur in the air.

Just offshore are several islets, notably **Yiali**, a huge pumice stone with a golden beach—a favorite destination on Saturdays when quarrying stops for the weekend.

GETTING AROUND

Symi: The road links Yialos, Horio, and Pedi. Taxis congregate near Symi Tours on the waterfront, from where a minibus leaves for Pedi. Tour buses run about four times a week in season to the monastery. In summer, boats make excursions to the best beaches around the island.

Tilos: There is a road from Livadia to Megalo Horio, beyond which it divides, going on to Ayios Antonios or Eristos. One bus daily links them. There are not many more than a dozen vehicles on the island. Bicycles can be rented in Megalo Horio.

Nisyros: Buses to the volcano synchronize with the arrival and departure of the tour boats from Kos. An erratic bus service links all the villages on the island. Motorcycles can be rented from the Romantzo Hotel in Mandraki.

Interisland: At least two weekly ferries link the islands with Piraeus in season. The eastern Aegean ferry links the three islands weekly throughout the year, visiting Rhodes–Symi–Tilos–Nisyros–Kos–Kalymnos and making the reverse trip the following day. One of these ferries, on return, links the islands to Rhodes, Kastellorizo, and the southern Dodecanese, Crete, and the Cyclades. Daily excursion boats in season visit Symi and sometimes Tilos from Rhodes, and Nisyros and Tilos from Kos.

—*Beryl Biggins*

KOS

Thirty miles long and about five across at its widest point, Kos lies on a northeast-to-southwest axis three miles from

Kos and Astypalaia

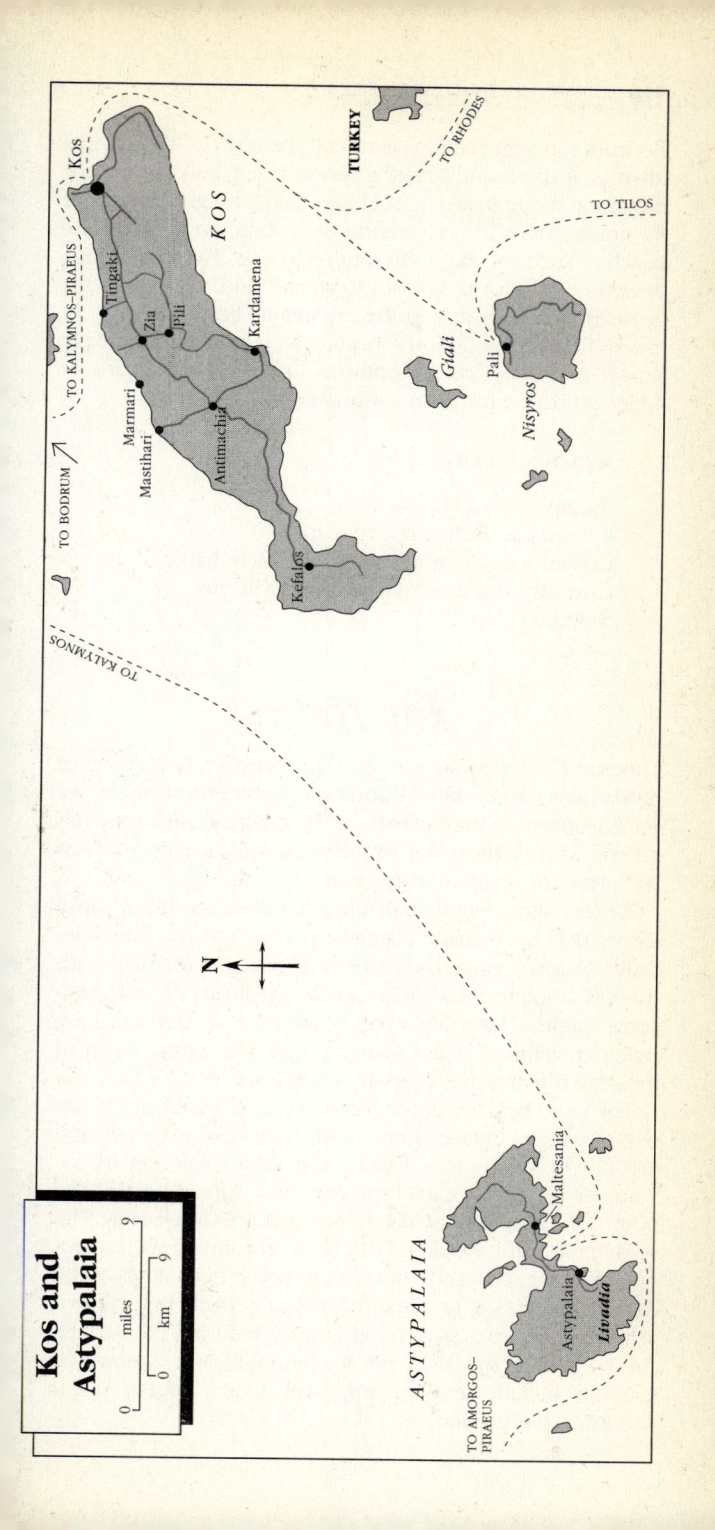

Bodrum (ancient Halicarnassus) on the coast of Turkey. Kos town is at the island's northernmost point, and the Dikeos mountain range forms a backbone along the greater part of its northeastern shore, ending in a long, wide sweep of beach at Kardamena on the southern coast. There are sandy beaches on both sides of Kos town and skirting the western coast. Between them and the mountains lies a flat plain of green fields. The island's beauty and mild climate have drawn visitors for many centuries, and the beaches are an added attraction for today's tourists.

MAJOR INTEREST

Asklepieion of Hippocrates
Roman and Hellenistic remains
Crusader castle and picturesque yacht harbor
Extensive beaches and mountain villages
Bicycling

KOS TOWN

Thousands of people arrive at Kos airport (just west of Kardamena) every week during the summer season, either on European charter planes or by Olympic Airways from Athens. Many visitors stay in the town, which caters to them and grows to accommodate them.

Writers often complain that Kos has been spoiled. It's true there have been many changes in recent years. The sidewalks in town, once mud, are now paved and bright with flowers (though the old trees still remain to provide welcome shade). The country roads have been surfaced, making easier travelling for the many cyclists who pedal down to their favorite beaches every morning.

The town beaches have changed, too. The factories to the west are gone; the tree-lined roads have been extended and are full of restaurants, hotels, and discos catering to the younger set. These establishments now spread around the point, which used to be the preserve of the Greek army. The soldiers are still there and can be seen sunning themselves outside their club, right next to the beach bungalows of the **Atlantis Hotel**. The first luxury hotel to be built west of town at Lambi, site of a new, huge holiday industry, the Atlantis was built when space was not at a premium, and its attractive grounds include a swimming pool, tennis courts, and a children's playground.

From the town beach, fringed with tamarisks, the hydrofoil leaves daily for Rhodes and, in season, for Patmos and other islands. Along the waterfront and in adjacent streets are many hotels of modest size, such as the older **Hara**, which has cool marble floors and spacious rooms, and the homey **Hotel Koala**, where there is always a big-hearted Australian welcome. A couple of miles beyond, standing in magnificent position on Cape Psalídi, is the **Hippocrates Palace**, one of the few hotels on Kos with air-conditioning, also with its own swimming pool and good conference facilities. Continuing past the cape of Ayios Fokás, the road reaches **Thermae**, with a fine beach and sulfur springs. Here the road ends and the Dikeos mountains sweep into the sea.

At the heart of Kos town the fishing boats now share **Mandráki harbor** with dozens of visiting yachts and tour boats headed for the islands of Nisyros, Pserimos (which we do not discuss), Astypalaia, Kalymnos, Leros, and Patmos, or for Bodrum in Turkey. The evening stroll has become an opportunity to compare tour prices, which vary considerably, and to choose the next day's outing. There is now bus service from the harbor to Ayios Fokas and Lambi beaches.

The harbor, flanked by restaurants, tour agencies, fountains, trees, and flowerbeds, is dominated by the large 15th-century **Castle of the Knights**, whose moat was long ago converted into a palm-lined avenue. This is the first sight of Kos for those who arrive by sea. Ferries and cruise ships, too large to enter the harbor, tie up under its walls.

Immediately behind the castle, beside the old mosque of Hadji Hassan, is the ancient **Hippocrates' plane tree**, which is really only about a half-dozen centuries old. Its center is hollow and its great branches seem to sprout from little more than the bark. Old marble columns are no longer sufficient to support them, and their weight is now supported by scaffolding.

A few steps lead down from beside the mosque to the foundations of the agora and harbor quarter of the **Hellenic town**, the buildings destroyed by an earthquake in A.D. 554 and the remains revealed by another quake in 1933. Stroll under palm trees along the ancient roads passing under the arch of the Crusaders' "Tax Gate" to reach Plateía Eleftherías, the modern town's Italianate central square, still called the Piazza by the Koans. To the right is the **museum**, exceptionally well endowed with statues from temples of various periods, perhaps because Xenophon, physician to the emperor Claudius, imported statues instead of carrying them off to Rome, as was usual during the Roman occupation of

Greece. Demeter and Persephone, Artemis, Aphrodite, and Athena—all are represented, with Hippocrates welcoming Asklepios as he steps ashore.

In Vas. Pavlou, off the square, is the Olympic Airways terminal, to the right of which is the road to the bus station. Improved services now run to the beaches and to the little villages that used to be isolated. In the center of town are the comfortable modern rooms of **Mustapha Tseleri**, each with bathroom and balcony access, at 29 Eleftherios Venizélou Street. On the same street, near the post office, is Kosland Tours, an extremely helpful source for accommodations for both individuals and groups; they also provide exchange and excellent car-rental facilities.

The Old Town

Iféstou, Apelou, and adjoining streets, in the center of Kos town, have been dubbed the Old Town and are now lined with shops selling tourist souvenirs, including excellent gold and silver jewelry. Look for the sign of Ifestos, the Jewellers Association of Kos, Kalymnos, and Leros, for guaranteed quality. There are fine ceramics to be bought in Filita Street, where **Gallerie Anemos** and **Gallery Katrin** sell ceramics by modern artists. Shops with marble figures, onyx, icons, perfumes, enamels, handmade embroideries and laces, silk-painted cushions, and many other items all vie for attention. Unlike most tourist shops, they close on Sundays.

At the end of the Old Town is a *plateía* with a small minaret, once lonely but now surrounded by touristy restaurants with pop music and fairy lights, behind which is hidden an old Turkish *hamám* (bath house). The **Hamam**, now a taverna serving simple grills and salads, is not easy to find, but there is a back entrance behind the minaret. Follow the path through a wilderness of dried wildflowers and grasses to the small, irregular courtyard; tables are set under the spreading branches of a Mouria tree, whose sweet fruits look like pale-green loganberries. Flowers bloom riotously, pines and cypresses form a backdrop, and stars can be seen overhead. In an earlier life the Hamam's proprietor, George, was a master butcher, and his expertise in choosing meat ensures that the quality cannot be bettered. He and his wife, Eva, work hard to cope with all the trade; customers who return—and most do—sometimes find themselves volunteering their services on busy nights.

The Hamam stands on the edge of another large archaeological site in Gregoriou Fifth Street, with mosaic pavements and scraps of wall paintings. On the opposite side of the road is a small but charming **Roman odeion** (concert hall) set in a grove of cypress trees. On the same road is a restored **Roman house**, the only antiquity in the town for which an entry fee is charged.

The Asklepieion

The most famous of the Koan antiquities, the Asklepieion, is a couple of miles southwest of town. There is no public bus, so take a tour or a taxi, rent a car or a bicycle, or walk—but go! This is something not to be missed.

Hippocrates, the most famous healer of ancient times and the father of modern medicine, was born in Kos about 460 B.C. He taught at the Asklepieion, though the present site wasn't completed until after his death, its predecessor having been destroyed in an earthquake.

This sanctuary, dedicated to Asklepios, the god of healing, was both a place of pilgrimage and a place of healing. Patients came from all over the ancient Greek world and would sacrifice to the god, pray for a cure, and put themselves into the hands of the doctor-priests. The sanctuary had temples, shops, water, and houses for the patients who, accompanied by relatives, would settle in for an extended stay. There was a stadium for the games, which were dedicated to the god, as were the various performances in the theater. Built on a series of wide terraces amid thick woods on the lower slope of the mountain, the sanctuary overlooks the fields and the sea, beyond which the Turkish coast can be seen.

The spring that provided water for the sanctuary still gushes, undiminished, into a stone trough around which the patients and their relatives congregated. On the upper terraces are the foundations of several temples. Here the ceremony of the Hippocratic oath is occasionally reenacted; flower-garlanded girls shower rose petals in the path of the young doctors newly admitted to the mysteries, while a goatherd plays his haunting tune on a reed pipe.

In addition to Hippocrates, another famous son of Kos was Ptolemy II. Other Ptolemies were regular visitors, including Cleopatra, who left her jewels at the Asklepieion for safekeeping. She wore the fine silk for which the island was renowned, and which was so transparent that the women of Messenia were forbidden to wear it at religious initiations. Ezra Pound described it as "a gleam of Cos . . . a slither of dyed stuff."

The approach to the Asklepieion is through the Turkish village of **Platáni**, where the spread of tables under the plane trees is another practice that has endured. The tavernas still serve only traditional dishes, and the prices are reasonable.

The Villages

The main artery of the island skirts Mount Dikeos. Side roads wind up its gentle lower slopes to small villages with stunning views over green fields to broad beaches, a white expanse of salt pans, and across to the Turkish coast.

Zia, 14 km (9 miles) southwest of town, where the tour companies take visitors for a Greek taverna night, is well worth a visit during the day. The gardens are bright with flowers, and it is possible to walk up through the trees to a little church where a prolific spring must have ensured this site as scared to earlier religions, too. The water is now piped down to the village of Zipári.

Pili, west of Zia, also has running water: a spring from which the cold, clear liquid gushes out of six pipes night and day throughout the year. Turn right above the plateia to the spring, or walk uphill and bear left to reach the ancient *tholos* with 12 crypts—believed to be the tomb of a mythical king, Harmylos.

Excellent wine is made in the villages, but the air alone can be intoxicating. Take the 7:00 A.M. bus up to Pili when the morning is fresh and the mountaintop is fringed with a puff of cloud. Have a coffee before walking down through the green fields to **Marmari** on the northern coast for an early swim. The cool, pleasant lounge of the **Panorama Hotel**, right on the beach in Marmari, offers welcome shade and refreshments.

The main road continues southwest down the length of the island as far as Kefalos on the craggy peninsula at the southern end, passing through a crossroads at **Antimáchia**, where there is a working windmill and a café selling delicious homemade ice cream. To the left, past the airport, is **Kardámena**. This old fishing village on the southern coast has now become a package holiday village with restaurants, furnished apartments, and hotels, where families take advantage of a safe beach for children and babysitter services. There are day trips from here to the island of Nisyros, though the local bus service into Kos town is poor.

To the right, on the northern coast, is another fishing village, **Mastihári**, which has become a small port for people travelling to Kalymnos direct from the airport. It has accommodations and food as well as a wide beach, mostly empty even in summer. This coast has many beaches, most of them nearer Kos town, such as the previously mentioned Marmari and **Tingáki**, with tavernas, one or two small hotels, and a few pensions here and there by the fields leading to the beach. Tingaki is fast becoming a suburb of Kos town.

The main road continues past Antimachia to **Kéfalos** through the neck of the island past a five-mile-long beach that begins at **Ayios Stéfanos**. The remains of a fifth-century basilica were discovered on the grounds of the Club Med complex in Kefalos, now due to be opened to a more general clientele. The water tends to be a bit warmer on the stretch known as **Bubble Beach**, where volcanic fumes bubble up from the seabed.

On each side of the road to Kefalos are numerous hotels and pensions. The **Kordistos Hotel**, almost on the beach itself, has cool rooms protected from the sun by arcaded balconies. This is a friendly, comfortable, relaxing hotel in pleasant surroundings. All manner of sea sports are available in the bay, and there are numerous tavernas along the beach. The **Skala** serves light snacks and is popular with the local residents—always a good sign.

Kefalos town stands very high near the entrance to the peninsula, little visited by tourists. There are several old windmills, and from the highest of them, a few minutes' walk from the center, the views are splendid. Due south there are some interesting caves that are used as stores by the villagers; turning counterclockwise it is possible to see the Knidos peninsula of Turkey, Nisyros, Yiali, the bay off Ayios Stefanos filled with sails, northern Kos, Kalymnos, and, on a good day, the end of the Bodrum peninsula.

Beaches in the Kefalos area are rugged and isolated, reachable over four or five miles of rough track. Suitable vehicles are for hire in the town, and most of the roads in Kos are safe for mopeds and scooters—but the most popular vehicle on the island is the humble bicycle. They are everywhere on the roads; the trees outside every hotel in town prop up a dozen or more. This is one island where bells are not associated with goats.

GETTING AROUND

In season there are daily ferries linking Piraeus and Rhodes via Patmos, Leros, Kalymnos, and Kos, as well as one or two via Paros, Amorgos, Astypalaia, Kalymnos, Kos, Nisyros, Tilos, and Symi. There is also a hydrofoil service from Rhodes to Kos, daily in summer. Another weekly boat visits the northeastern Aegean islands. Careful checking of the existence and times of all ferries is essential.

There are Olympic Airways flights to and from Athens (three daily), Rhodes (two daily), Leros (three weekly), and Samos and Thessaloniki (once weekly). Schedules are subject to change.

Ferry service connects Kos with Bodrum, Turkey. Kos is a port of entry for Greece.

—*Beryl Biggins*

ASTYPALAIA

Kalymnos, Leros, and Patmos, remnants of the same mountain chain, form a broken line. Astypálaia is over to the west, almost part of the Cyclades and sharing much of their architectural style. One of a number of islands served by a poor ferry service between Piraeus and Rhodes, it has recently been made more accessible by ferries from Kos and Kalymnos. As you approach the butterfly-shaped island from Piraeus, the first thing that strikes you is the number of rocks piercing the surface of the water; you can't help wondering how many lurk just below the surface! This is not an area for sailing without good charts. The first sight of the island is the castle, which appears to grow out of the craggy hill on which it stands.

MAJOR INTEREST

Cycladic architecture
Venetian castle
Good walking

The town, Astypalaia, or Skala, straggles up from the port, but the older houses huddle together beneath the castle walls. The **castle** was built in the 13th century by a Venetian, John Quirini, and stayed in the same family for many generations—the Crusaders didn't get this far. Above its vaulted gateway rises the **church of Our Lady of the Castle**, a wonderful confection of domes, arches, and planes. The **church of Ayios Theólogos**, another Cycladic gem, stands within the castle walls among derelict houses of three and four stories that have been occupied within living memory. It's a peaceful spot where lizards sun themselves on the stone walls. A few long-lived trees add a little shade, and here and there a section of marble column acts as a reminder that this was the site of the old acropolis.

On the saddle of the hill, below the castle, nine windmills stand abandoned. With panoramic views of the northern bays and the surrounding islands, they would make wonderful vacation homes.

The hotels are down by the port or on the road leading to it. The **Vivamare** has self-catering apartments; those at the front are rather noisy. (No one is left for long in ignorance of the most popular form of transport, the motorbike.) The **Paradissos Hotel** is rather quieter. Meanwhile, those who prefer private homes to modern amenities may find rooms in the village. (Contact Gournas Travel; Tel: 0243-613-34.)

The taverna by the ferry serves good Greek food and is the only place open out of season, except for the coffeehouses. **Nick's**, by the harbor's small pebble beach, serves drinks, generous helpings of octopus or squid, and salad.

The island is divided into two parts connected by a narrow strip of land. The town is in the western section facing south, as is the nearby beach of **Livádia** and the **monastery of Ayios Ioánnis**, a working farm in a well-watered valley a two-hour trek over the hills to the west.

Across the connecting strip is one other village, **Maltesania**, named for the Maltese pirates who were once based here. Its beach, **Análipsi**, is secluded enough for nude bathing. The road soon peters out but a quite reasonable track leads north to **Vathý**, a deep bay. Transport to the nearly landlocked bay is by taxi, the driver phoning ahead to arrange a boat for the last stretch. A single family farms the land and also runs a small taverna "on demand." The fish can be chosen on your arrival and cooked while your appetite is sharpened by a swim in the calm waters of the sea loch.

GETTING AROUND

Astypalaia is not well served by ferries. Up to three weekly from Piraeus go via several Cycladic islands, including Amorgos and Paros. Coming the other way, they visit Kalymnos, Kos, Nisyros, Tilos, and Symi once a week. Excursion boats run several times a week in season from Kos, Kalymnos, and Rhodes. In winter, ferries sometimes dock at Vathy, when winds are contrary. On such occasions, a bus runs to Astypalaia town.

There is a sporadic bus service. Four a day leave the port for Livadia. Two a day go east to Analipsi beach, near where the two wings of the butterfly meet. Gournas Travel (Tel: 0243-613-34) runs boat trips twice weekly to Vathy in season. Otherwise, travel is by taxi or on foot.

—*Beryl Biggins*

KALYMNOS

With two ferry lines from Piraeus and with its proximity to Kos and its convenient airport, Kálymnos is easy to get to. The island basically consists of three long mountain ranges on a southeast to northwest axis, with two valleys between. The capital and port, Pothia, lies at one end of a valley between two mountains on the south coast. At the other end of the valley, on the west coast, is a cluster of small resorts, including Myrties, which faces the offshore island of Telendos. Citrus plantations cover the second, parallel valley. The bare northern mountains reach almost to Leros.

MAJOR INTEREST

Untouristy atmosphere
Clinging mountain villages

Kalymnos has for centuries been an island of sponge divers. They would leave their homes after Easter and not return until the end of summer. Easter, the most important festival in the Orthodox year, had even greater meaning to these men, as it marked their last sight of home and loved ones for six months. They fasted through Lent, gloried in Christ's rising, and feasted for a week before leaving. When they returned with money earned they celebrated again. The women of the island, left alone for half the year, are reputed to be very independent. In recent times the Mediterranean sponges began to get very scarce, and the divers had to go first to Italy, then to the northwest African coast to harvest them. Now pollution has taken its toll and there are no more sponges in the Mediterranean. The islanders are having to find new ways to make a living.

Póthia is quite large and colorful and, though not particularly attractive, has a lively character. It continues well inland up the valley and spreads around the bay, which is dominated by a huge cross—an indication of a very religious island. The number of large and beautiful modern churches confirms this.

Visitors are surprised by the many lovely sculptures in the town and throughout Kalymnos, 44 in all. Forty-three of these are the work of Michael Kokkinos and his daughter Irene, who donated them to the island. The **museum** is housed in the charming Vouvalis villa, donated by the owner, and contains the villa's original 19th-century furnishings together with a small collection of archaeological remains found in various caves on the island. Houses large and small, with and without gardens, line the confusing back streets; there are private rooms of all descriptions to let. To the right of the harbor behind the cathedral is **Manoli's** restaurant, where the food is pure Greek. No English is spoken; walk into the kitchen and take a look.

From the cathedral the road leads to Plateía Kýprou, where the taxis wait, and continues, shaded by gum trees, to the villages and shingle beaches of the west coast. Laden with history, this road first passes a castle built by Crusaders high on its acropolis, then a much earlier citadel, ancient Damos, one of the largest settlements of the Mycenaeans. Only a few huge blocks remain from its mysterious past, along with the wells, down below by the roadside, which are still in use.

Near the wells a small path leads to remnants of two early Christian churches. A mosaic showing leaves and fishes is all that remains of **Ayía Iríni**. Part of the **church of Christ of Jerusalem** still stands, and Apollo's name from an earlier temple is still clear on one of the marble uprights.

Several of the resort villages, notably **Kandouni, Myrtiés**, and **Massoúri** on the west coast, have small hotels, guesthouses, and restaurants clinging to the steep sides of the road above the sea or below the mountain. Kandouni nestles below a tiny monastery, occupied by monks who have not only seen the empty beach below them develop into a small tourist resort, but are now having to endure the construction of an airstrip on the mountain top above their heads. The beach is a small crescent of sand, separated by a huge rock from Linaria beach, where an old *ouzerí* still offers grilled octopus and other fishy snacks (evenings only). On the road into Linaria, away from heavy traffic and close to the beach, is the very modern **Elies Hotel**, delightfully set in a well-planned garden around a pleasant swimming pool.

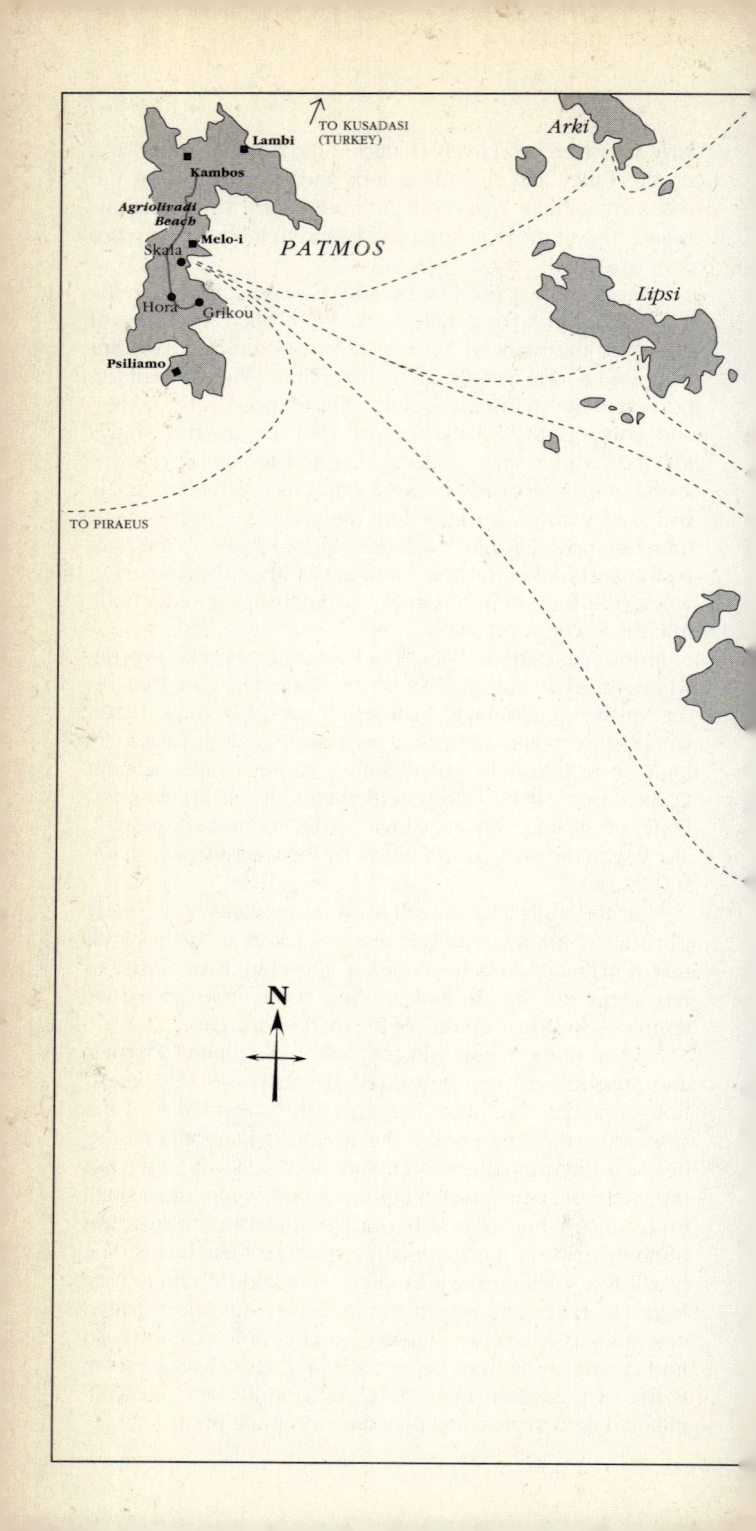

PATMOS

- Lambi
- Kambos
- Agriolivadi Beach
- Skala
- Melo-i
- Hora
- Grikou
- Psiliamo

TO KUSADASI (TURKEY)

Arki

Lipsi

TO PIRAEUS

N

Kalymnos, Leros, and Patmos

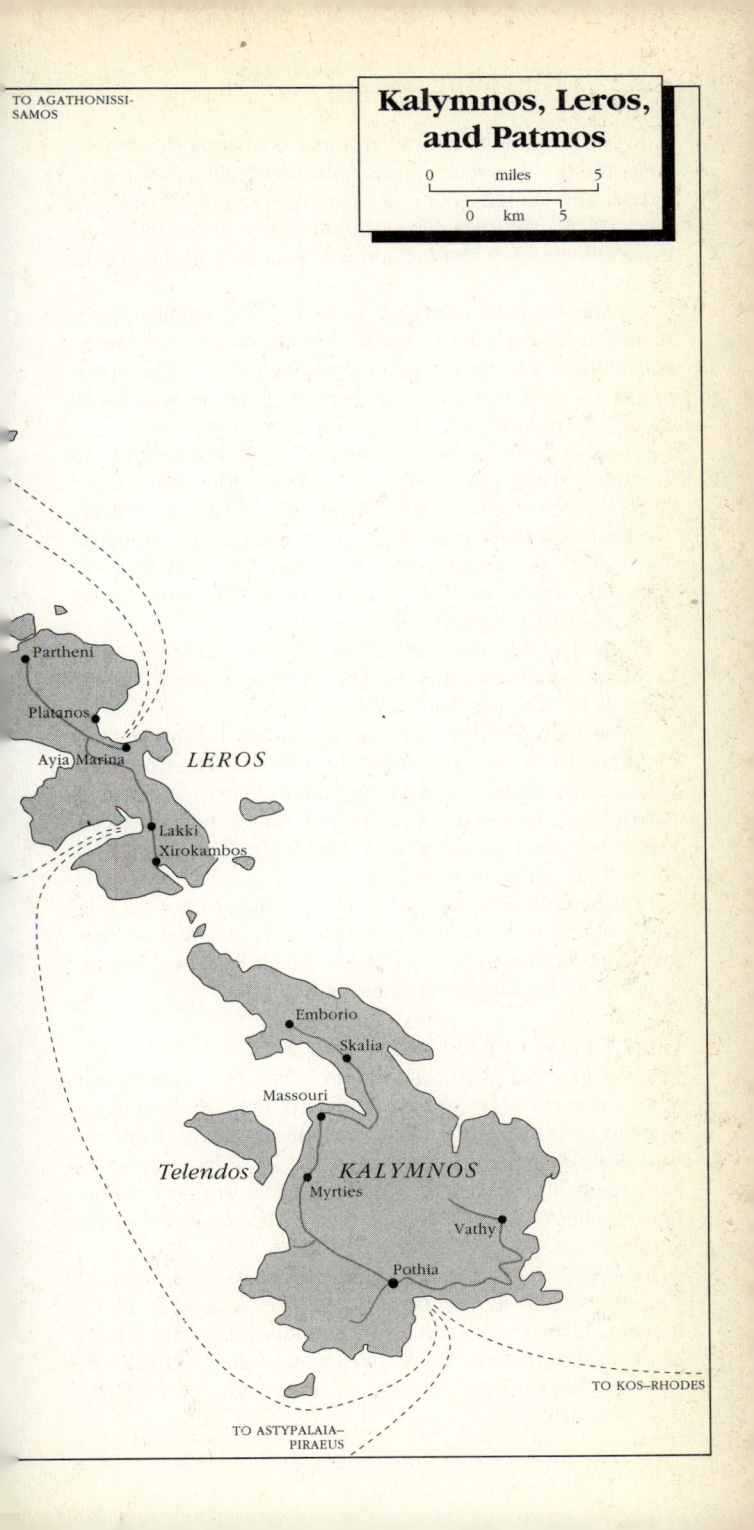

TO AGATHONISSI-SAMOS

TO KOS–RHODES

TO ASTYPALAIA–PIRAEUS

LEROS
- Partheni
- Platanos
- Ayia Marina
- Lakki
- Xirokambos

KALYMNOS
- Emborio
- Skalia
- Massouri
- Myrties
- Vathy
- Pothia

Telendos

In Myrties, on the landward side, the **Atlantis Hotel** has a welcoming atmosphere and a substantial library of paperbacks. The dining room is open to the public, and the terrace has extensive views of the coast in either direction, especially lovely when the sun is setting behind the islet of Telendos.

On the seaward side, also in Myrties, the **Agelika Apartments** have spacious rooms, each with kitchen, bathroom, and terrace. The gardens run down to the sea. The apartments are owned and run by a charming family who speak excellent English.

Little boats run a constant shuttle service from Myrties to **Télendos**, which has a very good beach, and a daily caïque runs between Myrties and Xirokambos on Leros (see below). The **Restaurant Myrties** by the pier is a good place to watch all the coming and going. Under the water lies a city that was buried by seismic activity in A.D. 554 during the same 14-day earthquake that destroyed Roman Kos.

From Massouri, just north of Myrties, the road runs north between mountains and sea as far as **Emborió**, where several tavernas have rooms with private showers.

Once a day the bus runs east and then north over the mountain from Pothia to **Vathý**. This pleasant little tree-lined village is set at the end of a large valley of citrus orchards. A narrow fjord connects it with the sea. Above the fjord is the Daskaleios cave, inhabited in Neolithic times and used as a shrine through many centuries.

From Pothia or from Myrties it is possible to book a full-day boat trip around the island, including a stop at the larger **grotto of Kefalas** in the southwest, which has considerable stalactite and stalagmite formations.

GETTING AROUND

Buses run from the cathedral in Pothia to Myrties and Massouri every hour and a half and continue three times a week to Emborio. The daily bus to Vathy also leaves from the waterfront near the cathedral. Taxi fares are by tariff or by agreement, and are usually very reasonable. For more information, check with Blue Islands Travel, Charalambos Square, Pothia; Tel: (0243) 230-55.

In season there is a daily ferry to Piraeus via Leros and Patmos, usually in the evenings. There is a daily early-morning ferry going south to Kos and Rhodes. A weekly boat heads back to Piraeus via Astypalaia, Amorgos, and Patmos. Another weekly boat travels north through most of the islands to Samos.

Excursion boats go in season to Kos town (at least daily), Mastihari on Kos (twice daily), Leros, Patmos, and Nisyros. One small boat leaves Myrties daily for Xirokambos (Leros). There is an all-day shuttle between Myrties and Telendos. An excursion boat from Pothia visits the islet of Pserimos to the southeast.

—*Beryl Biggins*

LEROS

Leros has never been a tourist island, and so is discovered with delight by people who find the countryside beautiful and who enjoy staying in one of the island's old mansions, now restored and modernized.

A green island just north of Kalymnos and southeast of Patmos, with rolling hills, country paths, and a jagged coastline full of little coves and long beaches, it is ideal for walking; every turn brings a new view.

MAJOR INTEREST

Swimming
Good walking

On two of Leros's several bays are the ports of **Lakkí**, where the main ferries stop, and Ayia Marina, just below Platanos, the capital. The Italians built submarine pens in the huge, deep bay of Lakki, along with a new town of villas and gardens set on wide, straight avenues. To the new arrival the town of Lakki appears to sleep amid its palm trees. Only two of the little shops in the old Italian market are still open; the others have closed, not for lack of business but because they have been replaced by large, modern emporiums scattered rather haphazardly around the town. The sports shop has a most imposing entrance, and an elegant shoe store is furnished with deep armchairs, potted plants, and floor-to-ceiling mirrors. The seeming lack of customers is due to the fact that most people are at work, employed in the large psychiatric hospital housed in buildings once used by the Italian navy.

Just out of town on a byroad is the delightfully situated **Angelou Pension**, part of a working farm. Its apartments are spacious and well furnished; terraces overlook a citrus grove, the wide bay, and the distant hills. Handier for a short stay is the modest but comfortable **Hotel Katerina**, on the same road as the Italian market; at the side of the market the simple taverna **Sotos** offers good Greek food. Farther back in the town, at 7 Ayias Olgas Street, is **Pension Zorzou**, a large, modern, private establishment totally in keeping with its elegant surroundings. The rooms are pleasant and well appointed, the house stands in a large garden with walks and benches, and there is a very nice swimming pool.

In the same class is the secluded **Koulouki** restaurant, set on terraces by the water, just past the quay. The half-hidden road here leads through the trees to the village of Kouloúki and along the northern side of the bay.

The road south leads to the village of **Xirókambos**, hemmed in by high cliffs, from which you can take fine walks over the mountains both east and west.

The road north from Lakki, and many footpaths, lead to Platanos, passing **Pantéli**, a bayside resort town where chickens and goats still outnumber the tourists for most of the year.

Ponteli can be reached by field paths from Lakki or from **Ayía Marína**, just around the headland, which is used by local interisland ferries, excursion boats from Kos, fishing boats, and yachts. Ayia Marina is a quiet place with several good tavernas, presided over by a statue of Papa Anastasis, archimandrite and fighter for independence. His first 65 years (he was born in 1880) spanned three different foreign occupations—but happily he lived for 10 more years to enjoy the freedom he had struggled for.

From Ayia Marina two roads lead up to Platanos; the post and telephone offices are on the one on the right. On the left at the fork is a well-stocked (unnamed) craft shop with many unusual items: wise-looking puppets; gourds painted to resemble Russian dolls, devout priests, and demure maidens; and delicate batiks.

The roads meet at **Plátanos** (Hora) in the plateia, a tiny space hardly big enough for the vehicles to edge around the central plane tree. The Venetian **Kastro** perches high above the houses. Access is by steps—one for each day of the year—or hair-raising taxi ride. But it's worth it, both for the **Byzantine museum** in the castle, established by the bishop of Leros after several years of hard work, and for the magnificent views, so magnificent that the army uses the inner fortress for observation, as the Italians did during their occupation in World War II.

When the Italian army surrendered, British troops occupied the islands but were without air cover and were driven out by German airborne forces. Almost the entire British force on Leros was wiped out; there is a small English cemetery at **Alinda**, just north of Platanos. The village straggles around a long tamarisk-fringed shore; there are a few hotels here, including the best on the island, the **Malleas Beach**, a stonefaced, well-designed building, with all rooms facing the sea; shady terraces; a relaxed, comfortable air; and an efficient and obliging staff. The **Gianna Hotel**, a little way in from the shore, has excellent views.

Alinda also has a museum, **Belleni's Tower**, open 9:00 A.M. to noon and 6:00 to 9:00 P.M. The curator accompanies visitors and is extremely knowledgeable about the exhibits, which include musical instruments, kitchen equipment, an old ouzo still, and many other items of interest. There is also a splendid collection of old printing machines operated by hand or foot, pressers and binders, a guillotine, and page layouts, in addition to an array of old printed books (one handwritten from the 17th century), a selection of newspapers, including one dated 1941 with a beautifully printed full-color map, and many political and war cartoons from the same period.

Roads and footpaths lead to other bays on the ragged coast, and there is a bus that serves many of them. The times are listed at the bus stops, but the drivers do not seem to read the notices. The army occupies a large camp in the north of the island, past the airport, and uses much of the surrounding countryside for maneuvers, sharing it with innumerable goats. Photography is forbidden in much of the area.

GETTING AROUND

Travelling on Leros is by bus and taxi, moped and bike, or on foot. Buses leave from the main square in Platanos, visiting Lakki and Xirokambos six times daily and Partheni (near the airport) via Alinda three times daily. Service is erratic. Taxis congregate in the main square in Platanos (Tel: 230-70) and at Lakki (Tel: 225-50). Mopeds and bikes can be rented in both centers.

Olympic Airways flies to and from Athens at least three times a week, and there are flights two or three times a week to Kos in season.

The big ferries dock at Lakki. In season there are daily ferries to Piraeus, Patmos, Kalymnos, Kos, and Rhodes. The interisland ferry visits twice weekly, first going north as far as Samos, then south the following day, ending up in Rhodes.

Excursion boats to and from Patmos and Lipsi to the north leave from Ayia Marina. There is at least one a day in season to Lipsi, and there are one or two weekly to Patmos. Excursion boats run according to demand.

—*Beryl Biggins*

PATMOS

Once known vaguely as the spot where Saint John wrote the Revelation (in Greek, *apokálipsi*), and conjuring up visions of crags, caves, and austere dark-stoned monasteries, Patmos, the northernmost of the larger islands of this group, has recently been gaining a reputation as the Mykonos of the Dodecanese. This in turn has evoked alternative images of sun-browned bodies, Beautiful People, a sparkling sea lapping golden beaches, and labyrinthine streets of blinding white Cubistic architecture. Throughout its history (at least the part that began with the still-disputed visit of Saint John in A.D. 95) the island has maintained a delicate balance between the sacred and the profane, with both profiting from the other's presence and doing so with a judicious amount of respect. It is a combination, too, that works greatly in the favor of visitors in search of both riotous fun and restful quiet, a twosome rarely found together elsewhere.

MAJOR INTEREST

Monastery of St. John the Theologian
Monastery of the Apocalypse
Town of Hora
Beaches

Patmos's size—it is seven miles long and three miles across at its widest—is both convenient and deceptive. In outline it resembles a sea horse floating upon its side, head to the north, nose pointing toward Turkey, and its navel the eastward-facing port of Skala, nerve center of the island. From here connections are easily made via the north–south spine of Patmos's only road or by sea with the outlying farming and fishing communities and major beaches, all in coves and bays on the eastern side. These are reachable by car in five to ten minutes or by caïque in twice that time.

In the meantime, in the "pouch" of the seahorse, dominating Skala and its harbor from a hillside to the south, is the brooding mass of the fortress-like monastery of St. John. Rising from the midst of the capital town of Hora and providing a striking contrast to the commercial bustle of the port below, the monastery is just a ten-minute drive up the winding road from Skala. On the way is the monastery of the Apocalypse, which covers the hillside cave where Saint John prayed and then received his revelations.

With a car or even a fast motor launch, it is possible to see most of Patmos in a day. On the other hand, exploring its many coves, bays, and tiny, secluded beaches can absorb an entire or even several summers.

The same can be said for the intricate reaches of its history. For an island so seemingly out of the well-trodden marches of time, Patmos has had an extraordinarily eventful past, more suitable to a historical romance than a tiny, monkish hideaway in the Aegean. Aside from having been the site of the writing of the Apocalypse, Patmos has been protected by kings, popes, and pashas, sacked by the Venetians, annexed by the Italians, occupied by the Nazis, and, most recently, chosen as a summer retreat by some of the most powerful men of the contemporary world, including the Aga Khan and Axel Springer, the late German press lord. Patmos has also been the home of one of the wealthiest Mediterranean merchant fleets of the 16th and 17th centuries, the repository of some of the most valuable ecclesiastical treasures in the Orthodox world, the site of a theological school so important to Ottoman-occupied Greece that it was called a "substitute for ancient Athens," and the birthplace of three of the most prominent leaders of Greece's War of Independence against the Turks.

For visitors from cruise ships with only a few hours to spend on the island, visits to the monasteries of the Apocalypse and St. John are essential, if only to see from outside the latter the extraordinary view of the island and the vast expanse of the Aegean spread out below (with Samos often visible in the north and Turkey to the east). Also recommended is a stroll through the whitewashed, maze-like streets of Hora with its 16th- and 17th-century mansions, the former homes of wealthy ship-owning merchants now beautifully restored by the wealthy and not-so-wealthy artists, actors, and business people who came to cherish their crumbling elegance in the 1960s and 1970s. If time permits, also visit the enchanting nunnery of Zoodochos Pigi nestled in Hora's southeastern corner.

Those with days or weeks to spare will have an opportunity to savor the more hedonistic side of Patmian life: the nightlife of Skala and Hora; the wonderful variety of the island's beaches, from the multicolored pebbles of Lambi to the fine, pure sand of Psiliamo; the surprisingly high-quality food, from the lunchtime fare on the beach at Kambos to the quiet decorum of dinner in a restored mansion at the hilltop town of Hora; and, finally, excursions to the nearby islands of Arki and Lipsi and to the Turkish port of Kuşadası and its magnificent nearby ruins of Ephesus (the site of one of the schools of pre-Socratic Greek philosophy), from which Saint John embarked on his exile to Patmos.

Staying on Patmos

Finding accommodations from which to begin these explorations can often be an adventure in itself, particularly at the height of the season, in July and August. Patmos's sudden emergence in the 1970s as a resort as well as a religious center took most of the islanders by surprise, and only recently has there been a boom in hotel construction. Before that a search for a bed for the night often ended on a beach or a makeshift cot in the living room of one of the Patmian women who await arriving ships with offers of a "room"; as this scenario occasionally has been played out even in recent years, it is imperative to book accommodations in advance.

The only hotels not in Skala or its outskirts are the remote but small and charming **Dolphin Hotel** on the pebble beach of the northern coast at Lambi, and the **Xenia** in Grikou, a secluded and picturesque bayside location on the southeastern coast. Set on the beach in a grove of tamarisk trees, the clean and well-serviced Xenia offers considerable peace and quiet but somewhat limited access to the rest of the island, with infrequent bus and caïque connections throughout the day. Also available in Grikou are modern, well-appointed rooms and apartments rented out by the owners of the beautifully situated **Flisvos Taverna**, set on a rocky promontory overlooking the center of the bay.

Skala tends to be packed in summer, as it is both the site of the island's major hotels and the hub of its communications network, including the post office, banks, and telecommunications office. The recent boom has resulted in the construction of several new hotels, two of them with the very welcome inclusion of salt-water swimming pools (considered redundant only by those visitors who have never been stranded at midday in Skala without a taxi or caïque in sight). These are the **Skala** and **Romeo** hotels, equally well appointed and recommended, with the latter also renting apartments. On a slightly less luxurious level but still with all the modern conveniences (and cleanliness and charm as well) are the **Captain's House**, **Plaza**, and **Kastelli** hotels in the center of Skala just off the seafront.

There are also various rooms and houses to be rented near the beaches of Melo-i, Agriolivadi, and Kambos, some of them little more than a bed and chair, others luxury villas. For information about these, ask either the local café or taverna owners or, for rooms only, the tourist police in Skala.

Although in Hora there are a few rooms to rent, and luxury villas as well, these are very hard to come by and even to inquire about. The tourist police may have some information, but often the rooms must be sought by asking around in the town's byways, and the villas by looking for advertisements in the best travel magazines and newspapers. It is possible that the island's premier travel agent, Yannis Stratis, may know of something, but he should be consulted months in advance at the Skala office of his Apollon Travel Agency; Tel: (0247) 313-56 or 313-24. Also of help in renting villas in Hora as well as Kambos and other areas is Dolly Contoyiannis, who speaks English and French and can be reached in Patmos or Athens; in Athens, Tel: (01) 779-3150; on Patmos, Tel: (0247) 310-71.

The Monasteries

In planning a visit to the monasteries, it is best to consider taking a bus or taxi up to Hora and see the monastery of St. John first. From there a ten-minute walk down the old road will bring you to the monastery of the Apocalypse, after which it is only another ten minutes' walk (part of it through the small pine woods outside the Apocalypse monastery) to the port town of Skala.

The **monastery of St. John** is the theologian's most visible worldly monument. Its 900th anniversary, which took place in 1988, was attended by as prestigious a group of ecclesiastical, scholarly, political, and other secular notables as Christianity has gathered together in many a century.

The monastery's inception in 1088 had a similar weighty

eminence to it, both worldly and religious. Its founder, a prominent monk and abbot named Ioannis Christodoulos (now referred to as Osios, or Blessed, Christodoulos, an honor just below sainthood), had had a long-standing passion to "possess" this island of the Apocalypse and erect a monastery to the saint who wrote it. At the age of 67 he achieved his initial goal with the approval of the great Byzantine emperor Alexios I Komnenos, who saw in Christodoulos's plans a way of maintaining a precarious but nonetheless important foothold for both empire and Christianity in territory under the threat of Muslim annexation.

Thus, when asked by Christodoulos for permission to build the monastery, Alexios responded enthusiastically by not only giving Christodoulos the island outright but also making him its ruler in perpetuity. He also exempted the island from taxes, gave it sovereignty and land holdings in Asia Minor and Crete (where it still has property), and, perhaps most important, gave it the coveted right to possess ships, a factor that would eventually result in Patmos's becoming one of the leading maritime powers in the Mediterranean. The 1088 chrysobull (imperial decree) granting these privileges, a most impressive document, is proudly on display in the monastery museum.

Upon receiving the decree, Christodoulos hurried to the island with a group of Cretan workmen, wrote admiringly of the "great art" of a Temple of Artemis standing on the hilltop, had it razed (parts can still be seen in the monastery's church), and rushed to have his men construct the first walls, "urged on by one thought," he wrote, "now, the soonest, to protect ourselves from a sea swarming with Arabs and pirates by raising them as high as our strength allowed."

The walls were raised within two years and, over the centuries, have been strengthened again and again to form the buttressed, brooding mass of grayish stone that so impresses visitors today. Also completed by 1090 were the main church and the chapel enclosing the front of the grotto of the Apocalypse. Christodoulos dedicated the chapel to the mother of the Virgin Mary, Saint Anne, which also happened to be the name of the emperor Alexios's mother and first child. This is only a small but relevant example of the way in which Christodoulos laid the foundations not only of his "workshop of virtue" but also of a political fortress that was to become, over the next 800 years, one of the most influential of its kind in the Mediterranean.

Christodoulos, forced to abandon the island after his

workers and monks had fled the attacks of Seljuk Turks, died in Evia in 1093. His remains, upon instructions in his will, were returned to Patmos and almost immediately began working miraculous cures. In the 17th century a small chapel dedicated to Christodoulos was built adjacent to the main church, and within the chapel, to the right of the main church's inner narthex, can be seen the silver-covered reliquary containing his bones.

Also part of the complex of the main church are the **chapel of the Virgin**, set to the rear of Christodoulos's chapel, where parts of the ancient temple to Artemis as well as a fourth-century basilica have been visibly incorporated into the structure; and the monastery's **ancient treasury**, hidden behind the rear wall of the main church, in which are kept more than 60 of the monastery's relics, including pieces of the True Cross and a portion of the skull of Saint Thomas. This cannot be visited without special permission, nor can the monastery's **library**, which holds one of the most valuable collections of manuscripts in the Orthodox world.

Some of the most important and beautiful of the monastery's treasures can be seen in the recently refurbished **treasury museum**, done up as part of the 900th anniversary celebration and in conjunction with the publication of an excellent catalogue and illustrated book on the monastery and its holdings.

Of particular note in the museum are the above-mentioned 12th-century chrysobull (more than six feet long); an inscribed marble tablet commemorating a visit to Patmos by Orestes and his founding there, on the site of the present monastery, of a temple to Artemis; the monastery's oldest manuscript, 33 pages from a silver-lettered, 6th-century Gospel of St. Mark; a small, diamond-shaped liturgical embroidery showing Christ washing his disciples' feet at the Last Supper, worn by the abbot of the monastery during the Niptiras Ceremony when he reenacts this event in a public square in Hora each year on Maundy Thursday; and various icons from the 11th to the 17th centuries, one of which, by Theodorus of Tyrus (12th to 13th century), is considered a masterpiece.

The **monastery of the Apocalypse** sits about halfway up the hill from Skala, just below the white expanse of the modern seminary and the ruins of the original 18th-century school abutting the monastery's upper wall. The upper section of the monastery, completed in the 17th century, was the last to be built and is part of an accumulation of rooms that gradually extended uphill from the original chapel of St.

Anne, raised in 1090 across the front of the grotto where Saint John is said to have received his vision.

While biblical scholars have expressed doubts about both John's writing of the book entirely on Patmos and the presence of his amanuensis, Prochoros, to transcribe the revelation, the latter's account and the subsequent accretion of local legends around it seem to have won the day; it is so marvelous a story that people have from the outset most willingly suspended their disbelief about its accuracy.

Prochoros (who seems to have written his account, *The Travels and Miracles of Saint John the Theologian,* in the fourth or fifth century) not only is portrayed at John's side in most icons, but his versions of some of the events of John's stay on Patmos (the saint's saving a young Patmian from drowning and his triumphant battle with the island's magus, Kynops) are pictured on the walls of the church at the monastery of St. John. So never mind that Prochoros describes Patmos as being nine days' voyage from Ephesus (a rowboat could probably get there in two) or about as big as Sicily. These are mere details.

According to Prochoros and tradition, when the Patmians learned that John was planning to leave the island and return to Ephesus following the assassination of the emperor Domitian in A.D. 96 and the subsequent revocation of edicts persecuting the Christians, they begged him first to write down the teachings of Jesus, with whose help he had conquered the magus and converted them to Christianity. So John and Prochoros retired to a quiet spot on the hillside above the harbor where, after a long period of fasting and prayer, John dictated to Prochoros first his Gospel and then later, in the holy grotto, the Apocalypse.

The **grotto** is reached by entering the monastery through a charming roofed courtyard, to the left of which are exterior flights of stairs leading down to the chapel of St. Anne (which assumed its present, vaulted form in 1703) and the grotto itself.

The word "grotto" is misleading, conjuring up something magnificent and gloomy receding deep into the bowels of the earth. Instead, it is so shallow that it barely qualifies as a cave, indented only about four yards at its deepest point. In its rear wall are sanctified impressions where John is said to have laid his head and placed his hand to help him rise in the mornings. At first the visitor thinks, "Is this all?" But then there is something about the cave's upper lip—a thick outjutting of rock curled menacingly over the mouth of the cave like a petrified thundercloud—that begins to satisfy expectations. The priest points out a three-part cleft that cuts deeply into the lip and roof of the grotto. And here, with only a little help from the imagination, a feeling of awe does begin to arise. It was through this massive cleft, split by the sound of his "great voice, as of a trumpet," that God spoke to John and vouchsafed his revelation, beginning, "I am Alpha and Omega, the first and the last: and what thou seest, write in a book..."

Hora

As noted above, Hora, the town surrounding the monastery of St. John, is very much worth a stroll. Its winding streets are full of rich visual surprises afforded not only by its architecture but also by the varying views of the island, the Aegean, and the local inhabitants: adults, children, monks, cats, and an occasional donkey or chicken. Worth visiting are the nunnery of **Zoodóchos Pigí** (Source of Life) and the **Simandiris House**, a former merchant's mansion now converted into a folk museum. For excellent basic island fare, try lunch at **Vangelis's Taverna**, which has a tree-shaded garden in back, or the **Olympia** opposite. Both face onto the quiet elegance of Plateía Levkás, with its town houses and the tiny church of Ayia Lefká, and are a refreshing respite from the glaring whitewashed walls of midday Hora.

Sunset in Hora can be spectacular, as the great orange globe sinks out of sight at the edge of the Aegean somewhere beyond Mykonos. Nightlife in Hora is also something special, in spite of the presence of the monastery, although the sidewalks do tend to roll up at about 11:00 P.M., no matter how much the shank of the evening may still be bouncing upon them. Vangelis's evening fare also sometimes includes a small group of musicians, most of them moonlighting Patmian shipwrights playing, for the most part, authentic music of the Dodecanese. For a touch of something gentler after a strenuous day at the beach, there is the truly fine cuisine and lovingly cared-for atmosphere of the **Patmian House** and the **Pirgos** restaurants (the latter sometimes only a café-bar, sometimes serving food), both of them situated in beautifully restored Hora mansions.

Skala

Below, in the harbor town of Skala, life assumes a much livelier and more contemporary configuration. During the day Skala is a town of services, crisscrossed by the traffic of people going to and from the market, banks, post and telephone offices, travel agencies, and, as the day approaches noon, the bus and caïque stations that will take them either home or to the island's various beaches. By 2:00 P.M. Skala looks as deserted as an outpost in the Sahara, with taxis just about as hard to come by as they would be there.

Nightlife in Skala and some of the outlying beaches and towns, principally Kambos (Upper and Lower), Melo-i, and Grikou (to some extent), revolves around a selection of tavernas, bars, discos, and, rarely, live Greek music and dancing. For the last, the **Aloni**, just below Hora on the Grikou side, offers occasional evenings (usually Wednesdays and Saturdays) of costumed traditional Greek dancing with dinner. The clientele consists mostly of Patmians and their friends, and the atmosphere is festive and genuine. In Skala, two tavernas that have become local traditions because of their good food and camaraderie are **Grigoris's** for grilled dishes and **Pantelis's** for fish and various prepared dishes. The habitués of the island then rendezvous at the **Arion** café on the waterfront (next to the Apollon travel agency) for some more imbibing or coffee or both, and, if the spirit descends, some dancing inside. It is almost invariably here that the last stragglers gather and evening closes down all over the island, while up above, sitting stolidly among the stars of Hora's streetlamps, the monastery presides—and continues.

The Beaches of Patmos

To the north there are **Meló-i**, the nearest to Skala, with a campsite; **Agriolivádi**, with a single taverna and a quiet, family atmosphere; **Kambos**, perhaps the most-frequented beach on the island, with windsurfing, waterskiing, and three good tavernas, with one, **George's Place**, of particular quality; and **Lambi**, the beach of the famous multicolored volcanic stones, so distinctive and beautiful that even the most jaded traveller cannot resist pocketing a few.

To the south the lovely bay of **Grikou** curves for more than half a mile in a graceful arc around the uninhabited island of Traonisi and the curious rock of Kalikatsou (meaning "cormorant") which, as it sits out on the end of a narrow spit of sand, seems to float on the water like a seabird and is hewn with caves and dwelling places, perhaps made by fourth-century monks. Last but certainly not least is the exceptional beach of **Psiliámmo**. The name means "fine sand," and Psiliammo is the only beach on Patmos where such a marvel exists unadulterated by stones or pebbles. The beach is about 220 yards long and has a single, jerry-built taverna and few shade trees, but the swimming is excellent and the ride, about 45 minutes by a fast caïque from Skala, offers an opportunity to see the south side of the island. (There is a similar ride of equal length to Lambi in the north.)

GETTING AROUND

From Piraeus, one ship a day leaves around noon for Patmos and the rest of the Dodecanese. Conversely, there is a ship leaving from Rhodes for Piraeus at about the same time. As Patmos is equidistant between the two ports, these ships often arrive at the island within minutes of each other, occasionally causing some confusion. Depending upon the weather and the speed of the ship, the trip from Patmos to either Rhodes or Piraeus can take anywhere from 9 to 12 hours.

It is possible to reach Patmos from Athens in a much shorter period of time (three to four hours) by flying to either Kos or Samos and then taking a fast motor launch or hydrofoil (the latter only from Kos) to the island. There are at least two flights daily from Athens to both Samos and Kos.

On the island there is regular bus service from the port of Skala to the major points on the island's main road—Hora, Grikou, and Upper and Lower Kambos—at various times throughout the day. A schedule is posted on the bulletin board outside the police station at the port's administration building.

At the corner of this building is a taxi stand at which people are expected to wait their turn for one of these rarely seen vehicles to appear. Attempting to hail a taxi before it reaches this point is greeted with utter scorn by the drivers, who are thoroughly schooled in the way things should be done.

Throughout the morning and occasionally during the mid-afternoon in season, there are regular caïque runs from Skala to and from the major beaches to the north and south. Fares vary according to the distance. The longest runs—to Lambi and Psiliammo—take about 45 to 60 minutes, while those to Kambos and Grikou are about 25 minutes or less, depending on the boat.

Walking is not only a possibility but, if the weather is right, highly recommended. It takes 30 to 40 minutes to walk from Skala to Hora via the old stone road and about 20 minutes to come back down again. The trip by foot to the bay of

Kambos takes a bit more than an hour, while to Grikou it is 40 to 50 minutes. For a detailed breakdown of the various hiking possibilities on the island, see this writer's guidebook, *Patmos*.

—*Tom Stone*

ACCOMMODATIONS REFERENCE

Rhodes
▶ **Faliraki Beach Hotel. Faliraki,** 851 00 Rhodes. Tel: (0241) 854-03.
▶ **Fantasia.** 1 Demosthenous Street, **Rhodes Old Town,** 851 00 Rhodes. Tel: (0241) 262-09.
▶ **Kava d'Oro Hotel.** 15 Kistiniou Street, **Rhodes Old Town,** 851 00 Rhodes. Tel: (0241) 369-80.
▶ **Lindos Bay Hotel. Vliha Bay,** 851 00 Rhodes. Tel: (0241) 422-11.
▶ **Miramare Beach Hotel.** Trianton Avenue, **Ixia,** 851 00 Rhodes. Tel: (0241) 242-51.
▶ **Olympic Palace Hotel.** Trianton Avenue, **Ixia,** 851 00 Rhodes. Tel: (0241) 287-55.
▶ **Rodos Palace.** Trianton Avenue, **Ixia,** 851 00 Rhodes. Tel: (0241) 252-22.
▶ **Steps of Lindos Hotel. Vliha Bay,** 851 00 Rhodes. Tel: (0244) 422-62/67.
▶ **Sunwing Hotel. Kallithea,** 851 00 Rhodes. Tel: (0241) 286-00 or 627-13.
▶ **Thomas Hotel. Monolithos,** 851 00 Rhodes. Tel: (0246) 612-91; Telex: 9604.

Kastellorizo
▶ **Hotel Megisti.** 851 11 Kastellorizo. Tel: (0241) 290-72.

Kasos
▶ **Hotel Anagenessis. Phri,** 858 00 Kasos. Tel: (0245) 413-23.
▶ **Ekaterini Markou Apartments. Phri,** 858 00 Kasos. Tel: (0245) 414-40.

Karpathos
▶ **Kanaki Pension. Pigadia,** 857 00 Karpathos. Tel: (0245) 229-08.
▶ **Neohori Pension. Pigadia,** 857 00 Karpathos. Tel: (0245) 225-19.
▶ **Romantica Hotel. Pigadia,** 857 00 Karpathos. Tel: (0245) 224-61.

▶ **Seven Stars Hotel. Pigadia**, 857 00 Karpathos. Tel: (0245) 221-01.

Chalki
▶ **Xenonas Halki**. 851 10 Chalki. Tel: (0241) 572-08.

Symi
▶ **Aliki Hotel**. 856 00 Symi. Tel: (0241) 716-65.
▶ **Dorian Hotel**. 856 00 Symi. Tel: (0241) 711-81 or 713-07 (Simi Tours).
▶ **Grace Hotel**. 856 00 Symi. Tel: (0241) 714-15.
▶ **Hotel Village. Horio**, 856 00 Symi. Tel: (0241) 718-00.
▶ **Pedi Beach Hotel. Pedi**, 856 00 Symi. Tel: (0241) 718-70.
▶ **Villa Marina**. C/o Les Katerinettes Restaurant, 856 00 Symi. Tel: (0241) 716-71.

Tilos
▶ **Irini Hotel. Livadia**, 850 02 Tilos. Tel: (0241) 532-93.

Nisyros
▶ **Ipapandi Hotel**. 853 03 Nisyros. Tel: (0242) 314-85.
▶ **Porfyris Hotel. Mandraki**, 853 03 Nisyros. Tel: (0242) 313-76.
▶ **Romantzo Hotel. Mandraki**, 853 03 Nisyros. Tel: (0242) 313-40.

Kos
▶ **Atlantis Hotel. Lambi Beach**. 853 00 Kos. Tel: (0242) 287-31.
▶ **Hara Hotel**. 6 Halkonos Street, **Kos Town**, 853 00 Kos. Tel: (0242) 225-00.
▶ **Hippocrates Palace Hotel**. Kalidi Street, **Kos Town**, 853 00 Kos. Tel: (0242) 244-01.
▶ **Hotel Koala**. Harmilou Street, 853 01 Kos. Tel: (0241) 228-97.
▶ **Kordistos Hotel. Kefalos**, 853 01 Kos. Tel: (0242) 712-51.
▶ **Mustapha Tseleri Rooms**. 29 Eleftherios Venizelou Street, **Kos Town**, 853 00 Kos. Tel: (0242) 288-96.
▶ **Panorama Hotel. Marmari**, 853 00 Kos. Tel: (0242) 410-03.

Astypalaia
▶ **Paradissos Hotel**. 859 00 Astypalaia. Tel: (0243) 612-24.
▶ **Vivamare Apartments**. 859 00 Astypalaia. Tel: (0243) 613-28.

Kalymnos

- Agelika Apartments. Myrties, 852 00 Kalymnos. Tel: (0243) 478-64.
- Atlantis Hotel. Myrties, 852 00 Kalymnos. Tel: (0243) 474-97.
- Elies Hotel. Panormos, 852 00 Kalymnos. Tel: (0243) 471-60.

Leros

- Angelou Pension. Lakki, 854 00 Leros. Tel: (0247) 225-14.
- Gianna Hotel. Alinda, 854 00 Leros. Tel: (0247) 231-53.
- Hotel Katerina. Lakki, 854 00 Leros. Tel: (0247) 224-60.
- Malleas Beach Hotel. Alinda, 854 00 Leros. Tel: (0247) 233-06.
- Pension Zorzou. 7 Ayias Olgas, Lakki, 854 00 Leros. Tel: (0247) 224-00.

Patmos

- Captain's House. Skala, 855 00 Patmos. Tel: (0247) 317-93.
- Dolphin Hotel. Lambi, 855 00 Patmos. Tel: (0247) 320-60; in Athens, (01) 959-1387.
- Flisvos Taverna. Grikou, 855 00 Patmos. Tel: (0247) 313-80.
- Kastelli. Skala, 855 00 Patmos. Tel: (0247) 313-61.
- Plaza. Skala, 855 00 Patmos. Tel: (0247) 314-98.
- Romeo. Skala, 855 00 Patmos. Tel: (0247) 319-62.
- Skala. Skala, 855 00 Patmos. Tel: (0247) 313-43.
- Xenia. Grikou, 855 00 Patmos. Tel: (0247) 312-19.

THE NORTH-EASTERN AEGEAN ISLANDS

By J. A. Lawrence

J. A. Lawrence is an American who has lived in Athens for 15 years. She writes science fiction, children's books, and historical fiction and has contributed to several guidebooks on her adopted country. She has co-authored a guide to Athens, produced a compendium of information for newcomers intending to live in Greece, and written a guide to Cyprus.

The islands of Limnos, Lesvos (also called Mytilini after its capital), Chios, Samos, and Ikaria are very close to the coast of what is now Turkey, which was once Byzantium and earlier the Ionian coast of Greece. These islands, sometimes called the Eastern Sporades, came under Greek jurisdiction only a generation ago, and their people have little to do with distant Athens. Yet the islanders here have been Greeks for thousands of years.

There are ferries from Athens, and planes as well. Among the islands smaller boats weave their routes, unbeknownst to anyone in Athens, so you can't plan until you get there. You may find, for example, that the ferry goes from Chios to

Samos and back—but not to the same port you left—on Tuesday and Friday (this week)—and to Turkey on Monday and Saturday. The local buses run only on weekdays until 1:00 P.M.—one way each day, so you must stay overnight in the village or call a taxi to come from the port 30 miles away to fetch you back. As a rule, be there 15 minutes ahead of time—and bring something to read in case of delay.

Travelling by small ferryboat is pleasant, easy, and not expensive. You can sunbathe, read, chat with your companions, exclaim at the odd wave splashing the deck—unless the wind rises, in which case be prepared with the Dramamine that dock kiosks sell in packets of two. Travel by caïque, a very small boat usually loaded with crates and sacks of bread and islanders who have been shopping, all packed into two benches and a passageway, is rather more adventurous.

The sunset over the glittering sea takes your breath away as the red glow illuminates the rolled-up sails on fishing boats, and a few lights drift out through the dusk toward the Asian shore. The fishermen will probably mingle and exchange greetings, and maybe quarrel over tangled nets. You can get oxygen poisoning from the fresh air here; the vegetables are newly picked; the eggs come from free-ranging hens (a road hazard); and there are monasteries cared for by one lonely little old nun who smiles eagerly and opens doors but can't explain anything in English.

A few places have been developed for tourism, alas. This does not mean that the plumbing is better, although the transportation certainly is, and the beaches may even have changing rooms and showers and refreshment stands. But once there are umbrellas and pedalos, the goats have to be penned and the chickens cooped, and the paved roads fill with traffic.

Undeveloped means, for example, that women in the remote villages stare at you with what seems to be bitter, implacable hostility, but if you smile and say hello, they begin to bring sweets, coffee, and presents. Their ideas of foreigners come from television, and they are shy. Once tourist development takes place, they smile first and then *sell* you sweets, coffee, and presents. However, it is still possible in Limnos, Lesvos, Ikaria, and some parts of Chios to find the real Greek countryside with the old-fashioned hospitality that has not yet been abused by too many weird demands by strangers.

Accommodation in these islands consists of hotels and rooms to rent. These designations are official and have to do with such mysteries as, of all things, hotels must have white sheets but rooms may use printed ones. For the traveller it depends on the establishment: Some rooms may have private bathrooms, marble floors, and walk-in closets while some hotels can be shabby, cramped, and share a bath. Or vice versa. Most beds in the islands tend to be on the firm side, not designed for the sort of princess who can detect a pea six feet below. The authorities have recently decreed that new buildings for guest accommodation must be built in "the traditional island style" with white or beige stucco trimmed with wooden shutters and doors, so they all look pretty much alike. It should be noted that prices can always be negotiated, especially in months other than July and August.

A word about dress: Greek families are straitlaced. Not even the children are likely to go about without shirts, much less adult men and women. And when they find naked people on the beaches, country people feel that they dare not bring their kids to their own seaside, which tends to short-circuit hospitality: They become resentful about tourists. Ask at your hotel or at a tour office where you may bathe topless or nude. And, of course, bare shoulders and legs are not permitted when you visit monasteries; bring a wrap on island tours. In fact, even trousers on women cause frowns.

Bus drivers are often helpful. Sometimes they'll arrange a rendezvous with another bus. If there are no other passengers, or just a few, they may even stop and let you take pictures. Most tour buses will stop for a tourist in distress.

For most of human history, communication on these islands has been limited by the same things that protected a community from danger—mountains, risky seas, and, at best, the speed of a horse. Isolated communities tend to be both vulnerable and suspicious. Even the oldest ruins are found in places that could easily have been fortified; only the new towns dare occupy open spaces. Watchtowers dot the coasts, ready to send signals of invasion. Castles ancient, Byzantine, Genoese, and Turkish stand over the villages; other villages huddle tightly walled in the fold of a mountain.

Traces of Neolithic human habitation are found on the islands, and there is evidence of Minoan and Mycenaean civilizations as well. The Greeks defeated Troy around 1190 B.C., stopping on the islands en route, fighting their own battles regardless of the islanders, who from then on desperately tried to ally themselves with anybody who would stop the constant piratical traffic on their shores. Unfortunately they often picked the losers. With the collapse of Mycenae and the ensuing Dark Ages of Greek culture, the islands were a convenient stopping place for everyone who wanted to go back and forth from Europe to mainland Asia.

In the ninth century B.C. Ionians colonized the Aegean islands and the coast of Asia, and by the seventh century the Greek city-state was a reality, which meant that every town regarded itself as a separate country. Even on small islands there were struggles until one city became dominant. Leagues and alliances were sworn and forsworn, grew and foundered, while these fertile dots in the sea struggled to make a living.

The Persians swept through the islands on their way to fight the Athenians, and the Athenians swept back to punish rebels who took the wrong side in the Peloponnesian Wars.

Somehow, trade continued and flourished until the Roman Empire fell. Then the islands bounced back and forth from Byzantium to Seljuk Turks to Cretan Arabs to pirates. Lost markets for olives meant abandoning the farm and turning to piracy. The Mediterranean was awash in Egyptian, Italian, Syrian, and Greek hit-and-run thieves, in Crusaders and Venetians, until at last the Ottoman Turks captured Byzantium, wiping out all other claims. The islands resisted hopelessly and watched the pashas settle in, patching up the castles (more or less) that they had damaged, and conducting a ramshackle administration. All that was asked of the Greeks was that they pay their taxes and send a certain number of children to be Janissaries. The people, left pretty much to their own devices, gathered around the priests and pursued their fortunes. Many Greeks wormed their way through the system to high positions.

A feeling for community remained, but the growth of national feeling was slow in spite of the language and ancient culture shared with other islands and the mainland. For reasons of their own (such as wanting that foothold in the Mediterranean), other countries had been making various efforts to stir up the Greeks against the Turks, but they didn't have much effect until the late 18th century when the Russians, by invoking a common religion, managed to ignite the spark of revolution.

Many islanders wanted to join the revolution, and their harbors were used by Greek generals. Samos subverted Chios, and the Ottoman Empire struck back. Whole populations were wiped out in reprisals. In 1822 thousands were executed and enslaved. Limnos had a brief moment of

Greekness but was given back to Turkey in exchange for Evia in 1829. Samos and Chios were devastated.

In 1908 the Young Turks' rebellion against the Ottoman throne resulted in the Balkan Wars and treaties about Macedonia. The wheeling and dealing among Greece, Bulgaria, and Serbia caused the islands to be joined to the Greek Republic in 1912. Many present islanders are descendants of Greeks who left Asia Minor in 1922 and earlier.

Samos, just northeast of Patmos in the Dodecanese, is the softest of these islands, with crowds of tourists. **Ikaría**, northwest of Patmos, is grittier, with the same elegant natural beauty. **Chios**'s strong contrasts of atmosphere are suffused with melancholy light. **Lesvos** and **Limnos**, the farthest north in this group, are harsher and almost untouched by the modern world.

Times are changing too fast, and much of the wonder in these islands is likely to be lost each year. A real traveller enjoys the contrasts, and there are still adventures to be found in these hills.

IKARIA

Charter tours have not yet overrun the resources of Ikaría. Small, undeveloped, and enchanting, Ikaria has only about 8,000 inhabitants. It lazily begins to attend to tourism, more or less, in mid-June.

The island can be reached only by sea, and with a few exceptions accommodations are modest. The roads are rough and the landscape wild. Transportation is difficult and expensive. In fact, hoteliers complain that they dare not build large hotels because there is always some doubt about whether the guests will be able to get here. There are no remarkable archaeological sites or great Byzantine monuments.

But the island is worth any effort it takes. The wild landscape is breathtakingly beautiful. On closer inspection it is not exactly wild: Thousands of years of hand-scarring care have gone into building the stone terraces that save the hillsides from erosion. The tiny villages are open, spread out

Ikaria, Fourni, and Samos

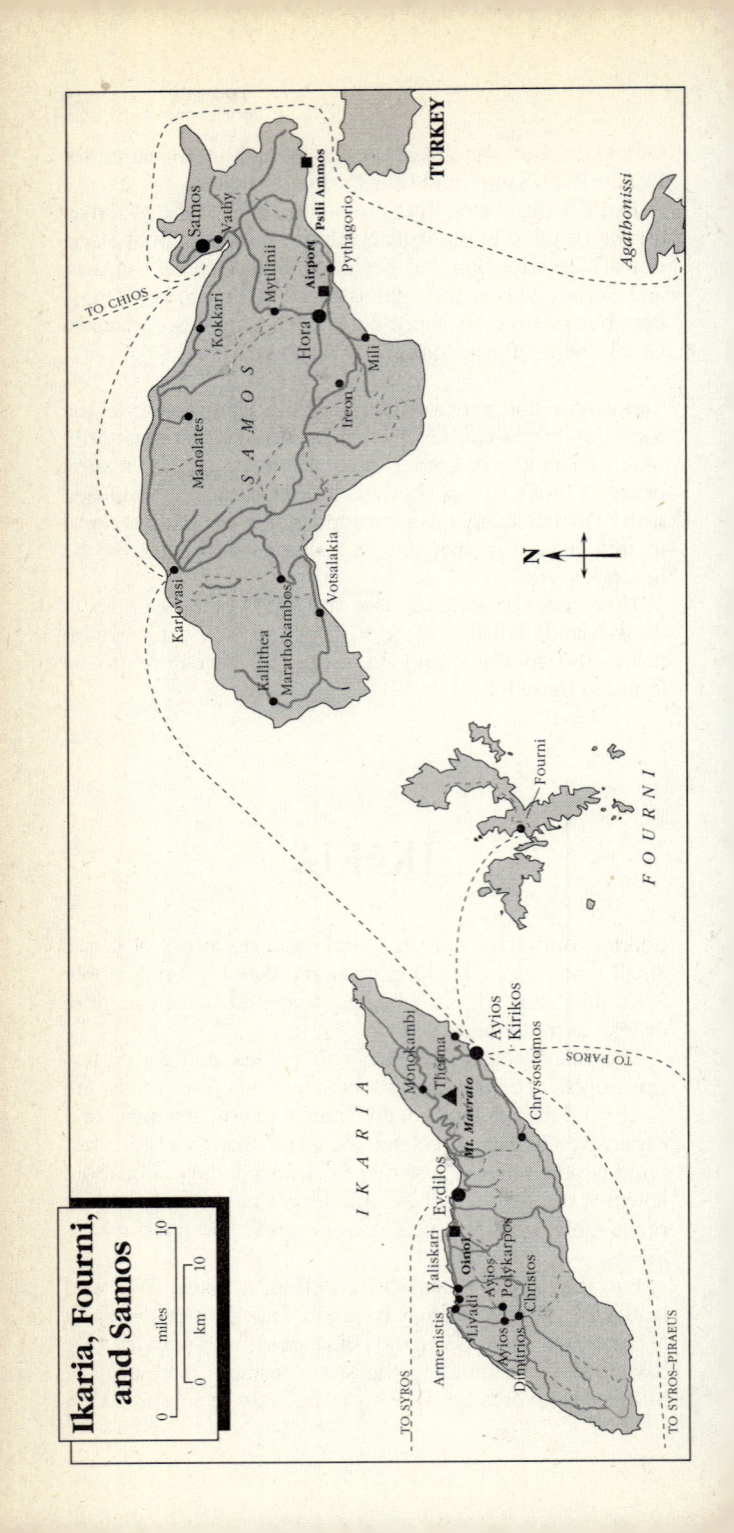

along the hills. Mountain springs offer pure water and hot, radiant springs provide therapeutic baths, while the seawater is almost as clear as the air. Steep mountainsides are clothed in silver olives, dark cypresses, pines, and apple trees. A wait for your food at the local fish taverna doesn't mean poor service, but that the catch is only just being unloaded from the boat.

MAJOR INTEREST

Beautiful unspoiled countryside
Climbing
Hospitality
Fresh seafood
Day trip to the island of Fourni

Ikaria was probably first occupied by Pelasgians and Carians from Asia Minor. Icarius, king of Caria, may have given the island its name, but most favor another story, the legend of Daedalus and Ikaros: That after Ikaros's wax-held wings gave way on his escape with his father from Crete, and Ikaros fell into the sea near Paros, the grieving Daedalus buried him on the nearest island, naming it Ikaria.

After the Trojan War, Ionians settled in. The Persian king Darius held Ikaria, and later it paid tribute to Athens. It was abandoned in early Christian times, after which Ikaria was used as a pirates' hideout and a place of exile. As a Byzantine province, it was used for out-of-favor officials. When the Franks were ousted by the Turks, Ikaria quietly thrived.

On July 16, 1912, the Ikarians declared independence from the Turks, issued coins and stamps, and even wrote a national anthem to celebrate their freedom. The composer of the Greek national anthem set it to music.

But in November the Greek fleet arrived and claimed Ikaria, and the islanders feel that very little advantage has come of it. In the 1960s and 1970s offenders against the junta government were exiled here, and as there were sometimes twice as many new left-wing residents as there were native Ikarians, Ikaria became known as the "red" island.

Ayios Kirikos

The capital and port, Ayios Kírikos, on the south coast near the eastern tip, is called simply Ayios, which is equivalent to calling San Francisco "San." It's an ordinary town, but friendly. Right at the dock is a clean little umbrella-shaped café, a perfect spot to have a snack or drink if you're waiting for a boat. Dolichi Tours (Tel: 0275-220-68 or 223-46; Fax: 223-46) at the far end of the waterfront is run by **Mr. Mitikas** and his family, who know all about the island and handle local tours, boat tickets, and jeep or motorcycle rentals. The family also offers clean, comfortable, and inexpensive rooms to rent on the high ground toward Therma. Mrs. Mitikas may provide you with a clove-studded apple, an ecologically sound device to deter flying bugs from your room. Ikariada Tours (233-11 or 222-77), recently opened on the waterfront road, also organizes excursions and sells boat tickets. Summer trips around the island and to the nearby islands of Fourni and Patmos are now available. But note that excursions often depend on demand and may be canceled at the last minute. Don't wait to tell the travel agent of your interest.

There are more rooms to rent and a couple of hotels in town. The charming, whitewashed **Pension Maria Elena**, with wood shutters and a tile roof, is well signposted, up Artemídos Street from the dock. It offers lovely, light, and clean rooms—all likely to have a fine harbor view—with breakfast, at very low rates; studio apartments are also available. This place is a real bargain.

The **Climataria**, a taverna hidden among the little streets of the tiny market, charcoal-grills fresh fish and meats and offers wine by the glass. The *ouzerí* on the dockside near Dolichi Tours prepares delicious *mezédes*.

The dock is decorated with a large metal sculpture representing Ikaros falling between gigantic wings (the islanders have a rude name for it). Past the **Ta Adelphia** taverna on the seafront, the pebbly town beaches are now equipped with salt showers. Farther down the Chrysóstomos road two discos vie for trade by offering dance contests and alternating business hours. The **Flic Flac** is said to have a slight edge over the **Take It Easy**.

The main road runs from Ayios along the north coast, and, potholes notwithstanding, the islanders are very glad to have it. The other roads are unpaved and often horrendous. On the *good* road the bus is able to make 20 miles per hour. In fact, the only practical vehicle for this island is a jeep (which can be rented in Ayios, Evdilos, and Armenistis). The roads are too steep and unreliable and the winds too strong and sudden for Ikaria to be safe for two-wheelers, and it's no place for unreliable brakes.

From Ayios the road north climbs amazingly quickly around Mount Mavrato, though not quite to its entire height of 3,400 feet. Ten minutes from the port you are driving at 2,000 feet and looking down at the bay and the neighboring resort of **Therma**, on a branch road just a few miles northeast of town. For years the hot baths of Therma—whose radioactivity was once proudly advertised—have been attracting the rheumatic and arthritic. The baths are huge, wonderful old stone tubs, filled from pipes running to the hot springs, whose water is filtered through nets tied over the enthusiastically spraying taps. Attendants clean the tubs with disinfectant between bathers, refill them, and advise you how long to soak—usually about ten minutes at first. The tiny amount of radioactivity in the salt water is no danger, and the therapeutic effects on painful joints and general aches is proven. Many elderly people visit Therma regularly, clutching their doctors' prescriptions for time and temperature. It feels wonderful even if you don't suffer from rheumatism! One spring is in a cave, with a very hot bath sunk into tiles and a steam bath as well; another occupies a pavilion in the square. These public baths cost only a few drachmas; the private **Kratsa** costs the price of a cup of coffee.

The town beach and small marina are nearby, and a caïque runs every half hour throughout the day between Ayios Kirikos and Therma. A bus also travels just as frequently between them.

Almost every building in Therma has some rooms to rent, and many of the hotels have elevators. The **Ikarion** is a sprawling, renovated, older hotel (read no elevator), well kept with large rooms, most of them with bath and telephone, at very low prices. The informal **Rena**'s flagstone courtyard is shaded by an old plane tree, and the hotel provides a refrigerator on every floor. The **Anthemis** is new and clean, with an elevator, and is somewhat more expensive. On the high ground is the inexpensive **Marina**, with a fine sea view and many steps. Rooms on the lower floor open on to public balconies, so, for privacy, ask for a room on the upper floor. There are facilities to make coffee and a refrigerator for guest use. (Dolichi Tours has another office in the main square if you need assistance.)

The view becomes more and more breathtaking as the road twists up along jagged cliffs and through steep terraced hills such as those you might find in Italian paintings. A mist seems to gather; the road advances up into the clouds. You can still see the low ground of the northeast peninsula, seemingly floating out to sea. Little rocks of islands dot the clear water. The temperature suddenly drops ten degrees. Far out to the northeast is **Fanari**, with its fine beaches. The

Ikarians hope to build an airport here, and a new road from Ayios Kirikos is currently under construction.

When the northern road, bordered by sharp precipices, slowly starts to descend, you pass traditional Ikarian houses built of stone, painted white, and roofed with rough plates of slate, with extra rocks to weigh them down. Gold, brown, and calico goats wander freely, and free-ranging donkeys pose a road hazard. Villages are not signposted, so you may want to buy a map in Ayios. The village of Monokámbi, not far from Ayios, is proud of its unique cork tree. The road wanders peacefully along the north coast to Evdilos, passing through olive trees and fruit groves (Ikaria produces excellent apricots).

The jam-packed bus for Evdilos leaves Ayios daily at noon, returning from Armenistis at 7:00 A.M. and Evdilos at 8:00 A.M. If you want a seat get there 20 minutes early. There are tourist buses in July and August.

The North Coast

Evdilos, where ferries from Samos and Piraeus sometimes dock, is 39 km (24 miles) north and west of Ayios Kirikos—a two-hour drive because of the twisting road. Narrow streets house about 700 residents, and there is an ouzeri, two *kafeneíos*, a pharmacy, a fast-food stand, a general store, and rooms to rent. High up is the very nice—comfortable, clean, and friendly—but expensive **Eudoxia Hotel**. A few steps downhill is the much less costly **Hotel Atheras**, a cool Neoclassical building with swimming pool, bar, and restaurant, and a friendly family management. The 22 rooms are clean and inviting, with individual wrought-iron balconies, some with a sea view. Rooms are available in a yellow Neoclassical house at the dock's end (see Mr. Rozos), or ask at the general store for Mr. Spanos, who also rents rooms. Avventura Travel and Tourism in Evdilos rents cars and jeeps and offers other services. Rates are higher here than in Ayios and Armenistis. West of Evdilos are fine sand beaches, and sometimes boats go from here or Armenistis over to Fourni for fish dinners.

Kambos, just a few kilometers west of Evdilos, has a tiny one-room **museum** containing a handsome male torso in marble, a lovely little horse's head made of bone, and vessels that were found in the sea. The guard, who speaks English, can often be found in the supermarket in Evdilos.

Inland from here are the enchanting little villages of the hills, some of which don't yet have electricity. Small, simple cottages, often with slate roofs, are surrounded by cultivated gardens, goats, rabbits, and chickens—food for the household.

The old center of wine-making was **Oinoi**, just west of Kambos, but these days most islanders make their own wine at home. Many houses have a vat where the grapes are crushed—by foot—and the juice runs through pipes into clay amphoras, where it is filtered three times. Thereafter it is aged for three to six months.

Nightlife is down the road a piece (west), at **Yaliskári**, where you'll also find a fine beach and **Manolis's** lively taverna. The **Kamares** restaurant, poised at the sea's edge, overlooks a lovely sand beach with a small lagoon. A disco and a *bouzoúki* club on the roadside open in July.

Along the coast west of Yaliskari is the popular seaside village of **Armenistís**. New buildings are climbing higher and higher up the hill here. The gorgeous 45-room **Cavos Bay Hotel** is cool, comfortable, and welcoming, with an excellent indoor and outdoor restaurant overlooking the sea, a swimming pool, and a bar. The spacious lounge, its white walls decorated with plants on upside-down ceramic roof decorations embedded in the wall, has a lovely feeling of breezes and restfulness. Friendly management, good service, and reasonable rates make it a favorite.

Up a longish hill is the **Armena Inn**, looking like a ship's prow, an informal—and low-priced—family-style pension with a fine view. The beige-trimmed-with-blue **Astachi**, up a dirt road, is very new, clean, and inexpensive, and also offers two-room family suites. There is no shortage of rooms in Armenistis, however: Even the harbor tavernas rent them out. The little **Delfini Restaurant**, built right over the rocky river delta (dry in summer) where tame ducks entertain visitors, offers delicious charcoal-grilled fish and home cooking, even coffee.

On the other side of the lane to the sea is a minimal minimarket and Marabou Travel, which has English books and magazines for sale and jeeps or cycles for rent, as well as providing the usual services. They will call you a taxi if you make the request in person, but not if by phone.

Unpaved roads lead from Armenistis to the interior through thyme and oregano, wild capers and grapevines. Here are the summer homes of people working off-island. The village of **Ayios Polýkarpos**, south of Livadi, is immaculate and rich, with beautifully maintained houses in bright stucco and wood. There are no tourist facilities, however. You may see hill women walking briskly to the shops, swinging their arms in unison right and left, wearing the unique Ikarian shopping bag—a goatskin tied by the feet—like a knapsack on their backs.

The road through the pines bumps on to **Ayios Dimítrios**, a completely different community of old stone houses and tall trees. These villages, collectively called "**Rachés**," also include **Christós**, a picture-book village of stone and wood adorned with silver and green leaves. On August 6 and 15 all the island gathers here for religious holidays and feasting on goat, and the dancing lasts all night. The lovely little **Hotel Raches** is a surprise indeed in this quiet, traditional village. Clean and modern, its cool underground lounge has a country oven and a small folk-implement museum, and its large veranda offers a terrific view. All rooms have bathrooms, unless you want a two-room suite (one bath). Prices are low, and downstairs is a little restaurant. At the edge of town is an old-fashioned *fournos* (bakery) with fantastic country bread.

Evangelístrias Monastery, a church built in three arched sections with separate altars, sanctuaries, and iconostases, is just past the pretty reservoir outside Raches among chestnut and cherry trees. The original wall paintings are in an excellent state of preservation.

Amid the running brooks and rocks just southwest of here is a sudden high point surrounded by sand called **Ammoudiá** (2,970 feet), from which you can see all of Ikaria and much of Samos. A ruined tenth-century Byzantine castle occupies another high point at **Nikariá**, a few kilometers northeast. Inside the castle's towers and bastions are goats and a ruined church.

"Welcome to Nas" says a sign between a taverna and a minimarket. Here on the northwest coast south of Armenistis was the city of **Tavropolion**, sacred to the goddess Artemis. From her great temple, of which only a few steps are left, worshipers would set off to celebrate on the island of Delos. The site is down at the shore, a stiff clamber—but the beach alone is worth the climb. Occasionally two separate groups can be observed here: those who are clothed, with backs turned huffily to those who are not.

The South Coast

From Ayios along the south coast the unpaved road—watch for falling rocks—leads to the **convent of Evangelismós**. White walls and cypresses protect a gently decaying, peaceful garden, invaded continually by a determined nannygoat and under the care of a lone nun. The church, dated 1775, has some fine icons mounted in a carved and painted iconostasis and a quiet, nostalgic atmosphere.

The road beyond the picturesque and peaceful coastal village of **Chrysóstomos** is impossible without a jeep.

FOURNI

Of the tiny sprawl of islands between Samos and Ikaria only Fourni has any public transport connection to the outside world. It is served by caïque from Samos, and in summer there are excursions from Ikaria (Ayios Kirikos) as well.

The port, also called Fourni, is famous for its fish tavernas—fish is expensive anywhere in Greece, however. Fourni is crowned with old windmills, and its little streets wander inland among the few shops—just supplied from the caïque you came on. Simple rooms can be rented on the harbor and more substantial apartments inland. And unless you have your own boat or have come with an excursion, you must stay the night.

It is a fishing village, and what it has are boats. The people are talkative and informal. In the evening, an old man comes down from a day tending goats in the hills. He makes fresh cheese and offers it in a basket at the tavernas; it is delicious.

GETTING AROUND

Ferries from Piraeus to Samos, which stop at Ayios Kirikos, run at least daily in summer, three to six times a week in winter. A caïque to Fourni meets the ferry every other day—or every day if the captain feels like it. Some boats stop at Evdilos if there is enough traffic. Local boats run back and forth to Fourni, Patmos, and Samos, unpredictably. There is no airport yet.

The following boats travel to Ikaria this summer, on the following routes: *Milena:* Paros, Naxos, Ikaria, Samos (Karlovasi and Vathy); *Dimitra:* Syros, Tinos, Mykonos, Donoussa, Koufonissi, Amorgos, Astypalaia, Syros, Tinos, Mykonos, Ikaria, Fourni, Samos (Karlovasi and Vathy).

On Ikaria there are taxis whose fares are 3,000 drachmas between Ayios and Evdilos and 1,000 drachmas between Evdilos and Armenistis. The best thing to do is hire a jeep. The roads are dangerous for motorcycles.

Local buses are few. They run weekdays only, from Ayios south to Chrysostomos; north to Perdiki, Monokambi, Ploumari, and Mileopo; northwest via Mavrato, Mavrikato, and Ploumari to Karavostamo, Evdilos, and sometimes Armenistis.

SAMOS

It is hard to believe from the seaward approach that Samos hasn't been purposely landscaped by an artist: a terraced Italian garden punctuated by exclamation points of cypress against all the colors of green, embroidered with white villages with red-tile roofs, crowned by the turquoise domes of churches. The scalloped coastline alternates tiny beaches with dramatic rocks. In the slight haze the high ridge of mountains that forms the island's spine seems painted in pale watercolors.

Plentiful mountain springs make the 184 square miles of Samos one of the greenest places in Greece. The rocky shores are broken by pebble and sand beaches that range greatly in size. It is a gracious landscape, topped by Mount Kerkis and fruitful with trees and vines. In the summer of 1990, however, Samos suffered a calamitous fire that burned about 7,000 acres of the pine forests, hillsides, pastures, and farms of the southeastern part of the island.

Samos wine, usually red and rather sweet, has been famous from ancient times. The wine got a great boost from the Crusaders, who took it back to Rome where it became very popular as communion wine. *Kavas* (wine shops) display dozens of kinds of locally made wine and ouzo.

MAJOR INTEREST

Archaeological sites: Heraion (Temple of Hera), Roman baths, and Tunnel (Aqueduct) of Evpalinos
Archaeological museum in Vathy
Paleontological museum in Mytilinii
Wine
Beauty of the landscape

Early Anatolian settlers were followed by Ionians from Epidaurus, Lesvos, and other places. By the seventh century B.C. Samos was a leading commercial center, utilizing ships bought from Corinth. Its navy was unrivaled during the sixth century; Samian seamen claimed to be the first Greeks to reach Gibraltar. By 535 B.C. Samos had achieved considerable prosperity. A great harbor, an extraordinary aqueduct tunnel, and the Temple of Hera (the Heraion) were among the outstanding achievements of the tyrant Polykrates.

But at his death the Persians came. In the fifth century B.C. Samos joined a revolt against Persia and thereafter remained loyal to the Athenians until Athens made a displeasing decision in a dispute with another island. Samos rebelled again and held off the ships and Pericles for some time. Samos and Athens lived in accord until the fourth century, when Samian history becomes blurred. The island was occupied by Ptolemaic Egypt, Syria, and Pergamum. True to form, after a brief period under Mark Antony, Samos rebelled against the Romans as well and was allowed autonomy after Augustus. Under the Byzantines Samos headed the Aegean military district.

After the coming of the Genoese, Samos, like Chios, became the property of the Giustinianis. But after the fall of Constantinople to the Turks in 1453 Samos was abandoned. Two centuries later it was resettled with newcomers, many from Albania; perhaps this is why so many Samians have fair complexions. The island was governed by archbishops for many years as an asylum for Christians.

For 100 years Samos paid no taxes to the Ottomans, and Turkish families never settled here. When the Turks finally asked permission of the archbishop to build a mosque, it was granted, on condition that it be built on the site of the former mosque. There was no former mosque, and therefore no mosques are to be found in Samos.

During the Greek War of Independence Samos was in the forefront, coercing Chios into joining the revolution. When the Great Powers were drawing up the treaty granting independence to the Greek state, Samos was among the islands that somehow were given right back to the Turks. Samos protested passionately; Europe sympathized and negotiated a special status: The island was granted self-government. A Greek "Prince of Samos" was designated by the Turks and governed with a Greek council and assembly.

Samos was one of the first islands to accept tourism after the war, and the results are mixed. In some areas there is little left of the original character of the island.

Vathy

The port and capital of Samos is a sizable town (population 5,500) sprawling over the harbor on the northeastern coast of the island and up the surrounding hills. Once, in the heyday of the tobacco trade, the port at the deep bay was called Lower (Kato) Vathy. The village on the hill, safe from marauders, was Upper (Ano) Vathy. Over the years the two parts have merged, although on road signs only the upper part is still called Vathy. The whole town has been called Vathý or Samos interchangeably for the last ten years.

When the painted shutters of Vathy's buildings are closed for the afternoon siesta, it looks like a heap of dice with bright, different-colored pips. The waterfront is largely given over to tourists, with a hotel and a tourist shop every ten feet, plus numerous bars and restaurants. Prices are generally relatively high in Samos. The town tourist information office is in a side street a few yards from central Pythagoras Square.

Along the waterfront are tour and travel agencies such as Samos Tours, Ireon Tours, and the well-organized Rhenia Tours. Trips to Kuşadası (near Ephesus in Turkey) and Patmos, and excursions by jeep, bus, boat, and even on foot are offered. A public bus to any of the beaches may be crowded enough to have standing room only. The excursion buses cost double, but you get a seat.

The city hall, the large **church of Ayios Spyridon** (where the first Samian parliament met in the winter of 1912), OTE (telecommunications), the post office, and the **Archaeological Museum** are clustered around the small municipal garden, two streets back at the center of the port. The museum has a fine, well-explained (in English), and well-displayed collection housed in two buildings, one modern, for the Heraion statues from the archaeological site on the south coast, and one Neoclassical, for everything else. In the former, among the statues of the Archaic period, are a colossal *kouros* (a very large young man for whom the ceiling had to be raised) and the Geneleo group from the sanctuary at Heraion—a family portrait in stone of worshipers at the shrine of Hera. Originally six figures occupied the base; now the seated Philia, the figures of Philippi and Ornithi (their names are inscribed), and a seated woman remain, all headless. (A copy has been set up on the site.)

Across the court is the Neoclassical building devoted to works of all ancient periods, which show the extent of Samian trade from the eighth through the sixth centuries B.C.—objects from Egypt, Cyprus, and Syria, many found at the Heraion. There are some fine, solid, Hellenistic draped ladies, pottery from all periods, and even some amazingly well-preserved fragments of wooden furniture more than 2,500 years old. One wonderful vessel, used for offerings, is shaped like a doughnut. On it sit a frog, a sheep's head, a snake, two cups, a bull's head, an unidentifiable creature, and two small pots. Objects of devotion were marked as the property of a deity, to make them unsuitable for other uses. Among the bronzes is a roomful of gryphons from the eighth century B.C. For a couple of centuries these heads were used on everything—perhaps to avert evil—and then they suddenly became unfashionable, around 600 B.C.

The **Byzantine Museum**, housed in the Bishop's Palace on 28 Oktovríou Street, displays icons, embroidery, manuscripts, and other treasures.

Restaurants line the harbor. Most are more anxious to collect your currency than to please your palate. The Ireon cafeteria at the corner of the square does try to serve what you order, however. The best eating places are not on the waterfront, but behind it. Ranging from the very simple, 1950s-style garden taverna with good food and microscopic prices of **Manolis**, off Kanári Street one block west of the Olympic Airways office, to the fine food of the **Kouros Restaurant**, in the garden of a tall, rather battered old mansion flanked by giant palm trees at the far end of town—with surprisingly reasonable prices (they have an undeserved reputation for being too expensive)—there are some really pleasant places to eat. **Stamatis**, a two-level garden decorated with plants and a minuscule fish pond, has "real Samian cooking." The **Steps**, up a flight and open for lunch and dinner, has two wooden verandas overlooking the bay and friendly waiters who serve a varied menu. **La Calma**, directly downstairs from the Kouros, has a romantic perch right on the water. Near the launderette is **Alekos**, a grill with plain, well-cooked food, low prices, and no stairs.

The luxurious, air-conditioned **Christiana Hotel** is high up in the heart of Vathy, with a generous veranda wrapping its marble way around to a swimming pool, the sort of accommodation that brings to mind the phrase "gracious living." You will pay less than you might expect for this elegance. At the other end of the price scale is the inexpensive and charming pension **Avli**, housed in an old Catholic convent. A few rooms have private bathrooms, others have numbered chambers at the end of a hall. But any inconvenience is offset by its engaging character and friendly proprietor, Spyros, and his delightful wife and sons. They have invested time and care in restoring and maintaining the peaceful, antique character of the cloister.

In between is the little cluster of clean, inviting, small hotels—**Helen**, **Ellenis**, and the rooms called **Themis**—all on Grammou Street leading from the port next to the church. A step away from the boats, the street is unexpectedly quiet after the waterfront bustle.

Rodítses and **Gangou** beaches are past the Customs House and the hospital. Along the shore road on the way is the Neoclassical (1815) **Eleana Hotel**, cherished by its proprietor and offering a family-run pension accommodation. The house has high ceilings, and pine floors, and smells of fresh pine. Guests share the kitchen and the laundry.

This area is filled with new buildings and many hotels and rooms. Up the hill past the army base is the picturesque and interesting **Ino Hotel** (70 rooms), its multilevel structure commanding a panoramic view on all sides, its courtyard, with jigsaw puzzle–shaped swimming pool, surrounded by whitewashed arches, little tables, and chairs and lounges. The bar serves breakfast, drinks, and snacks, adding to the general feeling of above-it-all comfort. Minibus transportation to town (only about a ten-minute walk) is available mornings and evenings. If you can't get a room here, try the more modest but similarly "traditional island"–style **Pension Evdoxia** on the way downhill.

On Captain Stamatos Street off Pythagoras Square is the **Voulgaris** bookshop, where you can buy secondhand paperbacks.

Pythagorio

Pythagório (Ancient Samos), on the coast south of Vathy and just west of Psilí Ammos, is the most popular of resorts and also the island's main archaeological area. Once tobacco was a main export of Samos; then it was olives. Now there are more tourists than trees (especially since the devastation of the hillsides above town brought on by the 1990 fire). If you haven't booked in advance, summer accommodation becomes a matter of taking whatever you can get. The biggest hotel in Samos, the 334-room **Doryssa Bay**, with tennis, a pool, and miniature golf, is just outside Pythagorio. To the west are three miles of beach, both pebble and sand. Overlooking the beach on one side and the harbor on the other are the two pleasant medium-sized and medium-priced **Labito Hotels**, opposite one another, just out of earshot of the racket. Although the black wrought-iron balconies overlooking the marble terrace bar look expensive, the prices are moderate and the atmosphere comfortable and friendly. One of the two hotels is a little older and a shade less expensive.

About ten yards to the right of the hotels is the beach taverna **Nikos**, serving charcoal-grilled specialties and displaying a little model of itself in a corner of the room.

Fully 25 percent of Pythagorio is rental accommodation.

Two kilometers (about a mile) outside town toward Vathy, perched on a steep rock at the shoreline, is the outrageously deluxe **Princessa Hotel**, with a swimming pool (which at these prices should be filled with Champagne), a bus, and an air of grandeur. For more subdued elegance and immaculate cleanliness in a family atmosphere—with equally good views—the graceful little **Hera II** on the edge of town has just been renovated and is now air-conditioned. The same nice people run the **Hera** (I) on Iras (Hera's) Street in town, a bit cozier and more modest in price, and just as clean.

The lively harbor is crowded with boats. Many carry signs offering day trips to beaches, to Samiópoula and other even tinier offshore islands, and to Turkey, Patmos, and Leros. Boats usually leave at 9:00 A.M. and return at 5:00 P.M. Prices may vary with the number of passengers.

Lights garland the row of cafés, coffee bars, tavernas, restaurants, and pizzerias. Tourist shops fill every available space. There is plenty of action, the evening *volta* (promenade) being fraught with budding relationships—and plenty of noise.

On the main street, opposite Regina Tours, is the local tourist office, which dispenses free information, maps, and booklets, handles room reservations and foreign exchange, and provides a metered phone for overseas calls—all with the pleasantest manners. A complete bus schedule is posted outside.

The small **Archaeological Museum**, containing Archaic, Hellenistic, and Roman sculptures and mosaics, is situated in tiny, delightful Peace Square. (Also in the square are rooms to rent and a minute produce market.) You may encounter obstacles to the enjoyment of the museum and ancient monuments most often because of a shortage of personnel. With only one or two guards available to cover all the antiquities as well as the museums, there's always a chance that the sites will not be open.

In ancient times the island was dedicated to the goddess Hera. Zeus courted her unsuccessfully for many years, but finally the courtship resulted in marriage. Thereafter mythology is replete with stories of his strayings and her schemings. Hera's temple, the **Heraion**, became a center for family therapy and marriage counseling. The oldest remains date from the Bronze Age, and the sanctuary was continually being extended and improved. Polykrates built a **Sacred Way** from the port; running five miles along the coastline and lined with 2,000 statues, it led to a new and magnificent temple to the goddess, a wonder of the Hellenic world. The building was supported by 134 pillars, only one of which has survived the centuries of earthquakes, Samos being very prone to seismic disturbances.

The precincts are only slowly being restored, although it is easy to see their vast extent; a copy of the dedicatory Geneleo group is placed along the Sacred Way. There are parts of many temples to many gods, including an early Christian basilica. Fallen stones have been stacked to await further developments in the science of archaeology. The capitals are decorated with the egg-and-dart motif, an ancient eastern symbol of life and death, the dart representing the head of a serpent. The site, when not crawling with tour groups, would be a peaceful place to meditate—but you are asked not to sit or stand on carefully balanced stones, and there are snakes in the grass.

The ruins of a sizable **Roman bath**, with standing columns, hypocausts, and waterworks, which may well have been used by Antony and Cleopatra, are next to the Doryssa Bay Hotel on the modern road parallel to the Sacred Way leading to the village of Ireon.

In the sixth-century B.C. Polykrates made Samos a famous port and held court nearby. A pirate by calling, he had no financial problems; among his expensive projects were the construction of a huge harbor mole on which modern Pythagorio is built, the building of a fleet of galleys, and the expansion of the sanctuary of Hera. When Polykrates became power-mad, the great Samian geometer Pythagoras left Samos for Italy.

Polykrates later turned his attention to the matter of water supplies in case of siege. He summoned the engineer Evpalinos, who designed an aqueduct, known as the **Tunnel of Evpalinos**, to cut right through a mountain to the northern springs. Polykrates ordered 4,000 prisoners from Naxos to get to work. Half dug from the south, half from the north; they met within a few inches of one another, even maintaining the ten-foot slope. (A recent similar effort in France resulted in a half-mile difference at the center.)

The tunnel, more than 3,000 feet long, may be visited—take a flashlight. The entrance is inside a stone hut (see the door of the Archaeological Museum in town for opening times, if any). The entry is very narrow, but the tunnel widens out. If you are claustrophobic, wait for your friends outside—or hike up the hillside to the small **monastery of the Madonna of the Caves**, which hides the entrance to a group of caves used by refugees in times of trouble.

Polykrates, true to his piratical nature, was finally brought down by his insatiable greed. A certain ruler of Lydia in Asia Minor offered him some cases of gold and jewels. Suspicious, Polykrates sent his secretary to inspect the loot. The secretary said it was all there. The tyrant sped across the 4,800-foot gap between Samos and Asia and was captured, killed, and crucified on a cross facing Samos. His secretary took over his job.

Visible from this hill, to the west of the harbor, the **church of the Transfiguration** occupies a small promontory in Pythagorio, displaying a banner that proclaims "Saved by Christ August 24, 1824" in giant letters. Inspired by the French Revolution, Lykourgos Logothetis organized and led the uprising of 1821 to 1824, which ended in a bloody naval battle. The Samians, saved by a combination of intelligent resistance and the arrival of Greek ships, celebrated their delivery by raising the church within the ruins of the castle of Logothetis. A bust of the hero is mounted in the church courtyard. The church overlooks the bay as the freedom fighters must have done when the Turkish fleet was sailing inexorably toward the island.

Just up the road are three popular tavernas, the **Esperides**, the **Elias**, and the pretty, new **Avli**, which opens as early as 5:00 P.M.

On the Mytilinii road just past the T-junction for Pythagorio is **Zorba's Bouzouki**, for food, drink, dancing, and performances. Between Hora and Mili, past the airport and closer to Mili, is the popular **Kotopoula** bouzouki.

Iréon, at the opposite end of the Sacred Way from Pythagorio, is a little fishing village of about 400 inhabitants who eagerly welcome visitors. Large hotel complexes are prohibited, but there are many small hotels and rooms. Off the beaten track, dusty with unpaved roads, Ireon grows on you. It is not elegant or beautiful, but it has a relaxed atmosphere and friendly people who want you to be here. There is none of the touristic whoop-de-do of Pythagorio—and it's less expensive. The travelling department store—a colorful heap of miscellaneous goods on a three-wheeled rattletrap—visits Ireon and sells dish towels, pillows, and clothes.

Rent a horse for 2,000 drachmas an hour (with guide), or a car or motorcycle. A delicious pension, the **Venetia** "Motel," is built inside a leafy bower, where birds feed their young outside the window of your large, light room. There is a beachside restaurant and bar across the lane as well as the rustic stone bar in the lounge.

Farther along is a sandier beach, and at the jetty is the

Heraion Hotel, also with restaurant and bar. The manager, whose English is excellent after his years abroad, also arranges excursions, picnics, and boat trips—a fine way to explore the island and the many unfrequented beaches. Both the Venetia and the Heraion are inexpensive.

The **Karabopetra** restaurant in the plateia has a good stuffed zucchini. At the Pythagorio end of town is **Persephone's** shop, with a long-distance phone and foreign papers, open from 8:00 A.M. to 11:00 P.M. **Evelyn's** is said to have the best coffee on the island; try the cappucino.

Mytilinii

Eight to ten million years ago a number of animals gathered around a drying lake and perished as the climate changed. Among them were the samotherion, an outsize giraffe-like creature first found here, and the little three-toed Mediterranean horse. Their remains may be seen in the small **Paleontology Museum** at the village of Mytilinií, 8 km (5 miles) northwest of Pythagorio. Mythology once attributed the bones to giant monsters called Neades, whose wailing voices were powerful enough to shake the earth.

Monasteries in Samos all date from the 16th and 17th centuries, when the island was repopulated. Most are hidden among the trees in the hills, to escape the prying eyes of pirates. The church of the white-painted **monastery of Megáli Panayía** (the Great Madonna), just south of Mytilinii, was built in 1593 (its outbuildings were damaged recently by fire). One story tells of two monks who came from Turkey to Samos, upon hearing of its revival; one monk was overcome by the vision of a miraculous icon buried a dozen yards down, where holy water now springs from the ground. This icon was burned in a great fire in the 18th century, but the church's frescoes are outstanding. The monks didn't get along together, because of the machinations of the Devil, so one departed, discovered many springs of water elsewhere, and founded the **monastery of Tímios Stavros** (Holy Cross) a few miles farther north.

Timios Stavros, with its wonderfully carved wood iconostasis, was named to honor a fragment of the True Cross brought by Saint Helen, mother of Constantine—an errand she seems to have repeated throughout the Christian world. The Crusaders seized the relic, broke it up, and distributed the pieces among European monasteries.

Northern Samos

Kokkári, 10 km (6 miles) and a 20-minute bus ride west of Vathy, blends into Kokkari beach, both built on the seaside. There are rooms to rent everywhere, and its shore is lined with bars and eating places. This old fishing village has expanded rapidly to accommodate tourists. Some houses, with their tiny, enclosed balconies, remain from the Turkish era. The church, stuccoed o'er with the pale cast of concrete, overlooks old roofs weighed down with stones and far, far too much of what the authorities think is correct island architecture.

The large and fairly pricey **Venus Hotel**, on high ground, is very clean and new, with an impressive collection of cactus plants around the bar and dining room and views from the balconies. The **Kokkari Beach**, a big hotel with all amenities, is right on the shore. More modest prices can be found at the **Dimitra**, a pleasant wood-and-tile hotel also near the beach, or at the very inexpensive, clean **Synaheris** rooms, with or without private baths.

Picturesque Kokkari is a bit too popular to be cozy. In full spate, your eardrums can be blasted by the Top Ten pop tunes as you enjoy a delectable fresh fruit salad platter at a harbor café.

On the windward side around the bend, the waves are heavier and the pebbles thicker on the ground. Sailboats can be rented at the Cavos Bar café on the shore for about 2,000 drachmas an hour. The **Memory Tourist** shop offers some unusual items: hand-painted scarves and cushions, pottery, cards, and courteous service.

Inland from Kokkari is the oldest of the new monasteries: the **monastery of Vrondianí**, with fine 17th- to 19th-century icons and wood carvings. South of it is a ruined Medieval monastery.

The north coast is full of beaches—**Tzabo, Lemonákio, Tzamádou** (the last being the most crowded). One of the most appealing coastal villages is gentle **Ayios Konstantínos**, not yet developed, with pretty stone houses and gardens. The town spreads out a long way on the coast and is rapidly acquiring rooms. Morning glories the size of soup plates decorate stone fences.

The **Paradiso Taverna** here is a favorite for "Greek Night" excursions. The tradition of performing for guests is not artificial, but very old. Here you'll find fantastic local wine, good food, cheerful if slow service, guitar and bouzouki music, and colorful characters.

The **Ariadne Hotel** just down from the taverna is named for the little daughter of the owners. This is a modest and friendly hotel with nine rooms. Rooms are also available at **Irini's**, newly finished and clean. Also new, the **Koala Hotel** has just been built by a returnee from Australia who's eager to please. The hotel is large, light, and attractive.

Locals are apologetic about the beach: It's rocky or walled-off by cement. But you can stay cheaply and peacefully here and go to Kokkari to swim, or swim off the rocks at the far end of town, a newer area. Near the wild wood, **Brinias's** rooms are modern and clean, with baths. You can also get studios or two-room apartments at very reasonable prices.

From here roads lead inland and up into the verdant Ambelos (Karvoúni) hills to picturesque villages such as **Manolátes**. You may pass through the romantically designated Valley of the Nightingales, which has two tourist pavilions among the ivy-twined trees, where the nightingales still sing on spring evenings. The road climbs steeply into tall forest.

Karlovasi

Karlóvasi, 33 km (20 miles) west of Samos, is actually five separate towns. **Neo Karlovasi** is a modern, bustling market town with shops, schools, the University of the Aegean, libraries, a modern medical center, and the bus terminal. It is well supplied with new hotels. **Meseo Karlovasi** is a sprawling area of houses, buildings, and a sports stadium. Its attractive plateia, occupied mostly by huge shade trees and complete with village fountain, enjoys breezes from all sides and has a restaurant that offers charcoal grills in the evening.

The road continues 2 km (about a mile) down to the sea toward the port, past the charming **Nepheli Hotel**. White, rough plaster walls lead into a cool white cave of a lobby filled with green plants. The 24 modern rooms with bath are air-conditioned, and the management is building a swimming pool. Also on the way to the port is the **Samos Wine** works, where visitors are welcome during working hours to watch the wine-making process and, of course, taste the wine.

At the sea is the old **Ormos** (Bay) town, with abandoned golden-stone mansions and beautiful, slowly deteriorating old warehouses once used by the local leather industry, opposite the beach. You can swim at Karlovasi beach outside the harbor. For the kids there is a little fair down by the beach where you can hire a horse and carriage for the same price as a taxi. Day trips to Fourni, the offshore island of Samiopoula, and Patmos leave from the harbor once a week each between 7:00 and 9:00 A.M.; get tickets and information at the Trata Snack Bar.

Cheerful ceramic faces grin at you from a workshop just behind the loading dock where ferries come in. Lanterns at the end of the harbor decorate **Ta Adelphia** restaurant, serving charcoal grills and pizza. The **Samaina Bay** is a large (75 rooms), modern hotel at the port, with a pool, bar, and restaurant.

Old Karlovasi, a lovely old village built in a horseshoe shape overlooking the valley and the sea, is accessible from the port by a cool, leafy road, which divides at the top of the hill at a *kafeneío*, famous for its *loukoumádes* (freshly made honey-soaked doughnuts). The left-hand fork leads along a path among well-tended old houses with flower-filled balconies and past a church with a complicated little bell tower. About a 20-minute walk brings you to a tiny, white, birthday cake of a church decorated with pink and blue icing and topped by a candle-like cross. From its marvelous perch it surveys a dream world at sunrise or sunset. A 20-minute walk down the right fork from the kafeneio brings you to the church of Ayios Antónios, built inside a stalactite cave.

One and a half kilometers (1 mile) from the port is **Potámi** (River), a splendid, large pebble-and-sand beach with shade trees. In the shrubbery on the roadside are tavernas along the curve of the beach. Umbrellas, sunbeds, and rooms may be rented. A caïque runs from Potami to the beaches of **Megálo Seitani** and **Mikró Seitani**. For 3,000 drachmas the caïque will take four to five passengers and wait one to two hours; for 5,000 drachmas it will drop you off and return later. Megalo Seitani is larger, has calmer waters, and is more popular—even among the Mediterranean seals. Mikro Seitani is smaller and windier, with choppier waves; the trip here costs as much as to Megalo Seitani because it is difficult to land. However, from Mikro Seitani it is possible to reach the 11th-century Byzantine **church of the Transfiguration** (the walk takes less than an hour via a footpath) to see the underground escape tunnel between the church and the castle above.

Wade or swim up the river from Potami through waterfalls or walk along the coast to reach these and other fine—and unfrequented—beaches.

Western Samos

From Karlovasi the roads—and buses—go to the south and west, where tourism is only just beginning to make a mark. The lovely big village of **Marathókambos** perches on high ground among vineyards. The road, not as good as elsewhere, descends from here to the fishing village of **Ormos Marathókambos** on the south coast. With about 20 pleasant, clean rooms, the **Kerkis Bay Hotel** here is attached to a seaside restaurant. Prices are moderately high; negotiate.

The sea on the south side of Samos is calmer than on the north, so there are more water sports here. This coast is lined with beaches: West of Ormos is the long beach of **Kambos**, which merges with **Votsalákia** (Little Pebbles). The **Votsalakia Hotel** has self-catering bungalows and is very reasonably priced. Rooms, maisonettes, and apartments may also be rented from **A. Prodromos**'s new complex just down the road. A little farther west is **Psilí Ammos**, a lovely, fine sand beach, where the water is clean enough to be shared by little fish. (There are a lot of beaches on Samos with this name; the best known is near Vathy.) A new pavilion is opening. Umbrellas are expensive to rent; it might pay to buy your own. Beaches continue around the coast, some of which are likely to be yours alone, accessible by dirt road. **Limonias**, just west of Psili Ammos, has a yacht club and windsurfing facilities.

An interesting drive west and then north from Votsalakia over poor roads (use caution) to Mount Kerkis twists past gray rock, dark trees, and silver olives against a brilliant sky, punctuated by the dotted lines of fences and terraces among the groves. This is the wild side of Samos, amid the harshness of bare scree and mountain scrub. Soon it is too high for trees. Looking down from the heights you see fire-burnt hills, forests, and the sea dotted with neighboring islands—Fourni, Ikaria, Samiopoula, and many more. The color of the now-inactive volcanic peak, **Mount Kerkis**, is a glowing sand-gray, spotted with dark flecks of vegetation that produce an eerie effect against blue sky. Some of its flowers and herbs are unique. Pythagoras (of the theorem) was imprisoned by Polykrates in one of its many caves.

The bus route ends in the undistinguished village of **Kallithéa**, where you may only be able to get a coffee or a cold drink. But the view is terrific.

GETTING AROUND

The airport on Samos is on the road to Hora, just west of Pythagorio. There are flights from Athens twice daily in summer (45 minutes) and from Lesvos, Chios, Mykonos, and Kos at least weekly. There is a weekly air link with Thessaloniki. Ferryboats run from Piraeus once or twice per day in summer and six times per week in winter. The trip takes 12 hours. There is also a ferry once a week from Kavala.

Local boats connect Samos with Chios and Ikaria. Caïques frequently go to Leros, Patmos, Turkey (Kuşadası), and the tiny nearby islands. There are two harbors, Karlovasi and Vathy, and most boats stop at both. There is a price difference, so choose your closest destination.

The local tourist office is at 25 Martíou 4, Vathy, 83 100; Tel: (0273) 285-30. The Community of Pythagorio Tourist Office is at Pythagorio, 83 103; Tel: (0273) 612-38.

Three reliable tour operators are Samos Tours, 1 Sofoúli Street, Samos; Tel. (0273) 277-15 or 289-15; Telex: 0294176 HORI-GR; Rhenia Tours, 15 Sofouli Street, P.O. Box 10, Samos; Tel: (0273) 226-41/45; and Ireon Tours, Karlovasi; Tel: (0273) 335-00 or 333-90; Telex: 0294109 IREO GR or 0294190 IRKA GR.

There are laundromats at Vathy, Pythagorio, Kokkari, and Karlovasi.

CHIOS

The 325 square miles of Chios are crammed with contrasts, from the worldly, sophisticated capital of Chios town (a.k.a. Hora) to dim and sacred caverns, from primitive huts to the rich jewels of the church and the arched cells of feudal strongholds—to the simple pleasures of sand and clear water.

This was always a rich island, producing crops, wine, mastic, silk—and merchant seamen. Instead of establishing colonies, Chios established trading depots, or *embória,* around the Mediterranean. Homer claimed that a descendant of Minos the Cretan brought wine to the island. Chios was an island state by the eighth century B.C. In the seventh and sixth centuries B.C. trade and the arts flourished.

Chios

| 0 | miles | 6 |
| 0 | km | 6 |

- Ayia Gala
- Viki
- Amades
- Yiossonas
- Nagos
- Ano Kardamyla
- Marmaro
- *Inousses*
- Volissos
- Pityous
- Lagada
- Limnia
- Daskalopetra
- Anavatos
- Vrontados
- Avgonima
- **Nea Moni**
- Hora
- **Airport**
- Bella Vista
- Kambos
- Koudari
- Vavyli
- Karfas
- Limani
- Sklavia
- Thymiana
- Ayia Ermioni
- Mesta
- Olymbi
- Katavaktis
- Pyrgi
- Komi
- Emborio

TO PSARA
TO LESVOS
TO SAMOS
TO PIRAEUS

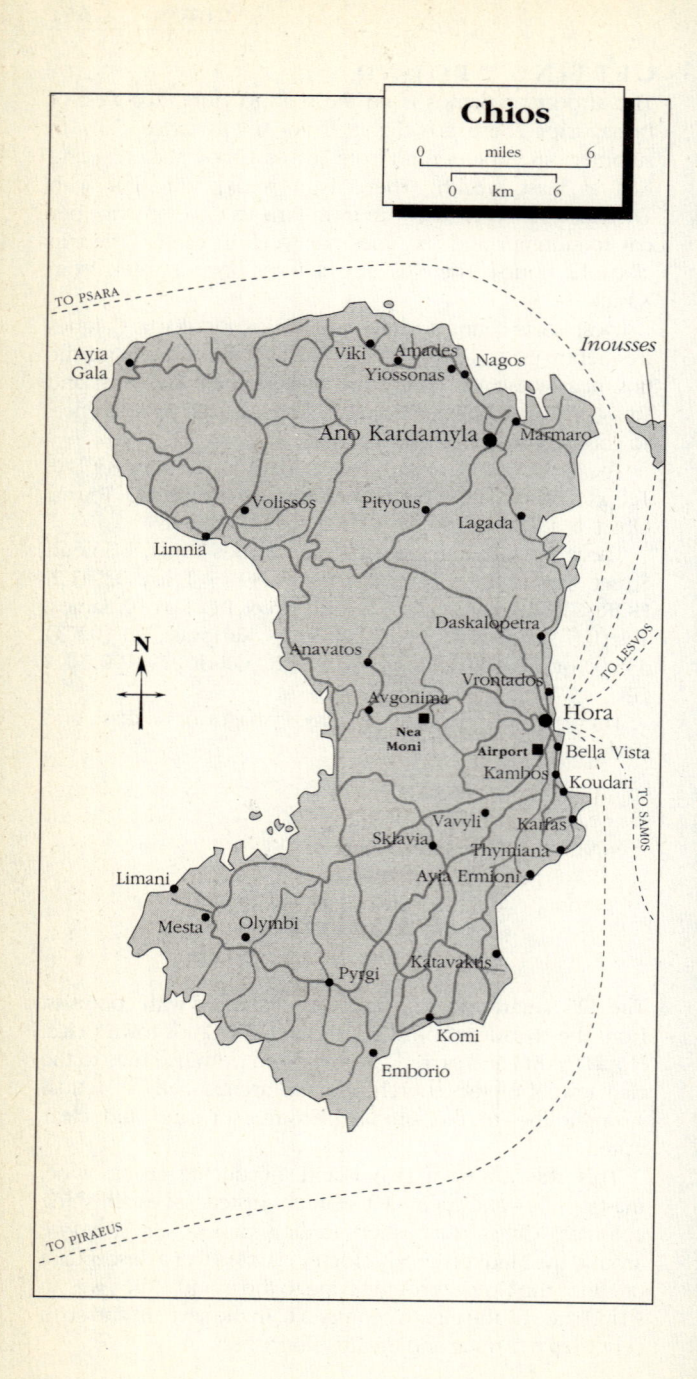

N

The wars between the Persians and the Athenians caught Chios in the middle, though her sympathies were with Athens. For a short while there was peace, but in the Peloponnesian Wars Chios aligned herself with Sparta. Chios even rebelled against Alexander—talk about David and Goliath—forcing him to leave a garrison on the island. Everybody wanted a piece of the action; the wars of Alexander's heirs and the Roman wars left Chios depleted and in ruins. Many Chiots were exiled, earthquakes toppled what was left of the main city, and they say the arch-pirate Moawiya destroyed anything left on the coasts.

With the Byzantines came peace and new settlements. But as Byzantium declined, it was unable to protect the islands from the Turks. The Genoese stepped in and sternly maintained the good times for two centuries. The Giustiniani family pounced on the profitable mastic trade, and arts and architecture flourished. Christopher Columbus studied navigation with Vrontados sea masters before his voyage to the "Indies."

Piali Pasha snatched the island in 1566 but left only a small garrison, leaving the islanders to thrive. Chiots began once more to establish trade abroad, and the island still boasts many shipowners. Seafarers brought contact with the wider world and its books, learning, and the arts. Chiots became famous for food and drink, big beds, and foolish, even smug, attitudes. It was all roses until the Greek War of Independence, when the Samians, insisting that the Chiots join them in rebellion, invaded the island and stirred up the peasants. On March 11, 1822, Lykourgos Logothetis landed on Chios and announced the revolution. With less than wild enthusiasm, the contented Chiots joined in. But Logothetis's men were ill-armed, with only homemade bayonets. On March 30, Kara Ali Pasha's fleet attacked Chios and took a bitter revenge. The furious sultan ordered mass executions. At least 25,000 (some say 60,000) Chiots were massacred; the survivors were enslaved, the women taken off to harems. The incident enraged the world; poems and paintings such as Delacroix's *Massacre of Chios* expressed sympathy. The French tried and failed to liberate the island. On June 19, the patriot Kanaris made a noble stab at the pasha: By night he crept up on the Turkish flagship, planted an explosive charge, and jumped into the water, barely escaping the Turkish guns. The ship blew up, with hundreds of Turkish casualties—as well as a number of Greek captives.

By 1832 many of the old families were gone for good. The island never quite recovered, and in 1881 a terrible earthquake wreaked havoc, causing thousands of fatalities and knocking down almost every building. In 1912 the Greek army drove out the pashas.

MAJOR INTEREST

Hora
Kastro
Museums: Archaeological, Byzantine, Argentis

Stately homes of Kambos
"Teacher's Rock" (Daskalopetra) near Vrontados
Nea Moni
Ruined village of Anavatos
The mastic villages
Day trips to islands of Psara and Inousses

Hora

The port (also called Chios) is a busy modern town in the middle of the island's east coast, with boutiques, restaurants, coffee bars, and plenty of hotels, ranging from the elegant Chandris (see below) to shabby rooms. There is even a tiny red-light district. The modern city has grown around the port, engulfing the Medieval **Kastro**—the fortress originally built by Byzantines in the tenth century and enriched by the subsequent tenants. Most of it was ruined either in the struggles of revolution or the earthquakes. Now you walk through an arch near the Dimarchío (Town Hall) and find yourself inside an old, dusty village of Turkish balconies and crumbling houses, in sharp contrast to the modern town. But now and then a house is lovingly restored, suddenly transforming the street from decayed to picturesque. A tiny graveyard of monuments topped by Turkish turbans contains the remains of an admiral blown up by Kanaris, in a wreathed sarcophagus.

The round tower to the right of the entrance to the Kastro through the Porta Maggiore was built by the Venetians. Standing here you can see the 15th-century **Palace of the Giustiniani**. In the high-vaulted small cellar of the palace a group of martyrs was held in April 1822. Up the steps the **Byzantine Museum**—labeled "Ephorate of Byzantine Antiquities Giustiniani"—contains a collection of frescoes from Nea Moni, west of Hora (see below). From Olymbi to the south have come icons, frescoes, folk-art gates, and a handsome floor mosaic. Some wall paintings by well-known Byzantine artists are remarkably expressive.

The castle is being extensively repaired. Museum hours are Tuesdays through Sundays 9:00 A.M. to 8:00 P.M.

A statue of Kanaris stands in the Municipal Gardens in front of the town hall by the main town square, Vounáki. Coffee and ice cream are available at shaded tables near the taxi stands in the square. Far up and to the right, off the main shopping street of Aplotarias, is a super taverna called **Hotzas** (74 Steftsoúris Street), with fine *mezédes,* the only barrel wine in town, good cooking, and reasonable prices.

The courtyard of the old mosque is littered with fragments of marble—bearing inscriptions in Turkish, Arabic, Greek, Armenian, and Hebrew, the latter from memorials to Jews who emigrated from Spain in the 15th century—cannonballs and cannon, and a sarcophagus of the Giustinianis. Through the door of the mosque you can see a tapestry version of the Delacroix painting of the Chiot massacre. Unfortunately the door is locked—scholars are doing research here.

The **Homerion Conference Center**, a state-of-the-art exhibition gallery, auditorium (462 seats), and conference hall, also serves as a community center. An old Turkish bath next to the bus station may or may not become a municipal art gallery.

The **Koraïs Library**, on Korai Street in a Chian building that is a characteristic blend of Byzantine, Renaissance, and local taste, contains 150,000 volumes and exhibits such as the first Greek flag, a unique brass astrolabe, and editions of Homer in many languages. Upstairs is the **Argentis Museum**, a room or two of which are devoted to nicely displayed folk arts, costume dolls, and prints. The most interesting section is the vast space devoted to the Argentis family, a monument to an obsession: portrait after expert portrait, records of doings, needlework samplers—every detail of their lives. The saddest display is a family tree with medallion portraits of prolific generations gradually culminating in a lone, unmarried writer and scholar of Chian history.

Just opposite the stadium, on Michalon Street in the new (south) part of town, is the very modern **Archaeological Museum**. One wing is set aside for research; the others display (with English labels) statues, pottery, and marbles. An inscribed edict of Alexander the Great calls back the exiles of 320 B.C. to establish a democratic constitution in Chios and details the taxes and the garrison to be supported locally. There are some nice quotations from ancient literature about Chios, which claims—as do other islands—to be the homeland of Homer.

Off the harbor, in back of the Iviskos café, is a milk bar

serving luscious fresh yogurt and cheese pitas, and the **Byzantium**, an inexpensive authentic taverna. If you don't mind being in the middle of the action—and the traffic in Hora is very heavy—you might stay at the tiny, shiny **Apollonion**, right on the corner of the square near the yogurt shop, up Roidou Street. Rooms have baths and are very clean. Refrigerators are available on each floor and the prices are low.

The waterfront is the place to be after dark. Cafés abound, some inexplicably jammed and others inexplicably deserted. Far to the northern end, past the port authority and under the jetty wall, is a very good *ouzerí* called **Icthyoskala** with fish *mezédes*, plenty for a meal. Try the dried mackerel. The disco-bar **En Plo** upstairs in the center of the waterfront is wildly popular.

At the far (south) end of town, away from the madding crowd, is the hospitable **Chandris Hotel** with swimming pool and cool dignity. You may well run into visiting VIPs—members of Parliament, electoral candidates, or TV stars, with their respective entourages. Prices aren't as high as you might expect. Across the street is the more relaxed **Hotel Kyma**, with an all-day coffee pot and orange juice jug, a wraparound sea-view veranda on each floor, and a friendly, homey atmosphere. Both will help arrange tours and offer their own excursions.

At this end of town are the **Symposium Restaurant**, offering Italian and French—*à la grecque*—dishes in a little garden, and the sea-view terrace of the large, clean **Bella Vista**, which specializes in fresh fish. Ask for *pikilía,* a wonderful sampling of everything.

Closer to the center of town, the pretty **Phaidra Traditional Pension**, or Phaidra "Motel" if you read the other sign, is a restored Neoclassical house with a small bar and rooms of interesting shapes and sizes.

Up from the port on Koundouriótou Street (by the Kahlua café) is the **Neoclassical Pension**, an old mansion with various-size rooms being lovingly restored by its young managers. Some of the high ceilings have had the whitewash removed from the lovely old paintings that the former occupant had hidden. Here you may have to share a bathroom. This pension has a hidden glory: Behind it is an enchanted garden that serves as a bar, where little tables are hidden among trees in a world of their own.

The **Ionic Center**, located in a 19th-century stately mansion converted to classrooms and dormitories, offers summer courses in Greek for visitors, as well as cultural and study groups.

Kambos and South

From the 14th century until 1822, Kambos, the area south of the port, was cultivated by rich merchants. Orange trees and orchards drew water from the hills to the west. All you see from the road are high stone walls, occasionally pierced by an elaborate gate or a studded wooden door. Behind these walls are the *archontiká,* the stately homes. These may have begun as individual fortress towers, but they developed a unique architecture, combining Italian, Byzantine, and early Christian styles with native stone and artistry. Oddly, the houses are not large; emphasis is on the thousands of trees, the rose gardens, the pergolas, the cisterns, the waterwheels drawn by donkey power bringing well water to the pools and lily ponds, and the marble statuary decorating arbors of flowers. The courtyards are paved with hand-cut tiles or with the Chian black-and-white pebble mosaic in floral, animal, and geometric patterns. These places were intended to display wealth—but only to the chosen who were allowed behind the walls. The 1881 earthquake destroyed the upper floors, and many homes have been left in ruin.

A few have been restored. Among these, one contains the beautiful **Perivoli,** a popular restaurant in the huge enclosed garden among old stone water cisterns and orange trees. Not only is the restaurant charming, but you can actually rent rooms (with bath and shower, or shared at a lower cost) in the romantic golden-stone mansion, exquisitely restored and furnished with handwoven rugs and curtains, local paintings, and simple good taste. Some of the large rooms, with high pine ceilings and polished wood floors, can be connected as suites. Rent a moped or use the minibus to town or airport. Enjoy "Greek Night," hosted once or twice a week by the restaurant. In winter the restaurant is in a sort of conservatory with fireplaces, oak tables, and Renaissance arches. No wonder people keep coming back.

Another welcoming restored mansion, painted white, a bit simpler and less expensive, is concealed in a quiet road at Frangovouni (on the Thymiana bus route): the **Pension Voulamadis.** Not quite so dramatic, the rooms are clean, comfortable, and peaceful, and the friendly family will let you use the refrigerator.

Farther south on the coast road are charming villages and

beaches, and the famous frescoes of the **church of Panayía Krina** at Vávyli—not far from a village called Sklaviá (Slavery). Close to the airport is the popular **Acroyiali Disco**; the **Roxy** is at Bella Vista just south of Hora.

At the beach resort of **Kondári**, just south of Bella Vista, the new **Golden Odyssey** is an elegant 150-bed hotel in a garden 100 yards from the beach, with a drugstore, a beauty parlor, a huge swimming pool, and surprisingly low rates for its clean, white perfection. The town swimming pool, housed in a white, tent-shaped building, is on the Karfas road at Kondari.

Karfás, just down the coast a piece, is a very popular beach resort, somewhat overwhelmingly inundated with grand hotels. The 107-room **Golden Sands** is one example, with a swimming pool next to the beach, extensive terraces, and local motifs adapted to a modern marble decor. Here you get the full treatment—valet services, beauty parlors, air-conditioning—at a cost. At the opposite end of the price scale, Mr. **Zevgios** rents 16 rooms (with bath) in a new but traditionally styled seaside house down the road. If you like a very Greek atmosphere with lots of life, kids, and the sound of human activity, the **Yiamos** restaurant, cafeteria, and hotel on the beach is popular and cheerful. It's fairly simple, but the adequate rooms have a sea view behind a series of pillars on the veranda.

Thymiana, just to the south, is a center for handmade toys, crafts, and needlework. Shop here at the **Popular Art Cooperative**; Tel: 511-80 or 518-20.

Ayia Ermióni, mostly new and with many apartments to let, is quieter than Karfas; see the Chios Travel Office for rentals here. A restaurant, a little marina, many new rooms to let, half a mile away from the beach of Megali Limnionas—all this as well as the odd hovel. The first pine-shuttered white house situated on the rocky shore as you come from Hora belongs to the **Papanikolaos** family, who rent small but clean and new apartments at reasonable rates. Here you swim from flat rocks. At the nearby little resort of **Ayia Fotiní**, the **Esperides** is a comfortable new hotel with excellent prices, its rooms and apartments on a long, clean, pebble beach. Book early for high season. Inland from here and 9 km (6 miles) southwest of Hora on the Kallimasía road is **Stelios's Taverna**, well known for delicious *mezedákia*.

Kataráktis, on the coast just south of Kallimasia, has been said to have underwater ruins, but archaeologists have recently searched to no avail. It is a very, very quiet seaside village with a small marina and pebbly beach.

Beaches continue down the coast, while inland are farms

and villages. A characteristic modern Greek country sight is a tethered goat, a truck garden under a clump of olive trees—and a ghostly scarecrow made of tattered plastic bags.

One of the prettiest of beaches is sandy **Komi**, on Kala Motis Bay, still undeveloped and simple. There are one or two eating places, a few private houses, and a couple of buildings with apartments to let (try those of Mr. **Lambrakis**). Or you can rent an adequate, inexpensive room at the **Komi Hotel** and restaurant at the bus stop.

On the way south to the fine pebble beach of Emborio the landscape is rather stark. Then one of the *xysta* (*xysta* is a graffito technique by which whitewash is painted over a dark surface and scraped away, leaving designs of leaves and flowers and geometric shapes in horizontal bands) houses in a garden comes into view, looking like a white lace frill on a bouquet. Once the site of a temple to Athena (middle of the sixth century B.C.) that was rebuilt frequently until its final incarnation as a basilica in the sixth century A.D., **Emborió** has developed recently and quickly as a tiny seaside resort. Camping and nudity are forbidden; the small beach is immaculate. Scramble over the rocks to finer and finer shingles. In the harbor are a few rooms and eating places.

Southwest of Hora

To the southwest of Hora are some charming villages, old churches with fine paintings—and the **mastichóhora**, the mastic towns.

The products of Chios have always been related to pleasures: wine, sweets, mastic (a resin used for chewing gum), candy, and varnish for paintings. Once the mainstay of the Chian economy, mastic comes from the lentisk tree, which grows here exclusively. Now it's sold as gum under the name Elma and as plain unsweetened *mastíca*. It was so popular among the harem ladies that the pashas treated the Chiots of the mastic villages like diamond miners: body searches as they left work, isolation of the workers' townships, rigorous penalties for theft. But the mastic villages were spared the terrors of 1822.

These Medieval fortress villages were established under the Genoese from the 11th to the 14th centuries. Far from the dangerous coastline, they were always independent, huddled around defensive towers, closing their gates from sunset to sunrise. They have changed very little. The streets leading to the towers are narrow and twisted—the widest are only wide enough for a loaded mule. Streets stop suddenly, ending in a triangular corner house, to confuse invaders. Houses are very close together, and often the top stories overhang enough to connect to the house opposite, making the street into an arcade. The ground floor indeed may still be used as a byre for the donkeys or the goats. Upstairs, the living quarters surround an open court, and everything is built of stone. Roofs are the same height, to facilitate escape.

In **Pyrgí**, 35 km (22 miles) southwest of Hora, the walls are decorated with *xysta*. Women sit on their steps in skirts, aprons, and kerchiefs, chatting and embroidering. Farm women come in with donkeys loaded with potatoes and vegetables to market here. The **church of the Assumption of the Virgin** (1694) in the square is decorated with xysta crosses and angels. Shops sell reproductions of graffiti—cheap ones machine-made, expensive ones handmade. Mr. **Alexopoulos**'s balcony restaurant hangs over the charming square; the helpful proprietor speaks English.

A post office in the square hides behind a dark red door, two doors from the Agrotikí Trápeza (Agricultural Bank). The OTE (a simple public telephone in this case) is just outside the tiny, beautifully preserved Byzantine **church of Ayioi Apóstoli** (another of Pyrgí's 30 churches), whose entrance is buried under an archway. The interior is decorated with fine wall paintings by a local painter of the 16th century.

Not far from Pyrgí is the site of the **Temple to Apollo**, at **Phanai**, whose first remains date from the ninth century B.C. On the hill are traces of a Byzantine fortress, and beneath those, remains from the Bronze Age. There are other remnants of ancient temples and palaces on the hill of Profitas Iliás to the north.

Sparse trees dot the farmland; the village of **Olýmbi** west of Pyrgi resembles a pueblo furnished with stone corrals. At first the town of **Mestá**, just west of Olymbi, seems to consist of stone huts gathered around a red-roofed church; then you see it as a wide, short castle, with balconies and flowers clinging to its outer walls and broken towers at the corners. You plunge into a maze of tunnels, with vistas of stone arches dappled with light coming through the openings above. The word "hidden" takes on a new dimension inside this stone shell as you wander through a narrow maze, the world shut out and far away.

The inhabitants have suddenly wakened to the fact that

this is a unique environment. Property prices have soared and everybody is doing up the old homes as rooms to rent. The family inheritance is turning into a gold mine. Few people in this village speak English, but their children are learning. Both Pyrgi and Mesta offer special accommodation. You'll love the clean white-painted stables with a few pieces of embroidery on the wall, the patent afterthought of the bathroom, with the shower stuck on the wall anywhere and likely to spray wildly, and the kids sleeping happily in what used to be a hayloft.

The **Women's Tourist and Agricultural Cooperative** for both towns has an office outside the entrance to Pyrgi; Tel: (0271) 724-96. The Coop lets rooms and sells handicrafts and herbs, and stray books left by tourists make up a little foreign-language library. The **GNTO** (Greek National Tourist Organization) lets rooms and apartments in restored village houses and operates out of the office of Mr. Dimitris Pipidis in Mesta's central plateia.

The iconostasis of the deserted **church of the Taxiárchis** (A.D. 1200) in Mesta is carved wood, with marvelous detailed legends depicted among foliage and grotesque creatures (1833; school of Chios). The major icons are in the new church. The modern **church of the Archangels**, one of the largest in Chios, is very grand and overdecorated, a combination in style of folk art and Rococo. Everybody in town wanted to contribute something, so gold and crystal crosses dangle in front of the bright triple iconostasis and paintings litter the walls. The two old icons are buried in silver and laden with votive offerings.

North of Mesta, the **Limáni** (Harbor) is charming. There are excellent fish tavernas and rooms to rent. Try **Maria's Labyrinth**, constructed in conventional plaster and wood; with Mariette Braun as landlady your stay is bound to be interesting. The rocky beach is a scramble away beyond the tavernas past the lighthouse. The watchtower is still whole, if you like climbing.

West of Hora

Along a beautiful, peaceful dirt road west out of Hora, among olive and pine groves, is the **Nea Moní** (New Monastery)—new in 1042. Tall cypresses, crumbling stone, and the sound of goat bells greet you. A sign at the door requests respectful behavior.

For most of its life Nea Moni was a wealthy, important

institution with a famous library. It began to decline early in the 19th century. In 1822 when the Turks were slashing their way through the island, they slaughtered the monks and searched for treasure, eventually putting the church to the torch. The final blow was the earthquake of 1881, which toppled all the domes. Too much has happened here: It's said that the cistern where refugee women were imprisoned still echoes with ghostly laments, and the bishop whose tomb is in the garden rises at night to pray in the church. The monastery was recently miraculously preserved from fire. You can see the circle where the fire was stopped by a procession of women carrying the holy icon.

The skulls and bones of the martyrs are carefully kept in cupboards in a chapel at the entrance, tended by two very old nuns, who live by a calendar 13 days behind the rest of the world and who sing psalms and often demonstrate—with accompanying chants—the ancient wooden alarm paddle that woke the monks.

Lately efforts have been made to restore and preserve the monastery's glorious gold Chian-style mosaics, with colors as bright as yesterday. Many pieces are missing, but some walls are almost complete. Fine marble decorations still exist. Display cases hold relics and a scrap of silk altar cloth, the only remaining sample from the silk industry of Chios. In a tiny chapel is a delectable wall painting of three priests carrying an icon of the Panayía (Virgin), which is itself on the wall.

Along the same road, **Avgónima**, a ruined hamlet where a handful of people still live as if inside a castle wall, has a school and even a taverna. In the new church is an interesting icon of Christ sitting in a chalice.

Anávatos, just north of Avgonima, perches at the top of a steep cliff that rises suddenly out of a wilderness. All colors of rock and sand splatter down the mountainside. The villagers were massacred in 1822 along with refugees who had sought a last shelter in this fort. Many threw themselves from the cliff.

At the top of the cliff the church of the Archangels is being restored at a pace set by low funds and the few climbs a cement-bearing donkey can make in a day. Traces of frescoes remain like memories of a dream. The church is held together with new iron; the rest of the village is broken arches and doorways and stairs and ruined floors—and a dizzying drop protected by absolutely nothing. Walk with care and don't let the kids run loose. Down at the back are little stone walls, fig and olive trees, and some sad houses.

North of Hora

Pebble beaches dotted with tavernas and rooms to let line the shore north of Hora. At **Daskalópetra** (Teacher's Rock), five minutes from Hora, the bus drops you in a pretty plateia with two snack bars and a playground; continue uphill to the poet's classroom, a circular site complete with seats and altar reputed to be where Homer conducted classes. A marine museum called Love of Progress is located here, and a monument to Yannis Psycharis, a famous champion of the demotic Greek language, faces Asia Minor. (Should you observe a six-foot cube made of screen dangling from a tree, you are not hallucinating. It's a container for drying octopus.)

Lo beach, along the coast road, is a private pebble beach to which admission is charged (70 drachmas). There are showers, pedalos, and a million people, especially in August.

Among the better buys of the island are the well-designed self-catering apartments and maisonettes in **Vrontádos** (Vrontados actually surrounds Daskalopetra) called **Kyveli** (Cybele), bright and shiny clean, a few feet from the beach, with one- and two-bedroom units and a swimming pool. One child up to 12 years of age is free, the rest of your kids half price. Less expensive small apartments are rented by **P. Karapournos**. The pleasant, middle-range **Hotel Xenios** has a hillside terrace, a pool, and a fireplace in the lobby for winter, and almost all rooms have a sea view. Venetia is the disco here, or you could visit the peaceful convent of Our Lady of the Myrtles (**Panayía Myrtidiótissa**).

Near the village of Sikiáda is a proud new campsite, with eating places around the little bay below. But the favorite place to go for dinner is the pretty harbor village of **Langáda**, large enough to offer minimarkets, cafés, and a row of fish tavernas offering octopus (*ktapódi*).

By and large, roads in Chios are very good, although the planner seems to have had a passion for the S-curve even when there is nothing to go around. A magnolia tree with flowers as big as dinner plates decorates the road leading north to the pleasant tree-shaded plateia in the center of the engaging village of **Pityoús**, "Homer's birthplace." The remains of Medieval watchtowers guard the village from above.

Twenty-seven kilometers (17 miles) from Hora is **Ano** (Upper) **Kardámyla**, a quiet farm village resting below the Tower of the Old Woman, a remnant of the Medieval town. There are older remains of a temple of Delphian Apollo and of an ancient road on the same hill as well. The shady plateia has a little bank, one kafeneio, a church, and a few houses. Down at **Marmaro**, or Kato (Lower) Kardámyla, you'll find the sea. Little houses dream in the sun, new paint dries on boats, and the new café **Makaki** sits in the tiny square—and bus station—dominated by a giant sundial. The streets are narrow between foot-deep wooden balconies. At night several cafés and a taverna are open, but if you want lunch, don't wait until 2:00 here—the proprietor may have already gone to siesta.

At the far end of town is the **Kardamyla Hotel**, recently acquired by the same hospitality-prone management as the Kyma in Hora. With a veranda right on top of a private sandy beach lined with trees, this establishment is undergoing daily improvements. Something about certain hosts affects the atmosphere and leads their guests to make friends; the management of the Kyma and Kardamyla has this rare quality. Impromptu parties, excursions, boat rides—anything can happen. The hotel is in sight of the church of St. Mark's of the Lovers, to which sweethearts make special pilgrimages. Across the street is the newly built **Chiona,** in the white-plaster-and-wood tradition, with a restaurant and a very great interest in ecology—including special discounts to ecologists!

To the northwest, the character of the landscape changes from rock to high rolling hills. Past Pityous, something heartbreaking has happened: Endless acres of pathetic tree trunks lie like burnt matchsticks on the barren ground. Not long ago it was beautiful pine forest. All across the center of the island the hills have been savaged. Sad, scorched signs among the devastation say "Please be careful of forest fires."

The destruction of the foliage has revealed village after village that nobody loves. The paint has dropped from the brown walls and the tile roofs have fallen in. Collected in little pockets in the hills, a few residents still keep their houses painted white. Here and there an old man or woman tends a few goats and chickens. Once these were important farmlands. But even then most of these houses were only huts: one room for the animals downstairs, one for the family upstairs. People slept on a raised step by the fireplace. Old Genoese protective walls can be seen occasionally. Some villages were abandoned in 1822, others more recently, as Chiots went abroad, made their fortunes, and bought property elsewhere. The villages are labeled, but not signposted, and there are a number of dirt branch roads.

Along the rocky landscape of the northern shores pink oleanders fill the river beds. Glyfáda, Nagos, and Yióssonas (named for Jason, whose ship *Argo* was said to have landed here) are clean pebble-and-sand beaches. As the roads become more difficult, the beaches grow less crowded. **Nagos**, north of Kardamila, is a little garden village with a café. Just to the west of Nagos at **Amádes** you'll find a snack bar before the turn down to the beach as you go through nibbled mountain scrub on a twisting road. **Viki**, the starting place for a climb up Mount Profítas Iliás (4,215 feet), is still surrounded by trees.

About 60 km (37 miles) from Hora in the northwest corner of Chios is the enchanted village of **Ayías Galas**, unchanged for a thousand years. Old women shout as they shove the behinds of their two goats, while the donkey ambles back into his stall under the house. Elderly gentlemen surrounded by a mountain of greenery smile toothlessly as they crouch to duck under crumbling stone arches. Most people are too old to keep up the whitewashing. Although there are only 70 of the former 473 inhabitants left, the village is alive and well. The voices of American children astonish you in this setting: They come here to visit Granny in summer and are delighted to show you around. Tiny stone steps lead past the little tower down to the present village church, and then 114 more-comfortable steps go to an 11th-century Byzantine church built against the rock under the village, as if emerging from the earth. A bat-filled monk's cell guards the entrance to the outer church, where the oldest (1711) carved-wood iconostasis in Chios is still in place, with merry carved faces and plastic flowers decorating the painted wooden ones. Within the church is another church, and a cave—bring your flashlight. Frescoes can still be seen, though they are faded. Inside are more caves, and a few yards below is the entrance to a relatively unexplored stalactite-filled chamber. As you emerge from all this inwardness, the children assure you that if the metal cross, sticking into a rock above like King Arthur's sword, is ever removed, the whole village will vanish without a trace.

A few of the villages in the northwest are occupied; occasionally a house is even repaired or built. In general, mountain village means that what you get is mountain village: There are no extras. With luck there may be a *kafeneío,* even a telephone, but certainly no shopping, tourist goods, postcards, or handmade jewelry.

Volissós, back down toward Hora, was once an important

village, crowned with a castle with six round towers; it is another candidate for the birthplace of Homer. There are wonderful unfrequented beaches on this coast.

On the sand-and-pebble beach at **Limnos** (just west of Limniá, Volissos's port), under burned hills and a ruined castle, sits a resort with large shade trees, a modest taverna, pedalos and umbrellas, and even rooms to rent. On the coast is a little green spot, and in the green spot is a pretty bay, and in the curve of the bay, a few minutes' drive north, is the beautiful huge courtyard (complete with restaurant) of the **Ayia Markéllas Monastery**, on a lovely clean beach. Individuals and entire families can rent the monastic cells (about 12 feet by 12 feet, they are minimally furnished with one simple iron bed, two chairs, and a little table). Additional beds can be purchased at a central store, cooking is done on grills under the generous shade of plane trees, and washing is done in well water brought up by a *manganos* (waterwheel). There are 90 rooms and 24 new, Turkish-style toilets. The cost is minimal for this unique, if summer camp–like, accommodation, but you must book in advance—and bring your own beach umbrella.

PSARA

Psará is ideal for those who would like to withdraw from the world and meditate for a few days. It's a barren little place, and once you go you are stuck until the next day, probably in the old jail, now a GNTO (in Greek EOT) hostelry. At least the GNTO taverna is excellent. This is a fine place to stay if you really want a lot of nothing.

Boats go to Psara on alternate days from Hora (18 nautical miles, four hours) and from Limnia, so it is possible to leave from Hora and return the next day to Limnia. Admiral Konstantinos Kanaris was born on this isle of proud and independent mariners, and the Greek Revolution spoke to their souls. In 1824 the Turks, having devastated Chios, Samos, and Lesvos, turned to Psara. About 30,000 people, among them women and children who had fled from the other islands, desperately tried to defend themselves against an all-out attack. About 3,000 to 4,000 escaped in small boats, and many were rescued by the French fleet. Thereafter the island was deserted.

Since then the French apparently have had a special interest in the island. In the 1980s a Frenchman related to Kanaris, Michel Marbot, and a Greek, Michael Goutos, decided to restore the island. It is being resettled as a Franco-Greek project and even has a bilingual newspaper. Electricity was brought in and a water purification project started up. Old houses are being restored and summer amenities developed. Even plants and animals are being restocked. It is quiet, with pleasant beaches and some accommodations, including the **EOT Guesthouse** in a former prison.

INOUSSES

Inoússes is actually a group of nine islets off the northeast coast of Chios, but unless you have a private boat, all but one—the largest—are inaccessible. Caïques leave from Hora several times a day.

As you come into the main harbor, which is sheltered by tiny islands, at least seven churches are visible, each a different color. The hillsides are green, with large houses far apart from one another. Quiet and elegant, the island is inhabited by shipping magnates of such wealth that they eclipse a mere Onassis. Among the trees and villas, where glossy white goats browse, is a yacht club, a post office/bank, and a naval academy. Benefactors have endowed the island with statuary and a children's shelter for off-islanders. A charming bronze *Gulls in Flight* graces the waterfront, and a green bronze mermaid combs her hair on a rock in the harbor. An American nun has trained a fine choir, which performs on religious occasions.

In winter there are about 500 inhabitants; when the shipowners' families return for their holidays, there may be as many as 2,000. The town plans a museum to house an unusual collection of model ships, mostly built by prisoners in the time of Napoleon. One recent purchase was valued at £39,000 in London.

The **convent of the Evangelist** holds the body of a recently canonized young woman who was so pious that her prayers were answered when she offered to save her father from cancer by sacrificing her own life. The monastery, very luxurious and beautifully placed, is surrounded by cypress and is accessible by rough road or sea; there is a tiny jetty at the shoreline.

You may not be drowned in hospitality, but you will not be attacked with it either, as in parts of Samos. There is just one place to stay overnight here—**Thalassopolos** rooms—and a lone taverna. Inousses is a great place for anyone who is happy with his or her own company and who appreciates peace and gracious quiet.

GETTING AROUND

There are flights two to four times a day from Athens to Chios, and once or twice a week from Lesvos, Samos, and Mykonos. There are daily ferryboats in season to and from Piraeus (ten hours), three a week out of season, and frequent service to Lesvos. Ferryboats go twice weekly to Thessaloniki (change at Mytilini), as well as to Kavala/Alexandroupolis via Limnos. They run weekly to Volos and to Samos–Ikaria–Kos–Rhodes. The *Capitan Stamatis* goes alternately to Samos and Turkey (Çeşme). Normally a ferryboat departs from Hora to Psara on alternate days (four-hour trip), while a caïque travels back and forth from Psara to Volissos (Limnia) on the other days. In summer, a boat may go from Hora to Psara on Sundays, and there are occasional excursions.

On Chios there are nine bus routes that run daily to the villages, four days a week to Volissos, and once a week to Nea Moni. Blue local buses go from the opposite side of the gardens (11 Vas. Georgíou) to the beach at Karfas. The buses belong to the drivers, and it sometimes happens that they don't leave the main road to enter the villages unless a passenger asks to get off. This means that when returning, you are better off walking back to the main road to wave down the bus. Buy bus tickets for local rides from an agent before boarding, and punch in on the machine on board.

Chios now has radio taxi; Tel: 211-11. Car and motorcycle rentals are available almost everywhere.

A number of private tour agencies—such as Ionia Travel, Chios Tours, Dollar Tours, Chandris, and others—line the waterfront (Prokyméa) in Hora. Day trips are available to beaches, Inousses, Turkey, and around the island. For information, touring, and accommodation, a useful organization is the Chios island tourist office in Hora on Kansari Street; Tel: 242-17. The ELPA (automobile association) office is at 19 Rodokanáki Street in Hora; Tel: (0271) 224-45 or 230-76. The Union of Room Renters also publishes a leaflet directory, which you can pick up at the tourist office in Hora.

LESVOS

Hidden away in the northern hump of the island of Lesvos is Pelópi, the ancestral home of Michael Dukakis, whose inhabitants were hoping and praying that the new U.S. president would offer money to build a new road to the village. Once you have driven around in Lesvos you will sympathize: Most of the roads were surely built for Persian donkeys in 600 B.C.

Those donkeys' descendants are still around, faithfully lugging loads of goat fodder and fruit. Goats, chickens, and sheep wander freely in the roads, sometimes accompanied by a man with a handkerchief tied over his head or a woman in long skirts and an apron, tugging at the beaded bridle.

Village houses are made of stone or stucco with red-tile roofs, but the largest, most elaborate building in every village is the schoolhouse. The white boxes among the trees are beehives; sometimes you can see a keeper—barehanded, with only his eyes protected. Big red plastic containers of sheep's milk appear on the roadside in the morning, waiting for the yogurt-maker.

Lesvos (or Lesbos, also often called Mytilini after its principal city) is Greece's third-largest island (after Crete and Evia), shaped like a lumpy, sideways letter K split by the Gulf of Yeras in the southeast and the bigger Gulf of Kalloni more or less in the center. Its rocky, pine-forested landscape is highest at Mount Olympos to the south (3,160 feet), though there are steep wooded hills to the north as well. The western hills are rolling and scrubby.

MAJOR INTEREST

Mytilini castle
Teriade and Theophilos art museums
Church of the Archangel Michael in Mandamados
Beautiful towns of Molyvos, Petra, Ayiasos
Monasteries of Limonos and Perivoli
Beaches

Mytilini

Mytilíni, the capital and port on the eastern coast facing the Turkish port of Dikili and, farther inland, ancient Pergamum, is a busy town overlooked by a big, marvelous **castle**, built

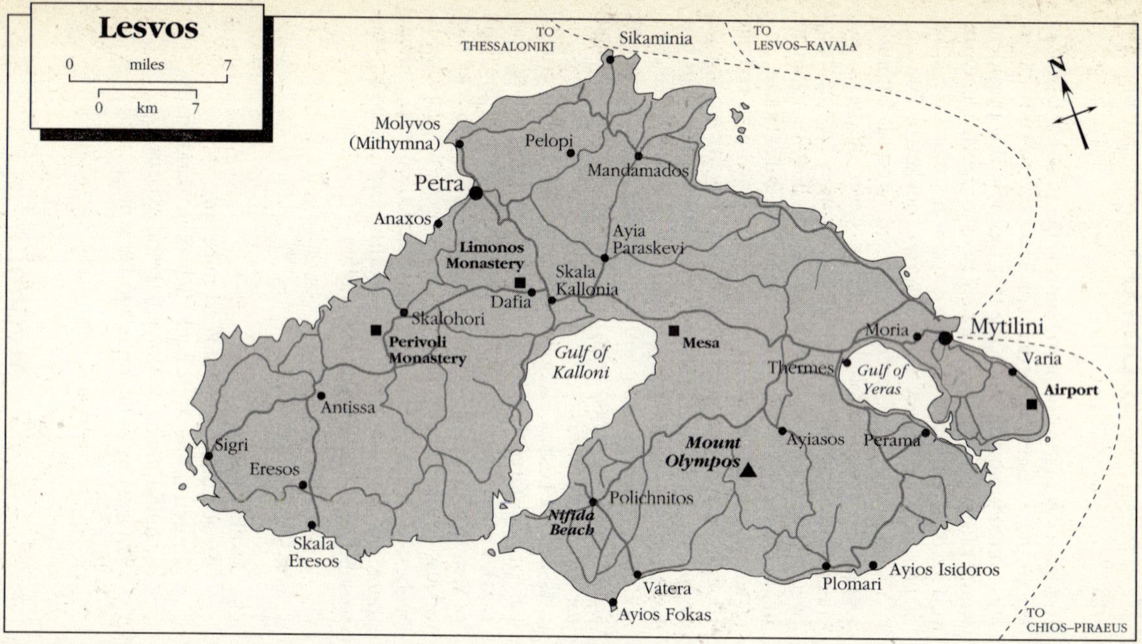

Lesvos
0 miles 7
0 km 7
N
TO THESSALONIKI
TO LESVOS–KAVALA
TO CHIOS–PIRAEUS
Sikaminia
Molyvos (Mithymna)
Pelopi
Mandamados
Petra
Anaxos
Limonos Monastery
Ayia Paraskevi
Skala Kallonia
Dafia
Skalohori
Perivoli Monastery
Gulf of Kalloni
Mesa
Moria
Mytilini
Varia
Airport
Thermes
Gulf of Yeras
Antissa
Sigri
Eresos
Skala Eresos
Mount Olympos
Ayiasos
Perama
Polichnitos
Nifida Beach
Vatera
Ayios Fokas
Plomari
Ayios Isidoros

in Byzantine times and rebuilt in 1374 by the Genoese Gattelusi family. It is one of the largest castles in the Mediterranean, and strange crypts and dungeons are hidden in its towers and bastions.

The southern curve of the port is lined with shipping offices (where day trips to Dikili in Turkey are sold at a whopping price), tour agencies, hotels, restaurants—and no doubt it always has had such commercial enterprises, because the island's naturally superior harbor is right on the trade routes between Asia and Europe. During the Athenian reign—and especially under the elected dictator Pittacus, who had a talent for soothing rival factions—Lesvos became a great commercial and cultural center.

The island always produced wine, oil, grain—and lyric poets, such as Arion, Terpander, and, later, Sappho. There must be something in the air, because artists and poets thrive here. Recent Lesvian notables are Nobel Prize winner Odysseus Elytis, author Stratis Myrivilis, and the incomparable primitive painter Theophilos. And as for spirits, local ouzo is famous for its potency.

In the fifth century B.C., during the Peloponnesian War, the city-state of Mytilini rebelled, and the annoyed Athenians sent a shipful of troops authorized to perform wholesale executions. Athens shortly thought better of it and sent another galley to change the orders. It arrived just in time, and only the ringleaders were killed. Thereafter, however, an Athenian garrison was stationed here. By the time of Alexander Lesvos was again in Persian hands. From then on the island changed owners with every wave of events: Romans, Seljuk Turks, Byzantines, Venetians, Genoese, and Ottoman Turks all played ball with it.

During the period of the Greek revolution in the 1820s, any signs of sympathy were violently quelled. Many churches hold the remains of local saints martyred by the Turks not so very long ago. **Mytilini Cathedral** has portraits of many of them, as well as the body of young Saint Theodore, who after his death appeared during a time of plague and miraculously stopped the epidemic. His darkened hands can be seen through the glass of his coffin, and his skull is separately cased—the workmen accidentally decapitated the body when exhuming it.

Around the bend near the ferryboat dock is the **Archaeological Museum**: a garden with some sculpture and one room displaying some fine late-Roman mosaics. It's open every day except Mondays from 8:00 A.M. to 1:00 P.M. A new museum is being constructed.

A statue of Liberty holds her torch high on a pedestal overlooking the sandy town beach—with all the comforts of umbrellas and lounge chairs and pedalos—under the castle walls. There are ruins under the water for the Cousteaux among us. Opposite the beach is a woodland recreation area with picnic tables and drinking water.

The extent of the castle can be seen clearly from the remains of an **ancient theater** on a nearby hillside, which consists of a grass bank and a stage circle. Long ago the castle and town were separated from the mainland, connected only by bridges. Constructed on Byzantine ruins by the Gattelusi, this crumbling fortress—both going under the ground and towering into the air, with bastions in the sea itself—is a delight for Dungeons and Dragons enthusiasts. Around it are the remains of the prehistoric city, where archaeologists are having a field day.

The strong radical tradition of the island didn't prevent 18th- and 19th-century merchants from thriving and building tall, narrow mansions of a type unique to Mytilini, with towers and niches for now-vanished statuary. Happily, the authorities began to think twice about demolishing these buildings and are even beginning to restore them.

Bus schedules for the day are posted on a blackboard at the city bus station at the northern end of the port (next to the old house of the Folk Museum). The very good village buses leave from the far southern end of the port; on the waterfront between the stations is the official tourist information office; Tel: (0251) 213-29. The main shopping district is in the market behind the harbor, especially around Ermoú Street. In the harbor is the completely renovated and air-conditioned **Lesvion Hotel**. Try the **Dimitrakis** fish taverna to the north of the port for lunch, and the **Asteria**, on the opposite side, for your evening meal.

In the suburb of **Variá**, 4 km (2.5 miles) south toward the airport, are the extraordinary **Teriade** and **Theophilos art museums** founded by M. Teriade (Eleftheriadis), a local gentleman who went to Paris as a law student and returned an art entrepreneur. He published prints by most of the great names of 20th-century art—Picasso, Matisse, Rouault, Chagall—and collected very fine contemporary Greek works, which are housed in an elegant building in an olive grove. In another building is his collection of the works of the Greek folk artist Theophilos, who trotted his paintbox through his native country recording festivals, customs, and scenes of patriotic fervor. Theophilos once had himself painted as Alexander the Great in gold armor and plumed helmet, with a giant paintbrush and palette as weapons. His massed paintings have the effect of a warped kind of illustrated travelogue—utterly authentic and highly personal.

West from Mytilini

The central road passes through plains, orchards, and olive groves. Hot-spring baths (*thermes*) still function at the edge of the Gulf of Yeras, 10 km (6 miles) from Mytilini, where men and women (separately) enjoy a communal bath of natural hot water—terrific in cold weather. The village on the gulf called **Thermes** also has baths, but is not developed as a spa. Nearby is the **Hotel Zaira**, an old, stone olive mill converted into a seaside hotel, although the beach here is not really that good for swimming. On the gulf, the large, luxurious **Silver Bay Hotel and Bungalows** with a roof garden and a swimming pool, is one of the best on the island.

Twenty kilometers (12.5 miles) farther west at a site called **Mesa**—very hard to find down a bumpy dirt road and guarded by sheep, barking dogs, and a wooden kiosk—is an extremely ruined **Temple of Aphrodite**. **Dáfia**, reputedly the home of the most beautiful women in Greece, is one of a cluster of plains villages near **Kallonί**, in the center of the island where the road branches in all directions.

Just a bit farther to the west is the **Limónos Monastery** (1523), cared for by a bibliophile monk who has accumulated well over 15,000 volumes. A **Folk Art and Ecclesiastical Museum** in the monastery displays dazzling antique manuscripts and votive jewelry, relics and icons, and *firmans* (decorative calligraphic orders in Arabic). One of its four rooms is devoted to old cooking utensils, such as the monastery's own former ouzo-making equipment.

There are rooms to let in **Skalohóri**, a pretty village among valleys with cypress trees and orchards about 15 km (9 miles) west of Limonos. The road winds through terraced hillsides and farms, where the famed horses of Lesvos are bred. Fifteen kilometers (9 miles) southwest of Skalohori, at the quiet **Perivóli Monastery**, now tended by one elderly lady, there are some lovely faded frescoes of monstrous sea things eating ships, glorious bands of angels silently shouting, and holy saints—matters connected with the Second Coming. The lighting is poor; bring a flashlight.

The road west passes through magnificent scenery, until it branches after **Antissa**; from then on the countryside is called the "Sahara": lichens and bare rocks, without a tree in sight. One branch leads to the far west coast at **Sigri**, whose attraction is the Petrified Forest. (Along this route, the **Ipsilon Monastery** commands a splendid view from the heights. Here are more churchly treasures: gold and jewels, reliquaries and hand-lettered Gospels.) The **Petrified Forest**, open during the day, is about a 25-minute drive south of Sigri along a very poor dirt road. Somewhere between 20 million and 500,000 (scholars differ) years ago, there was a volcanic eruption of Mount Ordymnos and pressure and heat converted this forest into wonderfully colored stone. A few of the multicolored stone trees are still upright, the tallest over 13 feet high; the longest fallen tree is 40 feet. No souvenirs, please: Too much of this unique stone has vanished already. Excavations continue.

Eleven kilometers (7 miles) south of Antissa is **Eresós**, in the plain between the village and the sea, the birthplace of the poet Sappho and the philosopher Theophrastos, and a very pretty village of old stone houses. Remains of a Byzantine castle rebuilt by the Genoese are under the acropolis, from which you can see orchards and fields in the distance. From here the end of the island looks like the end of the earth, bare hills floating out into an infinite sea. Four kilometers (2.5 miles) south, **Skala Eresos** is a resort beach with tourist shops, pensions, hotels, and lots of seaside tavernas. It is both charming and comfortable—it won an EC prize as one of the best in Europe—and for once topless is okay on the beach. Boat excursions go from here to other beaches in summer. A tiny **museum** has vases, statuettes, and marbles found by local diggers, right next to a deteriorated fifth-century **basilica** floored with mosaic. **Eresos Castle** peers down at the confusion of motorcycles and wooden-saddled donkeys.

The Eresos Travel Agency (0253-530-76/77 or 535-77; Fax: 0253-535-76) is abundantly equipped with accommodation; information; exchange and telephone facilities; car, motorcycle, and bicycle rentals; as well as tickets and tours.

The road north from Antissa goes via goat track to the remains of a castle and an ancient acropolis on the coast. (There are actually three Antissas a few kilometers apart. The ruined village is the former Antissa, but not *ancient* Antissa.) The drive over these awful roads must be its own reward unless you are a dedicated archaeologist, in which case you undoubtedly won't want to miss it. You can find some apparently secluded beaches here, though the sheep (and shepherds) may stare at you.

Northern Lesvos

North along the coast road are beaches and pretty settlements. A side road just north of Mytilini leads to **Mória**, near which stand the arches of a Roman aqueduct.

The village of **Mandámados**, 36 km (22 miles) north of Mytilini, is lovely, its red-tiled roofs spilling over the hillside. Locations with clay soil tend to develop ceramics, and this village is specially known for outsize pots. But there are ancient shadows here. In the courtyard of the important **church of the Taxiárchis** (Archangel) **Michael**, a bull is sacrificed every year shortly after Easter. Scorch marks on the walls mark the fires where the meat is cooked in great cauldrons for the feast the next day. Rooms around the courtyard are rented to pilgrims.

In the 17th century Turks massacred the brothers of the monastery. The only survivor crept out, gathered the clay soaked with the blood of his brothers, and formed an icon of great power. In the church, the strange, dark face modeled of blood and earth stares intently out of its frame of golden wings and crowns. An endless line of devoted worshipers passes by; they leave mounds of flowers and gold offerings to this angel, who leads the soul into deliverance at the time of death.

At the northern tip of the island the attractive village of **Sikaminiá** tumbles down the hillside to the *skala,* a wee harbor with fish tavernas and rooms to rent, delightful if you like quiet charm, a few shops, a sandy beach, and friendly people. The tourist shop sells, in addition to the characteristic blue pottery and glass, tapestries woven by the owner during the winter, depicting little vignettes of island scenery.

On the headland west along a rugged road through rugged countryside is the fortressed hill of **Mólyvos**, now officially called **Míthymna** (the ancient name) and rival city to Mytilini. Steep cobblestoned streets are arched with vines and flowers hanging from balconies that almost touch overhead. It is an enchanted town, where the beautiful traditional houses are unchanged, although a little self-consciousness has seeped into the charm. Modern buildings are not permitted. Artists abound, and the town is a center for arts and crafts.

There is a tourist office by the bus stop and hotels, rooms, and cars to rent. Not only is the village itself a treat, but it also has a fine **castle** with wonderful rolling views—the Asian coast is so close that a local saying declares that if you call your chickens in Molyvos, they come home from Turkey. The castle's outer walls were destroyed by the Turks; because it was so well defended, it took them longest of all to conquer. The defenders finally escaped to the sea through a tunnel at the bottom of the well. In the summer there are performances in the castle bailey. Some of ancient Mithymna is submerged in Molyvos, but most of it has never been excavated and is lying under those hills. The attractive **Delfinia** hotel on the beach offers bungalows, tennis, and a swimming pool, as well as a bar and restaurant.

Spiritual peace and quiet is offered by the **Karuna Meditation Center** just outside of town; contact Yiorgos and Yosoda Kassipides, Mithymna (Tel: 0253-811-08), for information about the summer program.

Seven kilometers (4 miles) south of Molyvos is **Petra**, with a good beach and the **church of the Panayía Glykophíloussa** (Virgin of the Sweet Kiss), 114 steps up at the top of a rock. This church served the castle when the Byzantine princess Maria Paleologos got Lesvos as her dowry, though it was rebuilt in the 18th and 19th centuries. It is almost as lovely a town as Molyvos, with winding stone streets and flowers everywhere. The enterprising **Women's Agricultural and Tourist Cooperative** runs a popular restaurant here and rents rooms in private houses, allowing the visitor to be part of a family. One of the best beaches on the island is just a bit to the southwest at **Anaxos**.

Southern Lesvos

The star of the southern peninsula is the lovely mountain village of **Ayiasós**, perched high up on **Mount Olympos**—a white-faced rock that sticks out of the surrounding shrubbery like a lighthouse, topped by a giant aerial. This area is hard to beat for natural forest beauty. Pines and chestnuts shade the winding road that reveals more and more panoramas: mountains with their tiny bright villages, white churches perched on impossible peaks, forest, and always, near or far, the sea. The road itself gleams through the woodlands like a river. This is bird watchers' paradise; signs proclaim "No hunting until 1992"! The air is so pure on this mountain that a sanatorium is located in the pine forest nearby.

Ayiasos, 28 km (17 miles) west of Mytilini, has charming old houses, a busy little *plateía* with two hotels, and the elaborate **church of the Panayía**, where an ancient icon reputedly painted by Saint Luke himself is honored (it is hidden in gold repoussé and glass and covered by a Medieval copy). Such objects of worship tend to get kissed away, and there is only a shadow of the real image left. In the precincts of the church are reasonable rooms to let with all modern conveniences (book through Plomari Travel; Tel: 0252-329-46 or 321-81), a folk-art museum, and a spectacular **Ecclesiastical Museum**. Treasures of enamel, gold, and ivory, illuminated Gospels, and medallions line the walls; there is yet another fragment of the True Cross mounted in enamel, plus yards of embroidered vestments. Offerings left at the icon include cases and cases of earrings, bracelets, and necklaces. August 15, the Assumption of the Virgin, brings hundreds here to celebrate. This was always a center of arts, with a high reputation for pottery going back for generations.

Other roads south from Mytilini skirt the peaceful Gulf of Yeras, lined with elegant, empty beaches among cypress trees and groves. Tempting—but the tanning factories of Perama have polluted the water, and it will take years to clear.

Swim instead at **Plomári**, the island's main ouzo center and a popular resort on the southern coast (Plomari Travel here is very helpful). Narrow streets with houses painted tan, red, and yellow climb up from the shore, which is a solid line of rentals: bike rentals, jeep rentals, car rentals, boat rentals. This is a popular area for package tours. The main swimming beach is at the little farm village of **Ayios Isídoros** to the east, also home to the **Dilini Restaurant**, with delicious food at good prices; the shorelines to the west are undeveloped.

An uneven road wanders more or less along the coast west to **Vaterá**, whose fine sand beach is said to be one of the best in Europe, with hotels, restaurants, vineyards, and gardens. The big, beautiful **Irini** hotel with its seaside veranda is very popular. Persist westward over a clattering plank bridge and bear left—you didn't really expect a signpost—and eventually you will bump into the delectable little harbor of **Ayios Fokás**: a couple of fish tavernas, newly supplied with water and power and still off the beaten track, each with a couple of rooms to rent—a nice quiet corner for a restful stay. Above is the site of the **Temple of Dionysus**, the overgrown bits of which will not add greatly to your understanding of ancient Greece, and a tiny white church replete with an iconostasis of laminated plastic.

From Vatera you can drive north to **Polichnítos**, a town whose harbor is a summer village with a marina and a beach, with rooms and apartments to rent at the waterfront; and thence west to pebbly and very attractive **Nifída** beach, which has secret sand a few yards in. This area is being developed—but there are charming villas and cottages here, some of which can be rented. There's even the odd bit of nightlife: *kafeneíos* and tavernas with entertainment.

GETTING AROUND
There are at least four daily flights from Athens, at least one daily from Thessaloniki, four weekly from Limnos, five weekly from Rhodes, three weekly from Mykonos, two weekly from Samos, and one weekly from Chios.

Ferries connect Mytilini (the only port) almost daily with Piraeus (sometimes via Chios; 14 hours), Kavala (sometimes via Limnos), and Thessaloniki.

There are many good car-rental firms, but the roads vary in quality. A good source of information on Lesvos is Plomari Travel, Plomari, 812 00 Lesvos; Tel: (0252) 329-46 or 321-81; Telex: 27147.

LIMNOS

This is an island where tourism is rare and hospitality is still alive. The people are farmers and fishermen, and the 186 square miles of land is fields and scrub in the east, rock in the west—the island is divided by two great bays—and there are some great beaches all around. Strong winds sweep down upon Limnos from the Dardanelles, and what with the free-ranging goats and sheep it's a brave tree that makes it through adolescence.

History from the Stone Age to World War II has left its mark. Limnos claims the most advanced Neolithic civilization of the Aegean. The island was dedicated to the god Hephaestus, the smith who was, for his sins, married to the irrepressible Aphrodite. He was lamed as a result of heavenly child abuse: He tried to break up a fight between his parents, Zeus and Hera, and Zeus threw him out of Heaven. He landed on Limnos.

At the start of the fifth century B.C. Limnos was taken over by Athenian "cleruches," who paid for Phidias's statue, called the Lemnian Athena, which stood on the Athenian Acropolis.

Legends accuse the islanders of having rather short tempers. Loyal Lemnians didn't think much of Aphrodite's virtue, an attitude that annoyed her. She cursed the island's women

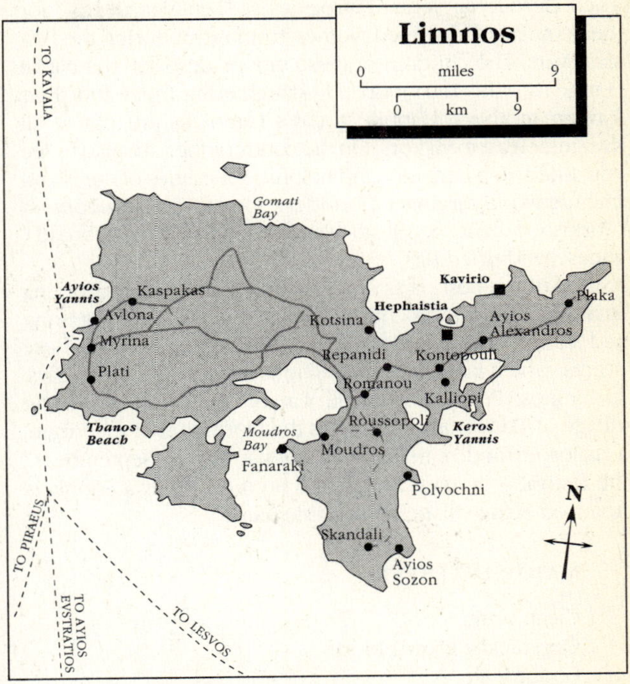

Limnos
0 miles 9
0 km 9
TO KAVALA
Gomati Bay
Ayios Yannis
Kaspakas
Avlona
Myrina
Plati
Thanos Beach
Kavirio
Hephaistia
Plaka
Ayios Alexandros
Kotsina
Repanidi
Kontopouli
Romanou
Kallioni
Roussopoli
Keros Yannis
Moudros Bay
Moudros
Fanaraki
Polyochni
Skandali
Ayios Sozon
N
TO PIRAEUS
TO AYIOS EVSTRATIOS
TO LESVOS

with a foul smell, and love withered. Men rejected their wives, who retaliated by murdering them. The Argonauts sailing with Jason stopped at Limnos and stayed to comfort the bereaved widows (their descendants were called Minyans). Then Herodotus defined atrocities as "Lemnian deeds," for the Lemnians kidnapped women from Attica during the Persian Wars. The children of these unions despised the native Lemnians, who responded by slaughtering them and their foreign mothers. Happily, today's Lemnians are not at all savage, at least to visitors. On the contrary, they are glad to see you, filled with curiosity, and helpful. Specialties of the island include wood carving, embroidery, local sweets, *loukoúmia* (Turkish delight, not at all like the kind you find abroad), cheese, and dried figs.

One of the best parts of an island vacation can be joining in a *panegyri,* a local church festival and fair. Feasting, song and dance, and a welcome to visitors characterize these events, which take place throughout the year on saints' days. In Limnos, Portianó goes all out on August 6, while the village of Tsimándria celebrates the Dormition of the Virgin, a major Orthodox holiday, on August 15. On September 7 the festival is at Ayios Sozos, and on the 17th Ayia Sophia is honored at the village of the same name.

MAJOR INTEREST

Clean water
Organically grown food
Country air
Hospitality
Archaeological sites at Poliochni, Kavirio, Hephaistia, and Myrina

Western Limnos

The capital and port of Limnos, **Mýrina**, is also called **Kastro** for the ruined castle standing sentinel over the harbor. Some of the walls are prehistoric; most were rebuilt in 1186 by the Byzantines and later by Venetians and Turks. It's worth the climb for the splendid view—and hidden passages, which invoke an atmosphere of age and mystery. On a clear day you can see Mount Athos, 36 miles to the northwest. But this is not Disneyland, and there are no safeguards, so it's best to go with a companion and nonskid shoes, a flashlight, and possibly a stout stick for probing dark places.

Myrina is a respectable-size town on the west coast, with

tavernas, garages, banks, and even a small hospital. Theodoros Petrides rents cars and Maria Petridou runs excursions from the same office (Tel: 0254-220-39 or 229-90). Cars may also be rented from Tzaneros near the port, or from Spyros Petrides in the middle of the agora. The Astron Hotel in the center has an automatic laundry service. On Ermoú Street (the main shopping street) are a couple of foreign bookshops.

The attractive wood-and-stone **Nefeli Apartments** on the cliff near the castle offer a great view at sunset; each apartment has a kitchen. In town, the self-catering **Afroditi Apartments** have reasonable rates, balconies, a cheerful garden, and a friendly management that also arranges excursions. But the stellar performance of hospitality in town comes from the deluxe **Akti Myrina Hotel**, which combines Swiss efficiency with Greek climate in a bungalow colony set in lovely gardens. This is sheer relaxation with privacy, beach, pool, excursions, excellent restaurants, bars, and perhaps the only full-size bathtubs in Greece—at an appropriate price. You even escape from television, and the hotel kiosk sells English books. **Tasos's** taverna, about 200 yards away, is very popular, with low prices and good *mezédes*. In fact, the food on Limnos is unusually tasty; the farmers claim that they do not use chemical fertilizers or insecticides. If you have never had a real fresh egg, it's a memorable experience.

The modest **Archaeological Museum** is in a lovely old house north of the center of town and contains artifacts found at the sites of Kavirio, Hephaistia Poliochni, and Myrina (see below). Nearby is the cathedral with a fine carved-wood iconostasis.

The port itself divides the developed "Romeïkós Yialós," Greek Beach, from the "Tourkikós Yialós," Turkish Beach (better sand), which tells you something about social distinctions in the last century. The new and cozy **Lotos** café-restaurant offers first-class service and repast on Romeïkos Yialos.

The most popular beach in the area is **Thanos**, 4 km (2.5 miles) south of town, where there is also camping. The western coast abounds in beaches: **Avlona, Plati,** and **"Hundred Heads" Bay** offer good swimming. At Plati there is a popular summer *bouzoúki* and café-restaurant—look for **Grigoris Taverna**. Just to the north of Myrina is **Káspakas**, a popular beach with a taverna that has live music on Saturdays. And far to the north around Cape Mourtzeflos is hidden **Gomáti Bay** for windy swimming.

The main road crosses the island from Myrina east to

Moudros, passing through farmland with an occasional wriggle through a picturesque, narrow-laned hill town. All the villages are nicely labeled in Greek and English.

Eastern Limnos

Moudros Bay, a fine natural harbor that divides the island, was the base for the disastrous British Dardanelles campaign of 1915. There is a very tidy British cemetery of 900 graves. Moudros, on the eastern shore of the bay, is the second most important city of Limnos, with a population of about 1,000. Local swimming is good at **Fanaráki Beach**, 4 km (2.5 miles) south of here. A fine taverna in the area is **Tzitzivakos** on the harbor.

Skandáli, the southernmost village of this peninsula, is tiny, with only 150 inhabitants. There are some big sandy beaches here, as well as the **church of Ayios Sozos**. At this church on September 7 there is a festival for the whole island, with song, dance, and feasting.

Offshore at **Charos Reef** blocks of marble were found belonging to an Archaic Temple to Apollo, which stood in ancient Chryse, a town mentioned by Herodotus as having been drowned by an earthquake. This suggests some interesting underwater exploring. Even if you don't find the lost city, Keros Bay is a good place for swimming.

As you head north by the eastern road you come upon one of the earliest cities of the Aegean—even older than Troy—which stood at **Polióchni** on the eastern coast near Voroskópos. Italian archaeologists have marked off tentative identifications of buildings as old as 2000 B.C. atop others dating back to the fourth millennium B.C. Tour buses from Myrina visit the impressive site, which includes some town walls that are still standing, 16 feet high. The stone remains of houses are very clear, even showing traces of plumbing—the earliest Aegean stone baths. The hoard of gold treasure found here is in the National Archaeological Museum in Athens. A small booklet in many languages is on sale here.

The road leads back to Moudros and through the enchanting little village of Romanou toward the northeast. **Mosychlos** (near Repanidi, just northeast of Moudros), now only a memory of a name, was the site of the legendary workshop of Hephaestus, inside a fiery mountain, where he created such bibelots as the chariot of the sun and the armor of Achilles, aided by golden robots. His chimneys spewed out continual fire and smoke—the word for volcano in ancient Greek is *hephaisteio* (*iféstio* is the modern version)—from a mountain that finally disappeared in a cataclysmic earthquake.

Red "Lemnian earth," containing a high proportion of silica, was approved by the early Christian physician Galen for snakebite and infections. It is found only near **Repanídi**, and from prehistoric times to the end of the 19th century was dug up once a year with due ceremony. Farther to the north, **Kotsina**, which was a busy center in Medieval times, is proud of the statue of the local heroine Maroula, who aided the Greek ships in defeating Suleyman Pasha in 1478. Below the church is a holy spring, deep in the earth. The large village of **Kontopoúli** east of Repanidi (where there is a disco) is known for sporting activity; it holds horse races on October 26. Nearby **Kalliópi** does the same in the spring, on April 21.

But the main attractions of this area are the archaeological sites of Hephaistia and Kavirio. A dirt road north from Kontopouli leads past blinding white salt flats called *alikí* to Ayios Aléxandros, once a picturesque village with a tiny schoolhouse, now a sad little heap of stones where goats browse. To the left is the road to **Kavirio**, a ruined pre-Classical sanctuary perched on a cliff overlooking Pournia Bay, dedicated to gods older than the Olympians. The remains of halls larger than the Parthenon, and of columns, streets, and houses, are now contemplated by the rabbits whose burrows overlook the site.

Down a rough path is the **cave of Philoctetes**, thought by some to have been connected to the sanctuary above by a secret passage. This hero inherited the bow and arrows of Herakles, against the wishes of the goddess Hera. She caused him to be wounded in the leg, either by one of the arrows or a snakebite. The wound became so infected that nobody could stand the smell, so his shipmates dumped the poor chap in this cave; some say he was cured by applications of Lemnian earth, after a long sojourn in the cave. Tourism may eventually scare away the wandering flocks of sheep. On the opposite side of the bay, where the road turns into a footpath, is the very extensive site of the great Classical city of **Hephaistia**, only a tiny part of which has yet been uncovered, though there are the ruins of a Classical theater. A sarcophagus is under shelter toward the back.

The farthest village to the north is **Plaka**, possibly the oldest village of the island, with rooms to rent and eating places. The **church of Ayios Charálambos** may even let visitors stay the night in a cell; under it is another holy fountain whose waters are supposed to be therapeutic.

GETTING AROUND

There are flights at least daily from Athens and Thessaloniki, and air service four times a week from Lesvos. The ferry runs twice a week from Rafina (15 hours) and four times a week from Kavala (5 hours and 30 minutes). There is irregular service to Lesvos. Local boats sometimes make trips to **Ayios Evstrátios**, a tiny nearby island with rooms to rent, fish tavernas, and a secluded coast.

Island buses run from the plateia in Myrina. The KTEL bus shelter posts daily routes; in general, there are two daily buses in each direction. There is a taxi stand in the plateia near the bus station. Cars and motorcycles may be rented in Myrina.

ACCOMMODATIONS REFERENCE

Ikaria

- **Anthemis. Ayios Kirikos**, 833 00 Ikaria. Tel: (0275) 231-56, 221-20, or 227-08.
- **Armena Inn. Armenistis**, 833 01 Ikaria. Tel: (0275) 414-15.
- **Astachi. Armenistis**, 833 01 Ikaria. Tel: (0275) 414-21.
- **Hotel Atheras. Evdilos**, 833 02 Ikaria. Tel: (0275) 314-34.
- **Cavos Bay Hotel. Armenistis**, 833 00 Ikaria. Tel: (0275) 414-49/00; in Athens, (01) 764-0235.
- **Eudoxia Hotel. Evdilos**, 833 02 Ikaria. Tel: (0275) 315-02/71; in Athens, (01)681-9969.
- **Ikarion. Therma**, 833 00 Ikaria. Tel: (0275) 224-81.
- **Pension Maria Elena.** Artemidos Street, **Ayios Kirikos**, 833 00 Ikaria. Tel: (0275) 228-35 or 225-43.
- **Marina. Therma**, 833 00 Ikaria. Tel: (0275) 221-88; in Athens, (01) 228-1775.
- **Mitikas** (Rooms). Contact Dolichi Tours, **Ayios Kirikos**, 833 00 Ikaria. Tel: (0275) 220-68 or 223-46; Fax: (0275) 223-46.
- **Hotel Raches. Christos Raches**, 833 01 Ikaria. Tel: (0275) 412-69.
- **Rena. Therma**, 833 00 Ikaria. Tel: (0275) 229-02.

Samos

- **Ariadne Hotel. Ayios Konstantinos**, 832 00 Samos. Tel: (0273) 942-05.
- **Avli Pension.** Areos Street, **Vathy**, 831 00 Samos. Tel: (0273) 229-39.

NORTHEASTERN AEGEAN ISLANDS

- ▶ **Brinias's** (Rooms). **Ayios Konstantinos**, 832 00 Samos. Tel: (0273) 942-41.
- ▶ **Christiana Hotel**. **Vathy**, 831 00 Samos. Tel: (0273) 271-49 or 230-84.
- ▶ **Dimitra Hotel**. **Kokkari**, 831 00 Samos. Tel: (0273) 923-00.
- ▶ **Doryssa Bay**. **Pythagorio**, 831 03 Samos. Tel: (0273) 613-60/90.
- ▶ **Eleana Hotel**. Roditses, **Vathy**, 831 00 Samos. Tel: (0273) 286-55 or 237-21.
- ▶ **Ellenis**. 4 Grammou, **Vathy**, 831 00 Samos. Tel: (0273) 288-28.
- ▶ **Pension Evdoxia**. **Vathy**, 831 00 Samos. Tel: (0273) 227-70 or 245-34.
- ▶ **Helen**. 2 Grammou, **Vathy**, 831 00 Samos. Tel: (0273) 282-15 or 228-66.
- ▶ **Hera** and **Hera II**. **Pythagorio**, 831 03 Samos. Tel: (0273) 614-28, 618-79, or 613-19.
- ▶ **Heraion Hotel**. **Ireon**, 831 03 Samos. Tel: (0273) 611-80.
- ▶ **Ino Hotel**. Kalami, **Vathy**, 831 00 Samos. Tel: (0273) 232-41/45.
- ▶ **Irini's**. **Kokkari**, 831 00 Samos. Tel: (0273) 940-12.
- ▶ **Kerkis Bay Hotel**. **Marathokambos**, 831 02 Samos. Tel: (0273) 372-02.
- ▶ **Koala Hotel**. **Ayios Konstantinos**, 832 00 Samos. Tel: (0273) 940-15.
- ▶ **Kokkari Beach Hotel**. **Kokkari**, 831 00 Samos. Tel: (0273) 922-38/63.
- ▶ **Labito Hotels**. **Pythagorio**, 831 03 Samos. Tel: (0273) 615-72/73.
- ▶ **Nepheli Hotel**. **Karlovasi**, 832 00 Samos. Tel: (0273) 340-01/02/03.
- ▶ **Princessa Hotel**. **Pythagorio**, 831 03 Samos. Tel: (0273) 616-98 or 615-01.
- ▶ **Prodromos Apartments**. Agrilionas Beach, **Marathokambos**, 831 02 Samos. Tel: (0273) 373-79.
- ▶ **Samaina Bay Hotel**. **Karlovasi**, 832 00 Samos. Tel: (0273) 340-04/09; Telex: 294224 SAMI GR.
- ▶ **Synaheris** (Rooms). **Kokkari**, 831 00 Samos. Tel: (0273) 923-17.
- ▶ **Themis** (Rooms). 3 Grammou, **Vathy**, 831 00 Samos. Tel: (0273) 226-86.
- ▶ **Venetia**. **Ireon**, 831 03 Samos. Tel: (0273) 611-95.
- ▶ **Venus Hotel**. **Kokkari**, 831 00 Samos. Tel: (0273) 922-30/60 or 923-04/05.

▶ **Votsalakia Hotel.** Marathokambos, 831 02 Samos. Tel: (0273) 372-32/29 or 373-55.

Chios, Psara, Inousses

▶ **Apollonion.** 15 Roidou, **Hora**, 821 00 Chios. Tel: (0271) 248-42.

▶ **Ayia Markellas Monastery.** 821 00 Chios. Reserve by mail only.

▶ **Chandris Hotel.** Hora, 821 00 Chios. Tel: (0271) 257-61/69; Telex: 294113.

▶ **Chiona.** Kardamyla, 823 00 Chios. Tel: (0271) 223-62.

▶ **EOT Guesthouse.** 821 00 Psara. Tel: (0272) 612-93 or (0251) 279-08.

▶ **Esperides Hotel.** Ayia Fotini, **Kondari**, 821 00 Chios. Tel: (0271) 516-91/95 or 311-31.

▶ **GNTO.** Mr. Pipidis, GNTO **Mesta**, 821 00 Chios. Tel: (0271) 763-19 or (for Pyrgi) 724-88.

▶ **Golden Odyssey.** Kondari, 821 00 Chios. Tel: (0271) 214-32; Telex: 294275.

▶ **Golden Sands.** Kondari, 821 00 Chios. Tel: (0271) 320-80/81 or 310-10.

▶ **P. Karapournos Apartments.** Vrontados, 821 00 Chios. Tel: (0271) 934-14.

▶ **Kardamyla Hotel.** Kardamyla, 823 00 Chios. Tel: (0272) 223-78; (0271) 255-51; Telex: 294141 KYMA GR; Fax: (0271) 252-53.

▶ **Komi Hotel.** Komi-Kalamoti, 821 02 Chios. Tel: (0271) 712-26.

▶ **Hotel Kyma.** Hora, 821 00 Chios. Tel: (0271) 255-51; Telex: 294141 KYMA GR; Fax: (0271) 252-53.

▶ **Kyveli Apartments.** Vrontados, 821 00 Chios. Tel: (0271) 931-44 or 929-19.

▶ **Lambrakis Apartments.** Komi, 821 02 Chios. Tel: (0271) 710-69; in Athens, (01) 251-3221.

▶ **Maria's Labyrinth.** Limani, **Mesta**, 821 00 Chios. Tel: (0271) 763-66.

▶ **Neoclassical Pension.** 6 Koundouriotou, **Hora**, 821 00 Chios. Tel: (0271) 232-97.

▶ **Papanikolaos Apartments.** Ayia Ermioni, 821 00 Chios.

▶ **Perivoli.** 9–11 Argenti, **Kambos**, 821 00 Chios. Tel: (0271) 315-13; (restaurant) 319-73.

▶ **Phaidra Traditional Pension.** 13 Livanou, **Hora**, 821 00 Chios. Tel: (0271) 411-29/30.

▶ **Thalassopolos** (Rooms). 821 00 Inousses. Tel: (0271) 514-75.

- Pension Voulamadis. Frangovouni, Kambos, 821 00 Chios. Tel: (0271) 317-33 or 925-64.
- Women's Tourist and Agricultural Cooperative. Pyrgi, 821 00 Chios. Tel: (0271) 724-96.
- Hotel Xenios. Vrontados, 821 00 Chios. Tel: (0271) 937-63/64.
- Yiamos Hotel-Restaurant. Kondari, 821 00 Chios. Tel: (0271) 312-02 or 314-21.
- Zevgios. Ayia Ermioni, Kondari, 821 00 Chios. Tel: (0271) 316-11.

Lesvos
- Delfinia. Molyvos, 811 09 Lesvos. Tel: (0253) 713-15/73 or 715-80.
- Irini Hotel. Vatera, 813 00 Lesvos. Tel: (0252) 614-10.
- Lesvion Hotel. Mytilini, 811 00 Lesvos. Tel: (0251) 281-77.
- Silver Bay Hotel and Bungalows. Gulf of Yeras, Mytilini, 811 00 Lesvos. Tel: (0251) 279-77 or 234-58.
- Women's Tourist and Agricultural Cooperative. Petra, 811 09 Lesvos. Tel: (0253) 412-38.
- Hotel Zaira. Loutra, Mytilini, 811 00 Lesvos. Tel: (0251) 911-00/02.

Limnos
- Afroditi Apartments. Myrina, 814 00 Limnos. Tel: (0254) 234-89 or 231-41.
- Akti Myrina Hotel. Myrina, 814 00 Limnos. Tel: (0254) 226-81/84; Telex: 297173 MYRI GR.
- Nefeli Apartments. Myrina, 814 00 Limnos. Tel: (0254) 234-15 or 235-51.

CHRONOLOGY OF THE HISTORY OF GREECE

Prehistory

A period during which man finally came to settle in Greece—some 70 million years after massive geological convulsions created the archipelago and cut off the area from easy access.

- c. 50,000 B.C.: Paleolithic hunters in northern Greece via Balkans.
- c. 7500–3000 B.C.: Neolithic farmers from Asia enter across Bosphorus, spread throughout mainland; first settlements in Crete, possibly from Asia Minor.
- c. 3000 B.C.: First Bronze Age weapons in Greece.
- c. 2500 B.C.: Mass land and sea migrations into Greece from the east; Early Cycladic culture; beginnings of the Minoan civilization; first settlements at Lerna, Mycenae, and Tiryns in northeastern Peloponnese.

The Minoan and Mycenaean Ages

The time of the great legendary kings and heroes of Greek tragedy and mythology, ended by a combination of natural catastrophe, attrition of war, invasion of the Dorians, and advent of the Iron Age.

- c. 2000 B.C.: Beginnings of Minoan palace culture on Crete. Meanwhile, first Greek-speaking peoples, called Hellenes by descendants, arrive in northern Greece; some—the Achaeans—move south to Peloponnese and become known as Mycenaeans.
- c. 1600 B.C.: Height of Minoan civilization: labyrinthine palace at Knossos in Crete; Minoan sea power dominates Aegean; cross-cultural contacts with emerging Greek-speaking Mycenaean civilization.
- c. 1500 B.C.: Massive volcanic eruption at Thira (Santorini) inundates Minoan coastal settlements and is perhaps initial cause of decline of Minoan power.
- c. 1400–1300 B.C.: Legendary dates for voyage of Jason and Argonauts, Oedipus at Thebes, and Theseus in Athens and at the palace of Minos.
- c. 1400–1200 B.C.: Mycenaean dominance of southern Greece and Aegean, including Crete.
- c. 1225 B.C.: The Trojan War, a Pyrrhic victory from which Mycenaeans would never fully recover.
- c. 1200 B.C.: Descent of Greek-speaking Dorian tribes from north. Gradual destruction and/or desertion of My-

cenaean power centers, with only Athens surviving. Approximate beginning of the Greek Iron Age.
- **c. 1050 B.C.**: Advent of protogeometric pottery in Athens.

The Greek Dark Ages

The years c. 1000 to 750 B.C. are an unsettled period of migration, realignment, and reconstruction in which the autocratic rule of Mycenaean citadels is gradually integrated with the more democratic ethos of the tribal village to create the basis for the Greek *polis,* or city-state. Displaced Mycenaeans colonize Ionia on the coast of Asia Minor, preserving legends of their heroic age in oral poetry. Power of kings declines with decrease in trade, replaced by councils of landowning *aristoi* (best men). However, recent excavations in Evia (Euboea) indicate strong power centers in Chalkis and Eretria (c. 1100–730 B.C.), which prospered from trade and colonization in Syria, Sicily, and the Black Sea area.

- **c. 1000 B.C.**: Ephesus founded on site of previous cities by Athenian colonists. Sparta founded by Dorians.
- **c. 900 B.C.**: Phoenician-based alphabet slowly introduced and adapted to Greek in many varied local forms.
- **813 B.C.**: Traditional date for founding of Carthage by Dido and Phoenicians.
- **776 B.C.**: Traditional date of the first games at Olympia in northwestern Peloponnese, the four-year intervals (uncertain in beginning) providing a basis for recorded history. About this time, Greek writing derived from the Phoenician alphabet replaces Mycenaean and is used to record both business matters and poetry. Athenian geometric pottery art begins to include human activity as a subject matter.
- **c. 750–700 B.C.**: Works of Homer (thought to have lived during the eighth or ninth century B.C. on the north coast of Asia Minor near Smyrna, maybe on Chios) are written down, possibly by Homer himself. Hesiod (from the Boeotian countryside outside Athens but of an Ionian-born father) writes first formalized Greek mythology (*Theogeny*) as well as moral treatise on life among mortals (*Works and Days*).

Archaic Greece: The Evolution of Hellenism

From c. 800 to 500 B.C., as population increases and living standards improve, there is a continuing development, through phases of tyranny and wars with Persia, of the city-state and its most important manifestations in Corinth, Athens, and Sparta. Abroad, Greek colonies are founded in Italy,

France, Spain, Syria, and the Black Sea area. In Ionia, which had contact with the civilizations of Persia and Lydia (east of the Ionian area in Asia Minor), there is a budding and then flowering of Greek art and thought, most particularly in the areas of philosophy and science, that would engender the golden fruits of the Classical Age in Athens.

- c. 800–750 B.C.: Evians found first Greek trading base in the East: Al Mina on the mouth of the Orontes river in northern Syria, perhaps source of Phoenician-based Greek alphabet.
- 753 B.C.: Roman author Varro's date for founding of Rome by Romulus.
- 750 B.C.: Evian cities of Chalkis and Eretria found first trading base in West at Cumae in southern Italy, site of previous Mycenaean and early Greek forays. A "new city" (*neo polis,* i.e., Naples) also established.
- 750–700 B.C.: Colonization of Magna Graecia (a Roman appellation) on the instep and sole of the boot of Italy and on the island of Sicily by various Greek city-states.
- 735 B.C.: Chalkis, with landless settlers from the Cycladic island of Naxos, establishes first Sicilian settlement, Naxos.
- 734–680 B.C.: Lelantine War, a territorial dispute between Chalkis and Eretria, widens to include most of Greek city-states and ends with dissolution of Evian power in Greece.
- 733 B.C.: Colonization of Corcyra (Corfu) and Syracuse by Corinth.
- 730–710 B.C.: Sparta subjugates neighboring Messenia, establishes colony of Taranto in Magna Graecia.
- 720 B.C.: Peninsula of Chalkidiki in northern Greece settled by Chalkis and Eretria; first Greek settlements in Hellespont; Sybaris founded in southern Italy by Achaeans. Beginning of Early Proto-Corinthian pottery.
- 710 B.C.: Crotona founded in southern Italy by Achaeans.
- c. 700 B.C.: Conjectural date for establishment of Spartan political system by semi-legendary lawgiver Lycurgus.
- c. 695 B.C.: Unification of Attica under Athens.
- 680 B.C.: Lydian attacks on Greek colonies in Ionia.
- 670–650 B.C.: Archilochus of Paros creates first truly personal lyric poetry, travels to Italy and Thasos as colonizer-soldier.
- 664 B.C.: Greeks in Egypt as traders and mercenaries.
- 655 B.C.: Proto-Corinthian pottery: Chigi vase.
- 650 B.C.: Paros colonizes island of Thasos in northern Greece. Beginnings of tyrannies in Greece proper with Theagenes at Megara and Kypselos at Corinth. The lyric poets Terpander of Lesvos, Kallinos of Ephesus, Tyrtaeus of Sparta, and Semonides of Amorgos active.

- **630 B.C.:** Greek settlements in Black Sea area, including Odessos, Chersonesos, and Trapezous (Trebizond).
- **c. 630 B.C.:** Megarian settlement at Bosphorus, traditionally called Byzantion because of its founder, named Byzas. At Athens, abortive first attempt at tyranny.
- **625–600 B.C.:** Thrasybulus establishes tyranny at Miletus in Asia Minor; Periander becomes tyrant at Corinth. First *kouroi;* early Corinthian pottery; beginning of Attic black figure pottery in the area of Kerameikos west of the Greek Agora in Athens, soon to become dominant influence in Greece, producing such masters as Execias (amphora in Vatican), Clitias, and Ergotimos (François vase at Florence). Establishment of Naucratis as Greek trading base in Egypt.
- **621 B.C.:** Draco issues Athens's first written laws.
- **610–575 B.C.:** Alcaeus and Sappho active as poets on Lesvos, where Sappho teaches the craft.
- **600 B.C.:** Founding of Massilia (Marseilles) by Phocaeans of Ionia, with daughter colonies at Antipolis (Antibes) and Nikaia (Nice). Temple of Hera built at Olympia. Athens takes Salamis from Megara.
- **594 B.C.:** Solon introduces radical democratic social and political changes in Athens.
- **c. 590 B.C.:** Aesop, a Phrygian slave on Samos, freed; travels throughout Greece and Persia telling tales; is killed by Delphians for embezzling funds intended for sacred shrine.
- **584–582 B.C.:** Thales, philosopher-scientist of Miletus, forms first school of philosophy and is said to have predicted eclipse of sun; theorizes that water is primary substance of universe.
- **583 B.C.:** Athens builds first major temple to Athena.
- **582 B.C.:** Pythian Games established at Delphi.
- **c. 582 B.C.:** Philosopher-mathematician Pythagoras is born on Samos.
- **572 B.C.:** Solon retires, binding Athens to obey his laws for ten more years.
- **570–550 B.C.:** Thales' disciple, Anaximander of Miletus, formulates first concepts of matter, creation of universe, and evolution. Postulates plurality of worlds, primary substance as Indefinite Something out of which pairs of opposites are formed. His pupil, the reforming poet and philosopher Xenophanes of Colophon (c. 570–475 B.C.), attacks conventional Homer-Hesiod theology; asserts existence of one god as basic substance of universe.
- **561 B.C.:** Pisistratus establishes short-lived tyranny.
- **560 B.C.:** Croesus of Lydia subjugates all Ionia except Miletus. Sparta forms Peloponnesian League.
- **556 B.C.:** Pisistratus again briefly seizes power but is overthrown by conservative-liberal alliance.

- **550 B.C.**: Pisistratus, under secret pact with liberals, once more becomes tyrant, only to be ousted again one year later as liberals turn against him.
- **546 B.C.**: Pisistratus uses armed force to establish a tyranny that will last until the ouster of his son in 510 B.C.
- **c. 540 B.C.**: Orpheus makes first appearances in Greek art and literature. Temple of Artemis, one of Seven Wonders of the World, built at Ephesus. Poets Theognis of Megara, Hipponax of Ephesus, and Ibycus of Rhegium (today Reggio di Calabria, Italy) active.
- **c. 535 B.C.**: Invention of technique for red-figure vase painting, which inspired Keats's "Ode on a Grecian Urn" and produced such Greek masters as Euphronias (krater of Herakles wrestling with Anteus) and Sosias (vase of Achilles and Patroklos). As villages gain political status, so too do their Dionysian rituals, sacrifices of goats (*trag*) accompanied by songs (*odia*), which together are called *tragodia*.
- **534 B.C.**: The poet and dramatist Thespis brings first tragedy to Athens's Dionysia festival from nearby Ikaria, in which he separates self from ritual chorus in part of "responder," thus becoming first actor.
- **530 B.C.**: Pythagoras, having emigrated from Samos, establishes school (Pythagorean Brotherhood) in Crotona, Italy; coins term "philosopher" (lover of wisdom); postulates theory that all things are finally reducible to numbers.
- **528 B.C.**: Pisistratus dies, succeeded by sons Hippias and Hipparchus, with the older Hippias as leader.
- **521 B.C.**: Darius I takes power in Persia.
- **520–468 B.C.**: Simeonides of Ceos writes poetry.
- **514 B.C.**: Hipparchus murdered.
- **512 B.C.**: Darius subjugates Thrace and Macedonia.
- **510 B.C.**: Hippias forced to abdicate. Building of temples at Acragas (Agrigentum today), Sicily.
- **509 B.C.**: Cleisthenes grants equal political rights to all citizens.
- **c. 502 B.C.**: Pindar begins writing poetry and music at courts of Alexander I of Macedonia, Theron of Acragas, Heiron I of Syracuse, and elsewhere.
- **500 B.C.**: Heraclitus of Ephesus in prime as philosopher; concerned with problem of change in world substance, states that all is in process of flux, postulating an identity of opposites in which all things are and are not what they are becoming, with fire as the basic world material.

The Persian Wars

Two conflicts spanning 21 years, beginning with the Athenian-aided revolt of Greek Ionian colonies (499–493 B.C.) against Darius. Subsequently (493 B.C.) Darius invades

Greece with large fleet, which is wrecked by a storm off peninsula of present-day Mount Athos.

- **499 B.C.:** In Athens, Aeschylus has first of his plays produced, introducing the second actor into Greek drama.
- **c. 497 B.C.:** Death of Pythagoras at Metapontum in southern Italy while fleeing Crotona uprising against attempts to make his Order the city's actual government.
- **496 B.C.:** Births of Pericles and Sophocles.
- **493 B.C.:** Themistocles elected archon at Athens.
- **490 B.C.:** New Persian invasion defeated by outnumbered Athenians at battle of Marathon; runner Phidippides, bringing news to Athens, gains immortal fame. In Elea, south of Naples, Parmenides establishes Eleatic school of philosophy, giving primary importance to reason and logic as ultimate judges of reality.
- **487 B.C.:** Performance of first comedy at Athens's Dionysia.
- **485 B.C.:** Darius dies and is succeeded by his son, Xerxes I, who begins four-year preparation to reinvade Greece with world's largest army, building boat bridges across Hellespont and digging a canal through peninsula of Athos.
- **480 B.C.:** In May, Xerxes' massive army enters Greece. In August, battle of Thermopylae; 300 Spartans, led by their king, Leonidas, die delaying Persian advance and allowing Athenians time to evacuate Athens and regroup at Salamis. In September, battle of Salamis; superior Persian fleet is crushed by smaller, more maneuverable Athenian navy.
- **479 B.C.:** Battles of Plataea (Thessaly) and Mycale (near Miletus, on the coast of Asia Minor); combined Greek forces defeat Persians and end war.

The Golden Age of Athens

The flowering of Classical Athenian culture, politics, philosophy, and science, lasting approximately 70 years, from the defeat of the Persians to the devasting Athenian loss at Sicily in 413.

- **477 B.C.:** Athens establishes Delian League, effectively creating Athenian Empire. Casting of *Charioteer* of Delphi.
- **476 B.C.:** Pindar writes *First Olympian Ode*.
- **475 B.C.:** Zeno of Elea succeeds Parmenides as head of Eleatic school in Italy; originates dialectic form of argument to be used by Socrates; poses paradoxes proving motion inconceivable in a divisible reality.
- **472 B.C.:** Aeschylus's *The Persians,* his earliest surviving work, is presented during Dionysia in Athens.
- **470 B.C.:** Sculptor Myron casts *Discus Thrower* at Athens. Pindar writes *First Pythian Ode*.

- 469 B.C.: Birth of Socrates.
- 468 B.C.: Aeschylus's playwriting supremacy challenged by first victory of young Sophocles, who introduces third actor into Greek drama.
- 467 B.C.: Aeschylus retakes playwriting crown with *Seven Against Thebes*.
- 462 B.C.: The philosopher Anaxagoras arrives in Athens; postulates universe made up of many differing forms of matter and other worlds and civilizations, all set in motion by a single, indivisible mind; also theorizes that the sun is a mass of burning stone, phases of the moon are caused by the earth's shadow; great influence on Pericles as well as a danger to him because of these "heresies."
- 461 B.C.: Leadership of democratic party falls to 33-year-old Pericles, a renegade aristocrat.
- 460 B.C.: Democritus, "Father of Physics," born at Abdera in Thrace.

The First Peloponnesian War

A series of minor skirmishes between Sparta and Athens, lasting from 460 to 451 B.C., after which a five-year armistice and then a shaky 30-year peace treaty are agreed upon.

- 460 B.C.: A series of provocative alliances and other acts by Athens causes Sparta to declare war on behalf of the Peloponnesian League.
- 460–420 B.C.: Polyclitus of Sikyon active as sculptor. Birth of the great physician Hippocrates of Kos c. 460.
- 458 B.C.: Aeschylus's *Oresteia* produced in Athens; the work is the only surviving ancient trilogy, a form introduced into the theater by Aeschylus.
- 456 B.C.: Temple of Zeus, one of Seven Wonders of the World, completed at Olympia.
- 455 B.C.: Euripides has first play produced, title unknown.
- 450 B.C.: Philosopher Empedocles of Agrigentum, Sicily, flourishes. First of pluralists, he tries to reconcile reason and sense-data; divides Parmedian plenum into Fire, Water, Earth, and Air, moved by Love and Strife.
- 447–438 B.C.: Parthenon built by architects Iktinos and Kallikrates and sculptor Phidias; first Corinthian column at Bassae.
- 446 B.C.: Evia and Megara secede from Athenian alliance; Sparta invades Athens, then inexplicably turns back, apparently having been promised large annual sum of money by Pericles. Pindar completes *Eighth Pythian Ode*.
- 445 B.C.: Athens and Sparta agree to Thirty Year Peace Treaty.
- 443 B.C.: Herodotus of Halicarnassus (present-day Bodrum, Turkey) joins in founding of Athenian colony at

Thurii, Italy. Completes his research (*historia*) into Persian Wars.
- **442 B.C.:** Sophocles' *Antigone* produced. Frieze of Parthenon begun under Phidias; completed 438. The Odeion (music hall) of Pericles constructed on side of Acropolis.
- **440 B.C.:** Revolt of Samos savagely repressed by Athenian forces. Temple of Poseidon at Sounion completed. Leucippus, philosopher and teacher of Democritus, postulates world made of tiny, undividable particles called atoms, from *a* (not) and *tome* (separation, cut).
- **437 B.C.:** Propylaea (portals) of Acropolis begun.
- **435–434 B.C.:** War breaks out between Corinth, a Spartan ally, and the independent Corcyrea (Corfu); Corcyra asks Athens for aid; Athens agrees to a defensive alliance (433), but, in breach of peace treaty with Sparta, ends up, perhaps purposefully, in offensive battle with Corinth to save Corcyra from defeat at sea and secure her alliance in anticipation of resumed hostilities with Sparta.
- **433 B.C.:** Potidaea, former Corinthian colony in Macedonia now part of Athenian alliance, is told by Athens to raze sea walls and expel Corinthians in city; she refuses, having received guarantees of aid from Sparta; Athens begins besieging city; in one battle, Socrates saves the life of young Alcibiades.
- **432 B.C.:** Sparta declares war on Athens for having violated the Thirty Year Peace Treaty.

The Second Peloponnesian War

The major war between Athens and Sparta, an off-and-on-again affair covering more than a quarter century in which several Athenian near-victories are squandered by tragic military and political miscalculations.

- **431 B.C.:** Athenians withdraw behind the Long Walls of Piraeus and Athens, leaving Spartans to ravage countryside to no avail. Meanwhile Athenian ships sail around Peloponnese attacking coastal cities. At end of first year of war, Pericles delivers his "Funeral Oration" for the fallen of Athens. Euripides' *Medea* performed in Athens.
- **430 B.C.:** Plague breaks out in densely populated Athens; Hippocrates of Kos called on for medical aid; Pericles, held responsible, is accused of misusing public funds, removed from power, and fined.
- **429 B.C.:** Popular demand results in Pericles' reinstatement, but he is very ill with plague and soon dies; Cleon takes leading government role. In Abdera, philosopher Democritus develops atomic theory of Leucippus; ends previous speculations and creates basis of modern science in area. A group of philosophers known as Sophists (Wise Ones) begin to teach practical philosophy, such as rhetoric, for

use in everyday life. Most famous is Protagoras of Abdera, who travels to Sicily and Magna Graecia before arriving in Athens; he originates the subjective philosophical stance "Man is the measure of all things."

- **428 B.C.:** Birth of Plato.
- **427 B.C.:** Sophist Georgias of Sicily arrives in Athens as diplomat; stays to teach rhetoric, argues that nothing is knowable by reason beyond what the senses communicate.
- **425 B.C.:** At Pylos, first-ever surrender of Spartan troops; Sparta sues for peace, but Cleon, the Athenian leader, rejects offer.
- **424 B.C.:** The Spartan general Brasidas takes over conduct of war. In Persia, Artaxerxes dies and is succeeded by Darius II. On the Acropolis, the exquisite Temple of Athena Nike, designed by the architect Kallikrates, is finished.
- **422 B.C.:** Brasidas takes Amphipolis in important timber and mining area north of Chalkidiki, causing the disgrace and retirement of the general of the Athenian fleet, Thucydides, who is exiled and goes off to finish his history. In subsequent battle with Athenians (421), both Brasidas and Cleon are killed. Nicias, leader of the opposition Oligarch party, takes over power in Athens; Alcibiades now leads opposition democrats. Aristophanes' *The Wasps* is performed.
- **421 B.C.:** The Peace of Nicias, a 50-year pact, is negotiated between Athens and Sparta, but is vigorously opposed by Alcibiades. Aristophanes' *Peace* is produced.
- **420 B.C.:** Alcibiades maneuvers Athenian Assembly into alliances with Spartan enemies, putting Athens and Sparta virtually at war again. Beginning of construction of the Erectheion on the Acropolis; completed 404. Temple of Apollo at Bassae begun; finished 400. Hippias of Elis, a Sophist, active in Athens.
- **418 B.C.:** Spartans defeat allied forces of Athens and Argos at battle of Mantinea.
- **416 B.C.:** Savage Athenian suppression of attempted revolt on Melos. Euripides' *Electra* is performed.

The Sicilian Expedition

During a pause in the war with Sparta, Athens moves to take over Sicilian tributes and resources and to cut off the main source of the Spartan food supply. Instead, political infighting and indecisive leadership by generals result in a catastrophic Athenian defeat.

- **415 B.C.:** After the Sicilian city of Segesta (Hellenized but non-Greek) requests military aid, the Athenian Assembly—at Alcibiades' urging—decides to send a fleet to conquer entire island and outflank Sparta. On eve of the fleet's departure, disfiguration of busts of god Hermes in Athens blamed on Alcibiades, who is ordered to sail to Sicily while the investigation continues. Arriving in Sicily, Alcibiades is told to return to Athens to stand trial. He jumps ship in southern Italy and flees to Sparta; the Athenians condemn him to death in absentia.

- **414 B.C.:** Nicias begins besieging Syracuse, Sicily's major city. The Spartans, following Alcibiades' advice, send "volunteer" forces to aid Syracuse, plus an officer to take command.
- **413 B.C.:** Utter destruction of Athenian forces at Syracuse. Meanwhile, Sparta, again heeding Alcibiades' advice, moves to cut off Athens's supply of food and silver in Attica. The Athenian theater festivals continue, with Euripides' *The Trojan Women* (415) and his *Iphigenia in Taurus* (414), Aristophanes' *The Birds* (414), and Euripides' *Electra* (413).

The Decline of Athens

Now seriously weakened, Athenian democracy becomes prey to extremist forces in and around the city.

- **412 B.C.:** Sensing Athenian defeat, various members of the Delian League defect. Persia enters war, financing Spartans.
- **411 B.C.:** A council of 400 so-called Oligarchs seizes power in Athens. Attempts to make peace with Sparta collapse as the Athenian army and fleet at Samos refuse to join revolt. Aristophanes' *Lysistrata* and *Thesmophoriazusae* performed.
- **410 B.C.:** Democracy restored in Athens; Alcibiades, having fled Sparta because of a dangerous liaison with the wife of the Spartan king, is recalled to Athens, then smashes Spartan fleet at Hellespont (Dardanelles).
- **408 B.C.:** Euripides' *Orestes* produced, after which he goes into voluntary exile at court of Macedonian king, Archelaus.
- **407 B.C.:** Alcibiades censured and removed from office after his fleet is defeated during his absence by Spartans under Lysander. Alcibiades retires to private castle on Gallipoli peninsula.
- **406 B.C.:** Athenian navy defeats Spartans at Arginusae. Sparta sues for peace but is rejected. Euripides, having written *The Bacchae* and *Iphigenia in Aulis* in exile in Macedonia, dies there. Death of Sophocles at age 90 in Athens.
- **405 B.C.:** Lysander and Spartans destroy virtually entire Athenian fleet at battle of Aegospotami and are now masters of the Aegean; 4,000 Athenian prisoners are executed; Alcibiades assassinated at instigation of Lysander, who sails

to and begins besieging Athens. Aristophanes' *The Frogs* and Euripides' *The Bacchae* performed.
- **404 B.C.**: Athens capitulates unconditionally. Oligarchs are returned from exile and established as the infamous Council of Thirty, instituting reactionary reign of terror.
- **403 B.C.**: Overthrow of Thirty by rebel democratic forces. Spartan king Pausanias overrules Lysander's wish to crush opposition, and democracy is restored in Athens. Darius II of Persia dies, succeeded by Artaxerxes II.
- **401 B.C.**: Spartan-backed Cyrus II, Persian prince, marches against his brother Artaxerxes and is defeated at battle of Cunaxa. Retreat of 10,000 Greek mercenaries (see Xenophon's *Anabasis*). Sophocles' *Oedipus at Colonus* performed posthumously.
- **c. 400 B.C.**: Pupils of Socrates found various schools: Antisthenes of Athens, a Cynic, advocates cultivation of inner virtue by freeing the self and body from dependence upon externals; Aristippus of Cyrene in northern Africa espouses opposing hedonist code that virtue lies in pleasure of the senses; Euclid of Megara forwards the idea that the Socratic "Good" is a reflection of the irreducible primary substance of the Eleatic philosophers. Praxiteles, the greatest sculptor of the fourth century B.C., born in Athens.
- **399 B.C.**: Trial and death of Socrates, almost 70; convicted of corrupting the young and attempting to introduce new gods (*daimonion*). Thucydides, returned from exile in 404 B.C., dies in Athens. Plato goes into 12-year exile in Megara, Sicily.

Classical Greece: The Fourth Century

The fourth century is marked in its first half by struggles for dominance among Sparta, Athens, and the newly emergent Thebes (in Boeotia, northwest of Athens), with Persia holding the balance of power; and in its second half by the sudden rise of Macedonia under Philip II and his son Alexander. Meanwhile, Athens continues as Greece's cultural center.

- **398 B.C.**: Agesilaus, king of Sparta, continues campaigns against Persia to free Ionian cities.
- **395 B.C.**: Publication of Thucydides' *History*.
- **395–386 B.C.**: Corinthian War: Sparta against Persian-backed alliance of Corinth, Athens, Thebes, and Argos. Lysander killed at outset. Athens rebuilds Long Walls.
- **394 B.C.**: Battle of Onidus, in Asia Minor: Sparta defeated by Persian fleet under Kronon, Athenian admiral. Xenophon, having fought on the Spartan side against an Athenian ally, is banned from Athens. Supported by the Spartans in Elis, he then has leisure to write his histories *Anabasis* and *Hellenica*.

- 387 B.C.: Plato returns to Athens, establishes his Academy.
- 386 B.C.: Corinthian War ends with Persian-imposed "King's Peace," leaving Sparta in power.
- 384 B.C.: Birth of philosopher Aristotle and of Demosthenes, the greatest orator of his day.
- 382–379 B.C.: Spartans hold citadel of Thebes, subdue Olynthos in Macedonia.
- 380 B.C.: Death of Aristophanes.
- 378 B.C.: Athens and Thebes in alliance; Athens again founds Naval Confederacy similar to Delian League.
- 373 B.C.: Temple at Delphi destroyed by earthquake.
- 371 B.C.: Thebes becomes dominant power in Greece by crushing Spartans at battle of Leuktra.
- 370–330 B.C.: Praxiteles active; sculpts *Hermes Carrying the Infant Dionysios*.
- 367 B.C.: Plato tutors Dionysus II in Syracuse; 17-year-old Aristotle joins Academy.
- 362 B.C.: Second battle of Mantinea; Thebes gains over Sparta-Athens alliance. End of Spartan supremacy. Xenophon allowed back in Athens.
- 360–323 B.C.: Career of Cynic philosopher Diogenes.
- 359 B.C.: Philip II regent, then king, of Macedonia.
- 358 B.C.: Philip takes Amphipolis and gold mines of Pangaion Mountains; founds Philippi at old mining town.
- 358–330 B.C.: Building of theater at Epidaurus.
- 357 B.C.: Athens declares war on Philip; also in "Social War" (357–355 B.C.) with members of Naval Confederacy.
- 356 B.C.: Philip takes Potidea. Birth of Alexander. Great Temple of Artemis at Ephesus burns down.
- 356–352 B.C.: Phocaeans seize Delphi, causing Third Sacred War that ends with Philip in control of sanctuary.
- 353–349 B.C.: Building of tomb of Mausolus, king of Caria, at Halicarnassus.
- 351 B.C.: First of many verbal assaults on Philip by Demosthenes.
- 348 B.C.: Philip takes and razes Olynthos in Macedonia.
- 343–342 B.C.: Philip engages Macedonian-born Aristotle to tutor Alexander.
- 338 B.C.: Battle of Chaeronea: Philip defeats forces of Athens, Thebes, and others, establishing Macedonian hegemony over all Greece except Sparta.
- 337 B.C.: Philip creates Corinthian League of Greek city-states, declares war on Persia.
- 336 B.C.: Philip is assassinated and is succeeded by his 20-year-old son, Alexander.

The Age of Alexander

Beginning his campaigns as a continuation of Philip's policy of uniting Greece through war with Persia, Alexander soon finds his own vision—a synthesis of the cultures of East and West—and sets out to accomplish this by conquering the entire known world from India to Spain, Italy, and Sicily.

- **335 B.C.**: Alexander razes Thebes for trying to revolt, sparing only the temples and the house of Pindar. In Persia, Darius III succeeds to throne. In Athens, Aristotle establishes his Lyceum, the so-called Peripatetic school of philosophy.
- **334 B.C.**: Alexander invades Asia, routs Persian force at Granicus river, liberates the former Greek colonies of Ionia from Persian rule.
- **333 B.C.**: Alexander cuts through famous chariot knot at Gordium, shatters Darius's forces at Issus.
- **332 B.C.**: Alexander takes Tyre, Gaza, and Jerusalem, founds the city of Alexandria in Egypt, visits oracle of the ram-headed god Ammon at Siwah.
- **331 B.C.**: At Gaugamela in Mesopotamia, Alexander again defeats Darius and is proclaimed king of Asia. Enters Babylon, Susa, Persepolis, and Pasargadae, and takes possession of fabulous hoard of Persian gold.
- **330 B.C.**: Burning of great palace at Persepolis by Alexander and soldiers. Darius murdered by followers. Alexander extends empire east into Bactria, captures and executes Darius's murderers.
- **327 B.C.**: Alexander marries Roxanne, said to be the most beautiful woman in all of Asia. Callisthenes, Alexander's official historian and nephew of Aristotle, executed for plotting to kill Alexander. Alexander enters India. Philosophers Anaxarchus and Pyrrho meet Indian ascetics, dubbed the Gymnosophists, or naked philosophers.
- **326 B.C.**: Alexander crosses Indus river and defeats Porus, but Bucephalus, his wonder horse, is wounded and dies. After conquering Punjab, his soldiers refuse to go farther away from home; Alexander sails them down Indus to chart new passage to Mediterranean.
- **325 B.C.**: Alexander leads support group across deadly Baluchistan desert as Nearchus follows coast with ships.
- **324 B.C.**: Alexander and forces at Susa rejoined by Nearchus. Mass wedding with Iranian women. Death of Alexander's friend and lover, Hephaistion, of fever on way to Babylon.
- **323 B.C.**: Death of Alexander in Babylon, probably of same type of fever that killed Hephaistion. He is 33 years old.

The Hellenistic Age

Alexander's political successors war over control of his empire while the bringing together of Eastern and Western cultures results in a profusion of scientific, philosophical, and artistic activity unmatched since the Golden Age of Athens.

Between 323 and 280 B.C. the Wars of the Diadochi (Alexander's successors) are waged for control of the empire. At the end, Alexander's half-brother, wife, son, and mother have been murdered and his empire abroad divided between the remaining successors: the Ptolemaic dynasty in Egypt and the Seleucid dynasty in the East, who continue to war for supremacy. On the Greek mainland, Macedonia, Sparta, and other city-states, principally the Achaean League, also fight for domination over the others. Weakened by decades of war, they are ripe for the picking by the emerging imperial power of Rome, freed in 202 B.C. from its battles with Hannibal and Carthage.

Because of the cultural unity of an empire in which Greek was now the common tongue (*koine*) of learning, commerce, and diplomacy, and because of the enormous stimulus of renewed contact with Oriental influences, the arts and the sciences flourish, most particularly in Alexandria. That city (made capital of Egypt by Ptolemy) with its massive museum (home of the muses) and library, is considered second only to Athens as a seat of learning and culture, while predominating as the Hellenistic center of scientific activity.

In the field of science, among the numerous figures to emerge are Euclid (c. 300 B.C.) and Archimedes (c. 287–212 B.C.); the astronomer Aristarchus of Samos (active c. 270 B.C.), who proposes a heliocentric universe; Eratosthenes, who correctly calculates the circumference of the earth; and the anatomist Herophilus of Chalcedon (active c. 285 B.C.) and physiologist Erasistratus of Ceos (in Alexandria c. 258 B.C.).

Cultural figures of the period include the Athenian playwright Menander (c. 343–281 B.C.), leading exponent of the New Comedy; Apolonius of Rhodes, author of *The Argonautica* (c. 260 B.C.); and the poets Callimachus and Theocritus (both active c. 270 B.C.).

Architecture and sculpture thrive. In 196 B.C. the library of Pergamum, in northwest Asia Minor near Lesvos, is built to compete with that of Alexandria, with its Great Altar of Zeus and Athena added c. 166 B.C. Other works of the period include the Pharos (Lighthouse) of Alexandria (300 B.C.), the Colossus of Rhodes (293 B.C.), the *Laocoön* (250 B.C.), and the *Farnese Bull* (190 B.C.).

In philosophy, Epicureans and Stoics seek to find a basis for leading a satisfying and self-sufficient life. Epicurus (c. 342–270 B.C.) advocates the cultivation of pleasure and serenity of mind and body through an avoidance of pain. Zeno, the head of the Stoics (active c. 310 B.C.), proclaims Reason as the way in which man can find himself in harmony with a predetermined universe.

The Roman Domination

Having at last defeated Hannibal and Carthage (202 B.C.), Rome turns its army's full force on Carthage's ally, Macedonia, and proceeds to turn all of Greece into a Roman province, in the process carting away or destroying much of its Classical art and architecture.

- **168 B.C.:** At battle of Pydna, Romans defeat last Macedonian king, Perseus, and divide his empire into four territories. Late Hellenistic works of art: the *Winged Victory (Nike) of Samothrace,* the *Aphrodite of Melos* (*Venus de Milo*), *The Dying Gaul*.
- **146 B.C.:** Macedonia and the rest of Greece are made a Roman province. Construction of Via Egnatia linking Rome with Thessaloniki.
- **138 B.C.:** The Stoa of Attalos II, king of Pergamum in Asia Minor, is finished in the Athens Agora.
- **131 B.C.:** In Athens, the Temple of Olympian Zeus, originally started in 515 B.C., is completed under the Roman emperor Hadrian.
- **67 B.C.:** Romans take Crete.
- **50 B.C.:** Lost works of Aristotle discovered by Andronicus of Rhodes.
- **49 B.C.:** Roman Civil War; Caesar crosses Rubicon; Pompey and some of Roman senate retreat to Greece.
- **48 B.C.:** Battle of Pharsalus (Thessaly). Caesar defeats Pompey, who flees to Egypt but is murdered as he lands. In subsequent war, library in Alexandria is burned down. Caesar restores Cleopatra, his 22-year-old lover and a Greek of Macedonian-Ptolemaic descent, as queen of Egypt; she had been joint ruler from 51 to 48 B.C., when she was driven out.
- **44 B.C.:** Caesar murdered; Brutus, one of assassins, goes into exile in Macedonia.
- **42 B.C.:** Brutus and Cassius, defeated by Mark Antony and Octavian in battles of Philippi, commit suicide.
- **41 B.C.:** Antony and Cleopatra become lovers.
- **40 B.C.:** Antony makes political marriage with Octavian's sister, Octavia. Pact of Brundesium gives Antony eastern provinces.
- **37 B.C.:** Antony and Cleopatra meet again. He then "marries" her, giving her Roman territories in east.
- **31 B.C.:** Antony and Cleopatra defeated by Octavian at battle of Actium near Lefkadia (Epirus).
- **30 B.C.:** Antony and Cleopatra commit suicide in Egypt as Octavian is about to invade.
- **29 B.C.:** Octavian becomes Caesar of the new Roman Empire and is given name Augustus.

The Pax Romana

Greek culture and language exercise a considerable influence on the Roman world during the Pax Romana and aid enormously in the dissemination of Christianity.

- **c. A.D. 30**: Crucifixion of Jesus, whose appellation "messiah" is, in Greek, *christos.*
- **49–51**: Paul, fluent in Greek, makes first missionary journey to Greece, visiting Neapolis (Kavala), Philippi, Thessaloniki, Veroea (Veria), Athens, and Corinth, and returns to Antioch via Ephesus.
- **57–58**: Paul in Macedonia, Corinth, then back to Middle East.
- **60–120**: The Four Gospels are written in the popular Greek of Alexander's empire.
- **61**: Paul, on way to Rome by ship, is forced by storm to land on Crete (Kali Limenes).
- **c. 95**: Saint John, exiled to Patmos, writes the Revelation (in Greek), recounting his vision. Epictetus, Greek Stoic, active in Rome.
- **105–115**: Publication of *Parallel Lives* by Plutarch (c. 46–120), a Greek of Theban ancestry. Greek historian Appian and satirist Lucian also active.
- **129–199**: Galen, Greek physician and philosopher, born at Pergamum, becomes doctor to Marcus Aurelius.
- **c. 160–180**: Pausanias travels in Greece.
- **250**: Invasion of the Goths, who capture and sack Athens, but are then pushed back beyond the Danube.
- **267**: Invasion of the Heruli through Bosphorus, burning Ephesus and then Athens.

The Age of Constantine

Increasing pressure by barbarians on border areas causes a shift of men, goods, money, and power to the peripheries of the Roman Empire, creating excessive bureaucracy and rampant inflation and corruption. To deal with this, the emperor Diocletian (284–306) restructures entire empire and, in 286, divides administration into eastern and western halves, with two emperors in each half: the Tetrarchy.

- **305**: Diocletian retires to his birthplace at what is now Split, Yugoslavia.
- **311**: Constantine becomes one of the four emperors.
- **312**: As Constantine prepares for battle for sole possession of western throne, he is said to have seen a sign of the Cross appear in the daytime sky with the inscription "In this sign, conquer." He does.

- **313**: With Constantine as undisputed western emperor, Edict of Milan legitimizes Christianity.
- **323**: Constantine becomes sole emperor of East and West.
- **324**: Following another sign of God, Constantine chooses site for new capital at small town of Byzantium (see entry for c. 630 B.C.).
- **325**: The Council of Nicaea, summoned by Constantine to establish firm basis for Christianity within empire, produces Nicene Creed.
- **330**: Constantine inaugurates the city of the New Rome, also called Constantinople, ushering in the Byzantine Empire, which is to last 1,122 years.

The Early Byzantine Age

Constantinople's power in political and religious spheres is consolidated as Rome falls to the Visigoths, and the center of pagan philosophy, Plato's Academy in Athens, is closed.

- **337**: As Constantine dies, he is finally baptized as a Christian.
- **360–363**: Brief return to paganism, with Julian the Apostate emperor.
- **380**: Byzantine emperor Theodosius I proclaims Christianity official state religion.
- **381**: Second Ecumenical Council, in Constantinople.
- **392**: Theodosius issues proclamations closing heathen temples, including Delphi, the Parthenon, and Olympia; Olympic games are forbidden because of their nudity.
- **395**: Death of Theodosius; division of empire by his sons Honorius and Arcadius, who receive the West and East respectively; end of Imperial Roman unity, each half following its own course. Honorius moves capital from Rome to Ravenna.
- **476**: Rome falls to Visigoths under Odoacer; this event commonly accepted as marking the end of the Western Roman Empire and the beginning of the Dark Ages.
- **527–565**: Justinian becomes Byzantine emperor. Rebuilding of fire-damaged Ayia Sophia in Constantinople in its present form, and (in 529) the closing of Plato's school of pagan philosophy, the Academy.
- **797**: Irene the Athenian becomes the first woman to rule the Byzantine Empire.

Middle Byzantine Age

A period characterized by two enormous dangers to the continuance of the Empire: the sudden explosion of Islamic armies out of the Arabian peninsula and the violent internal religious controversy between the Iconoclasts and Iconodules.

- **800**: Charlemagne's coronation as emperor of resurgent Holy Empire in Rome; as Irene is still emperor in Constantinople, this further widens East-West split.
- **843**: Final victory of Iconodules (icon venerators) over Iconoclasts after destructive 120-year controversy.
- **860–863**: Saints Cyril and Methodius, apostles of the Slavs, devise Cyrillic alphabet and translate Bible into Slavonic.
- **867**: Byzantine emperor Basil I founds Macedonian dynasty.
- **1025**: Death of Basil II; end of dynasty.
- **1054**: Final schism between Roman and Eastern churches over papal claims to absolute rather than relative authority and the wording of Nicene Creed.
- **1055**: The Seljuk Turks take Jerusalem and begin raids on Byzantine territory, while Normans do the same in Italy.

The Destruction of Byzantium

As predators from both the Western Crusades and the Eastern forces of Seljuk and then Ottoman Turks continually threaten to destroy the Empire, there is a concurrent final humanist flowering of Byzantine art inspired by its rich Classical Greek heritage.

- **1081**: Emperor Alexios I Comnenos founds new dynasty. Normans invade Greece.
- **1099**: The First Crusade retakes Jerusalem.
- **1147**: Second Crusade: Normans, in passing, attack and take Corfu, Corinth, and Thebes.
- **1187**: Muslims under the Kurdish leader Saladin capture Jerusalem.
- **1189**: Third Crusade.
- **1201–1204**: Venetian-led Fourth Crusade loots, burns, and desecrates Constantinople, establishing "Latin" control of empire as members of Byzantine court flee to surrounding principalities.
- **1210**: Mainland Greece and islands carved up into small duchies and states by leading members of the Crusade. Venetians begin 459-year occupation of Crete.
- **1261**: Michael VIII Paleologos retakes Constantinople and establishes the last Byzantine dynasty, the Paleologi.
- **1301**: Beginning of Ottoman conquests following collapse of Seljuk empire.
- **1309**: The Knights of St. John occupy Rhodes.
- **1326–1397**: The Ottoman Turks take virtually all of Byzantine Empire except for the Morea (in Peloponnese), Constantinople, and Thessaloniki.
- **1453**: In third siege of the city Turks take Constantinople. End of the Byzantine Empire.

The Ottoman Period

Lasting almost 400 years (1456–1830), this was a period in which Greece as a nation sank into oblivion, and the see of the Greek Orthodox church, tolerated by Islamic religious doctrine and designated by the Turks as a secular administrative body, became the principal repository and keeper of the identity of the Greeks as a people and as a political entity.

- **1648**: Turks begin 22-year siege of Herakleion, Crete.
- **1669**: Herakleion falls; Turks occupy all of Crete.
- **1683**: Turks fail in second attempt to take Vienna.
- **1684**: War between Venice and Ottoman Empire.
- **1686–1715**: Odyssean expedition of Venetian admiral, Morosini, against Ottomans throughout Greece, during which (1687) his troops fire upon the Parthenon, now a Muslim mosque, and touch off the explosives stored inside, blowing out its roof and interior walls.
- **1801**: Lord Elgin "saves" Parthenon sculptures by transporting them to Britain.
- **1809–1811**: First visit of poet Lord Byron to Greece.
- **1814**: Founding of the secret Greek revolutionary society, the Philikí Etaireía, in Odessa.
- **1820**: The *Venus de Milo* is "rescued" by a French officer from island of Milos and taken to the Louvre. With French backing, Ali Pasha revolts against sultan, deposing him.
- **1821**: On March 25, the Greek bishop Germanos raises the flag of revolt against Turks at the monastery of Ayia Lavra in northern Peloponnese; this day later becomes National Independence Day.

War of Independence

Various factors—the decline of Ottoman power, external pressure by Russia and the European Great Powers, rampages by Albanian warlords on the Greek mainland, and an increase in active organized resistance by Greeks within the Empire and abroad, abetted by foreign philhellenes and fueled by the emergence of the "Great Idea" of a reborn Classical Greece—come together and finally erupt in the Greek revolution.

- **1821–1822**: Greek rebels establish footholds in Peloponnese and some Aegean islands. Provisional Greek government organized in Epidaurus.
- **1824**: Byron arrives at Mesolongi, gets caught in a rainstorm, develops a fever, and abruptly dies.
- **1825–1826**: Egyptian forces cross to Peloponnese, crush rebellion everywhere except Nafplion, then help Turkish forces succeed in the siege of Mesolongi.

- **1827**: British, French, and Russians destroy Turkish-Egyptian fleet at the battle of Navarino.
- **1828**: Ioannis Kapodistrias arrives in Greece to become first president.
- **1829**: Sultan signs peace treaty. Greek Orthodox church begins separation from patriarchate of Constantinople, a process completed only in 1850.
- **1829–1832**: After Greece is officially liberated in 1830 and Kapodistrias is assassinated in 1831, the Kingdom of Greece is created by Britain, Russia, and France with 17-year-old Otto of Bavaria named as monarch. In May 1832 the Protocol of London declares independence for Greece, a country that does not yet include Crete, Thessaly, Macedonia, Thrace, or the Ionian and Dodecanese islands.

Modern Greece

A continuing struggle for a spiritual as well as geographical identity, as forces attempt to promulgate their visions of a modern Greece among a people in many ways still shackled by the 400-year Ottoman era.

- **1834**: The small, ruined town of Athens, totally unsuited for the task, becomes the new Greek capital.
- **1839**: French archaeologists take the *Winged Victory (Nike) of Samothrace* from Turkish hands and install it in the Louvre.
- **1843**: A bloodless coup forces the king to grant a constitution; after this event, the square in front of the palace is called Constitution Square (Syntagma).
- **1862–1863**: Otto I replaced by British-backed 17-year-old Danish prince, who becomes King George I. Britain cedes Ionian islands to Greece.
- **1866**: Cretans rebelling against Turks blow themselves up inside Arkadi Monastery.
- **1873**: Schliemann finds his Treasury of Priam at Troy.
- **1875–1881**: Olympia excavated by German archaeologists.
- **1876**: Schliemann uncovers tombs thought to be those of Agamemnon and Atreus at Mycenae.
- **1881**: Great Power convention following Russo-Turkish Wars grants almost all of Thessaly and Arta to Greece.
- **1883**: Nikos Kazantzakis, author of *Zorba the Greek,* born in Herakleion, Crete.
- **1884**: Schliemann unearths palace of Tiryns.
- **1892–1903**: Delphi excavated by French archaeologists.
- **1896**: First modern Olympic Games held at Athens.

- **1898**: Great Powers force Ottomans to relinquish Crete as "autonomous" entity.
- **1900**: Sir Arthur Evans uncovers Palace of Knossos. C. P. Cavafy, Greek poet from Alexandria, begins writing major works.
- **1909**: Venizelos, hero of the Cretan struggle for independence, named premier of Greece. Birth of poet Ioannis Ritzos, nominated ten times for Nobel Prize.
- **1911**: Italians take Dodecanese islands from Turks.
- **1912–1913**: Balkan Wars. By terms of peace treaty Epirus, Macedonia, Crete, and (later, in February 1914) all northeastern Aegean islands except Imbros and Tenedos become Greek territories.
- **1913**: King George I assassinated in Thessaloniki; succeeded by his son, Constantine I.
- **1914**: Turkey signs treaty with Germany as armed neutral; Britain, Russia, and France declare war on Turkey; Greece neutral. Britain, which had administered the island since 1878, annexes Cyprus.
- **1917**: Venizelos brings Greece into war on side of Allies; pro-German King Constantine goes into exile, leaving the throne to his second son, Alexander.
- **1919**: Peace Treaty of Neuilly grants western Thrace to Greece.
- **1920**: In August, Peace Treaty of Sèvres grants Greece eastern Thrace, Smyrna, and all Aegean islands except the Italian Dodecanese. In October, King Alexander dies. In November, Royalists win election. In December, Greeks vote in a plebiscite to bring back King Constantine and continue war with Turkey.
- **1920–1922**: The Greco-Turkish War, which ends in a disastrous massacre of Greek forces and civilians on the quay at Smyrna (now Izmir) by Turkish troops under rebel leader Mustafa Kemal Pasha, known as Atatürk. King Constantine abdicates; his son George II becomes king.
- **1923**: Peace of Lausanne; Turkey given eastern Thrace, Smyrna, and the islands Imbros and Tenedos; immense exchange of populations as some 1.35 million Greeks and 430,000 Turks are resettled.
- **1924**: On March 25, the parliament declares Greece a republic with a president.
- **1924–1935**: Years marked by parliamentary struggles and successful and unsuccessful coups d'état.
- **1935**: A plebiscite votes for restoration of the monarchy; George II recalled from exile.
- **1936**: Venizelos dies in exile after unsuccessful coup attempt. General Metaxas, named premier by king, abolishes constitution and establishes dictatorship.
- **1939**: As war breaks out in Europe, Metaxas proclaims Greek neutrality.

CHRONOLOGY

- **1940:** On October 28, Metaxas delivers his famous *"Okhi!"* ("No!") to Italian demand that he allow Mussolini's troops "right of passage" through Greece; date becomes a national holiday; Greece at war with Axis powers.
- **1941:** Metaxas dies. Hitler's troops invade Greece; king and government flee to Cairo.
- **1944:** British army and Greek army and navy units enter Athens. Rebellion by Greek Communist resistance groups refusing to turn in arms.
- **1946:** Full Civil War breaks out in Greece between Communist and anti-Communist forces. Plebiscite returns George II to the throne.
- **1947:** George II dies, succeeded by his brother Paul I. Truman Doctrine proclaimed to aid Greece against Communists.
- **1949:** Tito breaks with Moscow, closing border to Greek Communists. End of Civil War.
- **1952:** The conservative Greek Rally party wins elections. Greece and Turkey join NATO.
- **1954:** In Cyprus, Archbishop Makarios declares for union (*enosis*) with Greece.
- **1963:** Murder of leftist parliamentary deputy Grigoris Lambrakis (hero of the film and novel *Z*). Premier Constantine Karamanlis steps down, calls for new elections, loses, goes into exile in Paris. Poet George Seferis awarded Nobel Prize for literature.
- **1963–1964:** Civil war in Cyprus between Greek and Turkish nationalists; establishment of U.N. peace-keeping force.
- **1964:** Election of the leftist Center Union party led by George Papandreou. Paul I dies, succeeded by son, Constantine II.
- **1965:** Papandreou resigns when Constantine II refuses to sign his directive aimed at purging the army.
- **1967:** Coup d'état by army colonels preempts a contingency plan of the CIA for a takeover coup by Greek generals; Constantine and his family flee to Rome.
- **1972:** United States and junta sign agreement allowing Sixth Fleet a base in Piraeus.
- **1973:** Following a plebiscite abolishing the monarchy, the junta proclaims a "republic" with former colonel George Papadopoulos as president. At Metsovio, the Athens polytechnic university, a student revolt against the regime is brutally and bloodily put down by the army, but forces resignation of Papadopoulos.
- **1974:** Junta collapses after abortive attempt to assassinate Makarios and seize Cyprus. Karamanlis returns from Paris and forms new government. War with Turkey, as its troops occupy northern half of Cyprus, is barely avoided. A new plebiscite confirms abolition of monarchy. Ban on Communist party lifted.

- **1975:** Karamanlis's right-of-center party, New Democracy, wins elections by large majority, applies for membership in the EEC.
- **1977:** In early elections, the leftist PASOK party, headed by George Papandreou's son, Andreas, makes the largest gain and becomes official opposition. Death of Archbishop Makarios. Tomb believed to be that of Philip II, father of Alexander the Great, uncovered in Macedonia.
- **1979:** Nobel Prize won by poet Odysseus Elytis.
- **1980:** Karamanlis elected president, replaced as prime minister by his foreign minister, George Rallis.
- **1981:** Greece becomes tenth member of EEC. Andreas Papandreou's PASOK wins new election by a wide margin; becomes first socialist government in Greek history.
- **1985:** Karamanlis loses presidential election to PASOK candidate, Christos Sarzetakis; Shi'ites board and hijack TWA flight 847 at Athens, causing international uproar.
- **1988:** Credibility of Papandreou's government damaged by revelations of embezzlement of millions of dollars from government pension funds by Greek banker, George Koskotas, who flees Greece and is later arrested and jailed in Salem, Massachusetts.
- **1989:** Koskotas implicates Papandreou and ministers in embezzlement scheme; several ministers resign, some are jailed. Papandreou is later indicted for illegal phone tapping, bribe taking, and breach of faith. Nevertheless, the opposition New Democracy party is unable to gain ruling majority in two general elections and is forced into temporary coalitions with Communist-dominated left coalition first and then also with Papandreou and PASOK.
- **1990:** New Democracy finally wins election in coalition with single independent candidate, a former New Democracy member who subsequently rejoins the party. Constantine Mitsotakis becomes prime minister, institutes price increases and wage freezes to combat serious economic crisis, causing series of nationwide strikes.

—*Tom Stone*

INDEX

ABC Hotel, 275, 332
Abdera, 322
Achaia, 142, 186
Achaia Clauss winery, 187
Achilleion, 373
Acrocorinth, 148
Acropolis, 42
Acropolis Museum, 54
Acroyiali Disco, 658
Acteon Hotel, 527, 559
Adamas, 486
Adam's Greek Kitchen, 570
Adonis: Athens, 74; Naxos, 504
Adriatica, 377
Aegean Center for the Arts, 476
Aegean Maritime Museum, 449
Aegina, 6, 408
Aeolos, 326, 332
Aerides (Winds) Taverna, 83
Afandou, 572
Afroditi Apartments, 681, 687
Agapitos, 264
Aga's Fountain, 470
Agelika Apartments, 608, 624
Agnanti Hotel, 217, 220
Agnonta, 346
Agora, 54
Agrambeli, 377
Agrari, 448
Agriolefkes, 233
Agriolivadi, 620
Aigaion, 105, 112
Aiolos Beach Hotel, 371, 405
Akroathos, 304
Akrogialli, 550
Akropolis House, 74
Akrotiri, Crete, 552; Santorini, 495; Zakynthos, 398
Aktaion, 500
Akti Myrina Hotel, 681, 687
Alana, 169
Alatza Imaret, 268
Alekos, 641
Alexander Beach Bungalows, 315, 332
Alexander's Taverna, 339
Alexandroupolis, 325
Alexopoulos, 660
Alikambos, 545

Alikes, 230, 400
Aliki, Milas, 492; Poros, 419; Thasos, 316
Aliki Hotel, 587, 623
Alimia, 585
Alinda, 611
Alkyon Hotel, 294, 332
Alones, 415
Aloni, Alonnisos, 351; Patmos, 620
Alonia Hotel, 443, 502
Alonnisos, 8, 335, 348
Altana Apartments Traditional Settlement, 500, 504
Altis, 124, 183
Altis Hotel, 186, 192
Alykanas, 400
Alykes, 303
Alyko, 470
Amades, 665
Amalia Hotel: Athens, 74; Delphi, 119, 137
Amalia Hotel Olympia, 186, 192
Amari Valley, 542
Ammoudi, 500
Ammoudia, Epirus, 200; Ikaria, 636
Amopi, 582
Amorgos, 430
Amorgos, 74
Amouliani, 303
Amphipolis, 308
Anafonitria, 400
Analipsi, 603
Anapiros, 272
Anargyros Kafieris, 499
Anastasia/Siba, 99
Anatoli, 344
Anatolia Hotel, 323, 332
Anavatos, 662
Anaxos, 676
Andreas Theodorakis, 540
Andritsena, 190
Andromache Guesthouse, 345, 359
Andros, 9, 432
Anemos, 339
Anemo Theatro, 450
Angelos's Taverna, 341
Angelou Pension, 609, 624
L'Angolo Bar, 450
Anixi, 466, 504
Anna Gelou's White Shop, 450
Anna's, 356
Ano Boularioi, 177

Ano Kardamyla, 663
Ano Mera, 451
Ano Petali, 481
Ano Syros, 458
Anoyeia, 537
Anoyi, 393
Anthemis, 633, 684
Anthes, 96
The Anthropos, 85
Antimachia, 600
Antiparos, 478
Antipaxi, 374
Antissa, 673
Antonini's Restaurant, 450
Antonis O Magos, 404
Apaggio, 85
Aperi, 583
Aperitton, 345, 359
Apikia, 436
Apiranthos, 469
Apokalypsis, 72
Apokofto, 484
Apollo Hotel, 414, 425
Apollon, 469
Apollon Café, 476
Apollon Hotel, 218, 220
Apollonia, 481
Apollonia Beach, 518, 559
Apollonion, 656, 686
Apollon Theatre, 459
Apotsos, 89
Aproopto, 272
Aptera, 543
Arcadia, 142, 188
Archaeological Museum: Andros, 437; Argostoli, 386; Ayios Nikolaos, 532; Chania, 548; Chios, 655; Corfu Town, 369; Ermoupolis, 458; Herakleion, 522; Ioannina, 205; Ithaca, 392; Kassandra, 299; Kastellorizo, 576; Kastoria, 283; Komotini, 324; Larissa, 227; Lesvos, 671; Limnos, 681; Milos, 489; Mykonos, 449; Nafplion, 154; Naxos, 466; Parikia, 476; Pythagorio, 643; Rethymno, 538; Rhodes Town, 568; Siphnos, 485; Siteia, 534; Skyros, 355; Sparta, 160;

711

712 INDEX

Thessaloniki, 256; Tinos, 442; Vathy, 640; Volos, 228
Archanes, 524
Archipelago, 338
Archondiko, 282
Archontiko, 421
Arco Hotel, 341, 359
Arekia, 398
Areopagus, 43
Areopolis, 174
Arethusa's Fountain, 393
Aretsou, 272
Argentis Museum, 655
Argive Heraion, 150
Argo, 442, 502
Argo Hotel, 414, 425
Argolid, 142, 145
Argos, 134, 159
Argo-Saronic Gulf, 6
Argo-Saronic Gulf Islands, 408
Argostoli, 383
Ariadne Hotel, 648, 684
Arimondi Fountain, 538
Arion Hotel, Skala, 620; Vouliagmeni, 105
Aristi, 215
Aristokration, 100
Aristotelous, 265
Arkadi Monastery, 541
Arkasa, 583
Armathia, 581
Armena Inn, 635, 684
Armenaki Villas, 500, 504
Armeni, 500
Armenistis, 635
Armeos, 461
Armoloi, 345
Arnados, 443
Arnea, 305
Arta, 211
Artemona, 481
Artemona Xenon, 482, 504
Artemon Hotel, 482, 504
Artemos, 419
Artena, 404
Arvanitohori, 581
Arvi, 528
Asklepieion, Kos, 599; Poros, 419
Askyphou, 545
Aslanis, 99
Asomatos, 525
Asprovalta, 308
Assos, 389
Astachi, 635, 684
Asteria, 672
Asteros, 569
Astir Palace, 532, 559
Astir Palace Hotel, Athens, 72
Astir Palace Hotels: Aphrodite, Arion, Nafsika, 105, 112
Astoria, 518, 559

Astra Bar, 449
Astrofengia, 351
Astypalaia, 563, 602
Athena Andreadi, 99
Athenaeum, 90
Athenaeum Inter-Continental, 72
Athens, 6, 39
Athens Hilton, 73
Athens Tower, 94
Athos Palace, 299, 332
Atlantis Hotel: Kalymnos, 608, 624; Kos, 596, 623; Santorini, 498, 504
Atlantis Villas, 500, 504
Atrium Hotel, 341, 359
Atsitsa, 357
Atsitsa Centre, 357
Attaviros, 573
Attica, 6, 101
Avgonima, 662
Avgoustis's, 401
Avlaki, 593
Avlemonas, 404
Avli Pension, 641, 684
Avli Restaurant, 539
Avli Taverna, 645
Avlona, 681
Axos, 537
Ayia Anna, 470
Ayia Eleni, 317
Ayia Ermioni, 658
Ayia Fotin, 582
Ayia Fotini, 658
Ayia Galini, 527
Ayia Irini, 605
Ayia Lavra Monastery, 188
Ayia Marina: Aegina, 414; Kasos, 580; Leros, 610; Milos, 491; Spetses, 425
Ayia Markellas Monastery, 666, 686
Ayia Matrona, 422
Ayia Mavra, 400
Ayia Moni, 157
Ayia Paraskevi: Skiathos, 341; Spetses, 424
Ayia Pelagia, 403
Ayias Galas, 665
Ayia Sophia, 263
Ayiasos, 676
Ayia Triada, 488
Ayia Triada Monastery, 242
Ayia Varvara, 525
Ayioi Anargyroi, 424
Ayioi Deka, 520
Ayioi Theodori, 164
Ayios Antonios, 592
Ayios Athanasios, 344
Ayios Dimitrios, 636
Ayios Emilianos, 590
Ayios Evstratios, 684
Ayios Fokas, Lesvos, 677; Skyros, 357

Ayios Haralambos, 324
Ayios Ioannis, Crete, 542; Thessaly, 234
Ayios Ioannis Kerami, 468
Ayios Isidoros, 542, 677
Ayios Kirikos, 631
Ayios Konstantinos, 647
Ayios Mamas, 467
Ayios Menas, 377
Ayios Nikitas, 378
Ayios Nikitas Hotel, 379, 406
Ayios Nikolaos, 531
Ayios Nikolaos Anapafsas, 242
Ayios Nikolaos Bay, 401
Ayios Nikolaos beach, 590
Ayios Nikolaos Park, 290
Ayios Panteleimon, 177, 263
Ayios Polykarpos, 635
Ayios Prokopios, 470
Ayios Sostis, 448, 483
Ayios Spyridon, 377
Ayios Stephanos, Corfu, 372; Kos, 601
Ayios Stefanos Monastery, 242
Ayios Yeorgios, 529
Ayios Yiorgios, 576
Ayios Yiorgos Diasoritis, 468

Bajazzo, 87
The Balalaika, 88
Balthazar, 87
Banana Beach, 341
Barlaam, 241
Basilica of Ayios Dionysios, 396
Basilica of Paleopolis, 369
Basilica of Trion Ierarchon, 190
Bassae, 190
Batis Camping and Hotel, 311, 332
Batsi, 435
Bay of Phorcys, 393
The Beautiful Paleopolis, 436
Bella Venezia, 371, 405
Bella Vista, 372, 373, 656
Belle Helene, 150, 192
Belleni's Tower, 611
Bellonia Villas, 501, 504
Belou Hotel, 447, 503
Bembo Fountain, 520
Benaki Museum, 63, 98
Berlin, 97
Bextsinar, 270
"Bikini Red" Pub, 404
Le Bistro, 339
Bistrot Boh, 448
Blue Caves, 400

INDEX 713

Blue Grotto, 576
Blue Sky, 591
La Boheme, 339
Bokhali, 398
Bonsai, 414
Boschetto, 88
Bosphorus Hotel, 323, 332
Botsaris, 85
Bouboulina's, 424
Boufidis's, 238
Bouillabaisse, 85
Bourtzi, 153
Bourtzi Hotel, 338, 359
Breath of Zorba, 379
Brinias's, 648, 685
British Cemetery, 369
Bubble Beach, 601
Burgi, 230
Byzantine Café, 88
Byzantine Castle, 311
Byzantine Museum: Athens, 64; Chios, 654; Leros, 610; Samos, 641
Byzantion, 168
Byzantium, 656

Café Candouni, 500
La Calma, 641
Calypso, 371, 405
Camile Stefani, 501
Campiello, 368
Canaris, 84, 111
Cape Matapan, 177
Cape Sounion, 6
Cape Yerakas, 401
Capitol, 275, 332
Caprice, 521
Captain's Garden, 569
Captain's House, 615, 624
Capuchin Monastery and Guesthouse, 459, 503
Caravel, 401, 407
Carmela's, 549
Carnayio Fish Taverna, 339
Carnival, 358
Casablanca, 339
Casa Delphino, 549, 559
Casa Lucia, 373, 405
Castellania, 569
Castle of Angelokastro, 372
Castle of Passava, 174
Castle of Platamonas, 281
Castle of the Knights, Kastellorizo, 576; Koz, 597
Castle of St. George, 387
Castro, 466
Cathedral of Ayios Andreas, 187
Cathedral of Ayios Dimitrios, 164
Cathedral of the Dormition, 237
Cathedral of Saints Konstantinos and Eleni, 576
Cathedral of the Virgin Mary, 324
Cava d'Oro, 539
Cave of Antiparos, 479
Cave of Ayia Sophia, 404
Cave of Ellinikokamara, 580
Cave of Hades, 109
Cave of the Nymphs, 393
Cave of Paenia, 110
Cave of the Panayia Arkoudiotissa, 553
Cave of Philoctetes, 683
Cave of Polyphemus, 325
Cave of St. John the Hermit, 553, 556
Caves of Dirou, 175
Caves at Keri, 399
Cavos Bay Hotel, 635, 684
Cavo Tagoo Hotel, 448, 503
Center of Hellenic Tradition, 97
Cephalonia Star, 383, 406
Chalki, Naxos, 468
Chalki, 563, 585
Chalkidiki, 295
Chandris Hotel, 656, 686
Chania, Crete, 545; Thessaly, 545
Chapel of Ayios Yiorgos Mandilas, 238
Chapel of the Virgin, 617
Charos Reef, 682
Chateau Zevgoli, 466, 504
Chatzigeorgalis, 569
Chersonisos, 531
Chez Julian, 339
China Town, 540
Chiona, 664, 686
Chios, 8, 629, 651
Chris and Eve's, 323, 332
Chrisi, 558
Christiana Hotel, 641, 685
Christos, Ikaria, 636; Paros, 477
Christos Apartments, 501, 504
Christos Karageorgiou, 323
Chrysopigi, 484
Chrysostomos, 637
Chryssi Milia Beach, 351
Church of the Anastasis, 458
Church of the Archangel Michael, 542
Church of the Archangels, 661
Church of the Assumption, 459
Church of the Assumption of the Virgin, 660
Church of Ayia Aikaterini, 520
Church of Ayia Marina, 302
Church of Ayia Paraskevi, 243, 400
Church of Ayia Sophia, 166
Church of Ayia Triada, 232
Church of Ayioi Anargyri, 283
Church of Ayioi Apostoli, 660
Church of Ayios Charalambos, 683
Church of Ayios Dimitrios, 268
Church of Ayios Haralambos, 500
Church of Ayios Nikolaos, 475
Church of Ayios Nikolaos Kambinari, 174
Church of Ayios Nikolaos Kasnitzi, 284
Church of Ayios Nikolaos Orphanos, 268
Church of Ayios Nikolaos tou Molou, 397
Church of Ayios Sozos, 682
Church of Ayios Spyridon, 369, 640
Church of Ayios Stefanos, 283, 556
Church of Ayios Strategos, 177
Church of Ayios Theologos, 602
Church of Ayios Yanni Kastri, 347
Church of Ayios Yermanos, 287
Church of Ayios Yiorgios, 62
Church of Ayios Yiorgios of the Mountain, 576
Church of Ayios Yiorgos, 169
Church of Christ of Jerusalem, 605
Church of Christos Elkomenos, 167
Church of Eleousas, 286
Church of Episkopi, 177
Church of the Evangelistria, 424
Church of the First-Enthroned Virgin, 468
Church of the Heaven-Bearing Virgin, 481

INDEX

Church of a Hundred Doors, 474
Church of Iron St. John, 491
Church of the Metamorphosis, 155, 286
Church of Osios David, 267
Church of Our Lady, 573
Church of Our Lady of the Angels, 397
Church of Our Lady of the Castle, 602
Church of the Panayia, 676
Church of the Panayia Chalkeon, 269
Church of the Panayia Glykophiloussa, 676
Church of Panayia Kastriotissa, 284
Church of Panayia Krina, 658
Church of the Parigoritissa, 211
Church of Profitis Ilias, Hora, 465; Thessaloniki, 268
Church of Saint Anthony, 464
Church of St. Mark, 519
Church of St. Mary, 539
Church of Saints Jason and Sosipater, 369
Church of St. Titus, 519
Church of San Salvadore, 550
Church of the Taxiarchis, 661
Church of the Taxiarchis Michael, 675
Church of the Taxiarchoi, 174
Church of the Transfiguration, 645, 649
Church of the Virgin Koumoulos, 436
Church of the Virgin of Rodarios, 499
Church of the Virgin of the Troughs, 482
Church of Vlacherna, 177
Cifte Haman, 269
City Bar, 450
Climataria, 632
Clockwork Monkey Collectors' Corner, 97
Cochili, 372
Compendium Ltd., 98
Constantine Laskaris's, 437
Convent of Evangelismos, 636
Convent of the Evangelist, 667

Cooperative Artisanal of Lefkada, 378
Copacabana, 92
Coral Hotel, 532, 559
Corali, 488, 504
Corfu, 8, 363, 364
Corfu Palace Hotel, 371, 405
Corfu Villas Travel, 405
Corinth, 7, 116, 147
Corinth Canal, 146
Corinthia, 142, 145
Corto, 460
Coryialenios Historical and Cultural Museum 386
Costas, 415
Creta Maris, 531, 560
Cretan Historical Society 519
Creta Star Hotel, 541, 560
Creta Sun Hotel, 518, 560
Crete, 9, 506
Crete Chandris, 554, 560
Crystal Lounge, 73
Curry Palace, 89
Cyclades, 9, 427

Da Bruno, 88
Dadi, 321
Dafia, 673
Dakrotsides, 461
Damigos Tennis Club and Pool, 500, 504
Danae Hotel, 412, 425
Daphni, 6, 108
Dapia, 423
Daskalopetra, 663
Daskalopoulos Hotel, 217
Decor, 264
Delfinia, 676, 687
Delfini Beach, 461
Delfini Hotel, 488, 504
Delfini Restaurant, 635
Delicious, 88
Delion, 474
Delos, 9, 452
Delphi, 7, 113, 119
Delphi Museum, 123
Delphi Restaurant, 80
Dendrinos, 390
Despotiko Hotel, 447, 503
Devil's Gorge, 419
Dia, 558
Diafani, 584
Diakofto, 188
Diamantis, 232
Diana Hotel, 397, 407
Diaporos, 300, 332
Dias Hotel, 217, 221
Didimotiko, 320
Diktian Cave, 529
Dilini Restaurant, 677

Dilino Restaurant, 593
Dilofo, 218
Dimitra Hotel, 647, 685
Dimitrakis, 672
Dimitris Daskalopoulos Hotel, 217, 220
Dimitroulia Brothers, 233, 245
Dimitsana, 191
Dina Hotel, 476, 504
Diogenes, 205
Dio Horia, 443
Dion, 292
Dionysos, Athens, 76, 83; Skopelos, 345, 359
Dionysus Theater, 47
Divani Motel, 236, 245
Dodecanese, 8, 562
Dodona, 7, 208
Dolce Vita, 450
The Dolphin, 418
Dolphin Hotel, 614, 624
Doma, 552, 560
Domata, 387
Donoussa, 430
Dorian Hotel, 587, 623
Dormition, 488
Dormition of the Virgin, 485
Doryssa Bay, 642, 685
Dourabeis, 84
Dragonisi, 451
Drakolimni, 217
Drakona, 556
Drenia, 303
Drepano, 154
Driftwood Bar, 399
Drogarati Cave, 383
Drosia, 104
Drosiani, 468
Dzimakos's Taverna, 350

Eagles' Palace, 305, 332
Edem, 450
Edessa, 287, 289
Ee Oraia Mytilini, 311
Eftychia's, 377
Ekali, 104
Ekaterini Markou Apartments, 580, 622
Elafonisi, 557
Eleana Hotel, 642, 685
Electra Palace Hotel, Athens, 74; Thessaloniki, 275, 332
Eleftheroudakis, 98
Elenidis, 258
Eleni Kathourou, 500
Eleni Martinou, 96
Eleusis, 6, 109
Elia, 448
Eliana, 460
Elias, 645
Elias's Taverna, 338
Elies Hotel, 605, 624
Eliovasilema, 421
Elis, 142, 182

INDEX 715

Ellenis, 641, 685
Elli, 345, 359
Elounda, 532
Elounda Beach hotel, 532, 560
Elounda Mare hotel, 532, 560
Emborio, Chios, 659; Kalymnos, 608; Kasos, 580; Santorini, 501; Symi, 590
En Gavrio, 435
The Enotion, 153
En Plo, 656
EOT Guesthouse, 667, 686
EOT Traditional Houses, 500, 504
Epaminondas Holiday Apartments, 435, 502
Epidaurus, 7, 113, 135, 156
Epirus, 7, 194
Episcopal Palace, 164
Episkopi, Crete, 556; Hydra, 421
Erato, 233, 245
Erechtheion, 49
Eresos, 674
Eristos, 592
Ermones Beach Hotel, 373, 405
Ermoupolis, 457
Esperia Pension, 518, 560
Esperides, 645
Esperides Hotel, 658, 686
Etia, 535
Etz Hayyim, 548
Eucalyptus, 372
Eudoxia Hotel, 634, 684
Europa, 283, 333
Europe Hotel, 460, 503
Eva Grim, 521
Evangelistria, Nisyros, 593; Skiathos, 342
Evangelistrias Monastery, 636
Evdilos, 634
Evelyn's, 646
Every Day, 499
Evia, 104
Exambela, 483
Exo Gonia, 500
Exostis, 232
Exoyi, 393

Faggotto, 550
Faka, 548
Falasarna, 556
Faliraki, 571
Faliraki Beach Hotel, 571, 622
Faltaits Historical and Folklore Museum, 355
Family Coffee Shop, 264

Fanaraki Beach, 682
Fanári, 633
Fanari Camping, 322, 333
Fanari Hotel, 323, 333
Faneromeni Church, 413
Faneromeni Monastery, Naxos, 470; Lefkada, 378
Fani Mitropoulou, 304
Fanourakis, 95
Fantasia Pension, 569, 622
Far East, 87
Farouk Hanbali, 100
Felos, 435
Ferma Beach, 534, 560
Fetiye Mosque, 206
Filippo's, 99
Filoti, 469
Filoxenia Guesthouse, 390, 406
Fira, 498
Firostefani, 499
Fiscardona Guesthouse, 390, 406
Fish Tavern Scarus, 500
Fiskardo, 389
Flic Flac, 632
Flisvos Taverna, 614, 624
Folegandros, 430
Folk Art and Ecclesiastical Museum, 673
Folk Museum, Ayios Yeorgios, 529; Karpathos, 583; Kastoria, 283; Komotini, 324; Volos, 229; Xanthi, 321
Folklore Museum, Milos, 489; Siphnos, 481; Stemnitsa, 190
Forest Theater, 256
Fort Santa Maura, 375
Fortezza, 539
Fountain of Peirene, 148
Fourni, 637
Françoise Hotel, 461, 503
Franco's Bar, 499
Frangokastelo, 544
Frikes, 394
Frosso, 345
Frourion, 227

G. B. Corner, 81
Gaïdoronisi, 303
Galatas, 157
Galaxias, 518, 560
Galaxy Hotel, Alonnisos, 351, 360; Athens, 90; Ioannina, 204, 221; Kavala, 311, 333
Galerie Antiqua, 97
Galerie Iro, 97
Galerie Varsakis, 339
Galissas, 461

Gallerie Anemos, 598
Gallery Katrin, 598
Gangou, 642
The Garden, 421
Garden Restaurant Delfi, 498
Garden Theater, 256
The Gastra, 205
Gavdos, 558
Gavrion, 434
Geometric Cemetery, 468
George Goutis, 96
George's Place, 620
Germanos Papadapoulos, 286
Gerofinikas, 80
Gianna Hotel, 611, 624
Giel Haute Coiffure, 99
Gioura, 351
Glaros, 356
Glass House, 521
Glossa, 347
Glyf, 373
Glyfada, 105
Glyfada Beach, Corfu, 373; Skyros, 358
Glyfada Beach Hotel, 373, 405
Glyfada Hotel, 314, 333
GNTO, 661, 686
Golden, 478
Golden Coast Hotel, 107, 112
The Golden Fleece, 540
Golden Odyssey, 499
Golden Odyssey Hotel, 658, 686
Golden Sands, 658, 686
Gomati Bay, 681
Gondola, 383
Goni, 545
Gortys, 526
Goulandris Museum of Cycladic Art, 63, 98
Gounaki, 539
Gournia, 533
Gouverneto, 553
G. Passaris, 459
Grace Hotel, 587, 623
Gramos, 273
Gramvousa, 541
Grand Balcon, 73
Grand Chalet, 104, 112
Grande Bretagne, 72
Grand Hotel, 373, 405
Grazia Tower, 468
Great Meteoron, 241
El Greco, Karpathos, 582; Mykonos, 450
Greco Gold, 499
El Greco hotel, 541, 560
Greek Coast Hotel, 105, 112
Greek Islands Club, 403
Greenwich Village, 527
Gregory's, 392

INDEX

Grigori's, 120
Grigoris's, 620
Grigoris Taverna, 681
Grikou, 620
Grotta, 464
La Grotta Hotel, 400, 407
Grotto of Kefalas, 608
Gucci, 99
Gytheion, 173

Halakas, 491
Halandriani, 458
Halepa, 552
Hamam, 598
Hara Hotel, 597, 623
Havriata, 387
Helen hotel, 641, 685
Hellas Restaurant, 155
Hera hotel, 643, 685
Hera II, 643, 685
Heraion Hotel, 646, 685
Herakleia, 430
Herakleion, 516
Herb Shop, 540
Hermes, 532, 560
Hermes of Praxiteles, 183
Hermion, 83
Herodes Atticus Theater, 47
Hill of Cronus, 124
Hippocrates Palace Hotel, 597, 623
Hippocrates' plane tree, 597
Historical and Ethnographic Museum, Heraklelon, 520
Hivadolimani, 491
Homerion Conference Center, 655
Honey Tree, 415
Hora, Alonissos, 351; Andros, 437; Chios, 654; Kythira, 403; Mykonos, 447; Naxos, 465; Patmos, 619; Thrace, 329; Tinos, 439
Hora Sphakion, 544
Horefto, 233
Horio, Chalki, 585; Skyros, 353; Symi, 589
Hortiatis, 257
Hotel Adonis, 469, 504
Hotel Alexandra, 461, 503
Hotel Amfipolis, 314, 332
Hotel Anagenessis, 580, 622
Hotel Andros Holiday, 435, 502
Hotel Antoniadi, 236, 245
Hotel Atheras, 634, 684

Hotel Byzantino, 168, 192
Hotel Byzantion, 165, 192
Hotel City, 275, 332
Hotel Dimitsana, 191, 192
Hotel Egeo, 312, 332
Hotel Egli, 438, 502
Hotel Galaxy, 228, 245
Hotel Hermes, 460, 503
Hotel Homer, 460, 503
Hotel Ilion, 338, 359
Hotel Karalis, 181, 192
Hotel Kastoria, 283, 333
Hotel Kastraki, 238, 245
Hotel Katerina, 233, 245
Hotel Katerina, Leros, 610, 624
Hotel Kioni, 391, 406
Hotel Koala, 597, 623
Hotel Korthion, 438, 502
Hotel Kouneni, 447, 503
Hotel Kyma, 656, 686
Hotel Kypseli, 228, 245
Hotel Lucy, 311, 333
Hotel Megisti, 576, 622
Hotel Menelaion, 160, 192
Hotel Meteora, 236, 245
Hotel Myrto, 280, 333
Hotel Nefeli, 257, 276
Hotel Olympia, Syros, 461, 503; Thessaloniki, 237
Hotel Panorama, 257, 276, 333
Hotel Park, 280, 334
Hotel Pefka, 257, 276, 334
Hotel Pighi Sarisa, 436, 502
Hotel Platyialos, 484, 504
Hotel Princess of Mykonos, 448, 503
Hotel Raches, 636, 684
Hotel Timoleon, 315, 334
Hotel Trikolonion, 191, 193
Hotel Village, 590, 623
Hotel Vourlis, 460, 503
Hotel Xenia, 438, 502
Hotel Xenios, 663, 687
Hotel Zaira, 673, 687
Hotzas, 655
House Evi, 300
House of Mehmet Ali, 311
House of the Tiles, 158
Hundred Heads Bay, 681
Hydra, 6, 408, 420

Ia, 500
Iakovatos Mansion, 387
Ialysos, 573
Icthyoskala, 656

Idaean Cave, 526, 537
Ierapetra, 534
Ierissos, 303
Igoumenitsa, 195
I Kali Kardia, 353
Ikaria, 8, 629
Ikarion, 633, 684
Ikaros Village, 531, 560
Ikos Travel, 350, 360
Ilias Lalaounis, 94
Imborio, 438
Imerovigli, 500
Imvrou Ravine, 545
Ino Hotel, 642, 685
Inousses, 667
Ioanna Angelatou, 168
Ioannina, 7, 203
Ioannis Kostandoglou, 96
The Ionian Islands, 361
Ionic Center, Chios, 656
Ios, 430
Ipapandi Hotel, 592, 623
Iphigenia, 91
Ipsilon Monastery, 674
Ireon, 645
Irini, 677, 687
Irini Hotel, 591, 623
Irini Ravine, 555
Irini's, 648, 685
Isle of Ayios Achillios, 286
Isternia, 444
Itanos Taverna, 532
Ithaca, 8, 363, 391
Ixia, 571

Jean and It, 589
Jesuit Monastery and Guesthouse, 458, 503
Jewish Museum, Athens, 64
J. Vourakis & Fils, 95

Kabanera, 356
Kaity Pension, 403, 407
Kakodiki, 555
Kal, 372
Kalambaka, 236
Kalami, 372
Kalamitsa, 357
Kalathas, 553
Kalauria, 418
Kalavryta, 188
Kalligata, 387
Kalliope Ranga, 216, 221
Kalliopi, 683
Kallithea, Rhodes, 571; Samos, 650
Kalloni, 673
Kaloyeros, 542
Kalpaki, 212
Kalymnos, 563, 604
Kalypso Cretan Village, 544, 560
Kalyva, 383
Kamares, 480,

INDEX 717

Kamares Cave, 525
Kamares Restaurant, 635
Kamari, 501
Kamari Hotel, 501, 505
Kambos, 650
Kambos Beach, 620, 634, 650
Kameiros, 573
Kameiros Skala, 573
Kaminia, 473
Kanaki Pension, 582, 622
Kanapitsa Peninsula, 340
Kandanos, 555
Kandouni, 605
Kapetanakou Tower Hotel, 174, 192
Kapilio, 272
Kapsali, 403
Kara Musa Djami, 539
Karabopetra, 646
Karalis Beach Hotel, 181, 192
Karavomilos, 401
Kardaki, 542
Kardamena, 600
Kardamites Museum, 444
Kardamyla Hotel, 664, 686
Kardamyli, 174
Kardiani, 444
Kardiotissa, 529
Karfas, 658
Kargas, 477
Karlovasi, 648
Karnagio, 551
Karpathos, 563, 581
Karuna Meditation Center, 676
Karya, 379
Karytena, 190
Kasiotiko Spiti, 581
Kasos, 563, 579
Kaspakas, 681
Kassandra, 298
Kassiopi, 372
Kassopi, 201
Kasteli Hotel, 423, 426
Kastelli, 615, 624
Kastellorizo, 8, 562, 574
Kastoria, 282, 283
Kastraki, Naxos, 470; Peloponnese, 154; Thessaly, 237
Kastri, 404, 458
Kastro Bar, 449
Kastroperpatimata, 273
Kataraktis, 658
Les Katerinettes, 589
Kathara Monastery, 393
Kathisma, 379
Kathistres, 580
Kato Hora, 404
Kato Kastro, 437
Kato Katelio, 388
Kato Zakros, 535
Katoi-i, 451
Katrin's, 449

Katsanaki, 235
Kava d'Oro Hotel, 569, 622
Kavala, 310
Kavasila, 213
Kavirio, 683
Kaviros, 327, 333
Kavos, 272
Kavos Pension, 390, 406
Kavouria, 551
Kea, 430
Kechrias Monastery, 342
Kechrovouni Nunnery, 443
Kefallonia, 363, 382
Kefalos, Kefallonia, 383; Kos, 601
Kelefa, 174
Kelepouris, 461
Keramoti, 315
Kerdilia, 273
Keri, 399
Kerkis Bay Hotel, 650, 685
Kernos Beach, 531, 560
Khelathros, 581
Kiara, 99
Kifissia, 104
Kimolos, 492
King Maron Beach Hotel, 325, 333
King Otto, 154, 192
Kini, 461
Kioni, 394
Kionia, 442
Kipi, 218
Kira Fira Jazzbar, 498
Kissamos, 556
Kissamos Valley, 557
Kita, 176
Klemataria, 521
Klima, Milos, 490; Skopelos, 347
Klimataria, 284, 344
Klimatoria, 325
Knossos, 523
Knossos Beach Hotel, 518, 560
Knossos restaurant, 521
Koala Hotel, 648, 685
Kochi, 482
Kokkari, 647
Kokkari Beach Hotel, 647, 685
Kokkini Varka, 84
Kokkinokastro Beach, 351
Kolona, 412
Kolonaki, 61, 98
Kolonaki Tops, 81
Kolymbada, 358
Kolymbithres, 477
Komi, 659
Komi Hotel, 659, 686
Komos, 528
Komotini, 323

Kompos, 540
Kona Kai, 73, 87
Kondari, 658
Konitsa, 212
Konstantine Beslemes, 153
Kon Tiki, 339
Kontiki, 570
Kontopouli, 683
Kontou, 235
Koraïs Library, 655
Kordistos Hotel, 601, 623
Koroni, 177, 179
Korthion, 438
Kos, 563, 594
Kostas Akalestos's Parikia Tours, 476
Kostos, 478
Kotopoula, 645
Kotsina, 683
Koubelidiki, 284
Koufonisi, 558
Koukounaries Beach, 341
Koulis Christodoulou, 216, 220
Koulo, 372
Koulouki, 610
Kouloura, 372
Koum Kapi, 552
Kounelas Fish Taverna, 450
Kounistra Monastery, 342
Kounopetra, 387
Kounoupitsa, 424
Kourkoumelata, 387
Kourohori, 467
Kouros Restaurant, 641
Kratsa Baths, 633
Krikelas, 272
Krios, 473
Kristina's Restaurant, 356
Kriti Beach, 541, 560
Kritsa, 532
Kseri Elia, 421
Ktikados, 442
Kynigos, 488
Kyr Sotos, 345, 360
Kyra Panayia, 351
Kyria Kali's, 357
Kyriakopoulou, 235
Kyria Maria, 421
Kytheria Pension, 403, 407
Kythira, 8, 363, 402
Kyveli Apartments, 663, 686

Labito Hotels, 642, 685
Laconia, 142, 160
Laganas, 399
Lageri Beach, 477
Lake Avythos, 388
Lake Korissia, 372
Lake Koronia, 302
Lake Kournas, 543

718 INDEX

Lake Melissani, 383
Lake Pamvotis, 206
Lake Volvi, 302
Lake Vouliagmeni, 147
Lakki, 609
Lalaounis, Mykonos, 450; Rhodes, 568
Lalaria Beach, 341
Laloula, 477
Lambi, 620
Lambiotes, 542
Lambrakis Apartments, 659, 686
Langada, 663
Langada Pass, 165
Langadas, 317
Lara Hotel, 387, 406
Larissa, 159, 226
Lasithi Plateau, 528
Lassi, 386
Lato, 533
Lazaretto, 392
Lazaros's, 423
Leather Workshop, 374
Ledra Grill, 73
Ledra Marriott, 73
Lefkada, 363, 375
Lefkadia, 289
Lefkas Hotel, 377, 406
Lefkes, 477
Lefkimmi, 371
Lefkos, 583
Lemonakio, 647
Lena's House, 449
Lepeda, 387
Lerna, 134, 158
Leros, 563, 609
Leskhi, 99
Lesvion Hotel, 672, 687
Lesvos, 8, 629, 669
Leto Hotel, 447, 503
Lia, 212
Liadromia Hotel, 350, 360
Lichnos Beach Hotel, 199, 221
Lies, 593
Ligeri, 424
Likogiannis Furs, 284
Lilis, 460
Lilla's, 174
Limani, 661
Limaniotis, 273
Limenakia, 339
Limenas, 314
Limnos, 8, 629, 678
Limonari, 346
Limonias, 650
Limonos Monastery, 673
Lina Hotel, 399, 407
Linaria, 353
Lindos, 572
Lindos Bay Hotel, 572, 622
Liotrivi, 483
Liston, 367
Litharitza, 207

Litohoro, 280
Little Venice, 449
Little Venice Gallery, 450
Liuba Cottages, 401, 407
Livadaras, 459
Livadia, Astypalaia, 603; Tilos, 591
Livatho, 387
Lixouri, 387
Lofos Strani, 398
Logaras, 478
Loggia, 519, 538
Longovarda Monastery, 477
Loom, Naxos, 466; Rhodes, 569
Lotos, 681
Lotus, 450
Loukia Haute Couture, 99
Loulaki Bar, 421
Lourdata, 387
Louros Springs Hotel, 209, 221
Loutra, 327
Loutra Eleftheron, 309
Loutraki, 146, 347
Loutros, 327
Lukullus, 466
Lycabettus, 61
Lygia, 379
Lykovrisi, 81
Lyttos, 530

Macedonia Palace, 275, 333
Madro Travel, 345, 360
Magazia, 355
Maherado, 400
Maistrali, 390
Maistrali Café/Bar and Hotel, 461
Makaki, 664
Makedonia Grill House, 569
Makedonos, 556
Makrinitsa, 231
Makrinitsa Guesthouses: Mousli, Sisilianou, Xiradaki, 245
Makris, 325
Makry Yialos Beach, 386
Makryammos, 314, 333
Malleas Beach Hotel, 611, 624
Mallia, 531
Maltesania, 603
Malvasia Hotel, 167, 192
Mandamados, 675
Mandato, 274
Mandragoras, 271
Mandraki, Nisyros, 592; Skiathos, 341
Mandraki Harbor, Kos, 597; Rhodes, 569
Manesis Taverna, 86
Manganas, 482
The Mani, 7, 170

Manolates, 648
Manoli's, Kalymnos, 605; Vathy, 641
Manolis's, 635
Manoussi, 282
Manthos, 304
Maralinas, 88
Marathi, 477
Marathokambos, 650
Marathon, 107
Mare Nostrum Holidays, 340
Maria's Labyrinth, 661, 686
Maria Stavrokopoulou's Café, 451
Marina, 633, 684
Mariner Virgin, 489
Marinero, 528
Marinos, 540
Mario's, 500
Maritime Museum, Andros, 437; Santorini, 500
Mariva, 327, 333
Markopoulos, 388
Markos's Café, 442
Marmara, 478
Marmari, 600
Marmaro, 664
Maronia, 324
Maroulas, 537
Marpissa, 478
Marpounta Village Club, 351, 360
Massouri, 605
Mastihari, 600
Matala, 527
Mathew's, 450
Mathiassos's Sweetshop, 465
Mati, 96
Matoula's, 168
Mavrantzis Bay, 401
Maxim, 521
Mediterranea Bourse, 569
Medusa, 460
Megali Mourtia, 351
Megalohori, 501
Megalo Horio, 591
Megalo Papingo, 216
Megalos Aselinos, 341
Megalo Seitani, 649
Megan, 380
Meganisi, 380
Meganisi Hotel, 380, 406
Megaspileon Monastery, 188
Megisti, 575
The Melanes Valley, 467
Meliton Hotel, 301, 333
Melo-i, 620
Melos, 489
Meltemi, 549
Memories, 86
Memory Tourist, 647

INDEX 719

Menetes, 533
Menites, 436
Mentor Hotel, 391, 406
Mesa, 673
Mesa Kastro, 437
Meseo Karlovasi, 648
Mesopotamos, 200
Messenia, 142, 177
Mesta, 660
Metaxata, 387
The Meteora, 7, 236
Methana, 157
Methoni, 177, 294
Metropolitan Church of Chania, 548
Metropolitan Hotel, 275, 333
Mets, 65
Mets Bar, 86
Metsovo, 218
Metsovo Art Museum, 219
Metsovo Folk Art Cooperative, 219
Mezetzidiko, 339
Miaoulis Square, 458
Michaeli's, 442
Michalis, 95
Mikri Viglia, 470
Mikro, 216
Mikro Horio, 591
Mikrolimano, 84, 111
Mikro Seitani, 649
Milatos, 531
Milia Beach, 351
Milies, Skopelos, 347; Thessaly, 235
Milopotamos, 234
Milos, 486
Minion, 100
Minoa, 477
Minotaur Bar, 449
Miramare Beach Hotel, 571, 622
Miramare Hotel, 315, 333
Miranda Guest House, 421, 426
Mithymna, 675
Mitikas, 632, 684
Mocassino, 98
Molhos, 264
Molos, Hydra, 421; Skyros, 355
Molos Beach, 478
Molyvos, 675
Monastery of the Apocalypse, 617
Monastery of Ayia Mamas, 580
Monastery of Ayia Paraskevi, 217
Monastery of Ayia Triada, 553
Monastery of Ayios Andreas, 387
Monastery of Ayios Dionysos, 280

Monastery of Ayios Ioannis, 603
Monastery of Ayios Nektarios, 413
Monastery of Ayios Nikolaos, Metsovo, 219; Spetses, 423; Thrace, 322
Monastery of Ayios Nikolaos ton Philanthropinon, 207
Monastery of Ayios Panteleimonas, 207
Monastery of Ayios Yerasimos, 389
Monastery of Ayios Yiorgios, 580
Monastery Beach, 477
Monastery of the Chrysoskalitissa, 557
Monastery of Gonias, 556
Monastery of Great Lavra, 307
Monastery of John the Baptist, 585
Monastery of the Madonna of the Caves, 644
Monastery of the Mavriotissa, 284
Monastery of Megali Panayia, 646
Monastery of Moni Toplu, 534
Monastery of Panachrantos, 437
Monastery of the Panayia, Hydra, 420; Metsovo, 219
Monastery of Panayia Chrysoleontissa, 413
Monastery of Panayia Makrinitissa, 232
Monastery of Panayia Spiliani, 593
Monastery of Panormitis, 590
Monastery of Profitis Ilias, 501
Monastery of St. John, 615
Monastery of Timios Stavros, 646
Monastery of Vrondiani, 647
Monastery of Zalongo, 201
Monastiraki, 56, 96
Monastiraki Church, 542
Monemvasia, 7, 165
Moni, 415
Moni, 468
Moni Preveli, 544
Moni Valsamonero, 525
Moni Vrondisi, 525
Monodendri, 214, 217

Monoklissia, 317
Monolithos, 574
Montagna, 258, 271
Moondy Bay Hotel, 415, 426
Moria, 675
Morko, 345
Morosini Fountain, 519
Morpho, 338
Mosque of Aslan Pasha, 206
Mosque of Hasan Pasha, 550
Mosychlos, 682
Motel Astir, 325, 332
Moudros Bay, 682
Mouikis Hotel, 383, 406
Mouikis Village, 383, 406
Moumin Mehmet Mouhsin, 323
Mount Aetos, 393
Mount Ainos, 389
Mount Athos, 7, 306
Mount Dikti, 528
Mount Fengari, 329
Mount Ida, 526
Mount Kerkis, 650
Mount Kynthos, 453
Mount Olympos, 676
Mount Olympus, 7, 242, 277
Mount Parnassus, 119
Mount Pelion, 230
Mount Penteli, 104
Mount Profitis Ilias, 478
Mourayio, 424
Mousli, 232
Mprotolog, 444
Museum of Argos, 159
Museum of Modern Art, Andros, 437
Museum of Modern Greek History, Athens, 65
Museum of Post-Byzantine Art, Zakynthos, 397
Mustapha Tseleri Rooms, 598, 623
Mycenae, 7, 116, 150
Mykonos, 9, 445
Mykonos Bar, 450
Mykonos Beach Hotel, 447, 503
Mykonos Folk Museum, 449
Mylopotamos, 404
Myrdiotissa, 373
Myrina, 680
Myrtia, 86
Myrties, 605
Myrtos, 389
Mystra, 7, 162
Mytilini, 669
Mytilini Cathedral, 671
Mytilinii, 646

INDEX

Nafplion, 153
Nafplion Art Gallery, 155
Nafsika, 105
Nafsika Bungalows, 412, 426
Naftikos Omilos Androu, 438
Nagos, 665
Naousa, 477
Naoussa, 289, 290
Nasiotis, 100
National Archaeological Museum, 66, 98
National Gallery and Alexandros Soutzos Museum, 64
National Garden, 63
National Tourist Organization Hotel, 216, 221
National Welfare Organization shop, 97
Naval Museum, Chania, 549
Navy Out, 273
Naxos, 462
Nea Hora, 550
Nea Moni, 661
Nea Peramos, 309
Nea Roda, 303
Nefeli Apartments, 681, 687
Nefeli Hotel, 355, 360
Nekromanteion, 200
Nemea, 7, 116, 149
Neoclassical Pension, 656, 686
Neohori, 488
Neohori Pension, 582, 622
Neo Karlovasi, 648
Neokastro, 181
Neo Rion, 570
Neorion Bay, 418
Neos Marmaras, 301
Nepheli Hotel, 648, 685
Neraida, Athens, 92; Syros, 460
Nerantzopoulos, 282
Nestor's Palace, 179
New Fort, 367
New Gate, 520
Nick's, 603
Nicola's Garden, 390
Nifida, 677
Nikaria, 636
Nikia, 593
Nikiana, 379
Nikolaos Dakotros's Taverna, 498
Nikolaos Dragatsis, 95
Nikopolis, 202
Nikos, 351
Nikos Notonakis, 540
Nikos Saxonis Hotel, 216, 221
Nikos Taverna, 642
Nimborio, 585

Nine Muses, 92
Niricos Hotel, 377, 406
Nisyros, 563, 592
Nitsa's Women's Co-operative, 392
Nomia, 176
Nos, 589
Nostalgia, Athens, 97; Mykonos, 451
Nostos, 199
Nostos Hotel, Frikes, 391, 406; Tzaneria Beach, 340, 359
Nydri, 379
Nykterida, 553

O Adelfos tou Kosta, 401
Oasis, 570
Oasis Hotel, 528, 560
Oasis of Walnuts, 436
Oceanis Hotel, 311, 333
Odysseas Hotel, 391, 407
Odyssey, 154
Odyssey Hotel, 379, 406
Oia's Sunset, 500, 505
Oinoi, 635
Olga Hotel, 383, 406
Olive Tree, 380
Olive Wood Mini-Shop, 368
O Loutros Fish Taverna, 264, 273
Olymbi, 660
Olympia, 7, 113, 124, 182
Olympias, 302
Olympic Hotel, 204, 221
Olympic Palace Hotel, 571, 622
Olympos Naoussa, 265, 271
Olympos Village, 584
Omega, 98
Omonia Square, 65
Omorfi Ekklesia, 412
O Nestoras, 228
Oniro Roof Garden, 466
On the Rocks, 92
Opsis Art Gallery, 450
Oraia Ellas, 398
Orestiada, 320
Orestion, 283, 333
Orloff Guest House, 420, 426
Ormos, 648
Ormos Marathokambos, 650
Ormos Panayias, 300
Ornos, 448
Oscar's Taverna, 357
Osios Loukas Monastery, 117
Osteria del Pesce da Lu, 450
Ostria, 234
O Takis, 451
Othos, 583
O Ti Kalo, 436

O Tsounas, 370
Ouranopolis, 303
Our House, 539
Ouzeri, 404
Ovraiki, 548
Ozz, 99

Il Padrino, 424
Pafsilipou Taverna, 552
Pagoni, 99
Palace of the Despots, 162
Palace of the Giustiniani, 654
Palace of the Grand Masters, 567
Palace of St. Michael and St. George, 367
Palamidas, 421
Palatia, 464
Palea Epidavros, 157
Paleohora, Aegina, 413; Crete, 555
Paleohori, 490
Paleokastritsa, 372
Paleokastro, Nisyros, 593; Pylos, 181
Paleopolis, 436
Pali, 593
Palia Fabrika, 499
Pallini Beach, 299, 333
Pamvotis, 207
Pan Bar, 90
Panagiotopoulos Leather and Travel Goods, 100
Panayia, 118
Panayia Evangelistria, 441
Panayia Gouvernitissa, 528
Panayia Hodegetria, 164
Panayia Kyra, 533
Panayia Myrtidiotissa, 663
Pandrosos, 476, 504
Pangrati, 65
Panorama, 257
Panorama Bar, 73
Panorama Hotel, Kastro, 466, 504; Marmari, 600, 623
Panormos, 346
Panormos Beach Hotel, 346, 360
Panormos Hotel, 390, 406
Panos-Zafira, 311
Panteli, 610
Pantanassa Monastery, 164
Panteleimon, 281
Pantelis's, 620
Pantheon, 460
Papafrangas, 491
Papakis, 556
Papanikolaos Apartments, 658, 686

INDEX 721

Papingo, 216
Paradise Beach, 448
Paradise Beach Camping, 503
Paradise Hotel, 350, 360
Paradisos, 321
Paradiso Taverna, 647
Paradissos Hotel, 603, 623
Paralama, 274
Paraport, 351
Paraportiani, 449
Parga, 195
Parikia, 473
Park Hotel, 228, 245
Parliament, 57
Paros, 471
Parthenis, 99
The Parthenon, 50
Parthenon Hotel, 74
Paschalis, 264
Patitiri, 350
Patmian House, 619
Patmos, 8, 563, 612
Patralis, 424
Patras, 186
Patsoura's, 383
Paul G. Pylarinos, 96
Pavlos's, 346
Pavlou Hotel, 417, 426
Paxi, 199, 374
Pedi, 590
Pedi Beach Hotel, 590, 623
Pefkakia, 229
Pefkari, 315
Pefkos, 357
Pelican Hotel, 498, 505
Pella, 288
Peloponnese, 7
Peloponnesian Folklore Foundation, 154
Pension Evdoxia, 642, 685
Pension Istron, 532, 560
Pension Maria Elena, 632, 684
Pension Voulamadis, 657, 687
Pension Zorzou, 610, 624
Pentelikon, 104, 112
PentheRoudakiS, 95, 99
Perachora, 146
Perahori, 392
Perama, 212
Perasma Gallery, 153
Peratata, 387
Perdika, 415
Pergola Restaurant, 500
Perissa, 501
Peristera, 351
Perivleptos Monastery, 164
Perivoli, 657, 686
Perivoli Monastery, 673
Perivoli T'ouranou, 83

Perivolos, 501
Persephone's, 646
Petra, 676
Petralona, 298
Petalouda, 583
Petra Mare, 534, 560
Petros, 528, 560
Petros Dzafolias, 229
Phaidra Traditional Pension, 656, 686
Phaistos, 526
Phanai, 660
Philippi, 312
Phillipi's, 450
Philokalia, 98
Phloisbos, 488
Phri, 579
Phylakopi, 491
Piano Bar, 460
Pierros, 449
Pigada, 442
Pigadia, 582
Pikilasos, 555, 560
Piles, 583
Pili, 600
Pindos, 215
The Pink Panther, 155
Piraeus, 111
Pirgos, 619
La Piscine, 338
Piso Livadi, 478
Pitsidia, 528
Pityous, 663
Pizzeria Napoli, 522
P. Karapournos Apartments, 663, 686
Plaka, Athens, 56; Limnos, 683; Milos, 488
Planos, 401
Platamon Beach Hotel, 294, 334
Platani, 600
Plati, 681
Platania, 341
Platanos, Leros, 610; Skopelos, 344; Tinos, 445
Plateia Emmanouil, 284
Plateia Navarino, 263
Platy Ammos, 403
Platy Yialos Beach, Kefallonia, 386; Mykonos, 484
The Playboy, 92
Plaza, 615, 624
Plaza Hotel, 340, 359
Plekta Lanari, 99
Plomari, 677
Plomisti, 344
Plotinoupolis, 321
Pnyx, 46
Polaris Travel Agency, 331
Polatof, 99
Poli, 580
Polichnitos, 677

Poliochni, 682
Polis, 393
Pollonia, 492
Polybates, 593
Polygyros, 299
Polyrrenia, 556
Pop Eleven, 99
Popular Art Cooperative, 658
Porfyris Hotel, 592, 623
Poros, 6, 380, 416
Poros, Kefallonia, 388; Lefkada, 408
Poros Hotel, 417, 426
Porta, 199
Portaria, 233
Porto Carras, 301
Porto Corfu Pizzeria, 370
Porto Galini Hotel, 379, 406
Porto Kaio, 177
Porto Koufo, 301
Porto Lagos, 322
Porto Marino, 540
Porto Rio Hotel, 187, 192
Porto Veneziano, 552, 560
Porto Zoro, 401
Poseidon, 153
Possidonion Hotel, 423, 426
Possidonion Hotel/Bungalows, 461, 503
Potami, 387
Potami Beach, 649
Potamies, 467
Potamos, 403
Pothia, 604
Pothos Hotel, 338, 359
Potidaia, 298
Prassa, 492
Prassies, 542
Praxiteles, 186
Praxiteles Restaurant, 193
Preveza, 203
Princessa Hotel, 643, 685
Prince Stafylos, 345, 360
Prinkipo Nisia, 271
Prionia, 280
Prodromos, 478
Prodromos Apartments, 650, 685
Propodes, 207
Propylaea, Athens, 42; Eleusis, 109
Prunier, 88
Psara, 666
Psarades, 286
Psaropoulos, 105
Psarotaverna, 356
Psarrou, 448
Psathi, 492
Psathoura, 351
Psil, 467
Psiliammo, 620
Psili Ammos, 650

INDEX

Pydna, 294
Pylea Fish Tavernas: Gramos, Kerdilia, 273
Pylos, 179
Pyrgaki Point, 471
Pyrgi, 660
Pyrgos, Santorini, 500; Tinos, 444
Pythagorio, 642

Quartetto di Zante, 399
Queen Olga Hotel, 275, 334

Rachamos, 460
Raches, 636
Rafina, 104
Raikos Hotel, 403, 407
Ranga Paranga, 97
Ratatouille, 230
Rayias, 270
Regantos's, 377
Remember, 99
Remezzo, Athens, 87; Hydra, 421
Remvi, 229
Rena, 633, 684
Renes Beach, 358
Renos Prekas Wines, 499
Repanidi, 683
Restaurant Fay, 568
Restaurant Myrties, 608
Rethymna Beach, 541, 560
Rethymno, 538
Reymoundos, 98
Rheneia, 451
Rhodes, 8, 562, 564
Rhodes Tourist Office, 570
Rhodes Town, 567
Ritsi, 99
Riva District, 437
Rivari, 491
Rocco, 219
Roditses, 642
Rodos Palace, 571, 622
Romantica, 377
Romantica Hotel, 582, 622
Romantzo Hotel, 592, 623
Romeo, 615, 624
Rongotis, 271
Rooms in Kioni, 407
Rooms in Vathy, 407
Rotunda, 556
Rousanou, 241
Roussos Hotel, 501, 505
Roxy, 658
Royal Tombs, 291
Rustic Taverna, 573

The Sailor, 418
St. George Lycabettus Hotel, 73
St. John Chrysostom, 492
St. Mark's Square, 397
Saint Spyridon, 155
St. Titus's Church, 526
Saliagos, 478
Salamis, 42
Samaina Bay Hotel, 649, 685
Samaria, 539
The Samarian Gorge, 554
Sami, 383
Samos, 8, 629, 638
Samos Wine, 648
Samothrace, 326
Sanguin Hotel, 534, 561
San Stephanos, 448
Santa Maria Beach, 477
Santa Marina, 448, 503
Santorini, 9, 493
Santorini Image Hotel and Bungalows, 500, 505
Sapountzi, 283
Sappho's Leap, 380
Sarella, 99
Sarti, 300
Sarti Beach, 300, 334
Savva's, 576
Savvouras, 153
Schinoussa, 430
Sea Colors, 460, 503
Sedoni Cave, 537
Selai Cave, 580
Selene Restaurant/Bar, 498
Selini, 345
Selinos, 555
Seriphos, 430
Sesame Kitchen, 450
Sesklia, 590
Sesklo, 223
Seven Brothers, 83
Seven Brothers Hotel, 417, 426
Seven Stars Hotel, 582, 623
Sgoumbros, 373
Siatista, 281
Sid, 372
Sigma & Kappa Hellas, 300
Sigri, 673
Sikaminia, 675
Silivani, 460
Silver Bay Hotel and Bungalows, 673, 687
Silver Center, 99
Simandiris House, 619
Sioras, 424
Siphnos, 480
Sirapian Dikran, 96
Sirens Beach, 531, 561
Siroccos, 540
Sisilianou, 232
Siteia, 534
Siteia Beach, 534, 561
Sithonia, 300
Sithonia Beach Hotel, 301, 334
Sixties, 92
Skala, 619
Skala Eresos, 674
Skala Hotel, 615, 624
Skala Resort, 388
Skalohori, 673
Skandali, 682
Skaros, 497
Skiathos, 8, 335, 336
Skites, 304, 334
Skopelos, 8, 335, 343
Skopelos Village, 346, 360
Skoteino, 530
Skotinas, 281
Skyros, 8, 335, 352
Skyros Travel, 355, 360
Socrates Prison, 76
Solomos Museum, 397
Solomos Square, 396
Sotos, 610
Soto's Grotto, 414
Soufli, 321
Souipas, 230
Sounion, 105
Souyia, 555
Sparta, 160
Spetses, 6, 408, 422
Spetses Hotel, 423, 426
Sphinx Restaurant/Bar, 501
Spilia, 556
Spiliopoulos, 186
Spiliotissa Monastery, 216
Splantzia, 552
Sporades, 8, 335
Sportif, 99
Spyro's Rotisserie, 344
Stafylos Beach, 346
Stamatis, Andros, 436; Vathy, 641
Stamatis Ftoulis's, 356
Stamatopoulos, 83
State Theater of Northern Greece, 256
Stathis's Crete, 557, 561
Stathis's, Skiathos, 341
Stavri, 175, 177
Stavros, Chalkidiki, 302; Crete, 553; Ithaca, 393; Tinos, 442
Stavros Melissinos, 99
Stayira, 305
Stelios's Taverna, 658
Stelle's, 540
Stemnitsa, 190
Stenies, 438
Steni Vala, 351
Stephanos's, 356
Steps, 641
Steps of Lindos Hotel, 572, 622
Sternes, 553

INDEX 723

Stimadourakis Fish Restaurant, 556
Stoa of Attalos, 55
Stomiou Monastery, 213
Strada Marina Hotel, 397, 407
Strofi, 76
Studio Gallery, 373
Stylianos D. Damigos, 499
Sunwing Hotel, 571, 622
Super Paradise, 448
Symi, 563, 587
The Symposium, 76, 568
Symposium Restaurant, 656
Synaheris, 647, 685
Syntagma Square, 57
Syntrivani tou Syntagmatos, 80
Syros, 455
Syrtaki, 316
Syvota, 380

Ta Adelphia, Ayios Kirikos, 632; Karlovasi, 649; Thessaloniki, 263
Ta Agrimia, 539
Ta Delphinia, 435
Tagastiri, 549
Take It Easy, 632
Takis, 415
Takouni Expres, 100
Ta Kymata, 344
Tamarisko, 476
Ta Nissia, 271
Ta Palia Kalamakia, 228
Ta Phanaria, 155
Ta Plataria, 291
Ta Psaradika, 284
Tarsanas, 339
Tasos', 258
Tasos's, 425, 681
Tassos's, 539
Taverna, 83
La Taverna Italiana, 450
Taverna Maria, 540
Taverna Psara, 83
Taverna To Spitiko, 218
Ta Vrakakia, 301
Tavropolion, 636
Ta Yannena, 460
Telendos, 608
Tempe, 243
Temple of Athena Nike, 48
Teriade, 672
Thalassomylos, 386
Thalassopolos, 667, 686
Thanasis's, 264, 273
Thanos, 681
Thasos, 313
Thasos Hotel, 315, 334
Themis, 641, 685
Themistocles, 86

Theodore Rousounnellos, 450
Theophilos art museums, 672
Therma, 633
Thermae, 597
Thermes, 673
Thermi, 305
Thessaloniki, 7, 250
Thessaly, 7, 222
Thomas, 207
Thomas Hotel, 574, 622
Thrace, 318
Three Brothers, 421
Three Churches, 477
Thronos, 542
Thymiana, 658
Tilisos, 537
Tilos, 563, 591
Tingaki, 601
Tinos, 439
Tinos Beach, 443
Tinos Beach Hotel, 443, 502
Tiryns, 7, 134, 158
To Akrotiri, 398
To Allo, 345
To Brook, 354
To Gerani, 82
To Kandouni, 392
To Kanoni, 168
To Kastroperpatimata, 266
To Katoi, 390
Tolon, 154
Tomb of Nikos Kazantzakis, 520
To Nisaki, 322
Top Hana, 548
Top Hanas, 549
Topolia Ravine, 557
Tosca Beach Hotel, 311, 334
Tositsa family mansion, 219
To Stenaki, 273
Totti's Ouzerie, 265, 272
Tower, 257
Tower of Ayios Petros, 435
Tower of Markellos, 412
Tower of Proforion, 304
Tower of Trigoniou, 266
Tower of the Winds, 57
Tragaia, 468
Tramps, 460
Transfiguration Church, 263
Trapsetelli, 488
Trechandiri, 392
Trehandiri, 424
Treis Boukes, 358
Triandaros, 443
Tripa, 370
Trireme of Timocharis, 572

Troizen, 419
Troulos Bay Hotel, 341, 359
Trussardi, 99, 450
Trypiti, 489
Tsambia, 443
Tsangarada, 234
Tsardaki, 284
Tsavros, 373
Tsekouras Taverna, 82
Tseleniana, 555
Tsepelovo, 218
Tsiatsiapa, 283
Tsilivi, 401
Tsimiski Street, 258
Tsitsiris Castle Hotel, 175, 193
Tsougria, 341
Tsoukas Brothers, 284
Tunnel of Evpalinos, 644
Tzabo Beach, 647
Tzaki, 571
Tzamadou, 647
Tzaneria Beach, 340
Tzitzivakos, 682
Tzotzos's, 267

Vai, 535
The Vale Of Tempe, 242
Valide, 539
Valide Mosque, 520
Valley of the Butterflies, Paros, 476
Valley of Butterflies, Rhodes, 573
Valtos, 199
Vangelis, 311
Vangelis's Taverna, 619
Varia, 672
Vasilikaki, 550
Vasiliki, 380
Vasilikos, 401
Vassilena's, 85
Vassiliko Theatro, 256
Vassilis, 104
Vassilis's, 424
Vatera, 677
Vathia, 175
Vathia Tower Hotel, 175, 193
Vathy, Astypalaia, 603; Ithaca, 392; Kalymnos, 608; Samos, 639
Velanio Beach, 346
Venetia, 645, 685
Venus Hotel, 647, 685
Venus Village, 488, 504
Vergina, 291
Via Egnatia, 261
Victoria Hotel, 218, 221
Vienoula Kousathana, 450
Vienoula's Garden Hotel, 447, 503
Viki, 665
Vikos Gorge, 214, 216

INDEX

Vikos Guest House, 217, 221
Vilidiris, 264
Village Inn, 301, 398
Villa Marina, 587, 623
Villa Meltemi, 399, 407
Villa Orsa, 340, 359
Vinia, 445
Virgin of Mercy, 485
Virgin of the Rosary, 489
Vistonia, 322
Vivamare Apartments, 603, 623
Vizari, 542
Vizitsa, 235
Vizitsa Guesthouses, 245
Vlachos Kastraki, 238, 245
Vlatades Monastery, 258, 266
Volada, 583
Volimes, 400
Volissos, 665
Volos, 227
Vorres Museum, 110
Vostitsano, 412
Votsalakia, 650
Votsalakia Hotel, 650, 686
Voulgaris, 642
Vouliagmeni, 105
Vouzas, 119, 137
Vrisi, 483
Vrisi Monastery, 483
Vrisses, 542, 545
Vromolimni Bay, 340
Vrontados, 663
Vronti, 582
Vurgunda, 584

White House, 372
White Rocks Hotel and Bungalows, 386, 406
White Tower, 256
Wholesale, 120
Women's Agricultural and Tourist Cooperative, Chios, 661; Lesvos, 676, 687
Women's Cooperative, Zakynthos, 398

Xanc, 323
Xanthakou Brothers, 284
Xanthi, 321
Xanthippi, 322
Xanthopoulos, 95
Xenia, 211, 228, 322, 323, 327, 334, 377, 438, 476, 504, 614
Xenia Hotel, Andros, 438, 502; Arta, 211, 221; Chania, 549, 561; Epidaurus, 157, 193; Grikou, 614, 624; Herakleion, 518, 561; Ioannina, 205, 221; Komotini, 323, 334; Lefkada, 377, 406; Lefkes, 478, 504; Ourzanopolis, 305, 334; Paleopoli, 327, 334; Parikia, 476, 504; Rethymno, 541, 561; Volos, 228, 245; Xanthi, 322, 334
Xenia du Lac, 283, 334
Xenia Palace, 154, 193
Xenonas Halki, 585, 623
Xerxes' Canal, 303
Xi, 387
Xinos, 81
Xiradaki, 232
Xirokambos, 610
Xobourgo, 444

Yacht Club, 370
Yachting Club, 532
Yaliskari, 635
Yanko's, 488
Yannis Roussos's Restaurant, 478
Yeraki, 169
Yerolimena, 176
Yeros tou Morea, 83
Yeroulanou, 235
Yesterday's, 92
Yiali, 594
Yialos, 587
Yialyia, 438
Yiamos Hotel-Restaurant, 658, 687
Yiannis, 370
Yiannis Michaelidis, 450
Yria, 474
Yuri's, 271
Y. Voulgaris, 450

Zachlorou, 188
Zafiris, 82
Zagora, 233
Zagoria, 213
Zakynthos, 363, 394
Zalongo, 201
Zante Beach Hotel and Bungalows, 399, 407
Zappeion, 64
Zarkadas Hotel, 217, 221
Zazas, 418
Zephyria, 490
Zephyros, 73, 84
Zeses Hotel, 215, 221
Zevgios, 658, 687
Zia, 600
Ziogas Rooming House, 238, 245
Ziros, 535
Zogeria, 424
Zoi, 499
Zolotas, Athens, 94; Mykonos, 450
Zoodochos Pigi, 619
Zorba's, Delphi, 120; Kythira, 404
Zorba's Bouzouki, 645
Zoumboulakis Galleries, 96